YOUR STUDY OF

THE BOOK OF MORMON

• MADE EASIER •

FOR TEENS

PART TWO: 2

MOSIAH THROUGH ALMA

BOOKS BY DAVID J. RIDGES

THE GOSPEL STUDIES SERIES

- *Isaiah Made Easier, Second Edition*
- *The New Testament Made Easier, Part 1, Second Edition*
- *The New Testament Made Easier, Part 2, Second Edition*
- *Your Study of The Book of Mormon Made Easier, Part 1*
- *Your Study of The Book of Mormon Made Easier, Part 2*
- *Your Study of The Book of Mormon Made Easier, Part 3*
- *Your Study of The Doctrine and Covenants Made Easier, Part 1*
- *Your Study of The Doctrine and Covenants Made Easier, Part 2*
- *Your Study of The Doctrine and Covenants Made Easier, Part 3*
- *The Old Testament Made Easier, Part 1*
- *The Old Testament Made Easier—Selections from the O.T., Part 2*
- *The Old Testament Made Easier—Selections from the O.T., Part 3*
- *Your Study of the Pearl of Great Price Made Easier*
- *Your Study of Jeremiah Made Easier*
- *Your Study of The Book of Revelation Made Easier, Second Edition*
- *Gospel Studies Series Deluxe Sets*

ADDITIONAL TITLES BY DAVID J. RIDGES

- *Our Savior, Jesus Christ: His Life and Mission to Cleanse and Heal*
- *Mormon Beliefs and Doctrines Made Easier*
- *The Proclamation on the Family: The Word of the Lord on More Than 30 Current Issues*
- *100 Signs of the Times Leading Up to the Second Coming of Christ*
- *Doctrinal Details of the Plan of Salvation: From Premortality to Exaltation*
- *To This End Was I Born: Walking with the Savior in His Final Week*
- *Temples: Sacred Symbolism, Eternal Blessings*
- *Priesthood Power Unlocked*
- *Using the Signs of the Times to Strengthen Your Testimony*
- *The Red Porsche*
- *The Righteous Role of a Father*
- *A Mother's Perfect Hope*
- *Seasons of a Mother's Love*
- *Born to the Virgin Mary*
- *Gospel Questions, Gospel Answers*

YOUR STUDY OF

THE BOOK OF MORMON

• MADE EASIER •

FOR TEENS

PART TWO: 2

MOSIAH THROUGH ALMA

DAVID J. RIDGES

CFI

An imprint of Cedar Fort, Inc.
Springville, Utah

This is not an official publication of The Church of Jesus Christ of Latter-day Saints. The opinions and views expressed herein belong solely to the author and do not necessarily represent the opinions or views of Cedar Fort, Inc. Permission for the use of sources, graphics, and photos is also solely the responsibility of the author.

ISBN 13: 978-1-4621-3684-1 (Volume 2)
ISBN 13: 978-1-4621-3579-0 (Set)

Published by CFI, an imprint of Cedar Fort, Inc.
2373 W. 700 S., Springville, UT 84663
Distributed by Cedar Fort, Inc., www.cedarfort.com

LIBRARY OF CONGRESS CATALOGING-IN-PUBLICATION DATA

Names: Ridges, David J., author.
Title: The Book of Mormon made easier for teens / David J. Ridges.
Description: Springville, Utah : CFI, an imprint of Cedar Fort, Inc., [2019] | Includes bibliographical references.
Identifiers: LCCN 2019018562 (print) | LCCN 2019020853 (ebook) | ISBN 9781462135790 (perfect bound : alk. paper)
Subjects: LCSH: Book of Mormon--Commentaries. | Mormon youth--Religious life.
Classification: LCC BX8627 .R533 2019 (print) | LCC BX8627 (ebook) | DDC 289.3/22--dc23
LC record available at https://lccn.loc.gov/2019018562
LC ebook record available at https://lccn.loc.gov/2019020853

Cover design by Shawnda T. Craig

Edited by Nicole Terry

Printed in the United States of America

10 9 8 7 6 5 4 3 2 1

Printed on acid-free paper

CONTENTS

THE JST REFERENCES IN STUDY GUIDES BY DAVID J. RIDGES

Note that some of the JST (The Joseph Smith Translation of the Bible) references I use in my study guides are not found in our LDS Bible in the footnotes or in the Joseph Smith Translation section in the reference section in the back. The reason for this, as explained to me while writing curriculum materials for the Church, is simply that there is not enough room to include all of the JST additions and changes to the King James Version of the Bible (the one we use in the English-speaking part of the Church). As you can imagine, as was likewise explained to me, there were difficult decisions that had to be made by the Scriptures Committee of the Church as to which JST contributions were included and which were not.

The Joseph Smith Translation of the Bible in its entirety can generally be found in or ordered through LDS bookstores. It was originally published under the auspices of the Reorganized Church of Jesus Christ of Latter Day Saints in Independence, Missouri. The version of the JST I prefer to use is a parallel column version, Joseph Smith's "New Translation" of the Bible, published by Herald Publishing House, Independence, Missouri, in 1970. This parallel column version compares the King James Bible with the JST side by side and includes only the verses that have changes, additions, or deletions made by the Prophet Joseph Smith.

By the way, some members of the Church have wondered if we can trust the JST since it was published by a breakaway faction from our Church. They worry that some changes from Joseph Smith's original manuscript might have been made to support doctrinal differences between us and the RLDS Church. This is not the case. Many years ago, Robert J. Matthews of the Brigham Young University Religion Department was given permission by leaders of the RLDS Church to come to their Independence, Missouri, headquarters and personally compare the original JST document word for word with their publication of the JST. Brother Matthews was thus able to verify that they had been meticulously true to the Prophet's original work.

INTRODUCTION

Welcome to the Book of Mormon Made Easier for Teens (and adults who would like a bit more help studying the Book of Mormon). These three study guide volumes combined contain every verse in the Book of Mormon. So, as you read and study, you will be reading the entire Book of Mormon word for word.

This study guide series was written for you. It is designed to help you learn to see applications in your own life from what you are reading and learning in the Book of Mormon. That way, it will be more interesting for you to read and study.

One of the things that typically stands in the way of understanding the scriptures is the vocabulary and overall language used in the scriptures. And so, I am going to help you learn "Scriptureze," or, in other words, the language of the scriptures, as we go along. In effect, you will learn a new language. Especially at first, I will define many words as we come to them. As you get to the point that you no longer need some of the words defined, you can ignore my definitions, realizing that you are actually making good progress in learning the language of the scriptures.

The Prophet Joseph Smith taught that we can get closer to God by living according to the teachings of the Book of Mormon than through any other book. The exact quote is, "I told the brethren that the Book of Mormon was the most correct of any book on earth, and the keystone of our religion, and a man would get nearer to God by abiding by its precepts, than by any other book." (See Book of Mormon, Introduction, paragraph 6.) So, there is probably nothing more valuable that you can do than to read and study the Book of Mormon.

The difference between this version and the regular Book of Mormon Made Easier study guides published several years ago is that these three volumes have many more definitions of scriptural terms that can be difficult for younger readers and also for many adults. They also contain a number of additional explanations of the teachings and principles taught in the Book of Mormon, and some longer and more technical notes and commentary have not been included.

You will see as we go along that I have used bold for many words and phrases. You can use this as a guide to mark your own scriptures with colored pencils, or highlight them if you are using digital scriptures. Also, you will see that by marking certain key words and phrases in a verse, you can, in effect, make brief notes as to what the verse is about. Later, as you re-read and study your Book of Mormon, you can glance at a verse and quickly see what it is about because of what you have marked in it.

Most important of all, the Book of Mormon is true. It is the word of God. And it is a sure way to bring the Spirit into your heart and mind whenever you choose to read and study it.

—David J. Ridges

THE BOOK OF MOSIAH

As we begin our study of this portion of the Book of Mormon, we will step back from the details and look at the big picture for a moment. There are often major messages from the Lord in the scriptures, which we can more readily see when we take time out from looking at the "trees," so to speak, and pull back for a look at the "forest."

For instance, you could, in a general way, divide the Book of Mormon into three parts. In the first third, we see men and women who are righteous when we first meet them in the account and who remain righteous to the end. Examples would include Lehi and Sariah, Nephi, Sam, Jacob, and Zoram.

We are introduced to others who tend to be rebellious and wicked when we first meet them and who remove themselves further and further from God as the account continues, until they become extremely wicked and depraved. Examples would include Laman and Lemuel, the sons of Ishmael, and their wives.

In summary, in the first third or so of the Book of Mormon, we meet people who are righteous when we are first introduced to them, and we watch as they exercise faith and repentance and thus become stronger and stronger in following God throughout their lives. This is a great example and encouragement to each of us. On the other hand, we see rebellious and wicked souls who never seem to make a one hundred percent commitment to follow God and thus become less and less sensitive to the Spirit and more and more apt to follow Satan's ways. The righteous become more righteous, and the wicked become more wicked. This pattern fits many people today and is both an encouragement and a warning to members of the Church.

In the second third of the Book of Mormon, the portion that we are about to study, it seems that the Lord brings another group of people into the picture. The examples in this group are wicked when we first meet them, but they are successful in overcoming evil and rebellion in their lives. By the time we bid farewell to them in our study, they are deeply committed to God and are wonderful examples of faithful Saints.

Such people as Alma the Elder, Alma the Younger, the four sons of Mosiah, and Zeezrom fall into this category. Yet another example with a little different background is Amulek. When we first meet him, he is not necessarily wicked but is inactive in the Church. He has been encouraged many times by the Spirit to become a faithful member but has ignored the promptings. As we watch him meet Alma (Alma 8:18–32), the Lord's prophet, and minister to his needs, we witness true conversion take place in his heart and then observe as he is taught and prepared and becomes a mighty servant of the Lord.

Thus, a major "big picture" message comes to us in the first third of the Book of Mormon as the Lord encourages the righteous to remain righteous and warns the wicked to turn from their evil and rebellious ways. In the second third, the Savior reminds and teaches those who have had times of evil and wickedness in their lives that there is hope for them. Indeed, through the examples of key characters in the Book of Mormon account, the Lord assures such Saints that there is not only hope for them, but also the opportunity for absolute success in becoming righteous through Christ's Atonement.

In the last third of the Book of Mormon, we see the ultimate fate of the wicked as they are destroyed in the Americas at the time of the Savior's Crucifixion, as well as through the wars that follow their apostasy. We see the strengthening of the righteous as Christ ministers to the Nephites as recorded in Third Nephi. We watch the wonderful results of personal righteousness during the two hundred years of peace. Then we are startled to see how fast a once-righteous people, who get careless in living their religion, fall away from God and become extremely wicked.

In summary, there are several major messages to be received as we step back and look at the "big picture."

We will now turn our attention to the Book of Mosiah. By way of quick background and review, Lehi and his family left Jerusalem in 600 BC. After they arrived in the Americas, and after Lehi died (2 Nephi 4:12), Laman and Lemuel and their families and followers continued to grow in hatred for Nephi and his righteous followers. The time came that the Lord commanded Nephi and his people to flee (2 Nephi 5:5). They did so, and at the end of their travels, they settled in a place they called Nephi (2 Nephi 5:8), which came to be known as the land of Nephi.

A few hundred years later, a righteous man named Mosiah was commanded to lead the righteous out of the land of Nephi, away from the wicked (Omni 1:12). After fleeing into the wilderness, Mosiah and his people eventually came upon another civilization, known as the people of Zarahemla (Omni 1:14). These people (also known as the Mulekites, named after Mulek) had come from Jerusalem about the same time as Lehi and his people. Mosiah and his followers settled in the land of Zarahemla. The two peoples joined together, and Mosiah eventually became their king.

Mosiah's son, Benjamin, became the next king of Zarahemla. During his reign, the Lamanites came from the land of Nephi and waged war against King Benjamin and his people in the land of Zarahemla. But, with the help of the Lord, the righteous Nephites, with King Benjamin in the lead, drove the Lamanites out of the area. Benjamin also dealt successfully with problems of apostasy and rebellion among his own people. (See Words of Mormon 1:12–18.)

As we begin our study of the Book of Mosiah, it is a time of peace for righteous King Benjamin. He is getting old and is preparing to turn the government over to one of his sons.

MOSIAH 1

You may have noticed already that the first six books in the Book of Mormon are written in what we call "first person." This means that the author is giving the account himself and uses "I," "we," "us," etc. An example of this is "I, Nephi, having been born . . ." in 1 Nephi 1:1.

The Book of Mosiah, however, is told in what we call "third person." Someone else is telling the story. That "someone else" is Mormon. He has written a shortened version of the large plates of Nephi, called "an abridgment," and is now giving us his abridgment, or summary, of those plates. The books of Mosiah, Alma, Helaman, Third Nephi, Fourth Nephi, and Mormon are all abridgments made by Mormon of the large plates. Thus, he is our teacher as we now continue studying the Book of Mormon. The things he was inspired to include in his abridgment are the things the Lord knew we would need in our day in order to stay loyal to God.

1 AND now **there was no more contention** [*fighting, arguing, hurting each other, etc.*] in all the land of Zarahemla, among all the people who belonged to king Benjamin, so that king Benjamin had continual peace all the remainder of his days.

Just a quick mention of the word "and." You will notice that it is used much in the Book of Mormon text. Its use is very typical of ancient Near Eastern languages and is an internal evidence that the Book of Mormon is a translation from such an ancient language. We will **bold** the word "**and**" in verse 2, next, to illustrate this.

2 **And** it came to pass that he had three sons; **and** he called their names Mosiah, **and** Helorum, **and** Helaman. **And** he caused that they should be taught in all the language of his fathers [*ancestors*], that thereby they might become men of understanding; **and** that they might know concerning the prophecies which had been spoken by the mouths of their fathers, which were delivered them by the hand of the Lord.

We understand that the phrase "taught in all the language of his fathers," in verse 2, above, includes not only languages, grammar, writing, and vocabulary, etc., but also the language of the gospel, the plan of salvation, the Atonement of Christ, and the doctrines of the gospel, etc.

In verses 3–5, next, we are reminded of the importance of having and studying the scriptures.

3 And he also taught them concerning the records which were engraven on the plates of brass [*basically the Old Testament, up to the writings of Jeremiah*], saying: My sons, I would that ye should remember that **were it not for these plates, which contain these records and these commandments, we must have** [*would have*] **suffered in ignorance, even at this present time, not knowing the mysteries of God.**

"Mysteries," as used in verse 3, above, refer to the basics of the gospel, such as faith, repentance, baptism, the gift of the Holy Ghost, doctrines of the plan of salvation, etc. Such simple truths and principles are "mysteries" to those who do not have or understand the gospel of Christ. See Bible Dictionary under "Mystery" at the back of the LDS Bible.

4 For **it were not possible that our father, Lehi, could have remembered all these things, to have taught them to his children, except it were for the help of these plates**; for he having been taught in the language of the Egyptians therefore he could read these engravings, and teach them to his children, **that thereby they could teach them to their children, and so fulfilling the commandments of God, even down to this present time.**

5 I say unto you, my sons, **were it not for these things** [*the brass plates, scriptures*], which have been kept and preserved by the hand of God, **that we might read and understand of his mysteries, and have his commandments always before our eyes,** that even **our fathers would have dwindled in unbelief,** and **we should have been** [*would have been*] **like unto our brethren, the Lamanites, who know nothing concerning these things, or even do not believe them** when they are taught them, because of the traditions of their fathers, which are not correct.

We often refer to the scriptures as "the standard works." In other words, they are the standard by which all teachings, traditions, behaviors, philosophies, etc., should be measured in order for us to stay on the covenant path or reach the path leading back to God.

Next, Benjamin bears strong testimony to his sons that the scriptures on the brass plates, along with the plates kept by Nephi, are true.

6 O my sons, I would that ye should remember that **these sayings are true**, and also that **these records are true**. And behold, also the plates of Nephi, which contain the records and the sayings of our fathers [*ancestors*] from the time they left Jerusalem until now, and **they are true**; and we can know of their surety because we have them before our eyes.

Next, Benjamin reminds his sons as well as us that it is not enough just to read the scriptures. Rather, we must diligently search them. "Search" is a powerful word, and implies "looking for something." And what are we looking for? One major answer is exaltation, which means living in the highest degree of glory in the celestial kingdom and becoming gods.

We are studying to learn the things necessary for us to become Christlike and to become like Heavenly Father. There is, in fact, quite a difference between studying the scriptures to be able to discuss them with others and studying them to know what to do to obtain exaltation in the highest degree of the celestial kingdom. Such "searching" adds tremendous meaning to our personal scripture study.

7 And now, my sons, I would that ye should remember to **search them diligently**, that ye may profit

thereby; and I would that ye should keep the commandments of God, that ye may prosper in the land according to the promises which the Lord made unto our fathers.

8 And many more things did king Benjamin teach his sons, which are not written in this book.

9 And it came to pass that after **king Benjamin** had made an end of teaching his sons, that he **waxed old** [*grew old*], and he saw that he must very soon go the way of all the earth [*die*]; therefore, he thought it expedient [*necessary*] that he should **confer the kingdom upon one of his sons**.

10 Therefore, **he had Mosiah** [*his son, named after King Benjamin's father, Mosiah*] **brought before him**; and these are the words which **he spake unto him, saying**: My son, I would that ye should [*I want you to*] **make a proclamation** [*a major announcement*] throughout all this land among all this people, or the people of Zarahemla, and the people of Mosiah who dwell in the land, that thereby they may be gathered together; for on the morrow I shall proclaim unto this my people out of mine own mouth that thou art a king and a ruler over this people, whom the Lord our God hath given us.

Verse 11, next, is the "topic sentence" or key sentence introducing the main emphasis in chapters 2–5. King Benjamin tells his people that he is going to give them another name, a new name so-to-speak, which will set them apart from other people. Then, in chapters 2–5, he will explain to them how they can retain this "new name" forever. The name which he gives them is "Christ." See Mosiah 5:8. Keeping this name upon us, the name of Christ, is symbolic of living the gospel and earning exaltation.

11 And moreover, **I shall give this people a name, that thereby they may be distinguished above all the people** which the Lord God hath brought out of the land of Jerusalem; and this I do **because they have been a diligent people in keeping the commandments of the Lord.**

12 And I give unto them a name **that never shall be blotted out, except it be through transgression.**

There is important symbolism associated with the receiving of a new name here and elsewhere in the scriptures. Isaiah mentions "a new name, which the mouth of the Lord shall name." See Isaiah 62:2. The symbolism is that the person is making covenants with God. By making and keeping these covenants, the person becomes a new person (therefore, the "new name") with much increased opportunities for progressing to become like God. It is similar in concept to being "born again."

Abraham, in the Old Testament, is an example of a person who was given another name in conjunction with making covenants with the Lord. In the heading to the Joseph Smith Translation of the Bible (JST), Genesis 17, we read "*Abram's new name.*" You may recall that when we first meet him in Genesis 11:26, his name is "Abram." He is

"Abram" through Genesis, chapters 12–16. Then, in Genesis 17:1, God commands Abram to "be perfect," which would be a commandment emphasizing our opportunity to become like God (exaltation). In Genesis 17:3, Abram falls on his face before God, demonstrating (in his culture) his humility and acceptance of the commandment. Next, in verses 4 and 5, the Lord covenants with Abram and changes his name to "Abraham" in association with the covenant. The covenant is explained in verses 2–7 as well as in Abraham 2:9–11 in the Pearl of Great Price. It is a covenant that, when kept, will lead to exaltation. Thus, Abram's name was changed to Abraham in conjunction with making covenants of exaltation with God.

When we first meet Abraham's wife in Genesis 12:5, her name is "Sarai." In Genesis 17:15–16, her name is changed to "Sarah" in conjunction with the great blessings promised to her. Among other blessings associated with exaltation, the promise to Sarah that "she shall be a mother of nations; kings of people shall be of her" (Genesis 17:16) is a promise of posterity that extends to the next life for those who will be exalted. See the last two lines of D&C 132:19.

Jacob's name is changed to "Israel" in Genesis 32:26–28, again in conjunction with blessings. Saul's name was changed to Paul after he turned to Christ. See Acts 13:2–3, 9, 13.

In Revelation 2:17, we read of a "white stone" with a "new name" written on it. Joseph Smith explains, in D&C 130:11, that this new name is for people who attain celestial glory.

In summary, as the Lord gave Abram, Sarai, Jacob, and Saul the names Abraham, Sarah, Israel, and Paul, it symbolized that they were now "new people" with a new set of privileges and opportunities for progression, which they would not have had without making covenants with God.

We will now watch as King Benjamin uses similar symbolism as he prepares and instructs his people to receive another name, the name of Christ, and teaches them how to keep that name forever in order to attain exaltation. Therefore, you and I can study his sermon carefully and be taught how we, too, can retain the name of Christ, which we took upon us by covenant when we were baptized and which we take upon ourselves each time we take the sacrament. If we stay on this path or get back on it through repenting, we will eventually attain exaltation.

In order to better study King Benjamin's counsel on how to keep the name of Christ upon us, we will now list several verses in chapters 1–5, and **bold** the words and phrases that teach us things we must do to retain the name of Christ once it is given to us by covenant. When we are done, we will return to chapter one and pick up where we left off, beginning with verse 13.

Mosiah 2:16–18

(Serve one another.)

16 Behold, I say unto you that because I said unto you that I had spent my days in your **service**, I do not desire to boast, for I have only been in the service of God.

17 And behold, I tell you these things that ye may learn wisdom; that ye may learn that **when ye are in the service of your fellow beings ye are only in the service of your God.**

18 Behold, ye have called me your king; and if I, whom ye call your king, do labor to serve you, then **ought not ye to labor to serve one another?**

Mosiah 2:19

(Show gratitude to God.)

19 And behold also, if I, whom ye call your king, who has spent his days in your service, and yet has been in the service of God, do merit any thanks from you, **O how you ought to thank your heavenly King!**

Mosiah 2:22–24

(Remember that God does not owe you. Rather, you owe God.)

22 And behold, **all that he requires of you is to keep his commandments**; and he has promised you that if ye would keep his commandments ye should prosper in the land; and he never doth vary from that which he hath said; therefore, **if ye do keep his commandments he doth bless you and prosper you.**

23 And now, in the first place, he hath created you, and granted unto you your lives, for which **ye are indebted unto him.**

24 And secondly, **he doth require that ye should do as he hath commanded you; for which if ye do, he doth immediately bless you; and therefore he hath paid you. And ye are still indebted unto him, and are, and will be, forever and ever;** therefore, of what have ye to boast?

Mosiah 2:32

(Avoid contention among you.)

32 But, O my people, **beware lest there shall arise contentions among you,** and ye list to obey the evil spirit, which was spoken of by my father Mosiah.

Mosiah 2:34

(Dedicate yourselves completely to God.)

34 I say unto you, that there are not any among you, except it be your little children that have not been taught concerning these things, but what knoweth that ye are eternally indebted to your heavenly Father, to **render to him all that you have and are;** and also have been taught concerning the records which contain the prophecies which have been spoken by the holy prophets, even down to the time our father, Lehi, left Jerusalem;

Mosiah 2:41

(Keep in mind more and more the benefits of personal righteousness.)

41 And moreover, I would desire that ye should **consider on the blessed and happy state of those that keep the commandments of God.** For behold, they are blessed in all things, both temporal and spiritual; and if they hold out faithful to the end they are received into heaven, that thereby they may dwell with God in a state of never–ending happiness. O remember, remember that these things are true; for the Lord God hath spoken it.

Mosiah 3:4

(It is okay to rejoice and be happy as you strive to live the gospel.)

4 For the Lord hath heard thy prayers, and hath judged of thy righteousness, and hath sent me to declare unto thee that **thou mayest rejoice;** and that thou mayest declare unto **thy people,** that they **may also be filled with joy.**

Mosiah 3:17

(Avoid making your own rules to replace the gospel teachings and laws.)

17 And moreover, I say unto you, that **there shall be no other name given nor any other way nor means whereby salvation can come unto the children of men, only in and through the name of Christ,** the Lord Omnipotent.

Mosiah 3:18

(Keep yourself humble and believe that the Atonement will work for you.)

18 For behold he judgeth, and his judgment is just; and the infant perisheth not that dieth in his infancy; but men drink damnation to their own souls except they humble themselves and become as little children, and believe that salvation was, and is, and is to come, in and through the atoning blood of Christ, the Lord Omnipotent.

Mosiah 3:19

(Put off the "natural man" in yourself (the things that keep you from being close to God, and yield to the invitation of the Holy Ghost to become as a child before God. Do not become angry at God if things don't go the way you want them to.)

19 For the **natural man is an enemy to God,** and has been from the fall of Adam, and will be, forever and ever, **unless he yields to the enticings of the Holy Spirit, and putteth off the natural man and becometh a saint through the atonement of Christ the Lord, and becometh as a child, submissive, meek, humble, patient, full of love, willing to submit to all things which the Lord seeth fit to inflict upon him, even as a child doth submit to his father.**

Mosiah 3:22

(Remember, you are accountable to God for what you do and don't do.)

22 And even at this time, when thou shalt have taught thy people the things which the Lord thy God hath commanded thee, even **then are they found no more blameless in the sight of God,** only according to the words which I have spoken unto thee.

Mosiah 3:23–27

(Understand and accept the fact that there are severe consequences for intentional wickedness.)

23 And now **I have spoken the words which the Lord God hath commanded me.**

24 And thus saith the Lord: **They shall stand as a bright testimony against this people, at the judgment day;** whereof **they shall be judged, every man according to his works, whether they be good, or whether they be evil.**

25 And if **they be evil they are consigned to an awful view of their own guilt and abominations,** which doth cause them to shrink from the presence of the Lord into a state of **misery and endless torment,** from whence they can **no**

more return; therefore **they have drunk damnation to their own souls.**

26 Therefore, they have drunk out of the cup of the wrath of God, which justice could no more deny unto them than it could deny that Adam should fall because of his partaking of the forbidden fruit; therefore, **mercy could have claim on them no more forever.**

27 And **their torment is** as a lake of fire and brimstone, whose flames are **unquenchable**, and whose smoke ascendeth up forever and ever. Thus hath the Lord commanded me. Amen.

Mosiah 4:2

(Be willing to ask God for mercy and apply the Atonement of Christ to you.)

2 And **they had viewed themselves in their own carnal state**, even less than the dust of the earth. And **they all cried aloud** with one voice, saying: **O have mercy, and apply the atoning blood of Christ** that we may receive forgiveness of our sins, and our hearts may be purified; for we believe in Jesus Christ, the Son of God, who created heaven and earth, and all things; who shall come down among the children of men.

Mosiah 4:3

(Accept the joy and peace that comes with forgiveness of sins. In other words, let it happen. See Mosiah 3:4. Don't destroy it by constantly second guessing it.)

3 And it came to pass that after they had spoken these words the Spirit of the Lord came upon them, and **they were filled with joy, having received a remission of their sins, and having peace of conscience,** because of the exceeding faith which they had in Jesus Christ who should come, according to the words which king Benjamin had spoken unto them.

Mosiah 4:9–10

(Continue believing in God and having faith in Christ's Atonement working for you throughout your life.)

9 **Believe in God**; believe that he is, and that he created all things, both in heaven and in earth; believe that he has all wisdom, and all power, both in heaven and in earth; believe that man doth not comprehend all the things which the Lord can comprehend.

10 And again, **believe that ye must repent of your sins and forsake them, and humble yourselves before God; and ask in sincerity of heart that he would forgive you; and now, if you believe all these things see that ye do them.**

Mosiah 4:11–12

(Don't forget or ignore the blessings that God has already given you. Stay humble. Don't neglect your prayers. Keep your commitments to God. Continue progressing in knowledge of God and of Christ's Atonement.)

11 And again I say unto you as I have said before, that **as ye have come to the knowledge of the glory of God,** or if ye **have known of his goodness and have tasted of his love, and have received a remission of your sins,** which causeth such exceedingly great joy in your souls, even so I would

that ye should remember, and **always retain in remembrance, the greatness of God,** and your own nothingness [*in other words, don't forget your dependence on Him*], and his goodness and long-suffering towards you, unworthy creatures, and **humble yourselves** even in the depths of humility, **calling on the name of the Lord daily,** and **standing steadfastly in the faith** of that which is to come, which was spoken by the mouth of the angel.

12 And behold, I say unto you that **if ye do this ye shall always rejoice,** and be filled with the love of God, and always retain a remission of your sins; and **ye shall grow in the knowledge of the glory of him that created you,** or in the knowledge of that which is just and true.

Mosiah 4:13

(Be kind and be honest with others.)

13 And **ye will not have a mind to injure one another,** but to live peaceably, and to **render to every man according to that which is his due.**

Mosiah 4:14–15

(Be responsible parents.)

14 And ye will **not suffer** [*allow, cause through neglect*] **your children that they go hungry, or naked; neither will ye suffer that they transgress the laws of God, and fight and quarrel one with another,** and serve the devil, who is the master of sin, or who is the evil spirit which hath been spoken of by our fathers, he being an enemy to all righteousness.

15 But ye will **teach them to walk in the ways of truth and soberness; ye will teach them to love one another, and to serve one another.**

Mosiah 4:16–21, 26

(Be generous with others, remembering that God is generous with us. It would be hypocritical to accept God's generosity toward us to then be stingy with others whom we could help. Generosity is an attribute required for godhood. We are all beggars in the sense that we are dependent on God.)

16 And **also, ye yourselves will succor** [*rush to the aid of*] **those that stand in need of your succor** [*assistance*]; ye will administer of your substance unto him that standeth in need; and **ye will not suffer that the beggar putteth up his petition to you in vain, and turn him out to perish.**

17 Perhaps thou shalt say: The man has brought upon himself his misery; therefore I will stay my hand, and will not give unto him of my food, nor impart unto him of my substance that he may not suffer, for his punishments are just—

18 But I say unto you, O man, **whosoever doeth this the same hath great cause to repent; and except he repenteth of that which he hath done he perisheth forever, and hath no interest in the kingdom of God** [*will not attain celestial exaltation*].

19 For behold, **are we not all beggars**? Do we not all depend upon the same Being, even God, for all the substance which we have, for both food and raiment, and for gold, and for silver, and for all the riches which we have of every kind?

20 And behold, even at this time, **ye have been** calling on his name, and **begging for a remission of your sins.** And **has he suffered** [*allowed, permitted*] **that ye have begged in vain? Nay;** he has poured out his Spirit upon you, and has caused that your hearts should be filled with joy, and has caused that your mouths should be stopped that ye could not find utterance, so exceedingly great was your joy.

21 **And now, if God, who has created you, on whom you are dependent for your lives and for all that ye have and are, doth grant unto you whatsoever ye ask that is right, in faith, believing that ye shall receive, O then, how ye ought to impart of the substance that ye have one to another.**

26 And now, for the sake of these things which I have spoken unto you—that is, **for the sake of retaining a remission of your sins from day to day,** that ye may walk guiltless before God—I would that ye should **impart of your substance to the poor, every man according to that which he hath, such as feeding the hungry, clothing the naked, visiting the sick and administering to their relief, both spiritually and temporally, according to their wants.**

Mosiah 4:27

(Be aware that you don't have to be a "walking nervous breakdown" waiting to happen in order to be a faithful saint. Just do the best you can in wisdom, and keep improving.)

27 And **see that all these things are done in wisdom and order;** for **it is not requisite** [*not required; not necessary*] **that a man should run faster than he has strength.** And again, it is expedient [*necessary*] that he should **be diligent,** that thereby he might win the prize [*exaltation*]; therefore, **all things must be done in order.**

You may wish to read a talk given at the 1989 April general conference by Elder Marvin J. Ashton of the Quorum of the Twelve, in which he addressed the issues in verse 27, above. Among other things, he said, "The speed with which we head along the straight and narrow path isn't as important as the direction in which we are traveling."

Mosiah 4:28

(If you borrow something, return it.)

28 And I would that ye should remember, that **whosoever among you borroweth of his neighbor should return the thing that he borroweth, according as he doth agree,** or else thou shalt commit sin; and perhaps thou shalt cause thy neighbor to commit sin also.

Mosiah 4:30

(Keep your thoughts, words, and deeds in harmony with God. Keep the commandments and don't slack off on keeping your covenants to the end of your life.)

30 But this much I can tell you, that if ye do not **watch yourselves,** and **your thoughts,** and **your words,** and **your deeds,** and **observe the commandments of God,** and **continue in the faith** of what ye have heard concerning the coming of our Lord, **even unto the end of your lives,** ye must perish. And now, O man, remember, and perish not.

Mosiah 5:2

(With the help of the Holy Ghost, get to the point that you truly want to be righteous. Many of you are already to this point.)

2 And they all cried with one voice, saying: Yea, we believe all the words which thou hast spoken unto us; and also, we know of their surety and truth, because of **the Spirit of the Lord Omnipotent,** which **has wrought a mighty change in us, or in our hearts, that we have no more disposition to do evil, but to do good continually.**

Mosiah 5:5, 7

(Be willing to enter into covenants with God. Covenants open doors to heaven that would otherwise remain closed to you.)

5 And **we are willing to enter into a covenant with our God to do his will, and to be obedient to his commandments in all things that he shall command us, all the remainder of our days,** that we may not bring upon ourselves a never-ending torment, as has been spoken by the angel, that we may not drink out of the cup of the wrath of God.

7 And now, **because of the covenant which ye have made ye shall be called the children of Christ, his sons, and his daughters** [*another way of saying "exalted"*]; for behold, this day he hath spiritually begotten you [*you are "born again"*]; for ye say that your hearts are changed through faith on his name; therefore, ye are born of him [*His Atonement works for you*] and have become his sons and his daughters [*His children spiritually; you are qualifying for exaltation*].

Mosiah 5:12

(Always remember who you are.)

12 I say unto you, I would that ye should **remember to retain the name written always in your hearts,** that ye are not found on the left hand of God, but that ye hear and know the voice by which ye shall be called, and also, the name by which he shall call you.

Mosiah 5:15

(Don't let anything or anyone keep you from keeping your commitments to God.)

15 Therefore, I would that ye should **be steadfast and immovable,** always abounding in good works, that Christ, the Lord God Omnipotent, may seal you his, that you may be brought to heaven, that ye may have everlasting salvation and eternal life [*exaltation*], through the wisdom, and power, and justice, and mercy of him who created all things, in heaven and in earth, who is God above all. Amen.

Having reviewed many of King Benjamin's instructions for retaining the name of Christ upon us, in chapters 2–5, we will now return to Mosiah 1:13 and resume our study of the rest of King Benjamin's address and counsel to his people as he turns the throne over to his son, Mosiah. Remember that he is talking to Mosiah, his son, in verses 13 and 14, next. He tells Mosiah what the people will lose if they fall away from God.

13 Yea, and moreover I say unto you, that **if this highly favored people of the Lord should fall into transgression, and become a wicked and an adulterous** [*involved in a lot of sexual*

immorality] **people**, that **the Lord will deliver them up** [*will no longer protect them*], that thereby they become weak like unto their brethren; and he will no more preserve them by his matchless and marvelous power, as he has hitherto preserved our fathers [*ancestors*].

14 For I say unto you, that **if he had not extended his arm** [*shown His power*] in the preservation of our fathers **they must have** [*would have*] fallen into the hands of the Lamanites, and become victims to their hatred.

15 And it came to pass that after **king Benjamin** had made an end of these sayings to his son [*Mosiah*], that he **gave him charge concerning all the affairs of the kingdom**.

In verse 16, next, we see that the Nephites still have the brass plates, the large plates of Nephi, the sword of Laban and the Liahona. These things would now have been in their possession for about 470 years.

16 And moreover, he also gave him charge concerning the records which were engraven on **the plates of brass;** and also the **plates of Nephi;** and also, **the sword of Laban,** and **the ball or director** [*Liahona. See Alma 37:38*], which led our fathers through the wilderness, which was prepared by the hand of the Lord that thereby they might be led, every one according to the heed and diligence which they gave unto him [*symbolic of being guided by the Holy Ghost according to how well we listen and how well we obey and follow His promptings*].

There is an important message in verse 17, next. It reminds us that the only way we can truly progress is by being faithful to God. Remember, they were journeying toward the "promised land," which would be symbolic of the celestial kingdom.

17 Therefore, **as they were unfaithful they did not prosper nor progress** in their journey, but were driven back, and incurred the displeasure of God upon them; and **therefore they were smitten** with famine and sore afflictions, to stir them up in remembrance of their duty.

18 And now, it came to pass that **Mosiah went and did as his father had commanded him**, and proclaimed unto all the people who were in the land of Zarahemla that thereby they might gather themselves together, to go up to the temple to hear the words which his father should speak unto them.

MOSIAH 2

Chapters 2 through 5 contain what is known as King Benjamin's address. You will hear it referred to quite often in lessons and talks in church. It has many things to teach us as far as living the gospel in our daily lives is concerned. His actual sermon begins with verse 9 of this chapter.

So many people gathered to hear King Benjamin's talk that he had to have a tower built for him to stand on so that they could hear him. Even then, there were still so many gathered that all could not hear him, therefore he had his words written down and distributed among them.

1 AND it came to pass that after Mosiah had done as his father had commanded him, and had made a proclamation throughout all the land, that **the people gathered themselves together** throughout all the land, that they might go up to the temple **to hear the words which king Benjamin should speak unto them**.

2 And **there were a great number**, even so many that they did not number [*count*] them; for they had multiplied exceedingly and waxed [*grown*] great in the land.

As you will see in verse 3, next, King Benjamin and his people were still living under the Law of Moses. They knew of Christ, they believed in Christ, and they taught of Christ (compare with 2 Nephi 25:26). This is actually the purpose of the sacrifices and the rites in the Law of Moses in the Old Testament—to prepare people to understand and believe in the life and the Atonement of Christ, which was yet to come in the future. Thus, the Book of Mormon teaches very clearly what it was like among righteous people in Old Testament times (the times before the birth of Jesus). Unfortunately, much of this view of things has been removed from the Old Testament such that some members of the Church wonder if people in Old Testament times knew much if anything of the Savior. The Book of Mormon shows us that they did indeed, during times of righteousness.

3 And they also took of the firstlings [*firstborn*] of their flocks [*the firstborn males; symbolic of Christ*], that **they might offer sacrifice and burnt offerings according to the law of Moses**;

These animal sacrifices mentioned in verse 3, above, were symbolic of the sacrifice of the Son of God and were designed by the Lord to point their minds toward Christ and His Atonement. Similarly, the sacrament today is designed to point our minds to the Savior and his sacrifice for us.

4 And **also that they might give thanks to the Lord their God**, who had brought them out of the land of Jerusalem, and who had delivered them out of the hands of their enemies, and had appointed just [*"just" means living the gospel in righteousness and with exactness*] men to be their teachers, and also a just man to be their king, who had established peace in the land of Zarahemla, and who had taught them to keep the commandments of God, that they might rejoice and be filled with love towards God and all men.

When people, as a whole, are righteous, there is strong emphasis on the importance of the family. This is demonstrated in verse 5, next.

5 And it came to pass that when they came up to the temple, they pitched their tents round about, **every man according to his family**, consisting of his wife, and his sons, and his daughters, and their sons, and their daughters, from the eldest down to the youngest, every family being separate one from another.

6 And they pitched their tents round about the temple, every man **having his tent with the door thereof towards the temple**, that thereby they might remain in their tents and hear the words which king Benjamin should speak unto them;

7 For the multitude being so great that king Benjamin could not teach them all within the walls of the temple, **therefore he caused a tower to be erected**, that thereby his people might hear the words which he should speak unto them.

8 And it came to pass that he began to speak to his people from the tower; and **they could not all hear his words** because of the greatness of the multitude; **therefore he caused that the words which he spake should be written and sent forth** among those that were not under the sound of his voice, that they might also receive his words.

9 And **these are the words which he spake** and caused to be written, saying: My brethren, all ye that have assembled yourselves together, you that can hear my words which I shall speak unto you this day; for I have not commanded you to come up hither to trifle with the words which I shall speak, but that you should **hearken unto me, and open your ears that ye may hear, and your hearts that ye may understand, and your minds that the mysteries of God may be unfolded to your view.**

As mentioned elsewhere, the word "mysteries" in verse 9, above, means "the basic teachings and ordinances of the gospel." It does not mean mysterious and little-known things. See Bible Dictionary under "Mystery."

Next, you can see that King Benjamin is a kind and loving man.

10 **I have not commanded you to come up hither that ye should fear me**, or that ye should think that I of myself am more than a mortal man.

It was common in ancient times among some cultures, such as Egypt, for people to think of their kings as gods. It is obvious here that King Benjamin wants no part of such thinking.

11 But **I am like as yourselves**, subject to all manner of infirmities [*weaknesses*] in body and mind; yet I have been chosen by this people, and consecrated [*set apart*] by my father [*King Mosiah I*], and was suffered [*allowed*] by the hand of the Lord that I should be a ruler and a king over this people; and **have been kept and preserved by his matchless power**, to serve you with all the might, mind and strength which the Lord hath granted unto me.

12 I say unto you that as **I have been suffered** [*allowed*] **to spend my days in your service**, even up to this time, and **have not sought gold nor silver nor any manner of riches of you** [*I have not tried to become rich by getting tax money from you*];

Next, we see the kinds of laws and rules that a righteous nation would have. One of Satan's goals seems to be to promote the exact opposites in order to undermine and destroy stable societies.

13 **Neither have I suffered** [*permitted*] **that ye should be confined** [*put in*] **in dungeons**, nor that ye should **make slaves one of another**, nor that ye should **murder**, or **plunder** [*hurt, abuse, make miserable*], or **steal**, or **commit adultery**; nor even have I suffered that ye should **commit any manner of wickedness**, and **have taught you that ye should keep the commandments of the Lord**, in all things which he hath commanded you—

14 And even **I, myself, have labored with mine own hands** that I might serve you, and that ye should not be laden with taxes, and that there should nothing come upon you which was grievous [*painful, hard*] to be borne—and of all these things which I have spoken, ye yourselves are witnesses this day.

15 Yet, my brethren, I have not done these things that I might boast, neither do I tell these things that thereby I might accuse you; but **I tell you these things that ye may know that I can answer a clear conscience before God this day.**

Next, King Benjamin emphasizes the importance of serving one another. Concerning this topic, President Spencer W. Kimball said: "God does notice us and He watches over us. But it is usually through another mortal that He meets our needs. Therefore, it is vital that we serve each other in the kingdom . . ." (*The Teachings of Spencer W. Kimball,* edited by Edward L. Kimball [Salt Lake City: Bookcraft, 1982], 252).

Next, we are taught in very simple and beautiful terms one of the most common ways to serve God.

16 Behold, I say unto you that because I said unto you that I had **spent my days in your service,** I do not desire to boast, for **I have only been in the service of God.**

17 And behold, I tell you these things that ye may learn wisdom; that ye may learn that **when ye are in the service of your fellow beings ye are only in the service of your God.**

In a significant way, King Benjamin is a symbol of Christ. He is what we often refer to as a "type" of Christ. His unselfish service to his people is symbolic of the Savior's service to us.

18 Behold, ye have called me your king; and **if I, whom ye call your king, do labor to serve you, then ought not ye to labor to serve one another?**

19 And behold also, **if I, whom ye call your king, who has spent his days in your service, and yet has been in the service of God,** do merit any thanks from you, **O how you ought to thank your heavenly King!**

Near the end of verse 19, above, King Benjamin taught a powerful lesson on gratitude. It is interesting to note that gratitude is one of the most healing character traits of all. People who have gratitude seem to suffer far less than others in similar circumstances. Additionally, gratitude opens the door for people to see things as God sees them.

As he continues, King Benjamin masterfully teaches that we can never put God in the position of "owing us." He has taught us that we should have gratitude. Now he teaches us why we should have gratitude toward God.

20 I say unto you, my brethren, that **if you should render** [*give*] **all the thanks and praise which your whole soul has power to possess, to that God who has created you, and has kept and preserved you, and has caused that ye should rejoice, and has granted that ye should live in peace one with another—**

21 I say unto you that **if ye should serve him who** has created you from the beginning, and **is preserving you from day to day, by lending you breath** [*by giving you life*], **that ye may live and move** and do according to your own will, **and** even **supporting you from one moment to another—**I say, **if ye should serve him with all your whole souls yet ye would be unprofitable servants** [*you could not possibly put Him in your debt. You could not put Him into a position of being in debt to you*].

22 And behold, **all that he requires of you is to keep his commandments**; and he has promised you that **if ye would keep his commandments ye should prosper in the land;** and he never doth [*does*] vary from that which he hath said; therefore, **if ye do keep his commandments he doth bless you and prosper you.**

23 And now, **in the first place, he hath** [*has*] **created you, and granted unto you your lives, for which ye are indebted unto him.**

24 And **secondly, he doth require that ye should do as he hath commanded you; for which if ye do, he doth immediately bless you; and therefore he hath paid you. And ye are still indebted unto him, and are, and will be, forever** and ever; therefore, of what have ye [*you*] to boast?

25 And now I ask, **can ye say aught** [*anything*] **of yourselves?** I answer you, Nay. Ye cannot say that ye are even as much as the dust of the earth; yet ye were created of the dust of the earth; but behold, it belongeth to him who created you.

It would be easy to mistakenly conclude from verse 25, above, that we are worthless, that we are of less value than dust. That would be tragic false doctrine. Some philosophers and religions of the world have taken that approach and made the "worthlessness of man" into their main teaching. Such false thinking violates the teachings of D&C 18:10, wherein the Savior says, "Remember the worth of souls is great in the sight of God."

To understand what King Benjamin means, we must keep it within the context of his sermon. In other words, we must keep it within the setting in which he gave it. He has taught, leading up to verse 25, that we owe everything to God, even our very existence and our daily breath. Thus, without being sustained constantly by God, we would not even be here to discuss the topic of "dust." We are taught in D&C 88:5–13 that Christ is the power which holds all things together. This confirms what King Benjamin is teaching, as a setting in which to teach gratitude.

Spencer W. Kimball taught the following concerning this topic:

"This soul of man! Though it controls and organizes and programs and does so many mighty things, yet science tells us that without the spirit about all that is left is a quantity of water, fat enough to make about seven bars of soap, sulphur enough to rid one dog of fleas, iron enough for a large nail, magnesium for one dose, lime enough to whitewash a chicken coop, phosphorous sufficient to tip some 2200 matches, potassium enough to explode a toy cannon, sugar to fill a shaker, and little more. But with a spirit directing mental processes and physical maneuvers man is 'little lower than the angels' and is 'crowned . . . with glory and honour.' (Psalm 8:5.)

"And yet man in his vanity and impudence has taken unto himself the glory of all his accomplishments, set himself up as God and, as has been said, has even 'created God in his (man's) own image.' It is as if the Boulder Dam should say: 'I am powerful. I hold back great quantities of water. Parched land becomes fertile and productive because of me. There were no builders. I am the great cause and responsible to no power'" (Spencer W. Kimball, *The Teachings of Spencer W. Kimball*, edited by Edward L. Kimball [Salt Lake City: Bookcraft, 1982], 27).

26 And I, even **I, whom ye call your king, am no better than ye yourselves are**; for I am also of the dust. And ye behold [*can see*] that I am old, and am about to yield up this mortal frame to its mother earth [*I am about to die*].

27 Therefore, as I said unto you that I had served you, walking with a clear conscience before God, even so I at this time have caused that ye should assemble yourselves together, **that I might be found blameless, and that your blood** [*sins*] **should not come upon me**, [*in other words, I won't be responsible for your sins because I have taught you what the Lord told me to teach you*] when I shall stand to be judged of God of the things whereof he hath commanded me concerning you.

28 I say unto you that I have caused that ye should assemble yourselves together **that I might rid my garments of your blood** [*not be held accountable for your sins*], at this period of time when I am about to go down to my grave, that I might go down in peace, and my immortal spirit may join the choirs above in singing the praises of a just God.

29 And moreover [*in addition*], I say unto you that I have caused that ye

should assemble yourselves together, that I might declare unto you that **I can no longer be your teacher, nor your king**;

In the next verse, King Benjamin announces that his son, Mosiah, will be the next king. Thus, in order, the people have had King Mosiah I (who led the people out of the land of Nephi and into the land of Zarahemla; see Omni 1:12–14), then King Benjamin, son of Mosiah I, and now Mosiah II, son of King Benjamin.

30 For even at this time, my whole frame [*body*] doth tremble exceedingly while attempting to speak unto you; but the Lord God doth support me, and hath suffered [*allowed; blessed*] me that I should speak unto you, and hath commanded me that I should declare unto you this day, that **my son Mosiah is a king and a ruler over you.**

31 And now, my brethren, I would that ye should do as ye have hitherto done [*as you have done up to now*]. As ye have kept my commandments, and also the commandments of my father [*Mosiah I*], and have prospered, and have been kept from falling into the hands of your enemies, even so **if ye shall keep the commandments of my son, or the commandments of God which shall be delivered unto you by him, ye shall prosper in the land, and your enemies shall have no power over you**.

King Benjamin paid a high compliment to his son, Mosiah, in verse 31, above. He told the people that Mosiah would follow the Lord so closely that he would never give them commandments which were not in harmony with God's will. Next, he warns his people against one of Satan's most effective tools: contention. Contention (fighting, quarreling, arguing, being rude to each other, etc.) drives the Holy Ghost away and opens the door for the spirit of the devil.

32 But, O my people, **beware** [*watch out*] **lest there shall arise contentions among you**, and ye list to [*wish to, desire to*] obey the evil spirit, which was spoken of by my father Mosiah.

Next, King Benjamin will point out how serious it is to knowingly become an evil person.

33 For behold, **there is a wo** [*a very serious consequence*] **pronounced upon him who listeth** [*desires*] **to obey that spirit** [*the devil*]; for if he listeth to obey him, and remaineth [*does not repent*] and dieth in his sins, the same drinketh damnation to his own soul [*has chosen to be stopped in his eternal progression*]; for he receiveth for his wages an everlasting punishment [*in other words, he has earned everlasting punishment; see verses 38–39 for King Benjamin's definition of "everlasting punishment"*], having transgressed the law of God contrary to his own knowledge [*he knowingly chose evil*].

Verse 33, above, contains a powerful lesson on agency. King Benjamin emphasized the word "listeth" to follow Satan's ways, in other words, wanting to do evil and be wicked and not repenting of it. Such behavior brings "damnation." "Damnation," "damned," and other forms of this scriptural word mean "to be stopped." In other words, it means being stopped in terms of returning to the presence of God to live with Him forever.

Next, in verse 34, King Benjamin emphasizes that the people who are listening to him, except for their little children, are accountable because they have been taught.

34 I say unto you, that **there are not any among you, except it be your little children that have not been taught concerning these things**, but what knoweth that ye are eternally indebted to your heavenly Father, to render [*give*] to him all that you have and are; **and also have been taught concerning the records** [*the scriptures*] which contain the prophecies which have been spoken by the holy prophets, even down to the time our father, Lehi, left Jerusalem [*600 BC*]; [*In other words, his people had been taught what we would know basically as the Old Testament, down to and including the words of Jeremiah, who lived at the time Lehi left Jerusalem.*]

35 **And also, all that has been spoken by our fathers** [*ancestors, including Lehi, Nephi, Jacob, and others*] **until now**. And behold, also, they spake that which was commanded them of the Lord; therefore, they are just [*exactly on target*] and true.

Again, King Benjamin will emphasize the seriousness of sinning against knowledge and he will explain the consequences of so doing.

36 And now, I say unto you, my brethren, that **after ye have known** and have been taught all these things, **if ye should transgress** [*sin*] and go contrary to [*against*] that which has been spoken, that **ye do withdraw yourselves from the Spirit of the Lord, that it may have no place in you to guide you in wisdom's paths that ye may be blessed, prospered, and preserved—**

37 I say unto you, that the man that doeth this, the same **cometh out in open rebellion against God; therefore he listeth to** [*wants to*] **obey the evil spirit, and becometh an enemy to all righteousness** [*thinks and acts like Satan himself does; compare with D&C 76:31–35*]; therefore [*this is why*], **the Lord has no place in him, for he dwelleth not in unholy temples.**

In verse 33, King Benjamin used the term "everlasting punishment." In verses 38–39, next, he explains what he meant by that term.

38 Therefore **if** that man **repenteth not**, and remaineth **and dieth an enemy to God,** the demands of divine justice [*the law of justice*] do awaken his immortal [*resurrected*] soul to **a lively sense of his own guilt,** which **doth cause him to shrink from the presence of the Lord,** and doth fill his breast with **guilt**, and **pain**, and **anguish**, which is **like an unquenchable fire**, whose flame ascendeth up **forever and ever**.

39 And now I say unto you, that mercy hath no claim on that man; therefore his final doom is to endure **a never–ending torment.**

In verses 38 and 39, above, the terms "justice" and "mercy" are used. These are very important words and must be understood in order to comprehend the scriptures and the Atonement of Christ. Simply put, the eternal law of justice is that for every sin that is committed, a penalty must be paid. The law of mercy is that Christ's Atonement paid that penalty for all sins. This puts Him in a position to offer us mercy. Since Christ suffered for, and thus paid for, all sins (2 Nephi 9:21), He can offer us mercy so that we don't have to endure the suffering that would otherwise be required of us to pay for our sins ourselves. See D&C 19:15–17. Part of the law of mercy is that we must repent and truly change for the better in order for Christ's payment for our sins to satisfy the law of justice for us. If we don't repent, His payment for our sins cannot remain in force, and we must pay for them ourselves (see D&C 19:15–19).

In the next two verses, King Benjamin teaches a basic course in wisdom, common sense, and perspective. It is interesting that when we step back and look at the "big picture" (perspective), being righteous is indeed common sense. In other words, if people have any common sense at all, they will see that personal righteousness is best for society as a whole and for each individual within the society.

40 O, all ye old men, and also ye young men, and you little children who can understand my words, for I have spoken plainly unto you that ye might understand, I pray that ye should awake to a remembrance of **the awful situation of those that have fallen into transgression** [*sin*].

41 And moreover, I would desire that ye should **consider on the blessed and happy state of those that keep the commandments of God.** For behold, they are blessed in all things, both temporal [*physical*] and spiritual; and **if they hold out faithful to the end they are received into heaven, that thereby they may dwell with God in a state of never–ending happiness.** O remember, remember that **these things are true**; for the Lord God hath spoken it.

MOSIAH 3

As King Benjamin continues his talk to his people, he tells them that he is going to prophesy about the Savior. He tells them that an angel appeared to him and taught him what he is now going to teach them. We can imagine that his people, who have already been listening carefully to him, now focus even more intently on every word.

1 AND again my brethren, I would call your attention, for I have somewhat more to speak unto you; for behold, **I have things to tell you concerning that which is to come.**

2 And the things which I shall tell you are **made known unto me by an angel from God**. And he said unto me: Awake; and I awoke, and behold he stood before me.

3 And he said unto me: Awake, and hear the words which I shall tell thee; for behold, **I am come to declare** [*explain*] **unto you the glad tidings of great joy**.

We know that King Benjamin and his people already knew of the future birth and mission of Christ. We, too, know of His birth and mission. With this in mind, there is a very beautiful and significant message to us as well as to Benjamin and his people in what the angel tells this righteous king, next.

In order to give a background and setting to the point we are about to make, we will note that some good members of the Church are consistently too hard on themselves. Perhaps they forget that many of the temple recommend questions include the phrase, "Are you striving?" or some variation of it, rather than the question, "Are you perfect?" They tend to emphasize their imperfections and shortcomings at the expense of humbly acknowledging their strengths. This becomes very damaging to them and can hold them back from progressing. The truly righteous seem to have a healthy balance between knowing that they need to improve and accepting that they have much good in them, whether or not they are consciously aware of this balance.

With this in mind, a major message to us in this part of King Benjamin's address is that we should allow ourselves to be happy, to enjoy much, to "rejoice," as stated by the angel in verse 4, next. This is one of the sweet "fruits" of the Atonement of Christ, of which we can partake right now in this life.

4 For the Lord hath heard thy prayers, and hath judged of thy righteousness, and hath sent me to declare unto thee that **thou mayest rejoice**; and that **thou mayest declare unto thy people, that they may also be filled with joy**.

Just a bit more about the message, "thou mayest rejoice," in verse 4, above. While serving as a bishop and later as a stake president, I noticed that some members seem to have a hard time allowing themselves to "rejoice" after having properly and deeply repented of serious sin. In discussing this with a number of them, it appears to me that Satan has a very damaging tool of destruction designed especially for those Saints who have successfully returned to full membership privileges after having lost their way for a season.

At first, after having worked their way back, there was great joy and satisfaction coupled with peace. However, at some point, Satan seemed to instill in them a sense of guilt for feeling so good. He seemed to try to tell them that, because of their former serious sins, they would always be "second-class citizens" in the Church. As he furthers his evil cause, Lucifer successfully gets such Saints thinking that it is unfair that they should have the same blessings and happiness as members who have never gotten off of the path as far as they did. This, of course, is false! All who are on the covenant path, whether having recently returned or having been on it all their lives, are told, in effect, "thou mayest rejoice."

In the October 2000 general conference of the Church, Elder Richard G. Scott, of the Quorum of the Twelve Apostles, powerfully confirmed that, once a person has properly repented, there are no "second-class citizens" in the Church.

He said (**bold** added for emphasis), **"If you have repented from serious transgression and mistakenly believe that you will always be a second-class citizen in the kingdom of God, learn that is not true**. The Savior said: 'Behold, he who has repented of his sins, the same is forgiven, and I, the Lord, remember them no more. By this ye may know if a man repenteth of his sins—behold, he will confess them and forsake them' (D&C 58:42–43). Find encouragement in the lives of Alma the Younger and the sons of Mosiah. They were tragically wicked. Yet their full repentance and service qualified them to be considered as noble as righteous Captain Moroni (Alma 48:17–18)."

King Benjamin now continues, telling his people that the reason they can "rejoice" is because Christ will come to earth. Benjamin prophesies, using many powerful gospel terms. This is one of the finest descriptions of the Savior and His ministry anywhere in scripture. We will make many notes for the next several verses. You may wish to consider putting some of the notes we make here into your own scriptures.

First, in passing, we will just mention that the term "not far distant" in verse 5 turns out to be one hundred and twenty-four years, if you count the years from this time among the Nephites until the birth of Christ. If you count the years until the Savior begins His ministry, it is about one hundred and fifty-four years. The reason we mention this is that we live in the last days before the Second Coming and have several scriptures, such as D&C 106:4, in which we are told that the coming of the Lord is near. It is important for us to realize that a "short time" for the Lord can still be quite a few years for us.

5 For behold, **the time cometh, and is not far distant, that** with power, **the Lord** Omnipotent [*all-powerful*] who reigneth, who was, and is from all eternity to all eternity, **shall come down from heaven among the children of men** [*in other words, "among mortals"*], and shall dwell in a tabernacle of clay [*in a mortal body*], and shall go forth amongst men, **working mighty miracles**, such as healing the sick, raising the dead, causing the lame to walk, the blind to receive their sight, and the deaf to hear, and curing all manner of diseases.

The literal, physical miracles referred to in verse 5, above are all symbolic of the power of the Savior's Atonement to heal us spiritually. Therefore, every time you read of the Savior healing someone, it can remind you of His power to heal you spiritually.

6 And **he shall cast out devils**, or the evil spirits which dwell in the hearts of the children of men.

In addition to literally casting out devils and evil spirits, verse 6, above, can include "devils" such as anger, hatred, evil thoughts, grudges, etc., that "dwell in the hearts of the children of men."

Some have wondered if physical hunger, weariness, pain, etc., were really that hard on Jesus, or even if He was ever truly tempted, since He was the Son of God and could therefore choose not to suffer. King Benjamin addresses this issue next.

7 And lo, **he shall suffer temptations,** and **pain** of body, **hunger**, **thirst**, and **fatigue**, even **more than man can suffer,** except it be unto death [*in other words, it would kill a normal man*]; for behold, **blood cometh from every pore**, so great shall be his anguish [*suffering*] for the wickedness and the abominations of his people.

Another issue resolved in verse 7, above, is the question left by the Bible as to whether Jesus literally bled from every pore or if it was symbolic, rather than literal. The wording of Luke 22:44 is: "And being in an agony he prayed more earnestly: and **his sweat was as it were great drops of blood** falling down to the ground."

As you can see in verse 7, above, there is no question left after King Benjamin clearly stated that Jesus literally bled from every pore.

8 And **he shall be called Jesus Christ**, the Son of God, the Father of [*Creator of*] heaven and earth, the Creator of all things from the beginning; and **his mother shall be called Mary**.

In verse 8, above, these Nephite Saints are taught the Savior's name and some of His titles as follows:

His name: Jesus Christ

Titles

- The Son of God.
- The Father of heaven and earth (meaning, among other things, the Creator of our heavens and our earth).
- The Creator of all things.

King Benjamin's prophetic information is so specific that it even includes the name of the Savior's mortal mother, Mary! This is a reminder that the Lord's knowledge of the future is very specific. This great king continues with much more specific detail about the Savior's ministry and how all people can come unto Christ.

9 And lo, **he cometh** unto his own [*the Jews*], **that salvation might come unto the children of men** [*all people*] even **through faith on his name;** and even after all this **they** [*the Jews*] **shall consider him a man**, and **say that he hath a devil**, and shall **scourge him** [*whip Him*], and shall **crucify him.**

10 And **he shall rise the third day from the dead**; and behold, **he standeth to judge the world;** and behold, all these things are done that a righteous judgment might come upon the children of men. [*In other words, Christ's life and Atonement make it possible for all people to have a fair judgment.*]

11 For behold, and also his blood atoneth for the sins of those who have fallen by the transgression of Adam, **who have died not knowing the will of God concerning them, or who have ignorantly sinned**.

It is very important to keep verse 11, above, within the context of all the scriptures. Otherwise, we could come up with a false doctrine that those who die not knowing about Christ and the gospel are saved without any real effort on their part.

We might find ourselves thinking that they are lucky not to have had the gospel and wondering why we are so unfortunate as to have it in our lives, since it makes us accountable. Section 138 of the Doctrine and Covenants helps us to avoid such false thinking. and to understand that the people in verse 11, above, are not accountable for sins committed in ignorance. They still must repent and accept the gospel when given the opportunity in the spirit world mission field. Thus, they are ultimately not disadvantaged by not having had the gospel during their mortal lives (in other words, God is completely fair to them, too) and will have the opportunity to accept or reject it in the spirit world, which time comes before the Final Judgment Day. Therefore, all people will have a completely fair set of chances to accept or reject the full gospel, before the Final Judgment Day. We will use D&C 138:29–35 to explain this:

D&C 138:29–35

29 And as I wondered, my eyes were opened, and my understanding quickened, and I perceived that the Lord went not in person among the wicked and the disobedient who had rejected the truth, to teach them;

30 But behold, **from among the righteous, he organized his forces and appointed messengers, clothed with power and authority, and commissioned them to go forth and carry the light of the gospel to them that were in darkness, even to all the spirits of men;** and **thus was the gospel preached to the dead.**

31 And the chosen messengers went forth to declare the acceptable day of the Lord and proclaim liberty to the captives who were bound, **even unto all who would repent of their sins and receive the gospel.**

32 **Thus was the gospel preached to those who had died** in their sins, **without a knowledge of the truth, or in transgression,** having rejected the prophets.

33 These were taught **faith** in God, **repentance** from sin, vicarious **baptism** for the remission of sins, **the gift of the Holy Ghost** by the laying on of hands,

34 And **all other principles of the gospel** that were **necessary for them to know in order to qualify themselves that they might be judged according to men in the flesh,** but live according to God in the spirit.

35 **And so it was made known among the dead, both small and great, the unrighteous as well as the faithful, that redemption had been wrought through the sacrifice of the Son of God upon the cross.**

Now we will return to King Benjamin's address, in which he will remind those of us who have the gospel here during mortality how serious it is that we live it and that we use the gift of repentance and forgiveness.

12 **But wo, wo unto him who knoweth that he rebelleth against God!** For **salvation cometh to none such except it be through repentance and faith on the Lord Jesus Christ.**

13 And the Lord God hath sent his holy prophets among all the children of men, to declare these things to every kindred, nation, and tongue, that thereby whosoever should believe that Christ should come, the same might **receive remission of their sins, and rejoice with exceedingly great joy, even as though he had already come among them.**

In verse 13, above, we are taught that the Atonement of Christ worked for people before it was even performed. This is a wonderful aspect of the Atonement. It is indeed infinite! Thus, by some miraculous power that we may not understand, but certainly can gratefully accept, the power of the Atonement was in effect before the Savior entered mortality to perform it for all of us.

In fact, even though the Savior's Atonement was performed before we came to earth, we ourselves have great reason to be grateful that it worked before He accomplished it. Why? Because we needed it during our premortal lives, and it worked for us there also! Elder Jeffrey R. Holland spoke of this in the October 1995 general conference of the Church as follows (**bold** added for emphasis):

"We could remember that even in the Grand Council of Heaven He loved us and was wonderfully strong, that **we triumphed even there by the power of Christ and our faith in the blood of the Lamb**" (Jeffrey R. Holland, "This Do in Remembrance of Me," *Ensign*, Nov. 1995, 67).

A quote from the Institute of Religion student manual for the New Testament shows that we had agency in premortality and that we could exercise faith and repent from sins there. In it we read (**bold** added for emphasis):

"We were given laws and agency, and commandments to have faith **and repent from the wrongs that we could do there** . . . Man could and did in many instances, sin before he was born . . ." (Institute of Religion, *New Testament Student Manual*, 1979, Rel. 211–12, 336).

In conclusion, the Atonement of Christ has blessed our lives already, for eons of time during our premortal existence as spirit children of our Heavenly Parents, and it is blessing us now again as mortals.

Next, King Benjamin will explain to his people why the Law of Moses was necessary. The Law of Moses was the set of Old Testament "schoolmaster" laws, rituals, sacrifices and commandments (see Galatians 3:24; see also Bible Dictionary, pages 722–23 under "Law of Moses) given by God through Moses in order to prepare the prideful and rebellious Israelites to receive the gospel of Christ.

14 Yet the Lord God saw that his people [*the children of Israel*] were a stiffnecked [*prideful*] people, and he appointed unto them a law, even the **law of Moses**.

15 And many signs, and wonders, and **types, and shadows showed he unto them, concerning his coming**; and also holy prophets spake unto them concerning his coming; and **yet they hardened their hearts, and understood not that the law**

of Moses availeth nothing [*does not bring salvation*] **except it were through the atonement of his blood.** [*In other words, the Atonement of Christ is the only thing that can bring exaltation in the celestial kingdom.*]

The Jews became very set in their false traditions that taught that the Law of Moses could bring salvation. So much so, in fact, that they crucified Jesus when He taught otherwise.

In verse 15, above, King Benjamin used the terms "types and shadows." It is very important to understand what these words mean. Simply put, "types" and "shadows" mean "symbols," which include symbols depicting the Savior, designed to point people's minds toward Christ. For instance, the lambs without blemish, which were sacrificed by the shedding of their blood, under the requirements of the Law of Moses, were symbolic of Christ and His shedding of His blood for us. They were "types and shadows" of Christ.

Abraham was a "type" of the Father and Isaac was a "type" of the Son. See Genesis 22:1–13. Isaac carried the wood for his sacrifice (Genesis 22:6) and Christ carried the cross for His sacrifice (John 19:17). Abraham was very old, and so it is obvious that Isaac was obedient to his father and was willing to be sacrificed. Christ was obedient to the Father and voluntarily gave His life for us (John 10:18). Abraham and Isaac journeyed three days to get to the place where Isaac was to be sacrificed (Genesis 22:4). Christ's three-year mission culminated in His Crucifixion. The place designated by the Lord for Isaac to be sacrificed was Moriah (Genesis 22:2). This is part of the same mount upon which Christ was sacrificed. These parallels readily demonstrate that Isaac was a "type" of Christ.

Finally, the rituals and requirements of the Law of Moses were full of Atonement symbolism or "types and shadows" of Christ and His redeeming sacrifice for us. This sacrifice allows us to be freed from sin and become new persons, "born again," with new opportunities for progression. One excellent example of this aspect of the Law of Moses is found in Leviticus 14:1–9. We will include these verses here with notes and **bold** added for teaching purposes.

Leviticus 14:1–9

1 And the LORD spake unto Moses, saying,

2 This shall be the **law of the leper** [*leprosy, a very serious disease, can be symbolic of serious sin and great need for help and cleansing*] in the day of his cleansing: **He shall be brought unto the priest** [*symbolic of the need to have help from an authorized servant of God—bishop, stake president, etc.—in order to overcome grevious sin*]:

3 And **the priest shall go forth out of the camp** [*the person with leprosy did not have fellowship with the Lord's people and was required to live outside the main camp of the Children of Israel; the bishop, symbolically, goes out of the way to help sinners who want to repent*]; and **the priest shall look, and, behold** [*see*], **if the plague of leprosy be healed in the leper** [*the bishop serves as a judge to see if the repentant sinner is ready to return*

to full membership privileges and associate without restrictions with the Saints];

4 Then shall the priest command to take for him that is to be cleansed [*the person who has repented*] **two birds** [*one represents the Savior, the other represents the person who has repented*] **alive *and* clean** [*symbolizing that we can become clean and without sin, like the Savior, through His Atonement*], and **cedar wood** [*symbolic of the cross*], and **scarlet** [*associated with mocking Christ before his crucifixion, Mark 15:17*], and **hyssop** [*associated with Christ on the cross, John 19:29*]:

5 And the priest shall command that **one of the birds** [*symbolic of the Savior*] **be killed in an earthen vessel** [*Christ was sent to earth to die for us*] **over running water** [*Christ offers "living water," John 7:37–38, which cleanses us*]:

6 As for **the living bird** [*representing the person who has repented*], **he** [*the priest; symbolic of the bishop, stake president, etc.*] **shall take it** [*the living bird*], **and** the **cedar wood**, and the **scarlet**, and the **hyssop** [*all associated with the Atonement; see verse 4*], and shall **dip them and the living bird in the blood of the bird *that was* killed** over the running water [*representing the Savior's blood, which was shed for us*]:

7 And **he** [*the priest, symbolizing authorized priesthood holders performing ordinances of salvation for us*] **shall sprinkle** [*the blood*] **upon him that is to be cleansed from the leprosy** [*cleansed from sin, symbolically*] **seven times** [*seven is the number that, in numeric symbolism, represents completeness, perfection*], and **shall pronounce him clean,** and **shall let the living bird** [*the person who has repented*] **loose into the open field** [*representing the wide open opportunities again available in the kingdom of God for the person who truly repents*].

8 And **he that is to be cleansed shall wash his clothes, and shave off all his hair** [*symbolic of becoming like a newborn baby; fresh start*], and **wash himself in water** [*symbolic of baptism*], **that he may be clean**: and **after that he shall come into the camp** [*rejoin the Lord's people*], and shall tarry abroad out of [*outside of*] his tent seven days.

9 But it shall be on the seventh day, that **he shall shave all his hair off his head and his beard and his eyebrows, even all his hair he shall shave off** [*symbolic of being "born again"*]: and he shall wash his clothes, also **he shall wash his flesh in water** [*symbolic of baptism*], and **he shall be clean** [*a simple fact—namely, that we can truly be cleansed and healed by the Savior's Atonement*].

We will now return to King Benjamin's address. He will remind us that little children are not held accountable for sins because the Atonement takes care of them.

16 And even if it were possible that little children could sin they could not be saved; but I say unto you they are blessed; for behold, as in Adam, or by nature, they fall, even so **the blood of Christ atoneth for their sins.**

It is a common doctrine among some Christian religions that children are "conceived in sin" and are thus unclean. Therefore, they must be baptized as infants. If they are not, and they die, they are doomed forever and can never enter heaven. Verse 16, above, exposes this as a terrible false doctrine. Moroni, chapter 8, is a strong rejection of this evil doctrine. D&C 68:25 tells us that the age for children to be baptized is eight. And D&C 137:10 teaches that "all children who die before they arrive at the age of accountability are saved in the celestial kingdom of heaven."

Finally, President Joseph F. Smith taught that these little children will be exalted. He said that they "will inherit their exaltation," (*Gospel Doctrine,* Deseret Book, 1919 edition, page 453). From this, we understand that they will be given the chance to choose a mate, be married by the sealing power of the priesthood during the Millennium, and proceed to their exaltation on or before Final Judgment. In fact, Joseph Fielding Smith said that these children will choose companions during the Millennium and will then reveal this information to righteous mortals during that time who will be sealed by proxy for them (*Doctrines of Salvation*, Bookcraft Inc., 1956, volume 3, page 65).

As we continue with King Benjamin's address, remember that he has just taught his people that they cannot be saved through the Law of Moses. He now emphasizes that there is absolutely no other way to be saved, meaning celestial glory and exaltation, other than through Jesus Christ.

17 And moreover, I say unto you, that there shall be **no other name given nor any other way nor means whereby salvation can come unto the children of men, only in and through the name of Christ**, the Lord Omnipotent [*the Lord All-powerful*].

18 For behold he judgeth, and **his judgment is just** [*completely fair*]; and the infant perisheth not that dieth in his infancy [*see note for verse 16, above*]; but men drink damnation to their own souls [*men cause the destruction of their own souls*] except [*unless*] they humble themselves and become as little children, and believe that salvation was, and is, and is to come, in and through the atoning blood of Christ, the Lord Omnipotent.

The word "salvation," as used in this context, means exaltation in celestial glory.

Verses 18 and 19 contain what is known as "chiasmus." Chiasmus is a writing technique developed in ancient times that emphasizes certain words and phrases then lists these same words and phrases in reverse order. It is a literary style and technique that was discovered in ancient writings, including Isaiah, long after the Book of Mormon was published. Thus, discovering it in the Book of Mormon is strong internal evidence that Joseph Smith truly translated it from an ancient record.

Chiastic structure can be denoted by letters, for example: A B C D, and then the reverse order, D' C' B' A'. Chiastic structures can be any length. For instance: eyes, ears, hearts, hearts, ears, eyes. Normally, the middle word or words are the central focus of the thought. Thus, in our simple example above, "hearts" would be the main focus.

We will print verses 18 and 19 here for teaching purposes, and we will **bold** and **underline** the chiasmus contained in them. See if you can pick out the main focus or center of attention around which the other teachings and concepts revolve. We will denote each element of the chiasmus with a capital letter.

18 For behold he judgeth, and his judgment is just; and the infant perisheth not that dieth in his infancy; but men drink damnation to their own souls except they **humble (A)** themselves and **become as little children (B)**, and believe that salvation was, and is, and is to come, in and through **the atoning blood of Christ (C)**, the Lord Omnipotent.

19 For **the natural man (D)** is an enemy to God, and has been from the fall of Adam, and will be, forever and ever, unless he yields to the enticings of the Holy Spirit, and putteth off **the natural man (D')** and becometh a saint through **the atonement of Christ (C')** the Lord, and **becometh as a child (B')**, submissive, meek, **humble (A')**, patient, full of love, willing to submit to all things which the Lord seeth fit to inflict upon him, even as a child doth submit to his father.

As you can see, the central focus is avoiding the character traits of the "natural man." We will now continue by printing verse 19 again, which is a famous and often-quoted verse in the Book of Mormon. King Benjamin teaches us how to avoid becoming "natural men and women."

19 For the natural man is an enemy to God, and has been from the fall of Adam, and will be, forever and ever, **unless he yields to the enticings of the Holy Spirit**, and **putteth off the natural man** [*an intentional agency choice*] and **becometh a saint through the atonement of Christ the Lord**, and **becometh as a child, submissive, meek, humble, patient, full of love, willing to submit to all things which the Lord seeth fit to inflict upon him, even as a child doth submit to his father.**

As we study verse 19, above, we must understand that people are not "naturally" evil. In other words, the "natural man" is not born that way. Rather, people become that way by violating God's commandments. This is clearly taught in Alma as follows:

Alma 41:11

11 And now, my son, **all men that are in a state of nature**, or I would say, in a carnal state, are in the gall of bitterness and in the bonds of iniquity; they are without God in the world, and they **have gone contrary to the nature of God**; therefore, they are in a state contrary to the nature of happiness.

A similar reference is found in Moses as follows:

Moses 6:49

49 Behold Satan hath come among the children of men, and tempteth them to worship him; and **men have become carnal, sensual, and devilish**, and are shut out from the presence of God.

20 And moreover, I say unto you, that the time shall come when **the knowledge of a Savior shall spread throughout every nation, kindred** [*groups of related people*], **tongue, and people.** [*We understand that this will take place during the last days and the Millennium, and that those missed here on earth will get their opportunity in the spirit world.*]

21 And behold, when that time cometh [*after everyone has had fair opportunity to understand and accept or reject the gospel*], **none shall be found blameless** [*without accountability; see verse 22, below*] **before God**, except it be little children, **only** [*except*] **through repentance and faith on the name of the Lord God Omnipotent.** [*In other words, all, except little children, will eventually be held accountable for their behaviors, and all can become pure and clean through the Savior's Atonement.*]

> Remember that King Benjamin is telling his people what the angel mentioned in verse 2 of this chapter told him to teach his people. Therefore, in verse 22, next, we are reading the words of the angel, which began in verse 3.

22 And even at this time, when thou [*King Benjamin*] shalt have taught thy people the things which the Lord thy God hath commanded thee, **even then are they found no more blameless in the sight of God**, only [*except*] according to the words which I have spoken unto thee [*in other words, unless they repent*].

23 And now **I have spoken the words which the Lord God hath commanded me.**

> Again, in the next four verses, King Benjamin repeats to his people that they are accountable and warns them of the personal tragedy and misery that come from evil choices and the resulting behaviors. As he does this, he briefly reviews the laws of justice and mercy.

24 And thus saith the Lord: They [*the words which I have taught you*] shall stand as a bright testimony against this people, at the judgment day; whereof **they shall be judged, every man according to his works, whether they be good, or whether they be evil.**

25 And **if they be evil** they are consigned [*doomed*] to an awful view of their own guilt and abominations [*they will see themselves as they really are*], which doth cause them to shrink [*step back*] from the presence of the Lord into a state of misery and endless torment, from whence they can no more return; therefore they have drunk damnation to their own souls [*they are responsible for what they receive on Judgment Day*].

> Remember, as you read the next two verses, that King Benjamin clearly taught in verses 20–21, and we know from D&C 138, that before Final Judgment Day, everyone (who lived past age eight because little children are not accountable before God) will have had a completely fair opportunity to hear, understand, accept, or reject the gospel. This opportunity will either come here on earth or it will come to them in the spirit world mission field or beyond. Therefore, King Benjamin is speaking of those who willfully and intentionally rebel against God's commandments.

26 Therefore, they have drunk out of the cup of the wrath of God [*they have internalized behaviors that have led to their own damnation*], which **justice** [*the law of justice*] could no more deny unto them than it could deny that Adam should fall because of his partaking of the forbidden fruit; therefore, **mercy** [*the law of mercy*] could have claim on them no more forever.

27 And **their torment is as a lake of fire and brimstone** [*fire and molten sulphur*], whose flames are unquenchable [*can't be put out*], and whose smoke ascendeth up forever and ever. Thus hath the Lord commanded me. Amen.

MOSIAH 4

As we continue, we will see that King Benjamin's people took his words very seriously. Even though they are righteous, they have been made keenly aware of the serious dangers posed by sin and are very desirous that the Atonement work for them. We would likewise do well to pay close and serious attention to the words of our living prophets today. This is one of the major reasons Mormon was inspired to include these next verses in the stack of gold plates which Moroni gave to Joseph Smith to translate.

1 AND now, it came to pass that when king Benjamin had made an end of speaking the words which had been delivered unto him by the angel of the Lord, that he cast his eyes round about on the multitude, and behold **they had fallen to the earth, for the fear of the Lord had come upon them**.

2 And they had viewed themselves in their own carnal state [*they saw their vulnerability to temptation and sin*], even less than the dust of the earth. And they all cried aloud with one voice, saying: **O have mercy, and apply the atoning blood of Christ that we may receive forgiveness of our sins, and our hearts may be purified; for we believe in Jesus Christ, the Son of God**, who created heaven and earth, and all things; who shall come down among the children of men [*mortals*].

We need to be a bit careful not to misinterpret the phrase "even less that the dust of the earth" in verse 2, above, to mean "worthless." We know of the tremendous worth of each soul from reading D&C 18:10. Therefore, "less than the dust of the earth" would be an expression of humility.

Sometimes, members wonder how to tell whether their sins are forgiven and if they are in good standing with God. The answer is clearly given in verse 3, below.

3 And it came to pass that after they had spoken these words **the Spirit of the Lord came upon them**, and **they were filled with joy**, having received a remission of their sins, and having **peace of conscience**, because of the exceeding faith which they had in Jesus Christ who should come, according to the words which king Benjamin had spoken unto them.

Next, in loving kindness, King Benjamin tells his people to listen carefully to what he still has to say to them.

4 And king Benjamin again opened his mouth and began to speak unto them, saying: **My friends and my brethren, my kindred and my people**, I would again call your attention, that ye may **hear and understand the remainder of my words** which I shall speak unto you.

5 For behold, if the knowledge of the goodness of God at this time has awakened you to **a sense of your nothingness** [*compared to God; see Moses 1:10*], and your worthless and fallen state—[*without the Atonement constantly working in your lives*]

Next, King Benjamin will teach us how we can keep the Atonement constantly working in our lives.

6 I say unto you, if ye have come to a knowledge of the goodness of God, and his matchless power, and his wisdom, and his patience, and his long-suffering towards the children of men; and also, the atonement which has been prepared from the foundation of the world [*which was planned in the premortal councils*], that thereby salvation might come to him that should put his **trust in the Lord**, and should **be diligent** [*constant and steady*] **in keeping his commandments**, and **continue in the faith even unto the end of his life,** I mean the life of the mortal body—

7 I say, that **this is the man who receiveth salvation, through the atonement** which was prepared from the foundation of the world [*from the time of premortality*] for all mankind, which ever were since the fall of Adam, or who are, or who ever shall be, even unto the end of the world [*the Atonement is available to everyone*].

8 And this is the means whereby salvation cometh. And **there is none other salvation** save this which hath been spoken of; **neither are there any conditions whereby man can be saved except the conditions which I have told you**. [*In other words, there is no other way, to gain salvation, meaning, in this context, exaltation in the highest degree of glory in the celestial kingdom.*]

9 **Believe in God; believe that he is**, and **that he created all things**, both in heaven and in earth; **believe that he has all wisdom**, and **all power**, both in heaven and in earth; **believe that man doth not comprehend all the things which the Lord can comprehend**. [*Don't try to figure it all out intellectually or academically; rather, accept it on faith.*]

10 And again, **believe** [*this is an action word, not a passive intellectual state of being*] **that ye must repent of your sins and forsake them**, and **humble yourselves** before God; and **ask in sincerity of heart that he would forgive you;** and now, **if you believe all these things see that ye do them.**

Next, King Benjamin will teach us how to retain a remission of our sins on an ongoing basis throughout our lives.

11 And again I say unto you as I have said before, that **as ye have come to the knowledge of the glory of God,** or **if ye have known of his goodness and have tasted of his love,** and **have received a remission of your sins, which causeth such exceedingly great joy in your souls,** even so I would that ye should remember, and **always retain in remembrance, the greatness of God,** and **your own nothingness** [*your inability to save yourselves*], and his goodness and long-suffering towards you, unworthy creatures, and **humble yourselves** even in the depths of humility, **calling on the name of the Lord daily,** and **standing steadfastly in the faith** of that which is to come, which was spoken by the mouth of the angel [*having faith in Jesus Christ*].

12 And behold, I say unto you that **if ye do this ye shall** always rejoice, and be filled with the love of God, and **always retain a remission of your sins;** and ye shall grow in the knowledge of the glory of him that created you, or in the knowledge of that which is just and true.

13 And ye will **not have a mind to injure one another, but to live peaceably,** and to **render to every man according to that which is his due** [*be fair and honest with each other*].

14 [*You will be responsible parents.*] And **ye will not suffer** [*permit*] **your children that they go hungry, or naked** [*go without adequate food and clothing*]; **neither will ye suffer** [*allow*] **that they transgress the laws of God,** and **fight** and **quarrel** one with another, and **serve the devil,** who is the master of sin, or who is the evil spirit which hath been spoken of by our fathers [*ancestors; past prophets*], he being an enemy to all righteousness.

In verse 14, above, we are clearly taught that contention, fighting, quarreling, etc., are obvious ways of serving the devil.

15 But ye will **teach them to walk in the ways of truth and soberness** [*being serious about sacred things*]; ye will **teach them to love one another,** and **to serve one another.**

One of the most famous parts of King Benjamin's address is found in verses 16–25. It deals with our attitudes toward beggars. He reminds us that we are all beggars, so to speak, in critical need of help from God. Our attitudes and actions toward those whom we are in a position to help will in great measure determine how we are treated on Judgment Day.

16 And also, **ye yourselves will succor** [*rush to the aid of*] **those that stand in need** of your succor [*help*]; ye will administer of your substance [*give of your money, time, food, etc.*] unto him that standeth in need; and ye will not suffer [*allow*] that the beggar putteth up his petition to you [*begs for help from you*] in vain [*without success*], and turn him out to perish.

As King Benjamin continues his instruction and teaching regarding how we treat beggars, he teaches us to view them with kindness and patience, as God would. He is trying to help us learn to think the way God does. He is teaching us that God blesses us in spite of our foolishness and imperfections.

17 **Perhaps thou shalt say: The man has brought upon himself his misery; therefore I will stay my hand** [*hold back*], and will not give unto him of my food, nor impart [*give*] unto him of my substance that he may not suffer, for his punishments are just [*he deserves the trouble he is in*]—

18 But I say unto you, O man, **whosoever doeth this the same hath great cause to repent;** and except he repenteth of that which he hath done he perisheth forever, and hath no interest in the kingdom of God [*will not even come close to getting into heaven*].

19 For behold, **are we not all beggars?** Do we not all depend upon the same Being, even God, for all the substance which we have, for both food and raiment [*clothing*], and for gold, and for silver, and for all the riches which we have of every kind?

20 And behold, **even at this time, ye have been calling on his name, and begging for a remission of your sins**. And **has he suffered that ye have begged in vain? Nay;** he has **poured out his Spirit** upon you, and has caused that your **hearts** should be **filled with joy,** and has caused that your mouths should be stopped that **ye could not find utterance** [*you couldn't even speak*], **so exceedingly great was your joy**. [*In other words, God has been overwhelmingly generous with you, in spite of your shortcomings and imperfections.*]

21 And now, **if God**, who has created you, on whom you are dependent for your lives and for all that ye have and are, **doth grant unto you whatsoever ye ask that is right,** in faith, believing that ye shall receive, **O then, how ye ought to impart of the substance that ye have one to another.**

22 And **if ye judge the man** who putteth up his petition [*who begs*] to you for your substance that he perish not, **and condemn him** [*refuse to help him because you judge him as deserving the trouble he is in*], **how much more just will be your condemnation** for withholding your substance, which doth not belong to you but to God, to whom also your life belongeth; and yet ye put up no petition, nor repent of the thing which thou hast done.

In verses 23–25, King Benjamin points out that he is aware that some people do not have the means to give generously to others and explains that, in those cases, they will be judged by their attitudes.

23 I say unto you, wo be unto that man, for his substance shall perish with him; and now, **I say these things unto those who are rich as pertaining to the things of this world.**

24 And again, **I say unto the poor**, ye who have not and yet have sufficient, that ye remain from day to day [*you have just barely enough to stay alive*

yourselves]; I mean **all you who deny the beggar, because ye have not;** I would that ye **say in your hearts that: I give not because I have not, but if I had I would give.**

25 And now, **if ye say this in your hearts** [*in other words, if you really mean it*] **ye remain guiltless, otherwise ye are condemned;** and your condemnation is just [*fair*] for ye covet that which ye have not received.

Remember that King Benjamin has been teaching his people how to keep an ongoing remission of sins in their lives, since verse 11. He now summarizes what he has taught on this subject.

26 **And now**, for the sake of these things which I have spoken unto you—that is, **for the sake of retaining a remission of your sins from day to day,** that ye may walk guiltless before God—I would that ye should **impart of your substance to the poor, every man according to that which he hath, such as feeding the hungry, clothing the naked, visiting the sick and administering to their relief, both spiritually and temporally, according to their wants.**

Perhaps you noticed a very important teaching in verse 26, above—namely, that giving generously to "beggars" does not necessarily always have to do with money or material things. Rather, it can also have to do with time and effort, giving kindness, visiting the sick, etc.

It would obviously be possible for people to give everything to "beggars" such that they or their family could be reduced to abject poverty, or to the point that they don't have money to pay the rent or keep up with their other financial obligations, etc. Next, we are taught a vital lesson about the importance of wisdom and balance in such things.

27 And **see that all these things are done in wisdom and order; for it is not requisite** [*required*] **that a man should run faster than he has strength** [*the same message is found in D&C 10:4*]. And again, it is expedient [*necessary*] that he should be diligent, that thereby he might win the prize [*exaltation*]; therefore, **all things must be done in order.**

Next, King Benjamin summarizes the principle of honesty with a very simple example from everyday life.

28 And I would that ye should remember, that **whosoever** [*whoever*] among you **borroweth** of his neighbor **should return the thing** that he borroweth, **according as he doth agree, or else thou shalt commit sin; and perhaps thou shalt cause thy neighbor to commit sin also.**

Sometimes, members of the Church wish that the Church leaders would more specifically spell out what is sin and what is not. For instance, they wish that they would be more specific about what members should and should not do on the Sabbath. King Benjamin has a good answer for this in verse 29.

29 And finally, **I cannot tell you all the things whereby ye may commit**

sin; for there are divers [*various*] ways and means, even so many that I cannot number them.

30 But **this much I can tell you, that if ye do not watch** yourselves, and your **thoughts**, and your **words**, and your **deeds**, and **observe the commandments of God,** and **continue** in the faith of what ye have heard concerning the coming of our Lord, **even unto the end of your lives, ye must perish.** And now, O man, **remember, and perish not.**

MOSIAH 5

This is the final chapter of King Benjamin's address. In it, he will give his people another name, the name of Christ, as promised in Mosiah 1:11. He will also define what it means to become "sons" and "daughters" of Christ. We will be taught the importance of making and keeping covenants, such as baptism, taking the sacrament, temple marriage, etc. As we begin this chapter, we will be reminded that faith, commitment, and testimony are necessary for effective covenant making. As the chapter begins, King Benjamin wants to know whether or not his people believe in the talk he just gave them.

1 AND now, it came to pass that when king Benjamin had thus spoken to his people, **he sent among them, desiring to know of his people if they believed the words which he had spoken unto them**.

2 And they all cried with one voice, saying: **Yea, we believe** all the words which thou hast spoken unto us; and also, **we know of their surety and truth, because of the Spirit of the Lord Omnipotent** [*All-powerful*], **which has wrought** [*caused*] **a mighty change in us,** or in our hearts, that **we have no more disposition to do evil, but to do good continually.**

In verse 2, above, we are taught one way to tell if we have the Holy Ghost with us; namely, we do not desire evil and we want to do good.

In verse 3, next, we see the great value of having the companionship of the Holy Ghost in our lives. For instance, we can see where our choices will lead us. The Holy Ghost may also help us to see potential in another which other people can't see. Yet another manifestation of having the Holy Ghost with us would be knowing that the Second Coming of the Savior will absolutely happen.

3 And **we,** ourselves, also, **through** the infinite goodness of God, and **the manifestations of his Spirit, have great views of that which is to come;** and were it expedient [*necessary*], we could prophesy of all things.

In verse 4, next, we are taught the importance of faith in helping us learn and live the gospel.

4 And **it is** the **faith** which we have had on the things which our king has spoken unto us **that has brought us to this great knowledge,** whereby we do rejoice with such exceedingly great joy.

Next, we see the covenant which King Benjamin's people are willing to make, in order to be known as "children" of Christ. It is the same covenant which we make at baptism and each time we partake of the sacrament, as well as in other sacred covenant-making settings.

5 And **we are willing to enter into a covenant** with our God **to do his will**, and **to be obedient to his commandments** in all things that he shall command us, **all the remainder of our days**, that we may not bring upon ourselves a never–ending torment [*for instance, the torment of knowing that we could have achieved celestial glory but didn't*], as has been spoken by the angel, that we may not drink out of the cup of the wrath of God [*that we may not bring the punishments of God upon us*].

6 And now, these are the words which king Benjamin desired of them; and therefore he said unto them: **Ye have spoken the words that I desired; and the covenant which ye have made is a righteous covenant**.

Next, King Benjamin summarizes the results of making and keeping covenants with God. Being called "the children of Christ" is another way of saying "born again." And, if we qualify to be called "children of Christ" on the Final Judgment Day, it would be another way of saying that we have attained exaltation. Verse 7 has beautiful symbolism.

7 And now, **because of the covenant** which ye have made **ye shall be called the children of Christ, his sons, and his daughters;** for behold, this day **he hath spiritually begotten you** [*in other words, you are his "spiritual children," and you are "growing up" to become like Him*]; for ye say that your hearts are changed through faith on his name; therefore, **ye are born of him** [*spiritually*] **and have become his sons and his daughters.**

When you understand the phrase, "have become his sons and his daughters" in verse 7, above, it opens the door to understanding the meaning of other passages of scripture which use similar symbolism. For instance, Doctrine and Covenants 76:24, which reads as follows:

D&C 76:24

24 That by him [*Christ*], and through him, and of him, the worlds are and were created, and **the inhabitants thereof are begotten sons and daughters unto God.**

Understanding the meaning of the last phrase in verse 24, above, allows you to understand that the inhabitants of other earths can also achieve exaltation through the Atonement of Christ. In fact, Christ will visit them, also (see D&C 88:51–61), but he will not be born and crucified again on each of those worlds. Rather, His Atonement on our earth provides the same opportunities for them as it does for us.

At this point, some of you will have the question come up in your minds as to whether or not we will have to provide a savior for our own worlds if we become gods, or if we can use the Savior's Atonement for our spirit children as we send them to our worlds to work out their salvation as we had to do. The answer is, "We don't know." You may wish to come to the beginning of the Millennium (whether you are alive or recently resurrected), where we will find out the answers to all of our questions. See D&C 101:32–34.

8 And under this head [*Christ*] ye are made free [*compare with John 8:32*], and there is no other head whereby ye can be made free. **There is no other name given whereby salvation cometh** [*in other words, there is no other way to be saved, other than through Christ*]; therefore, **I would that ye should take upon you the name of Christ,** all you that have entered into the covenant with God that ye should be obedient unto the end of your lives.

Next, in verse 9, King Benjamin uses the term "right hand of God." In scriptural symbolism, "right hand" is the covenant hand. Being found on the "right hand of God" is another way of saying that you have kept your covenants and thus been saved in celestial glory. The phrase "left hand of God" means that you didn't make and keep covenants. Thus, you failed to have a pleasant Judgment Day. You did not make it to heaven. See verses 10 and 12.

9 And it shall come to pass that **whosoever doeth this** [*makes and keeps covenants with God*] **shall be found at the right hand of God,** for he shall know the name [*Christ*] by which he is called; for he shall be called by the name of Christ.

10 And now it shall come to pass, that **whosoever shall not take upon him the name of Christ** must be called by some other name; therefore, **he findeth himself on the left hand of God.**

11 And I would that ye should remember also, that this is the name [*the name of Christ*] that I said I should give unto you that **never** should be **blotted out, except it be through transgression**; therefore, take heed that ye do not transgress, that the name be not blotted out of your hearts.

12 I say unto you, I would that ye should remember to retain the name written always in your hearts [*your commitment to God must be deep, not superficial*], that ye are not found on **the left hand of God,** but that ye hear and know the voice by which ye shall be called, and also, the name by which he shall call you.

At the end of verse 12, above, as well as in the verses that follow, King Benjamin teaches that there is a great difference between knowing of Christ and knowing Christ. It is one thing to know about the Savior but quite another thing to know His "voice"; in other words, to be familiar with His gospel and to have felt the Holy Ghost bear witness of Him, and to be sincerely following Him through obedience to His commandments.

13 For **how knoweth a man the master whom he has not served** [*in other words, how could you know Christ if you have not served Him*], and who is a stranger unto him, **and is far from the thoughts and intents of his heart?**

14 And again, doth a man take an ass which belongeth to his neighbor, and keep him? I say unto you, Nay;

he will not even suffer [*permit*] that he shall feed among his flocks, but will drive him away, and cast him out. I say unto you, that **even so shall it be among you if ye know not the name by which ye are called**.

A major point in verse 14, above, is that if the Savior is basically a stranger to you on the Final Judgment Day, you will not be allowed to enter celestial glory.

Next, we are taught what we need to do to make sure that the Savior is not a stranger to us.

15 Therefore, I would that ye should **be steadfast and immovable** [*steady and solid*]**, always abounding in good works**, that Christ, the Lord God Omnipotent [*All-powerful*], may seal you his, that you may be brought to heaven, that ye may have everlasting salvation and eternal life [*exaltation*], through the wisdom, and power, and justice, and mercy of him who created all things, in heaven and in earth, who is God above all. Amen.

The phrase "eternal life" in verse 15, above, is another term for "exaltation," or living eternally in the highest degree of glory in the celestial kingdom. It means to become gods. Virtually every time and any time you see "eternal life" in the scriptures, it is referring to exaltation.

MOSIAH 6

The people of God have always been a record-keeping people. We see this now as King Benjamin records the names of those who have entered into the covenant to take upon them the name of Christ. This is similar to our membership records today. As he does this, we see again the doctrine that little children are not yet accountable.

1 AND now, king Benjamin thought it was expedient [*necessary*], after having finished speaking to the people, that he should **take the names** [*record the names*] **of all those who had entered into a covenant with God to keep his commandments.**

2 And it came to pass that there was not one soul, **except it were little children**, but who had entered into the covenant and had taken upon them the name of Christ.

3 And again, it came to pass that **when king Benjamin** had made an end of all these things, and **had consecrated** [*set apart*] **his son Mosiah to be a ruler and a king** over his people, and had given him all the charges [*responsibilities*] concerning the kingdom, **and also had appointed priests** [*Melchizedek Priesthood holders*] **to teach the people**, that thereby they might hear and know the commandments of God, and to stir them up in remembrance of the oath [*covenant*] which they had made, **he dismissed the multitude**, and they returned, every one, according to their families, to their own houses.

In verse 3, above, we put a note that indicated that the priests held the Melchizedek Priesthood. They did not have Aaronic Priesthood separate from Melchizedek Priesthood as we do today. Joseph Fielding Smith explained that from Lehi to the time of Christ's visit to the Nephites after His Crucifixion, the priesthood they had was Melchizedek. He said:

"The Nephites were descendants of Joseph. Lehi discovered this when reading the brass plates. He was a descendant of Manasseh, and Ishmael, who accompanied him with his family, was of the tribe of Ephraim [Alma 10:3]. Therefore there were no Levites who accompanied Lehi to the Western Hemisphere. Under these conditions the Nephites officiated by virtue of the Melchizedek Priesthood from the days of Lehi to the days of the appearance of our Savior among them. It is true that Nephi consecrated Jacob and Joseph that they should be priests and teachers over the land of the Nephites, but the fact that plural terms priests and teachers were used indicates that this was not a reference to the definite office in the priesthood in either case, but it was a general assignment to teach, direct, and admonish the people. Otherwise the terms priest and teacher would have been given, in the singular.

"From these and numerous other passages we learn that it was by the authority of the Melchizedek Priesthood that the Nephites administered from the time they left Jerusalem until the time of the coming of Jesus Christ" (Joseph Fielding Smith, *Answers to Gospel Questions*, Deseret Book, 1957, Vol. 1, 124–26).

Next, we see that twenty-nine-year-old Mosiah becomes the king. The time is one hundred and twenty-four years before the birth of Christ. King Benjamin lives three more years and dies.

4 And **Mosiah began to reign in his father's stead** [*in place of his father*]. And he began to reign **in the thirtieth year of his age** [*meaning that he was twenty-nine years old and was clicking off the 365 more days needed to become thirty*], making in the whole, about **four hundred and seventy–six years from the time that Lehi left Jerusalem** [*he left 600 BC.*].

5 And **king Benjamin lived three years and he died**.

6 And it came to pass that **king Mosiah did walk in the ways of the Lord,** and did observe [*keep*] his judgments [*rules*] and his statutes [*laws*], and did keep his commandments in all things whatsoever he commanded him.

In verse 7, next, a simple but important principle is illustrated—namely, the importance of having people earn their own living, where possible. You will notice in many different scriptural settings that this principle is in place when people in general are following God's commandments, but the further a nation wanders from the Lord, the further its citizens in general depart from this principle. It is commonly referred to as the principle of "self- sufficiency."

7 And **king Mosiah did cause his people that they should till the earth. And he also, himself, did till the earth**, that thereby he might not become burdensome to his people, that he might do according to

that which his father had done in all things. And there was **no contention among all his people for the space of three years.**

MOSIAH 7

Remember that King Mosiah and his people are living in the land of Zarahemla at this point in the Book of Mormon.

By way of background for these next chapters, about 79 years ago, from this point in the Book of Mormon chronology, a group of men left the land of Zarahemla in an attempt to return to the land of Lehi-Nephi, where their ancestors had once lived.

You may remember that Nephi had to flee from Laman and Lemuel and others who wanted to kill him. Nephi took the righteous people who wanted to follow him and, after traveling for many days, settled in an area that became known as the land of Nephi or the land of Nephi-Lehi. Over many more years and long after Nephi died, the Lamanites finally infiltrated the land where Nephi and his people settled and so Mosiah I, who was the king at the time, fled with his righteous people and eventually discovered the land of Zarahemla.

After King Mosiah I died, his son, Benjamin became king. It was during Benjamin's reign that this group of men set out to return to the land of Nephi. Sadly, that group fought among themselves, and all but 50 were killed in the wilderness before returning back to Zarahemla. After returning, they gathered another group and left again to find the land of Lehi-Nephi. That group had never been heard from again (see Omni 1:27–30) at the time that Mosiah II took over as king of the people in Zarahemla.

As we begin chapter 7, King Mosiah II is wondering what happened to the men in that group, especially since a number of his people have been constantly asking him to permit a party of men to attempt to discover their fate.

1 AND now, it came to pass that after king Mosiah had had continual peace for the space of three years, **he was desirous to know concerning the people who went up to dwell in the land of Lehi-Nephi**, or in the city of Lehi-Nephi; for his people had heard nothing from them from the time they left the land of Zarahemla; therefore, they wearied him with their teasings.

2 And it came to pass that king **Mosiah granted that sixteen of their strong men might go up to the land of Lehi-Nephi**, to inquire concerning their brethren [*the group of men who had left for Lehi-Nephi 79 years ago*].

3 And it came to pass that on the morrow [*the next day*] they started to go up, having with them one **Ammon**, he being a strong and mighty man, and a descendant of Zarahemla; and he **was also their leader**.

> The "Ammon" here is not the same as the Ammon we will meet in Mosiah 27, who is one of the sons of Mosiah II, and who will become a great missionary.

4 And now, they knew not the course they should travel in the wilderness to go up to the land of Lehi-Nephi;

therefore **they wandered many days in the wilderness**, even forty days did they wander.

5 And when they had wandered forty days **they came to a hill**, which is north of the land of Shilom, **and there they pitched their tents**.

6 And **Ammon took three** of his brethren, and their names were Amaleki, Helem, and Hem, **and they went down into the land of Nephi**.

As you perhaps just noticed, sometimes they call this land "the land of **Lehi-Nephi**" and other times, it is referred to as "the land of **Nephi**." The two terms seem to be interchangeable, and it is likely that they were used interchangeably by the people back then.

Next, Ammon and his three companions will be arrested immediately, which is no doubt a bit surprising to them since these people are also originally from the land of Zarahemla, and Ammon and his companions are not Lamanites. We will soon find out why the king and his guards were so quick to arrest them.

7 And behold, they met the king of the people who were in the land of Nephi, and in the land of Shilom; and **they were surrounded by the king's guard, and were taken, and were bound, and were committed to prison**.

8 And it came to pass when they had been **in prison two days** they were again **brought before the king** [*Limhi*], and their bands were loosed; and they stood before the king, and were permitted, or rather **commanded, that they should answer** the **questions** which he should ask them.

9 And he said unto them: Behold, **I am Limhi, the son of Noah, who was the son of Zeniff, who came up out of the land of Zarahemla** [*seventy-nine years ago*] to inherit this land [*the land of Nephi*], which was the land of their fathers [*ancestors*], who was made a king by the voice of the people.

Based on the information in verse 9, above, we will very briefly summarize what happened to the people who left the land of Zarahemla 79 years before. They were led by a good man whose name was Zeniff. They were welcomed by the Lamanites who had long since taken over the land of Nephi, and who secretly plotted to let Zeniff's colony settle and make the land productive, after which they would force these Nephites into bondage and live well off their labors.

Under Zeniff's righteous rule, these Nephites in Lamanite territory thrived, and thirteen years later (see Mosiah 9:9–14) when the Lamanites began efforts to work their plan to make the Nephites their slaves, Zeniff's colony fought them off successfully and maintained their freedom. This freedom was successfully defended and maintained throughout Zeniff's reign, which was probably about 40 years.

As Zeniff became old, he turned his kingdom over to his son, Noah (Mosiah 10:22; 11:1). Noah was a very wicked king. He did away with the righteous priests and chose wicked men to serve as priests for the people. One of these wicked priests was Alma. The corrupt and evil lifestyle of King Noah and his priests quickly spread to the people, which weakened the colony such that the Lamanites were able to work their plan and put Noah's people into bondage and live off their labors.

Noah was eventually burned to death by his own priests and one of his sons, Limhi, became the next king. Limhi inherited a kingdom which had to pay 50 percent of everything they had to the Lamanites. This bondage continued throughout King Limhi's reign up to the time that Ammon and his companions found him and his people. Thus, the Nephite colony in Lamanite territory had had three kings during the 79 years of their existence there: namely, Zeniff, Noah, and Limhi. We will now return to Mormon's account of what happened after Ammon's group found Limhi and his people.

In verse 10, next, we are given a clue as to why Ammon and his companions were arrested so quickly when they came down out of the hills and approached King Limhi and his guards. The king was very concerned for his own safety. We will find out why as the account continues and King Limhi gets to ask Ammon and the other prisoners some questions.

10 And now, **I desire to know the cause whereby ye were so bold as to come near the walls of the city, when I, myself, was with my guards without** [*outside of*] **the gate?**

11 And now, for this cause have I suffered [*permitted*] that ye should be preserved, that I might inquire of you [*so that I can ask you some questions*], or else I should have [*otherwise, I would have*] caused that my guards should have put you to death. **Ye are permitted to speak.**

12 And now, when **Ammon** saw that he was permitted to speak, he went forth and **bowed himself before the king; and rising again he said**: O king, I am very thankful before God this day that I am yet alive, and am permitted to speak; and I will endeavor [*attempt*] to speak with boldness;

Next, we will see that Ammon is skilled at understanding people and has the ability to make them curious, wanting to know more.

13 For I am assured that if ye had known me ye would not have suffered [*allowed*] that I should have worn these bands [*you wouldn't have allowed me to be tied up like this*]. **For I am Ammon,** and am a descendant of Zarahemla, **and have come up out of the land of Zarahemla** to inquire concerning [*find out what happened to*] our brethren, whom Zeniff brought up out of that land.

14 And now, it came to pass that after **Limhi** had heard the words of Ammon, he **was exceedingly** [*very*] **glad**, and said: Now, I know of a surety that my brethren who were in the land of Zarahemla are yet alive.

And now, I will rejoice; and on the morrow I will cause that my people shall rejoice also.

Limhi is greatly relieved that the people in the land of Zarahemla still exist. He and his people are facing very difficult times themselves as he will now explain to Ammon. In a way, perhaps, they remind us of the parable of the prodigal son (see Luke 15:11–32), in which the son did not appreciate how well off he was in the household of his father until he ventured far away and gained a true perspective of the blessings of home. Symbolically, among many other things, this can remind us to seek to return to the blessings of "home," meaning the blessings of returning to our Father in Heaven in the celestial kingdom.

King Limhi now explains the difficult circumstances he and his people are enduring. His hopes have been raised that Ammon and the people back in Zarahemla will rescue them.

15 For behold, **we are in bondage to the Lamanites**, and are taxed with a tax which is grievous [*difficult*] to be borne. And now, behold, **our brethren will deliver us out of our bondage** [*slavery*], or out of the hands of the Lamanites, and we will be their slaves [*this is similar to the prodigal son's feelings when he said he would rather be a servant in his father's household than continue living under the circumstances he was now facing*]; for it is better that we be slaves to the Nephites than to pay tribute [*taxes*] to the king of the Lamanites.

16 And now, **king Limhi commanded his guards that they should no more bind Ammon nor his brethren**, but caused that they should go to the hill which was north of Shilom, and bring their brethren into the city, that thereby they might eat, and drink, and rest themselves from the labors of their journey; for they had suffered many things; they had suffered hunger, thirst, and fatigue.

17 And now, it came to pass on the morrow that **king Limhi sent a proclamation among all his people**, that thereby they might **gather** themselves together **to the temple, to hear the words which he should speak unto them**.

We suspect that the temple, referred to in verse 17, above, was the one that Nephi and his people built in the land of Nephi, as recorded in 2 Nephi 5:16. That temple was patterned after the temple built by Solomon, except, according to Nephi, it was not as expensively furnished. Solomon's temple was thirty feet wide, thirty feet high, and ninety feet long. See 1 Kings 6:2.

Next, as we listen to King Limhi's address to his people (verses 18–33), we will see that he is a righteous man and has a good knowledge of the scriptures. And since we know that Mormon was inspired to select Limhi's sermon, out of many other things available to him as he made his abridgment, to include in what would become our Book of Mormon, we ought to look carefully for messages which apply to us in our day.

18 And it came to pass that when they had gathered themselves together that he spake unto them in this wise [*as follows*] saying: O ye, my people, **lift up your heads and be comforted**; for behold, the time is at hand, or is not far distant, when we shall no longer be in subjection to our enemies [*the Lamanites*], notwithstanding our many strugglings, which have been in vain; yet I trust there remaineth an effectual struggle to be made [*I suspect that we still have a difficult struggle ahead of us in order to gain our freedom*].

Perhaps one of Mormon's reasons for including Limhi's sermon here is that it contains a strong reminder that the only way to gain true freedom is through God, who has the power to redeem us. We will point out some possible symbolism as we continue. If you get good at picking out the symbolism that is so often contained in the scriptures, your scripture study will become much more rewarding to you.

19 Therefore, lift up your heads, and rejoice, and **put your trust in God**, in that God [*Jehovah, the premortal Jesus Christ, who was the God of the Old Testament*] who was **the God of Abraham, and Isaac, and Jacob** [*symbolism: the God who respects agency and thus makes covenants with His people, rather than forcing obedience*]; and also, that God who brought the children of Israel out of the land of Egypt [*Egypt is often used to symbolize the wickedness of the world and worldliness*], and caused that they should walk through the Red Sea on dry ground [*the Red Sea can be symbolic of baptism, passing through the water to get to the "promised land," or heaven*], and fed them with manna [*symbolic of spiritual nourishment from above*] that they might not perish in the wilderness [*symbolic also of the world*]; and many more things did he do for them.

20 And again, **that same God has brought our fathers** [*ancestors; Lehi, Nephi, etc.*] **out of the land of Jerusalem, and has kept and preserved his people even until now**; and behold, it is because of our iniquities [*wickedness*] and abominations [*terrible sins*] that he has brought us into bondage [*symbolism: sins and wickedness bring us into spiritual and literal slavery*].

21 And ye all are witnesses this day, that **Zeniff** [*the man who brought the original group from Zarahemla to the land of Lehi-Nephi*], **who was made king over this people**, he being over–zealous [*over anxious*] to inherit the land of his fathers, therefore being **deceived by the cunning and craftiness of king Laman** [*symbolic of Satan*], who having entered into a treaty with king Zeniff, and having yielded up into his hands the possessions of a part of the land, or even the city of Lehi-Nephi, and the city of Shilom [*symbolic of Satan's luring us into unrealistic security as we move toward him*]; and the land round about—[*perhaps symbolizing that Satan can seem rather "generous" as he lures us away from the true security of the covenant path*]

22 And **all this he did, for the sole** [*one*] **purpose of bringing this people into subjection or into bondage** [*symbolic of Satan's true motives as he

cunningly tempts us]. And behold, we at this time do pay tribute to the king of the Lamanites, to the amount of one half of our corn, and our barley, and even all our grain of every kind, and one half of the increase of our flocks and our herds; and even one half of all we have or possess the king of the Lamanites doth exact of us, or our lives [*symbolizing that Satan ultimately stops "smiling" and turns ugly*].

Remember that the various symbolisms suggested in the previous verses represent just one set of possibilities. No doubt, you can come up with other possible symbolism, for there is much of it in the scriptures. In fact, there is much symbolism in all things, both literal (temporal) events as well as in spiritual matters. Moses 6:63 confirms this fact and especially reminds us that there is symbolism of Christ in all things, as follows:

Moses 6:63

63 And behold, **all things have their likeness** [*all things have their symbolic meaning*], and **all things are created and made to bear record of me,** both things which are **temporal, and** things which are **spiritual; things** which are in the heavens above, and things which are on the earth, and things which are in the earth, and things which are under the earth, both above and beneath: **all things bear record of me.**

23 And now, is not this grievous to be borne? And is not this, our affliction, great? Now behold, how great reason we have to mourn [*be sorry for the situation we are in*].

24 Yea, I say unto you, **great are the reasons which we have to mourn**; for behold how many of our brethren have been slain, and their blood has been spilt in vain [*unnecessarily*], and all because of iniquity [*wickedness*].

Next, Limhi points out to his people how they got into such a fix.

25 For **if this people had not fallen into transgression** [*had not left the ways of God*] **the Lord would not have suffered** [*allowed*] **that this great evil should come upon them.** But behold, **they would not hearken unto his words**; but **there arose contentions among them,** even so much that they did shed blood among themselves.

26 And **a prophet of the Lord** [*named Abinadi*] **have they slain**; yea, a chosen man of God, **who told them of their wickedness and abominations** [*extremely evil attitudes and behaviors*], **and prophesied of many things which are to come, yea, even the coming of Christ.**

Limhi shows great understanding and testimony of Christ as he teaches and testifies to his people. By the way, on average, the Book of Mormon speaks of Christ, in one way or another, every 1.7 verses. The next verse of Limhi's talk is another example of this wonderful fact.

27 And because he said unto them that **Christ was the God, the Father** [*the Creator*] **of all things**, and said that **he should take upon him the image of man** [*He would be born into a mortal body*], and it should be

the image after which man was created in the beginning; or in other words, he [*Abinadi*] said that **man was created after the image of God** [*our bodies look like God's body*], and that **God should come down among the children of men** [*mortal people*], **and take upon him flesh and blood** [*a physical body*], **and go forth upon the face of the earth—**

28 And now, because he said this, **they did put him to death** [*they killed him*]; and many more things did they do which brought down the wrath [*anger*] of God upon them. Therefore, who wondereth [*it is no wonder*] that they [*Limhi's people*] are in bondage, and that they are smitten with sore afflictions [*very bitter and difficult problems*]?

29 For behold, the Lord hath said: **I will not succor** [*help and support*] **my people in the day of their transgression** [*when they turn wicked*]; but **I will hedge up their ways** [*I will get in their way, stop helping them, cause problems for them*] **that they prosper not**; and their doings shall be as a stumbling block [*things that cause them trouble, stop them from progressing*] before them.

Next, Limhi teaches what we often refer to as "the law of the harvest."

30 And again, he saith: **If my people shall sow** [*plant*] **filthiness they shall reap** [*harvest*] **the chaff** [*worthless outer husks of grain kernels*] thereof in the whirlwind; and the effect thereof is poison. [*In other words, sin and filthiness poison everything.*]

31 And again he saith: If my people shall sow filthiness they shall reap the **east wind**, which bringeth immediate destruction.

In the Bible, the "east wind" is the hot, dry, devastating wind that blows into the Holy Land from the east, having come across the hot desert sands. It is known to have dried up crops and ruined them, literally overnight. Thus, the "east wind" in scriptures represents devastating and rapid destruction.

32 And now, **behold** [*open your eyes and see*], **the promise of the Lord** [*that wicked living brings great trouble*] **is fulfilled, and ye are smitten and afflicted**.

Next, Limhi reminds his people that there is a way out of their painful situation. The same lesson applies to us and all other people.

33 But if ye will **turn to the Lord with full purpose of heart**, and **put your trust in him**, and **serve him with all diligence** of mind, **if ye do this, he will,** according to his own will and pleasure, **deliver you out of bondage** [*symbolic of being freed from the bondage of sin*].

MOSIAH 8

Next, King Limhi, having addressed his people, invites Ammon to speak to them and tell them what has happened in the Land of Zarahemla over the past 79 years.

1 AND it came to pass that after king Limhi had made an end of

speaking to his people, for he spake many things unto them and only a few of them have I [*Mormon*] written in this book [*in this part of the gold plates*], **he told his people all the things concerning their brethren** [*friends and relatives*] **who were in the land of Zarahemla.**

2 And **he caused that Ammon should** stand up before the multitude, **and rehearse** [*tell*] unto them **all that had happened** unto their brethren from the time that Zeniff [*the leader of the group that left Zarahemla about 79 years ago*] went up out of the land even until the time that he himself came up out of the land.

3 And **he also rehearsed unto them the last words which king Benjamin had taught them**, and explained them to the people of king Limhi, so that they might understand all the words which he spake. [*In other words, among other things, Ammon reviewed King Benjamin's address with them. That sermon, as you recall from Mosiah chapters 2–5, focused heavily on the Savior and the redemption; in other words, freedom from sin and other great blessings, which come from making and keeping covenants with God. Limhi's people need both physical and spiritual redemption from bondage.*]

4 And it came to pass that **after he had done all this, that king Limhi dismissed the multitude**, and caused that they should return every one unto his own house.

5 And it came to pass that **he caused that the plates which contained the record of his people from the time that they left the land of Zarahemla, should be brought before Ammon, that he might read them.**

It is interesting to observe that both Limhi (Mosiah 8:5) and Zeniff (Mosiah 8, heading) kept records, whereas there is no mention that wicked King Noah kept records. There seems to be a general pattern that the righteous are record-keepers, whereas the wicked are not. In fact, they often destroy the records of the righteous where possible (example: Alma 14:8).

6 Now, **as soon as Ammon had read the record**, the king inquired [*asked*] of him to know if he could interpret languages, and Ammon told him that he could not.

Next, King Limhi will tell Ammon about twenty-four gold plates and other items that were discovered when he sent several of his people to try to find Zarahemla. He had hoped to get help from people in the land of Zarahemla, if they still existed, to free his people from bondage in the land of Lehi-Nephi. His men got lost and couldn't find Zarahemla, but they did find ruins of the Jaredites (about whom they didn't know at the time). The twenty-four gold plates that they discovered and brought back to Limhi were written in a language that they could not understand, so Limhi wondered if Ammon could read them. The plates turned out to be the record of the Jaredites. Much later, Moroni will translate and abridge (make a shortened version of) these plates, and his abridgment will become the book of Ether in the Book of Mormon.

Next, Limhi will explain to Ammon why he was hoping that Ammon could understand the language in which the 25 gold plates were written.

7 And the king said unto him: Being grieved for the afflictions of my people, **I caused that forty and three of my people should take a journey into the wilderness, that thereby they might find the land of Zarahemla**, that we might appeal unto our brethren to deliver us out of bondage.

8 And **they were lost in the wilderness for the space of many days**, yet they were diligent, and found not the land of Zarahemla but returned to this land, having traveled in a land among many waters, having discovered a land which was covered with bones of men, and of beasts, and was also covered with ruins of buildings of every kind, having discovered a land which had been peopled [*populated*] with a people who were as numerous as the hosts of Israel. [*These were the ruins of the Jaredite civilization.*]

9 And for a testimony [*in order to prove*] that the things that they had said are true **they have brought twenty-four plates** [*the record of the Jaredites*] which are filled with engravings, and they are of pure gold.

10 And behold, **also**, they have brought **breastplates**, which are large, and they are of brass and of copper, and are perfectly sound.

11 And again, they have brought **swords**, the hilts [*handles*] thereof have perished, and the blades thereof were cankered with rust; and **there is no one in the land that is able to interpret the language or the engravings that are on the plates.** Therefore [*this is the reason*] I said unto thee: Canst thou translate?

12 And I say unto thee again: **Knowest thou of any one that can translate**? For I am desirous that these records should be translated into our language; for, perhaps, they will give us a knowledge of a remnant of the people who have been destroyed, from whence [*where*] these records came; or, perhaps, they will give us a knowledge of this very people who have been destroyed; and I am desirous to know the cause of their destruction.

Ammon's response to King Limhi's question above is fascinating and will bring up the subject of "seers" and what is known as a "Urim and Thummim."

13 Now Ammon said unto him: **I can assuredly** [*most certainly*] **tell thee, O king, of a man that can translate the records**; for he has wherewith that [*he has something with which*] he can look, and translate all records that are of ancient date; and it is a gift from God. And the things are called interpreters [*Urim and Thummim*], and no man can look in them except he be commanded, lest he should look for that he ought not

and he should perish. And **whosoever is commanded to look in them, the same is called seer.**

14 And behold, **the king** [*Mosiah II*] of the people who are in the land of Zarahemla **is the man that** is commanded to do these things, and **who has this high gift from God.** [*In other words, King Mosiah II is a seer.*]

We will take a moment here to consider the topic of "Urim and Thummin." As mentioned by Ammon, King Mosiah II has one. Then we will discuss the topic of "seers."

First, a question that often comes up at this point in the Book of Mormon: "Is there more than one Urim and Thummim?" The answer is "Yes." In our Bible Dictionary, near the end of our LDS Bible, under "**Urim and Thummim**," we read the following (**bold** added for emphasis):

"**Urim and Thummim**. Heb. term that means Lights and Perfections. An instrument prepared of God to assist man in obtaining revelation from the Lord and in translating languages. See Ex. 28:30; Lev. 8:8; Num. 27:21; Deut. 33:8; 1 Sam. 28:6; Ezra 2:63; Neh. 7:65; JS—H 1:35.

"Using a Urim and Thummim is the special prerogative (privilege) of a seer, and it would seem reasonable that such instruments were used from the time of Adam. However, the earliest mention is in connection with the brother of Jared (Ether 3:21–28). Abraham used a Urim and Thummim (Abr. 3:1–4), as did Aaron and the priests of Israel, and also the prophets among the Nephites (Omni 1:20–21; Mosiah 8:13–19; 21:26–28; 28:11–20; Ether 4:1–7). **There is more than one Urim and Thummim, but we are informed that Joseph Smith had the one used by the brother of Jared** (Ether 3:22–28; D&C 10:1; 17:1). (See Seer.) A partial description is given in Joseph Smith—History 1:35. Joseph Smith used it in translating the Book of Mormon and in obtaining other revelations.

"This earth in its celestial condition will be a Urim and Thummim, and many within that kingdom will have an additional Urim and Thummim (D&C 130:6–11)."

As mentioned above in the quote from the Bible Dictionary, a partial description of the Urim and Thummim that Joseph Smith used is given in Joseph Smith—History 1:35. It reads (**bold** added for emphasis):

Joseph Smith—History 1:35

35 Also, that there were **two stones in silver bows**—and these stones, fastened to a breastplate, constituted what is called the Urim and Thummim—deposited with the plates; and the possession and use of these stones were what constituted "seers" in ancient or former times; and that God had prepared them for the purpose of translating the book.

David Whitmer was one of the Three Witnesses of the Book of Mormon and it is interesting to read his description of the Urim and Thummim. When asked if he had seen the Urim and Thummim, he said, "I saw the Interpreters in the holy vision; they looked like whitish stones put in the rim of a bow—**looked like spectacles**, only much larger" (Richard Lloyd Anderson, *Investigating the Book of Mormon Witnesses* [Salt Lake City: Deseret Book, 1981], 81).

Now we will turn briefly to the topic of "seers." We are blessed to have "prophets, seers, and revelators" today in the First Presidency and the Quorum of the Twelve Apostles. We will pay special attention to some items that Ammon taught Limhi, in the next verses. In so doing, we can learn more about seers.

15 And the king said that **a seer is greater than a prophet.**

16 And Ammon said that **a seer is a revelator and a prophet also**; and **a gift which is greater can no man have**, except he should possess the power of God, which no man can; yet a man may have great power given him from God.

Pay special attention to verse 17, next, to be reminded of what our "seers" do today. They do this for us in general conference as well as in countless other settings as they fulfill their prophetic callings. They "see" dangers in our cultures, political trends, philosophies, media, etc. On the other hand, they "see" great opportunities for spiritual growth, joy, and happiness and point them out to us.

17 But **a seer can know of things which are past, and also of things which are to come,** and **by them shall all things be revealed,** or, rather, shall **secret things** be **made manifest**, and **hidden things shall come to light** [*will be revealed to us by them*], and **things which are not known shall be made known by them**, and also things shall be made known by them **which otherwise could not be known**.

The Prophet Joseph Smith emphasized the things that "seers" see, as they lead us in their prophetic callings. He said:

"Wherefore, we again say, search the revelations of God; study the prophecies, and rejoice that God grants unto the world Seers and Prophets. They are they who saw the mysteries of godliness; they saw the flood before it came; they saw angels ascending and descending upon a ladder that reached from earth to heaven; they saw the stone cut out of the mountain, which filled the whole earth; they saw the Son of God come from the regions of bliss and dwell with men on earth; they saw the deliverer come out of Zion, and turn away ungodliness from Jacob; they saw the glory of the Lord when he showed the transfiguration of the earth on the mount; they saw every mountain laid low and every valley exalted when the Lord was taking vengeance upon the wicked; they saw truth spring out of the earth, and righteousness look down from heaven in the last days, before the Lord came the second time to gather his elect; they saw the end of wickedness on earth, and the Sabbath of creation crowned with peace; they saw the end of the glorious thousand years, when Satan was loosed for a little season; they saw the day of judgment when all men received according to their works, and they saw the heaven and the earth flee away to make room for the city of God, when the righteous receive an inheritance in eternity" (Joseph Smith, *Teachings of the Prophet Joseph Smith*, selected and arranged by Joseph Fielding Smith [Salt Lake City: Deseret Book, 1977], pages 12–13).

We will now return to Ammon's words to King Limhi, as he finishes teaching about "seers."

18 Thus God has provided a means that man, through faith, might work mighty miracles; **therefore he** [*a seer, such as Mosiah II*] **becometh a great benefit to his fellow beings**.

Next, Mormon records Limhi's powerful closing testimony for us to read and to feel.

19 And now, when Ammon had made an end of speaking these words **the king rejoiced exceedingly**, and gave thanks to God, saying: Doubtless a great mystery is contained within these plates [*the twenty-four gold plates*], and these interpreters [*the Urim and Thummim*] were doubtless prepared for the purpose of unfolding all such mysteries to the children of men [*to mortal men and women*].

20 O **how marvelous are the works of the Lord**, and how long doth he suffer with his people [*how patient the Lord is!*]; yea, and **how blind and impenetrable are the understandings of the children of men**; for they will not seek wisdom, neither do they desire that she [*wisdom*] should rule over them!

Limhi finishes his testimony by pointing out how foolish people are to run away from God and into certain destruction.

21 Yea, **they are as a wild flock** which fleeth from the shepherd, and scattereth, and are driven, and are devoured by the beasts of the forest.

MOSIAH 9

THIS IS A FLASHBACK!

It is important to realize that Mormon is now taking us back 79 years in a "flashback" to the days of Zeniff and his people, as they left the land of Zarahemla to return to the land of Nephi, or else you could easily get confused chronologically at this point in your reading of the Book of Mormon. This chapter covers thirteen years, from approximately 200 BC to 187 BC.

By the way, you will see from the note in your Book of Mormon just before Mosiah chapter 9 that Mormon quoted directly from Zeniff's own records for chapters 9 and 10 here. He will now provide us with many more details about the Nephite colonists who left the land of Zarahemla to live in Lamanite territory, over their 79-year history, ruled over first by Zeniff, then by his son, wicked King Noah, and finally, by his son, righteous Limhi. Keep in mind, as always, that Mormon chose these details intentionally to teach us things we would especially need to know during our lives on earth in the last days before the Second Coming of Christ.

We will see in verse 1, next, that Zeniff, though obviously a tough and fearless explorer, has a strong sense of right and wrong as well as a tender heart.

First, Zeniff will tell us that he was part of the original group that left the land of Zarahemla to settle in Lamanite territory, who fought among themselves such that the majority of them were killed off. The remnant returned to Zarahemla. See also Omni 1:27–28.

1 **I, ZENIFF**, having been taught in all the language of the Nephites, and having had a knowledge of the land of Nephi, or of the land of our fathers' first inheritance [*our ancestors' original living place*], and **having been sent as a spy among the Lamanites** that I might spy out their forces, that our army might come upon them and destroy them—**but when I saw that which was good among them I was desirous that they should not be destroyed**.

2 Therefore, **I contended** [*debated and fought*] **with my brethren** in the wilderness, for I would [*wanted*] that our ruler should make a treaty with them; but he being an austere [*rough, severe, bitter*] and a blood-thirsty man commanded that I should be slain; **but I was rescued** by the shedding of much blood; for father fought against father, and brother against brother, until the greater number [*the majority*] of our army was destroyed in the wilderness; **and we returned**, those of us that were spared, **to the land of Zarahemla**, to relate that tale to their wives and their children.

3 And yet, **I being over–zealous** [*too anxious*] **to inherit the land of our fathers** [*to live where our ancestors had first settled*], collected as many as were desirous to go up to possess the land, and started again on our journey into the wilderness to go up to the land; but we were smitten with famine and sore afflictions; for we were slow to remember the Lord our God.

4 Nevertheless, **after many days' wandering in the wilderness** we pitched our tents in the place where our brethren were slain, which was near to the land of our fathers [*close to the land of Nephi*].

5 And it came to pass that **I went again with four of my men into the city, in unto the king**, that I might know of the disposition of the king [*in order to find out what the king of the Lamanites thought about our plan*], and that I might know if I might go in with my people and possess the land in peace.

We see immediately that the king of the Lamanites was cunning and could recognize opportunity when he saw it.

6 And I went in unto **the king**, and he **covenanted** [*made a promise*] **with me** that I might possess the land of Lehi-Nephi, and the land of Shilom.

7 And **he also commanded that his people should depart out of the land**, and I and my people went into the land that we might possess it.

In verse 8, we see typical members of the Church, who are industrious, hard-working people who turn ruins into a prosperous civilization. This approach to living is typical of righteous people.

8 And **we began to build buildings, and to repair the walls of the city**, yea, even the walls of the city of Lehi-Nephi, and the city of Shilom.

It is obvious from verse 8, above, that Nephi and his people once lived in this area.

9 And we began to till the ground, yea, even with all manner of seeds, with seeds of corn, and of wheat, and of barley, and with neas [*we don't know what this is*], and with sheum [*neither do we know what this is*], and with seeds of all manner of fruits; and **we did begin to multiply and prosper in the land**.

Next, as he looks back in time, Zeniff points out the plot in the cunning heart of King Laman and his people.

Also, it is interesting to note, in passing, that, just as the Nephites named their kings after Nephi (see Jacob 1:11), so also the Lamanites named their kings after Laman (see verse 10, next).

10 Now it was the **cunning** and the **craftiness** of **king Laman**, to bring my people into bondage, that he yielded up the land that we might possess it.

11 Therefore it came to pass, that **after we had dwelt in the land for the space of twelve years** that **king Laman began to grow uneasy**, lest by any means my people should wax [*grow*] strong in the land, and that they [*the Lamanites*] could not overpower them and bring them into bondage [*slavery and subjection*].

12 Now **they were a lazy and an idolatrous** [*idol-worshiping*] **people**; therefore they were **desirous to bring us into bondage, that they might glut themselves with the labors of our hands**; yea, that they might feast themselves upon the flocks of our fields.

13 Therefore it came to pass that **king Laman began to stir up his people** that they should contend [*argue and fight*] with my people; **therefore there began to be wars and contentions in the land**.

14 For, in the thirteenth year of my reign in the land of Nephi, away on the south of the land of Shilom, when my people were watering and feeding their flocks, and tilling their lands, **a numerous host of Lamanites came upon them and began to slay them, and to take off their flocks, and the corn of their fields**.

15 Yea, and it came to pass that **they fled**, all that were not overtaken, even **into the city of Nephi**, and did call upon me for protection.

16 And it came to pass that **I did arm them** with bows, and with arrows, with swords, and with cimeters [*broad, curved swords*], and with clubs, and with slings, and with all manner of weapons which we could invent, and I and my people did go forth against the Lamanites to battle.

Theirs was a righteous cause; therefore they could appropriately ask God for help in defeating their enemies.

17 Yea, in the strength of the Lord did we go forth to battle against the Lamanites; for **I and my people did cry** [*pray*] **mightily to the Lord that he would deliver us out of the hands of our enemies**, for we were awakened to a remembrance of the deliverance of our fathers.

In verse 17, above, there is an important message that remembering past blessings from God is a key to having faith for current needs and requests to Him.

18 And **God did hear our cries and did answer our prayers**; and we did go forth in his might; yea, we did go forth against the Lamanites, and in one day and a night **we did slay three thousand and forty–three**; we did slay them even until we had driven them out of our land.

19 And I, myself, with mine own hands, did help to bury their dead. And behold, to our great sorrow and lamentation, **two hundred and seventy–nine of our brethren were slain**.

Perhaps one of the reasons Mormon chose to preserve the part of Zeniff's record given in verses 18 and 19, above, is to remind us and teach us that faithful Saints, with the help of the Lord, can triumph over great odds and opposition, especially in terms of spiritual dangers.

MOSIAH 10

This chapter covers about twenty-seven years, from approximately 187 BC (before the birth of Christ) to 160 BC. One of the major messages here will be the warning that the further people stray from God, the more wild, vicious, and bloodthirsty they become.

In fact, you may have noticed even now, in our day, that, quite often, the farther people get from the teachings and standards of the gospel, the more bizarre and wild their clothing, hair styles, tattoos, body piercings, and general appearance become.

One of the sad things that happens as a result of the Lamanites attacking these Nephite colonists is that now, Zeniff and his people have to spend a lot of their time and resources preparing to defend themselves against future attacks. This is quite similar to our situation in our country today.

1 AND it came to pass that we [*Zeniff and his people*] again began to establish the kingdom and we again began to possess the land in peace. And **I caused that there should be weapons of war made of every kind**, that thereby I might have weapons for my people against the time the Lamanites should come up again to war against my people.

There is much debate in our world as to whether it is right to stockpile weapons of war in times of peace. Since the Book of Mormon was written for our day, an important message in verse 1, above, is that it is both permissible and wise for the righteous, when necessary, to maintain armies and manufacture and store up weapons of defense in times of peace.

2 And **I set guards round about the land**, that the Lamanites might not come upon us again unawares and destroy us; and thus I did guard my people and my flocks, and keep them from falling into the hands of our enemies.

3 And it came to pass that **we did inherit** [*live in*] **the land of our fathers** [*ancestors*] for many years, yea, **for** the space of **twenty and two years**.

4 And I did cause that the men should till the ground, and raise all manner of grain and all manner of fruit of every kind.

5 And I did cause that the women should spin, and toil, and work, and work all manner of fine linen, yea, and cloth of every kind, that we might clothe our nakedness; and thus **we did prosper** in the land—thus we did have continual peace in the land for the space of twenty and two years.

The above verses again remind us that righteous people tend to work hard and be productive. While we should not judge others unrighteously, we should be sure that the principle of self-reliance, as taught by our Church leaders, is used in our own lives.

6 And it came to pass that **king Laman died**, and **his son began to reign** [*rule*] **in his stead** [*in his place*]. And **he began to stir his people up in rebellion against my people** [*symbolic of the fact that Satan constantly stirs up the wicked against the righteous*]; therefore they began to prepare for war, and to come up to battle against my people.

7 **But I had sent my spies out** round about the land of Shemlon, that I might discover their preparations, that I might guard against them, that they might not come upon my people and destroy them.

8 And it came to pass that **they came** up upon the north of the land of Shilom, with their numerous hosts, men armed with bows, and with arrows, and with swords, and with cimeters [*relatively short, curved, thicker swords*], and with stones, and with slings; and **they had their heads shaved that they were naked; and they were girded** [*clothed*] **with a leathern girdle about their loins** [*their waists and hips*].

Verse 8, above, is certainly a reminder that wild appearance and fashions go hand in hand with personal and cultural distance from God.

9 And it came to pass that I caused that the **women and children** of my people should be **hid** in the wilderness; and I also caused that all my **old men** that could bear arms, and also all my **young men** that were able to bear arms, should gather themselves together to **go to battle** against the Lamanites; and I did place them in their ranks, every man according to his age.

10 And it came to pass that **we did go up to battle against the Lamanites**; and I, even I, in my old age, did go up to battle against the Lamanites. And it came to pass that **we did go up in the strength of the Lord** to battle. [*Only the righteous can do this.*]

11 Now, **the Lamanites knew nothing concerning the Lord**, nor the strength of the Lord, therefore they depended upon their own strength. Yet they were a strong people, as to the strength of men.

Next, Zeniff points out how damaging false and evil traditions can be, as they are handed down from generation to generation. We see much of this in our world today, as ethnic war and personal hatreds are passed down from one generation to another. Perhaps this is one of

Satan's most successful tools of destruction.

Also, there is another significant tactic of the devil that is pointed out in the next verses. It is perhaps a bit more subtle or sneaky than outright false traditions, but is very destructive to societies and individuals alike. It is what we might call "the victim syndrome." We have, in a very real sense, become a nation of "victims." This attitude has a crippling effect on people. They come to believe that society "owes" them. Thus, Satan, in his subtle way, destroys their productivity and work ethic and replaces it with bitterness and self-pity and even hatred of those who are productive.

12 They were a wild, and ferocious, and a blood-thirsty people, **believing in the tradition of their fathers** [*ancestors, including Laman and Lemuel*], which is this—Believing that they were driven out of the land of Jerusalem because of the iniquities [*wickedness*] of their fathers [*ancestors, such as Lehi*], and that **they were wronged** in the wilderness by their brethren [*Nephi and Sam, for instance*], and **they were also wronged** while crossing the sea;

13 And again, **that they were wronged** while in the land of their first inheritance, after they had crossed the sea, and all this because that Nephi was more faithful in keeping the commandments of the Lord—therefore he was favored [*blessed*] of the Lord, for the Lord heard his prayers and answered them, and he took the lead of their journey in the wilderness.

14 And **his brethren** [*Laman, Lemuel, etc.*] **were wroth** [*extremely angry*] with him **because they understood not the dealings of the Lord**; they were also wroth with him upon the waters [*as they crossed the ocean*] because they hardened their hearts against the Lord.

It is Satan's way to have us blame others for our own unrighteous behavior.

15 And again, **they were wroth with him** [*Nephi*] when they had arrived in the promised land, because they said that he had taken the ruling of the people out of their hands; and they sought to kill him.

16 And again, **they were wroth with him** because he departed into the wilderness as the Lord had commanded him, and took the records which were engraven on the plates of brass, for **they said that he robbed them.**

17 And thus **they have taught their children that they should hate them, and that they should murder them, and that they should rob and plunder them, and do all they could to destroy them; therefore they have an eternal hatred towards the children of Nephi.**

You may have noticed something else in verses 12–17, above, which you see a lot in our world today: the rewriting of history to satisfy personal agendas. No wonder Mormon included these things in the Book of Mormon. We need to be alerted to what is going on all around us under the sponsorship of the devil.

Now, back to Zeniff and his confession that he was deceived by King Laman. We probably should not be too critical of him for this since such things happen to us too.

18 For this very cause has **king Laman** [*symbolic of Satan*], by his cunning, and lying craftiness, and his fair promises, **deceived me**, that I have brought this my people up into this land [*the land of Nephi*], that they may destroy them; yea, and we have suffered these many years in the land.

19 And now **I, Zeniff**, after having told all these things unto my people concerning the Lamanites, I **did stimulate them to go to battle with their might, putting their trust in the Lord**; therefore, we did contend [*fight*] with them, face to face.

20 And it came to pass that **we did drive them again out of our land**; and we slew [*killed*] them with a great slaughter, even so many that we did not number [*count*] them.

21 And it came to pass that **we returned again to our own land**, and my people again began to tend their flocks, and to till their ground.

22 And now **I, being old, did confer the kingdom upon one of my sons** [*Noah*]; therefore, I say no more. And may the Lord bless my people. Amen.

MOSIAH 11

Many wonder why Zeniff would turn the kingdom over to his son, Noah, who will be a very wicked king. We don't know. Zeniff was certainly a good man, based on what we have read about him. Perhaps Noah was reasonably righteous at the time and quickly turned to wickedness when he received the power and authority that came with being the king. Perhaps Noah was already pursuing a wicked lifestyle but doing it in secret, unbeknown to his father.

Whatever the case, we will now see how quickly a wicked, corrupt, powerful leader can lead his people astray. No doubt this is a warning to us as we select government leaders today. The Lord has also warned us of this in the Doctrine and Covenants as follows:

D&C 98:9–10

9 Nevertheless, when the wicked rule the people mourn.

10 Wherefore, honest men and wise men should be sought for diligently, and good men and wise men ye should observe to uphold; otherwise whatsoever is less than these cometh of evil.

King Noah will rule for approximately fifteen years, from about 160 BC to 145 BC. As we study this chapter, we will meet Abinadi, a humble and fearless prophet who was sent by the Lord to Noah and his people to try to save them.

Mormon teaches us many lessons as he gives a brief account of Noah's reign. Remember that Mormon is the great Book of Mormon prophet who is abridging or summarizing all the various Nephite plates and records to provide the shortened version of the gold plates that his son, Moroni, gave to Joseph Smith to translate as the Book of Mormon.

1 AND now it came to pass that **Zeniff conferred the kingdom upon Noah**, one of his sons; therefore Noah began to reign in his stead; and **he did not walk in the ways of his father** [*he did not live the same standards as his father, Zeniff, did*].

As we continue our study, Mormon will point out many of the lifestyles and philosophies wicked King Noah used to swiftly lead his people into gross iniquity. We will go quickly through verses 2–19 and **bold** several of these tools of the devil with which people are led astray.

2 For behold, **he did not keep the commandments of God** [*personal wickedness*], but **he did walk after the desires of his own heart** [*made his own rules*]. And he had many wives and concubines [*he defiantly and openly violated God's commandment to Lehi and his people not to practice plural marriage; see Jacob 2:27; 3:5*]. And **he did cause his people to commit sin, and do that which was abominable** [*extra wicked*] **in the sight of the Lord** [*he openly and intentionally led his people into sin*]. Yea, and **they did commit whoredoms** [*he promoted widespread sexual immorality*] and **all manner of wickedness** [*he sponsored and promoted all kinds of evil*].

3 And he laid a tax of one fifth part of all they possessed, a fifth part of their gold and of their silver, and a fifth part of their ziff, and of their copper, and of their brass and their iron; and a fifth part of their fatlings; and also a fifth part of all their grain.

4 And **all this did he take to support himself**, and his wives and his concubines; and also his priests, and their wives and their concubines [*he selfishly placed heavy burdens upon his people to support his riotous lifestyle*]; thus **he** had **changed the affairs of the kingdom.**

5 For **he put down all the priests** [*got rid of all the righteous church leaders*] that had been consecrated by his father, and **consecrated new ones** in their stead [*replaced them with wicked ones*], such as were **lifted up in** the **pride** [*he promoted pride*] of their hearts [*he surrounded himself with other leaders who would join him and support him in personal and public wickedness*].

6 Yea, and thus they were supported in their **laziness**, and in their **idolatry**, and in their **whoredoms**, by the taxes which king Noah had put upon his people; **thus did the people labor exceedingly to support iniquity** [*the people had to work hard to support wickedness in their government*].

7 Yea, and **they** also **became idolatrous** [*the people followed their leaders*], because **they were deceived by the vain and flattering words of the king and priests; for they did speak flattering** things unto them [*the people became gullible and lost their common sense*].

Next, Mormon points out that the people were heavily burdened by government spending and waste.

This is the exact opposite of King Benjamin and other righteous leaders who worked hard to keep from being a burden to their people. See Mosiah 2:14.

8 And it came to pass that **king Noah built many elegant** [*fancy*] **and spacious** [*large and roomy*] **buildings;** and he ornamented [*decorated*] them with fine work of wood, and of all manner of precious things, of gold, and of silver, and of iron, and of brass, and of ziff [*we don't know what this is*], and of copper;

9 And **he also built him a spacious palace**, and a throne in the midst thereof, all of which was of fine wood and was ornamented with gold and silver and with precious things.

10 And he also caused that his workmen should work all manner of fine work within the walls of the temple, of fine wood, and of copper, and of brass.

11 And the **seats which were set apart for the high priests**, which were above all the other seats, **he did ornament with pure gold;** and he caused a **breastwork** to be built before them, **that they might rest their bodies and their arms upon while they should speak lying and vain words to his people.**

12 And it came to pass that he built a tower near the temple; yea, a very high tower, even so high that he could stand upon the top thereof and overlook the land of Shilom, and also the land of Shemlon, which was possessed by the Lamanites; and he could even look over all the land round about.

13 And it came to pass that he caused many buildings to be built in the land Shilom; and he caused a great tower to be built on the hill north of the land Shilom, which had been a resort for the children of Nephi at the time they fled out of the land; **and thus he did do with the riches which he obtained by the taxation of his people.**

14 And it came to pass that **he placed his heart upon his riches** [*materialism*], and he spent his time in **riotous living** with his wives and his concubines [*servant wives*]; and so did also his priests spend their time with **harlots** [*prostitutes*].

15 And it came to pass that he planted vineyards round about in the land; and he built wine–presses, and **made wine in abundance**; and therefore he **became a wine–bibber** [*a drunkard*], and **also his people** [*his people followed him in this too*].

16 And it came to pass that the Lamanites began to come in upon his people, upon small numbers, and to slay them in their fields, and while they were tending their flocks.

17 And king Noah sent guards round about the land to keep them off; but he did not send a sufficient number [*inadequate military*], and **the Lamanites came upon them and killed them**, and drove many of their flocks out of the land; thus the Lamanites

began to destroy them, and to exercise their hatred upon them.

18 And it came to pass that king Noah sent his armies against them, and they were driven back, or **they drove them back for a time**; therefore, they returned rejoicing in their spoil [*pride destroys wisdom and perception of reality*].

19 And now, because of this great victory they were lifted up in the **pride** of their hearts; they did **boast** in their own strength, saying that their fifty could stand against thousands of the Lamanites; and thus they did boast, and did **delight in blood, and the shedding of the blood** of their brethren [*they have gone from depending on God for help, under King Zeniff, to having murder in their hearts, under Noah*], and this **because of the wickedness of their king and priests.**

In 1 Nephi 13:4–6, Nephi saw in vision the formation of the "great and abominable church," meaning the church of the devil (1 Nephi 14:10; 22:22). In 1 Nephi 13:7–9, he was shown three major tools that the devil uses to "convert" people to his "church": namely, materialism, sexual immorality, and pride. We have now seen these tools used effectively to convert King Noah and his people to the church of the devil.

It is important to note, as we continue, that one of King Noah's wicked priests was a young man named Alma. He, therefore, is very wicked when we meet him. We will be privileged to watch as he is converted back to the church of God and is cleansed completely of his sins by the Atonement of Christ as he deeply repents of them. The power of the Atonement to cleanse and heal is a most vital message for us in the Book of Mormon.

Next, we will watch and learn as Abinadi is sent by the Lord to teach Noah and his people and call them to repentance.

20 And it came to pass that there was a man among them whose name was **Abinadi**; and he **went forth among them, and began to prophesy**, saying: Behold, thus saith the Lord, and thus hath he commanded me, saying, Go forth, and say unto this people, thus saith the Lord—Wo be unto this people, for I have seen their abominations [*extremely wicked sins*], and their wickedness, and their whoredoms [*sexual sins*]; and except [*unless*] they repent I will visit [*punish*] them in mine anger.

21 And **except they repent and turn to the Lord their God, behold, I will deliver them into the hands of their enemies** [*the Lamanites; symbolically, "enemies" can be all sorts of sin*]; yea, and they shall be brought into bondage [*literal bondage to the Lamanites as well as literal bondage to Lucifer*]; and they shall be afflicted by the hand of their enemies.

22 And it shall come to pass that they shall know that **I am the Lord their God, and am a jealous God**, visiting the iniquities of my people.

The word "jealous" as used in verse 22, above, must be kept in the context of the scriptures. It means that

God does not want His children worshiping anyone or anything other than Him, because all other loyalties that lead us away from Him will ultimately hurt or damage us. And He doesn't want that to happen to us because He loves us. Compare with Exodus 20:3.

23 And it shall come to pass that **except this people repent and turn unto the Lord their God, they shall be brought into bondage**; and none shall deliver them, except it be the Lord the Almighty God.

24 Yea, and it shall come to pass that when they shall cry unto me **I will be slow to hear their cries**; yea, and I will suffer [*allow*] them that they be smitten by their enemies.

The phrase "slow to hear their cries" in verse 24, above, is an important guideline for parenting. If children are rescued too soon from the consequences of their inappropriate behavior, they do not learn the lesson.

25 And **except they repent** in sackcloth and ashes [*a sign of deep humility in Bible culture as well as Nephite culture*], **and cry mightily to the Lord their God, I will not hear their prayers** [*I will not give them the blessings they request*], neither will I deliver them out of their afflictions; and thus saith the Lord, and thus hath he commanded me.

Satan is a master of deception. He is a master psychologist. Let's watch now as Mormon points out a pattern that the devil uses to persuade people to avoid repenting.

Step 1: Get angry at whoever is telling you to repent.

26 Now it came to pass that **when Abinadi had spoken these words** unto them **they were wroth** [*angry*] **with him,** and sought to take away his life; but the Lord delivered him out of their hands.

Step 2: Discredit the messenger.

27 Now when king Noah had heard of the words which Abinadi had spoken unto the people, he was also wroth; and he said: **Who is Abinadi**, that I and my people should be judged of him, or **who is the Lord**, that shall bring upon my people such great affliction?

Step 3: Get rid of the messenger. Get him out of your life. One way to do this is to ignore him. Accuse him of having other motives for "attacking" you.

28 I command you to bring Abinadi hither, that I may **slay him**, for **he has said these things that he might stir up my people to anger one with another, and to raise contentions among my people**; therefore I will slay him.

Step 4: Avoid facing your need for repentance.

29 Now the **eyes of the people were blinded;** therefore **they hardened their hearts against** [*refused to believe*] **the words of Abinadi**, and they sought from that time forward to take [*capture*] him. And **king Noah** hardened his heart against the word of the Lord, and he **did not repent** of his evil doings.

MOSIAH 12

In this chapter, you will see many examples of how Satan deceives people in their thought processes and attitudes. We will see King Noah's wicked priests quoting scripture and arguing against the Prophet, Abinadi, much the same as people in our day argue against the true gospel.

After two years, Abinadi came among the people again and apparently spent some time among them in disguise. Then, when the time was right, he revealed his identity and began to preach. This is a reminder that the Lord doesn't give people just one chance; rather, He tries again and again to get us to use our agency to follow Him and be happy. These people are again receiving a fair warning to repent of their sins and live the gospel.

1 AND it came to pass that **after the space of two years that Abinadi came among them in disguise**, that they knew him not, **and began to prophesy** among them, saying: Thus has the Lord commanded me, saying—Abinadi, go and prophesy unto this my people, for **they have hardened their hearts against my words**; they have **repented not** of their evil doings; therefore, I will visit [*punish*] them in my anger, yea, in my fierce anger will I visit them in their iniquities and abominations.

As a true prophet of God, Abinadi now gives specific details as to what will happen to these people if they do not repent. Our prophets today do the same thing for us, for example, in "The Family: A Proclamation to the World," given in 1995. We are seeing many of the prophecies in this proclamation already coming true in our day. Let's look at one particular paragraph from it as an example:

"We warn that individuals who violate covenants of chastity, who abuse spouse or offspring, or who fail to fulfill family responsibilities will one day stand accountable before God. Further, we warn that the disintegration of the family will bring upon individuals, communities, and nations the calamities foretold by ancient and modern prophets."

Now watch, in verses 2–8, what Abinadi warns will happen to these people who are following King Noah's terribly bad example if they don't repent.

2 Yea, **wo be** [*trouble is coming*] **unto this generation!** And the Lord said unto me [*Abinadi*]: Stretch forth thy hand and prophesy [*tell what is going to happen in the future*], saying: Thus saith the Lord, it shall come to pass [*it will surely happen*] that **this generation** [*the people who are now alive*], because of their iniquities [*wickedness*], **shall be brought into bondage**, and **shall be smitten** [*hit, slapped*] **on the cheek**; yea, and shall be **driven** [*pushed around, herded, beat up*] by men, and shall be **slain** [*killed*]; and the **vultures** of the air, **and** the **dogs**, yea, **and** the **wild beasts, shall devour** [*eat*] **their flesh.**

3 And it shall come to pass that **the life of king Noah shall be valued even as a garment in a hot furnace** [*King Noah will be burned to death*]; for he shall know that I am the Lord.

4 And it shall come to pass that **I will smite** [*punish*] **this my people with sore** [*very difficult*] afflictions [*troubles*], yea, with **famine** and with **pestilence** [*serious things like crop failure, diseases, etc.*]; and I will cause that they shall **howl all the day long.**

Did you notice that the Lord still calls these wicked people "my people" in verse 4, above? This is a tender reminder to the reader that He still loves them.

5 Yea, and I will cause that they shall have **burdens lashed upon their backs; and they shall be driven before like a dumb ass.**

6 And it shall come to pass that I will send forth **hail** among them [*which will bring crop failure and famine*], and it shall smite them; and they shall also be smitten with the **east wind** [*terrible destruction; a reference to the destruction caused by the dreaded east wind coming of the deserts to the east of the Holy Land, which caused overnight crop failures*]; and **insects shall pester their land also, and devour their grain**.

7 And they shall be smitten with a great **pestilence** [*plagues and troubles of all kinds*]—and all this will I do because of their iniquities [*wickedness*] and abominations [*extra bad sins and evil behaviors*].

You may have noticed that the punishments of God are designed first to save souls and lastly to destroy the wicked when it becomes absolutely necessary.

8 And it shall come to pass that **except they repent I will utterly destroy them from off the face of the earth**; yet they shall leave a record behind them, and I will preserve them [*the written accounts of these people*] for other nations which shall possess the land; yea, even this will I do that I may discover [*reveal*] the abominations of this people to other nations. And many things did Abinadi prophesy against this people.

We will once again see the "pattern" for avoiding repentance as the people react to Abinadi's message. Instead of looking at themselves and their wicked lives, and humbly repenting, they will **get mad at him**, tie him up, and take him to King Noah.

9 And it came to pass that they were **angry with him**; and they took him and carried him bound before the king, and said unto the king: Behold, we have brought a man before thee who **has prophesied evil concerning thy people** [*they are "calling evil good and good evil;" compare with 2 Nephi 15:20; Isaiah 5:20*], and saith that God will destroy them.

10 And he also prophesieth evil concerning thy life, and **saith that thy life shall be as a garment in a furnace of fire.**

In a sad sense, King Noah is a "type" of the burning of the wicked at the second coming of Christ. Remember that the word "type," as used in the scriptures, means "symbolic of."

As wicked King Noah hears what Abinadi said would happen to him, in the next verses, he becomes frightened and almost lets Abinadi go.

11 And again, he saith that **thou shalt be as a stalk** [*a piece of straw*], **even as a dry stalk of the field, which is run over by the beasts and trodden under foot.**

12 And again, he saith **thou shalt be as the blossoms of a thistle, which, when it is fully ripe, if the wind bloweth, it is driven forth upon the face of the land.** And **he pretendeth the Lord hath spoken it.** And he saith all this shall come upon thee except thou repent, and this because of thine iniquities.

By intentionally surrounding himself with wicked peers, Noah sealed his doom. Watch, next, as his peers support him and prevent him from doing what is right regarding Abinadi. Remember, also, that Noah's father, Zeniff, was a righteous man, so we know that Noah had at least been taught the gospel. You can almost hear the smooth, cunning voices of these priests in King Noah's court, as they flatter him.

13 And now, **O king, what great evil hast thou done, or what great sins have thy people committed**, that we should be condemned of God [*in trouble with God*] or judged of this man?

14 And now, O king, behold, **we are guiltless**, and **thou, O king, hast not sinned**; therefore, this man has lied concerning you, and he has prophesied in vain [*what he prophesied will not happen*].

The spiritual blindness demonstrated by Noah's wicked priests in verse 13, above, is typical of the spiritual insensitivity and being "past feeling" of many in the world today. They do not consider their evil ways to be wicked at all. Again, Satan is a tragically successful master of deception, and perhaps one of the most significant deceptions is to get people to ignore their conscience to the point that they truly believe that evil is good and good is evil and what they are doing and thinking is actually okay.

15 And behold, **we are strong, we shall not come into bondage** [*slavery; perhaps symbolic of the "we can handle it" attitude of sinners*], or be taken captive by our enemies; yea, and thou hast prospered in the land, and thou shalt also prosper [*the way you are leading us is just fine*].

16 Behold, here is the man, **we deliver him into thy hands; thou mayest do with him as seemeth thee good**.

Did you notice the role reversal in verse 16, above? The priests are giving the king permission, rather than the other way around.

17 And it came to pass that **king Noah caused that Abinadi should be cast into prison**; and he commanded that the priests should gather themselves together that he might hold a council with them what he should do with him.

18 And it came to pass that they said unto the king: Bring him hither [*here*] that we may question him; and the

king commanded that he should be brought before them.

19 And **they began to question him**, that they might cross him [*trap him in his words so that they would have the "legal" right to execute him*], that thereby they might have wherewith to accuse him; but **he answered them boldly**, and withstood [*skillfully answered*] all their questions, yea, to their astonishment; for he did withstand them in all their questions, and did confound them [*successfully rebutted them*] in all their words.

Remember that a wicked priest named Alma, who was a young man at the time (Mosiah 17:2), was there also in King Noah's court, listening to the words of Abinadi. While we don't know at what point Abinadi's words began touching Alma's heart so that he began believing Abinadi, we do know that Abinadi will have at least one convert before the trial is over. In fact, Alma will almost lose his own life for trying to defend Abinadi.

Next, we will watch as these wicked priests skillfully pretend to be righteous in order to cover up their evil ways. One of them will now pretend to be asking sincere questions, quoting Isaiah 52:7–10, to appear all the more holy. It would seem that the priest is implying, "True prophets publish peace. You are not promoting peace among our people. Instead, you are scaring them and predicting all kinds of terrible things. Therefore, you can't possibly be a true prophet sent from God." He, of course, is missing the point completely, which Abinadi will point out after the priest is through quoting Isaiah.

20 And it came to pass that **one of them said** unto him: What meaneth the words which are written [*in the scriptures*], and which have been taught by our fathers [*ancestors*], saying:

21 **<u>How beautiful upon the mountains are the feet of him</u> that bringeth good tidings; that publisheth peace**; that **bringeth good tidings of good**; that publisheth salvation; that saith unto Zion, Thy God reigneth;

22 Thy watchmen shall lift up the voice; with the voice together shall they sing; for they shall see eye to eye when the Lord shall bring again Zion;

23 **Break forth into joy**; sing together ye waste places of Jerusalem; for the Lord hath **comforted his people**, he hath redeemed Jerusalem;

24 The Lord hath made bare his holy arm [*shown His power*] in the eyes of all the nations, and all the ends of the earth shall see the salvation of our God?

The priests of Noah think that they are in charge during this trial (one of Satan's successful deceptions), but Abinadi is actually in charge, working under the inspiration of the Lord. Watch now, as he takes over and conducts a question and answer session with them. Remember that in verses 20 and 21, the priest asked Abinadi a question—namely, what does Isaiah 52:7–10 mean? Abinadi will now ask a question in response.

Question

25 And now Abinadi said unto them: **Are you priests**, and pretend to teach this people, and to understand the spirit of prophesying, **and yet desire to know of me what these things mean?**

Answer

26 I say unto you, wo be unto you for perverting [*twisting, corrupting*] the ways of the Lord! For **if ye understand these things ye have not taught them**; therefore, ye have perverted the ways of the Lord.

Question

27 Ye have not applied your hearts to understanding; therefore, ye have not been wise. Therefore, **what teach ye this people?**

Answer

28 And they said: **We teach the law of Moses** [*the Old Testament laws and commandments that Moses gave the people to prepare them to accept Christ and His gospel*].

Question

29 And again he said unto them: **If ye teach the law of Moses why do ye not keep it?** Why do ye set your hearts upon riches? Why do ye commit whoredoms [*sexual immorality*] and spend your strength with harlots [*prostitutes*], yea, and cause this people to commit sin, that the Lord has cause to send me to prophesy against this people, yea, even a great evil against this people?

Question and Answer

30 **Know ye not that I speak the truth?** Yea, **ye know that I speak the truth;** and **you ought to tremble before God.**

Question

31 And it shall come to pass that ye shall be smitten for your iniquities, for ye have said that ye teach the law of Moses. And **what know ye concerning the law of Moses? Doth salvation come by the law of Moses? What say ye?** [*In other words, can people return to the presence of God by keeping the Law of Moses? The answer is definitely "No." We can only be saved through Christ's gospel and the Atonement, with the Melchizedek Priesthood ordinances that go with it.*]

Answer

32 And **they answered and said that salvation did come by the law of Moses.** [*Wrong answer.*]

Abinadi has the priests on the defensive. He will take time now to be a teacher. Remember, Alma is listening, probably very carefully and focused now. Abinadi will now begin teaching the role of the Law of Moses in preparing people to accept Christ's gospel. He will mention two of the Ten Commandments and then will continue teaching the role of the Law of Moses, beginning with Mosiah 13:11.

Notice that Abinadi becomes gentler as he offers them an opportunity to change their thinking and repent.

33 But now Abinadi said unto them: **I know if ye keep the commandments of God ye shall be saved**; yea, if ye keep the commandments which the Lord delivered unto Moses in the mount of Sinai, saying:

34 **I am the Lord thy God**, who hath brought thee out of the land of Egypt, out of the house of bondage.

35 **Thou shalt have no other God before me.**

36 **Thou shalt not make unto thee any graven image, or any likeness of any thing in heaven above, or things which are in the earth beneath.**

Questions and Answers

37 Now Abinadi said unto them, **Have ye done all this?** I say unto you, **Nay**, ye have not. And **have ye taught this people that they should do all these things?** I say unto you, **Nay, ye have not.**

MOSIAH 13

Remember that one of wicked King Noah's wicked priests is a young man named Alma. We know that he is a young man because Mosiah 17:2 tells us so. We can imagine at this point that Alma is listening to Abinadi very intently. As we watch and listen to what happens next, we have to wonder what is taking place in Alma's mind and heart. Has his heart already been touched by the Spirit? Is he beginning to wonder if there is any hope for him? Has he already realized that Abinadi is a true prophet sent by God or is that transition in his thinking just beginning to take place? Hopefully, we will be privileged to attend a "fireside" in the next life where Alma will be the speaker and will tell us all about his experience here.

Watch now as King Noah tries to get rid of Abinadi right now. It doesn't work.

1 AND now when **the king** had heard these words, he **said unto his priests: Away with this fellow, and slay him**; for what have we to do with him, for he is mad [*has lost his mind*].

2 And **they** stood forth and **attempted to lay their hands on him**; but he withstood [*stopped*] them, and said unto them:

3 **Touch me not, for God shall smite you if ye lay your hands upon me**, for I have not delivered the message which the Lord sent me to deliver; neither have I told you that which ye requested that I should tell [*I haven't finished answering your question yet (Mosiah 12:20)*]; therefore, God will not suffer [*permit*] that I shall be destroyed at this time.

4 But I must fulfil the commandments wherewith God has commanded me; and **because I have told you the truth ye are angry with me**. And again, because I have spoken the word of God ye have judged me that I am mad [*crazy*].

5 Now it came to pass **after Abinadi had spoken these words that the people of king Noah durst not** [*did not dare*] **lay their hands on him**, for the Spirit of the Lord was upon him; and his face shone [*shined*] with exceeding luster [*light*], even as Moses' did while in the mount of Sinai, while speaking with the Lord.

6 And **he spake** [*spoke*] **with power and authority from God**; and he continued his words, saying:

Have you noticed that when our prophets and Church leaders speak to us, you often feel the "power and authority from God" in them as they speak, as mentioned in verse 6, above? This is one way you experience the help of the Holy Ghost bearing testimony to you that the Church is true.

In the next verses, you will see that Abinadi can read their minds by the power of the Spirit so that he knows exactly what they are thinking and feeling in their hearts.

7 Ye see that ye have not power to slay me, therefore I finish my message. Yea, and **I perceive** [*I see*] that it cuts you to your hearts because I tell you the truth concerning your iniquities [*wickedness*].

8 Yea, and **my words fill you with wonder and amazement, and with anger.**

9 **But I finish my message**; and then it matters not whither I go, if it so be that I am saved.

10 But this much **I tell you, what you do with me, after this, shall be as a type and a shadow of things which are to come** [*what you do to me will be a predictor of what will happen to you*].

In Mosiah 12:33–36, Abinadi started, but did not finish quoting the Ten Commandments to Noah and his priests. Now he will finish.

11 **And now I read unto you the remainder of the commandments of God**, for I perceive [*I can see*] that they are not written in your hearts [*you do not want to keep God's commandments*]; I perceive that ye have studied and taught iniquity the most part of your lives.

The phrase at the end of verse 11, above, points out clearly what is going on in the hearts of many today. They are intentionally studying how to be more wicked and how to involve more people in wickedness. Most often, it is for financial gain, and sometimes it is to justify their own evil doings and satisfy their own egos.

There is a strong trend in our world today to reduce the Ten Commandments to "suggestions" or even to ignore the Bible completely. The Book of Mormon sustains the Bible here by confirming that the Ten Commandments were indeed commandments, and that they are still commandments from God in our day.

12 And now, ye remember that I said unto you: **Thou shall not make unto thee any graven image**, or any likeness of things which are in heaven above, or which are in the earth beneath, or which are in the water under the earth.

13 And again: **Thou shalt not bow down thyself unto them, nor serve them**; for I the Lord thy God am a jealous God, visiting the iniquities of the fathers upon the children, unto the third and fourth generations of them that hate me;

14 And showing mercy unto thousands of them that love me and keep my commandments.

15 **Thou shalt not take the name of the Lord thy God in vain**; for the Lord will not hold him guiltless that taketh his name in vain.

16 **Remember the sabbath day, to keep it holy.**

17 Six days shalt thou labor, and do all thy work;

18 But the seventh day, the sabbath of the Lord thy God, thou shalt not do any work, thou, nor thy son, nor thy daughter, thy man–servant, nor thy maid–servant, nor thy cattle, nor thy stranger that is within thy gates;

19 For in six days the Lord made heaven and earth, and the sea, and all that in them is; wherefore the Lord blessed the sabbath day, and hallowed it.

20 **Honor thy father and thy mother**, that thy days may be long upon the land which the Lord thy God giveth thee.

21 **Thou shalt not kill.**

22 **Thou shalt not commit adultery. Thou shalt not steal.**

23 **Thou shalt not bear false witness** against thy neighbor.

24 **Thou shalt not covet** thy neighbor's house, thou shalt not covet thy neighbor's wife, nor his man–servant, nor his maid–servant, nor his ox, nor his ass, nor anything that is thy neighbor's.

Watch now as Abinadi asks Noah and his priests some more questions. And remember, Alma is listening.

Question

25 And it came to pass that after Abinadi had made an end of these sayings that he said unto them: **Have ye taught this people that they should observe to do all these things for to keep these commandments?**

Answer

26 I say unto you, **Nay**; for if ye had, the Lord would not have caused me to come forth and to prophesy evil concerning this people.

Next, Abinadi will explain the relationship between the Law of Moses and the Gospel of Christ. He will tell them that it is necessary for the people to continue living the Law of Moses until the Savior comes to earth. And he will clearly teach his listeners that the Law of Moses alone does not have the power to save us. Rather, it is Christ and His Atonement that have power to save us.

27 And now ye have said that salvation cometh by the law of Moses. I say unto you that **it is expedient**

[*necessary*] **that ye should keep the law of Moses as yet; but** I say unto you, that **the time shall come when it shall no more be expedient to keep the law of Moses.**

What Abinadi teaches above is clearly what was taught in Old Testament times to righteous people; namely, that the time would come that they would no longer be living the Law of Moses. As you know, somehow the scribes and Pharisees and chief priests, etc., among the Jews, failed to understand this message when the Savior came among them. Thus, they were extremely angry with Jesus for replacing what their main prophet, Moses, taught them with the higher laws and ordinances that could actually save them and get them in to heaven.

28 And moreover, I say unto you, that **salvation doth not come by the law** [*the Law of Moses*] **alone**; and **were it not for the atonement, which God himself shall make for the sins and iniquities of his people, that they must unavoidably perish,** notwithstanding [*even though they had*] the law of Moses.

Next, Abinadi explains to these priests why the Law of Moses was given in the first place. This is one of the clearest explanations of this subject anywhere.

29 And now I say unto you that **it was expedient** [*necessary*] **that there should be a law given to the children of Israel,** yea, even **a very strict law;** for **they were a stiffnecked** [*stubborn, proud, not humble*] **people,** quick to do iniquity [*quick to commit sins*], and slow to remember the Lord their God;

30 Therefore there was a law given them [*the Law of Moses*], yea, **a law of performances** [*things they had to do exactly right*] **and of ordinances,** a law which they were **to observe strictly from day to day, to keep them in remembrance of God and their duty towards him.**

31 But behold, I say unto you, that **all these things were types of** [*symbolic of*] **things to come.** [*In other words, the whole Law of Moses was designed to point the peoples' minds toward Christ and get them ready to live His higher gospel.*]

Question and Answer

32 And now, **did they understand the law?** I say unto you, **Nay**, they did not all understand the law; and this **because of the hardness of their hearts**; for **they understood not that there could not any man be saved except it were through the redemption of God** [*they did not understand that no one could be saved except through the Atonement of Christ*].

Question and Answer

33 For behold, **did not Moses prophesy unto them concerning the coming of the Messiah,** and **that God should redeem his people? Yea,** and **even all the prophets** who have prophesied ever since the world began—**have they not spoken more or less concerning these**

things? [*In other words, Moses taught of Christ and every other Old Testament prophet also taught about the Savior and the Atonement. This is an indicator as to how much was lost as the "plain and precious things" (1 Nephi 13:26–29) were systematically taken out of what became our Bible.*]

Question

34 **Have they not said that God** [*Christ*] **himself should come down among the children of men, and take upon him the form of man, and go forth in mighty power upon the face of the earth?**

Question

35 **Yea**, and **have they not said also that he** [*Christ*] **should bring to pass the resurrection of the dead, and that he, himself, should be oppressed and afflicted?**

MOSIAH 14

In this chapter, Abinadi is saying, in effect, "Haven't you read Isaiah? Don't you understand that he was prophesying about Christ?" He will then quote what we know as Isaiah, chapter 53, to Noah and his priests.

Mosiah 14 compares to Isaiah, chapter 53 in the Bible, and is a wonderful chapter, showing that teaching and prophesying about Christ was a major part of the Old Testament. Abinadi, in effect, brings Isaiah in as a "second witness" to what he has been teaching the priests of Noah.

1 Yea, even **doth not Isaiah say: Who hath believed our report** [*"Who listens to us prophets, anyway?"*], and **to whom is the arm of the Lord revealed** [*"Who sees God's hand in things"*]?

Isaiah gave these prophecies about Jesus and His mortal mission here on earth over 600 years before the Savior's birth. He is definitely an Old Testament prophet and Abinadi is showing Noah and his priests that the Old Testament definitely prophesied of Christ.

Isaiah is speaking of these things as though they had already taken place. Also, notice that Isaiah repeats the same ideas and teachings many times in these verses. This is confusing to some people as they read and study Isaiah's writings because they don't realize that he is repeating things for emphasis as he teaches.

2 For **he** [*Jesus*] **shall grow up** before him [*Heavenly Father*] **as a tender plant** [*a new plant, a restoration of truth*], and as a root **out of dry ground** [*symbolic of false religions among the Jews at the time of Christ*]; **he hath no form nor comeliness** [*He has no special appearance or beauty*]; and when we shall see him **there is no beauty that we should desire him** [*normal people couldn't tell he was the Son of God just by looking at Him*].

3 **He is despised and rejected of men; a man of sorrows** [*sensitive to peoples' troubles*], and **acquainted with grief**; and **we hid as it were our faces from him** [*wouldn't even look at him*]; **he was despised**, and **we** [*people in Judea*] **esteemed him not** [*didn't believe that He was the Son of God; even his own siblings rejected him at first; John 7, heading and verse 5*].

4 Surely **he has borne our griefs, and carried our sorrows**; yet **we did esteem him stricken, smitten of God, and afflicted** [*we didn't recognize him as the Great Atoner, rather thought he was being appropriately punished by God*].

5 But **he was wounded for our transgressions** [*He paid for our sins*], he was **bruised for our iniquities** [*He suffered the pain for our sins*]; **the chastisement of our peace was upon him** [*he was punished so that we could have peace*]; and **with his stripes** [*punishments*] **we are healed** [*we are healed from the effects of our sins; the Atonement and its effects*].

6 **All we, like sheep, have gone astray**; we have turned every one to his own way [*every one of us has sinned; we all need the Atonement*]; and **the Lord hath laid on him the iniquities of us all** [*Heavenly Father sent His Son to take our sins upon Himself*].

7 **He was oppressed**, and he was **afflicted** [*He was badly treated*], **yet he opened not his mouth**; he is brought as a lamb to the slaughter, and **as a sheep** before her shearers is dumb [*can't speak*] so **he opened not his mouth**.

8 **He was taken from** prison and from **judgment** [*He was not given fair treatment*]; and **who shall declare his generation** [*who even cared about what happened to him*]? For he was cut off [*killed*] out of the land of the living; **for the transgressions of my people was he stricken** [*He paid for our sins*].

9 And **he made his grave with the wicked** [*died with convicted criminals hanging on crosses on both sides of His cross*], and **with the rich in his death** [*a rich man donated his tomb, John 19:38–42*]; because **he had done no evil, neither was any deceit** [*lying, deception, not telling the truth*] **in his mouth** [*Christ was perfect*].

10 **Yet it pleased the Lord** [*it was the Father's will*] **to bruise him** [*to allow Him to perform the Atonement*]; **he hath put him to grief**; when thou shalt make his soul an offering for sin **he shall see his seed** [*his loyal followers, success; Mosiah 15:10–12*], he shall prolong his days, and **the pleasure of the Lord** [*the will of the Father*] **shall prosper in his hand** [*will be accomplished by the Son's Atonement*].

11 **He shall see the travail** [*labor to bring forth the Atonement*] **of his soul, and shall be satisfied** [*He will look upon the Atonement with satisfaction*]; **by his knowledge shall my righteous servant justify** [*save*] **many; for he shall bear their iniquities**.

12 Therefore will I divide him a portion with the great, and **he shall divide the spoil** [*Jesus will receive His reward*] **with the strong** [*the righteous*]; **because he hath poured out his soul unto death** [*because He gave His life*]; and **he was numbered with the transgressors** [*people thought He was a sinner and deserved to be crucified*]; and **he bore the sins of many** [*He suffered for the sins of all people; see 2 Nephi 9:21*], and **made intercession for the transgressors** [*atoned for our sins*].

MOSIAH 15

As you might have noticed already, many members of the Church have difficulty reading and understanding the writings of the prophet Isaiah in the scriptures. One of the great contributions of the Book of Mormon is that it helps us better understand Isaiah's writings. This chapter, Mosiah, chapter 15, is a good example of this. Abinadi will now explain the words of Isaiah which he read to Noah and his priests, as recorded in Mosiah 14. As we study what Abinadi says about Isaiah's writings, we learn much ourselves about how to understand the words of Isaiah.

The nest verses get us off to a good start by explaining to us that one of Isaiah's major teachings was that Heavenly Father's Son, Jesus Christ, would come and be born on earth and would perform His Atonement, which would make it possible for all of us to be redeemed, in other words, set free from our sins if we repent and also be redeemed from the effects of physical death.

1 AND now Abinadi said unto
them: I would that ye should understand that **God himself** [*Jesus*] **shall come down among the children of men, and shall redeem his people** [*Jesus will come to earth and carry out the Atonement*].

Book of Mormon students often find themselves a bit confused after reading the next three verses. It will help if you understand that Jesus has several titles, or "name titles," many of which describe certain aspects of His role as Redeemer. For instance, "Son of God," "Jehovah," "Holy One of Israel," "I AM," "Father" (of our salvation), "Creator," "Son of Man of Holiness," "Good Shepherd," "Firstborn," "Deliverer," "Redeemer," "Judge," "Rock," etc. Watch for several of these titles or names used by Abinadi as he taught Alma and the other priests of wicked King Noah about Christ.

2 And because he [*Christ*] dwelleth
in flesh he shall be called **the Son of God** [*He will literally be the Son of Heavenly Father when He comes to earth as a mortal*], and having subjected the flesh to the will of the Father, being **the Father** [*the "Father" of our salvation, the author of our salvation, in the same sense that George Washington is the "father" of our nation*] and **the Son** [*literally, the Son of God*]—

3 **The Father** [*of our salvation*], because
he was conceived by the power of God [*because He was literally the Son of God, which gave Him power over death and hell and all other things that would stand in the way of our gaining exaltation*]; and **the Son**, because of the flesh [*because He was born as a mortal to the Father and Mary*]; thus becoming **the Father** [*of our salvation*] **and Son** [*of God by way of His mortal birth*]—

For more concerning the use of the term "Father" to refer both to Heavenly Father and Jesus, you may wish to read pages 465–73 in *The Articles of Faith*, by James E. Talmage, 12th edition, published by Deseret Book.

4 And **they** [*the Father and Jesus*] **are one**
God [*they work in perfect unity, "one" in purpose*], yea, **the very Eternal Father of**

heaven and of earth [*the Creator; refers to Jesus; see Mosiah 16:15; also see the next note, below*].

We will quote from James E. Talmage to explain the bolded part of verse 4, above.

"God is not the Father of the earth as one of the worlds in space, nor of the heavenly bodies in whole or in part, nor of the inanimate objects and the plants and the animals upon the earth, in the literal sense in which He is the Father of the spirits of mankind. Therefore, scriptures that refer to God in any way as the Father of the heavens and the earth are to be understood as signifying that God is the Maker, the Organizer, the Creator of the heavens and the earth.

"With this meaning, as the context shows in every case, Jehovah who is Jesus Christ the Son of Elohim, is called 'the Father,' and even 'the very eternal Father of heaven and of earth' (see Mosiah 15:4 . . . and also Mosiah 16:15). With analogous meaning Jesus Christ is called 'The Everlasting Father' (Isaiah 9:6; compare 2 Nephi 19:6). The descriptive titles 'Everlasting' and 'Eternal' in the foregoing texts are synonymous" (James E. Talmage, *Articles of Faith* [Salt Lake City: Deseret Book, 1981], 421).

We now turn again to Abinadi as he teaches about the coming of Christ into mortality. He explains that Christ will become mortal and will humbly submit to the Father in all things as He works out the Atonement in perfect unity and harmony with Him.

5 **And thus the flesh** [*the Mortal Christ*] **becoming subject** to the Spirit, or the Son **to the Father**, being **one God** [*completely united in purpose*], suffereth temptation, and yieldeth not to the temptation, but suffereth [*allows*] himself to be mocked, and scourged [*whipped*], and cast out, and disowned by his people.

6 And after all this, after working many mighty miracles among the children of men [*among mortals*], **he shall be led, yea, even as Isaiah said** [*in Mosiah 14:7*], **as a sheep before the shearer** is dumb [*does not bleat*], so he opened not his mouth [*when Herod questioned him; see Luke 23:7–9*].

7 Yea, even so **he shall be led, crucified, and slain**, the flesh becoming subject even unto death, **the will of the Son being swallowed up in the will of the Father** [*Christ submitting completely to the will of His Father*].

8 And **thus God breaketh the bands of death** [*overcomes physical death for everyone ever born*], having gained the victory over death; giving the Son [*Christ*] power to make intercession for [*to atone for the sins of*] the children of men—

Next, Abinadi teaches King Noah and his wicked priests that after Jesus has finished His mortal life and mission on earth—in other words, after He has been crucified and resurrected—He will return to heaven, having done everything Heavenly Father asked Him to do. Remember, the young priest, Alma, is listening to all this.

9 **Having ascended into heaven** [*Jesus returned to heaven*], having the

bowels of mercy [*being full of mercy for us; hopefully, Alma is listening carefully to this*]; being filled with compassion towards the children of men [*Jesus has very tender feelings for us*]; standing betwixt them and justice [*the law of justice, which demands that payment be made for sins*]; **having broken the bands of death** [*having overcome death for all people*], **taken upon himself their iniquity** [*evil behaviors*] **and their transgressions** [*sins*], **having redeemed them, and satisfied the demands of justice** [*paid the penalty for our sins required by the law of justice*].

10 And now I say unto you, who shall declare his generation [*who, in his generation, will even care what happens to Him*]? Behold, I say unto you, that when his soul has been made an offering for sin [*when Christ has given His life for our sins*] **he shall see his seed** [*Christ's "children," meaning His followers who qualify to be redeemed from their sins; referring back to what Isaiah said, quoted in Mosiah 14:10; see also Mosiah 5:7*]. And now what say ye? And **who shall be his seed?** [*In other words, "What is your answer? What did Isaiah mean when he referred to Christ's "seed?"*]

Abinadi has no doubt stumped King Noah and his priests with his question, above, as to what Isaiah meant when he referred to Christ's seed. They don't know the answer. Having their full attention, he now answers his own question. Watch carefully as he defines the Savior's seed as those who believe in Christ, who live the gospel, and who ultimately attain exaltation in the celestial kingdom.

11 Behold I say unto you, that **whosoever has heard the words of the prophets**, yea, all the holy prophets who have prophesied concerning the coming of the Lord—I say unto you, that **all those who have hearkened** [*listened and obeyed*] **unto their words, and believed that the Lord would redeem his people,** and have looked forward to that day [*Christ's Atonement*] for a remission of their sins, I say unto you, **that these are his seed**, or **they are the heirs of the kingdom of God** [*they are the ones who will receive celestial glory, exaltation*].

12 For **these are they whose sins he has borne** [*these are the ones who are forgiven of sins*]; **these** [*Christ's seed*] **are they for whom he has died, to redeem them from their transgressions.** And now, are they not **his seed**?

13 Yea, and are not the prophets, every one that has opened his mouth to prophesy, that has not fallen into transgression, I mean **all the holy prophets** ever since the world began? I say unto you that they **are his seed.**

14 And **these are they** who have published peace, who have brought good tidings of good, who have published salvation; and said unto Zion: Thy God reigneth!

Now Abinadi has come full circle back to the question posed by the cunning priest of Noah, starting in Mosiah 12:21, who intended to trap him with his question. Abinadi will explain that there are many interpretations of those whose "feet" are "beautiful upon the mountains." In other words, there are many who teach of Christ, including Christ Himself.

15 And **O how beautiful upon the mountains were their feet!**

16 And again, **how beautiful upon the mountains are the feet of those that are still publishing peace** [*who are still teaching of Christ and His gospel*]!

17 And again**, how beautiful upon the mountains are the feet of those who shall hereafter publish peace**, yea, from this time henceforth and forever!

18 And behold, I say unto you, **this is not all** [*this is not the only interpretation of "beautiful feet upon the mountains" or messengers whose feet have brought them upon the mountains where they can be more easily heard by the people below*]. For O **how beautiful upon the mountains are the feet of him** [*Christ*] that bringeth good tidings, that is **the founder of peace**, yea, even **the Lord**, who has redeemed his people; yea, him **who has granted salvation unto his people**;

19 For **were it not for the redemption which he hath made for his people**, which was prepared from the foundation of the world [*which was planned and implemented in premortality*], I say unto you, were it not for this, **all mankind must have** [*would have*] **perished**.

20 **But** behold, **the bands of death shall be broken** [*all will be resurrected*], **and the Son** [*Christ*] reigneth, and hath power over the dead; therefore, he **bringeth to pass the resurrection of the dead**.

Next, Abinadi will set the stage to preach the doctrine that everyone, whether good or evil, will be resurrected and that the wicked will be subject to the law of justice, rather than the law of mercy. We would suspect that Alma's heart has been deeply touched by now and that the Spirit is bearing witness to him that even he can become clean through the Savior's Atonement.

Abinadi will teach several specific doctrines about the Resurrection. We will give some explanations as we proceed. To begin with, he will use the phrase "first resurrection." This is another way of saying "the resurrection of the just," meaning the righteous who will come forth in celestial bodies to enter celestial glory. He is referring specifically to all those from Adam and Eve down to the time of Christ's Resurrection, who are worthy of celestial glory, and who will be resurrected with Christ. See D&C 133:54–55.

21 And there cometh a resurrection, even a **first resurrection**; yea, even **a resurrection of those that have been, and who are, and who shall be, even until the resurrection of Christ**—for so shall he be called.

22 And now, the resurrection of all the prophets, and all **those that have believed in their words, or all those that have kept the commandments of God, shall come forth in the first resurrection;** therefore, they are the first resurrection.

23 **They are raised** [*resurrected*] **to dwell with God who has redeemed them**; thus they have eternal life

[*exaltation in celestial glory*] through Christ, who has broken the bands of death.

Verse 24, next, is an example of the importance of interpreting specific verses within the context of all the scriptures. For instance, verse 24 must be seen in connection with D&C 138, where those who did not have an opportunity to hear the gospel on earth will be taught in the spirit world mission field. And, depending on whether they accept it or reject it, they may also come forth in the "first resurrection," meaning, in this case, the resurrection of those who will receive celestial glory, which will take place at the beginning of the Millennium.

24 And **these are those who have part in the first resurrection**; and these are they that have died before Christ came, in their ignorance, not having salvation declared unto them. And **thus the Lord bringeth about the restoration of these; and they have a part in the first resurrection, or have eternal life, being redeemed by the Lord** [*as explained in D&C 138*].

In verse 25, next, Abinadi's words remind us that in all ages, when the truth was available to people, they knew that little children who die before the age of accountability will attain exaltation in celestial glory. It is a very simple statement of fact.

25 **And little children also have eternal life.**

The term "eternal life" as used in the scriptures always means "exaltation in celestial glory." In other words, living in the highest degree of glory in the celestial kingdom, where families are forever and husbands and wives become gods over their own worlds. Again, "eternal life" means "exaltation." For example, D&C 14:7 says (**bold** added for emphasis), "And, if you keep my commandments and endure to the end you shall have **eternal life**, which gift **is the greatest of all the gifts of God.**"

Some members of the Church wonder how this can be, since little children were not married, and marriage is required for exaltation. The answer is simple. They are, of course, adult spirits after they die. As such, they can meet, fall in love, and choose eternal companions in the spirit realm or in the Millennium. Joseph Fielding Smith tells us that they will then be permitted to inform mortals living during the Millennium as to whom they wish to marry. (See *Doctrines of Salvation*, Joseph Fielding Smith, 1956, Bookcraft, vol. 3, page 65.) These mortals can then be sealed by proxy in a temple. Thus, "little children . . . have eternal life," plain and simple. Next, Abinadi addresses the plight of the wicked who refuse to repent. Remember, Alma is listening.

26 But behold, and **fear, and tremble** before God, for **ye ought to tremble;** for **the Lord redeemeth none such that rebel against him and die in their sins;** yea, even all those that have perished in their sins ever since the world began, **that have wilfully rebelled against God, that have known the commandments of God, and would not keep them; these are they that have no part in**

the first resurrection [*they will not attain celestial glory*].

We know from D&C 138 that God is completely fair and that for a person to qualify for the judgment spoken of by Abinadi in verse 26, above, he or she must have had a completely fair opportunity before the Final Judgment Day, to use agency to accept or reject the gospel, knowing full well what it is all about and having had a witness from the Holy Ghost that it is true. This must take place either here on earth or in the spirit world.

27 **Therefore ought ye not to tremble? For salvation cometh to none such; for the Lord hath redeemed none such**; yea, **neither can the Lord redeem such**; for he **cannot** deny himself; for he **cannot** deny justice when it has its claim.

It is interesting to pose the following question to students and then see how they answer:

Question: Is it that God **will not** forgive unrepentant sinners **or that He cannot**?

Question: What did Abinadi teach on this matter?

Answer (according to verse 27, above): He cannot. "**Neither can the Lord redeem such**; for he **cannot** deny himself; for he **cannot** deny justice when it has its claim." (Compare with Alma 42:13, 22, 25.)

28 And now I say unto you that **the time shall come that the salvation of the Lord shall be declared to every nation, kindred, tongue, and people.** [*Everyone will ultimately hear the gospel. God is completely fair. This includes the work in the spirit world.*]

Finally, Abinadi summarizes and repeats again the answer to the question that King Noah's priest asked him in Mosiah 12:20–24.

29 Yea, Lord, **thy watchmen** [*prophets*] **shall lift up their voice**; with the voice together shall they sing; for they shall see eye to eye, when the Lord shall bring again Zion.

30 Break forth into joy, sing together, ye waste places of Jerusalem; for the Lord hath comforted his people, **he hath redeemed Jerusalem** [*Israel will be gathered and Jerusalem will be restored*].

31 **The Lord hath made bare his holy arm in the eyes of all the nations** [*the Lord will show His power in the last days, Second Coming, and Millennium*]; and **all the ends of the earth shall see the salvation of our God** [*everyone will eventually know of Christ*].

MOSIAH 16

Two chapters ago, in Mosiah 14, Abinadi quoted from the prophet Isaiah's writings, teaching about the Savior and His Atonement. In Mosiah 15, he explained the words of Isaiah to King Noah and his court. Next, in chapter 16, he adds his own testimony to the testimony of Isaiah. Thus, Noah and his wicked priests have two witnesses against them, unless they repent—namely Abinadi and Isaiah. Hopefully, by now young Alma, who has been listening all along, has been deeply touched and is very worried about his own soul. We can feel the Spirit bearing witness to him and to us of the truthfulness of Abinadi's words. His testimony offers bright hope to all who are willing to call upon the Lord (see Mosiah 16:12). On the other hand, as Abinadi explains, the wicked who refuse to repent have great cause for concern.

As he continues, he points his listeners' minds to the end, meaning to the Millennium and Final Judgment, so that no question remains as to the fact that all who are accountable will answer to God for their actions.

1 AND now, it came to pass that after Abinadi had spoken these words [*his explanation of Isaiah's teachings*] he stretched forth his hand and said: **The time shall come when all shall see the salvation of the Lord**; when every nation, kindred, tongue, and people shall see eye to eye [*Millennium; see D&C 84:98*] and shall confess before God that his judgments are just [*everyone will ultimately have to acknowledge that God's judgment is correct and fair; see D&C 76:110*].

Next, Abinadi speaks of the outcome for the wicked on the Final Judgment Day.

2 And **then shall the wicked be cast out**, and they shall have cause to howl, and weep, and wail, and gnash their teeth [*grind their teeth together; a sign of extreme suffering in biblical language*]; and **this because they would not hearken unto the voice of the Lord; therefore the Lord redeemeth them not** [*they cannot be freed from sin by Christ's Atonement*].

3 For **they are carnal** [*they have become carnal, meaning given to worldly lusts and pleasures that violate God's commandments*] **and devilish** [*they think and act much like the devil does*], and the devil has power over them; yea, even that old serpent that did beguile [*deceive*] our first parents [*Adam and Eve*], which was the cause of their fall; which was the cause of all mankind becoming carnal [*worldly, sinful*], sensual [*lustful*], devilish, knowing evil from good [*they know they are sinning against God's laws and commandments*], subjecting themselves to the devil [*choosing to follow the devil*].

As taught in 2 Nephi 2:22–23, the Fall was good. It was absolutely necessary to open the door to our progression to exaltation. With it, as Abinadi teaches here, came the opportunity for us to choose good or evil. Many choose to "become" carnal, sensual, and devilish, as Abinadi points out in verse 3, above. Many do not. But without the Atonement, we would all be lost (see 2 Nephi 9:7–9). The point is that the Fall of Adam and Eve and the Atonement of Christ go hand in hand in preparing the way for exaltation.

4 Thus **all mankind** were lost; and behold, they **would have been endlessly lost were it not that God redeemed his people** from their lost and fallen state.

5 But remember that **he that persists in his own carnal nature** [*does not repent*], and goes on in the ways of sin and rebellion against God, **remaineth in his fallen state** [*after Judgment Day*] and the devil hath all power

over him. Therefore, **he is as though there was no redemption made** [*for sins*], **being an enemy to God**; and also is the devil an enemy to God.

6 And now **if Christ had not come** into the world, speaking of things to come as though they had already come, **there could have been no redemption** [*no Atonement*].

7 And **if Christ had not risen from the dead**, or have broken the bands of death that the grave should have no victory, and that death should have no sting, **there could have been no resurrection.**

8 **But there is a resurrection,** therefore the grave hath no victory, and **the sting of death is swallowed up in Christ** [*Christ overcame physical death completely for all of us; we will all be resurrected*].

9 **He is the light and the life of the world;** yea, a light that is endless, that can never be darkened [*Satan and evil can never triumph over Christ*]; yea, and also a life which is endless, that there can be no more death [*people who are resurrected can never die again*].

Next, Abinadi teaches us that everyone ever born (which leaves out Satan and the one third who followed him—they will never be born, therefore, never resurrected) will be resurrected and will face Christ (see John 5:22) at His judgment bar; in other words, Final Judgment.

10 Even **this mortal** [*physical body*] **shall put on immortality** [*will become immortal and live forever because of resurrection*], and this corruption [*mortal body which decays in the grave*] shall put on incorruption [*will be resurrected and never die and decay again*], **and shall be brought to stand before the bar of God** [*Christ; John 5:22*], **to be judged** of him according to their works whether they be good or whether they be evil—

11 **If they be good**, to the resurrection of endless life and happiness [*celestial glory and eternal life, exaltation*]; and **if they be evil**, to the resurrection of endless damnation [*being stopped forever from returning to live with God*], being delivered up [*turned over*] to the devil, who hath subjected them, which is damnation—

In verse 12, next, Abinadi gives us and King Noah and his priests a very clear definition of what leads to damnation.

12 **Having gone according to their own carnal** [*worldly, wicked*] **wills and desires; having never called upon the Lord while the arms of mercy were extended towards them**; for the arms of mercy were extended towards them, and they would not; **they being warned of their iniquities** [*wickedness*] **and yet they would not depart from them; and they were commanded to repent and yet they would not repent.**

13 And now, ought ye not to tremble and repent of your sins, and remember that **only in and through Christ ye can be saved**?

14 Therefore, **if ye teach the law of Moses, also teach that it is a**

shadow of those things which are to come— [*In other words, if you are going to teach the Law of Moses, teach all of it, most especially the fact that it points toward Christ and His gospel and Atonement. Also, the Law of Moses is a "shadow" of Christ's gospel, meaning that when you see a shadow of something, you know there is much more to whatever is casting the shadow.*]

15 **Teach them that redemption cometh through Christ the Lord**, who is the very Eternal Father [*the Creator of all things and the Father of our salvation*]. Amen.

MOSIAH 17

In this chapter we will officially meet Alma for the first time in the Book of Mormon. For many years, critics of the Book of Mormon pointed to the name "Alma" and claimed that Joseph Smith had made a serious mistake by using this name in the book, which they considered to be a fake and a fraud anyway. They claimed that "Alma" was a Spanish name for girls and that no such name existed in ancient Holy Land territory. Not so. In 1971, the name Alma was discovered on ancient writings in the Near East. A brief quote follows:

"It was not until 1971, 141 years after the publication of the Book of Mormon, that the name *Alma* turned up in an English translation of documents from Palestine. In that year Yigael Yadin described in the English version of his book, *Bar-Kokhba,* the discovery, careful excavation, and preliminary evaluation of objects found in caves west of the Dead Sea, particularly in the Nahal Hever area, from the period of the Bar-Kokhba revolt against the Romans about A.D. 130. Among the documents dealing with land transactions at nearby En-gedi the name *Alma* appears, written *aleph, lamed, mem, aleph.* Here, discovered in the Judean desert in 1961, is the confirmation that the Book of Mormon name *Alma*, at which critics of that sacred book have scoffed since its publication in 1830, is an authentic entry in the ancient Near Eastern Hebrew/Aramaic onomasticon" (Monte S. Nyman and Charles D. Tate, Jr., eds., *First Nephi: The Doctrinal Foundation* [Provo: BYU Religious Studies Center, 1988], 288–89).

We have already mentioned Alma several times in our notes and comments during Abinadi's teaching. He is an example of the power of the Atonement to cleanse and heal, completely. He is one of King Noah's wicked priests but will be forgiven and cleansed completely of his sins.

As mentioned previously, in this middle portion of the Book of Mormon, it appears that the Lord wants us to learn, among many other things, a major message regarding those who are very serious transgressors, who repent completely. In addition to Alma, we will meet several others in this section of the Book of Mormon, including Alma the Younger and the sons of Mosiah, whose repentance will lead to such lasting righteousness that they are compared to Captain Moroni by Mormon, in Alma 48:17–18. In other words, there is great and wonderful hope for the wicked who truly repent. They can become completely clean and worthy of exaltation in the highest degree of glory in the celestial kingdom.

Mosiah 11:2, 4–6, and 14 describe Noah's priests, which include Alma, as very wicked men, like Noah himself was. We will repeat these verses and **bold** the phrases which describe these men. Our purpose in doing so is to remind you of very serious sins from which Alma successfully repented.

Mosiah 11:2, 4–6, 14

2 For behold, **he** [*Noah*] **did not keep the commandments of God, but he did walk after the desires of his own heart.** And he **had many wives and concubines**. And **he did cause his people to commit sin,** and do that which was abominable [*extremely wicked*] in the sight of the Lord. Yea, **and they did commit whoredoms** [*sexual immorality*] **and all manner of wickedness.**

4 And all this did he take to support himself, and his wives and his concubines; and also **his priests, and their wives and their concubines**; thus he had changed the affairs of the kingdom.

5 For he put down all the priests that had been consecrated by his father, and consecrated new ones in their stead, such as were **lifted up in the pride of their hearts.**

6 Yea, and thus they were supported in their **laziness**, and in their **idolatry** [*idol worship; prioritizing on other things rather than worshiping God*], and in their **whoredoms** [*sexual immorality*], by the taxes which king Noah had put upon his people; thus did the people labor exceedingly to support iniquity.

14 And it came to pass that he **placed his heart upon his riches,** and he spent his time in **riotous living** with his wives and his concubines; and **so did also his priests spend their time with harlots** [*prostitutes*].

As we return now to Mormon's account of Abinadi and Alma, we have an indicator of the depth of Alma's conversion during Abinadi's preaching. In the next verses, Alma risks his life to try to save Abinadi.

1 AND now it came to pass that **when Abinadi had finished** these sayings, that **the king commanded** that the priests should take him and cause **that he should be put to death**.

2 But there was one among them [*King Noah's priests*] whose name was **Alma**, he also being a descendant of Nephi. And he **was a young man, and he believed the words which Abinadi had spoken**, for he knew concerning the iniquity which Abinadi had testified against them; **therefore he began to plead with the king that he would not be angry with Abinadi, but suffer** [*allow*] **that he might depart in peace**.

3 **But the king was more wroth** [*angry, enraged*], and caused that Alma should be cast out from among them, and sent his servants after him that they might slay him.

You may have wondered how we know what Abinadi preached. The answer is given in the next verse. We will **bold** it.

4 But he [*Alma*] fled from before them and hid himself that they found him not. And **he being concealed for many days did write all the words which Abinadi had spoken.**

5 And it came to pass that the king caused that his guards should surround **Abinadi** and take him; and they bound him and **cast** him **into prison**.

6 And **after three days**, having counseled with his priests, he caused that he should again be **brought before him**.

It is a common pattern for bullies and wicked people to seek some kind of justification for their behavior. They attempt to put the blame for their own evil behaviors onto their victims. Perhaps this is because it is too painful for them to face their own wickedness. Whatever the case, Satan's way seems to be to blame others for one's own current inappropriate behavior. Noah seeks justification in his own corrupt legal system for his actions against Abinadi.

7 And he said unto him: **Abinadi**, we have found an accusation against thee [*we have found a legal reason to execute you*], and **thou art worthy of death**.

We see the hypocrisy of King Noah, and his priests who support him, as they claim to be shocked that God would stoop so low as to come to earth and associate with mortals. It is an offense to their pretended righteous worship of God. In effect, they are accusing Abinadi of blasphemy against God ("blasphemy" means doing something terribly offensive against God) for suggesting such a thing, and thus offending God. It is insightful to note that blasphemy against their pretended righteousness was the same justification that the "righteous" Jewish leaders claimed as they stoned Stephen to death. See Acts 7:51–58, in the Bible.

8 For **thou hast said that God himself should come down among the children of men; and now, for this cause thou shalt be put to death unless thou wilt recall all the words which thou hast spoken evil concerning me and my people.**

9 Now **Abinadi said** unto him: I say unto you, **I will not recall the words which I have spoken unto you concerning this people, for they are true**; and that ye may know of their surety I have suffered myself that I have fallen into your hands. [*Abinadi allowed them to capture him so that he could testify directly to them.*]

10 Yea, and **I will suffer even until death, and I will not recall my words, and they shall stand as a testimony against you**. And if ye slay me ye will shed innocent blood, and this shall also stand as a testimony against you at the last day [*Judgment Day*].

King Noah is an example of a wicked person who may be on the verge of repenting, but who is encouraged and emboldened in evil by corrupt peers. We see this next as he orders that they proceed with Abinadi's execution.

11 And now **king Noah was about to release him,** for he feared his word; **for he feared that the judgments of God would come upon him.**

Verse 12, next, reminds us how dangerous corrupt peers and friends can be.

12 **But the priests lifted up their voices against him**, and began to accuse him, saying: He has reviled the king. **Therefore the king was stirred up in anger against him**, and he delivered him up that he might be slain.

13 And it came to pass that **they took him and bound him, and scourged** [*whipped*] **his skin with faggots** [*bundles of small sticks, bound together, often used as kindling to start fires*], yea, even unto death [*this alone nearly killed him*].

14 And now when the flames began to scorch him, **he cried unto them, saying**:

15 Behold, **even as ye have done unto me**, so shall it come to pass that **thy seed** [*your descendants*] **shall cause that many shall suffer the pains that I do suffer**, even the pains of death by fire; and this because they believe in the salvation of the Lord their God.

In verse 15, above, we see the devastation that the wicked can pass on to their posterity who often follow in their evil footsteps. Just before he dies, Abinadi prophesies that many of these wicked men's posterity will be as evil and corrupt as they are and, consequently, will take satisfaction in burning other righteous people. We see the fulfillment of this prophecy in Alma 25:5.

16 And it will come to pass that **ye shall be afflicted with all manner of diseases because of your iniquities** [*wickedness*].

17 Yea, and **ye shall be smitten on every hand**, and shall be driven and scattered to and fro, even as a wild flock is driven by wild and ferocious beasts.

18 And in that day **ye shall be hunted**, and ye shall be taken by the hand of your enemies, and then **ye shall suffer, as I suffer, the pains of death by fire**.

We see the fulfillment of Abinadi's prophecy in verses 16–18, above, in Alma 25:8–12.

19 Thus God executeth vengeance [*punishment*] upon those that destroy his people. **O God, receive my soul**.

20 And now, **when Abinadi had said these words, he fell, having suffered death by fire**; yea, having been put to death because he would not deny the commandments of God, **having sealed the truth of his words by his death**.

One who seals "the truth of his words by his death" is called a "martyr." There have been many martyrs, including Joseph Smith, who have sealed their testimonies with their blood. Abinadi gave his life so that Alma might be saved. And because Alma was saved, countless others who followed him were saved. Alma lived to be 82

(Mosiah 29:45) and thus had many years to do much good. It is sweet to picture in our minds the reunion in the spirit world paradise between Alma and Abinadi.

MOSIAH 18

In this chapter we are taught clearly the things we covenant to do when we are baptized. We make and renew the same covenants each time we partake of the sacrament worthily.

1 AND now, it came to pass that **Alma**, who had fled from the servants of king Noah, **repented of his sins and iniquities**, and went about privately among the people, and began to teach the words of Abinadi—

It is encouraging to note that Alma was ultimately forgiven completely of his sins. We know this from Mosiah 26:20, which reads (**bold** added for emphasis):

Mosiah 26:20

20 Thou art my servant; and **I covenant with thee that thou shalt have eternal life** [*exaltation; the highest degree of glory in the celestial kingdom. Another way of saying this is that Alma's "calling and election was made sure"*]; and thou shalt serve me and go forth in my name, and shalt gather together my sheep.

This verse verifies that Alma's calling and election was made sure. Thus, we know that it is possible to be completely forgiven from very serious sin. Now we will return to Alma's brief summary of Abinadi's teachings about Christ and His Atonement.

2 Yea, **concerning that which was to come** [*including the coming of the Messiah*], and also concerning **the resurrection of the dead**, and **the redemption of the people, which was to be brought to pass through the power, and sufferings, and death of Christ, and his resurrection and ascension into heaven.**

3 And **as many as would hear his word he did teach**. And he taught them privately, that it might not come to the knowledge of the king. And many did believe his words.

In the next verse, we are introduced to the word "Mormon." Joseph Smith explained the meaning as follows (**bold** added for emphasis):

The Prophet's Definition of the Word "Mormon." *Editor of the Times and Seasons:* Sir—Through the medium of your paper I wish to correct an error among men that profess to be learned, liberal and wise; and I do it the more cheerfully because I hope sober-thinking and sound-reasoning people will sooner listen to the voice of truth than be led astray by the vain pretensions of the self-wise. The error I speak of is the definition of the word "Mormon." It has been stated that this word was derived from the Greek word *mormo.* This is not the case. There was no Greek or Latin upon the plates from which I, through the grace of the Lord, translated the Book of Mormon. Let the language of the book speak for itself.

On the 523rd page of the fourth edition, it reads: "And now, behold we have written this record according to our knowledge in the characters which are called among us the Reformed Egyptian, being handed down and altered by us, according to our manner of speech; and if our plates had been sufficiently large, we should have written in Hebrew; but the Hebrew hath been altered by us also; and if we could have written in Hebrew, behold, ye would have had no imperfection in our record. But the Lord knoweth the things which we have written, and also that none other people knoweth our language; therefore He hath prepared means for the interpretation thereof."

Here, then, the subject is put to silence; for "none other people knoweth our language;" therefore the Lord, and not man, had to interpret, after the people were all dead. And, as Paul said, "The world by wisdom know not God;" so the world by speculation are destitute of revelation; and as God in His superior wisdom has always given His Saints, wherever he had any on the earth, the same spirit, and that spirit, as John says, is the true spirit of prophecy, which is the testimony of Jesus. I may safely say that the word "Mormon" stands independent of the wisdom and learning of this generation.

The word "Mormon" means, literally, more good.

Yours,

Joseph Smith

(Joseph Smith, *History of The Church of Jesus Christ of Latter-day Saints,* 7 vols., introduction and notes by B. H. Roberts [Salt Lake City: The Church of Jesus Christ of Latter-day Saints, 1932–51], 5: 399).

Next, the people who believed Alma's teachings went to a place where he could teach them without being caught by the King's servants.

4 And it came to pass that **as many as did believe him did go forth to a place which was called Mormon,** having received its name from the king, being in the borders of the land having been infested, by times or at seasons, by wild beasts.

5 Now, **there was in Mormon a fountain** [*a spring*] **of pure water, and Alma resorted thither** [*Alma went there*], there being near the water a thicket of small trees, **where he did hide himself** in the daytime from the searches of the king.

6 And it came to pass that **as many as believed him went thither** [*there*] **to hear his words.**

7 And it came to pass **after many days there were a goodly number gathered together at the place of Mormon, to hear the words of Alma.** Yea, all were gathered together that believed on his word, to hear him. And **he did teach them,** and did preach unto them **repentance,** and **redemption, and faith on the Lord.**

Alma's followers are now to the point of desiring baptism, because of his teachings and the power of the Holy Ghost upon them. By way of final preparation for baptism, Alma will list at least eight things that we covenant to do when we are baptized. We will number these in **bold ( )** and underline them as we study verses 8–10, next.

8 And it came to pass that he said unto them: **Behold, here are the waters of Mormon** (for thus were they called) and now, **(1) as ye are desirous to come into the fold of God** [*since you want to join the Church*], and **(2) to be called his people** [*want to take upon you the name of Christ*], and **(3) are willing to bear one another's burdens,** that they may be light;

9 Yea, and **(4) are willing to mourn with those that mourn**; yea, and **(5) comfort those that stand in need of comfort**, and to **(6) stand as witnesses of God at all times and in all things, and in all places** that ye may be in, even until death, that ye may be redeemed of God, and be numbered with those of the first resurrection [*those who attain celestial glory*], that ye may have eternal life [*exaltation*]—

10 Now I say unto you, if this be the desire of your hearts, what have you against being baptized in the name of the Lord, as a witness before him that **ye have entered into a covenant with him**, (7) **that ye will serve him** and **(8) keep his commandments**, that he may pour out his Spirit more abundantly upon you?

Did you notice the wonderful promises in the above verses that the Lord gives those who are worthily baptized and continue faithful? They are:

1. You will "be redeemed of God" (verse 9).

2. You will "be numbered with those of the first resurrection" (attain celestial glory; verse 9).

3. You will "have eternal life" (attain exaltation, become gods, and be in a family unit forever; verse 9).

4. You will have "his Spirit more abundantly upon you" (verse 10; the Gift of the Holy Ghost is a powerful companion).

Parley P. Pratt described the effects of the Gift of the Holy Ghost as follows:

"The gift of the Holy Spirit adapts itself to all these organs or attributes. It quickens all the intellectual faculties, increases, enlarges, expands and purifies all the natural passions and affections; and adapts them, by the gift of wisdom, to their lawful use. It inspires, develops, cultivates and matures all the fine-toned sympathies, joys, tastes, kindred feelings and affections of our nature. It inspires virtue, kindness, goodness, tenderness, gentleness and charity. It develops beauty of person, form and features. It tends to health, vigor, animation and social feeling. It develops and invigorates all the faculties of the physical and intellectual man. It strengthens, invigorates, and gives tone to the nerves. In short, it is, as it were, marrow to the bone, joy to the heart, light to the eyes, music to the ears, and life to the whole being" (Parley P. Pratt, *Key to the Science of Theology/A Voice of Warning* [Salt Lake City: Deseret Book, 1965], 101).

11 And **now when the people had heard these words, they clapped their hands for joy, and exclaimed: This is the desire of our hearts.**

Many people are curious about two things in the next verses; namely, where did Alma get his authority to baptize, and why did he go under water himself when he baptized Helam? Joseph Fielding Smith (who was an Apostle and became President of the Church in 1970) addresses these two issues as follows:

Question: "Who baptized Alma, and where did he get his priesthood?"

Answer: **We may conclude that Alma held the priesthood before he, with others, became wicked with King Noah.** Whether this is so or not makes no difference because in the Book of Mosiah it is stated definitely that he had authority (Mosiah 18:13).

Mosiah 18:13

13 And when he had said these words, the Spirit of the Lord was upon him, and he said: Helam, I baptize thee, having authority from the Almighty God, as a testimony that ye have entered into a covenant to serve him until you are dead as to the mortal body; and may the Spirit of the Lord be poured out upon you; and may he grant unto you eternal life, through the redemption of Christ, whom he has prepared from the foundation of the world.

The fact that he had authority to baptize, is evidence that he had been baptized. Therefore, when Alma entered the water with Helam, it was not a case of Alma baptizing himself; he was merely offering a token to the Lord of his humility and full repentance. In Alma 5:3 we learn that Alma was consecrated the high priest over the Church under his father. Now **Alma did not organize the Church with the idea that they had no church before that time. They had a church from the days of Lehi. Alma only set things in order** (Joseph Fielding Smith, *Answers to Gospel Questions*, 5 vols. [Salt Lake City: Deseret Book, 1957–66], 3: 203).

12 And now it came to pass that **Alma took Helam, he being one of the first, and went and stood forth in the water**, and cried, saying: O Lord, pour out thy Spirit upon thy servant, that he may do this work with holiness of heart.

Watch verse 13 for the promises of the Lord to those who are faithful to their baptismal covenants.

13 And when he [*Alma*] had said these words, the Spirit of the Lord was upon him, and he said: Helam, **I baptize thee**, having authority from the Almighty God, **as a testimony that ye have entered into a covenant to serve him until you are dead** as to the mortal body; and **may the Spirit of the Lord be poured out upon you**; and may he grant unto you **eternal life** [*exaltation*]**, through the redemption of Christ**, whom he has prepared from the foundation of the world.

14 And after Alma had said these words, **both Alma and Helam were buried in the water**; and they arose and came forth out of the water rejoicing, being filled with the Spirit.

15 And again, **Alma took another**, and went forth a second time into the

water, **and baptized him** according to the first, **only he did not bury himself again in the water.** [*He had already demonstrated his recommitment to his own baptismal covenant by going under the water with Helam.*]

16 **And after this manner** [*this is how*] **he did baptize every one** that went forth to the place of Mormon; and they were in number **about two hundred and four souls**; yea, and they were baptized in the waters of Mormon, and were filled with the grace [*the help of the Atonement*] of God.

17 **And they were called the church of God, or the church of Christ**, from that time forward. And it came to pass that whosoever was baptized by the power and authority of God was added to his church.

This whole situation, about which we have been reading, was an apostasy (under King Noah's rule) and a restoration (under Alma) with a prophet (Abinadi) giving his life to spread the gospel (similar to the Savior and Joseph Smith). You have probably seen this pattern many times in the work of the Lord here on earth.

Based on the next verse, there is no question as to whether or not Alma had the priesthood and authority to baptize. As mentioned above in the quote from Joseph Fielding Smith, we don't know for sure how he got it.

18 And it came to pass that **Alma, having authority from God, ordained priests**; even one priest to every fifty of their number did he ordain **to preach unto them, and to teach them** concerning the things pertaining to the kingdom of God.

As the prophet of the Lord for these people, Alma gives the new leaders and teachers of this "restored" church instructions similar to the instructions given by the Brethren today including to stick with the First Presidency and the Quorum of the Twelve as to what you teach in your stewardships. There is great power in this, because it brings harmony and unity, which brings the Spirit of the Lord upon the people, which brings light, truth, intelligence, etc. This is the only way to avoid apostasy.

19 And he commanded them that they should **teach nothing save it were the things which he had taught, and which had been spoken by the mouth of the holy prophets**.

20 Yea, even he commanded them that they should **preach nothing save it were repentance and faith on the Lord, who had redeemed his people**.

We are reminded in verse 20, above, of the importance of keeping our gospel message simple as we take it to all the world.

Next, Alma teaches his newly baptized followers some basic requirements that they must fulfill if they want to be considered "children of God," or those who qualify for celestial glory. These things, of course, apply to us today also.

21 And he commanded them that there should be **no contention** [*no mean-spirited arguing, quarreling, etc.*] **one**

with another, but that they should **look forward with one eye** [*in harmony and unity*], **having one faith and one baptism** [*having doctrinal unity, not breaking off into separate churches, etc.*], **having their hearts knit together in unity and in love one towards another.**

22 And thus he commanded them to preach. **And thus they became the children of God** [*worthy members of the Lord's Church; see Mosiah 5:7 where "sons and daughters" of Christ is another term for exaltation*].

23 And he commanded them that they should **observe the sabbath day, and keep it holy**, and also **every day they should give thanks to the Lord their God** [*have true gratitude for their blessings; see D&C 59:21*].

24 And he also commanded them that **the priests** whom he had ordained **should labor with their own hands for their support** [*they should not have "paid" ministers, priests, etc.*].

25 And **there was one day in every week** [*a Sabbath*] that was **set apart** that they should gather themselves together **to teach** the people, and to **worship the Lord their God**, and also, as often as it was in their power, to assemble themselves together.

26 And **the priests were not to depend upon the people for their support** [*no paid ministry*]; but for their labor they were to receive the grace of God, that they might wax strong in the Spirit, having the knowledge of God, that they might teach with power and authority from God.

Next, we see a type of "consecration," or welfare system, set up among the people by Alma. The same principles are used in the Lord's true Church today. Note that Alma's instructions in these matters are "principle-based," rather than having numerous rules and formulas for calculating how much one should give to others in need.

27 And again Alma commanded that **the people of the church should impart** [*share*] **of their substance**, every one according to that which he had [*according to their individual ability to give*]; **if he have more abundantly he should impart more abundantly;** and **of him that had but little, but little should be required**; and **to him that had not should be given.**

28 And thus they should **impart of their substance of their own free will** and good desires towards God [*as a matter of the heart*], and to those priests that stood in need, yea, and to every needy, naked soul.

As mentioned previously, a very important principle is given in verses 27 and 28, above. Perhaps you've heard members from time to time who have expressed a desire to have the Brethren spell out exactly how much fast offering a person should pay or even give exact rules for calculating tithing, or give more precise instructions for what are proper and improper Sabbath day activities. Instead, we have what are referred to as "principle-based" commandments and instructions.

The closer people come to Christ, the less rules they need. The Prophet Joseph Smith said, in reference to how he governed his people, "I teach them correct principles, and they govern themselves" (*Millennial Star,* 13:339). Alma is doing the same with his people. Our Church leaders do the same with us.

When a member is truly converted, he or she will want to help others, and will do so generously, but within his or her means, because that is wisdom. And the Spirit will give guidance in the process. Thus, numerous rules are not needed, and would in fact be damaging.

29 And this he said unto them, having been commanded of God; and **they did walk uprightly before God, imparting to one another both temporally and spiritually** according to their **needs** and their **wants**.

Just a quick comment about the word "wants" in verse 29, above. Perhaps you've noticed that the Lord is not interested only in our "bare bones" needs. Rather, in the true gospel, and through the Spirit, much attention is given to individual wants, talents, abilities, etc. It is probable that many of the sweet blessings and "tiny miracles" in your life have had to do with your wants and desires, not just your needs for survival. Thus, you have the knowledge that the Lord is interested in you as an individual, and that He knows you well, and enjoys blessing you in ways that are unique, intimate, warm, and special to you.

30 And now it came to pass that **all this was done** in Mormon, yea, **by the waters of Mormon**, in the forest that was near the waters of Mormon; yea, the place of Mormon, the waters of Mormon, the forest of Mormon, how beautiful are they to the eyes of them who there came to the knowledge of their Redeemer; yea, and how blessed are they, for they shall sing to his praise [*have gratitude to Him*] forever.

31 And **these things were done in the borders of the land, that they might not come to the knowledge of the king** [*King Noah, who was constantly trying to find Alma and his group so he could destroy them*].

32 **But** behold, it came to pass that **the king**, having **discovered a movement among the people**, sent his servants to watch them. **Therefore** on the day that they were assembling themselves together to hear the word of the Lord **they were discovered unto the king**.

33 And now the king said that Alma was stirring up the people to rebellion against him; therefore **he sent his army to destroy them**.

34 And it came to pass that **Alma and the people of the Lord were apprised** [*were told*] of the coming of the king's army; **therefore they took their tents and their families and departed into the wilderness**.

35 And they were in number **about four hundred and fifty souls**.

MOSIAH 19

As stated in chapter 18, Alma and his 450 converts were alerted to the fact that King Noah had discovered their whereabouts, so they escaped into the wilderness. Thus, the king's army had no success locating them. King Noah is about to meet the fate of most tyrants. His wicked lifestyle and bad example have weakened his kingdom and many of his subjects are fed up with him. They are now much easier for their enemies, the Lamanites, to attack.

Many wicked dictators, terrorists, tyrants, etc., today show no mercy toward women, children, and other innocent victims when it comes to accomplishing their wicked schemes. This is Satan's way. You will see that King Noah fits this evil pattern, sponsored by Lucifer, as Mormon continues his abridgement of the Book of Mormon records.

1 AND it came to pass that **the army of the king returned, having searched in vain** [*unsuccessfully*] **for the people of the Lord**.

2 And now behold, the forces of the king were small, having been reduced, and **there began to be a division among the remainder of the people**.

3 And **the lesser part began to breathe out threatenings against the king**, and there began to be a great contention among them.

4 And now there was a man among them whose name was **Gideon** [*a good man*], and he being a strong man and **an enemy to the king**, therefore he drew his sword, and swore in his wrath that he would slay the king.

5 And it came to pass that **he fought with the king**; and when **the king** saw that he was about to overpower him, he **fled and ran and got upon the tower which was near the temple**.

6 And **Gideon pursued after him** and was about to get upon the tower to slay the king, and the king cast his eyes round about towards the land of Shemlon, and behold, the army of the Lamanites were within the borders of the land.

Next, Mormon points out that Noah pretends to be concerned about the safety of his people, even though his only real concern is for his own life. Mormon is our teacher here and he wants us to learn to see beyond the false motives of such men as King Noah.

7 And now **the king cried** out in the anguish of his soul, saying: **Gideon, spare me,** for the Lamanites are upon us, and they will destroy us; yea, **they will destroy my people.**

8 And now **the king was not so much concerned about his people as he was about his own life**; nevertheless, Gideon did spare his life.

9 And **the king commanded the people that they should flee before the Lamanites, and he himself did go before them**, and they did flee into the wilderness, with their women and their children.

10 And it came to pass that **the Lamanites** did pursue them, and **did overtake them**, and began to slay them.

Next, we see Noah's true colors as well as those of the men who will continue fleeing with him, as they desert their wives and children in order to save their own lives. But you will see that even some of these vile men repent, a reminder of the vast reach of the Atonement.

11 Now it came to pass that **the king commanded them that all the men should leave their wives and their children**, and flee before the Lamanites.

12 Now **there were many that would not leave them**, but had rather stay and perish with them. And **the rest left their wives and their children and fled.**

13 And it came to pass that **those who tarried** [*remained*] with their wives and their children **caused that their fair daughters should** stand forth and **plead with the Lamanites that they would not slay them**.

14 And it came to pass that **the Lamanites had compassion on them**, for they were charmed with the beauty of their women.

By way of review, remember, in Mosiah, chapter 7, when Ammon and his fifteen companions finally found the Nephites in the land of Nephi, who had been gone from Zarahemla for seventy-nine years, it was Limhi and his people whom they found. King Limhi's people were in bondage to the Lamanites, paying 50 percent of all they had, in order to survive. Verse 15, next, explains how this bondage came to be.

15 Therefore **the Lamanites did spare their lives, and took them captives** and carried them back to the land of Nephi, and granted unto them that they might possess the land, under the conditions that they would deliver up king Noah into the hands of the Lamanites, and deliver up their property, even **one half of all they possessed**, one half of their gold, and their silver, and all their precious things, and thus they should pay tribute to the king of the Lamanites from year to year.

16 And now there was one of the sons of the king [*King Noah*] among those that were taken captive, whose name was **Limhi**.

17 And now **Limhi was desirous that his father** [*King Noah*] **should not be destroyed**; nevertheless, Limhi was not ignorant of the iniquities of his father, he himself being a just [*righteous*] man.

18 And it came to pass that **Gideon sent men into the wilderness secretly, to search for the king and those that were with him**. And it came to pass that **they met the people** [*who had left their wives and children and fled with King Noah*] **in the wilderness**, all save [*except*] the king and his priests.

These wicked men were beginning the repentance process by facing what they had done, and determining to accept the consequences, no matter what.

19 Now **they had sworn** [*promised*] in their hearts **that they would return to the land of Nephi**, and if their wives and their children were slain, and also those that had tarried with them, that they would seek revenge, and also perish with them.

20 And **the king** [*Noah*] **commanded them that they should not return**; and **they were angry with the king, and caused that he should suffer, even unto death by fire** [*they burned King Noah to death with fire, which fulfilled Abinadi's prophecy, given in Mosiah 12:3*].

21 And they were about to take **the priests** also and put them to death, and they **fled** before them.

Keep these wicked priests of Noah in mind. They are cowards of the worst sort and will soon be the source of much trouble and death for Limhi's people, who are in bondage to the Lamanites.

22 And it came to pass that **they** [*the people who destroyed King Noah with fire*], **were about to return to the land of Nephi and they met the men of Gideon**. And the men of Gideon told them of all that had happened to their wives and their children; and that the Lamanites had granted unto them that they might possess the land by paying a tribute [*tax*] to the Lamanites of one half of all they possessed.

23 And **the people told the men of Gideon that they had slain the king, and his priests had fled** [*escaped*] from them farther into the wilderness.

24 And it came to pass that after they had ended the ceremony [*the celebrating at having found each other, etc.*], that **they returned to the land of Nephi**, rejoicing, because their wives and their children were not slain; and they told Gideon what they had done to the king.

25 And it came to pass that **the king of the Lamanites made an oath unto them**, that his people should not slay them.

An oath in ancient cultures was a most serious and sacred promise that, once made, was not to be broken. This Lamanite king had high integrity, as far as this oath was concerned. Therefore, the Nephites could trust it completely.

26 And **also Limhi**, being the son of the king, having the kingdom conferred upon him by the people, **made oath unto the king of the Lamanites** that his people should pay tribute unto him, even one half of all they possessed.

27 And it came to pass that **Limhi began to establish the kingdom and to establish peace among his people.**

28 And **the king of the Lamanites set guards round about the land,** that he might keep the people of Limhi in the land, that they might

not depart [*escape*] into the wilderness; and he did support his guards out of the tribute which he did receive from the Nephites.

29 And now king Limhi did have **continual peace in his kingdom for the space of two years**, that the Lamanites did not molest them nor seek to destroy them.

Don't forget that the wicked priests of King Noah, who escaped, are still around. Amulon is their leader. They are extremely selfish and focused only on their own needs, as Mormon will point out next, in chapter 20. Remember, Mormon is the Book of Mormon prophet who is compiling the main set of gold plates that his son, Moroni, will eventually give to the Prophet Joseph Smith on the Hill Cumorah.

MOSIAH 20

Amulon and his companion priests of King Noah now find themselves without wives, since they deserted their own wives and children for the Lamanites to kill while they escaped (Mosiah 19:11–12). Since they desire to have wives and children but are embarrassed to return to their own, they now seek to solve that problem another way.

Remember that Limhi and his people live in the midst of Lamanite territory in the land of Nephi, and that they have a treaty with the Lamanite king and his people that they will not be killed if they continue to pay the Lamanites the agreed-upon fifty percent tax and do not cause the Lamanites any trouble. Amulon and his wicked companions are now going to do something that will cause Limhi and the Nephites in Lamanite territory terrible trouble!

1 NOW **there was a place in Shemlon** [*a place in Lamanite territory*] **where the daughters of the Lamanites did gather themselves together** to sing, and to dance, and to make themselves merry.

2 And it came to pass that there was **one day a small number of them gathered together** to sing and to dance.

3 And now the **priests of king Noah**, being ashamed to return to the city of Nephi, yea, and also fearing that the people would slay them, therefore they **durst not** [*didn't dare*] **return to their wives and their children.**

4 And having tarried in the wilderness, and **having discovered the daughters of the Lamanites, they laid and watched them**;

5 And when there were but few of them [*Lamanite's daughters*] gathered together to dance, **they** [*the priests*] **came forth out of their secret places and took them** [*kidnapped them*] and carried them into the wilderness; yea, **twenty and four of the daughters of the Lamanites** they carried into the wilderness.

Imagine the trouble this will cause for Limhi's people when the Lamanites discover that twenty-four of their young women have been kidnapped!

6 And it came to pass that when **the Lamanites** found that their daughters had been missing, they **were angry with the people of Limhi**, for they thought it was the people of Limhi.

7 **Therefore they sent their armies forth; yea, even the king himself** went before his people; and they went up to the land of Nephi **to destroy the people of Limhi**.

8 And **now Limhi had discovered them from the tower** [*the tall watchtower they had built*], even all their preparations for war did he discover; **therefore he gathered his people together, and laid wait for them** in the fields and in the forests [*to ambush the Lamanites*].

9 And it came to pass that **when the Lamanites had come up, that the people of Limhi began to fall upon them from** their waiting places, and began to slay them.

10 And it came to pass that **the battle became exceedingly sore** [*very severe*], for they fought like lions for their prey.

11 And it came to pass that **the people of Limhi began to drive the Lamanites before them**; yet they were not half so numerous as the Lamanites. But **they fought for their lives, and for their wives, and for their children**; therefore they exerted themselves and like dragons did they fight.

12 And it came to pass **that they found the king of the Lamanites among the number of their dead; yet he was not dead**, having been wounded and left upon the ground, so speedy was the flight of his people.

13 And **they** [*members of Limhi's army*] **took him and bound up his wounds, and brought him before Limhi**, and said: Behold, here is the king of the Lamanites; he having received a wound has fallen among their dead, and they have left him; and behold, we have brought him before you; and now let us slay him.

14 But **Limhi said unto them: Ye shall not slay him**, but bring him hither that I may see him. And they brought him. And Limhi said unto him: **What cause have ye to come up to war against my people? Behold, my people have not broken the oath** that I made unto you; therefore, **why should ye break the oath which ye made unto my people?**

Remember that the breaking of an oath (a covenant, promise) is an extremely serious matter in the Nephite and the Lamanite culture.

15 And now **the king said: I have broken the oath because thy people did carry away the daughters of my people**; therefore, in my anger I did cause my people to come up to war against thy people.

16 And now **Limhi had heard nothing concerning this matter**; therefore he said: I will search among my people and whosoever has done this

thing shall perish [*will be executed*]. Therefore he caused a search to be made among his people.

17 Now when **Gideon** had heard these things, he being the king's captain, he went forth and **said unto the king: I pray thee forbear** [*don't go ahead with what you have planned*], and do not search this people, and lay not this thing to their charge [*don't blame your people for what has happened to the Lamanite daughters*].

18 For **do ye not remember the priests of thy father** [*the priests of Noah*], whom this people sought to destroy? And are they not in the wilderness? And **are not they the ones who have stolen the daughters of the Lamanites?**

19 And now, behold, and **tell the king** [*of the Lamanites*] **of these things, that he may tell his people that they may be pacified towards us**; for behold they are already preparing to come against us; and behold also there are but few of us [*we are badly outnumbered*].

20 And **behold, they come with their numerous hosts**; and except the king [*of the Lamanites*] doth pacify them towards us we must [*will*] perish.

21 **For are not the words of Abinadi fulfilled, which he prophesied against us**—and all this because we would not hearken unto the words of the Lord, and turn from our iniquities [*repent from out wickedness*]?

22 And now **let us pacify the king**, and we fulfil the oath which we have made unto him; for **it is better that we should be in bondage than that we should lose our lives**; therefore, let us put a stop to the shedding of so much blood.

23 And **now Limhi told the king all the things concerning his father** [*Noah*], **and the priests** [*Amulon and the others*] that had fled into the wilderness, and attributed the carrying away of their daughters to them.

24 And it came to pass that **the king was pacified** towards his [*Limhi's*] people; and he [*the king of the Lamanites*] said unto them: **Let us go forth to meet my people** [*the Lamanites who are coming to attack you; see verse 20*], without arms [*weapons*]; and **I swear** [*promise*] unto you **with an oath** that my people shall not slay thy people.

25 And it came to pass that they followed the king, and went forth without arms to meet the Lamanites. And it came to pass that **they did meet the Lamanites**; and the king of the Lamanites did bow himself down before them [*his own people*], and did plead in behalf of the people of Limhi.

26 And when **the Lamanites** saw the people of Limhi, that they were without arms, they **had compassion on them and were pacified towards them**, and returned with their king in peace to their own land.

Verse 21, above is a good reminder that other people besides those of us who believe in God can have kindness and compassion in them also. We are all God's children and have His attributes in us.

MOSIAH 21

Chapters 21 and 22 will conclude the account of Limhi and his people. They will go through more misery and bloodshed while in bondage to the Lamanites. They will finally escape and go with Ammon and his fifteen men (who came from the land of Zarahemla to find them) back to the land of Zarahemla to join Mosiah and his people there.

Chapters 21 and 22 complete the "flashback in time" begun in Mosiah 9, as far as the history of Limhi and his people are concerned (the 79 years of Zeniff, Noah, and Limhi, who built up a Nephite colony in Lamanite territory). Chapters 23 and 24 will finish the flashback as far as Alma and his colony of converts are concerned. They, too, will arrive in the land of Zarahemla and join righteous King Mosiah II and his people.

1 AND it came to pass that **Limhi and his people returned to the city of Nephi**, and began to dwell in the land again in peace.

2 And it came to pass that **after many days the Lamanites began again to be stirred up in anger against the Nephites**, and they began to come into the borders of the land round about.

3 Now **they durst not slay them** [*did not dare kill the Nephites*], **because of the oath which their king had made unto Limhi**; but they would smite [*hit*] them on their cheeks, and exercise authority over them; and began to put heavy burdens upon their backs, and drive them as they would a dumb ass [*a donkey that is "dumb," in other words, unable to talk or talk back; this is a direct fulfillment of the prophecy of Abinadi in Mosiah 12:5*]—

4 Yea, **all this was done that the word of the Lord** [*the prophecies of Abinadi in Mosiah 12:2, etc.*] **might be fulfilled.**

5 And now the afflictions of the Nephites were great, and t**here was no way that they could deliver themselves** out of their hands, for the Lamanites had surrounded them on every side.

There is a major message developing here: we must ultimately turn to the Lord for deliverance from our enemies, including sin and shortcomings. Limhi's people will try to take care of the situation themselves in the next few verses, but will not succeed. Finally, they will humble themselves and turn to the Lord, beginning in verses 13 and 14. You will see also that the Lord in His wisdom will not rescue them too soon. Rather, He waits until genuine internal change has taken place, and then provides for the needed rescue.

6 And it came to pass that the people [*King Limhi's people*] began to murmur with the king because of their afflictions; and **they began to be desirous to go against them** [*the Lamanites*] **to battle**. And they did afflict the king

sorely [*they continued to weary him*] with their complaints; therefore **he granted unto them that they should do according to their desires**.

7 And **they** gathered themselves together again, and **put on their armor, and went forth against the Lamanites** to drive them out of their land.

8 And it came to pass that the **Lamanites** did **beat them,** and drove them back, and slew many of them.

9 And **now there was a great mourning and lamentation** [*crying and howling*] **among the people of Limhi**, the widow mourning for her husband, the son and the daughter mourning for their father, and the brothers for their brethren.

10 Now there were a great many widows in the land, and they did cry mightily from day to day, for **a great fear of the Lamanites had come upon them**.

11 And it came to pass that their continual cries did stir up the remainder of **the people of Limhi** to anger against the Lamanites; and they **went again to battle**, but they were **driven back again,** suffering much loss.

12 Yea, **they went again even the third time, and suffered in the like manner;** and those that were not slain returned again to the city of Nephi.

Some people, under severe circumstances of defeat, seem to grow angry and bitter, even more rebellious. Others humble themselves and sincerely draw closer to God and seek His help. This seems to be an agency choice. Limhi's people chose to turn to God for help, just as we can turn to the Savior's Atonement for help in overcoming things we can't defeat by ourselves.

13 And **they did humble themselves even to the dust**, subjecting themselves to the yoke of bondage, submitting themselves to be smitten, and to be driven to and fro, and burdened, according to the desires of their enemies.

14 And **they did humble themselves even in the depths of humility**; and **they did cry mightily to God;** yea, even all the day long [*they kept praying day after day*] did they cry unto their God that he would deliver them out of their afflictions.

15 And now **the Lord was slow to hear** [*answer*] their cry **because of their iniquities** [*they needed to make genuine changes*]; **nevertheless the Lord did hear their cries, and began to soften the hearts of the Lamanites** that they began to ease their burdens; **yet the Lord did not see fit** [*did not consider it wise*] **to deliver them out of bondage.**

There is an important message for us in verses 15 and 16. It is that even though the Lord may not consider it wise to free us from our problems according to our timetable, He is quick to encourage us in discernable ways in the meantime.

16 And it came to pass that they began to **prosper by degrees** in the land, and began to raise grain more

abundantly, and flocks, and herds, that **they did not suffer with hunger.**

17 Now **there was a great number of women, more than there was of men** [*because so many men had been killed in battle*]; therefore king Limhi commanded that every man should impart [*give*] to the support of the widows and their children, that they might not perish with hunger; and this they did because of the greatness of their number that had been slain.

18 Now **the people of Limhi kept together** in a body [*for protection*] as much as it was possible, and secured their grain and their flocks;

19 And **the king himself did not trust his person** [*did not feel safe*] **without** [*outside of*] **the walls of the city** [*of Nephi*], **unless he took his guards with him, fearing that he might by some means fall into the hands of the Lamanites.**

Limhi and his people are still trying to find the remainder of King Noah's wicked priests and capture them because of the trouble they had caused. You will see that these priests had caused trouble in addition to kidnaping the Lamanite daughters.

20 And **he caused that his people should watch the land round about, that by some means they might take those priests** that fled into the wilderness, **who had stolen the daughters of the Lamanites,** and that had caused such a great destruction to come upon them.

21 For they were desirous to take them that they might punish them; for **they** [*Amulon and the other priests of Noah*] **had come into the land of Nephi by night, and carried off their grain and many of their precious things**; therefore they laid wait for them [*they watched for a chance to capture them*].

22 And it came to pass that **there was no more disturbance between the Lamanites and the people of Limhi, even until the time that Ammon and his brethren came into the land** [*from Zarahemla*].

Now, we are about to be told why King Limhi was so quick to have Ammon and his companions arrested, tied up, and thrown in prison when they approached him and his guards, after having come from the land of Zarahemla to try to find the Nephite colony. See Mosiah 7:7.

23 And **the king** having been without [*outside of*] the gates of the city with his guard, discovered Ammon and his brethren; and **supposing them to be priests of Noah** therefore he **caused that they should be taken, and bound, and cast into prison**. And had they been the priests of Noah he would have caused that they should be put to death.

24 **But when he found that they were not, but that they were his brethren**, and had come from the land of Zarahemla, **he was filled with exceedingly great joy**.

The next verses repeat what Limhi told Ammon in Mosiah 8, starting with verse 7. It is the account of Limhi's men finding the ruins of the Jaredite civilization. The record of the Jaredites is found in the book of Ether in the Book of Mormon.

25 Now king **Limhi had sent, previous to the coming of Ammon, a small number of men to search for the land of Zarahemla;** but **they could not find it**, and they were lost in the wilderness.

26 Nevertheless, **they did find a land which had been peopled** [*inhabited*]**;** yea, a land which was **covered with dry bones**; yea, a land which had been peopled and which had been destroyed; and they, having **supposed it to be the land of Zarahemla** [*this would be very discouraging to them*], returned to the land of Nephi, having arrived in the borders of the land not many days before the coming of Ammon.

27 And **they brought a record** [*see Mosiah 8:9; it is the twenty-four gold plates which will become the Book of Ether in the Book of Mormon, after Moroni translates it*] with them, even a record of the people whose bones they had found; and it was **engraven on plates of ore.**

28 And now Limhi was again filled with joy on learning from the mouth of Ammon that **king Mosiah had a gift from God** [*including a Urim and Thummim; see Mosiah 8:13–19*], **whereby he could interpret such engravings**; yea, and Ammon also did rejoice.

29 **Yet Ammon and his brethren were filled with sorrow** because so many of their brethren had been slain;

30 And also **that king Noah and his priests had caused the people to commit so many sins and iniquities** [*wickednesses*] against God; and **they also did mourn for the death of Abinadi**; and **also for the departure of Alma and the people that went with him**, who had formed a church of God through the strength and power of God, and faith on the words which had been spoken by Abinadi.

31 Yea, they [*Ammon and his men*] did mourn for their departure, for they knew not whither they had fled. Now **they would have gladly joined with them**, for they themselves had entered into a covenant with God to serve him and keep his commandments [*possibly meaning the covenant of baptism that Ammon and his companions would have made back in Zarahemla*].

32 And now since the coming of Ammon, **king Limhi had also entered into a covenant with God, and also many of his people, to serve him and keep his commandments**.

33 And it came to pass that **king Limhi and many of his people were desirous to be baptized**; but there was none in the land that had authority from God [*probably because King Noah did away with all the worthy, righteous priests many years ago; see Mosiah 11:5*]. And

Ammon declined doing this thing, considering himself an unworthy servant. [*This informs us that Ammon had the priesthood, but did not consider himself worthy to perform ordinances at this time.*]

34 **Therefore they did not at that time form themselves into a church**, waiting upon the Spirit of the Lord. Now they were desirous to become even as Alma and his brethren, who had fled into the wilderness.

Next, in verse 35, Mormon points out once again the basic covenant we make at baptism.

35 They were desirous to **be baptized as a witness and a testimony that they were willing to serve God with all their hearts**; nevertheless they did prolong the time [*they temporarily put it off*]; and an account of their baptism shall be given hereafter. [*They will eventually be baptized by Alma, in the land of Zarahemla, after he has taught them; see Mosiah 25:15–18.*]

From now on, every effort and thought of these people will be to determine a way to escape from bondage under the Lamanites.

36 And **now all the study of Ammon and his people, and king Limhi and his people, was to deliver themselves out of the hands of the Lamanites and from bondage.**

MOSIAH 22

We will take just a moment here and point out again that both Limhi's people and the people of Alma will ultimately escape from captivity and end up in Zarahemla. It is worth noting the difference between the two escapes.

Limhi and his people will have to figure out a way to distract their Lamanite guards (Mosiah 22:6–8), whereas the Lord will put Alma's captors to sleep (Mosiah 24:19) while he and his people escape.

Perhaps one lesson we could learn from this is that there are some situations in our lives in which we need to use our own initiative and come up with a solution and work to carry it out, with the Lord's help. (See D&C 58:26–28.) Whereas, in other situations, the Lord takes over and we are set free by His power over our enemies.

1 AND now it came to pass that **Ammon and king Limhi began to consult with the people how they should deliver themselves out of bondage**; and even they did cause that all the people should gather themselves together; and this they did that they might have the voice of the people concerning the matter.

2 And it came to pass that **they could find no way to deliver themselves out of bondage, except it were to take their women and children, and their flocks, and their herds, and their tents, and depart into the wilderness**; for the Lamanites being so numerous, it was impossible for the people of Limhi to contend with them, thinking to deliver themselves out of bondage

by the sword [*there was no chance for a military victory*].

3 Now it came to pass that **Gideon** [*the man who fought against King Noah in Mosiah 19:4–8*] went forth and **stood before the king, and said** unto him: Now O king, thou hast hitherto [*up to now*] hearkened unto my words many times when we have been contending with our brethren, the Lamanites.

4 And now O king, if thou hast not found me to be an unprofitable servant, or if thou hast hitherto listened to my words in any degree, and they have been of service to thee, even so I desire that thou wouldst listen to my words at this time, and **I will be thy servant and deliver this people out of bondage**.

Watch the key elements of Gideon's plan, which he presents, next, to King Limhi.

5 And the king granted unto him that he might speak. And **Gideon said** unto him:

6 Behold the back pass, through the back wall, on the back side of the city. The Lamanites, or **the guards of the Lamanites, by night are drunken;** therefore **let us send a proclamation among all this people** that they gather together their flocks and herds, that they may drive them into the wilderness by night.

7 And **I will** go according to thy command and **pay the last tribute** [*tax or gift*] **of wine to the Lamanites, and they will be drunken**; and **we will pass through the secret pass on the left of their camp when they are drunken and asleep.**

8 **Thus we will depart** with our women and our children, our flocks, and our herds into the wilderness; and **we will travel around the land of Shilom**.

9 And it came to pass that **the king hearkened unto the words of Gideon**.

10 And king Limhi caused that his people should gather their flocks together; and he sent the tribute of wine to the Lamanites; and **he also sent more wine, as a present unto them; and they did drink freely of the wine which king Limhi did send unto them.**

11 And it came to pass that **the people of king Limhi did depart by night** into the wilderness with their flocks and their herds, and they went round about the land of Shilom in the wilderness, **and bent their course towards the land of Zarahemla**, being led by Ammon and his brethren.

12 And **they had taken all their gold, and silver, and their precious things, which they could carry**, and **also their provisions** with them, into the wilderness; and they pursued their journey.

13 And **after being many days in the wilderness they arrived in the land of Zarahemla,** and joined

Mosiah's people, and became his subjects.

14 And it came to pass that **Mosiah received them with joy**; and **he also received their records** [*the records started by Zeniff and finished by Limhi; see heading before Mosiah, chapter 9*], and **also the records which had been found by the people of Limhi** [*the twenty-four gold plates giving the history of the Jaredites*].

15 And now it came to pass when **the Lamanites** had found that the people of Limhi had departed out of the land by night, that they **sent an army into the wilderness to pursue them**;

16 And after they had pursued them two days, they could no longer follow their tracks; therefore **they were lost in the wilderness**.

These Lamanites, who can't find their way back to their homes, will stumble onto Amulon and the other priests of Noah, who kidnapped the twenty-four Lamanite daughters. A bit later, they will stumble onto Alma and his people, who have had many years of peace in the area in which they settled.

MOSIAH 23

Chapters 23 and 24 now take us back about 24 years in history to where Alma and his people fled into the wilderness and eventually settled in a pleasant area that they named Helam. They built a city, which they also named Helam (see Mosiah 23:19–20). Helam must have been a prominent member among them. He was the first person Alma baptized (see Mosiah 18:12–14). They lived in this area, in the wilderness, for a total of about twenty-four years. You can calculate this by looking at the chronology note at the end of the heading for Mosiah 23, in your Book of Mormon, if you have a newer Book of Mormon or an electronic copy, or on the bottom right corner of the page if you have an older copy of the Book of Mormon. Thus, these faithful Saints will live in peace for many years before Amulon and the Lamanites find them and put them into bondage. Mormon will teach us many lessons in these next two chapters, as he gives us a brief account of Alma and his people.

1 NOW **Alma, having been warned of the Lord that the armies of king Noah would come upon them**, and having made it known to his people, therefore they gathered together their flocks, and took of their grain, and departed into the wilderness before [*ahead of*] the armies of king Noah.

2 And **the Lord did strengthen them**, that the people of king Noah could not overtake them to destroy them.

Some possible symbolism in verses 1 and 2, above, could be that the Lord warns us of danger and we often have to flee the situation to avoid being harmed. This includes spiritual danger. As we do so, we receive strength from the Lord, including increased strength of character.

3 And they fled **eight days' journey** into the wilderness.

4 And **they came to** a land, yea, even **a very beautiful and pleasant land, a land of pure water** [*perhaps symbolizing that when we follow the promptings of the Spirit, we end up in a much better situation. This could even symbolize heaven*].

5 And they pitched their tents, and began to till [*cultivate and farm*] the ground, and began to build buildings; yea, **they were industrious,** and did labor exceedingly [*a characteristic of righteous people*].

6 And **the people were desirous that Alma should be their king**, for he was beloved by his people.

7 **But he said** unto them: Behold, **it is not expedient** [*not necessary; not a good idea*] **that we should have a king**; for thus saith the Lord: **Ye shall not esteem one flesh above another** [*you should not consider one person to be more important than another*], or **one man shall not think himself above another**; therefore I say unto you it is not expedient that ye should have a king.

8 Nevertheless, **if it were possible that ye could always have just men** [*righteous men who live the gospel with exactness*] to be your kings it would be well for you to have a king [*as during the Millennium when the Savior will be our King; see Revelation 19:16*].

Next, we are reminded again of the power of the Atonement to cleanse even from very serious wickedness. We are also reminded that it takes real effort and sincere repentance and change to be cleansed.

9 But remember the iniquity [*wickedness*] of king Noah and his priests; and **I myself** was caught in a snare [*a trap*], and **did many things which were abominable** [*very wicked*] in the sight of the Lord, which caused me **sore** [*very deep*] **repentance** [*godly sorrow; compare with 2 Corinthians 7:8–11*];

10 Nevertheless, **after much tribulation, the Lord did hear my cries, and did answer my prayers,** and has made me an instrument in his hands in bringing so many of you to a knowledge of his truth [*a reminder that a once wicked and rebellious person can repent thoroughly and do much good in the Lord's work*].

11 Nevertheless, in this I do not glory, for **I am unworthy to glory of myself**.

Watch the "power words" that Alma uses as he describes the effects of sin in verse 12, next. You may even wish to underline or mark them in your own scriptures.

12 And now I say unto you, ye have been **oppressed** by king Noah, and have been in **bondage** to him and his priests, and have been **brought into iniquity** by them; therefore ye were **bound with the bands of iniquity**.

13 And now **as ye have been delivered by the power of God** out of these bonds; yea, even **out of the hands of king Noah** and his people, and also **from the bonds of iniquity** [*through the Atonement of Christ*], even so I desire that ye should **stand fast in**

this liberty wherewith ye have been made free, and that ye trust no man to be a king over you.

Being freed from the "bonds of iniquity" in verse 13, above, is even more significant in the eternal scheme of things than being set free from physical enemies.

Next, Alma will give vital instruction to all of us; namely, that we should pay very close attention to the qualifications of the messenger before listening to the message.

14 And also **trust no one to be your teacher nor your minister, except he be a man of God**, walking in his ways and keeping his commandments.

15 **Thus did Alma teach his people**, that every man should **love his neighbor as himself**, that there should be **no contention among them** [*the first major message of the Savior to the Nephites as he appeared to them after His crucifixion and resurrection; see 3 Nephi 11:22–29; avoiding contention is a celestial attribute*].

16 And now, **Alma was their high priest**, he being the founder of their church.

17 And it came to pass that **none received authority to preach or to teach except it were by him** [*Alma*] from God. Therefore he consecrated [*ordained and set apart*] all their priests and all their teachers; and none were consecrated except they were just men.

The word "just," as used in verse 17, above, means "exact in living the gospel personally."

18 Therefore **they did watch over their people**, and did nourish them with things pertaining to righteousness.

19 And it came to pass that **they began to prosper exceedingly** [*very much*] in the land; and they called the land Helam.

20 And it came to pass that **they did multiply** [*increased in population*] and prosper exceedingly in the land of Helam; and they built a city, which they called the city of Helam.

Next, Mormon speaks to us personally and points out what the Lord wants us to learn from what is included next in the gold plates which he is compiling. One of the major messages he gives us is that personal righteousness does not entirely eliminate lessons and trials that can lead to growth. Note that Mormon is quick to point out that those who remain faithful to the Lord through trials and tribulations will be exalted in celestial glory.

21 **Nevertheless** [*even when things are going well and the people are living the gospel*] **the Lord seeth fit to chasten** [*to discipline, humble, purify*] **his people**; yea, he trieth [*tests*] their patience and their faith.

22 **Nevertheless—whosoever putteth his trust in him the same shall be lifted up** [*exalted*] at the last day [*on Judgment Day*]. Yea, and thus it was with this people.

23 For behold, I [*Mormon*] will show unto you that **they were brought into bondage** [*captivity and slavery*], **and none could deliver them but the Lord their God**, yea, even the God of Abraham and Isaac and of Jacob.

You have probably noticed the phrase "the God of Abraham and Isaac and of Jacob" or something very similar, many times in the scriptures. It means the true God, as opposed to the countless other gods or idols, etc., which people have come to worship over the ages.

24 And it came to pass that **he did deliver them, and he did show forth his mighty power unto them, and great were their rejoicings.**

Next, Mormon tells us what happened to Alma and his righteous followers to bring them into bondage.

25 For behold, it came to pass that **while they were in the land of Helam**, yea, in the city of Helam, while tilling the land round about, behold **an army of the Lamanites was in the borders of the land.**

26 Now it came to pass that **the brethren of Alma fled from their fields, and gathered themselves together in the city of Helam**; and they were much frightened because of the appearance of the Lamanites.

27 But **Alma went forth and stood among them** [*his people*], **and exhorted** [*counseled*] **them** that they should not be frightened, but that they should remember the Lord their God and he would deliver them.

28 **Therefore they hushed their fears, and began to cry** [*pray*] unto the Lord that he would soften the hearts of the Lamanites, that they would spare them, and their wives, and their children.

29 And it came to pass that **the Lord did soften the hearts of the Lamanites**. And **Alma and his brethren** went forth and **delivered themselves up** [*surrendered*] **into their hands**; and the Lamanites took possession of the land of Helam.

There is a very important message for all of us in verses 27–29, above. It is that we should follow our prophet, no matter what. It may have been a surprise to some of his people when Alma told them to surrender. It may have been very difficult for some of Alma's people to surrender, since they were in the right and knew that the Lord can support His people in righteous causes, including battles. But, when the prophet speaks, the decision has been made and the only decision left for each individual is whether or not to follow the prophet. Mormon will show us some significant and rather tender outcomes for Alma's people as they followed their beloved prophet.

30 Now **the armies of the Lamanites,** which had followed after the people of king Limhi [*who escaped to Zarahemla after getting their guards extra drunk*], **had been lost in the wilderness for many days.**

31 And behold, **they had found those priests of king Noah**, in a place which they called Amulon [*who was their wicked leader*]; and they had begun to possess the land of

Amulon and had begun to till the ground [*plant crops and farm the ground*].

32 Now the name of **the leader of those priests was Amulon** [*one of King Noah's chief wicked priests*].

33 And it came to pass that **Amulon did plead with the Lamanites;** and **he also sent forth their wives,** who were the daughters of the Lamanites, **to plead** with their brethren [*their own people*], **that they should not destroy their husbands.**

34 And **the Lamanites had compassion** on Amulon and his brethren, and did not destroy them, because of their wives.

It is rather amazing that Amulon was able to secure the safety of himself and his priests, especially after they kidnapped these twenty-four Lamanite daughters and married them. Perhaps there is a bit of symbolism in this to the effect that Satan can slick-talk people into many ridiculous things.

35 And **Amulon and his brethren did join the Lamanites**, and they were traveling in the wilderness in search of the land of Nephi when **they discovered the land of Helam, which was possessed by Alma and his brethren**.

Again, we will point out that the Lord could have prevented this trial of faith for Alma and his righteous people. But, as Mormon will show, the Lord had a purpose in allowing it. In fact, the Lord could have inspired Alma that the Lamanites were lying in verses 36–37, next, but He didn't. Again, as Mormon has told us, the Lord had a purpose in what happens here.

36 And it came to pass that **the Lamanites promised** unto Alma and his brethren, **that if they would show them the way** which led **to the land of Nephi** that **they would grant unto them their lives and their liberty**.

37 But **after Alma had shown them the way** that led to the land of Nephi **the Lamanites would not keep their promise;** but they set guards round about the land of Helam, over Alma and his brethren.

38 And **the remainder of them went to the land of Nephi; and a part of them returned to the land of Helam**, and also brought with them the wives and the children of the guards who had been left in the land.

39 And the **king of the Lamanites had granted unto Amulon that he should be a king and a ruler over his people, who were in the land of Helam** [*including Alma and his people; this would appear to be one of the worst things that could happen to these righteous Saints*]; nevertheless he [*Amulon*] should have no power to do anything contrary to the will of the king of the Lamanites.

In a very real sense, what has just happened to Alma and his people is a "miniature" of what is going on here on earth. The Lord's people try to do right, yet Satan is allowed to cause trouble for them. Nevertheless, the devil has limits placed on him (see D&C 129). Those who remain loyal to God, no matter what, grow in faith and testimony, as will be pointed out next, in chapter 24.

MOSIAH 24

Although it is not a pleasant symbolism, in a sense, Amulon is a "type" of Satan. In other words, his behaviors of lying and delighting in persecuting the righteous can be symbolic of what Satan and his evil followers do.

Perhaps you've noticed that the Lord often turns the evil attempted by the devil into something very beneficial. This was certainly the case in the Garden of Eden. This must be frustrating to Satan and his evil hosts. Watch as Amulon and his wicked priests teach the Nephite language to the Lamanites (verse 4). This will be a great blessing in thirty years or so when the four sons of Mosiah go on missions to the Lamanites in the land of Nephi (see Mosiah 28:5–9). They will also teach the Lamanites to keep good records and to write to one another (Mosiah 24:6). All of this will ultimately benefit missionary work among the Lamanites at a later date.

1 AND it came to pass that **Amulon did gain favor in the eyes of the king of the Lamanites**; therefore, **the king of the Lamanites granted unto him and his brethren that they should be appointed teachers over his people**, yea, even over the people who were **in the land of Shemlon,** and in the land of **Shilom**, and in the land of **Amulon**.

2 For **the Lamanites had taken possession of all these lands**; therefore, the king of the Lamanites had appointed kings over all these lands.

3 And now **the name of the king of the Lamanites was Laman**, being called after the name of his father [*an imitation of the people of the Lord, who named their kings Nephi, after righteous Nephi; see Jacob 1:11*]; and therefore he was called king Laman. And he was king over a numerous people.

4 And he appointed teachers of the brethren of Amulon [*the priests of King Noah*] in every land which was possessed by his people; and **thus the language of Nephi began to be taught among all the people of the Lamanites.**

5 And they were a people friendly one with another; nevertheless **they knew not God; neither did the brethren of Amulon teach them anything concerning the Lord their God**, neither the law of Moses; nor did they teach them the words of Abinadi;

6 But **they taught them that they should keep their record, and that they might write one to another.**

7 And thus the **Lamanites began to increase in riches**, and began to **trade** one with another and wax [*grow*] great, and began to be a **cunning** and a **wise people, as to the wisdom of the world,** yea, a very cunning people, **delighting in all**

manner of wickedness and plunder, except it were among their own brethren.

8 And now it came to pass that **Amulon** [*a "type" of Satan, as mentioned in the note at the beginning of this chapter*] **began to exercise authority over Alma and his brethren** [*"types" of the Saints of God throughout history*], and began to **persecute** him, **and cause that his children should persecute their children** [*the root cause of ethnic hatred in the world today*].

9 For **Amulon knew Alma**, that he had been one of the king's priests [*one of King Noah's priests*], and that it was he that believed the words of Abinadi and was driven out before the king, and therefore he was wroth [*very angry*] with him; for he was subject to king Laman [*implying that Amulon was all the more angry and hateful toward Alma because he had limits set by King Laman as to what he could and could not do to Alma*], yet he exercised authority over them [*Alma's people*], and put tasks upon them, and put task–masters [*slave drivers*] over them.

10 And it came to pass that **so great were their afflictions that they began to cry** [*pray*] **mightily to God**.

> We have suggested above that Amulon was a "type" of Satan. In 2 Nephi 32:8, we are taught, "The evil spirit teacheth not a man to pray, but teacheth him that he must not pray." In verse 11, next, Amulon exhibits the same behavior as the devil.

11 And **Amulon commanded them that they should stop their cries** [*their praying*]; and he put guards over them to watch them, that whosoever should be found calling upon God should be put to death.

12 And Alma and his people did not raise their voices to the Lord their God [*did not pray out loud*], but did pour out their hearts to him; and **he did know the thoughts of their hearts.**

> We are taught in D&C 6:16 that Satan is not granted the power to read our thoughts. This privilege is limited to the Godhead and those righteous servants who are inspired by the Holy Ghost.
>
> Next, we are taught the power of covenants to free us from bondage.

13 And it came to pass that **the voice of the Lord came to them** in their afflictions, **saying: Lift up your heads and be of good comfort** [*cheer up, be happy*], **for I know of the covenant which ye have made unto me**; and **I will covenant with my people** and deliver them out of bondage [*symbolic of the power of covenants, made and kept, to deliver us from the bondage of sin*].

14 And **I will also ease the burdens** which are put upon your shoulders, **that even you cannot feel them** upon your backs, **even while you are in bondage**; and **this will I do that ye may stand as witnesses for me hereafter**, and **that ye may know of**

a surety that I, the Lord God, do visit [*bless*] **my people in their afflictions.**

Verse 14 has important messages for us from the Lord. For instance, as you know, many good people carry heavy burdens, yet they are cheerful and don't seem to realize how bad off they are. This is a direct blessing from the Lord. And, in reality, they are not as bad off as they appear to be to others because of the blessings and help of the Lord.

When the Lord pours out blessings while we are undergoing severe trials of our faith, it strengthens our testimonies and afterwards we stand as strong witnesses for Him. This was the case with the survivors of the pioneer Willie and Martin handcart companies of 1856.

15 And now it came to pass that **the burdens which were laid upon Alma and his brethren were made light;** yea, **the Lord did strengthen them that they could bear up their burdens with ease**, and **they did submit cheerfully and with patience** to all the will of the Lord.

16 And it came to pass that so great was their faith and their patience that **the voice of the Lord came unto them again, saying**: Be of good comfort, for **on the morrow** [*tomorrow*] **I will deliver you out of bondage.**

17 And **he said unto Alma: Thou shalt go before this people, and I will go with thee** and deliver this people out of bondage. [*Symbolic of the Lord leading the prophet and the people following the prophet to safety.*]

18 Now it came to pass that **Alma and his people in the night–time gathered their flocks together, and also of their grain**; yea, even all the night–time were they gathering the flocks together [*symbolism: it takes preparation and work to follow the prophet*].

19 And **in the morning** the Lord caused a deep sleep to come upon the Lamanites, yea, and all their task–masters were in a profound sleep. [*Perhaps symbolic of the fact that the people of the Lord will ultimately leave the wicked behind who are so spiritually asleep that they do not even comprehend that righteousness is desirable.*]

20 And **Alma and his people departed into the wilderness**; and when they had traveled all day they pitched their tents in a valley, and they called the valley Alma, because he led their way in the wilderness.

21 Yea, and in the valley of Alma **they poured out their thanks to God** because he had been merciful unto them, and eased their burdens, and had delivered them out of bondage; for they were in bondage, and none could deliver them except it were the Lord their God [*gratitude is always a character trait of the truly righteous*].

22 And **they gave thanks to God**, yea, all their men and all their women and all their children that could speak lifted their voices in the praises of their God.

23 And now **the Lord said unto Alma: Haste thee and get thou and this people out** of this land, **for the Lamanites have awakened** and do pursue thee; therefore get thee out of this land, and **I will stop the Lamanites** in this valley that they come no further in pursuit of this people.

24 And it came to pass that **they departed** out of the valley, and took their journey into the wilderness.

25 And after they had been in the wilderness twelve days **they arrived in the land of Zarahemla; and king Mosiah did also receive them with joy.**

Now, everyone is back home in Zarahemla, and Mormon's account continues from there.

MOSIAH 25

This chapter is a transition between the reuniting of the people of Limhi and the people of Alma with the people in the land of Zarahemla, and the calling of Alma to be the President of the Church. In this chapter, Mormon ties together several details before moving on to Alma's ministry over all the Church.

Mormon gives us a bit more information about the original people of the Land of Zarahemla, who were Mulekites (descendants of Mulek who was the son of wicked King Zedekiah, King of Jerusalem and Judah when Lehi and his family fled Jerusalem). He reports the uniting of the Mulekites and the Nephites in Zarahemla. He also gives some details about the feelings of the sons and daughters of Amulon and the other wicked priests of King Noah, who no longer want to be known as their children. They are ashamed of their fathers. Furthermore, he gives information about the relative sizes of the various groups now populating the land of Zarahemla.

Remember that King Mosiah II (the son of King Benjamin and the grandson of King Mosiah I) is the righteous king of the land of Zarahemla at this point in Book of Mormon history.

1 AND now **king Mosiah caused that all the people should be gathered together.**

2 Now **there were not so many of the children of Nephi**, or so many of those who were descendants of Nephi, **as there were of the people of Zarahemla, who was a descendant of Mulek**, and those who came with him into the wilderness [*from Jerusalem*].

As mentioned in the note at the beginning of this chapter, Mulek was a son of King Zedekiah, who was the unrighteous king of Jerusalem at the time Lehi and his family left Jerusalem in 600 BC. According to the Bible, when Jerusalem was captured about 588 BC, the Babylonian armies captured Zedekiah and killed his sons before his eyes, then put out his eyes (see Jeremiah 39:6–7; 52:1–11). The Book of Mormon informs us that they missed one of the sons of Zedekiah, namely, Mulek. He came with a group from Jerusalem and they ended up in the land of Zarahemla (see Omni 1:14–15; Helaman 6:10).

3 And **there were not so many of the people of Nephi and of the people of Zarahemla as there were of the Lamanites**; yea, they were not half so numerous [*there were twice as many Lamanites as all the other people put together*].

4 And now **all the people of Nephi** were assembled together, **and also all the people of Zarahemla**, and they **were gathered together in two bodies** [*groups*].

5 And it came to pass that **Mosiah did read, and caused to be read, the records of Zeniff** [*the father of King Noah and the grandfather of King Limhi, who led a group from the land of Zarahemla to settle in the land of Nephi among the Lamanites, about 79 years ago*] **to his people**; yea, he read the records of the people of Zeniff, from the time they left the land of Zarahemla until they returned again.

6 And **he also read the account of Alma and his brethren**, and all their afflictions, from the time they left the land of Zarahemla until the time they returned again.

7 And now, when Mosiah had made an end of reading the records, **his people** who tarried in the land [*who had remained in the land of Zarahemla all these 79 years*] **were struck with wonder and amazement.**

8 For **they knew not what to think**; for when they beheld those that had been delivered out of bondage [*Limhi's people and Alma's people*] they were **filled with exceedingly great joy**.

9 And again, when they thought of their brethren who had been slain by the Lamanites they were **filled with sorrow**, and even shed many tears of sorrow.

10 And again, when they thought of the immediate goodness of God, and his power in delivering Alma and his brethren out of the hands of the Lamanites and of bondage, **they did raise their voices and give thanks to God**.

11 And again, **when they thought upon the Lamanites**, who were their brethren, of their sinful and polluted state, **they were filled with pain and anguish for the welfare of their souls.**

In Ezekiel, chapter 18, we are taught that the sins of the fathers do not extend to the children into the third and fourth generation, if the children do not follow the wicked lifestyle of their parents. The children of Amulon and the other wicked priests of Noah are an example of this principle. Mormon talks about them next. It appears that they rejected the teachings of their wicked fathers and joined either Limhi or Alma as they escaped to the land of Zarahemla.

12 And it came to pass that **those who were the children of Amulon and his brethren**, who had taken to wife the daughters of the Lamanites, **were displeased with the conduct**

of their fathers, and they would no longer be called by the names of their fathers, therefore they took upon themselves the name of Nephi, that they might be called the children of Nephi and be numbered among those who were called Nephites.

13 And now **all the people of Zarahemla** [*the descendants of Mulek*] **were numbered** [*counted*] **with the Nephites**, and this because the kingdom had been conferred upon none but those who were descendants of Nephi.

14 And now it came to pass that **when Mosiah had made an end of speaking and reading to the people, he desired that Alma should also speak to the people.**

15 And **Alma did speak unto them**, when they were assembled together in large bodies, and he went from one body to another, **preaching** unto the people **repentance and faith on the Lord.**

> You may recall that back in the land of Nephi, after Ammon and his fifteen companions had found Limhi and his people, they had asked Ammon to baptize them. He declined to do so, considering himself to be unworthy, and Mormon told us that he would tell us later about their baptism (see Mosiah 21:33–35). He does so next.

16 And **he** [*Alma*] **did exhort** [*teach and counsel*] the people of Limhi and his brethren, all those that had been delivered out of bondage, **that they should remember that it was the Lord that did deliver them**.

17 And it came to pass that **after Alma had taught the people** many things, and had made an end of speaking to them, that **king Limhi was desirous that he might be baptized; and all his people were desirous that they might be baptized also.**

18 Therefore, **Alma did go forth into the water and did baptize them**; yea, he did baptize them after the manner he did his brethren in the waters of Mormon; yea, **and as many as he did baptize did belong to the church of God**; and this because of their belief on the words of Alma.

> With this sudden increase in the number of members of the Church in the land of Zarahemla, Mosiah turns the running of the Church over to Alma and retains the political government himself. Thus, Alma becomes the President of the Church. Considering what Mormon taught us about Alma's past, this is a wonderful confirmation and testimony of the power of the Savior's Atonement to cleanse and heal completely.

19 And it came to pass that **king Mosiah granted unto Alma that he might establish churches** [*wards, branches, stakes, or whatever they were called*] **throughout all the land of Zarahemla**; and **gave him power to ordain priests and teachers over every church.**

20 Now this was done because **there were so many people that**

they could not all be governed by one teacher; neither could they all hear the word of God in one assembly;

This sounds very much like the organization of the Church today, wherein the Saints are organized into branches and districts, wards, and stakes, with bishops and stake presidents to preside over each, and with each leader turning to the prophet and the Apostles for guidance in how they should lead.

21 Therefore they did assemble themselves together in **different bodies**, being **called churches; every church having their priests and their teachers, and every priest preaching the word according as it was delivered to him by the mouth of Alma.**

22 And thus, **notwithstanding there being** [*even though there were*] **many churches** [*units of the Church, like wards and branches*] **they were all one church**, yea, even the church of God; for there was nothing preached in all the churches except it were repentance and faith in God [*in other words, the basic doctrines and principles of the gospel*].

23 And now there were **seven churches in the land of Zarahemla**. And it came to pass that whosoever were desirous to take upon them the name of Christ, or of God, they did join the churches of God;

24 And **they were called the people of God. And the Lord did pour out his Spirit upon them, and they were blessed, and prospered in the land.**

MOSIAH 26

As mentioned previously, Mormon now turns our attention to the ministry of Alma as the President of the whole Church. He is faced with the problem of how to deal with members of the Church who are involved in very serious sin. The difficulty for Alma is no doubt increased by the fact that his own son and the sons of his dear friend Mosiah are among the transgressors, as we will see in chapter 27.

In this chapter, the Lord will give us all some counsel and understanding of how He expects his church leaders to deal with those who commit serious sin.

1 NOW it came to pass that there were **many of the rising generation** [*the younger generation*] that could not understand the words of king Benjamin, being little children at the time he spake unto his people; and they **did not believe the tradition** [*the righteous tradition*] **of their fathers.**

2 **They did not believe** what had been said concerning **the resurrection of the dead, neither** did they believe concerning **the coming of Christ.**

3 And now **because of their unbelief they could not understand the word of God; and their hearts were hardened** [*they were not sensitive to spiritual things*].

4 And **they would not be baptized; neither** would they **join the church.** And **they were a separate people**

as to their faith, and remained so ever after, even in their carnal and sinful state; for they would not call upon the Lord their God.

5 And now in the reign of Mosiah they were not half so numerous as the people of God [*members of the Church*]; but **because of the dissensions** [*apostasy*] **among the brethren they became more numerous.**

> What comes next sounds like what Satan is prompting nonmembers and unfaithful members to do to faithful members of the Church today.

6 For it came to pass that **they did deceive many with their flattering words**, who were in the church, and **did cause them to commit many sins**; therefore it became expedient [*necessary*] that those who committed sin, that were in the church, should be admonished [*counseled and disciplined as needed*] by the church.

> Next, we see the local leaders bringing the serious transgressors to Alma. This is a learning process for him.

7 And it came to pass that **they were brought before the priests** [*Melchizedek priesthood leaders; see* Answers to Gospel Questions, *vol. 1, by Joseph Fielding Smith, 124–26*], and delivered up unto the priests by the teachers; and **the priests brought them before Alma, who was the high priest**.

8 Now **king Mosiah had given Alma the authority over the church** [*in other words, Alma had been made President of the Church*].

9 And it came to pass that Alma did not know concerning them; but **there were many witnesses against them**; yea, the people stood and testified of their iniquity in abundance.

10 Now there had not any such thing happened before in the church; therefore **Alma** was troubled in his spirit [*was very concerned as to how to handle the situation*], and he **caused that they should be brought before the king**.

11 And **he said unto the king** [*King Mosiah II*]: Behold, here are many whom we have brought before thee, who are accused of their brethren; yea, and they have been taken in divers iniquities [*various forms of serious sin*]. And **they do not repent** of their iniquities; **therefore we have brought them before thee, that thou mayest judge them according to their crimes**.

> The word "crime" in verse 11, above, is an interesting term to use for sin. It points out that "sin" weakens a people and a nation. By definition, "crime" is something that is damaging to society. Therefore, in a significant sense, "sin" is "crime." Unfortunately, many governments throughout the world today have laws protecting some serious sins while prosecuting other serious sins. One of Satan's very effective deceptions is to legalize many sins, which quickly leads to the disintegration of a society.

12 But **king Mosiah said unto Alma: Behold, I judge them not; therefore I deliver them into thy hands to be judged.**

Alma had hoped that King Mosiah II would handle the situation, but this was not the case. For one thing, this identifies the difference between what governments can do and what churches can do to their disobedient people as pointed out in D&C 42:79. Alma now turns to the Lord for counsel on how to handle transgressors in the Lord's church. He is deeply worried that he might handle this situation incorrectly.

13 And now the spirit of **Alma was again troubled; and he** went and **inquired of the Lord what he should do** concerning this matter, **for he feared that he should do wrong in the sight of God**.

14 And it came to pass that after he had poured out his whole soul to God, **the voice of the Lord came to him, saying**:

The answer from the Lord to Alma comes in two parts. First, Alma, himself, is acceptable to the Lord (verses 15–20). This gives him confidence in carrying out the second part (verses 21–32) of the answer—namely, how to proceed in handling transgressors, even to the point of excommunicating them if necessary.

Regarding the first part of the answer, perhaps one of Alma's concerns was that he, himself, had been caught up in serious transgression when he was one of King Noah's priests (see Mosiah 11:5–7, 14), and it might seem hypocritical for him to be passing judgment upon others who are involved in wickedness. There may be a major message for us here; namely, that a person who has truly repented is not a "repentant sinner." Rather, he or she is a worthy saint of God.

It may also be that Alma is wondering where he went wrong as a parent, or what he could have done more for his rebellious son, Alma the Younger.

Whatever the case, the word of the Lord to him in verse 15, next, put his mind at ease as to whether or not he was acceptable before God.

15 **Blessed art thou, Alma,** and blessed are they who were baptized in the waters of Mormon. **Thou art blessed because of thy exceeding faith in the words alone of my servant Abinadi**.

16 **And blessed are they** because of their exceeding faith in the words alone which thou hast spoken unto them.

17 And **blessed art thou** because thou hast established a church among this people; and they shall be established, and they shall be my people.

18 Yea, blessed is this people who are willing to bear my name; for in my name shall they be called; and **they are mine** [*they are also acceptable to the Lord*].

19 And **because thou hast inquired of me concerning the transgressor, thou art blessed.**

From verse 20, next, we understand Alma's calling and election to be made sure. In other words, the Lord assures him at this point that he will be exalted in the highest degree of the celestial kingdom and become a god. The term "eternal life" means exaltation.

20 Thou art my servant; and **I covenant with thee that thou shalt have eternal life;** and thou shalt serve me and go forth in my name, and shalt gather together my sheep.

21 [*Now, the second part of the Lord's answer, verses 21–32.*] And **he that will** [*wants to*] **hear my voice shall be my sheep** [*My faithful follower*]; and him shall ye receive into the church, and him will I also receive.

22 For behold, **this is my church**; whosoever is baptized shall be baptized unto repentance. And **whomsoever ye receive** shall believe in my name; and **him will I freely forgive.**

23 For **it is I** [*the premortal Jesus Christ*] **that taketh upon me the sins of the world**; for it is I that hath created them; and it is I that granteth unto him that believeth unto the end **a place at my right hand** [*symbolic of celestial glory; Christ is the final judge, according to John 5:22*].

24 For behold, **in my name are they called** [*they have taken upon themselves the name of Christ through baptism*]; and **if they know me** [*are faithful to Me*] they shall come forth [*in the resurrection of the righteous*], and **shall have a place eternally at my right hand.**

25 And it shall come to pass that when the second trump [*the resurrection of those who did not accept Christ, either on earth or in the spirit world or Millennium*] shall sound **then shall** they that never knew me [*were not faithful*] **come forth and shall stand before me** [*to be judged*].

26 And **then shall they know that I am the Lord their God**, that I am their Redeemer; **but they would not be** [*did not want to be*] **redeemed.**

27 And then I will confess unto them that I never knew them [*in other words, "they never knew me"; see Joseph Smith Translation, Matthew 7:23*]; and **they shall depart into everlasting fire prepared for the devil and his angels** [*they will not gain celestial glory*].

At this point in the Book of Mormon, it appears that they have not received the details we have been given about the three degrees of glory and outer darkness. Rather, the main considerations are heaven and hell. Perhaps they did have this knowledge, but it is not in our portion of the Book of Mormon. Or perhaps the Lord had chosen not to give them these doctrinal details. Alma the Younger indicates that he does not understand all we know about the order of resurrection. See Alma 40:19.

The Lord, having taught Alma the doctrinal background of what He will say next, now gives specific instructions as to how to deal with sinners in the Church.

28 Therefore **I say unto you, that he that will not** [*does not want to*] **hear my voice**, the same **shall ye not receive into my church**, for **him I will not receive** [*accept as worthy for exaltation*] at the last day [*on Judgment Day*].

29 Therefore I say unto you, Go; and **whosoever transgresseth against me, him shall ye judge** according to the sins which he has committed; and **if he confess** his sins before thee

and me, **and repenteth** in the sincerity of his heart, **him shall ye forgive, and I will forgive him also** [*similar to the authority and stewardship of bishops and stake presidents*].

30 **Yea, and as often as my people repent will I forgive them their trespasses against me.**

If we want to be forgiven, we must do the following:

31 And **ye shall also forgive one another your trespasses**; for verily I say unto you, **he that forgiveth not his neighbor's trespasses** when he says that he repents, the same hath brought himself under **condemnation** [*his progression is stopped*].

32 Now I say unto you, Go; and **whosoever will not repent of his sins the same shall not be numbered among my people** [*you will have to excommunicate them*]; and this shall be observed from this time forward.

33 And it came to pass when Alma had heard these words **he wrote them down** that he might have them, and that he might judge the people of that church according to the commandments of God.

34 And it came to pass that **Alma went and judged those that had been taken in iniquity** [*serious sins*], according to the word of the Lord.

35 And **whosoever repented of their sins and did confess them**, them he did number among the people of the church [*they retained their membership in the Church*];

36 And **those that would not confess their sins and repent of their iniquity, the same were not numbered among the people of the church**, and their names were blotted out [*they were excommunicated and their names were removed from the records of the Church*].

Verse 37, next, shows the results of appropriate church disciplinary action. If these procedures were not in place, the Church would eventually disintegrate and disappear.

37 And it came to pass that **Alma did regulate all the affairs of the church**; and **they began again to have peace and to prosper exceedingly in the affairs of the church**, walking circumspectly [*righteously*] before God, **receiving many, and baptizing many.**

38 And now **all these things did Alma and his fellow laborers do** who were over the church, walking in all diligence, teaching the word of God in all things, suffering all manner of afflictions, being persecuted by all those who did not belong to the church of God.

39 And **they did admonish** [*teach, counsel; discipline*] **their brethren**; and they were also admonished, every one by the word of God, according to his sins, or to the sins which he had committed, being commanded of God to pray without ceasing, and to give thanks in all things.

MOSIAH 27

This is one of the better-known chapters in the Book of Mormon. It contains the account of the conversion of Alma the Younger and the four sons of Mosiah. Perhaps you remember that they were very wicked young men, and were going around secretly among the people trying to destroy the Church. An angel appeared to them and called them to repentance. The events in this chapter remind us again of the power of the Atonement to grant newness of life. Many other things are taught here, including the power of the prayers of righteous parents and others.

To begin with, we are taught the importance of having good laws in governments in order to have religious liberty.

1 AND now it came to pass that **the persecutions** [*pain and suffering*] **which were inflicted on** [*caused to*] **the church by the unbelievers became so great that the church began to murmur, and complain to their leaders concerning the matter**; and they did complain to Alma. And Alma laid the case before their king, Mosiah. And Mosiah consulted [*discussed it*] with his priests.

2 And it came to pass that **king Mosiah sent a proclamation throughout the land round about that there should not any unbeliever persecute any of those who belonged to the church of God.** [*Good, sound, civil law.*]

3 And there was **a strict command throughout all the churches that there should be no persecutions among them**, that there should be an equality among all men; [*Religious law within the Church.*]

4 That they should let **no pride** nor **haughtiness** disturb their peace; that **every man should esteem** [*consider and treat*] **his neighbor as himself** [*the "Golden Rule"*], **laboring with their own hands for their support** [*work ethic*].

5 Yea, and **all their priests and teachers should labor with their own hands for their support** [*no paid ministers*], in all cases save it were in sickness, or in much want; and doing these things, they did abound in the grace [*help*] of God.

6 And **there began to be much peace again in the land**; and the people began to be very numerous, and began to scatter abroad upon the face of the earth, yea, on the north and on the south, on the east and on the west, building large cities and villages in all quarters of the land.

7 And **the Lord did visit** [*bless*] **them and prosper them**, and they became a large and wealthy people.

Next, we see that Alma the son of Alma (who fled from King Noah and baptized many and led them to Zarahemla), who is now the president of the whole Church, is causing a lot of trouble among members of the Church. He is very good at speaking and debating and many members are believing him and following him in his wicked ways.

8 Now **the sons of Mosiah were numbered** [*found, counted*] **among the unbelievers; and also one of the sons of Alma** [*Alma the Younger*] **was numbered among them, he being called Alma,** after his father; nevertheless, he became **a very wicked and an idolatrous man**. And he was **a man of many words**, and did speak **much flattery** to the people; therefore **he led many of the people to do after the manner of his iniquities** [*he was a powerful leader in wickedness*].

9 And he became **a great hinderment** [*opposition*] to the prosperity of the church of God; stealing away the hearts of the people [*many church members admired him and followed him*]; **causing much dissension** [*disagreement and arguing*] among the people; giving a chance for the enemy of God [*the devil*] to exercise his power over them.

Next comes the account of the conversion of Alma and the four sons of Mosiah. Perhaps you can imagine how the angel might have felt who was assigned to appear to them on this occasion. This is an angel with tender feelings and lots of love, as we will see in Alma 8:15, yet he is very strict, even to the point of commanding them to stand up and face him while he is speaking to them. This is truly a case of "reproving betimes with sharpness . . . and then showing forth afterwards an increase of love" (D&C 121:43).

10 And now it came to pass that while he was going about to destroy the church of God, for **he did go about secretly with the sons of Mosiah seeking to destroy the church**, and to lead astray the people of the Lord, **contrary to the commandments of God, or even the king—**

11 And as I said unto you, **as they were going about rebelling against God, behold, the angel of the Lord appeared unto them**; and he descended as it were in a cloud; **and he spake as it were with a voice of thunder**, which **caused the earth to shake** upon which they stood;

12 And so great was their astonishment [*great surprise*], that **they fell to the earth,** and understood not the words which he spake unto them.

13 Nevertheless he cried again, saying: **Alma, arise and stand forth,** for **why persecutest thou the church of God?** [*why are you fighting against the Lord's church?*] For the Lord hath said: This is my church, and I will establish it; and nothing shall overthrow it, save it is the transgression of my people.

One can imagine that Alma, King Mosiah, and others had prayed countless times for these young men. Now, finally, their prayers of faith and their patience with the Lord as He follows His timetable, are being answered.

14 And again, **the angel said: Behold, the Lord hath heard the**

prayers of his people, and also the prayers of his servant, Alma, who is thy father; for he has prayed with much faith concerning thee that thou mightest be brought to the knowledge of the truth [*not forced to repent, rather, taught the truth so that he could use his agency knowingly*]; therefore, for this purpose have I come to convince thee of the power and authority of God, that the prayers of his servants might be answered according to their faith.

15 **And now** behold, **can ye dispute the power of God?** For behold, **doth not my voice shake the earth?** And **can ye not also behold** [*see*] **me before you?** And I am sent from God.

Alma (the sons of Mosiah are seeing and hearing this too; see verse 18) is being "brought to the knowledge of the truth," verse 14, so that he can use his agency under fair circumstances. Every accountable individual who has ever lived will also have the privilege of being taught the truth, whether on earth or in the spirit world, so that they can use their agency to choose between good and evil. Thus, everyone will have been treated completely fairly by God before Final Judgment Day. See D&C 138.

The scriptures teach that "every knee shall bow," and every tongue will "confess" that Jesus is the Christ. See Philippians 2:10–11, D&C 76:110, Mosiah 27:31, etc. The word "confess" does not necessarily mean to accept Jesus as the Christ. Rather, it means to acknowledge that Jesus is who He claimed to be. They still have their agency and can choose not to follow Christ, but it will be with "a knowledge of the truth" such as Alma and the sons of Mosiah were given.

16 Now I say unto thee: Go, and remember the captivity of thy fathers in the land of Helam, and in the land of Nephi; and remember how great things he has done for them; for they were in bondage, and he has delivered them. **And now** I say unto thee, Alma, **go thy way**, and **seek to destroy the church no more**, that their prayers may be answered, and this **even if thou wilt of thyself be cast off** [*even if you, yourself, want to be cast out from the presence of God forever*].

17 And now it came to pass that **these were the last words which the angel spake unto Alma**, and he departed.

18 And now **Alma and those that were with him fell again to the earth** [*they had all stood up when the angel said to*], for great was their astonishment; for **with their own eyes they had beheld** [*seen*] **an angel of the Lord**; and his voice was as thunder, which shook the earth; and **they knew that there was nothing save the power of God that could shake the earth and cause it to tremble as though it would part asunder.**

19 And now **the astonishment of Alma was so great that he became dumb** [*unable to speak*], that he could not open his mouth; yea, and he became **weak**, even that he could not

move his hands; therefore he was taken by those that were with him, and carried helpless, even until **he was laid before his father**.

20 And they rehearsed unto his father all that had happened unto them; and **his father rejoiced, for he knew that it was the power of God**.

21 And he caused that a multitude should be gathered together **that they might witness what the Lord had done for his son, and also for those that were with him**.

Did you notice in verse 21, above, that Mormon used the word "for" rather than "to" when referring to the Lord's treatment of his son and the sons of Mosiah? There is an important difference between the two words. "For" emphasizes that this was a great opportunity for them, rather than a punishment "to" them.

22 And he caused that the priests should assemble themselves together; and **they began to fast, and to pray to the Lord** their God that he would open the mouth of Alma, that he might speak, and also that his limbs might receive their strength—that the eyes of the people might be opened to see and know of the goodness and glory of God.

As we continue, we will be taught a great lesson about what the Savior's Atonement can do for each of us. You may wish to pay special attention to how fast Alma changed and why it could happen so completely in such a brief time.

23 And it came to pass after they had fasted and prayed for the space of two days and two nights, the limbs of **Alma** received their strength, and he **stood up and began to speak unto them**, bidding them to be of good comfort:

24 For, said he, **I have repented of my sins**, and **have been redeemed of the Lord**; behold I am born of the Spirit [*I am born again. I am a new person*].

25 And the Lord said unto me: Marvel not that **all mankind,** yea, men and women, all nations, kindreds, tongues and people, **must be born again**; yea, born of God, **changed from their carnal** [*worldly*] **and fallen state, to a state of righteousness** [*deep, personal goodness and righteousness*], being redeemed of God, becoming his sons and daughters [*being true followers of Christ, and through Him, followers of Heavenly Father*];

Being "sons and daughters" of God is a synonym for being true followers of Christ and eventually being exalted in the highest degree of glory in the celestial kingdom. See Mosiah 5:7; D&C 76:24.

26 And thus **they become new creatures**; and unless they do this, they can in nowise inherit the kingdom of God [*enter celestial exaltation*].

27 I say unto you, **unless this be the case** [*unless they are born again*], **they must be cast off** [*cannot return to the presence of God*]; and this I know, because I was like [*just about*] to be cast off.

Next, in verse 28, we find out why Alma was able to repent completely in such a short time.

28 Nevertheless, after wading through much tribulation, **repenting nigh unto death**, the Lord in mercy hath seen fit to snatch me out of an everlasting burning, and **I am born of God**.

Alma had true "godly sorrow" for his sins, which was so intense that it nearly killed him. It may be that most people take longer to truly repent, because they are either unwilling or incapable of seeing their sinful behaviors in such stark contrast to the things of God. Whether such repentance happens quickly or takes much longer, "godly sorrow" must be a major factor in a person's being "born again." Paul speaks of this godly sorrow as follows:

2 Corinthians 7:10–11

10 For **godly sorrow worketh repentance** [*causes us to repent*] to salvation [*and thus obtain exaltation*] not to be repented of [*and leaves us with no regrets*]: but **the sorrow of the world** [*being sorry you got caught, or sorry because you are embarrassed, or sorry that your opportunity to continue committing that sin has been taken away, etc.*] **worketh death** [*leads to spiritual death*].

Now, Paul describes some components of godly sorrow, which make it so effective in cleansing us from sin and leading us to truly change and become more righteous.

11 For behold this selfsame thing [*this godly sorrow, the very thing I'm teaching you about, namely*], that ye sorrowed [*were sorry for sins*] after a godly sort [*in the way God wants you to be*], what **carefulness** [*sincerity, anxiety*] it wrought [*caused*] in you, yea, what **clearing of yourselves** [*eagerness to become clear of the sin*], yea, what **indignation** [*irritation, anger at yourself for committing the sin*], yea, what **fear** [*alarm*], yea, what vehement desire [*strong desire to change*], yea, what **zeal** [*enthusiasm to change*], yea, what **revenge** [*punishment; suffering whatever is necessary to make permanent change*]! In all things ye have approved yourselves to be clear in this matter [*in everything you have done you have demonstrated that you understand godly sorrow*].

Now we will return to Alma's account of his marvelous conversion as he contrasts his prior spiritual darkness with the intense spiritual light that is now filling his whole soul.

29 **My soul hath been redeemed** from the gall of bitterness [*the bitterness of wickedness; "gall" is a very bitter liquid*] and bonds of iniquity [*the chains of sin*]. I was in the darkest abyss [*the deepest spiritual darkness*]; but now I behold [*see*] the marvelous light of God. My soul was racked with eternal torment; but I am snatched, and **my soul is pained no more**.

The word "**snatched**" is a wonderful description of what happened to Alma through the Atonement. The term reflects tremendous relief and amazement at being rescued so quickly and so completely from the jaws of hell. Enos used the phrase "my guilt was **swept away**" to describe his feelings after his sins were forgiven (Enos 1:5–6). Such is the power of the Atonement. This can happen to each of us as we deeply repent from our sins.

30 **I rejected my Redeemer** [*this is not the same as "denying Christ;" see D&C 76:31–35 for a description of those who deny Christ and become sons of perdition*], and **denied that which had been spoken of by our fathers**; but now that they may foresee that he will come, and that he remembereth every creature of his creating, **he will make himself manifest unto all** [*everyone will have a completely fair chance before Judgment Day*].

31 Yea, **every knee shall bow, and every tongue confess** [*acknowledge, whether they accept Him or not*] before him. Yea, even at the last day [*Final Judgment Day*], when all men shall stand to be judged of him, **then shall they confess** [*acknowledge*] **that he is God**; then shall they confess, who live without God in the world, that the judgment of an everlasting punishment is just [*fair and appropriate*] upon them; and they shall quake, and tremble, and shrink beneath the glance of his all–searching eye.

A very important and often forgotten component of true repentance is the principle of restitution. "Restitution" means doing everything within your own power to right the wrongs that you have caused. Alma and the sons of Mosiah are examples of this principle.

32 And now it came to pass that **Alma began from this time forward to teach the people, and those who were with Alma** at the time the angel appeared unto them, **traveling round about through all the land, publishing to all the people the things which they had heard and seen, and preaching the word of God in much tribulation, being greatly persecuted by those who were unbelievers, being smitten by many of them.**

33 But notwithstanding all this [*in spite of persecution*], **they did impart much consolation** [*comfort and help*] to the church, confirming their faith, and exhorting them with long-suffering and much travail to keep the commandments of God.

34 And four of them were the **sons of Mosiah**; and their names were **Ammon**, and **Aaron**, and **Omner**, and **Himni**; these were the names of the sons of Mosiah.

35 And **they traveled throughout all the land** of Zarahemla, and among all the people who were under the reign of king Mosiah, zealously **striving to repair all the injuries which they had done to the church** [*the principle of restitution in action*], confessing all their sins, and publishing all the things which they had seen, and explaining the prophecies and the scriptures to all who desired to hear them.

36 **And thus they were instruments in the hands of God** in bringing many to the knowledge of the truth,

yea, to the knowledge of their Redeemer.

Next, Mormon assures us that Alma and the sons of Mosiah repented successfully.

37 And **how blessed are they!** For they did publish peace; they did publish good tidings of good; and they did declare unto the people that the Lord reigneth.

MOSIAH 28

Alma and the four sons of Mosiah are examples of true repentance. One of the signs of true conversion to Christ is that a person begins to think as the Savior thinks. This includes deep concern for the welfare of all people, whether they are righteous, wicked, or somewhere in between. As Mormon continues, we now see this aspect of true conversion in the lives of the sons of Mosiah.

1 NOW it came to pass that after **the sons of Mosiah** had done all these things [*mentioned in chapter 27, verses 32–36*], they took a small number with them and **returned to their father, the king, and desired of him** that he would grant unto them **that they might**, with these whom they had selected [*there were others who went on this mission with them; see Alma 17:12*], **go up to the land of Nephi** [*Lamanite territory, a very dangerous place for Nephites to go; see Alma 17:20*] that they might preach the things which they had heard, and **that they might impart the word of God to their brethren, the Lamanites**—

2 **That perhaps they might bring them to the knowledge of the Lord their God**, and convince them of the iniquity [*wickedness*] of their fathers [*ancestors*]; and that perhaps they might cure them of their hatred towards the Nephites [*the only cure for ethnic hatred is true conversion to Christ*], that they might also be brought to rejoice in the Lord their God, that they might become friendly to one another, and that there should be no more contentions in all the land which the Lord their God had given them.

3 Now **they were desirous that salvation should be declared to every creature, for they could not bear that any human soul should perish**; yea, even the very thoughts that any soul should endure endless torment did cause them to quake and tremble.

4 And **thus did the Spirit of the Lord work upon them**, for they were the very vilest of sinners. And the Lord saw fit in his infinite mercy to spare them; nevertheless they suffered much anguish of soul because of their iniquities, suffering much and fearing that they should be cast off forever.

5 And it came to pass that **they did plead with their father many days that they might go up to the land of Nephi**.

You can perhaps imagine the fears and worries that his sons' request brought up in King Mosiah's heart. No doubt the Lamanites in the land of Nephi were full of hatred toward Nephites. Their hatred probably increased after Limhi and Alma and their people escaped from them many years ago. They had been taught by their parents and leaders to hate Nephites (see Mosiah 24:8). Therefore, it is no wonder that Mosiah hesitated to give permission to his sons and the others to go and preach to these Lamanites. But when he prayed to the Lord about it, he got his answer as follows:

6 And **king Mosiah went and inquired of the Lord if he should let his sons go up among the Lamanites to preach the word.**

7 **And the Lord said** unto Mosiah: **Let them go up,** for **many shall believe** on their words, and **they shall have eternal life** [*exaltation*]; and **I will deliver thy sons out of the hands of the Lamanites**.

There is an important lesson to be learned in the phrase "I will deliver thy sons out of the hands of the Lamanites" in verse 7, above. Often, when people are in the service of God, on His errand, they feel that they should be protected and blessed such that all will go well all of the time. As we study the missions of these men, in Alma, chapters 17–26, we will see that they sacrificed much and some of them suffered much in order to fulfill this mission. Yet the Lord did bring them back to Mosiah when their missions were completed. Being called of God and serving Him does not mean that there won't be trials, tribulations, disappointments, suffering, etc., along with the joys and satisfactions that go along with such work.

8 And it came to pass that **Mosiah granted that they might go and do according to their request.**

9 And **they took their journey into the wilderness** to go up to preach the word among the Lamanites; and I [*Mormon*] shall give an account of their proceedings [*doings, missions*] hereafter [*in Alma, chapters 17–26*].

With his sons gone on missions to the Lamanites, King Mosiah does not have a son to be the next king as he approaches the end of his life. As a result, the whole system of government among his people will be changed to what is called "the reign of the judges." Mormon will describe this to us in Mosiah 29.

10 Now **king Mosiah had no one to confer the kingdom upon, for there was not any of his sons who would accept of the kingdom.**

With his sons gone, Mosiah has another problem, namely, what to do with the sacred records, the sword of Laban, and other things entrusted to his care by his father, King Benjamin. In verse 20, Mormon tells us that Mosiah turns these things over to Alma the Younger. Verses 11 through 20 give more details about these items.

11 **Therefore he took** the records which were engraven on **the plates of brass,** and also **the plates of Nephi** [*the large plates and the small plates of Nephi*], and **all the things which he**

had kept and preserved according to the commandments of God, **after having translated and caused to be written the records which were on the plates of gold** [*the twenty-four gold plates which contained the history of the Jaredites*] which had been found by the people of Limhi, which were delivered to him by the hand of Limhi;

12 And this he did because of the great anxiety of **his people**; for they **were desirous** beyond measure **to know concerning those people** [*the Jaredites; see Ether*] **who had been destroyed.**

13 And now **he translated them by the means of those two stones** [*the Urim and Thummim*] which were **fastened into the two rims of a bow**.

14 Now **these things** [*the Urim and Thummin; by the way, there is more than one Urim and Thummim. Joseph Smith had the one used by the Brother of Jared; see Bible Dictionary, under "Urim and Thummim"*] **were prepared** from the beginning, and were handed down from generation to generation, **for the purpose of interpreting languages**;

15 And **they have been kept and preserved by the hand of the Lord**, that he should discover [*reveal*] to every creature who should possess the land the iniquities and abominations of his people;

16 And **whosoever has these things is called seer**, after the manner of old times.

For more about "seers," see the notes in this book after Mosiah 8:16.

17 Now after Mosiah had finished translating **these records** [*the twenty-four gold plates*], behold, it **gave an account of the people** [*the Jaredites*] **who were destroyed, from the time that they were destroyed back to the building of the great tower** [*the Tower of Babel; see Genesis 11:1–9*], at the time the Lord confounded the language of the people and they were scattered abroad upon the face of all the earth, yea, **and even from that time back until the creation of Adam**.

18 Now this account did cause the people of Mosiah to mourn exceedingly, yea, they were filled with sorrow; **nevertheless it gave them much knowledge**, in the which they did rejoice.

19 And **this account shall be written hereafter** [*as the Book of Ether*]; for behold, it is expedient [*necessary*] that all people should know the things which are written in this account [*the account of the Jaredites*].

20 And now, as I [*Mormon*] said unto you, that after **king Mosiah** had done these things, he **took the plates of brass, and all the things which he had kept, and conferred them upon Alma, who was the son of Alma;** yea, **all the records**, and **also the interpreters** [*the Urim and Thummim*], and conferred them upon him, and commanded him that he should keep and preserve them, and

also keep a record of the people, handing them down from one generation to another, even as they had been handed down from the time that Lehi left Jerusalem.

MOSIAH 29

As you read in verse 10 of chapter 28, none of King Mosiah's sons wanted to be the next king. And so, King Mosiah will establish a type of democratic government to replace the type of government they have, which has a king to rule. Among other things, this chapter is a major document on how to set up righteous governments for the fair and proper governing of all of the citizens of a nation.

As he nears the end of his life, King Mosiah gives a clear and masterful explanation to his people of how such a government must be established. As mentioned above, he recommends that they no longer have kings. He points out the dangers of having leaders who have too much power and whose lifestyles reject the commandments of God. He emphasizes citizen involvement in running the country, the vital role of free elections and the responsibility of citizens to elect leaders whose lives reflect respect for God's laws. We will highlight the basic teachings and principles involved in establishing such a government.

1 NOW when Mosiah had done this [*turned the records, Urim and Thummim, etc., over to Alma the Younger*] he sent out throughout all the land, among all the people, **desiring to know their will concerning who should be their king.**

2 And it came to pass that **the voice of the people** came, saying: We are desirous that **Aaron thy son should be our king and our ruler.**

3 Now **Aaron had gone up to the land of Nephi** [*on a mission to the Lamanites with his brothers and others; see Mosiah 28:5–9*], therefore the king could not confer the kingdom upon him; **neither would Aaron take upon him the kingdom; neither were any of the sons of Mosiah willing to take upon them the kingdom.**

4 Therefore **king Mosiah sent again among the people**; yea, even a written word sent he among the people. And these were the words that were written, saying:

5 Behold, O ye my people, or **my brethren, for I esteem you as such,** I desire that ye should **consider the cause which ye are called to consider** [*this is a good example of citizen involvement in a democracy*]—for ye are desirous to have a king.

6 Now I declare unto you that **he** [*Aaron*] **to whom the kingdom doth rightly belong** [*according to the voice of the people (elections); see verses 1–2*] **has declined**, and will not take upon him the kingdom.

Next, in verses 7–8, King Mosiah teaches an important principle, namely, that we should not unnecessarily place ourselves or anyone else in a position which could cause us to lose our souls.

7 And now **if there should be another appointed** [*to be king*] in his stead [*in his place*], behold I fear there

would rise contentions among you. And who knoweth but what my son, to whom the kingdom doth belong, should turn to be angry and draw away a part of this people after him, which would cause wars and contentions among you, which would be the cause of shedding much blood and perverting the way of the Lord, yea, and destroy the souls of many people.

8 Now I say unto you **let us be wise** and consider these things, for **we have no right to destroy my son, neither should we have any right to destroy another** if he should be appointed in his stead.

Remember that Aaron was one of the rebellious sons of King Mosiah (Mosiah 27:8–10, 34). Next, his father, Mosiah, expresses concern that Aaron not be exposed to the temptation to return to his old, wicked lifestyle. There is an important message in this for us also—namely, to stay away from past sins of which we've repented.

9 And **if my son should turn again to his pride and vain things** he would recall the things which he had said, and claim his right to the kingdom, which would cause him and also this people to commit much sin.

10 And **now let us be wise** and look forward to these things [*let's think ahead*], and do that which will make for the peace of this people.

Next, King Mosiah proposes to his people that they change their form of government from a kingdom with a king to a democracy. This is a drastic change from what they are used to. It is a change from their tradition. It is different from what their parents and grandparents had. It will require much more involvement on their part. Sensing their concern, this great, righteous king does a masterful job of teaching them in preparation for changing their form of government to what will become known as "the reign of the judges."

11 Therefore **I will be your king the remainder of my days**; nevertheless, **let us appoint judges** [*elected officials and leaders; see verse 39*], to judge this people according to our law; and we will newly arrange the affairs [*change the system of government*] of this people, for **we will appoint wise men to be judges, that will judge** [*govern*] **this people according to the commandments of God.**

12 Now **it is better that a man should be judged of God** [*according to God's standards*] **than of man**, for the judgments of God are always just, but the judgments of man are not always just.

13 Therefore, **if it were possible that you could have just men** [*men whose lives are in harmony with God's laws*] **to be your kings**, who would establish the laws of God, and judge this people according to his commandments, yea, if ye could have men for your kings who would do even as my father Benjamin did for this people—I say unto you, if this could

always be the case then it would be expedient [*a good idea*] that ye should always have kings to rule over you.

14 And even **I myself have labored with all the power and faculties which I have possessed, to teach you the commandments of God** [*civil government officials should uphold the standards of God, rather than attempting to put them completely out of the affairs of government, like King Noah did, and like many are doing in our day*], and to establish peace throughout the land, that there should **be no wars nor contentions** [*this does not refer to defending the nation against outside enemies; King Benjamin did, according to Omni 1:24; rather it refers to wars and contentions among the citizens of the nation*], **no stealing, nor plundering, nor murdering, nor any manner of iniquity;**

15 And whosoever has committed iniquity, him have I **punished according to the crime which he has committed, according to the law** which has been given to us by our fathers.

16 Now I say unto you, that because all men are not just **it is not expedient** [*wise*] **that ye should have a king or kings to rule over you** [*it is not wise to have leaders with absolute power over you*].

17 For behold, **how much iniquity** [*sin and wickedness*] **doth one wicked king** [*or any powerful leader*] **cause** to be committed, yea, and what great destruction!

18 Yea, **remember king Noah**, his wickedness and his abominations [*extreme evil*], and also the wickedness and abominations of his people. Behold what great destruction did come upon them; and also **because of their iniquities they were brought into bondage** [*to the Lamanites and to Satan*].

19 And **were it not for the interposition** [*intervention, help*] **of their all–wise Creator, and** this because of **their sincere repentance**, they must [*would*] unavoidably remain in bondage until now.

20 But behold, **he** [*the Lord*] **did deliver them because they did humble themselves before him**; **and because they cried** [*prayed*] **mightily unto him he did deliver them out of bondage**; and thus doth the Lord work with his power in all cases among the children of men, extending the arm of mercy towards them that put their trust in him.

21 And behold, now I say unto you, **ye cannot dethrone an iniquitous** [*wicked*] **king save** [*except*] **it be through much contention, and the shedding of much blood.**

22 For behold, **he has his friends in iniquity** [*a wicked leader surrounds himself with wicked friends and associates*], and he keepeth his guards about him; and **he teareth up the laws of those who have reigned in righteousness before him** [*wicked leaders destroy the laws of the nation that were established and based upon God's laws*]; and **he trampleth under his feet the commandments of God;**

These teachings of Mosiah are very revealing and powerful. They clearly point out what is happening to the laws and legal systems of many nations today. Next, Mosiah shows us that such wicked leaders replace sound and righteous laws with laws that support evil and wickedness.

23 And **he** [*a wicked king; a wicked leader*] **enacteth laws, and sendeth them forth among his people**, yea, **laws after the manner of his own wickedness** [*laws that reflect his own wickedness*]; and **whosoever doth not obey his laws he causeth to be destroyed**; and whosoever doth rebel against him **he will send his armies against them to war** [*sometimes this is done by the legal system, by the courts, judges, lawyers, and juries, etc., rather than by armies*], and if he can he will destroy them; and **thus an unrighteous king doth pervert** [*corrupt*] **the ways of all righteousness.**

24 And now behold I say unto you, **it is not expedient** [*necessary*] **that such abominations should come upon you.** [*In other words, you can prevent this.*]

25 Therefore, **choose** you **by the voice of this people** [*by the process of free elections*], **judges** [*elected officials*], **that ye may be judged according to the laws which have been given you by our fathers** [*the righteous laws established by Nephi, Mosiah I, Benjamin, etc.*], which are correct, and **which were given them by the hand of the Lord.**

26 Now **it is not common that the voice of the people** [*the majority of voters*] **desireth anything contrary to that which is right**; but it is common for the lesser part [*the minority*] of the people to desire that which is not right; therefore this shall ye observe and make it your law—to do your business by the voice of the people. [*In other words, usually, there is safety in democracy.*]

27 And **if the time comes that the voice of the people** [*the majority of voters*] **doth choose iniquity** [*vote for evil leaders and laws*], **then is the time that the judgments** [*punishments*] **of God will come upon you**; yea, then is the time he will visit [*punish*] you with great destruction even as he has hitherto [*previously*] visited this land.

Next, King Mosiah points out safeguards, the checks and balances, which must be in place in the constitution of a land that is based upon principles established by God.

28 And now **if ye have judges, and they do not judge you according to the law which has been given** [*if they don't abide by the original intent of the law*], **ye can cause that they may be judged of a higher judge.**

29 **If your higher judges do not judge righteous judgments**, ye shall cause that **a small number of your lower judges** should be gathered together, and they **shall judge your higher judges, according to the voice of the people.**

30 And I command you to do these things in the fear of the Lord; and I command you to do these things, and that ye have no king; that **if these people commit sins and iniquities they shall be answered upon their own heads** [*accountability of elected officials*].

31 For behold I say unto you, **the sins of many people have been caused by the iniquities** [*wickedness*] **of their kings**; therefore their iniquities are answered upon the heads of their kings.

32 And now I desire that this inequality [*between the rulers and the people they rule over*] should be no more in this land, especially among this my people; but **I desire that this land be a land of liberty,** and **every man may enjoy his rights and privileges alike** [*with equality*], so long as the Lord sees fit that we may live and inherit the land, yea, even as long as any of our posterity remains upon the face of the land.

33 And **many more things did king Mosiah write unto them**, unfolding [*explaining*] unto them all the trials and troubles of a righteous king, yea, all the travails of soul [*worries*] for their people, and also all the murmurings of the people to their king; and he explained it all unto them.

34 And he told them that these things ought not to be; but that **the burden should come upon all the people, that every man might bear his part** [*the individual responsibility of citizens to be involved in their government*].

35 And **he also unfolded** [*explained*] unto them all the **disadvantages** they labored under, by **having an unrighteous king to rule over them**;

36 Yea, **all his iniquities and abominations**, and all the **wars**, and **contentions**, and **bloodshed**, and the **stealing**, and the **plundering**, and the committing of **whoredoms** [*sexual immorality*], and all manner of iniquities which cannot be enumerated [*listed*]—telling them that these things ought not to be, that they were expressly repugnant [*revolting, disgusting*] to the commandments of God.

37 And now it came to pass, **after king Mosiah had sent these things forth among the people they were convinced of the truth of his words.**

38 **Therefore they relinquished** [*gave up*] **their desires for a king**, and became exceedingly anxious that every man should have an equal chance throughout all the land; yea, and every man expressed a willingness to answer for his own sins [*rather than blaming others*].

39 Therefore, it came to pass that **they assembled** themselves together in bodies throughout the land, **to cast in their voices** [*to vote*] **concerning who should be their judges**, to judge them according to the law which had been given them; and they were exceedingly **rejoiced because of the liberty which had been granted unto them.** [*Active involvement of individuals is how individual freedom is preserved.*]

40 And **they did wax** [*grow*] **strong in love towards Mosiah**; yea, they did esteem [*respect and look up to*] him more than any other man; for they did not look upon him as a tyrant who was seeking for gain [*personal benefit at their expense*], yea, for that lucre [*money; wealth*] which doth corrupt the soul; for he had not exacted [*taken*] riches of [*from*] them, neither had he delighted in the shedding of blood; but he had established peace in the land, and he had granted unto his people that they should be delivered from all manner of bondage; therefore they did esteem him, yea, exceedingly, beyond measure.

41 And it came to pass that **they did appoint judges to rule over them**, or to judge them according to the law; and this they did throughout all the land. [*In other words, they followed counsel and established a democracy.*]

42 And it came to pass that **Alma** [*Alma the Younger*] **was appointed to be the first chief judge** [*basically, the president of the country*], **he being also the high priest** [*he was also the President of the Church*], his father [*Alma the Elder*] having conferred the office upon him, and having given him the charge concerning all the affairs of the church.

43 And now it came to pass that **Alma did walk in the ways of the Lord**, and he did keep his commandments, and he did judge righteous judgments; and there was continual peace through the land.

44 And **thus commenced the reign of the judges** throughout all the land of Zarahemla, among all the people who were called the Nephites; and **Alma was the first and chief judge.**

The burden of being the chief judge as well as the President of the Church will become too much, after nine years, and Alma will step down as president of the country and devote all his time and energy to his church responsibilities. See Alma 4:15–20.

Next, we will say farewell to Alma's father, Alma, who was converted by the prophet Abinadi in King Noah's court, and to Mosiah II, who followed in the righteous footsteps of King Benjamin, his father. It will be a choice privilege to meet them in the next life. Alma will die at age 82, and Mosiah will die at age 63.

45 And now it came to pass that **his father** [*Alma the Younger's father*] **died, being eighty and two years old**, having lived to fulfil the commandments of God.

46 And it came to pass that **Mosiah died** also, in the thirty and third year of his reign, **being sixty and three years old**; making in the whole, **five hundred and nine years from the time Lehi left Jerusalem**

[*so there are ninety-one years left before the birth of Christ in Bethlehem, and about one hundred and twenty-four years before the wicked are destroyed and the righteous spared immediately prior to the appearance of the resurrected Savior to the Nephites in the Americas*].

47 And **thus ended the reign of the kings** over the people of Nephi; and thus ended the days of Alma, who was the founder of their church.

THE BOOK OF ALMA

THE SON OF ALMA

This book is the record of Alma the Younger. Remember that, when we first met him, Alma the Younger was a very wicked young man, secretly going around with his friends, the four sons of King Mosiah II, trying to destroy the Church (Mosiah 27:8-9). His father, Alma the Elder, was a young but wicked priest in King Noah's court when we first met him (Mosiah 17:2), but he was converted by the prophet Abinadi and had eventually become the President of the Church (Mosiah 26:8). One of the problems he faced as President was that his own son, Alma the Younger, and the four sons of Mosiah were a serious problem for the Church. But, as you will recall, an angel appeared to these young men and they were converted and repented of their wickedness (Mosiah 27). Now, many years later, Alma the Younger has become the President of the Church and is also the chief judge (basically, the president of the nation). His father has died at age 82 (Mosiah 29:45). A very important message for all of us at this point of the Book of Mormon is that repentance works. The Atonement of Christ cleanses us from our sins and we become new people, like in the case of Alma the Elder and Alma the Younger and the sons of Mosiah.

The book of Alma covers only 39 years, yet it takes up about one third of the Book of Mormon. When you finish reading it, you will have read a major portion of this book of scripture. As with the rest of the Book of Mormon, the book of Alma is rich in teachings relevant to us and our day. For example, in chapter 1, an evil man named Nehor takes advantage of the freedoms provided by the new Nephite democratic government, established by King Mosiah, to attempt to disguise his evil motives. In chapter 30, we will encounter another such man, an anti-Christ named Korihor, who will likewise take advantage of freedom of speech and religion to attempt to destroy the very system of which he takes advantage. We see much of this today.

Another very relevant aspect of the book of Alma for us in our day is what is often referred to as the "war years." These are especially chapters 43 through 62, in which Captain Moroni leads the Nephites through many years of warfare. Many readers of the Book of Mormon wonder why there are so many chapters dealing with war. They find themselves wishing that Mormon had summarized these down to one or two chapters and then moved on to other matters.

There is certainly a message in this for us. The fact that Mormon takes the time to meticulously engrave so many plates is a major message that the "war years" chapters contain vital information and counsel for us who are living under similar circumstances today. Perhaps one such message is to see what our military leaders should do in like matters. In other words, what would Captain Moroni do?

Another message is that "there never was a happier time" (Alma 50:23) among the righteous Nephites than during this time of constant war. We, too, can lead happy lives in our day even though we live in a world of much trouble and political arguing, etc. Mormon will teach us how this can be.

ALMA 1

In chapters 1 through 4, you will read about attacks against the government as well as the Church. It is much like in the world we live in. First, in chapter 1, a powerful man named Nehor enters the scene, teaching false doctrines and introducing "priestcraft" for the first time among Alma's people (Alma 1:12). "Priestcraft" means preaching false doctrine in order to gain "riches and honor." See Alma 1:16. You see this today when preachers become popular and wealthy by teaching what people want to hear, even if it does not agree with the Bible. An example could be when a preacher teaches that premarital sex is okay as long as you are seriously in love, despite the fact that the Bible teaches that it is serious sin. Another example is when a preacher teaches that marriage between same sex couples is okay, even though the Bible teaches that it is not.

You will see that Nehor's teachings are the same as many of the false philosophies that we see and hear today. The result of following Nehor's teachings is the destruction of society, as you will see in Alma, chapter 14, especially verse 16, where the rulers of Ammonihah had adopted the philosophies of Nehor. Also read Alma 16:9–10, where the city of Ammonihah is destroyed.

1 NOW it came to pass that **in the first year of the reign of the judges** [*the first year of Alma the Younger's service as chief judge or "president" of the country*] over the people of *Nephi*, from this time forward, king Mosiah having gone the way of all the earth [*having died*], having warred a good warfare, walking uprightly [*righteously*] before God, leaving none to reign [*rule as king*] in his stead [*in his place*]; nevertheless he [*Mosiah II*] had established laws, and they were acknowledged by the people; therefore they were obliged [*obligated, required*] to abide by [*obey*] the laws which he had made.

2 And it came to pass that **in the first year of the reign of Alma** in the judgment-seat [*the office of chief judge*], **there was a man** [*Nehor; see verse 15*] **brought before him to be judged**, a man who was large, and was noted for his much strength.

> Watch, now, as we are told what Nehor taught. You will see similarities to much of what is taught in today's world.

3 And he had gone about among the people, **preaching to them that which he termed to be the word of God, bearing down against the church; declaring** unto the people **that every priest and teacher ought**

to become popular; and **they ought not to labor with their hands** [*a paid clergy*], but that they ought to be supported by the people.

In verse 4, next, Nehor basically redefines God.

4 And he also testified unto the people that **all mankind should be saved at the last day** [*on Judgment Day*], and that **they need not fear nor tremble** [*for so-called sins*], but that they might lift up their heads and rejoice; for **the Lord had** created all men, and had also **redeemed all men**; and, **in the end, all men should have eternal life.** [*In other words, there is no such thing as sin, or need for godly sorrow, or fear of wickedness. Everyone will ultimately be saved and return to heaven.*]

5 And it came to pass that he did teach these things so much that **many did believe on his words**, even so many that they **began to support him and give him money.**

Whenever we attend inappropriate concerts, buy or rent unwholesome videos, buy or support any media that promote values that are contrary to the lifestyle of the Saints of God, we are, in effect, supporting Satan and giving him money, just as these people did for Nehor.

6 And **he began to be lifted up in the pride of his heart**, and to wear very costly apparel, yea, and even **began to establish a church** after the manner of his preaching. [*Nehor really is of the opinion that he is above the laws of God and the laws of man.*]

7 And it came to pass as he was going, to preach to those who believed on his word, **he met a man** [*Gideon, the man who fought King Noah; see Mosiah 19:4–6*] who belonged to the church of God, yea, even **one of their teachers**; and he [*Nehor*] **began to contend with him** [*Gideon*] sharply, that he might lead away the people of the church; **but the man withstood him** [*stood up to him*], admonishing [*teaching and warning*] him with the words of God.

8 Now **the name of the man was Gideon**; and it was he who was an instrument in the hands of God in delivering the people of Limhi out of bondage.

9 Now, **because Gideon withstood him with the words of God he was wroth** [*very angry*] with Gideon, and drew his sword and **began to smite him**. Now Gideon being stricken with many years [*being very old*], therefore he was not able to withstand [*fight off*] his blows, **therefore he was slain by the sword**.

10 And **the man who slew him** was taken by the people of the church, and **was brought before Alma**, to be judged according to the crimes which he had committed.

11 And it came to pass that **he** stood before Alma and **pleaded for himself with much boldness** [*no remorse at having murdered a righteous elderly man*].

In the next verses, we are taught the dangers of "priestcraft" or preaching what people want to hear instead of what they need to hear, in order to make money. We often think of priestcraft as having to do with ministers and evangelists who study what people desire to hear and then teach it, becoming powerful and wealthy in the process. But to limit it to professed teachers of religion is too narrow. In a broad sense, it applies to Hollywood, television, and any media producers who study what people want to hear, which is opposite God's laws, and then produce and sell their wares in order to become popular and gain wealth.

12 But **Alma said** unto him: Behold, **this is the first time that priestcraft has been introduced among this people.** And behold, **thou art not only guilty of priestcraft, but hast endeavored to enforce it by the sword** [*media producers today often defend their wares with the "sword" of legal action*]; and **were priestcraft to be enforced among this people it would prove their entire destruction** [*a direct warning as to what is happening to societies throughout the world today*].

Occasionally, a member of the Church will ask whether the Church believes in capital punishment (being executed) for first degree murder. The answer is given in verses 13–14, next.

13 And **thou hast shed the blood of a righteous man**, yea, a man who has done much good among this people; and **were we to spare thee his blood would come upon us** for vengeance.

14 **Therefore thou art condemned to die, according to the law which has been given us by Mosiah**, our last king; and it has been acknowledged by this people; therefore this people must abide by the law.

15 And it came to pass that **they took him; and his name was Nehor**; and they carried him upon the top of the hill Manti, and there he was caused, or rather did acknowledge, between the heavens and the earth, that what he had taught to the people was contrary to the word of God; and **there he suffered an ignominious** [*humiliating*] **death**.

Next, in verse 16, we are given the definition of priestcraft.

16 Nevertheless, this did not put an end to the spreading of **priestcraft** through the land; for there were many who loved the vain things of the world, and they went forth **preaching false doctrines;** and this they did **for the sake of riches and honor.**

17 Nevertheless, they durst not [*did not dare*] lie, if it were known, for fear of the law, for liars were punished; therefore **they pretended to preach according to their belief;** and now the law could have no power on any man for his belief. [*In other words, they took advantage of freedom of speech, guaranteed by their government, to preach their lies.*]

18 And they durst not steal, for fear of the law, for such were punished; neither durst they rob, nor murder, for **he that murdered was punished unto death** [*capital punishment*].

The Book of Mormon teaches us much about cause and effect in the rise and fall of nations and societies. It is the Lord's classroom for His people. There seems to be a warning for us in these verses about what happens when prideful and self-serving people begin abusing righteous laws of civil government in order to promote their own selfish and evil agendas. They subtly or obviously hide behind constitutional guarantees and rights in order to persecute those who are trying to follow God. We see this in the next verses.

19 But it came to pass that **whosoever did not belong to the church of God began to persecute those that did belong to the church of God**, and had taken upon them the name of Christ.

20 Yea, **they did persecute them, and afflict them with all manner of words** [*freedom of speech*], and this because of their humility; because they were not proud in their own eyes, and because they did impart the word of God, one with another, without money and without price [*which bothered those who preached for personal popularity and money, in other words, those who practiced priestcraft*].

21 Now **there was a strict law among the people of the church, that there should not any man, belonging to the church, arise and persecute those that did not belong to the church,** and that there should be no persecution among themselves.

Next, we are taught what happens when members ignore the counsel of Church leaders to not argue with those who speak against the Church.

22 Nevertheless, **there were many among them** [*members of the Church*] **who began to be proud, and began to contend warmly with their adversaries** [*enemies of the Church*], even unto blows; yea, they would smite one another with their fists.

23 Now this was in the second year of the reign of Alma, and it was a cause of much affliction to the church; yea, **it was the cause of much trial with the church**.

24 For **the hearts of many were hardened, and their names were blotted out** [*they were excommunicated*], that they were remembered no more among the people of God. And also many withdrew themselves from among them [*many left the Church by their own choice*].

25 Now **this was a great trial to those that did stand fast in the faith** [*who remained faithful to the Church*]**;** nevertheless, **they were steadfast and immovable** in keeping the commandments of God, and they bore with patience the persecution which was heaped upon them.

26 And when the priests left their labor to impart the word of God unto the people, the people also left their labors to hear the word of God. And when the priest had imparted unto them the word of God they all

returned again diligently unto their labors; and the priest, not esteeming himself above his hearers [*like Nehor and those who practiced priestcraft*], **for the preacher was no better than the hearer**, neither was the teacher any better than the learner; and thus **they were all equal,** and they did all labor, every man according to his strength.

27 And **they did impart of their substance** [*they shared what they had*], every man according to that which he had, **to the poor, and the needy, and the sick, and the afflicted**; and they did not wear costly apparel, yet they were neat and comely [*pleasantly dressed*].

28 And thus they did establish the affairs of the church; and thus **they began to have continual peace again, notwithstanding** [*in spite of*] **all their persecutions.**

29 And now, **because of the steadiness of the church they began to be exceedingly rich,** having abundance [*lots of*] of all things whatsoever they stood in need—an abundance of flocks and herds, and fatlings [*healthy young animals*] of every kind, and also abundance of grain, and of gold, and of silver, and of precious things, and abundance of silk and fine-twined linen, and all manner of good homely cloth.

In effect, verse 30, next, describes a "Zion" society, as briefly described in Moses 7:18, which described Enoch's people as "Zion, because they were of one heart and one mind, and dwelt in righteousness; and there was no poor among them."

30 And thus, in their prosperous circumstances, **they did not send away any** who were **naked** [*without adequate clothing*], or that were **hungry**, or that were **athirst** [*thirsty*], or that were **sick**, or that had **not** been **nourished**; and **they did not set their hearts upon riches;** therefore they were **liberal** [*generous*] **to all,** both old and young, both bond and free, both male and female, **whether out of the church or in the church**, having no respect to persons as to those who stood in need.

We see verse 30, above, in action today, exemplified by the Church's humanitarian aid donations throughout the world.

It is interesting that the prosperity which comes through the united efforts of unselfish, righteous Saints, seems to be wonderfully unavoidable. It happens repeatedly throughout the scriptures every time the members of the Church abide collectively by the laws of a Zion society.

31 And **thus they did prosper and become far more wealthy than those who did not belong to their church.**

It seems that for every righteous behavior that is in harmony with the laws of God, Satan promotes a "mirror image," or opposite, as pointed out in verse 32, next.

32 For **those who did not belong to their church did indulge themselves in sorceries**, and in **idolatry**

or **idleness**, and in **babblings**, and in **envyings** and **strife**; **wearing costly apparel;** being **lifted up in the pride of their own eyes; persecuting, lying, thieving, robbing, committing whoredoms** [*sexual immorality*], and **murdering**, and **all manner of wickedness;** nevertheless, the law was put in force upon all those who did transgress it, inasmuch as it was possible.

33 And it came to pass that **by thus exercising the law upon them** [*by enforcing the laws of the land*], **every man suffering according to that which he had done**, they became more still, and durst not commit any wickedness if it were known; therefore, there was much peace among the people of Nephi until the fifth year of the reign of the judges [*until Alma's fifth year as the chief judge*].

ALMA 2

The Nephite government at the time of Alma the Younger's service as chief judge was based on God's laws. It was set up by King Mosiah II (see Mosiah 29). People who do not want to be righteous and live according to God's commandments often have trouble living under this type of government. Therefore, they either seek to overthrow the government or to drastically change the laws of the land, so that the laws support their wicked behaviors.

In Alma, chapters 2 and 3, Mormon shows us attempts to overthrow a government based on God's laws and gospel principles, which support true and lasting individual freedom. We will also be shown the destructive results of following the philosophies of Nehor (Alma 1:2–12).

1 AND it came to pass in the commencement of the fifth year of their reign [*the Nephite democracy was just over four years old*] there began to be a contention among the people; for **a certain man, being called Amlici**, he being a very cunning man, yea, a wise man as to the wisdom of the world, he being after the order of the man [*Nehor*] that slew Gideon by the sword, who was executed according to the law [*in other words, Amlici had adopted Nehor's philosophies, teachings, and support of priestcraft*]—

2 Now **this Amlici had, by his cunning, drawn away much people after him**; even so much that they began to be very powerful; and **they began to endeavor to establish Amlici to be a king over the people** [*they wanted to overthrow Alma's democratic government and install a king instead*].

3 Now **this was alarming to the people of the church**, and also to all those who had not been drawn away after the persuasions of Amlici; for they knew that according to their law that such things must be established by the voice of the people [*by public elections*].

4 Therefore, **if it were possible that Amlici should gain the voice of the people** [*if he could get the majority vote in an election*], he, being a wicked man, would deprive them of their rights

and privileges of the church; for **it was his intent to destroy the church of God**.

5 And it came to pass that **the people assembled themselves together throughout all the land** [*a democracy in action*], every man according to his mind, whether it were for or against Amlici, in separate bodies, having much dispute and wonderful [*intense*] contentions one with another.

6 And **thus they did assemble themselves together to cast in their voices** [*votes*] **concerning the matter**; and they [*the election results*] were laid before the judges.

7 And it came to pass that **the voice of the people came against Amlici**, that he was not made king over the people.

8 Now this did cause much joy in the hearts of those who were against him; but **Amlici did stir up those who were in his favor to anger against those who were not in his favor.**

9 And it came to pass that **they gathered themselves together, and did consecrate Amlici to be their king**.

10 Now **when Amlici was made king over them** [*the people who had voted for him and who had rebelled against the national government led by Alma*] **he commanded them** [*his followers*] **that they should take up arms** [*weapons*] **against their brethren**; and this he did that he might subject them to him [*this is Satan's way*].

11 Now **the people of Amlici were** distinguished by the name of Amlici, being **called Amlicites**; and **the remainder were called Nephites, or the people of God**.

In verse 12, next, we are taught that it is sometimes necessary for a peaceful people to arm themselves with weapons of war in order to defend themselves against enemies.

12 Therefore the people of the Nephites were aware of the intent of the Amlicites, and therefore **they did prepare to meet them;** yea, **they did arm themselves with swords,** and with **cimeters** [*curved, broad-bladed swords*], and with **bows**, and with **arrows**, and with **stones**, and with **slings**, and with **all manner of weapons of war, of every kind**.

13 And **thus they were prepared** to meet the Amlicites at the time of their coming. And there were appointed captains, and higher captains, and chief captains, according to their numbers [*they had an organized army*].

14 And it came to pass that **Amlici did arm his men** with all manner of weapons of war of every kind; and he also appointed rulers and leaders over his people, to lead them to war against their brethren.

15 And it came to pass that **the Amlicites came** upon the hill Amnihu, which was east of the river Sidon, which ran by the land of Zarahemla, and there they began **to make war with the Nephites**.

16 Now **Alma**, being the chief judge and the governor of the people of Nephi, therefore he **went** up with his people, yea, with his captains, and chief captains, yea, **at the head of his armies**, against the Amlicites to battle.

17 And **they began to slay the Amlicites** upon the hill east of Sidon. And **the Amlicites did contend with** [*fight against*] **the Nephites with great strength**, insomuch that **many of the Nephites did fall** [*were killed*] before the Amlicites.

18 Nevertheless **the Lord did strengthen the hand of the Nephites,** that they slew the Amlicites with great slaughter, that they began to flee before them.

19 And it came to pass that the Nephites did pursue the Amlicites all that day, and did slay them with much slaughter, insomuch that **there were slain of the Amlicites twelve thousand five hundred thirty and two souls**; and **there were slain of the Nephites six thousand five hundred sixty and two souls**.

20 And it came to pass that **when Alma could pursue the Amlicites no longer** he caused that his people should pitch their tents in the valley of Gideon, the valley being called after that Gideon who was slain by the hand of Nehor with the sword; and in this valley **the Nephites did pitch their tents for the night**.

21 And **Alma sent spies** to follow the remnant of the Amlicites, that he might know of their plans and their plots, whereby he might guard himself against them, that he might preserve his people from being destroyed.

These spies that Alma sent out will return with very bad news for Alma and his soldiers.

22 Now those whom he had sent out to watch the camp of the Amlicites were called Zeram, and Amnor, and Manti, and Limher; these were **they** who **went out with their men to watch the camp of the Amlicites**.

23 And it came to pass that on the morrow **they returned** into the camp of the Nephites in great haste, being greatly astonished, and struck **with much fear, saying:**

24 Behold, we followed the camp of the Amlicites, and to our great astonishment, in the land of Minon, above the land of Zarahemla, in the course of the land of Nephi, **we saw a numerous host** [*a large number*] **of the Lamanites; and behold, the Amlicites have joined them**;

25 And **they are upon our brethren in that land**; and they are fleeing before them with their flocks, and their wives, and their children, towards our city; and except we make haste they obtain possession of our city, and our fathers, and our wives, and our children be slain.

26 And it came to pass that **the people of Nephi** took their tents, and **departed out of the valley of Gideon towards their city**, which was the city of Zarahemla.

27 And behold, **as they were crossing the river Sidon, the Lamanites and the Amlicites**, being as numerous almost, as it were, as the sands of the sea, **came upon them to destroy them**.

One lesson to be learned from this situation is that, even though the faithful followers of the Lord seem to be badly outnumbered by their enemies, which can include evil philosophies, false doctrines, etc., as well as physical enemies, they are actually never "outnumbered" because they have the Lord on their side.

28 Nevertheless, **the Nephites being strengthened by the hand of the Lord, having prayed mightily to him** that he would deliver them out of the hands of their enemies, therefore the Lord did hear their cries, and did strengthen them, and **the Lamanites and the Amlicites did fall before them**.

In a sense, Alma is symbolic of Christ and the powers of righteousness, and Amlici is symbolic of Satan and the forces of evil. Another way to describe this symbolism would be to say that Alma is a "type" or "shadow" of Christ, and Amlici is a "type" or "shadow" of Satan.

Verse 29, next, would make an exciting and dramatic scene in a movie about this part of the Book of Mormon.

29 And it came to pass that **Alma fought with Amlici with the sword, face to face;** and they did contend mightily, one with another.

30 And it came to pass that **Alma, being a man of God**, being exercised [*enlivened*] **with much faith, cried, saying: O Lord, have mercy and spare my life, that I may be an instrument in thy hands to save and preserve this people**.

31 Now when **Alma** had said these words he contended [*fought*] **again with Amlici**; and he **was strengthened, insomuch that he slew** [*killed*] **Amlici with the sword.**

32 And **he also contended with the king of the Lamanites**; but the king of the Lamanites fled back from before Alma and sent his guards to contend with Alma.

33 But **Alma, with his guards**, contended with the guards of the king of the Lamanites until he **slew and drove them back**.

34 And **thus he cleared the ground, or rather the bank**, which was on the west of the river Sidon, throwing the bodies of the Lamanites who had been slain into the waters of Sidon, that thereby his people might have room to cross and contend with the Lamanites and the Amlicites on the west side of the river Sidon.

Internal evidence shows that Joseph Smith indeed was translating from engravings on metal plates as he brought forth the Book of Mormon by the gift and power of God.

In the first lines of verse 34, above, it appears that Mormon changed his mind after having engraved "thus **he cleared the ground**" and decided instead to engrave "**the bank**." For us, on a computer, this would be a simple matter of backspacing, deleting, and re-typing. However, when painstakingly engraving thin metal plates, there is no "backspacing." Therefore, he had to make his change or correction by engraving the word "rather," followed by his correction.

There are a number of such instances that appear to be little engraving errors or changes of mind. Joseph Smith was faithful to what was on the plates even to the point of preserving these things. You might wish to look at some of them in the following references: Mosiah 7:8, Alma 24:19, Alma 35:15, Alma 43:38, and Alma 50:32. They are all strong evidence that the Book of Mormon came from ancient engravings on metal plates.

35 And it came to pass that when they had all crossed the river Sidon that **the Lamanites and the Amlicites began to flee before them**, notwithstanding [*even though*] they were so numerous that they could not be numbered [*counted*].

36 And **they fled before the Nephites** towards the wilderness which was west and north, away beyond the borders of the land; **and the Nephites did pursue them with their might, and did slay them**.

37 Yea, **they were met on every hand, and slain and driven**, until they were scattered on the west, and on the north, **until they had reached the wilderness**, which was called Hermounts; and it was that part of the wilderness which was infested by wild and ravenous beasts.

38 And it came to pass that **many died in the wilderness** of their wounds, and were devoured by those beasts and also the vultures of the air; and their bones have been found [*this comment is by Mormon, who is engraving this record about 500 years after this battle*], and have been heaped up on the earth.

ALMA 3

Mormon is a great teacher and is thinking of us as his students as he compiles the plates of the Book of Mormon that Joseph Smith will eventually translate. He will now teach us a number of lessons based on what he wrote in chapter 2. Over nineteen thousand people died in battles (Alma 2:19) as a result of the wickedness of one man, Amlici, and there must have been many more, to the point that, according to verse 1, next, they didn't even try to count the total who died.

1 AND it came to pass that the Nephites who were not slain by the weapons of war, after having buried those who had been slain—**now the number of the slain were not numbered** [*counted*], **because of the greatness of their number**—after they had finished burying their dead they all returned to their lands, and to their houses, and their wives, and their children.

2 Now **many women and children had been slain with the sword,** and also many of their flocks and their herds; and **also many of their fields of grain were destroyed**, for they were trodden down by the hosts of men.

3 And now as **many of the Lamanites and the Amlicites** [*the apostate Nephites who were joined by the Lamanites to fight Alma and his people*] who **had been slain upon the bank of the river Sidon** were cast into the waters of Sidon; and behold their bones are in the depths of the sea, and they are many.

4 And **the Amlicites** were distinguished from the Nephites, for they **had marked themselves with red in their foreheads** after the manner of the Lamanites; nevertheless they had not shorn [*shaved*] their heads like unto the Lamanites.

The forehead was symbolic of loyalty in Biblical culture. See Revelation 13:16; 14:1. Thus, it may be that the Amlicites chose to mark their foreheads with red as a symbol of loyalty to their Lamanite allies, who's skins would have been somewhat that color.

Next, in verse 5, we are reminded that immodesty and wild fashions accompany falling away from God.

5 Now **the heads of the Lamanites were shorn**; and **they were naked, save it were skin which was girded about their loins**, and also their armor, which was girded about them, and their bows, and their arrows, and their stones, and their slings, and so forth.

6 And **the skins of the Lamanites were dark, according to the mark** which was set upon their fathers [*Laman and Lemuel*], **which was a curse** upon them **because of their transgression and their rebellion** against their brethren, who consisted of Nephi, Jacob, and Joseph, and Sam, who were just and holy men.

Joseph Fielding Smith explains the "mark" and the "curse" mentioned in verse 6, above, as follows (**bold** added for emphasis):

Question: "The question I have is concerning the present status of the Lamanites. I know that Laman and Lemuel and their families were cursed, but to what extent is this curse carried today? Was the darker skin all or just part of the curse? Will this curse be completely forgotten and taken away by the Lord on the basis of repentance and complete acceptance of the gospel?"

Answer: The dark skin was placed upon the Lamanites so that they could be distinguished from the Nephites and to keep the two peoples from mixing. **The dark skin was the sign of the curse. The curse was the withdrawal of the Spirit of the Lord** and the Lamanites becoming a "loathsome and filthy people, full of idleness and all manner of abominations" (I Nephi 12:23). The Lord commanded the Nephites not to intermarry with them, for if they did they would partake of the curse.

At the time of the Savior's visit to the Nephites all of the people became united, and **the curse and the dark skin, which was its sign, were removed.** The two peoples became one and lived in full harmony and peace for about two hundred years.

There were no robbers, nor murderers, neither were there Lamanites, nor any manner of -ites; but they were in one, the children of Christ, and heirs to the kingdom of God. (4 Nephi, verse 17.)

The dark skin of those who have come into the Church is no longer to be considered a sign of the curse. (Joseph Fielding Smith, *Answers to Gospel Questions,* 5 vols. [Salt Lake City: Deseret Book, 1957–66], 3: 122.)

Next, Mormon explains the purposes of the mark and the curse.

7 And **their brethren** [*Laman and Lemuel*] **sought to destroy them** [*Nephi, Sam, Jacob, and Joseph*], **therefore they were cursed; and the Lord God set a mark upon them,** yea, upon Laman and Lemuel, and also the sons of Ishmael, and Ishmaelitish women.

8 And **this was done that their seed** [*posterity*] **might be distinguished from the seed of their brethren,** that thereby the Lord God might preserve his people, **that they might not mix and believe in incorrect traditions which would prove their destruction.**

9 And it came to pass that **whosoever did mingle his seed with that of the Lamanites did bring the same curse** [*the withdrawal of the Spirit of the Lord*] **upon his seed.**

10 Therefore, **whosoever suffered himself to be led away by the Lamanites was called under that head** [*was called a Lamanite*], **and there was a mark** [*the dark skin; 2 Nephi 5:21*] **set upon him**.

11 And it came to pass that **whosoever** would not believe in the tradition of the Lamanites, but **believed those records** [*the brass plates; the scriptures*] which were brought out of the land of Jerusalem, **and also in the tradition of their fathers** [*Lehi, Nephi, etc.*], **which were correct**, **who believed in the commandments of God and kept them, were called the Nephites**, or the people of Nephi, from that time forth—

12 And **it is they who have kept the records** which are true of their people, and also of the people of the Lamanites.

13 Now we will return again to **the Amlicites**, for they **also had a mark set upon them;** yea, **they set the mark upon themselves, yea, even a mark of red upon their foreheads.**

Next, Mormon explains how the prophecies of God were fulfilled in this matter.

14 **Thus the word of God is fulfilled,** for these are the words which he said to Nephi: Behold, the Lamanites have I cursed [*by the withdrawal of the Spirit because of their intentional wickedness*], and **I will set a mark on them**

that they and their seed may be separated from thee and thy seed, from this time henceforth and forever, except [*unless*] they repent of their wickedness and turn to me that I may have mercy upon them.

15 And again: **I will set a mark upon him that mingleth his seed with thy brethren** [*the Lamanites*], **that they may be cursed also**.

16 And again: **I will set a mark upon him that fighteth against thee and thy seed**.

17 And again, I say he that departeth from thee shall no more be called thy seed; and **I will bless thee, and whomsoever shall be called thy seed**, henceforth [*from now on*] and forever; and these were the promises of the Lord unto Nephi and to his seed.

There is an important general message in the above verses: anyone who leaves the association of the Saints of God through personal wickedness will suffer the "curse" or, the withdrawal of the Spirit of the Lord from them. Their minds become "dark" and their behaviors begin to reflect the goals of Satan rather than the blessings of God. This is a choice made with agency.

18 Now t**he Amlicites** knew not that they were fulfilling the words of God when they began to mark themselves in their foreheads; nevertheless they **had come out in open rebellion against God**; therefore it was expedient [*necessary*] that the curse should fall upon them [*in order for the word of God to be fulfilled*].

Next, Mormon emphasizes that it was an agency choice that brought the Amlicites to this status.

19 Now I [*Mormon*] would that ye should see [*I want you to understand*] that **they brought upon themselves the curse** [*the withdrawal of the Spirit*]; and **even so doth every man that is cursed bring upon himself his own condemnation.**

20 Now it came to pass that not many days after the battle which was fought in the land of Zarahemla, by the Lamanites and the Amlicites, that there was **another army of the Lamanites came in upon the people of Nephi**, in the same place where the first army met the Amlicites.

21 And it came to pass that **there was an army sent to drive them out of their land**.

22 Now **Alma himself being afflicted with a** wound did not go up to battle at this time against the Lamanites;

23 **But he sent up a numerous army against them**; and they went up and slew many of the Lamanites, and drove the remainder of them out of the borders of their land.

24 And **then they returned again and began to establish peace in the land**, being troubled no more for a time with their enemies.

25 Now **all these things** were done, yea, all these wars and contentions were **commenced and ended in the fifth year of the reign of the judges**.

Next, in verses 26–27, Mormon summarizes what he wants us to learn from what he recorded in this chapter.

26 And **in one year were thousands and tens of thousands of souls sent to the eternal world** [*killed*], that they might **reap their rewards according to their works, whether they were good or whether they were bad,** to **reap eternal happiness or eternal misery**, according to the spirit which they listed [*chose*] to obey, whether it be a good spirit or a bad one.

Next, in verse 27, Mormon tells us one especially important message that he does not want us to miss.

27 For **every man receiveth wages of him** [*either God or Satan*] **whom he listeth** [*chooses*] **to obey**, and this according to the words of the spirit of prophecy; therefore let it be according to the truth [*this is the truth of the matter*]. And thus endeth the fifth year of the reign of the judges.

ALMA 4

In this chapter, Mormon points out to us how Satan destroys the spirituality of some members of the Church. It also shows how other members remain true and faithful and thus retain a remission of their sins on a daily basis.

It has been six years since King Mosiah II changed the form of government among the Nephites from rule by kings to a type of democracy governed by judges, with a chief judge, much like a president over the nation. Alma is the chief judge.

1 NOW it came to pass in the sixth year of the reign of the judges over the people of Nephi, there were **no contentions nor wars in the land of Zarahemla**;

2 **But the people were afflicted**, yea, greatly afflicted for [*had big problems and troubles because of*] the loss of their brethren, and also for the loss of their flocks and herds, and also for the loss of their fields of grain, which were trodden under foot and destroyed by the Lamanites.

3 And so great were their afflictions that **every soul had cause to mourn; and they believed that it was the judgments of God sent upon them because of their wickedness and their abominations**; therefore they were awakened to a remembrance of their duty [*they had truly been humbled by the tragedy of war with the Amlicites and the Lamanites*].

4 And **they began to establish the church more fully**; yea, and **many were baptized** in the waters of Sidon and were joined to the church of God; yea, they were baptized by the hand of Alma, who had been consecrated the high priest [*the President of the Church*] over the people of the church, by the hand of his father Alma.

5 And it came to pass in the seventh year of the reign of the judges there were **about three thousand five hundred souls that united themselves to the church of God and were baptized**. And thus ended the seventh year of the reign of the judges

over the people of Nephi; and there was continual peace in all that time [*they had had two years of peace and serious rethinking of lifestyles since the tragic war*].

> Watch as Mormon shows us Satan's methods of leading righteous members of the Church astray. This is sometimes referred to as "The Cycle of Apostasy." You may wish to mark these things in your own scriptures.

6 And it came to pass in the eighth year of the reign of the judges, that **the people of the church began to wax** [*grow*] **proud, because of their exceeding riches,** and their **fine silks**, and their **fine-twined linen**, and because of their **many flocks and herds**, and their **gold and their silver, and all manner of** [*all kinds of*] **precious things,** which they had obtained by their industry; and **in all these things were they lifted up in the pride of their eyes,** for they began to wear very costly apparel.

> So far, we are seeing two major tools of the devil: pride and materialism. "Materialism" means being focused on your possessions and things, money and stuff, rather than being focused on God and how you can help others.

7 Now **this was the cause of much affliction** [*worry and concern*] **to Alma**, yea, **and to many** of the people **whom Alma had consecrated to be teachers, and priests, and elders over the church**; yea, many of them were sorely grieved for the wickedness which they saw had begun to be among their people.

8 For they saw and beheld [*saw*] with great sorrow that **the people of the church began to be lifted up in the pride of their eyes,** and to **set their hearts upon riches** [*materialism*] and upon the vain [*not important*] things of the world, that **they began to be scornful,** one towards another, and **they began to persecute** those that did not believe according to their own will and pleasure.

9 And thus, in this eighth year of the reign of the judges, **there began to be great contentions** [*arguments*] **among the people of the church**; yea, there were **envyings** [*they were jealous of each other*], and **strife**, and **malice** [*evil thinking and plots against each other*], and **persecutions**, and **pride**, even to exceed the pride of those who did not belong to the church of God.

> The bad example of members of the Church was beginning to take a toll on convert baptisms and respect for the Church.

10 And thus ended the eighth year of the reign [*rule*] of the judges; and **the wickedness of the church was a great stumbling–block to those who did not belong to the church;** and thus the church began to fail in its progress.

> One of Satan's greatest satisfactions is to have members of the Church lead others into wickedness, as shown next in verse 11.

11 And it came to pass in the commencement of the ninth year, Alma saw the wickedness of the church, and he saw also that **the example**

of the church began to lead those who were unbelievers on from one piece of iniquity to another, thus bringing on the destruction of the people.

12 Yea, he saw great **inequality** among the people, some **lifting themselves up with their pride, despising others, turning their backs upon the needy and the naked** [*those who did not have adequate clothing*] **and those who were hungry, and those who were athirst, and those who were sick and afflicted.**

Next, in verse 13, we see how many members remained faithful and kept their covenants of baptism (Mosiah 18:8–10).

13 Now this was a great cause for lamentations among the people, while others were **abasing** [*humbling*] **themselves, succoring** [*providing help and hurrying to the aid of*] those who stood in need of their succor, such as **imparting their substance to the poor and the needy, feeding the hungry,** and **suffering all manner of afflictions, for Christ's sake**, who should come according to the spirit of prophecy;

Next, Mormon points out to us that these people knew much about the future birth and mission of the Savior, including understanding the Atonement, which provides forgiveness of sins and resurrection.

14 **Looking forward to that day** [*the coming of the Savior for His birth and mission on earth*], **thus retaining a remission of their sins;** being **filled with great joy because of the resurrection of the dead**, according to the will and power and deliverance of Jesus Christ from the bands of death.

Next, Alma will give up his position of chief judge and spend all his time and effort preaching the gospel. This is the only way that a nation can be brought back to God.

15 And now it came to pass that **Alma**, having seen the afflictions of the humble followers of God, and the persecutions which were heaped upon them by the remainder of his people, and seeing all their inequality, **began to be very sorrowful** [*worried*]; nevertheless the Spirit of the Lord did not fail him [*did not leave him*].

16 And **he selected a wise man** [*to become the chief judge*] who was among the elders of the church, **and gave him power according to the voice of the people** [*the people voted for this*], that he might have power to enact laws according to the laws which had been given, and to put them in force according to the wickedness and the crimes of the people.

17 Now **this man's name was Nephihah,** and **he was appointed chief judge; and he sat in the judgment-seat to judge and to govern the people.**

18 Now **Alma did not grant unto him the office of being high priest over the church,** but he retained the office of high priest [*the President of the Church*] unto himself; but he delivered the judgment-seat unto Nephihah.

Next, we are taught the power of the word of God, which is the only force that can bring lasting positive change among people corrupted by the things mentioned earlier in this chapter. Our church leaders and missionaries and righteous members are applying the "power of the word" throughout the world now, as the final scenes unfold before the coming of the Lord.

19 And **this he did** that he himself might go forth among his people, or among the people of Nephi, **that he might preach the word of God** unto them, **to stir them up in remembrance of their duty**, and **that he might pull down, by the word of God**, all the **pride** and **craftiness** and all the **contentions** which were among his people, **seeing no way that he might reclaim them save it were in bearing down in pure testimony against them.**

20 And thus in the commencement of the ninth year of the reign of the judges over the people of Nephi, **Alma** delivered up the judgment-seat to Nephihah, and **confined** [*limited*] **himself wholly** [*completely*] to the high priesthood of the holy order of God, to the testimony of the word [*gospel*], according to the spirit of revelation and prophecy.

ALMA 5

Alma, chapter 5, is a direct quote from Alma's own record, as indicated in the paragraph directly preceding Alma, chapter 5 in your Book of Mormon. It is a major talk given by Alma to both faithful members as well as members of the Church who are starting to fall away.

Many different approaches can be used as we study this much-quoted chapter. For instance, Alma 5:14 is one of the most famous verses in the Book of Mormon. Alma asks the question to his people (and to us), "Have ye spiritually been born of God?" As we begin our study, we will use his question as a reference point and first go through the whole chapter, **bolding** indicators as to whether or not a person is being successfully "born of God." In other words, are you successfully being "celestialized"? You may wish to use this approach to Alma 5 as a sort of check-off list to see how you, personally, are doing. We will also use a series of underlined questions for each of Alma's main points about being "born of God" to help point them out to you.

After we have gone through the whole chapter, **bolding** some key indicators as to whether or not we are on the path to exaltation, we will repeat the chapter, making notes and pointing out other things.

Indicators given by Alma to his people as to whether or not they had been spiritually born of God, (indicated by **bold**).

1 NOW it came to pass that Alma began to deliver the word of God unto the people, first in the land of Zarahemla, and from thence throughout all the land.

2 And these are the words which he spake to the people in the church

which was established in the city of Zarahemla, according to his own record, saying:

3 I, Alma, having been consecrated by my father, Alma, to be a high priest over the church of God, he having power and authority from God to do these things, behold, I say unto you that he began to establish a church in the land which was in the borders of Nephi; yea, the land which was called the land of Mormon; yea, and he did baptize his brethren in the waters of Mormon.

4 And behold, I say unto you, they were delivered out of the hands of the people of king Noah, by the mercy and power of God.

5 And behold, after that, they were brought into bondage by the hands of the Lamanites in the wilderness; yea, I say unto you, they were in captivity, and again the Lord did deliver them out of bondage by the power of his word; and we were brought into this land, and here we began to establish the church of God throughout this land also.

<u>Do you remember and appreciate past blessings from God?</u>

6 And now behold, I say unto you, my brethren, you that belong to this church, have you sufficiently retained in **remembrance** the captivity of your fathers? Yea, and have you sufficiently retained in **remembrance** his mercy and long-suffering towards them? And moreover, have ye sufficiently retained in **remembrance** that he has delivered their souls from hell?

<u>Do you consider the teachings of the gospel to bring light into your soul?</u>

7 Behold, he changed their hearts; yea, he awakened them out of a deep sleep, and they awoke unto God. Behold, they were in the midst of darkness; nevertheless, **their souls were illuminated by the light of the everlasting word**; yea, they were encircled about by the bands of death, and the chains of hell, and an everlasting destruction did await them.

8 And now I ask of you, my brethren, were they destroyed? Behold, I say unto you, Nay, they were not.

<u>Do you love the gospel? Does it cause your soul to expand and grow? Can you feel it?</u>

9 And again I ask, were the bands of death broken, and the chains of hell which encircled them about, were they loosed? I say unto you, Yea, they were loosed, and **their souls did expand, and they did sing redeeming love.** And I say unto you that they are saved.

10 And now I ask of you on what conditions are they saved? Yea, what grounds had they to hope for salvation? What is the cause of their being loosed from the bands of death, yea, and also the chains of hell?

Do you believe in the words of our prophet today?

11 Behold, I can tell you—did not my father Alma **believe in the words** which were **delivered by** the mouth of Abinadi? And was he not **a holy prophet**? Did he not speak the words of God, and my father Alma believe them?

Do you truly want to be righteous?

12 And according to his faith there was **a mighty change wrought in his heart.** Behold I say unto you that this is all true.

Are you teachable? Are you being consistently faithful to God?

13 And behold, he preached the word unto your fathers, and a mighty change was also wrought in their hearts, and they **humbled themselves** and **put their trust in the true and living God**. And behold, they were **faithful until the end**; therefore they were saved.

Do you really want to do right and are you making noticeable progress? Can people tell that you are a member of the Church by watching you**?**

14 And now behold, I ask of you, my brethren of the church, **have ye spiritually been born of God? Have ye received his image in your countenances? Have ye experienced this mighty change in your hearts?**

Do you repent quickly, as needed? Do you look forward to being resurrected and being made clean so you can meet the Savior with humble confidence on the Final Judgment Day?

15 **Do ye exercise faith in the redemption of him who created you?** Do you look forward with an eye of faith, and **view this mortal body raised in immortality**, and this **corruption raised in incorruption, to stand before God to be judged** according to the deeds which have been done in the mortal body?

Can you humbly picture the Lord at the Final Judgment welcoming you to live with Him forever?

16 I say unto you, **can you imagine to yourselves that ye hear the voice of the Lord, saying unto you, in that day: Come unto me ye blessed**, for behold, your works have been the works of righteousness upon the face of the earth?

17 Or do ye imagine to yourselves that ye can lie unto the Lord in that day, and say—Lord, our works have been righteous works upon the face of the earth—and that he will save you?

18 Or otherwise, can ye imagine yourselves brought before the tribunal of God with your souls filled with guilt and remorse, having a remembrance of all your guilt, yea, a perfect remembrance of all your wickedness, yea, a remembrance that ye have set at defiance the commandments of God?

19 I say unto you, can ye look up to God at that day with a pure heart and clean hands? I say unto you, can you look up, having the image of God engraven upon your countenances?

20 I say unto you, can ye think of being saved when you have yielded yourselves to become subjects to the devil?

Are you in the process of gradually but noticeably improving and being cleansed from sins by the Atonement?

21 I say unto you, ye will know at that day that ye cannot be saved; for there can no man be saved except his garments are washed white; yea, his garments must be **purified until** they are **cleansed from all stain, through the blood of him of whom it has been spoken by our fathers, who should come to redeem his people from their sins.**

22 And now I ask of you, my brethren, how will any of you feel, if ye shall stand before the bar of God, having your garments stained with blood and all manner of filthiness? Behold, what will these things testify against you?

23 Behold will they not testify that ye are murderers, yea, and also that ye are guilty of all manner of wickedness?

24 Behold, my brethren, do ye suppose that such an one can have a place to sit down in the kingdom of God, with Abraham, with Isaac, and with Jacob, and also all the holy prophets, whose garments are cleansed and are spotless, pure and white?

25 I say unto you, Nay; except ye make our Creator a liar from the beginning, or suppose that he is a liar from the beginning, ye cannot suppose that such can have place in the kingdom of heaven; but they shall be cast out for they are the children of the kingdom of the devil.

Do you realize that you can't get to celestial glory on past deeds alone? Are you still truly converted to Christ?

26 And now behold, I say unto you, my brethren, **if ye have experienced a change of heart**, and if ye have felt to sing the song of redeeming love, I would ask, **can ye feel so now?**

Are you constantly improving, repenting as needed, and keeping yourself clean? Are you humble enough to let this continue to happen?

27 **Have ye walked, keeping yourselves blameless before God?** Could ye say, if ye were called to die at this time, within yourselves, that ye have been **sufficiently humble?** That your garments have been **cleansed and made white through the blood of Christ**, who will come to redeem his people from their sins?

Do you avoid unrighteous pride?

28 Behold, **are ye stripped of pride?** I say unto you, if ye are not ye are not prepared to meet God. Behold ye must prepare quickly; for the kingdom of heaven is soon at hand, and such an one hath not eternal life.

Do you avoid envy and jealousy of others?

29 Behold, I say, is there one among you who is not **stripped of envy?** I say unto you that such an one is not prepared; and I would that he should prepare quickly, for the hour is close at hand, and he knoweth not when the time shall come; for such an one is not found guiltless.

Do you avoid making fun of others who live the gospel better than you do? Do you refrain from persecuting others? Are you kind to others?

30 And again I say unto you, is there one among you that doth **make a mock of his brother, or that heapeth upon him persecutions?**

31 Wo unto such an one, for he is not prepared, and the time is at hand that he must repent or he cannot be saved!

32 Yea, even wo unto all ye workers of iniquity; repent, repent, for the Lord God hath spoken it!

33 Behold, he sendeth an invitation unto all men, for the arms of mercy are extended towards them, and he saith: Repent, and I will receive you.

34 Yea, he saith: Come unto me and ye shall partake of the fruit of the tree of life; yea, ye shall eat and drink of the bread and the waters of life freely;

35 Yea, come unto me and bring forth works of righteousness, and ye shall not be hewn down and cast into the fire—

36 For behold, the time is at hand that whosoever bringeth forth not good fruit, or whosoever doeth not the works of righteousness, the same have cause to wail and mourn.

37 O ye workers of iniquity; ye that are puffed up in the vain things of the world, ye that have professed to have known the ways of righteousness nevertheless have gone astray, as sheep having no shepherd, notwithstanding a shepherd hath called after you and is still calling after you, but ye will not hearken unto his voice!

38 Behold, I say unto you, that the good shepherd doth call you; yea, and in his own name he doth call you, which is the name of Christ; and if ye will not hearken unto the voice of the good shepherd, to the name by which ye are called, behold, ye are not the sheep of the good shepherd.

39 And now if ye are not the sheep of the good shepherd, of what fold are ye? Behold, I say unto you, that the devil is your shepherd, and ye are of his fold; and now, who can deny this? Behold, I say unto you, whosoever denieth this is a liar and a child of the devil.

40 For I say unto you that whatsoever is good cometh from God, and whatsoever is evil cometh from the devil.

Are you living the gospel that you claim to believe?

41 Therefore, if a man **bringeth forth good works** he hearkeneth unto the voice of the good shepherd, and he doth follow him; but whosoever bringeth forth evil works, the same becometh a child of the devil, for he hearkeneth unto his voice, and doth follow him.

42 And whosoever doeth this must receive his wages of him; therefore, for his wages he receiveth death, as to things pertaining unto righteousness, being dead unto all good works.

43 And now, my brethren, I would that ye should hear me, for I speak in the energy of my soul; for behold, I have spoken unto you plainly that ye cannot err, or have spoken according to the commandments of God.

44 For I am called to speak after this manner, according to the holy order of God, which is in Christ Jesus; yea, I am commanded to stand and testify unto this people the things which have been spoken by our fathers concerning the things which are to come.

45 And this is not all. Do ye not suppose that I know of these things myself? Behold, I testify unto you that I do know that these things whereof I have spoken are true. And how do ye suppose that I know of their surety?

46 Behold, I say unto you they are made known unto me by the Holy Spirit of God. Behold, I have fasted and prayed many days that I might know these things of myself. And now I do know of myself that they are true; for the Lord God hath made them manifest unto me by his Holy Spirit; and this is the spirit of revelation which is in me.

47 And moreover, I say unto you that it has thus been revealed unto me, that the words which have been spoken by our fathers are true, even so according to the spirit of prophecy which is in me, which is also by the manifestation of the Spirit of God.

48 I say unto you, that I know of myself that whatsoever I shall say unto you, concerning that which is to come, is true; and I say unto you, that I know that Jesus Christ shall come, yea, the Son, the Only Begotten of the Father, full of grace, and mercy, and truth. And behold, it is he that cometh to take away the sins of the world, yea, the sins of every man who steadfastly believeth on his name.

49 And now I say unto you that this is the order after which I am called, yea, to preach unto my beloved brethren, yea, and every one that dwelleth in the land; yea, to preach unto all, both old and young, both bond and free; yea, I say unto you the aged, and also the middle aged, and the rising generation; yea, to cry unto them that they must repent and be born again.

50 Yea, thus saith the Spirit: Repent, all ye ends of the earth, for the kingdom of heaven is soon at hand; yea, the Son of God cometh in his glory,

in his might, majesty, power, and dominion. Yea, my beloved brethren, I say unto you, that the Spirit saith: Behold the glory of the King of all the earth; and also the King of heaven shall very soon shine forth among all the children of men.

51 And also the Spirit saith unto me, yea, crieth unto me with a mighty voice, saying: Go forth and say unto this people—Repent, for except ye repent ye can in nowise inherit the kingdom of heaven.

52 And again I say unto you, the Spirit saith: Behold, the ax is laid at the root of the tree; therefore every tree that bringeth not forth good fruit shall be hewn down and cast into the fire, yea, a fire which cannot be consumed, even an unquenchable fire. Behold, and remember, the Holy One hath spoken it.

53 And now my beloved brethren, I say unto you, can ye withstand these sayings; yea, can ye lay aside these things, and trample the Holy One under your feet; yea, can ye be puffed up in the pride of your hearts; yea, will ye still persist in the wearing of costly apparel and setting your hearts upon the vain things of the world, upon your riches?

Do you avoid thinking that you are better than others?

54 Yea, **will ye persist in supposing that ye are better one than another;** yea, will ye persist in the persecution of your brethren, who humble themselves and do walk after the holy order of God, wherewith they have been brought into this church, having been sanctified by the Holy Spirit, and they do bring forth works which are meet for repentance—

55 Yea, and will you persist in turning your backs upon the poor, and the needy, and in withholding your substance from them?

56 And finally, all ye that will persist in your wickedness, I say unto you that these are they who shall be hewn down and cast into the fire except they speedily repent.

Do you find that there are many things in the world that you must avoid in order to remain loyal to Christ?

57 And now I say unto you, all you that are desirous to follow the voice of the good shepherd, come ye out from the wicked, and **be ye separate, and touch not their unclean things**; and behold, their names shall be blotted out, that the names of the wicked shall not be numbered among the names of the righteous, that the word of God may be fulfilled, which saith: The names of the wicked shall not be mingled with the names of my people;

58 For the names of the righteous shall be written in the book of life, and unto them will I grant an inheritance at my right hand. And now, my brethren, what have ye to say against this? I say unto you, if ye speak

against it, it matters not, for the word of God must be fulfilled.

59 For what shepherd is there among you having many sheep doth not watch over them, that the wolves enter not and devour his flock? And behold, if a wolf enter his flock doth he not drive him out? Yea, and at the last, if he can, he will destroy him.

Do you take the words and counsel of the leaders of the Church seriously?

60 And now I say unto you that the good shepherd doth call after you; and if you will **hearken unto his voice** he will bring you into his fold, and ye are his sheep; and he commandeth you that ye suffer no ravenous wolf to enter among you, that ye may not be destroyed.

61 And now I, Alma, do command you in the language of him who hath commanded me, that ye observe to do the words which I have spoken unto you.

62 I speak by way of command unto you that belong to the church; and unto those who do not belong to the church I speak by way of invitation, saying: Come and be baptized unto repentance, that ye also may be partakers of the fruit of the tree of life.

In chapter five, you will no doubt find more indicators as to how you are doing in working toward exaltation, which we did not point out. As mentioned previously, we will now repeat Alma, chapter 5 and do a few more things with it.

ALMA 5

1 NOW it came to pass that **Alma began to deliver the word of God unto the people**, first in the land of Zarahemla, and from thence throughout all the land.

2 And **these are the words which he spake** to the people in the church which was established in the city of Zarahemla, **according to his own record** [*this is a direct quote from Alma's own writing, copied to the gold plates by Mormon*], saying:

3 **I, Alma, having been consecrated by my father**, Alma [*Alma the Elder*], to be a high priest over the church of God [*the President of the Church*], he having power and authority from God to do these things, behold, I say unto you that he [*my father, Alma*] began to establish a church in the land which was in the borders of Nephi [*after he and his people escaped from King Noah*]; yea, the land which was called the land of Mormon; yea, and he did baptize his brethren in the waters of Mormon.

4 And behold, I say unto you, **they were delivered out of the hands of the people of king Noah, by the mercy and power of God**.

5 And behold, **after that, they were brought into bondage by the hands of the Lamanites in the wilderness**;

yea, I say unto you, they were in captivity, and **again the Lord did deliver them out of bondage** by the power of his word; and **we** [*it sounds like Alma the Younger was with them at this point, perhaps as a younger child*] **were brought into this land** [*the land of Zarahemla*], and here we began to establish the church of God throughout this land also.

6 And now behold, I say unto you, my brethren, you that belong to this church, **have you sufficiently retained in remembrance the captivity of your fathers?** Yea, and have you sufficiently retained in remembrance **his mercy and long-suffering** [*patience*] towards them? And moreover [*in addition*], have ye sufficiently retained in remembrance **that he has delivered their souls from hell** [*the power of the Atonement*]?

7 Behold, **he changed their hearts**; yea, he awakened them out of a deep sleep [*spiritual sleep*], and they awoke unto God. Behold, they were in the midst of darkness; nevertheless, their souls were illuminated by the light of the everlasting word; yea, they were encircled about by the bands of death, and the chains of hell [*the captivity of Satan*], and an everlasting destruction did await them.

8 And now I ask of you, my brethren, **were they destroyed?** Behold, I say unto you, **Nay, they were not**.

9 And again I ask, **were the bands of death broken, and the chains of hell which encircled them about, were they loosed?** I say unto you, **Yea**, they were loosed, and their souls did expand, and they did sing redeeming love [*they had great gratitude to God*]. And I say unto you that they are saved.

10 And now I ask of you **on what conditions are they saved?** Yea, what grounds had they to hope for salvation? **What is the cause of their being loosed from the bands of death** [*what did they have to do to be saved*], yea, and also the chains of hell?

11 Behold, **I can tell you**—did not my father Alma **believe** [*faith is the first principle of the gospel because it motivates to action*] **in the words which were delivered by the mouth of Abinadi**? And was he not a holy prophet? Did he not speak the words of God, and my father Alma believe them?

12 And **according to his faith** [*that he could still be saved*] **there was a mighty change wrought** [*that took place*] **in his heart**. Behold I say unto you that this is all true.

13 And behold, **he** [*my father*] **preached the word unto your fathers** [*parents, ancestors*], and a mighty change was also wrought [*caused*] in their hearts, and **they humbled themselves and put their trust in the true and living God**. And behold, **they were faithful until the end; therefore they were saved**.

14 And now behold, I ask of you, my brethren of the church, **have ye**

spiritually been born of God? Have ye received his image in your countenances? Have ye experienced this mighty change in your hearts?

When we are "born of God" or "born again" as taught in verse 14, above, we are not merely "as good as new," rather, we are **new**! We are not even the same person that we were before repenting, because of the power of the Atonement of Christ. This means that if you have committed sins, even big, serious sins, that, after you sincerely and honestly repent, whatever it takes, even confessing to your bishop, if required, you are no longer the same person you were. Rather, you are a new person, literally. You are a new person, "born" of God" like Alma said in verse 14. In effect, you are "newly born" with a whole new life ahead of you.

Alma asks these people (and us) several more questions in the next verses to make sure we understand what it means to be "born of God."

15 **Do ye exercise faith** in the redemption of him who created you? **Do you look forward with an eye of faith** [*do you look forward, not backward*], and **view this mortal body raised in immortality** [*the resurrection*], and **this corruption raised in incorruption** [*your sinful nature being changed to a pure and clean soul*], **to stand before God to be judged** according to the deeds which have been done in the mortal body?

16 I say unto you, **can you imagine to yourselves that ye hear the voice of the Lord, saying unto you, in that day: Come unto me ye blessed**, for behold, your works have been the works of righteousness upon the face of the earth?

Alma now warns against several behaviors and attitudes that are opposite to the underlined "checklist items" we pointed out in this chapter the first time through. Remember, those "checklist items" were questions you can answer for yourself to see how you are doing on the path to return to live with Heavenly Father.

Be aware that Alma adds several more good things you want to be doing also.

17 Or **do ye imagine to yourselves that ye can lie unto the Lord** in that day [*on the final day of judgment*], and say—Lord, our works have been righteous works upon the face of the earth—and that he will save you? [*Many religions and philosophers are saying exactly this—that sin is not sin.*]

18 **Or** otherwise, **can ye imagine yourselves brought before the tribunal** [*the judgment*] **of God** with your souls **filled with guilt and remorse** [*regret*]**, having a remembrance of all your guilt,** yea, **a perfect remembrance** of all your **wickedness**, yea, a remembrance **that ye have set at defiance the commandments of God?**

19 I say unto you, **can ye look up to God at that day with a pure heart and clean hands?** I say unto you, **can you look up, having the image of God engraven upon your countenances** [*do you "glow" with the Spirit of God on your face, so to speak*]**?**

20 I say unto you, **can ye think of being saved when you have yielded yourselves to become subjects to the devil**? [*the answer is obviously "No"*]

21 I say unto you, **ye will know at that day that ye cannot be saved**; for there can no man be saved except his garments [*symbolic of your life*] are washed white [*unless his life is made clean by the Atonement*]; yea, **his garments** [*his deeds, thoughts, and actions*] **must be purified until they are cleansed from all stain** [*sin*], **through the blood of him** [*Christ*] of whom it has been spoken by our fathers [*ancestors*], **who should come to redeem his people from their sins**.

22 And now I ask of you, my brethren, **how will any of you feel, if ye shall stand before the bar of God, having your garments** [*your life*] **stained with blood** [*sins*] **and all manner of filthiness**? Behold, what will these things testify against you?

Just a quick mention of the symbolism of "garments stained with blood and . . . filthiness." In ancient times in desert climates, you can imagine what a task it was to wash clothes. They, of course, did not have modern washing machines nor laundry detergents and stain removers. Consequently, many people wore the same clothes over an extended time, without washing them. Thus, you could tell much about the persons past life simply by looking at his garments (clothing) and seeing the stains from food, blood (from slaughtering animals), dirt, etc., which had collected. Therefore, "having your garments stained with blood and all manner of filthiness" (verse 22, above) means that your sins have not been washed away by the Savior's Atonement because you have not repented. Thus, you are not clean and pure on Judgment Day.

23 Behold **will they not testify that ye are murderers**, yea, and also that ye are **guilty of all manner of wickedness**?

24 Behold, my brethren, **do ye suppose that such an one can have a place to sit down in the kingdom of God**, with Abraham, with Isaac, and with Jacob [*who have already become gods; see D&C 132:37; in other words, exaltation*], and also all the holy prophets, whose garments [*lives*] are cleansed and are spotless, pure and white?

25 **I say unto you, Nay**; except ye make our Creator a liar from the beginning [*if God let you in without your repenting, He would be a liar, because He would be going against His own word that you have to repent and be made clean by the Atonement of Christ before you can come into heaven*], or suppose that he is a liar from the beginning, **ye cannot suppose that such can have place in the kingdom of heaven**; but they shall be cast out for they are the children of the kingdom of the devil [*they are followers of the devil*].

26 And now behold, I say unto you, my brethren, **if ye have experienced a change of heart**, and if ye have felt to sing the song of redeeming love [*if you have great gratitude to God because of the gospel and the Atonement*], I would ask, **can ye feel so now?** [*In other words, you*

have to maintain your righteousness by living the gospel; you can't get into heaven on past righteousness alone; see Ezekiel 18:24.]

27 **Have ye walked** [*through life*], **keeping yourselves blameless before God** [*are you constantly evaluating your life and changing and repenting as needed*]? **Could ye say, if ye were called to die at this time**, within yourselves, **that ye have been sufficiently humble**? That your garments have been [*that your life has been*] **cleansed and made white through the blood of Christ**, who will come to redeem his people from their sins?

Next, Alma points out that how you treat others is a major key to your own exaltation.

28 Behold, **are ye stripped of pride?** I say unto you, if ye are not ye are not prepared to meet God. Behold ye must prepare [*repent*] quickly; for the kingdom of heaven is soon at hand [*your lives will be over relatively soon and you will have to face the consequences of your choices*], and such an one hath not eternal life [*exaltation*].

29 Behold, I say, **is there one among you who is not stripped of envy?** I say unto you that such an one is not prepared; and I would that he should prepare quickly, for the hour is close at hand, and he knoweth not when the time shall come; for such an one is not found guiltless.

30 And again I say unto you, **is there one among you that doth make a mock of** [*make fun of or ridicule in cruel ways*] **his brother, or that heapeth upon him persecutions?**

31 **Wo** [*trouble is coming*] **unto such an one** [*such a person*], **for he is not prepared**, and the time is at hand that he must repent or he cannot be saved!

32 Yea, even **wo unto all ye workers of iniquity** [*sin and wickedness*]; **repent, repent**, for the Lord God hath spoken it!

As you can see, Alma has been very clear to these people who are listening to him, who need to repent, that they can't keep living wicked lives if they want to be saved in heaven. Next, he gives them the very happy message that they can still repent!

33 Behold, **he** [*the Lord*] **sendeth an invitation unto all men**, for **the arms of mercy are extended towards them** [*it is still not too late for you to repent*], and **he saith: Repent, and I will receive you.**

34 Yea, **he saith: Come unto me** and ye shall partake of the fruit of the tree of life [*the gospel, the love of God, and salvation*]; yea, **ye shall eat and drink of the bread and the waters of life** [*symbolic of Christ, His gospel and Atonement*] **freely** [*spiritual nourishment and salvation*];

35 Yea, **come unto me and bring forth works of righteousness, and ye shall not be hewn down and cast into the fire** [*you will not be destroyed with the wicked*]—

36 For behold, the time is at hand [*is getting close*] that whosoever bringeth

forth not good fruit, or **whosoever doeth not the works of righteousness, the same have cause to wail and mourn**.

37 **O ye workers of iniquity** [*evil and wickedness*]; ye that are puffed up in the vain things [*things of no lasting value*] of the world, ye that have professed to have known the ways of righteousness nevertheless have gone astray, as sheep having no shepherd, **notwithstanding** [*even though*] **a shepherd** [*Christ*] **hath called after you and is still calling after you** [*is still inviting you to repent*], but ye will not hearken unto [*listen to and obey*] his voice!

38 Behold, I say unto you, that **the good shepherd** [*Christ*] **doth call you**; yea, and in his own name he doth call you, which is the name of Christ; and **if ye will not hearken unto the voice of the good shepherd, to the name by which ye are called, behold, ye are not the sheep of the good shepherd.**

The imagery in verses 38 and 39 recalls the shepherds in the Holy Land who know their sheep individually by name, and whose sheep know them by voice and only come when their own shepherd calls them. For instance, at night it was the custom for several shepherds to bring their own sheep into a common corral or enclosure where one or two guards would watch over all the sheep. The next morning, as each shepherd came to get his sheep, he would call them individually and they would come from the herd and go with him. If another shepherd called them, they would not come.

39 And now **if ye are not the sheep of the good shepherd, of what fold are ye?** Behold, I say unto you, that **the devil is your shepherd, and ye are of his fold;** and now, who can deny this? Behold, I say unto you, whosoever denieth this [*anyone who would teach you something contrary to what I have taught concerning this*] is a liar and a child [*a follower*] of the devil.

Verse 40 is a vital and simple statement of truth regarding the ultimate source of good and evil.

40 For I say unto you that **whatsoever is good cometh from God, and whatsoever is evil cometh from the devil**.

In the next verse, Alma gives us a very simple test to see who is on the Lord's side and who is on the devil's side.

41 Therefore, **if a man bringeth forth good works he hearkeneth unto the voice of the good shepherd** [*Christ*], **and he doth follow him; but whosoever bringeth forth evil works, the same becometh a child of** [*belongs to*] **the devil, for he** hearkeneth unto his voice, and **doth follow him**.

42 And **whosoever doeth this** [*follows the devil and continues in sin*] **must receive his wages** [*reward*] **of him** [*from the devil*]; therefore, for his wages he receiveth death, as to things pertaining unto righteousness, being dead unto all good works. [*In other words, he dies spiritually.*]

43 And now, my brethren, **I would that ye should** [*I want you to*] **hear me**, for I speak in the energy of my soul; for behold, **I have spoken unto you plainly** [*just like our general authorities do today*] **that ye cannot err** [*you cannot misunderstand what I have said*], or have spoken according to the commandments of God.

Next, Alma bears his testimony to us that he has been called by God to teach what he has taught to these people and to us.

44 For **I am called to speak after this manner, according to the holy order of God, which is in Christ Jesus**; yea, I am commanded to stand and testify unto this people the things which have been spoken by our fathers concerning the things which are to come.

In the next verses there is an important lesson about how we gain a testimony. We know that Alma had seen an angel (Mosiah 27:11–17), yet in verses 45–47 he doesn't once mention this as the basis for his testimony. Rather, his testimony came through the power of the Holy Ghost (verse 46).

45 And **this is not all**. Do ye not suppose that I know of these things myself? Behold, **I testify unto you that I do know that these things whereof I have spoken are true. And how do ye suppose that I know** of their surety?

46 Behold, I say unto you **they are made known unto me by the Holy Spirit of God.** Behold, I have fasted and prayed many days that I might know these things of myself. And now I do know of myself that they are true; for **the Lord God hath made them manifest unto me by his Holy Spirit; and this is the spirit of revelation** which is in me.

47 And moreover, I say unto you that **it has thus been revealed unto me** [*by the power of the Holy Ghost*], **that the words which have been spoken by our fathers** [*ancestors, including past prophets*] **are true**, even so according to the spirit of prophecy which is in me, which is also **by the manifestation of the Spirit of God**.

If you ever find your own testimony sagging a bit, you may well want to strengthen it by reading Alma's testimony in these verses and letting the Holy Ghost bear witness to you that what he says is true.

48 I say unto you, that **I know** of myself that whatsoever I shall say unto you, concerning that which is to come, is true; and I say unto you, that **I know that Jesus Christ shall come**, yea, **the Son, the Only Begotten of the Father, full of grace** [*ability and desire to help us*], **and mercy, and truth.** And behold, it is **he** that **cometh to take away the sins of the world,** yea, **the sins of every man who steadfastly believeth on his name**.

The phrase "the Only Begotten of the Father" in verse 48, above, sometimes causes students to be a bit confused. They know that all of us are "begotten" as spirit sons and daughters of Heavenly Parents. In other words, we are literally the spirit offspring of God (Acts 17:28–29). Yet, the scriptures teach that Christ is the "Only" Begotten of the Father. So, which is correct? Answer: Both. They are context sensitive. All of us, including Jesus, are spirit offspring of God, in other words, "begotten of God." However, Jesus is the only child of the Father who was also "begotten" of the Father in the flesh. In other words, Heavenly Father was Jesus's father and Mary was His mother. Elder James E. Talmage explains it as follows: "That Child to be born of Mary was begotten of Elohim, the Eternal Father . . ." (*Jesus the Christ,* by James E. Talmage, page 81).

Next, Alma explains to these people that, as President of the Church, he has the responsibility to teach the gospel to everyone in the land.

49 And now I say unto you that this is the order after which **I am called**, yea, **to preach unto** my beloved brethren, yea, and **every one that dwelleth in the land**; yea, to preach unto all, both old and young, both bond and free; yea, I say unto you the aged, and also the middle aged, and the rising generation; yea, **to cry unto them that they must repent and be born again** [*"born again" means becoming new, righteous, worthy people by repenting, being baptized if they haven't already been, and living the gospel sincerely and carefully from that time on*].

50 Yea, thus saith the Spirit: **Repent, all ye ends of the earth** [*everyone*], for the kingdom of heaven is soon at hand; yea, the Son of God cometh in his glory, in his might, majesty, power, and dominion. Yea, my beloved brethren, I say unto you, that the Spirit saith: Behold the glory of the King of all the earth; and also the King of heaven shall very soon shine forth among all the children of men.

51 And also the Spirit saith unto me, yea, crieth unto me with a mighty voice, saying: Go forth and say unto this people—**Repent, for except ye repent ye can in nowise inherit the kingdom of heaven**.

52 And again I say unto you, the Spirit saith: Behold, the ax is laid at the root of the tree [*you don't have much time left to repent*]; therefore **every tree that bringeth not forth good fruit shall be hewn down and cast into the fire** [*the wicked will be destroyed*], yea, a fire which cannot be consumed, even an unquenchable fire [*the punishments of God cannot be stopped, except by repentance*]. Behold, and remember, the Holy One hath spoken it.

53 And now my beloved brethren, I say unto you, **can ye withstand** [*reject; fight against*] **these sayings**; yea, can ye lay aside these things [*ignore what I have taught you*], and trample the Holy One [*the Savior*] under your feet; yea, **can ye be puffed up in the pride of your hearts**; yea, will ye still persist in the wearing of costly apparel **and setting your hearts upon the vain things of the world, upon your riches?**

54 Yea, **will ye persist in supposing that ye are better one than another**; yea, will ye persist **in the**

persecution of your brethren, who humble themselves and do walk after the holy order of God, wherewith they have been brought into this church, having been **sanctified by the Holy Spirit,** and they do bring forth works which are meet for repentance—

> Being "sanctified by the Holy Spirit" as used in verse 54, above, means that you have followed the promptings of the Holy Ghost faithfully and thus have been made clean, pure, and holy by the Atonement of Christ. Thus, you are "sanctified," or made fit to be in the presence of God in celestial glory. One of the major functions of the Holy Ghost is to lead us to being cleansed and healed by the Atonement.

55 Yea, and **will you persist in turning your backs upon the poor, and the needy, and in withholding your substance from them?**

56 And **finally, all ye that will persist** [*continue*] **in your wickedness**, I say unto you that these are they who shall be **hewn down and cast into the fire** [*they will be destroyed*] **except** [*unless*] **they speedily repent.**

> As Alma summarizes his sermon to the people of Zarahemla, remember that they are caught in a tug of war between the teachings of Nehor (in Alma, chapter one) and the laws of God.

57 And now **I say unto you, all you that are desirous to** [*who want to*] **follow the voice of the good shepherd** [*Christ*], **come ye out from the wicked, and be ye separate, and touch not their unclean things**; and behold, their names shall be blotted out [*their names will be taken off of the list in heaven of those who will get to come to heaven*], that the names of the wicked shall not be numbered among the names of the righteous, that the word of God may be fulfilled, which saith: The names of the wicked shall not be mingled with the names of my people;

58 For **the names of the righteous shall be written in the book of life** [*the records in heaven in which the names of the exalted are kept; symbolic of exaltation in the highest degree in the celestial kingdom*], and unto them will I grant an inheritance at my right hand [*covenant hand; in other words, they have successfully made and kept their covenants with God*]. And now, my brethren, what have ye to say against this? I say unto you, if ye speak against it, it matters not, for the word of God must be fulfilled.

59 For **what shepherd is there among you having many sheep doth not watch over them**, that the wolves enter not and devour his flock? And behold, if a wolf enter his flock doth he not drive him out? Yea, and at the last, if he can, he will destroy him. [*In other words, don't be offended that God will ultimately destroy the wicked. You yourselves destroy wolves who destroy your flocks.*]

60 And now I say unto you that **the good shepherd** [*Jesus*] **doth call after you; and if you will hearken** [*listen and obey; see verse 41*] unto his voice

he will bring you into his fold [*the Church; ultimately, heaven*], and ye are his sheep; and he commandeth you that ye suffer [*allow*] no ravenous wolf [*vicious apostates and any other things that keep you from following Christ*] to enter among you, that ye may not be destroyed.

61 And now **I, Alma, do command you** in the language of him who hath commanded me, **that ye observe to do the words which I have spoken unto you**.

In verse 62, next, you will notice that Alma addresses members of the Church differently than non-members. This is because members are more accountable to God because they have made covenants, including baptism. He uses a softer approach to non-members, inviting them to be baptized and receive the highest blessings of God.

62 **I speak by way of command unto you that belong to the church; and unto those who do not belong to the church I speak by way of invitation,** saying: Come and be baptized unto repentance, that ye also may be partakers of the fruit of the tree of life [*all the blessings of the gospel*].

ALMA 6

This chapter is a brief transition between two major talks given by Alma, one to members and non-members in Zarahemla, which you just read (Alma 5), and one to faithful members of the Church and some other good and humble people in the valley of Gideon (Alma 7). In it Mormon tells us that Alma ordained additional priesthood leaders in Zarahemla and that converts were added to the membership there.

He also reports that members of the Church who continued in their wicked ways despite the urgent pleading of the President of the Church (Alma) to repent, lost their membership. This is a reminder that there is a balance between continuing to work with imperfect Saints and excommunicating those whose lifestyles constitute a serious threat to the stability of the Church.

1 AND now it came to pass that after Alma had made an end of speaking unto the people of the church, which was established in the city of Zarahemla, **he ordained priests and elders** [*Melchizedek Priesthood leaders; see note accompanying Mosiah 6:3 in this book*], by laying on his hands according to the order of God, **to preside and watch over the church.**

2 And it came to pass that **whosoever did not belong to the church who repented of their sins were baptized unto repentance, and were received into the church.**

3 And it also came to pass that **whosoever did belong to the church that did not repent** of their wickedness and humble themselves before God—I mean those who were lifted up in the pride of their hearts—the same **were rejected, and their names were blotted out** [*taken off the records of the Church*], that their names

were not numbered among those of the righteous [*they were no longer members of the Church*].

4 And **thus they began to establish the order of the church in the city of Zarahemla.**

Next, Mormon points out that all were welcome to attend the general meetings of the Church, whether they were members or not. This is an important guideline that is followed by the Church today.

5 Now I would that ye should understand that the word of God was liberal [*was given freely*] unto all, that **none were deprived of the privilege of assembling themselves together to hear the word of God.**

6 Nevertheless the children of God [*members of the Church*] were commanded that they should **gather themselves together oft, and join in fasting and mighty prayer in behalf of the welfare of the souls of those who knew not God**.

7 And now it came to pass that **when Alma had made these regulations he departed from** them, yea, from **the church** which was **in the city of Zarahemla, and went** over upon the east of the river Sidon, **into the valley of Gideon,** there having been a city built, which was called the city of Gideon, which was in the valley that was called Gideon, being called after the man who was slain by the hand of Nehor [*in Alma, chapter 1*] with the sword.

8 And **Alma went and began to declare the word of God unto the church which was established in the valley of Gideon**, according to the revelation of the truth of the word which had been spoken by his fathers [*ancestors*], and according to the spirit of prophecy which was in him, according to the testimony of Jesus Christ, the Son of God, who should come to redeem his people from their sins, and the holy order by which he was called. And thus it is written. Amen.

ALMA 7

As previously mentioned, this chapter is a talk given by Alma to faithful members of the Church as well as to some humble and good people who will join the Church. Because they are prepared for it, he is able to preach what are often referred to as "the peaceable things of the kingdom" to them; in other words, he does not have to call them to repentance. Rather, he can emphasize and teach the beautiful blessings that accompany personal righteousness. Again, as was the case with chapter 5, Mormon is giving us a direct quote from Alma's own record of this talk.

First, Alma explains why he has not been able to come personally to these people before this.

1 BEHOLD my beloved brethren, seeing that I have been permitted to come unto you, therefore I attempt to address you in my language; yea, by my own mouth, seeing that **it is the**

first time that I have spoken unto you by the words of my mouth [*in person*], I having been wholly confined to the judgment-seat [*my time was completely taken up by my duties as chief judge*], **having had much business that I could not come unto you**.

2 And even **I could not have come now at this time were it not that the judgment-seat** [*serving as president of the country*] **hath been given to another** [*Nephihah; see Alma 4:16–17*], to reign in my stead [*to rule in my place*]; and the Lord in much mercy hath granted that I should come unto you.

3 And behold, **I have come having great hopes and much desire that I should find that ye had humbled yourselves before God**, and that ye had continued in the supplicating of his grace, that I should find that ye were blameless before him, that I should find that ye were not in the awful dilemma that our brethren were in at Zarahemla. [*In other words, I came hoping that I would find you faithful in the Church, which I did, rather than having many prideful and unfaithful members, as was the case in Zarahemla.*]

4 But blessed be the name of God, that he hath given me to know, yea, hath given unto me the exceedingly great joy of knowing that **they** [*the Church in Zarahemla*] **are established again in the way of his righteousness**.

5 And **I trust, according to the Spirit of God which is in me, that I shall also have joy over you**; nevertheless [*however*] I do not desire that my joy over you should come by the cause of so much afflictions and sorrow which I have had for the brethren at Zarahemla, for behold, my joy cometh over them after wading through much affliction and sorrow.

Next, Alma lists several things that could lead members of the Church astray as well as attitudes and actions that will lead toward salvation.

6 But behold, I trust that ye are not in a state of so much **unbelief** as were your brethren; I trust that ye are not lifted up in the **pride** of your hearts; yea, I trust that ye have not **set your hearts upon riches** [*materialism*] and the **vain things** [*unimportant things*] of the world; yea, **I trust that you do not worship idols, but that ye do worship the true and the living God,** and that ye **look forward for the remission of your sins** [*being forgiven of your sins*], **with an everlasting faith,** which is to come [*the Atonement of Christ is soon to be performed; see verse 7*].

In the next verses, Alma prophesies about Christ, who will be born in Bethlehem in about 83 years. In so doing, he will teach us many things about Christ, His mortal ministry, and the Atonement. In verse 7, next, he will remind us that the Atonement is indeed the central focus of everything.

7 For behold, I say unto you there be many things to come [*there are many things ahead*]; and behold, **there is one thing which is of more importance than they all**—for behold, the time

is not far distant that **the Redeemer liveth and cometh among his people**.

Some people seem to be of the belief that prophets of God know everything. This is not the case. They know only what the Lord chooses to reveal to them to reveal to their people. An example of this is found in verse 8, next.

8 Behold, I do not say that he will come among us at the time of his dwelling in his mortal tabernacle [*body*]; for behold, the Spirit hath not said unto me that this should be the case. Now **as to this thing I do not know;** but this much I do know, that the Lord God hath power to do all things which are according to his word.

9 But behold, the Spirit hath said this much unto me, saying: Cry unto this people, saying—**Repent ye, and prepare the way of the Lord, and walk in his paths** [*the covenant path*], which are straight; for behold, the kingdom of heaven is at hand, and the Son of God cometh upon the face of the earth [*the time is getting close for the Savior to be born*].

10 And behold, **he shall be born of Mary, at Jerusalem** which is the land of our forefathers [*ancestors*], **she being a virgin**, a precious and chosen vessel, **who shall be overshadowed and conceive by the power of the Holy Ghost,** and **bring forth a son, yea, even the Son of God.**

Verses 11–12, next, contain very important doctrine about the Atonement, namely, that it does not only overcome physical death and work for our sins, but also for our shortcomings, weaknesses, and imperfections.

11 And **he shall go forth, suffering pains and afflictions and temptations of every kind;** and this that the word might be fulfilled which saith **he will take upon him the pains and the sicknesses of his people**.

12 And **he will take upon him death, that he may loose the bands of death** which bind his people; and **he will take upon him their infirmities**, that his bowels may be filled with mercy, according to the flesh, that he may know according to the flesh how to succor [*help, nourish*] his people according to their infirmities.

Elder Neal A. Maxwell taught the above concepts and even included that the Atonement can work for our stupidity, as follows (**bold** added for emphasis):

"**In Alma 7:12**, the only place in scriptures, to my knowledge, that it appears, **there seems to have been yet another purpose of the Atonement**, speaking again of the Savior and His suffering, 'and he will take upon him death, that he may loose the bands of death which bind his people; and he will take upon him their infirmities, that his bowels may be filled with mercy,' **have you ever thought that there was no way that Jesus could know the suffering which we undergo as a result of our stupidity and sin (because He was sinless) except He bear those sins of ours in what I call the awful arithmetic of the**

Atonement?" (Neal A. Maxwell, *A Symposium on the Old Testament,* p. 17, quoted in *Doctrines of the Gospel Student Manual,* Institutes of Religion, 1986 and 2000 editions, p. 24–25).

13 Now the Spirit knoweth all things; nevertheless **the Son of God suffereth** according to the flesh [*will become mortal*] **that he might take upon him the sins of his people, that he might blot out their transgressions** according to the power of his deliverance [*by the power He will gain by performing the Atonement*]; and now behold, this is the testimony which is in me.

Next, Alma teaches that we must be "born again." This is a way of saying that, by being baptized and continuing to repent throughout our lives, we become new people, different people, not who we were before. It is very comforting to know that we are not the person anymore who committed sins, even very serious sins. The Atonement of Christ is so powerful that it literally gives us the gift of many fresh starts throughout our lives.

14 Now I say unto you that **ye must repent, and be born again** [*become new people through the Atonement as guided by the Holy Ghost*]; for the Spirit saith **if ye are not born again ye cannot inherit the kingdom of heaven** [*celestial glory*]; therefore **come and be baptized unto repentance, that ye may be washed from your sins, that ye may have faith on the Lamb of God** [*Christ*], **who taketh away the sins of the world, who is mighty to save and to cleanse from all unrighteousness.**

15 Yea, I say unto you come and **fear not, and lay aside every sin**, which easily doth beset you [*that troubles you*], which doth bind you down to destruction, yea, come and go forth, and show unto your God that ye are willing to repent of your sins and **enter into a covenant with him to keep his commandments, and witness it unto him this day by going into the waters of baptism.**

16 And **whosoever doeth this, and keepeth the commandments of God from thenceforth** [*from the time of your baptism on*], the same will remember that I say unto him, yea, he will remember that I have said unto him, **he shall have eternal life** [*exaltation*], according to the testimony of the Holy Spirit, which testifieth in me.

Verses 17–19, next, are one of the main ways we know that these people in Gideon, to whom Alma is giving this "gentler sermon," were, in general, more righteous and ready to hear than other groups.

17 And now my beloved brethren, do you believe these things? Behold, I say unto you, yea, **I know that ye believe them; and the way that I know that ye believe them is by the manifestation of the Spirit which is in me.** And now **because your faith is strong** concerning that, yea, concerning the things which I have spoken, **great is my joy.**

18 For as I said unto you from the beginning, that I had much desire that ye were not in the state of dilemma like your brethren [*in Zarahemla*], even so **I have found that my desires have been gratified**.

19 For **I perceive that ye are in the paths of righteousness** [*you are on the covenant path*]**; I perceive that ye are in the path which leads to the kingdom of God; yea, I perceive that ye are making his paths straight** [*you are following Him with exactness in your personal lives*].

Next, Alma teaches us that the standards and requirements of the gospel always remain the same.

20 I perceive that it has been made known unto you, by the testimony of his word, that **he** [*God*] **cannot walk in crooked paths**; neither doth he vary from that which he hath said; neither hath he a shadow of turning from the right to the left, or from that which is right to that which is wrong [*God is absolutely dependable*]; therefore, **his course is one eternal round.**

The phrase "one eternal round" in verse 20, above, can have many definitions. The one that seems to fit here is that the same plan of salvation, including faith, repentance, baptism, and the Gift of the Holy Ghost, working in harmony with the Atonement of Christ, will bring anyone, anywhere, anytime, who follows the laws of God back into the presence of God to live with Him eternally. Thus, in effect, we come from God (from premortality, to earth, and then "full circle" back to Him, if we follow the gospel.)

21 And **he doth not dwell in unholy temples** [*unholy people*]; **neither can filthiness or anything which is unclean be received into the kingdom of God**; therefore I say unto you the time shall come, yea, and it shall be at the last day [*Judgment Day*], that **he who is filthy shall remain in his filthiness**.

22 And now my beloved brethren, **I have said these things** unto you **that I might awaken you to a sense of your duty to God, that ye may walk blameless before him, that ye may walk after the holy order of God** [*according to the covenants that you have made*], after which ye have been received [*after which you have become members of the Church*].

Next, Alma teaches us how to continue and grow as faithful members.

23 And now I would that ye should **be humble**, and **be submissive and gentle; easy to be entreated** [*easily taught*]; **full of patience and long-suffering**; being **temperate in all things**; being **diligent in keeping the commandments of God at all times; asking** [*praying*] **for whatsoever things ye stand in need, both spiritual and temporal; always returning thanks** unto God for whatsoever things ye do receive [*having and showing gratitude; compare with D&C 59:21*].

24 And **see that ye have faith, hope, and charity,** and then ye will always **abound in** [*do lots of*] **good works.**

25 And **may the Lord bless you, and keep your garments spotless** [*keep your lives clean*], that ye may at last be brought to sit down with Abraham, Isaac, and Jacob [*who are already in heaven and have become gods; see D&C 132:37*], and the holy prophets who have been ever since the world began, having your garments [*lives*] spotless [*through the Atonement of Christ*] even as their garments are spotless, in the kingdom of heaven to go no more out [*they have made it to heaven; they are there permanently*].

26 And now my beloved brethren, I have spoken these words unto you according to the Spirit which testifieth in me; and **my soul doth exceedingly rejoice, because of the exceeding diligence and heed which ye have given unto my word.** [*Such people make a prophet very happy.*]

As he concludes, Alma does something that, on special occasions, our church leaders do for us—he leaves a special blessing upon a whole group of people. Perhaps you have been in such a group or heard of such an occasion.

27 **And now, may the peace of God rest upon you**, and upon your houses and lands, and upon your flocks and herds, and all that you possess, your women and your children, according to your faith and good works, from this time forth and forever. And thus I have spoken. Amen.

ALMA 8

After having had wonderful success in the land of Gideon (Alma 7) as well as in Zarahemla (Alma 5), Alma now returns home to rest up. In this chapter, we will see him go next to the land of Melek and there, he will likewise have great success and acceptance among those people.

However, when he goes from there to the city of Ammonihah, he has a very disappointing opposite experience. He is treated horribly!

It is quite difficult, and almost a shock, after having great success in the work of the Lord to which you are called, to run into a terrible experience, where your efforts in your calling from the Lord are unsuccessful and you are openly rejected by those whom you desire to help. Such is the case with Alma in this chapter. We will watch and learn some encouraging and tender lessons as we continue.

1 AND now it came to pass that **Alma returned from the land of Gideon**, after having taught the people of Gideon many things which cannot be written, having established the order of the church, according as he had before done in the land of Zarahemla, yea, he returned **to his own house at Zarahemla to rest himself** from the labors which he had performed.

2 And **thus ended the ninth year of the reign of the judges** over the people of Nephi.

3 And it came to pass in the commencement of the tenth year of the reign of the judges over the people of Nephi, that **Alma departed from thence** [*from there*] **and took his journey over into the land of Melek,** on the west of the river Sidon, on the west by the borders of the wilderness.

4 And **he began to teach the people in the land of Melek** according to the holy order of God, by which he had been called; and he began to teach the people throughout all the land of Melek.

5 And it came to pass that **the people came to him throughout all** the borders of **the land** which was by the wilderness side. **And they were baptized** [*much success*] throughout all the land;

6 So that **when he had finished his work at Melek he departed thence, and traveled** three days' journey on the north of the land of Melek; and he came **to a city which was called Ammonihah.**

We will pause for a moment to talk about the city of Ammonihah. It was a very wicked group of people, arrogant and prideful, full of lawyers. We will be dealing with this city directly, from chapter 8, verse 18, through chapter 14. There will be some wonderful converts but the majority will remain caught up in their evil attitudes and wicked lives. We will meet an inactive member named Amulek, whom the Lord will ask to feed a tired, hungry prophet (Alma), and we will watch as he is brought back into activity in the Church and becomes a powerful missionary companion for Alma.

Ammonihah is heavily involved with lawyers who keep things stirred up so that they can get wealthy. We will meet a lawyer named Zeezrom, who will viciously and cunningly attack Alma and Amulek in public debate. Then we will be reminded that the "Lord loves stinkers" too, and we will watch as Zeezrom is converted and becomes a great blessing to the Lord's work.

We will be taught much about the gospel and the plan of salvation, including the fact that worthy men held the priesthood in the premortal life.

We will hurt as convert men are driven out of the city and their wives and children are martyred (killed because they are members of the Church) in a fire kindled in part by scriptures being burned.

We will see a prison crumble around Alma and Amulek, killing their tormentors, but not harming them. And we will be disappointed when the people of the city of Ammonihah run away in fear from Alma and Amulek, rather than shaking off their fear and pride and asking them to teach them the gospel.

Now, we will continue with chapter 8.

7 **Now it was the custom** of the people of Nephi to call their lands, and their cities, and their villages, yea, even all their small villages, after the name of him who first possessed them; and thus it was with the land of Ammonihah.

8 And it came to pass that **when Alma had come to the city of Ammonihah he began to preach the word of God unto them.**

9 Now **Satan had gotten great hold upon the hearts of the people of the city of Ammonihah**; therefore they would not hearken unto the words of Alma.

Verse 10, next, is sometimes called "a missionary's prayer."

10 Nevertheless Alma labored much in the spirit, wrestling with God in mighty prayer [*not superficial prayer, rather very strong and deep prayer*], that he would **pour out his Spirit upon the people who were in the city; that he would also grant that he might baptize them unto repentance.**

Watch now as the residents of Ammonihah display sarcasm and arrogance as they reply to Alma and his efforts to teach them the gospel. In effect, they say to him that they know who he is, but he is not the president of the country anymore so they don't have to listen to him.

11 Nevertheless, **they hardened their hearts, saying** unto him: Behold, **we know that thou art Alma; and we know that thou art high priest over the church** [*we know that you are President of the Church*] which thou hast established in many parts of the land, according to your tradition; and **we are not of thy church** [*we don't belong to your church*], and **we do not believe in such foolish traditions.**

12 And now we know that because we are not of thy church we know that **thou hast no power over us;** and thou hast delivered up the judgment-seat unto Nephihah; therefore **thou art not the chief judge over us** [*you are not the president of our nation anymore*].

Imagine Alma's disappointment and discouragement as the very people whom he wants to save abuse him and drive him away.

13 Now when **the people** had said this, and **withstood** [*rejected*] **all his words**, and **reviled** [*ridiculed*] **him**, and **spit upon him**, and caused that he should be **cast out of their city**, he departed thence [*from there*] and took his journey towards the city which was called Aaron.

Next, we have a very tender scene. The same angel who appeared to Alma and the sons of Mosiah in Mosiah 27:11, when they were rebellious young men and were seeking to destroy the Church, now appears to Alma to comfort him and instruct him to return to Ammonihah.

14 And it came to pass that while he was journeying thither, being weighed down with sorrow [*very discouraged*], wading through much tribulation and anguish of soul, because of the wickedness of the people who were in the city of Ammonihah, it came to pass while Alma was thus weighed down with sorrow, behold **an angel of the Lord appeared unto him**, saying:

15 **Blessed art thou, Alma**; therefore, **lift up thy head and rejoice,** for **thou hast great cause** [*reason*] **to rejoice**; for **thou hast been faithful in keeping the commandments of God from the time which thou receivedst thy first message from him. Behold, I am he that delivered it unto you** [*I am the same angel who appeared to you back then*].

The angel's message in verse 15, above, may seem a bit different than what Alma might have expected. He had been rejected, spit upon, and thrown out of the city of Ammonihah, and the angel says "Rejoice." The first part of the angel's message has nothing to do with the people of Ammonihah and everything to do with Alma's current standing before the Lord. And this is the message: no matter what circumstances or people do to you in a negative way, what really counts is how you stand with God. Alma can rejoice, because he has "been faithful in keeping the commandments of God" from the time when he was called to repentance by the angel.

The next part of the angel's message is for Alma to go back to Ammonihah and tell the people to repent or they will be destroyed. The angel tells Alma that these wicked people are actually studying ways at this very time to destroy the freedoms of Alma's people.

16 And behold, **I am sent to command thee that thou return to the city of Ammonihah,** and **preach again** unto the people of the city; yea, **preach unto them**. Yea, **say unto them, except** [*unless*] **they repent the Lord God will destroy them**.

17 For behold, **they do study at this time that they may destroy the liberty of thy people** (for thus saith the Lord), which is contrary to the statutes, and judgments, and commandments which he has given unto his people [*they are studying ways to get Alma's people to weaken their own government's laws and regulations, which were based upon the laws of God as set up by Mosiah II; see Mosiah 29*].

Alma is a very good example for us, because he wastes no time in doing what the Lord has commanded.

18 Now it came to pass that after **Alma** had received his message from the angel of the Lord he **returned speedily** to the land of Ammonihah. And he entered the city by another way [*using wisdom to avoid unnecessary confrontation*], yea, by the way which is on the south of the city of Ammonihah.

Next, we see the kindness and tenderness of the Lord again. He has sent an angel to a man (Amulek) who knows he should be active in the Church, but isn't (see Alma 10:5–6), and has asked the man to serve another man (Alma). This service will lead to true conversion and complete dedication to the Lord.

19 And as he entered the city **he was an hungered** [*hungry; an understatement, since he had fasted many days; see verse 26*], and he said to a man [*Amulek; see verse 21*]: Will ye give to an humble servant of God something to eat?

20 And the man said unto him: I am a Nephite, and I know that thou art a holy prophet of God, for **thou art**

the man whom an angel said in a vision: Thou shalt receive [*offer hospitality to*]. Therefore, go with me into my house and I will impart unto thee of my food; and **I know that thou wilt be a blessing unto me and my house.**

21 And it came to pass that **the man received him into his house**; and **the man was called Amulek**; and he brought forth bread and meat [*food*] and set before Alma.

We will take just a moment to get better acquainted with Amulek using excerpts from his own words found in Alma 10:4–6. "And behold, I am also a man of no small reputation among all those who know me (I am a rather important man in Ammonihah); yea, and behold, I have many kindreds (relatives) and friends, and I have also acquired much riches by the hand of my industry (I have worked hard and am rather wealthy). Nevertheless, after all this, I never have known much of the ways of the Lord, and his mysteries and marvelous power (I've never been particularly active and committed in the Church). I said I never had known much of these things; but behold, I mistake, for I have seen much of his mysteries and his marvelous power; yea, even in the preservation of the lives of this people (I actually had a pretty good testimony but ignored it). Nevertheless, I did harden my heart, for I was called many times and I would not hear (the Lord tried to get through to me several times, but I resisted); therefore I knew concerning these things, yet I would not know (but, really, I didn't want to know); therefore I went on rebelling against God, in the wickedness of my heart, even until the fourth day of this seventh month, which is in the tenth year of the reign of the judges."

Now, we will return to what happens next with Alma and Amulek.

22 And it came to pass that **Alma ate bread and was filled**; and **he blessed Amulek and his house**, and he **gave thanks unto God**.

23 And **after he had eaten and was filled he said unto Amulek: I am Alma**, and am the high priest over the church of God throughout the land. [*In other words, I am the President of the Church.*]

24 And behold, I have been called to preach the word of God among all this people, according to the spirit of revelation and prophecy; and I was in this land and they would not receive me, but **they cast me out and I was about to set my back towards this land forever.**

25 But behold, **I have been commanded that I should turn again and prophesy unto this people**, yea, and to testify against them concerning their iniquities [*wickedness*].

26 And now, Amulek, because thou hast fed me and taken me in, thou art blessed; for **I was an hungered, for I had fasted many days.**

We could think of verse 27 as "Amulek's MTC (Missionary Training Center). When Amulek begins preaching with Alma, we will see that this must have been a very effective time of training and learning for him.

27 And **Alma tarried** [*stayed*] **many days with Amulek** before he began to preach unto the people.

28 And it came to pass that **the people** [*of Ammonihah*] **did wax** [*grow*] **more gross in their iniquities** [*increased in wickedness*].

29 And **the word came to Alma, saying: Go;** and **also say unto my servant Amulek, go** forth and **prophesy unto this people**, saying—**Repent** ye, for thus saith the Lord, except ye repent I will visit [*punish*] this people in mine anger; yea, and I will not turn my fierce anger away.

30 And **Alma went forth, and also Amulek, among the people, to declare the words of God unto them**; and **they were filled with the Holy Ghost**.

In verse 31, next, we see that Alma and Amulek had special power granted to them for self-protection. However, as we continue reading, we will note that they put up with an awfully lot before they exercised this special power. Similarly, the Lord has special, absolute power, yet He puts up with much misbehavior before He exercises His power. Thus, Alma and Amulek had the power of God given to them but they did not misuse it.

31 And **they had power given unto them,** insomuch that **they could not be confined in dungeons** [*they couldn't be kept in jails or prisons*]**; neither was it possible that any man could slay** [*kill*] **them; nevertheless they did not exercise their power until they were bound in bands** [*tied up*] **and cast into prison.** Now, this was done that the Lord might show forth his power in them [*Mormon is telling us why the Lord gave them this power*].

32 And it came to pass that **they went forth and began to preach and to prophesy unto the people**, according to the spirit and power which the Lord had given them.

ALMA 9

Chapters 9–14 tell us about Alma and Amulek as they preached the gospel to the citizens of the city of Ammonihah. Remember, they are the people who rejected Alma, spit on him, and threw him out of their city when he first came to preach the gospel to them. Now, Alma is back in the city with Amulek, who invited him to stay in his home and fed him. Amulek is a citizen of the city and has been inactive in the Church, but now will join Alma as his missionary companion.

They will teach some very important doctrines of the gospel and will meet with a lot of opposition. But, as they teach, we will be taught many of the most important parts of the gospel of Jesus Christ.

Near the end of this group of chapters, Alma and Amulek will be put in prison and badly abused. The men of the city who are converted by the preaching of Alma and Amulek will be driven out of town and their wives and children will be destroyed.

These chapters, chapters 9-14, contain direct quotes from Alma's own record and also contain words of Amulek as they preached and dealt with the inhabitants of Ammonihah.

As is the case with many who fight against the gospel, the leading citizens of Ammonihah will oppose the gospel, hiding behind technicalities in their laws in order to appear valid in their opposition to truth. As mentioned above, we are reading Alma's own words as we continue here.

1 AND again, **I, Alma, having been commanded of God that I should take Amulek and go forth and preach** again unto this people, or the people who were **in the city of Ammonihah**, it came to pass **as I began to preach unto them, they began to contend** [*argue*] **with me, saying:**

2 **Who art thou? Suppose ye that we shall believe the testimony of one man** [*in other words, our law requires two witnesses*], although he should preach unto us that the earth should pass away?

3 Now they understood not the words which they spake; for **they knew not that the earth should pass away** [*they didn't know that eventually, the earth will be terrestrialized (will be like the Garden of Eden was), during the Millennium—tenth article of faith—and then celestialized for eternity, D&C 130:9–11*].

4 And they said also: **We will not believe thy words** if thou shouldst prophesy that this great city should be destroyed in one day [*which will happen; see Alma 16:9–10; this is called a "type," symbolic of what will happen to the wicked at the Second Coming*].

5 Now they knew not that God could do such marvelous works, for **they were a hard–hearted and a stiffnecked** [*not humble*] **people**.

6 And they said: **Who is God, that sendeth no more authority than one man** among this people [*in other words, what kind of a god do you have who doesn't even know the law of witnesses?*], to declare unto them the truth of such great and marvelous things? [*Sarcasm.*]

7 And **they stood forth to lay their hands on me** [*to grab me*]; **but behold, they did not.** [*It will be interesting to get the rest of the story on this.*] And I stood with boldness to declare unto them, yea, **I did boldly testify unto them, saying:**

You may recall that one of the things Alma taught about how to be saved, in Alma 5, was that of remembering past blessings from God. Here, he will point out to the Ammonihahites the dangers of forgetting such blessings.

8 Behold, O ye wicked and perverse generation [*twisting truth to justify sin, calling evil good and good evil, etc.*], **how have ye forgotten** the tradition [*the righteous heritage*] of your fathers [*ancestors*]; yea, **how soon ye have forgotten** the commandments of God.

9 **Do ye not remember** that our father [*ancestor*], Lehi, was brought out

of Jerusalem by the hand of God? **Do ye not remember** that they were all led by him through the wilderness [*symbolic of God's leading us through life*]?

10 And **have ye forgotten** so soon how many times he delivered our fathers out of the hands of their enemies, and preserved them from being destroyed, even by the hands of their own brethren?

11 Yea, and **if it had not been for his matchless power, and his mercy, and his long-suffering** [*patience*] towards us, **we should** [*would*] **unavoidably have been cut off from the face of the earth** long before this period of time, and perhaps been consigned to a state of endless misery and woe.

12 Behold, now **I say unto you** that he commandeth you to **repent**; and except ye repent, ye can in nowise inherit the kingdom of God [*the celestial kingdom*]. But behold, this is not all—he has commanded you to repent, **or he will utterly destroy you from off the face of the earth** [*a "type" of the destruction at the Second Coming*]; yea, he will visit [*punish*] you in his anger, and in his fierce anger he will not turn away [*He cannot repeal the law of justice*].

13 Behold, **do ye not remember** the words which he spake unto Lehi, saying that: Inasmuch as ye shall keep my commandments, ye shall prosper in the land? And again it is said that: Inasmuch as ye will not keep my commandments ye shall be cut off from the presence of the Lord [*simple, basic doctrine that the people of Ammonihah need to hear*].

14 Now I would that ye should **remember**, that inasmuch as [*since*] the Lamanites have not kept the commandments of God, they have been cut off from the presence of the Lord [*they have lost the Spirit of the Lord*]. Now we see that the word of the Lord has been verified in this thing, and the Lamanites have been cut off from his presence, from the beginning of their transgressions in the land. [*In other words, we have obvious proof that the word of the Lord comes to pass.*]

From the next verses, we understand that the Ammonihahites are more accountable than the Lamanites. They are apostates (meaning people who have rejected the gospel and left the Church) who know the truth and have rebelled against it, whereas the Lamanites have grown up with false teachings and don't know better than to believe them.

15 Nevertheless I say unto you, that **it shall be more tolerable for them** [*the Lamanites will be better off*] **in the day of judgment than for you, if ye remain in your sins**, yea, and even more tolerable for them in this life than for you, **except ye repent**.

16 For **there are many promises which are extended to the Lamanites**; for **it is because of the traditions of their fathers that caused them to remain in their state of ignorance** [*condition of not knowing about God and the gospel*]**;** therefore the Lord

will be merciful unto them and prolong their existence in the land.

17 And **at some period of time** [*whether in this life or in the spirit world; see D&C 138*] **they will be brought to believe in his word, and to know of the incorrectness of the traditions of their fathers**; and **many** [*not all, because it is an agency choice*] **of them will be saved**, for the Lord will be merciful unto all who call on his name [*who repent and come to Christ*].

The simple doctrine about the fairness of God, taught in verse 17, above, is very comforting for anyone who is concerned about anyone who did not or has not yet had a fair opportunity to understand and accept the gospel in this life. The fact is, God is completely fair. All who have lived beyond the years of accountability (age 8) will have a completely fair chance to completely understand, then accept or reject the gospel, before the Final Judgment Day.

Next, Alma gives a pure prophecy about the fate of the rebellious residents of Ammonihah. It is similar to the prophecy about the wicked in the last days before the Coming of the Lord. If they do not repent, they will be destroyed completely. The prophecy for Ammonihah will be fulfilled in Alma 16:9–10. The prophecy for the wicked in the last days will be fulfilled when the Savior comes to the earth for the Second Coming.

18 But behold, I say unto you that **if ye persist in your wickedness** that your days shall not be prolonged in the land, for the Lamanites shall be sent upon you; and if ye repent not they shall come in a time when you know not, and **ye shall be visited with utter** [*complete*] **destruction**; and it shall be according to the fierce anger of the Lord [*the law of justice will rule in your case*].

19 For he will not suffer [*allow*] you that ye shall live in your iniquities, to destroy his people. I say unto you, Nay; he would rather suffer that the Lamanites might destroy all his people who are called the people of Nephi, if it were possible that they could fall into sins and transgressions, **after having had so much light and so much knowledge given unto them of the Lord their God;** [*In other words, it would be better for them to be killed because of their righteousness than to revert back to their sinful ways.*]

20 Yea, **after having been such a highly favored people of the Lord;** yea, after having been favored above every other nation, kindred, tongue, or people; **after having had all things made known unto them, according to their desires, and their faith, and prayers**, of that which has been, and which is, and which is to come;

21 **Having been visited by the Spirit of God** [*having testimonies via the Holy Ghost*]; having **conversed** [*talked*] **with angels**, and having been **spoken unto by the voice of the Lord**; and having **the spirit of prophecy**, and the **spirit of revelation**, and also **many gifts** [*of the Spirit; see D&C 46:8–26; 1 Cor. 12:3–11; Moroni 10:9–18*], the

gift of **speaking with tongues**, and the gift of **preaching** [*the gift of teaching*], and **the gift of the Holy Ghost**, and the gift of **translation**;

In verse 21, above, Alma summarized for us many of the rich gifts of the Spirit that attend the faithful Saints in our day. He goes on to remind the citizens of Ammonihah of past blessings of the Lord to their ancestors.

22 Yea, and after having been **delivered of God out of the land of Jerusalem,** by the hand of the Lord; having been **saved from famine**, and from **sickness**, and all manner of **diseases** of every kind; and they **having waxed strong in battle** [*having been helped in battles*], that they might not be destroyed; having been **brought out of bondage time after time,** and having been kept and preserved until now; and they have been **prospered until they are rich in all manner of things**—

23 And now behold I say unto you, that **if this people** [*the Nephites, including the people of Ammonihah*], **who have received so many blessings from the hand of the Lord, should transgress contrary to the light and knowledge which they do have,** I say unto you that if this be the case, that **if they should fall into transgression, it would be far more tolerable for the Lamanites than for them.**

24 For behold, **the promises of the Lord are extended to the Lamanites** [*the Lamanites will be reclaimed*], but **they are not unto you if ye transgress** [*because you know better*]; for has not the Lord expressly promised and firmly decreed, that **if ye will rebel against him that ye shall utterly be destroyed** from off the face of the earth?

25 And now for this cause, that ye may not be destroyed, the Lord has sent his angel to visit many of his people, declaring unto them that they must go forth and cry mightily unto this people, saying: **Repent ye, for the kingdom of heaven is nigh at hand** [*your "day of facing God" is getting close; similar to what is happening to the world now, in the last days*];

Next, Alma gives a brief description of the Savior and His mission.

26 And not many days hence [*not long from now*] **the Son of God shall come** in his glory; and his glory shall be the glory of **the Only Begotten of the Father** [*in the flesh*], **full of grace** [*authority, power, and tenderness, to help us*], **equity** [*complete fairness*], and **truth, full of patience, mercy, and long-suffering, quick to hear the cries of his people and to answer their prayers.**

27 And behold, he cometh **to redeem those who will be baptized unto repentance, through faith on his name.**

28 Therefore, prepare ye the way of the Lord, for the time is at hand that all men shall reap a reward of their works [*the "law of the harvest"*], according to that which they have been—**if they have been righteous they shall reap** [*harvest*] **the salvation of their souls, according to the power and deliverance of Jesus Christ; and if they have been evil they shall reap the damnation** [*being stopped in their eternal progress*] **of their souls, according to the power and captivation of the devil.**

Alma continues now by bearing witness to these people that they are having their "chance" now, and would do well to listen and obey.

29 Now behold, **this** [*what you are hearing from me*] **is the voice of the angel**, crying unto the people.

30 And now, my beloved brethren, for ye are my brethren [*Alma loves these people*], and ye ought to be beloved [*you should work to qualify for the mercy of God*], and **ye ought to bring forth works which are meet for** [*needed for; required for*] **repentance**, seeing that your hearts have been grossly hardened against the word of God, and seeing that ye are a lost and a fallen people [*as you now stand*].

31 Now it came to pass that **when I, Alma, had spoken these words, behold, the people were wroth** [*furious*] **with me** because I said unto them that they were a hard-hearted and a stiffnecked people [*similar to people today who get angry at anyone who holds up or even mentions God's standards in public debate*].

32 And also **because I said unto them that they were a lost and a fallen people they were angry with me**, and sought [*tried*] to lay their hands upon me, that they might cast me into prison [*they tried to arrest Alma*].

33 **But** it came to pass that **the Lord did not suffer** [*allow*] **them that they should take me at that time and cast me into prison**.

34 And it came to pass that **Amulek went and stood forth, and began to preach unto them also**. And now the words of Amulek are not all written, nevertheless a part of his words are written in this book.

ALMA 10

Amulek now speaks to the people. In verse 2, he will refer to some writing in the temple, "written by the finger of God." Another instance of writing on a wall of a temple is found in Daniel 5:5–28. We don't have any more information about this so we will have to wait for further revelation about these two incidents. In verses 2–3, Amulek gives important information about Lehi's genealogy.

1 NOW **these are the words which Amulek preached** unto the people who were in the land of Ammonihah, saying:

2 **I am Amulek**; I am the son of Giddonah, who was the son of Ishmael, who was a descendant of Aminadi; and it was the same Aminadi who interpreted **the writing which was upon the wall of the temple**, which was **written by the finger of God**.

3 And Aminadi was a descendant of **Nephi**, who **was the son of Lehi,** who came out of the land of Jerusalem, **who was a descendant of Manasseh, who was the son of Joseph who was sold into Egypt** by the hands of his brethren.

Next, in verses 4-6, Amulek gives a bit of background information about himself. Among other things, he tells us that up to the time he met Alma, he was inactive in the Church and also that he has many relatives and friends and that he is quite wealthy.

4 And behold, I [*Amulek*] am also a man of no small reputation among all those who know me [*Amulek was well-known in Ammonihah*]; yea, and behold, **I have many kindreds** [*relatives*] **and friends**, and I have also acquired **much riches** by the hand of my industry [*through my hard work*].

5 Nevertheless, after all this, I never have known much of the ways of the Lord, and his mysteries and marvelous power. **I said I never had known much of these things; but behold, I mistake, for I have seen much of his mysteries and his marvelous power**; yea, even in the preservation of the lives of this people.

6 Nevertheless, **I did harden my heart, for I was called many times** [*to become active in the gospel*] **and I would not hear;** therefore I knew concerning these things, yet I would not know; therefore **I went on rebelling against God**, in the wickedness of my heart, even **until** the fourth day of this seventh month, which is in the tenth year of the reign of the judges.

7 As I was journeying to see a very near kindred [*a close relative*], behold **an angel of the Lord appeared unto me** and said: Amulek, return to thine own house, for thou shalt feed a prophet of the Lord; yea, a holy man [*Alma*], who is a chosen man of God; for he has fasted many days because of the sins of this people, and he is an hungered [*hungry*], and thou shalt receive him into thy house and feed him, and he shall bless thee and thy house; and the blessing of the Lord shall rest upon thee and thy house.

Obedience is sometimes referred to as "the first law of heaven." When we obey the Lord, blessings follow. Amulek is a great example of this principle, as we will see next.

8 And it came to pass that **I obeyed** the voice of the angel, and returned towards my house. And as I was going thither [*there*] I found the man whom the angel said unto me: Thou shalt receive into thy house—and behold it was this same man [*Alma*] who has been speaking unto you concerning the things of God.

Amulek now bears witness of the prophetic calling of Alma, and thus becomes a second witness to the things Alma has taught to these people. This will anger some of the lawyers (verse 14) and leaders of Ammonihah, because it defeats their initial attack against Alma on the grounds that he was the only witness to what he was saying. See Alma 9:2 and 6.

9 And **the angel said unto me he is a holy man;** wherefore **I know he is a holy man** because it was said by an angel of God.

10 And again, **I know that the things whereof he hath testified are true**; for behold I say unto you, that **as the Lord liveth,** even so has **he sent his angel to make these things manifest unto me**; and this he has done while this Alma hath dwelt at my house.

In verse 11, next, Amulek testifies that there are many more witnesses in the city that can bear witness that Alma is a prophet of God.

11 For behold, he hath blessed mine house, he hath blessed **me**, and **my women,** and **my children**, and **my father** and **my kinsfolk**; yea, even **all my kindred** hath he blessed, and the blessing of the Lord hath rested upon us according to the words which he spake [*We have witnessed Alma's prophetic calling firsthand*].

12 And now, when Amulek had spoken these words **the people began to be astonished, seeing there was more than one witness** who testified of the things whereof they were accused, and also of the things which were to come, according to the spirit of prophecy which was in them.

Next, you will see that some of the city leaders, especially some of the leading lawyers, are starting to worry that some of the people might believe what Alma and Amulek are saying. So they start plotting questions to ask and ways to get them arrested and killed or at least put in prison, to stop them.

13 Nevertheless, there were some [*lawyers; verse 14*] among them who thought to question them, that by their cunning devices they might catch them [*Alma and Amulek*] in their words, that they might find witness against them, that they might deliver them to their judges that they might be judged according to the law [*they want to get rid of Alma and Amulek, but they want it to look legal*], and **that they might be slain or cast into prison, according to the crime which they could make appear or witness against them.**

14 Now it was **those men** who sought to destroy them, who **were lawyers**, who were hired or appointed by the people to administer the law at their times of trials, or at the trials of the crimes of the people before the judges.

15 Now **these lawyers were learned in all the arts and cunning of the people** [*they were well educated in*

accomplishing whatever their clients wanted them to achieve and making it appear legal]; and this was to enable them that they might be skilful in their profession.

It is significant that Mormon gives so much detail about the role of unscrupulous and self-serving lawyers in achieving their goals and their clients' goals in a wicked society. We see much of the same today.

16 And it came to pass that **they began to question Amulek**, that thereby they might make him cross his words, or contradict the words which he should speak. [*They want to quickly destroy his credibility by getting him to contradict himself.*]

Amulek no doubt startles these men with his not-so-gentle response to their plots, including telling them that they are working for the devil.

17 Now they knew not that Amulek could know of their designs [*know of their plots and plans*]. But it came to pass as they began to question him, **he perceived their thoughts** [*by the power of the Holy Ghost*], **and he said** unto them: **O ye wicked and perverse generation** [*people who twist and distort the truth to achieve their own corrupt goals*], **ye lawyers and hypocrites,** for **ye are laying the foundations of the devil** [*you work for the devil*]; for **ye are laying traps and snares to catch the holy ones of God** [*similar to many groups and their lawyers who attempt to stop the work of the Church today, by using the law*].

18 **Ye are laying plans to pervert** [*corrupt and change*] **the ways of the righteous, and to bring down the wrath of God upon your heads,** even **to the utter destruction of this people.** [*You are going to get these people completely destroyed!*]

There is another strong warning for us today, in verse 19, namely, that if and when the time comes that the majority of voters in a nation support corrupt leaders and corrupt laws, at the ballot box, it is because the people themselves have become wicked.

19 Yea, **well did Mosiah say**, who was our last king, when he was about to deliver up the kingdom, having no one to confer it upon, causing that this people should be governed by their own voices—yea, well did he say that **if the time should come that the voice of this people** [*the majority of voters*] **should choose iniquity,** that is, **if the time should come that this people should fall into transgression, they would be ripe** [*ready*] **for destruction.**

20 And now I say unto you that **well doth the Lord judge of your iniquities; well doth he cry** unto this people, by the voice of his angels: **Repent ye, repent**, for the kingdom of heaven is at hand [*the justice of God is about to come upon you*].

21 Yea, well doth he cry, by the voice of his angels that: **I will come down among my people, with equity and justice in my hands.**

Next, we are told that there are some good and righteous people, even in Ammonihah. Later, in chapter 14, when the wicked in Ammonihah drive out the righteous or burn them, they are setting things in motion for their own destruction.

A positive and upbeat message found in verse 22, next, is that the righteous in a society play a significant role in holding back destruction.

22 Yea, and I say unto you that **if it were not for the prayers of the righteous, who are now in the land, that ye would even now be visited with utter** [*complete*] **destruction;** yet it would not be by flood, as were the people in the days of Noah, but it would be by famine, and by pestilence, and the sword [*the types of destruction going on in the world today*].

23 But **it is by the prayers of the righteous that ye are spared**; now therefore, **if ye will cast out the righteous from among you then will not the Lord stay his hand** [*the Lord will not hold back any longer from destroying you*]; but in his fierce anger he will come out against you; then ye shall be smitten by famine, and by pestilence, and by the sword; and **the time is soon at hand except** [*unless*] **ye repent**.

There is an important message for all people at the end of verse 23, above, namely, that despite how wicked and corrupt these Ammonihahites are, they are still invited to repent. They can still repent. It is not too late.

Next, we see the psychology of wickedness in action. Satan is a master at using this. Among other things, it includes avoiding the real issue by claiming to be insulted by the words of God's servants and by supporting peers in their wickedness.

24 And now it came to pass that **the people were more angry with Amulek**, and they cried out, saying: **This man doth revile against our laws which are just** [*proper and righteous*], **and our wise lawyers whom we have selected.**

25 But **Amulek** stretched forth his hand, and **cried the mightier** unto them, saying: **O ye wicked and perverse generation** [*people*], **why hath Satan got such great hold upon your hearts?** Why will ye yield yourselves unto him that he may have power over you, to blind your eyes, that ye will not understand the words which are spoken, according to their truth?

26 For behold, **have I testified against your law?** Ye do not understand; **ye say that I have spoken against your law; but I have not, but I have spoken in favor of your law,** to your condemnation. [*In other words, the government of Ammonihah had good laws, a good "constitution," but it was being ruined by lawyers.*]

Next, we have a strong warning about what a corrupt judicial system can do to a nation.

27 And now behold, I say unto you, that **the foundation of the destruction of this people is beginning to**

be laid by the unrighteousness of your lawyers and your judges.

28 And now it came to pass that **when Amulek had spoken these words the people cried out against him**, saying: Now we know that this man is a child of the devil [*a servant of the devil*], for he hath lied unto us; for he hath spoken against our law. And now he says that he has not spoken against it.

Verses 26 and 28, above, are further evidence that the city of Ammonihah had basically sound laws, set up by Mosiah II in Mosiah, chapter 29. Amulek was speaking in support of their laws, but they twisted things and called him a liar. Sometimes, Satan's way is to project onto others your own misbehavior.

29 And again, **he has reviled against our lawyers, and our judges**.

30 And it came to pass **that the lawyers put it into their hearts** [*for future use*] that they should remember these things against him.

Next, we meet one of the most skilled of all the wicked lawyers in Ammonihah, namely, Zeezrom. To see how to pronounce his name, you may wish to turn to the Pronunciation Guide at the back of your Book of Mormon. We suspect that he was one of the "noble and great ones" spoken of in Abraham 3:22, but just doesn't know it yet.

31 And **there was one among them whose name was Zeezrom.** Now he was **the foremost to accuse Amulek and Alma**, he being **one of the most expert among them**, having much business to do among the people [*a highly successful lawyer*].

32 Now **the object of these lawyers was to get gain** [*their goal was to get wealthy, rather than to uphold the purpose and integrity of the law*]; and they got gain according to their employ [*they got paid according to how much work they had]*.

ALMA 11

One of the wonderful messages in this part of the Book of Mormon is that Amulek went from a "less active," noncommitted member of the Church to a very powerful servant of the Lord with one hundred percent commitment to living the gospel in a short time. Anyone who will make the same commitment can do the same. The problem some members have is that they keep "re-deciding" whether or not to go to church, pay their tithing, live the Word of Wisdom, or whatever; thus, they never reach the complete commitment level.

As the confrontation between Zeezrom and Amulek develops in this chapter, we will be taught some powerful doctrines of the gospel and will watch as these doctrines begin to change Zeezrom's attitude. We will become more aware of the power of pure doctrine to change our lives. Elder Boyd K. Packer said, "True doctrine, understood, changes attitudes and behavior. The study of the doctrines of the gospel will improve behavior quicker than a study of behavior will improve behavior" (Oct. 1986 general conference). We will watch this principle in action with Zeezrom. But first, we will be taught about the money system used in Ammonihah, which will allow us in verse 22 to calculate, roughly, that Zeezrom tries to give Amulek about a $70,000 to $90,000 bribe (in 2019 US dollars) to deny his testimony of God. It is a foolish thing to try.

1 NOW **it was in the law** of Mosiah that every man who was a judge of the law, or those who were appointed to be **judges, should receive wages according to the time which they labored** to judge those who were brought before them to be judged.

2 Now if a man owed another, and he would not pay that which he did owe, he was complained of to the judge; and the judge executed authority, and sent forth officers that the man should be brought before him; and **he judged the man according to the law** and the evidences which were brought against him, and thus the man was compelled to pay that which he owed, or be stripped, or be cast out from among the people as a thief and a robber.

3 And **the judge received for his wages according to his time**—a senine of gold for a day, or a senum of silver, which is equal to a senine of gold; and this is according to the law which was given.

4 Now **these are the names of the different pieces of their gold, and of their silver, according to their value**. And the names are given by the Nephites, for they did not reckon after the manner [*according to the monetary system*] of the Jews who were at Jerusalem; neither did they measure after the manner of the Jews [*neither was their system of weights and measures the same as the Jews'*] but they altered their reckoning and their measure, according to the minds and the circumstances of the people, in every generation, until the reign of the judges, they having been established by king Mosiah.

5 Now **the reckoning is thus** [*the monetary system is as follows*]—a senine of gold, a seon of gold, a shum of gold, and a limnah of gold.

6 A senum of silver, an amnor of silver, an ezrom of silver, and an onti of silver.

7 A senum of silver was equal to a senine of gold, and either for a measure of barley, and also for a measure of every kind of grain.

8 Now the amount of a seon of gold was twice the value of a senine.

9 And a shum of gold was twice the value of a seon.

10 And a limnah of gold was the value of them all.

11 And an amnor of silver was as great as two senums.

12 And an ezrom of silver was as great as four senums.

13 And an onti was as great as them all.

14 Now this is the value of the lesser numbers of their reckoning—

15 A shiblon is half of a senum; therefore, a shiblon for half a measure of barley.

16 And a shiblum is a half of a shiblon.

17 And a leah is the half of a shiblum.

18 Now this is their number, according to their reckoning.

19 Now an antion of gold is equal to three shiblons.

Next, the motives and goals of the lawyers in Ammonihah are pointed out by Mormon as he tells us how they stirred up the people against each other so the lawyers could get more work and, as a result, get more pay.

20 Now, **it was for the sole** [*only*] **purpose to get gain** [*to gain wealth*], because they received their wages according to their employ [*work*], therefore, **they did stir up the people to riotings, and all manner of disturbances and wickedness, that they might have more employ,** that they might get money according to the suits [*cases; lawsuits*] which were brought before them; therefore they did stir up the people against Alma and Amulek.

Watch now as Zeezrom steps in and starts debating with Amulek, trying to make him look bad in front of the people.

21 And this **Zeezrom began to question Amulek**, saying: Will ye answer me a few questions which I shall ask you? Now **Zeezrom was a man who was expert in the devices of the devil, that he might destroy that which was good**; therefore, he said unto Amulek: Will ye answer the questions which I shall put unto you?

Perhaps you can sense Zeezrom's cockiness as he begins to carefully lay his trap for Amulek. First, Zeezrom tests him to see if he will compromise his standards for a substantial bribe. In other words, Zeezrom offers to pay Amulek a large amount of money if he will deny the existence of God.

22 And **Amulek said unto him: Yea** [*yes*]**, if it be according to the Spirit of the Lord**, which is in me; for I shall say nothing which is contrary [*against*] to the Spirit of the Lord. And **Zeezrom said unto him: Behold, here are six onties of silver** [*about $70,000 to $90,000, based on verse 3 and the description of their monetary system*], and **all these will I give thee if thou wilt deny the existence of a Supreme Being** [*God*].

In D&C 121:43, we are taught that there are times for "reproving betimes (immediately) with sharpness when moved upon by the Holy Ghost," and this is obviously one of those occasions, as you will see in verse 23, next. Not only that, but the Holy Ghost is telling Amulek what Zeezrom is thinking.

23 Now **Amulek said: O thou child of hell, why tempt ye me?** Knowest thou that the righteous yieldeth to no such temptations?

24 **Believest thou that there is no God?** I say unto you, Nay, **thou knowest that there is a God, but thou lovest that lucre** [*money*] **more than him.**

25 And now **thou hast lied** before God unto me. **Thou saidst unto me—Behold these six onties,** which are of great worth, **I will give unto thee—when thou hadst it in thy heart to retain them from me** [*you weren't really going to give the bribe money to me*]; and **it was only thy desire that I should deny the true and living God**, that thou mightest have cause to destroy me. And now behold, for this great evil thou shalt have thy reward [*you will get what you deserve*].

As Zeezrom keeps pressing Amulek, he will be taught true doctrines about the Atonement, Christ, spiritual death, repentance, forgiveness, physical death and resurrection, Judgment Day, and unavoidable accountability until, at the end of the chapter, you will see these pure doctrines beginning to penetrate Zeezrom's heart and mind. We will watch as his soul begins to be saved by "true doctrine, understood."

26 And **Zeezrom said** unto him: **Thou sayest there is a true and living God?**

27 And **Amulek said**: **Yea,** there is a true and living God.

28 Now **Zeezrom** said: **Is there more than one God?**

29 And he answered, **No**.

We know that there are three Gods in the Godhead—namely, the Father, the Son, and the Holy Ghost. However, John 17:3 in the Bible says, "And this is life eternal, that they might know thee **the only true God,** and Jesus Christ, whom thou has sent." Thus, we understand that Heavenly Father is the one Supreme God for us (1 Corinthians 8:6). Jesus and the Holy Ghost work under the direction of the Father, who is the Supreme Being.

Watch as Zeezrom cleverly tries to discredit Amulek by making it appear to the people who are listening that Amulek is limiting God's power by saying that there are things God can't do, and also that there is more than one God because the Son of God will come to earth.

30 Now **Zeezrom said** unto him again: **How knowest thou these things?**

31 And he said: **An angel hath made them known unto me.**

32 And **Zeezrom said** again: **Who is he that shall come? Is it the Son of God?**

33 And **he said** unto him, **Yea**.

34 And **Zeezrom said** again: **Shall he save his people in their sins?** And **Amulek answered** and said unto him: I say unto you **he shall not**, for **it is impossible** for him to deny his word.

35 Now **Zeezrom said unto the people: See that ye remember these things; for he said there is but one God; yet he saith that the Son of God shall come, but he shall not save his people—as though he had authority to command God.**

36 Now **Amulek saith** again unto him: Behold **thou hast lied**, for thou sayest that I spake as though I had authority to command God because I said he shall not save his people **in** their sins.

37 And I say unto you again that **he cannot save them in their sins**; for I cannot deny his word, and he hath said that no unclean thing can inherit the kingdom of heaven; therefore, how can ye be saved, except ye inherit the kingdom of heaven? **Therefore, ye cannot be saved in your sins.**

It is absolutely essential that we understand the point made in verses 34–37, above, namely, that we cannot be saved **in** our sins. We can only be saved **from** our sins **by** the Atonement of Christ through repentance.

Many in the world today have fallen into the trap of wanting to be saved **in** their sins. For instance, many Christian churches have changed the rules so that same-sex marriages can be performed by their ministers, and so that such couples can supposedly have acceptance before God. Many churches approve of premarital sex, provided that those involved have true feelings of love for each other. There has been much pressure put on the leaders of our Church to change the rules so that members who deliberately choose to go the way of the world and commit grievous sin can still retain full membership privileges. They want to be saved **in** their sins, rather than **from** their sins. Satan has many convinced not only that it should be possible, but that it is possible. It is not.

38 Now **Zeezrom saith** again unto him: **Is the Son of God the very Eternal Father?**

39 And **Amulek** said unto him: **Yea, he is the very Eternal Father of heaven and of earth, and all things which in them are** [*in other words, Christ is the Creator of the heavens (sky, planets, etc., and earth. Sort of like George Washington is the "father" of our country*]; **he is the beginning and the end, the first and the last** [*Christ is in charge of all things for our salvation (thus, He is the "Father" of our salvation), under the Father's direction, from His premortal calling to be our Redeemer to the Final Judgment Day, at which time he will turn things back over to the Father; see D&C 76:107*];

40 And **he shall come into the world to redeem his people**; and he shall **take upon him the transgressions of those who believe on his name**; and these are they that shall have eternal life [*exaltation*], and **salvation cometh to none else.**

41 Therefore **the wicked remain as though there had been no redemption made, except it be the loosing of the bands of death** [*except that they will be resurrected*]; for behold, the day

cometh that **all shall rise from the dead and stand before God, and be judged according to their works** [*everyone will be held accountable before God*].

42 Now, **there is a death which is called a temporal death** [*physical death*]; and the death of Christ shall loose the bands of this temporal death, that **all shall be raised from this temporal death.**

Next, Amulek teaches what Christ did for all of us with respect to physical death. Since none of us has a perfect physical body, there is much comfort in what he teaches. Our resurrected bodies will be in "perfect form." Many are inclined to speculate as to what age a "perfect" body will be. Eighteen? Twenty-five? Thirty-five? Will we be large-boned or small-boned? What height is perfect? No doubt we have never had a "perfect" body during our own mortal lives and no doubt, we will be very pleasantly surprised and satisfied when we finally get a perfect, resurrected body. We suspect, though, that there will be a large variety of "perfect" sizes, heights, weights, etc., to our entire satisfaction, among resurrected individuals, because of the obvious laws of God designed to preserve individuality.

43 **The spirit and the body shall be reunited** [*our spirit will join our body again when we are resurrected*] **again in its perfect form**; both limb and joint shall be **restored to its proper frame,** even **as we now are at this time** [*implying individuality in our resurrected bodies*]; and **we shall be brought to stand before God, knowing even as we know now, and have a bright recollection of all our guilt.**

44 Now, this restoration [*resurrection*] shall come to all, both old and young, both bond and free, both male and female, both the wicked and the righteous; and even there shall not so much as a hair of their heads be lost; but **every thing shall be restored to its perfect frame**, as it is now, or in the body, and **shall be brought and be arraigned** [*brought before a judge; a legal term that Zeezrom would understand*] **before the bar** [*the judgment bar*] **of Christ** the Son, and God the Father, and the Holy Spirit, which is one Eternal God [*a perfectly united Godhead, in purpose and goals*], **to be judged according to their works,** whether they be good or whether they be evil.

45 Now, behold, **I have spoken unto you concerning the death of the mortal body, and also concerning the resurrection of the mortal body**. I say unto you that this mortal body is raised to an immortal body, that is from death, even from the first death [*physical death*] unto life [*immortality; living forever as resurrected beings*], that **they can die no more; their spirits uniting with their bodies, never to be divided** [*separated*]; thus the whole [*body*] becoming spiritual [*perhaps meaning permanent, in the sense that our spirits are a permanent part of us*] and immortal, that they can no more see corruption [*cannot die again*].

In summary, Zeezrom has been taught with pure doctrine that there is absolutely no way that he, personally, can avoid being brought before the judgment bar of God to answer for his behaviors on earth. He does secretly believe in God, as Amulek was told by the Holy Ghost in verse 24, therefore, these doctrines have real impact on him.

46 Now, when Amulek had finished these words the people began again to be astonished, and also **Zeezrom began to tremble.** And thus ended the words of Amulek, or this is all that I have written.

ALMA 12

Alma now takes over. A large crowd has gathered (verse 2) and the people are surprised at what is happening (Alma 11:46). You will see that Zeezrom's heart is beginning to soften. He has been deeply shaken by the realization that Alma and Amulek know what he is thinking, and will ask a very sincere question (verse 8). In the process of responding to Zeezrom and Antionah (verse 20), Alma will teach all of us some very important doctrines of the plan of salvation.

1 NOW **Alma, seeing that the words of Amulek had silenced Zeezrom,** for he beheld that **Amulek had caught him in his lying** and deceiving to destroy him, and seeing that **he began to tremble under a consciousness of his guilt** [*Zeezrom's conscience still works, a good sign that there is hope for him*], he opened his mouth and began to speak unto him, and to establish [*support, confirm*] the words of Amulek, and to explain things beyond, or to unfold the scriptures beyond that which Amulek had done. [*We are about to see more of the power of pure, true doctrine to change people's hearts and behaviors.*]

2 Now **the words that Alma spake unto Zeezrom were heard by the people** round about; for the multitude was great [*large*], and he spake on this wise [*this is what Alma said*]:

3 Now Zeezrom, seeing that thou hast been taken [*caught*] in thy lying and craftiness, for thou hast not lied unto men only but thou hast lied unto **God**; for behold, he **knows all thy thoughts** [*see D&C 6:16*], and thou seest that thy thoughts are made known unto us by his Spirit; [*The Holy Ghost can let us know what others are thinking when necessary in doing the Lord's work.*]

4 And thou seest that we know that **thy plan was a very subtle** [*cunning and sneaky*] **plan,** as to the subtlety of the devil, for to lie and to deceive this people that thou mightest set them against us, to revile [*mock and reject*] us and to cast us out—

Next, in verses 5 and 6, Alma teaches us a very important principle in dealing with individuals who oppose us as we try to teach them the gospel. Alma gives Zeezrom a way out, a way to save face, so to speak. Alma puts the heat on the devil, rather than pushing Zeezrom farther into a corner. Thus, Zeezrom can more easily make the transition from attacker to student (verse 8). We would do well to remember this approach and use it where possible when people become confrontational with us.

5 Now **this was a plan of thine adversary**, and he hath exercised his power in thee. Now I would that ye should remember that what I say unto thee I say unto all.

6 And behold I say unto you all that **this was a snare of the adversary, which he has laid to catch this people, that he might bring you into subjection unto him, that he might encircle you about with his chains, that he might chain you down to everlasting destruction, according to the power of his captivity.**

7 Now when Alma had spoken these words, **Zeezrom began to tremble more exceedingly**, for he was convinced more and more of the power of God; and he was also convinced that Alma and Amulek had a knowledge of him, for he was convinced that they knew the thoughts and intents of his heart; for power was given unto them that they might know of these things according to the spirit of prophecy [*the Holy Ghost*].

As mentioned previously, Alma has skillfully and kindly left the door open for Zeezrom to make the transition from attacker to student. In verse 8, Zeezrom voluntarily walks through that door, so to speak.

8 And **Zeezrom began to inquire** [*ask questions*] **of them diligently, that he might know more concerning the kingdom of God.** And he said unto Alma: What does this mean which Amulek hath spoken concerning the resurrection of the dead, that all shall rise from the dead, both the just [*the righteous*] and the unjust, and are brought to stand before God to be judged according to their works?

Zeezrom's sincere question in verse 8, above, paves the way for one of the great sermons in the Book of Mormon on the "big picture," a wonderful overview of the plan of salvation, including: agency, accountability, Judgment Day, physical death, spiritual death, Satan's goals, the fall of Adam and Eve, the Atonement of Christ, resurrection, faith, repentance, works, the second death, justice, and mercy. We will make many notes in these next verses. You may want to transfer several of them into your own scriptures for future reference.

9 And now **Alma began to expound** [*teach and explain*] **these things unto him**, saying: It is given unto many to know the mysteries of God [*the simple, main, teachings, doctrines, principles and ordinances of the gospel*]; nevertheless they are laid under a strict command that they shall not impart only according to the portion of his word which he doth grant unto the children of men, according to the heed and diligence which they give unto him [*God reveals His gospel to us in accordance to what we are willing to live*].

The word "mysteries," as used in verse 9, above, does not mean strange or hidden doctrines such as how many angels can stand on the head of a pin, how do dinosaurs fit in, how does God's foreknowledge affect our agency, how do angels go through solid walls, etc. Rather, it means the basic truths, ordinances, laws, principles, and doctrines of the gospel, which are indeed "mysteries" to those whose lifestyles are foreign to them or who have no knowledge of them. (See Bible Dictionary, under "Mystery.")

10 And therefore, **he that will harden his heart** [*refuses to listen to and live the gospel*], the same **receiveth the lesser portion of the word** [*the gospel*]; and **he that will not harden his heart, to him is given the greater portion of the word, until it is given unto him to know the mysteries of God until he know them in full** [*until he knows everything God knows; see D&C 88:49, where it tells us that such people will get to the point that they "comprehend even God."*]

From what Alma says in verses 10 and 11, we understand that he is referring to a process, either negative or positive. In the next verses, he goes on to explain that for hard-hearted persons, it is possible, over time, to get to the point where they know nothing of the gospel, which leaves them under Satan's dominion.

11 And **they that will harden their hearts,** to them is **given the lesser portion of the word until they know nothing concerning his mysteries**; and **then they are taken captive by the devil**, and **led by his will down to destruction**. Now this is what is meant by **the chains of hell**.

12 And **Amulek hath spoken plainly concerning death** [*physical death*], **and being raised from this mortality to a state of immortality** [*resurrection*], and **being brought before the bar of God, to be judged according to our works**.

13 Then **if our hearts have been hardened**, yea, if we have hardened our hearts against the word [*if we have rejected the gospel, having had opportunities to receive it*], insomuch that it has not been found in us [*if we have not lived the gospel*], **then will our state be awful**, for then we shall be condemned [*damned; stopped from eternal progression*].

14 For **our words will condemn us**, yea, all our **works will condemn us**; we shall not be found spotless [*pure and clean; cleansed by the Atonement*]; and **our thoughts will also condemn us**; and in this awful state **we shall not dare to look up to our God**; and we would fain be glad if [*we will wish that*] we could command the rocks and the mountains to fall upon us to hide us from his presence.

Next, Alma reminds Zeezrom that there is no way at all to avoid standing and facing Christ (see John 5:22) on Judgment Day.

15 But this cannot be [*you can't avoid it*]; **we must come forth and stand before him** in his glory, and in his power, and in his might, majesty, and dominion, **and acknowledge to our everlasting shame that all his judgments are just** [*fair*]; that he is just in all his works, and that he is merciful unto the children of men [*who repent*], and that he has all power to save every man that believeth on his [*Christ's*] name and bringeth forth fruit [*lives; words, works, thoughts (see verse*

14)] meet [*necessary*] for repentance.

Next, Alma defines what is meant by the terms "second death" and "spiritual death." Since a spirit can't die, second death or spiritual death means something other than extinction of the spirit. **We will bold the definition.**

16 And now behold, I say unto you **then cometh a death, even a second death**, which is a **spiritual death**; then is a time that whosoever dieth in his sins, as to a temporal death, shall also die a spiritual death; yea, he shall **die as to things pertaining unto righteousness** [*will no longer have the rewards of the righteous, including celestial glory and exaltation, available to them; see verse 32, also D&C 76:112*].

17 Then is the time when **their torments shall be as a lake of fire and brimstone** [*molten sulphur, in other words, very painful*], whose flame ascendeth up **forever and ever**; and then is the time that they shall be chained down to an everlasting destruction, according to the power and captivity of Satan, he having subjected them according to his will [*as explained in Alma 34:35*].

18 Then, I say unto you, **they shall be as though there had been no redemption made** [*for our sins*]; for they cannot be redeemed according to God's justice; **and they cannot die**, seeing there is no more corruption [*no more death after you are resurrected*]. [*In other words, they will be as if there had been no Atonement for sin. They will live forever as resurrected beings, but not able to return to the presence of God, and sons of perdition will be subject to Satan's power forever; see verse 17.*]

19 Now it came to pass that when Alma had made an end of speaking these words, **the people began to be more astonished**;

Watch now, as Antionah, a clever leading ruler of Ammonihah, steps forward and cunningly attempts to trip Alma up. In effect, he will say, "You have said that all of us will live forever. But God placed cherubim and flaming sword so Adam and Eve couldn't live forever. So, who is right, you or God?"

20 But there was one **Antionah**, who was **a chief ruler** among them, **came forth and said** unto him: **What is this that thou hast said, that man should rise from the dead and be changed from this mortal to an immortal state that the soul can never die?**

Just by way of information, the "soul," as referred to in verse 20, above, means a resurrected person. D&C 88:15 says, "And the spirit and the body are the soul of man." Thus, the "soul," in this Book of Mormon context, consists of intelligence, spirit, and resurrected physical body, permanently joined together such that they will never be separated again by death or any other means.

Next, Antionah continues setting his trap for Alma. He even quotes scripture.

21 **What does the scripture mean**, which saith that **God placed cherubim and a flaming sword** on the east of the garden of Eden, **lest our**

first parents [*Adam and Eve*] **should** enter and **partake of the fruit of the tree of life, and live forever?** And thus we see that there was no possible chance that they should live forever. [*In other words, Antionah is saying that God made sure that there was no possible chance for them to live forever.*]

Alma is a master at tipping his opponent off balance. In effect, he says, "Excellent question! Thanks for asking. That's exactly where I wanted to go next." We will be taught much doctrine about the fall of Adam as we listen to his answer. Keep in mind that the Fall and the Atonement go hand in hand in opening doors for us to gain salvation.

22 Now Alma said unto him: **This is the thing which I was about to explain.** Now we see that **Adam did fall by the partaking of the forbidden fruit**, according to the word of God; and thus we see, that **by his fall, all mankind became a lost and fallen people** [*meaning that everyone needs the Atonement*].

23 And now behold, I say unto you that **if it had been possible for Adam to have partaken of the fruit of the tree of life at that time** [*after eating the forbidden fruit*], **there would have been no death,** and **the word** [*of God*] **would have been void** [*nullified*], making God a liar, for he said: If thou eat thou shalt surely die.

Next, Alma will speak of physical death. It is a great blessing. Satan and the one third who followed him will never die because they will never get physical bodies. Without gaining physical bodies, eventually dying and being resurrected, we would have no chance, ever, of becoming like our Heavenly Father, with a glorified, resurrected, celestial body. See D&C 130:22.

24 And we see that **death comes upon mankind** [*it is part of the plan*], yea, the death which has been spoken of by Amulek, which is the temporal death [*physical death*]; nevertheless **there was a space** [*mortality*] **granted unto man in which he might repent** [*learn to use the Atonement*]; **therefore this life became** a probationary state [*a time of learning and testing*]; **a time to prepare to meet God**; a time to prepare for that endless state [*eternity*] which has been spoken of by us, which is after the resurrection of the dead.

25 Now, **if it had not been for the plan of redemption** [*the plan of salvation*], which was laid from the foundation of the world [*in other words, was presented to us in premortality*], **there could have been no resurrection of the dead**; but there was a plan of redemption laid, which shall bring to pass the resurrection of the dead, of which has been spoken.

Alma now addresses the question, "What would have happened if Adam and Eve had eaten the fruit of the tree of life?"

26 And now behold, **if** it were possible that **our first parents** [*our first ancestors; Adam and Eve*] **could have** gone

forth and **partaken of the tree of life they would have been forever miserable,** having **no preparatory state** [*no time to grow, be taught, exercise agency, repent, progress, etc.*]; and **thus the plan of redemption would have been frustrated** [*defeated*], and the word of God would have been void [*no good*], taking none effect.

27 But behold, **it was not so**; but it
was appointed unto **men** that they
must die; and **after death, they
must come to judgment**, even that
same judgment of which we have
spoken, **which is the end** [*Final Judgment*].

Next, Alma explains that, in order for the plan of salvation to work, as it was set up for us in our premortal life, we had to be taught the gospel here on earth so that we could use our agency to make choices and thus "own" the final outcome for us on Judgment Day. God respects our individual agency and will never take it from us. Satan does not respect it and tries to take it from us. We increase or decrease our potential options and consequences by the choices we make. Thus, gods are the freest people in the universe because they have the most choices available to them still. Sons of perdition have lost their freedom completely to Satan and thus, are completely not free. See Alma 34:35. Being taught the gospel, either here on earth or in the spirit world mission field, is the first step in allowing us to exercise our agency to determine our final destiny, eternally.

28 And **after God had appointed
that these things** [*the plan of salvation, including death, Resurrection, and Final Judgment*] **should come unto man**, behold, then he saw that it was expedient [*necessary*] that man should know [*be taught*] concerning the things whereof he had appointed unto them [*the gospel and the plan of salvation*];

29 Therefore **he sent angels to converse with them**, who caused men to behold of his glory [*to understand the plan of salvation and the glory of God, which could be theirs if they make the right agency choices*].

30 And they [*righteous people*] began from that time forth to call on his name; therefore **God** conversed with men, and **made known** [*taught*] **unto them the plan of redemption**, which had been prepared from the foundation of the world [*which was planned and which they had been taught in the premortal life*]; and this [*plan of salvation, including gospel doctrines, ordinances, etc.*] **he made known unto them according to their faith and repentance and their holy works** [*this is how we attain exaltation, if we don't harden our hearts as warned against in verses 10–11*].

As Alma continues by explaining the fall of Adam and Eve, we come to realize that the partaking of the fruit was not a slip up or a mistake (see 2 Nephi 2:24). It was all part of the plan to allow Adam and Eve to exercise their God-given agency. The fall was good. They "fell forward" so to speak, and opened the door for all of us to come to earth and obtain mortal bodies and work out our salvation. See 2 Nephi 2:15–25.

31 Wherefore, **he gave commandments** [*knowledge, choices, and consequences*] unto men, they [*Adam and Eve*] having first transgressed the first commandments as to things which were temporal [*"Don't eat the forbidden fruit."*], and becoming as Gods, knowing good from evil, **placing themselves in a state to act, or being placed in a state to act according to their wills and pleasures, whether to do evil or to do good** [*the whole strategy in the Garden of Eden was to place Adam and Eve in a position where they not only could use their agency, but where they had to use their agency*]—

Pay attention to the sequence given in verse 32, next. First, God taught them the plan of redemption, the plan of salvation, the "big picture." Then, He gave them commandments. That way, they could understand why the commandments were important, and they could use their agency wisely, if they wanted to.

32 Therefore **God gave unto them commandments** [*commandments are teaching tools as well as rules for happy living*], **after having made known** [*taught*] **unto them the plan of redemption,** that they should not do evil, the penalty thereof being a second death [*spiritual death; being cut off from the presence of God forever*], which was an everlasting death as to things pertaining unto righteousness; for on such the plan of redemption could have no power, for the works of justice could not be destroyed, according to the supreme goodness of God [*the law of justice could not be overruled by the tender mercy of God; in other words, people are free to choose good or evil, and God cannot reward them for good if they choose evil*].

Next, Alma teaches the Atonement of Christ.

33 But God did call on men, in the name of his Son (this being the plan of redemption which was laid), saying: **If ye will repent and harden not your hearts, then will I have mercy upon you, through mine Only Begotten Son** [*through the Atonement of Christ*];

34 Therefore, **whosoever repenteth, and hardeneth not his heart, he shall have claim on mercy through mine Only Begotten Son, unto a remission of his sins** [*in other words, they can keep learning and repenting until they become worthy of celestial exaltation*]; **and these shall enter into my rest** [*exaltation; see D&C 84:24*].

35 And **whosoever will harden his heart and will** [*wants to*] **do iniquity** [*evil*], behold, I swear in my wrath [*anger; justice looks like anger to the wicked*] that **he shall not enter into my rest.**

36 And now, my brethren, behold I say unto you, that **if ye will harden your hearts ye shall not enter into the rest of the Lord**; therefore your iniquity [*wickedness*] provoketh him that he sendeth down his wrath upon you as in the first provocation [*as in the case of the forty years in the wilderness for the Children of Israel because they provoked God to anger by choosing wickedness; see Hebrews*

3:8–11], yea, according to his word in the last provocation [*Final Judgment*] as well as the first, to the everlasting destruction of your souls [*the "second death" or "spiritual death," meaning living forever as resurrected beings but being cut off forever from returning to the presence of God in celestial glory*]; therefore, according to his word, unto the last death, as well as the first [*everything will be done according to the word of the Lord; you can't get around it*].

37 And now, my brethren, **seeing we know these things** [*you and I have been taught the truths of the plan of salvation*], **and they are true, let us** [*Alma humbly includes himself in this category*] **repent, and harden not our hearts**, that we provoke not the Lord our God to pull down his wrath upon us in these his second commandments [*to repent and come unto the Father through Christ; see verses 32–36*] which he has given unto us; but let us enter into the rest of God [*heaven*], which is prepared according to his word.

The "second commandments" referred to in verse 37 are, as given in the note in parentheses, the commandments which are given to us here on earth which, if obeyed, will lead to exaltation. The "first commandments" are mentioned in verse 31, and refer to the two commandments given to Adam and Eve in the Garden of Eden, namely, have children (Genesis 1:28) but don't eat the forbidden fruit (Genesis 2:17).

Joseph Fielding Smith explained that partaking of the forbidden fruit was not a sin, as follows:

"I'm very, very grateful that in the Book of Mormon, and I think elsewhere in our scriptures, **the fall of Adam has not been called a sin. It wasn't a sin. . . . What did Adam do? The very thing the Lord wanted him to do**; and I hate to hear anybody call it a sin, for it wasn't a sin. Did Adam sin when he partook of the forbidden fruit? I say to you, no, he did not! Now, let me refer to what was written in the book of Moses in regard to the command God gave to Adam (Moses 3:16–17).

"Now this is the way I interpret that: The Lord said to Adam, here is the tree of the knowledge of good and evil. **If you want to stay here, then you cannot eat of that fruit. If you want to stay here, then I forbid you to eat it. But you may act for yourself, and you may eat of it if you want to. And if you eat it, you will die.**

"I see a great difference between transgressing the law and committing a sin" ("Fall, Atonement, Resurrection, Sacrament," by Joseph Fielding Smith, in Charge to Religious Educators, p. 124. Institute of Religion *Doctrines of the Gospel Student Manual,* 1986 and 2000, p. 20).

ALMA 13

Having taught the crowd in Ammonihah, including Zeezrom, the basic doctrines of the plan of salvation, including the fact that everyone will be resurrected and stand before Christ on Judgment Day, Alma now emphasizes the importance of righteous priesthood leaders and teachers, who will teach correct doctrines and principles as received from God, rather than false priests and teachers like those in Ammonihah with corrupt teachings which reflect corrupt lifestyles and beliefs.

Among other things, Alma will teach us that righteous priesthood holders here on earth held the priesthood in premortality.

1 AND again, my brethren, I would cite your minds forward to the time [*back to the time*] when the Lord God gave these commandments unto his children; and **I would that ye should remember that the Lord God ordained priests, after his holy order** [*the Melchizedek Priesthood*], which was after the order of his Son [*which is the same priesthood that Christ holds*], **to teach these things unto the people.**

2 And **those priests were ordained after the order of his Son** [*they held the Melchizedek Priesthood*], in a manner that thereby the people might know in what manner to look forward to his Son for redemption [*they were authorized servants of God, so they could be trusted to teach how to live the gospel and be saved through Christ*].

3 And this is the manner after which **they were ordained**—being called and prepared **from the foundation of the world** [*in the premortal life*] according to the foreknowledge of God [*they were foreordained*], **on account of their exceeding faith and good works**; in the first place [*in premortality; see* Mormon Doctrine, *page 477, quoted below*] being left to choose good or evil [*we had agency in premortality*]; therefore **they having chosen good** [*in premortality*], and exercising exceedingly **great faith** [*in premortality*], are called with a holy calling, yea, with that holy calling which was prepared with, and according to, a preparatory redemption for such.

Apostle Bruce R. McConkie explained that worthy men held the priesthood in their premortal lives. He said:

"Alma says that those 'ordained unto the high priesthood of the holy order of God' were 'in the first place,' that is in pre-existence, 'on the same standing with their brethren,' meaning that initially all had equal opportunity to progress through righteousness. But while yet in the eternal worlds, certain of the offspring of God, 'having chosen good, and exercising exceeding great faith,' were as a consequence 'called and prepared from the foundation of the world according to the foreknowledge of God' to enjoy the blessings and powers of the priesthood. These priesthood calls were made 'from the foundation of the world,' or in other words faithful men held priesthood power and authority first in pre-existence and then again on earth (Alma 13). Every man who has a calling to minister to the inhabitants of the world was ordained to that very purpose in the Grand Council of heaven before this world was" (Bruce R. McConkie, *Mormon Doctrine,* 2d ed. [Salt Lake City: Bookcraft, 1966], 477).

4 And thus **they have been called to this holy calling** [*to hold the priesthood and teach us the gospel*] **on account of**

their faith, while others would reject the Spirit of God on account of the hardness of their hearts and blindness of their minds, while, if it had not been for this they might have had as great privilege as their brethren. [*In other words, false priests and false teachers could be righteous, authorized priesthood bearers and teachers, but they have hard hearts and have chosen not to be so.*]

5 Or in fine [*in summary*], in the first place [*in premortality*] **they were on the same standing with their brethren** [*they started out equal with those who have become righteous priesthood holders*]; thus **this holy calling being prepared from the foundation of the world** [*existed in premortality*] **for such as would not harden their hearts** [*for worthy, righteous men in premortality*], being in and through the atonement of the Only Begotten Son [*the righteous achieved this status in premortality through the Atonement of Christ*], who was prepared—

Among other things in verse 5, Alma taught that the Atonement worked for us even in premortality. This is most significant. Elder Jeffrey R. Holland taught this in the October 1995 general conference. Speaking of the Savior and what we might think about during the sacrament, he said (**bold** added for emphasis):

"We could remember that **even in the grand council of heaven He loved us and was wonderfully strong**, that **we triumphed even there** [*in premortality*] **by the power of Christ and our faith in the blood of the Lamb**" (Jeffrey R. Holland, "This Do in Remembrance of Me," *Ensign*, Nov. 1995, 67).

6 And thus being called by this holy calling, and ordained unto the high priesthood of the holy order of God [*the Melchizedek Priesthood*], to teach his commandments unto the children of men, that they also might enter into his rest [*achieve exaltation; see D&C 84:24*]—

Watch, next, as Alma teaches that the Melchizedek Priesthood is the same priesthood that Christ holds, and it is eternal.

7 **This high priesthood** being after the order of his Son, which order was from the foundation of the world [*which priesthood existed in premortality*]; or in other words, **being without beginning of days or end of years**, being prepared **from eternity to all eternity**, according to his foreknowledge of all things—

8 Now they [*the righteous men spoken of at the beginning of the chapter*] **were ordained** after this manner [*in this way*]—being **called** with a holy calling, and **ordained** with a holy ordinance [*by the laying on of hands*], and taking upon them the high priesthood [*the Melchizedek Priesthood*] of the holy order, which calling, and ordinance, and high priesthood, is **without beginning or end**—

Next, Alma teaches that worthy men will hold the priesthood forever.

9 **Thus** [*by worthily exercising their priesthood; see verse 6*] **they become high priests forever,** after the order of the Son, the Only Begotten of the Father, who is without beginning of days or

end of years, who is full of grace, equity, and truth. And thus it is. Amen.

As Alma continues, we learn how mortal men can become worthy and effective priesthood holders.

10 Now, as I said concerning the holy order, or this high priesthood, **there were many who were ordained and became high priests of God;** and it was **on account of their exceeding faith** and **repentance**, and their **righteousness** before God, they **choosing to repent and work righteousness** rather than to perish;

11 **Therefore they were** called after this holy order, and were **sanctified** [*made clean and worthy to exercise their priesthood*], and their garments [*lives*] were washed white through the blood of the Lamb [*were made clean through the Atonement of Christ*].

12 Now they, after being sanctified by the Holy Ghost, having their garments made white, **being pure and spotless before God,** could not look upon sin save it were with abhorrence [*they saw how ugly sin really is*]; and there were many, exceedingly great many, who were made pure [*by the Atonement*] and entered into the rest [*exaltation; for example, Abraham, Isaac, and Jacob, who have already become gods; see D&C 132:37*] of the Lord their God.

Having given a marvelous discourse to the people of Ammonihah about the importance of having worthy priesthood holders as their leaders and teachers, Alma now invites them all to repent and humble themselves before God, in order to obtain the "rest" of God (exaltation in celestial glory; see D&C 84:24).

13 And now, my brethren, I would that ye should **humble yourselves** before God, and **bring forth fruit meet** [*needed*] **for repentance**, that ye may also **enter into that rest.**

Verse 14, next, mentions Melchizedek, a great and righteous man in the Bible. We are indebted to Alma and the Book of Mormon for teaching us much more about Melchizedek than we can learn from the Bible. This is another example of how the Book of Mormon and the Bible have come together in the last days according to Ezekiel 37:15–17.

Alma will give us some background on Melchizedek and how, as king of Salem (Jerusalem) anciently, he brought his people from extreme wickedness to righteousness.

14 Yea, **humble yourselves even as the people in the days of Melchizedek,** who was also a high priest after this same order which I have spoken [*who held the same priesthood the Savior holds*], who also took upon him the high priesthood forever.

15 And **it was this same Melchizedek to whom Abraham paid tithes**; yea, even our father [*ancestor*] Abraham paid tithes of one–tenth part of all he possessed [*see Genesis 14:18–20*].

16 Now these ordinances were given after this manner, that thereby [*through the ordinances of the priesthood*] the people might look forward on the Son of God, it being a type [*symbolic or representative*] of his order, or it being

his order, and this **that they might look forward to him for a remission of their sins**, that they might enter into the rest of the Lord.

17 Now this **Melchizedek** [*about 2000 BC*] **was a king over the land of Salem** [*Jerusalem; see Bible Dictionary, page 768, under "Salem"*]; and **his people had waxed** [*grown*] **strong in iniquity** [*sin*] **and abomination** [*gross wickedness*]; yea, they had all gone astray; they were full of all manner of wickedness;

18 But **Melchizedek** having **exercised mighty faith**, and **received the office of the high priesthood** according to the holy order of God, **did preach repentance** unto his people. And behold, **they did repent**; and **Melchizedek did establish peace** in the land in his days; **therefore he was called the prince of peace** [*a "type" of Christ*], for he was the king of Salem; and he did reign under his father.

19 Now, there were many before him, and also there were many afterwards, but **none were greater; therefore, of him they have more particularly made mention.**

20 Now I need not rehearse the matter; what I have said may suffice. Behold, **the scriptures are before you; if ye will wrest** [*intentionally twist and misinterpret them*] **them it shall be to your own destruction**.

In the final verses of this chapter, Alma gives a powerful summary of what he has taught these people in Ammonihah. He basically tells them that this is their opportunity to live the gospel and that they must accept it if they want to be saved. In verses 27 through 29, especially, he tells them how to go about accepting it.

21 And now it came to pass that when Alma had said these words unto them, he stretched forth his hand unto them and cried with a mighty voice, saying: **Now is the time to repent, for the day of salvation draweth nigh** [*your chance is here; this can also refer to the coming birth of Jesus, in about 82 years*];

Alma emphasizes that everyone will ultimately get a completely fair chance to hear and understand the gospel. This, of course, can include hearing it in the spirit world mission field. See D&C 138.

22 Yea, and **the voice of the Lord, by the mouth of angels, doth declare it** [*the gospel message*] **unto all nations**; yea, doth declare it, that they may have glad tidings of great joy; yea, and **he doth sound these glad tidings among all his people**, yea, even to them that are scattered abroad upon the face of the earth; wherefore they have come unto us.

23 And **they are made known unto us in plain terms, that we may understand, that we cannot err** [*so that we can't not understand them*]; and this because of our being wanderers in a strange land [*a land far from Jerusalem*]; therefore, we are thus highly favored, for we have these glad tidings declared unto us in all parts of our vineyard [*our land*].

24 For behold, **angels are declaring it unto many at this time in our land**; and this is for the purpose of preparing the hearts of the children of men to receive his word at the time of his coming in his glory [*at the time of Christ's mortal mission*].

25 And now we only wait to hear the joyful news declared unto us by the mouth of angels [*it will still be eighty-two years before angels announce the birth of the Christ Child*], of his coming; for **the time cometh, we know not how soon**. Would to God that it might be in my day; but let it be sooner or later, in it I will rejoice.

26 And **it shall be made known unto just and holy men, by the mouth of angels, at the time of his coming** [*example: the shepherds and wise men; also, Nephi was told by the voice of the Lord, in 3 Nephi 1:13*], that the words of our fathers may be fulfilled, according to that which they have spoken concerning him, which was according to the spirit of prophecy which was in them.

Next, Alma teaches these people and all of us how we can successfully come unto Christ.

27 And now, my brethren, I wish from the inmost part of my heart, yea, with great anxiety even unto pain, that ye would hearken unto my words, and **cast off your sins**, and **not procrastinate** [*put it off until later*] **the day of your repentance**;

28 But that ye would **humble yourselves** before the Lord, and **call on his holy name**, and **watch and pray continually, that ye may not be tempted above that which ye can bear**, and thus **be led by the Holy Spirit**, becoming **humble, meek, submissive, patient, full of love and all long-suffering**;

29 Having **faith on the Lord**; having a **hope** [*strong, humble confidence; see 2 Nephi 31:20*] that ye shall receive eternal life [*exaltation*]; **having the love of God always in your hearts**, that ye may be lifted up [*exalted*] at the last day [*on Judgment Day*] and enter into his rest [*celestial exaltation*].

30 And **may the Lord grant unto you repentance**, that ye may not bring down his wrath upon you, that ye may not be bound down by the chains of hell, that ye may not suffer the second death [*being cut off from the presence of God forever; see Alma 12:32*].

31 And **Alma spake many more words** unto the people, which are not written in this book.

ALMA 14

Alma and Amulek have now taught the basics of the plan of salvation to the people of Ammonihah, with great power and authority. Many will believe and begin to study the gospel and change their ways, but, unfortunately, the majority will not. As is the case with many wicked people, their basic motive is to continue doing what they want to do and to get rid of those who stand in their way, in this case Alma and Amulek, but they want it to appear legal.

Such people often resort to stirring up the citizens into a frenzy, creating a mob mentality to support their evil goals. "Anger against that which is good" (2 Nephi 28:20) is also a major tool of the devil, and we see it used effectively by Satan as Mormon continues his account about Alma and Amulek in Ammonihah.

It is a big disappointment to us what the people did to these humble servants of God next.

1 AND it came to pass after he had made an end of speaking unto the people **many of them did believe on his words, and began to repent, and to search the scriptures.**

2 But **the more part of them** [*the majority*] **were desirous that they might destroy Alma and Amulek**; for **they were angry** with Alma, **because of the plainness of his words** unto Zeezrom; and **they also said that Amulek had lied unto them, and had reviled against their law and also against their lawyers and judges.**

3 And they were also **angry** with Alma and Amulek; and **because they had testified so plainly against their wickedness**, they sought [*tried*] to put them away privily [*secretly*].

Remember, Alma and Amulek have had power given to them by God to escape such situations (Alma 8:31), but they will be very patient before using it (a reminder of the Lord's power to destroy the wicked and His patience before using it).

4 **But** it came to pass that **they did not** [*arrest them secretly*]; **but they** took them and bound [*tied*] them with strong cords, and **took them before the chief judge** of the land.

5 And **the people went forth and witnessed against them**—testifying that they had reviled against the law, and their lawyers and judges of the land, and also of all the people that were in the land; and also testified that there was but one God, and that he should send his Son among the people, but he should not save them [*as if Alma and Amulek were limiting God*]; and many such things did the people testify against Alma and Amulek. Now this was done before the chief judge of the land.

By now, Zeezrom has been truly converted, recognizes the damage he has caused, has a terribly guilty conscience (godly sorrow [*2 Corinthians 7:8–11*], which is a good sign that he can be saved) and does his best to stop the action against Alma and Amulek.

6 And it came to pass that **Zeezrom was astonished** at the words [*the accusations of the people*] which had been spoken; and **he** also **knew concerning the blindness of the minds, which he had caused among the people by his lying words**; and his soul began to be harrowed [*torn*] up under a **consciousness of his own guilt**; yea, he began to be **encircled about by the pains of hell.**

7 And it came to pass that **he began to cry unto the people, saying: Behold, I am guilty, and these men are spotless before God. And he began to plead for them from that time forth**; **but they reviled him**, saying: Art thou also possessed with the devil? And **they spit upon him, and cast him out from among them, and also all those who believed in the words which had been spoken by Alma and Amulek; and they cast them out**, and sent men to cast stones at them.

Having driven the men out of the city, who were converted by the preaching of Alma and Amulek, these wicked citizens now burn their wives and children, using the scriptures to help fuel the fire. Not only that, they bring Alma and Amulek to the site and make them watch. As we continue, a major question will be answered, namely, why God doesn't always stop such terrible things against innocent people and children.

8 And **they brought their wives and children together, and whosoever believed** or had been taught to believe in the word of God **they caused that they should be cast into the fire**; and they also brought forth their records which contained **the holy scriptures**, and **cast them into the fire also,** that they might be burned and destroyed by fire.

9 And it came to pass that **they took Alma and Amulek, and carried them forth to the place of martyrdom** [*the place where innocent people were being killed because of their belief in God*], **that they might witness the destruction of those who were consumed by fire.**

10 And **when Amulek saw the pains of the women and children** who were consuming [*being burned*] in the fire, he also was pained; and he said unto Alma: How can we witness this awful scene? Therefore **let us stretch forth our hands, and exercise the power of God which is in us, and save them from the flames.**

11 But Alma said unto him: **The Spirit constraineth me** [*is holding me back*] that I must not stretch forth mine hand; for behold **the Lord receiveth them up unto himself, in glory**; and **he doth suffer** [*permit*] **that they may do this thing**, or that the people may do this thing unto them, according to the hardness of their hearts, **that the judgments which he shall exercise upon them in his wrath may be just** [*fair*]; and **the blood of the innocent shall stand as a witness against them, yea, and cry mightily against them at the last day** [*on Judgment Day*].

As difficult as it may be to understand and accept the doctrine taught in verse 11, above, it is very important that we do so. Otherwise, it would be easy to become bitter against God as we see similar wicked things done against innocents today. What the Lord has done with this account in the Book of Mormon is invite us to see things from His perspective.

Over the years, I have had some students who just didn't feel that they could handle and accept the explanation in verse 11. In order to help them, I began asking them questions somewhat as follows:

Question

If you were God, how would you handle the situation?

Answer

Well, I wouldn't let them do such things.

Question

So, would you limit their agency?

Answer

Yes.

Question

Where would you draw the line and set limits to their agency?

Answer

When they started hurting someone who was innocent.

Question

And how would you let them know that they were about to cross the limits you set?

Answer

Maybe give them a severe muscle cramp or something that would drop them to the floor.

Question

Would you do anything like that to them if they were showing pornography to others, which is more damaging eternally than physical pain and suffering?

Answer

Well, I hadn't thought of that. Maybe not, but, I guess, probably yes. At least, I guess, I probably ought to.

Question

So what do you see happening to your whole agency thing, as soon as you start stopping them every time when someone crosses a limit you've set?

Answer

Well, it sort of ruins the whole thing. I guess people wouldn't really be free to choose between good and evil if I "zapped" them every time they did certain wicked things. I guess they really wouldn't have agency.

Question

Can you understand better now the tremendous respect that God has for individual agency and why He can't stop every cruel act and every spiritually devastating evil immediately? Can you see things a little more from His perspective now?

Answer

Yes. I just hadn't ever looked at it that deeply before. Thanks.

We will now continue with Mormon's account of Alma and Amulek. Watch as the wicked chief judge tries to make it sound like it is the fault of Alma and Amulek that the women and children were so horribly treated. It is Satan's way to blame others for your own bad behavior.

12 Now **Amulek said unto Alma: Behold, perhaps they will burn us also.**

13 And Alma said: **Be it according to the will of the Lord**. But, behold, our work is not finished; therefore **they burn us not**.

14 Now it came to pass that when the bodies of those who had been cast into the fire were consumed, and also the records which were cast in with them, **the chief judge of the land came and stood before Alma and Amulek,** as they were bound [*tied up*]; and **he smote** [*hit*] **them** with his hand upon their cheeks, and said unto them: **After what ye have seen, will ye preach again unto this people,** that they shall be cast into a lake of fire and brimstone?

15 Behold, **ye see that ye had not power to save those who had been cast into the fire; neither has God saved them because they were of thy faith.** And the judge smote them again upon their cheeks, and asked: **What say ye for yourselves?**

16 Now **this judge was after the order and faith of Nehor**, who slew Gideon. [*See Alma 1. In other words, this chief judge made his living and retained his popularity by telling the people what they wanted to hear, which is the definition of priestcraft. See Alma 1:12 and 16.*]

17 And it came to pass that **Alma and Amulek answered him nothing**; and he smote them again, and delivered them to the officers to be **cast into prison.**

18 And **when they had been cast into prison three days, there came many lawyers, and judges, and priests, and teachers, who were of the profession of Nehor** [*and their livelihood would be ruined if the people were converted to the Church*]; and they came in unto the prison to see them, and **they questioned them** about many words; but **they answered them nothing.**

19 And it came to pass that the judge stood before them, and said: **Why do ye not answer the words of this people?** [*He is justifying his actions by implying that he is merely doing what the people want him to do.*] Know ye not that I have power to deliver you up unto the flames? And **he commanded them to speak; but they answered nothing.**

20 And it came to pass that they departed and went their ways, but **came again on the morrow**; and **the judge also smote them again on their cheeks.** And **many came forth also, and smote them, saying: Will ye stand again and judge this people, and condemn our law? If ye have such great power why do ye not deliver yourselves?** [*They could, but choose not to use it yet.*]

21 And **many such things did they say unto them**, gnashing their teeth upon them [*biting them*], and spitting upon them, and saying: How shall we look when we are damned? [*In other*

words, we couldn't possibly look worse than you when we are damned by your supposed God.]

22 And many such things, yea, all manner of such things did they say unto them; and **thus they did mock them for many days.** And they did withhold food from them that they might hunger, and water that they might thirst; and they also did take from them their clothes that they were naked; and thus they were bound with strong cords, and confined in prison.

23 And it came to pass **after they had thus suffered for many days,** [*and it was on the twelfth day, in the tenth month, in the tenth year of the reign of the judges over the people of Nephi*] that **the chief judge over the land of Ammonihah and many of their teachers and their lawyers went in unto the prison** where Alma and Amulek were bound with cords.

24 And the chief judge stood before them, **and smote them again, and said unto them: If ye have the power of God deliver yourselves from these bands, and then we will believe that the Lord will destroy this people according to your words.**

25 And it came to pass that **they all went forth and smote them, saying the same words,** even until the last; and **when the last had spoken unto them the power of God was upon Alma and Amulek, and they rose and stood upon their feet.**

26 And **Alma cried, saying**: How long shall we suffer these great afflictions, O Lord? **O Lord, give us strength according to our faith** which is in Christ, even unto deliverance. And **they broke the cords** with which they were bound; and when the people saw this, they began to flee, for the fear of destruction had come upon them.

27 And it came to pass that so great was their fear that **they fell to the earth**, and did not obtain the outer door of the prison; and the earth shook mightily, and **the walls of the prison** were rent in twain [*torn in two*], so that they **fell to the earth**; **and the chief judge, and the lawyers, and priests, and teachers, who smote upon Alma and Amulek, were slain by the fall thereof.**

28 And **Alma and Amulek came forth out of the prison, and they were not hurt** [*similar to the righteous at the Second Coming*]; **for the Lord had granted unto them power, according to their faith** which was in Christ. And they straightway [*immediately*] came forth out of the prison; and they were loosed from their bands; and the prison had fallen to the earth, and **every soul within the walls thereof, save it were** [*except*] **Alma and Amulek, was slain; and they straightway came forth into the city.**

It would be nice if the large crowd of curious citizens who rushed toward the prison in verse 29, next, would have humbled themselves and asked Alma and Amulek to teach them. But, sadly, they seemed to be beyond this point in their wickedness, and instead, ran away.

29 Now **the people having heard a great noise came running** together by multitudes to know the cause of it; **and when they saw Alma and Amulek coming forth out of the prison**, and the walls thereof had fallen to the earth, **they were struck with great fear, and fled** from the presence of Alma and Amulek even **as a goat fleeth with her young from two lions;** and thus they did flee from the presence of Alma and Amulek.

ALMA 15

When we first met Zeezrom, he was a highly skilled wicked lawyer in the wicked city of Ammonihah. He "was a man who was expert in the devices of the devil, that he might destroy that which was good" (Alma 11:21). And he was one of the "foremost to accuse Amulek and Alma" (Alma 10:31). In other words, he was a skilled, wicked man who set out to destroy Alma and Amulek and the preaching of the gospel, which they were attempting to bring into Ammonihah.

As you recall, the pure doctrine taught by Amulek and then Alma, in chapters 11 through 13, brought conversion to Zeezrom and he was brought down to the depths of sorrow for his sins (Alma 14:6–7). He was driven out from the city after trying to defend Alma and Amulek. When we meet him here, in chapter 15, he is very sick because of his former wickedness. He will be healed, symbolic of the power of Christ's Atonement to cleanse and heal. This is a major message of this chapter.

We will also see Amulek give up basically everything he formerly possessed, including his wealth and good standing as a citizen of Ammonihah, in order to continue faithful in the Church. This is also an important message to all of us, namely, that we must change and give up whatever necessary in order to gain the far more valuable rewards of the gospel of Christ.

1 AND it came to pass that **Alma and Amulek were commanded to depart out of that city** [*a serious indicator of the coming destruction of the city because they would not have any righteous people in it now*]; and **they departed, and came out even into the land of Sidom**; and behold, there **they found all the people who had departed out of the land of Ammonihah**, who had been cast out and stoned, because they believed in the words of Alma.

2 And **they related unto them all that had happened** unto their wives and children [*who had been burned; Alma 14:8*], and also concerning themselves, and of their power of deliverance.

3 And also **Zeezrom lay sick** at Sidom, with a burning fever, which was **caused by the great tribulations** [*worries and pains*] **of his mind on account of** [*because of*] **his wickedness,** for **he supposed that Alma and Amulek were no more**; and he

supposed that they had been slain because of his iniquity. And **this great sin, and his many other sins, did harrow** [*tear*] **up his mind** until it did become exceedingly sore [*terribly painful*], having no deliverance; therefore he began to be scorched with a burning heat.

4 Now, **when he heard that Alma and Amulek were in the land of Sidom, his heart began to take courage;** and he sent a message immediately unto them, desiring them to come unto him.

5 And it came to pass that they went immediately, obeying the message which he had sent unto them; and **they went in unto the house unto Zeezrom**; and they found him upon his bed, sick, being very low with a burning fever; and his mind also was exceedingly sore [*worried and pained*] because of his iniquities; and when he saw them he stretched forth his hand, and besought [*asked*] them that they would heal him.

Watch, now, as the power of the Savior to heal us from the devastating effects of sin is demonstrated beautifully. Zeezrom is, in effect, "born again" as a new person, freed from past wickedness, with vast opportunities before him for the rest of mortality as well as into eternity. Watch the effect this has upon him.

6 And it came to pass that **Alma said** unto him, taking him by the hand: **Believest thou in the power of Christ unto salvation?**

7 And **he answered** and said: **Yea**, I believe all the words that thou hast taught.

8 And **Alma said: If thou believest in the redemption of Christ thou canst be healed.**

9 And **he said: Yea, I believe** according to thy words.

10 And then **Alma cried unto the Lord**, saying: O Lord our God, **have mercy on this man, and heal him according to his faith which is in Christ**.

11 And when Alma had said these words, **Zeezrom leaped upon his feet, and began to walk**; and this was done to the great astonishment of all the people; and the knowledge of this went forth throughout all the land of Sidom.

12 And **Alma baptized Zeezrom** unto the Lord; and he began from that time forth to preach unto the people.

13 And **Alma established a church in the land of Sidom**, and consecrated priests and teachers in the land, to baptize unto the Lord whosoever were desirous to be baptized.

14 And it came to pass that **they were many**; for they did flock in from all the region round about Sidom, and were baptized. [*Much success, not only among those who had been converted and evicted from Ammonihah, but also among the people who lived in the area around Sidom.*]

15 But as to **the people that were in the land of Ammonihah**, they yet **remained** a **hard–hearted** and a **stiffnecked** [*prideful, not humble*] people; and they **repented not of their sins**, ascribing all the power of Alma and Amulek to the devil [*in other words, calling good evil*]; for **they** were of the profession [*religion*] of Nehor [*see Alma 1*], and **did not believe in the repentance of their sins**.

Next, we see what Amulek gave up because of becoming active and faithful in the gospel of Christ.

16 And it came to pass that Alma and Amulek, **Amulek having forsaken all his gold, and silver, and his precious things**, which were in the land of Ammonihah, for the word of God, he being **rejected by those who were once his friends and also by his father and his kindred** [*relatives*];

17 Therefore, after Alma having established the church at Sidom, seeing a great check [*change in direction*], yea, **seeing that the people were checked** [*stopped*] **as to the pride of their hearts, and began to humble themselves before God**, and began to assemble themselves together at their sanctuaries [*they began to attend church*] to worship God before the altar, watching and praying continually, that they might be delivered from Satan, and from death, and from destruction—

18 Now as I said, **Alma** having seen all these things, therefore he **took Amulek** and came over **to the land of Zarahemla**, and took him **to his own house**, and did administer unto him in his tribulations, and strengthened him in the Lord.

19 And **thus ended the tenth year** of the reign of the judges over the people of Nephi.

ALMA 16

It seems to be Satan's way to have people be mad at someone. It is his way to have people blame someone else for their own bad behaviors and sins. This "tool of Satan" plays a role in what happens to the wicked city of Ammonihah in this chapter. You will see this tool of Satan in action as the Lamanites who are angry at someone else decide to kill the people of Ammonihah to work off their anger.

Perhaps you remember that when Alma and the sons of Mosiah were converted, the four sons of Mosiah requested the privilege of going on missions to the Lamanites. That permission was granted by their father, King Mosiah II (Mosiah 28:5–9). During all the time that Alma has been serving as the president of the Nephite church, confronting Nehor (Alma 1), fighting the attempted overthrow of the Nephite democracy and the ensuing wars with the rebels and the Lamanites (Alma 2–3), preaching to the people in Zarahemla (Alma 5), preaching in Gideon (Alma 7), preaching and spending time in prison with Amulek in Ammonihah, (Alma 9–14), traveling to Sidom and healing Zeezrom (Alma 15), and then returning to his home in Zarahemla with Amulek, during all this time, the four sons of Mosiah have been preaching the gospel to the Lamanites in the land of Nephi.

It has been many years for Alma, and in the meantime, the sons of Mosiah and their companions have had much success among the Lamanites (Alma 17–26). But many of the Lamanites are angry at the new converts among their own people and start killing them. Upon meeting no resistance, though, from the converts, who prefer to give up their lives rather than take up weapons and risk feeling good about killing in war (Alma 24:15–18), the angry Lamanites decide to quit killing their own people. But, being angry still, they decide to go kill some Nephites to satisfy their devil-inspired bloodlust. Thus, they move swiftly toward the land of Zarahemla and the first city they come to is Ammonihah, which, as previously mentioned, they destroy completely (Alma 16:9–10). We will get more detail about this as we begin Alma, chapter 16, now.

1 AND it came to pass **in the eleventh year of the reign of the judges** over the people of Nephi [*eleven years after Alma the Younger became the President of the Church*], on the fifth day of the second month, there having been much peace in the land of Zarahemla, there having been no wars nor contentions for a certain number of years, even until the fifth day of the second month in the eleventh year, there **was a cry of war heard throughout the land.**

2 For behold, **the armies of the Lamanites had come** in upon the wilderness side, into the borders of the land, even **into the city of Ammonihah, and began to slay the people and destroy the city.**

3 And now it came to pass, **before the Nephites could raise a sufficient army** to drive them out of the land, **they had destroyed the people who were in the city of Ammonihah,** and also some around the borders of Noah, and **taken others captive into the wilderness.**

Next, we will see that the Lord inspires Alma to tell the military leaders of the Nephites where the Lamanites took the captives.

4 Now it came to pass that **the Nephites were desirous to obtain** [*rescue*] **those who had been carried away captive into the wilderness.**

5 Therefore, he that had been appointed chief captain over the armies of the Nephites, [*and his name was Zoram, and he had two sons, Lehi and Aha*]—now **Zoram and his two sons, knowing that Alma was high priest over the church** [*the President of the Church*], **and having heard that he had the spirit of prophecy, therefore they went unto him and desired of him to know whither** [*where*] **the Lord would that they should go into the wilderness in search of their brethren, who had been taken captive by the Lamanites.**

6 And it came to pass that **Alma inquired of the Lord concerning the matter.** And Alma returned and said

unto them: Behold, the Lamanites will cross the river Sidon in the south wilderness, away up beyond the borders of the land of Manti. And behold there shall ye meet them, on the east of the river Sidon, and there the Lord will deliver unto thee thy brethren who have been taken captive by the Lamanites.

7 And it came to pass that **Zoram and his sons crossed over the river Sidon, with their armies, and marched away** beyond the borders of Manti into the south wilderness, which was on the east side of the river Sidon.

8 And **they came upon the armies of the Lamanites**, and the Lamanites were scattered and driven into the wilderness; **and they took their brethren who had been taken captive** by the Lamanites, and there was **not one soul of them had been lost** that were taken captive. And they were brought by their brethren to possess their own lands.

Next, we are told how completely the wicked in Ammonihah were destroyed. They had signed their death warrant, so to speak, by intentionally getting rid of all the righteous among them. Thus, they were ripe, or completely ready, for destruction. In a very real sense, they were a "type" or symbolic of the wicked at the Second Coming of Christ. They will be completely destroyed. None will survive.

9 And thus ended the eleventh year of the judges, the Lamanites having been driven out of the land, and **the people of Ammonihah were destroyed; yea, every living soul of the Ammonihahites was destroyed, and also their great city, which they said God could not destroy, because of its greatness.**

10 But behold, in **one day** [*symbolic of how quickly the wicked will be destroyed at the Coming of Christ*] **it was left desolate** [*empty of life*]; and the carcasses were mangled by dogs and wild beasts of the wilderness.

11 Nevertheless, **after many days their dead bodies were heaped up upon the face of the earth**, and they were covered with a shallow covering. And now so great was the scent [*so terrible was the smell*] thereof that the people did not go in to possess the land of Ammonihah for many years. And it was called Desolation of Nehors; for they were of the profession [*religion*] of Nehor [*see Alma 1*], who were slain; and their lands remained desolate.

12 And the Lamanites did not come again to war against the Nephites until the fourteenth year of the reign of the judges over the people of Nephi. And thus for **three years** did the people of Nephi have **continual peace** in all the land.

13 And **Alma and Amulek went forth preaching repentance** to the people in their temples, and in their sanctuaries, and also in their synagogues, which were built after the manner of [*like those built by*] the Jews.

14 And as many as would hear their words, unto them they did impart the word of God, **without any respect of persons** [*they preached to everybody who would listen, regardless of who they were*], continually.

15 And thus did Alma and Amulek go forth, and also many more who had been chosen for the work, to preach the word throughout all the land. And **the establishment of the church became general throughout the land,** in all the region round about, among all the people of the Nephites.

Perhaps you will recall that several years back, Alma was both the chief judge (the president of the nation) and the President of the Church. His people were gradually getting caught up in wickedness, and he finally decided that the only way to stop this trend was teaching the gospel and "bearing down in pure testimony against" the wickedness that was taking over (Alma 4:19). Thus, he called for an election, and another chief judge was elected to take his place (Alma 4:16–17), and he devoted himself entirely to the work of the Church, especially teaching. We begin to see the results of this in the next verses.

16 And **there was no inequality among them; the Lord did pour out his Spirit on all the face of the land** to prepare the minds of the children of men, or to prepare their hearts to receive the word which should be taught among them at the time of his coming—

17 **That they might not be hardened** [*resistant*] against the word [*the gospel*], that they might not be **unbelieving**, and go on to destruction, but **that they might receive the word with joy**, and as a branch **be grafted into the true vine** [*be joined to Christ by covenants*], that they might **enter into the rest** [*celestial exaltation; see D&C 84:24*] **of the Lord their God.**

Next, we are cautioned against many things that can pull us away from Christ.

18 Now **those priests** who did go forth among the people **did preach against** all **lyings**, and **deceivings**, and **envyings**, and **strifes**, and **malice** [*hatred, wanting to hurt*], and **revilings** [*fighting against that which is good*], and **stealing**, **robbing, plundering** [*taking other people's things*]**, murdering, committing adultery**, and all manner of **lasciviousness** [*any form of sexual immorality, including lustful thinking, pornography, immodesty, etc.*], crying that these things ought not so to be—

19 Holding forth [*teaching about*] things which must shortly come; yea, holding forth **the coming of the Son of God, his sufferings and death, and also the resurrection of the dead.**

20 And many of the people did inquire concerning the place where the Son of God should come; and **they were taught that he would appear unto them after his resurrection**; and this the people did hear with great joy and gladness.

21 And now **after the church had been established throughout all the land—having got the victory over the devil, and the word of God being preached in its purity in all the land**, and the Lord pouring out his blessings upon the **people—thus ended the fourteenth year of the reign of the judges** over the people of Nephi. [*Alma's friends, the sons of Mosiah, have now been on their missions among the Lamanites for fourteen years.*]

ALMA 17

Imagine Alma's surprise and joy one day, after all these years, as he ran into the sons of Mosiah, returning from their missions. Not only were they returning from missions among the Lamanites in the land of Nephi, but they had a large company of Lamanite converts with them, who were seeking refuge among the Nephites in the land of Zarahemla (Alma 27:14–19). We will learn more about what happens to them in Alma 27.

After telling us of the meeting of Ammon, Aaron, Omner, and Himni, who were the sons of Mosiah, Mormon gives us an account of their mission. This account is covered in Alma, chapters 17 through 26. These chapters contain many favorite Book of Mormon stories for adults and children alike, with many important lessons taught along the way.

1 AND now it came to pass that **as Alma was journeying** from the land of Gideon southward, away to the land of Manti, behold, **to his astonishment** [*surprise*]**, he met with the sons of Mosiah** journeying towards the land of Zarahemla.

2 Now **these sons of Mosiah were with Alma at the time the angel first appeared unto him**; therefore **Alma did rejoice exceedingly** [*a whole lot*] **to see his brethren**; and what added more to his joy, they were still his brethren in the Lord; yea, and they had waxed [*grown*] strong in the knowledge of the truth; for they were men of a sound understanding and **they had searched the scriptures** diligently, that they might know the word of God.

Next, Mormon points out that it is not enough to simply read the scriptures; rather, other things are required in order to teach the gospel with power and authority.

3 But **this is not all**; they had given themselves to **much prayer, and fasting; therefore they had the spirit of prophecy, and the spirit of revelation, and when they taught, they taught with power and authority of God.**

4 And they had been teaching the word of God for the space of **fourteen years among the Lamanites,** having had much success in bringing many to the knowledge of the truth; yea, by the power of their words many were brought before the altar of God, to call on his name and confess their sins before him.

Mormon now sets out to tell us about their missionary experiences and success among the Lamanites.

5 Now **these are the circumstances which attended them in their journeyings**, for they had many afflictions; they did suffer much, both in body and in mind, such as hunger, thirst and fatigue, and also much labor in the spirit.

6 **Now these were their journeyings:** Having taken leave of their father, Mosiah [*see Mosiah 28:9*], in the first year of the judges; having refused the kingdom which their father was desirous to confer upon them, and also this was the minds of the people [*the people also wanted one of them to be king*];

7 Nevertheless **they departed out of the land of Zarahemla**, and took their swords, and their spears, and their bows, and their arrows, and their slings; and this they did that they might provide food for themselves while in the wilderness.

8 And thus they departed into the wilderness with their numbers which they had selected [*others went with them also, on this mission*], **to go up to the land of Nephi, to preach the word of God unto the Lamanites**.

9 And it came to pass that they journeyed many days in the wilderness, and **they fasted much** and **prayed much** that the Lord would grant unto them a portion of his Spirit to go with them, and abide with them, that they might be an instrument in the hands of God **to bring, if it were possible, their brethren, the Lamanites, to the knowledge of the truth**, to the knowledge of the baseness [*crudeness*] of the traditions of their fathers, which were not correct.

10 And it came to pass that **the Lord did visit** [*bless*] **them with his Spirit**, and said unto them: Be comforted. And they were comforted.

An important message is given next for all who accept callings to serve the Lord. It is that being called of God to serve does not necessarily mean that everything will go smoothly.

11 And the Lord said unto them also: **Go forth among the Lamanites,** thy brethren, and establish my word; yet ye shall **be patient in long-suffering and afflictions** [*troubles and problems*], that ye may show forth good examples unto them in me, and I will make an instrument of thee in my hands unto the salvation of many souls.

12 And it came to pass that **the hearts of the sons of Mosiah, and also those who were with them, took courage** to go forth unto the Lamanites to declare unto them the word of God.

13 And it came to pass **when they had arrived in the borders of the land of the Lamanites**, that they separated themselves and departed one from another, trusting in the Lord that they should meet again at the close of their harvest; for they

supposed that great was the work which they had undertaken.

This was a very dangerous mission, as Mormon points out next.

14 And assuredly it was great, for **they had undertaken to preach the word of God to a wild and a hardened and a ferocious people; a people who delighted in murdering the Nephites, and robbing and plundering** [*robbing and stealing from*] **them;** and their hearts were set upon riches [*these Lamanites were materialistic*], or upon gold and silver, and precious stones; yet **they sought to obtain these things by murdering and plundering, that they might not labor for them with their own hands.**

15 Thus they were a very **indolent** [*lazy, didn't like to work hard*] people, many of whom **did worship idols,** and the curse [*the withdrawal of the Spirit of God; see 2 Nephi 1:18; 1 Nephi 12:23*] of God had fallen upon them because of the traditions of their fathers; notwithstanding [*nevertheless*] the promises of the Lord were extended unto them on the conditions of repentance.

16 Therefore, **this was the cause for which the sons of Mosiah had undertaken the work**, that perhaps they might bring them unto repentance; that perhaps they might bring them to know of the plan of redemption.

17 Therefore **they separated themselves one from another, and went forth among them, every man alone**, according to the word and power of God which was given unto him.

It sounds like Ammon, who was their leader, in effect, gave each of them a blessing and set them apart for their missions, much the same as is done today for missionaries as they leave for the mission field.

18 Now **Ammon** being the chief among them, or rather he **did administer unto them,** and he departed from them, after having **blessed them according to their several stations**, having imparted the word of God unto them, or **administered unto them before his departure**; and thus they took their several journeys throughout the land.

Mormon will now focus in on Ammon and his mission and will tell us about Aaron and others later. We find out from verse 19 that the sons of Ishmael (1 Nephi 7:6) remained loyal to Laman and Lemuel.

19 And **Ammon went to the land of Ishmael**, the land being called after the sons of Ishmael, who also became Lamanites.

20 And **as Ammon entered the land** of Ishmael, **the Lamanites took him and bound him** [*tied him up*], as was **their custom** to bind all the Nephites who fell into their hands, and **carry them before the king**; and thus it was left to the pleasure of the king to **slay** [*kill*] **them, or to retain them in captivity, or to cast them into prison, or to cast them out of**

his land, according to his will and pleasure.

21 And thus **Ammon was carried before the king** who was over the land of Ishmael; and his name was **Lamoni**; and he was a descendant of Ishmael.

Watch, now, as Ammon, under the direction of the Spirit, lays the foundation for Lamoni's conversion, being very careful not to give him too much all at once.

22 And **the king inquired of** [*asked*] **Ammon if it were his desire to dwell in the land among the Lamanites**, or among his people.

23 And **Ammon said** unto him: **Yea,** I desire to dwell among this people for a time; yea, and perhaps until the day I die.

24 And it came to pass that **king Lamoni was much pleased with Ammon**, and caused that his bands should be loosed; and he would that Ammon should take one of his daughters to wife.

25 But Ammon said unto him: Nay, but **I will be thy servant** [*both literally as a servant in the king's court, but more important, as a servant in bringing him the gospel, which Lamoni does not understand at this time*]. **Therefore Ammon became a servant to king Lamoni**. And it came to pass that he was set among other servants to watch the flocks of Lamoni, according to the custom of the Lamanites.

In the language of missionary work today, Ammon is "establishing a relationship of trust."

26 And after he had been in the service of the king three days, as **he was with the Lamanitish servants going forth with their flocks to the place of water**, which was called the water of Sebus, and all the Lamanites drive their flocks hither, that they may have water—

27 Therefore, **as Ammon and the servants of the king were driving forth their flocks to this place of water**, behold, a **certain** number of the **Lamanites**, who had been with their flocks to water, stood and **scattered the flocks of Ammon and the servants of the king**, and they scattered them insomuch that they fled many ways.

28 Now the **servants of the king** began to **murmur**, saying: **Now the king will slay us**, as he has our brethren because their flocks were scattered by the wickedness of these men. And **they began to weep** exceedingly, saying: Behold, our flocks are scattered already.

You can tell that the Spirit is with Ammon, because he recognizes the opportunity that this real trouble is providing.

29 Now **they wept because of the fear of being slain**. Now **when Ammon saw this his heart was swollen within him with joy**; for, said he, I will show forth my power unto these my fellow–servants,

or the power which is in me, in restoring these flocks unto the king, **that I may win the hearts of these my fellow–servants, that I may lead them to believe in my words**.

30 And now, **these were the thoughts of Ammon**, when he saw the afflictions of those whom he termed to be his brethren.

31 And it came to pass that he flattered them by his words, saying: My brethren, be of good cheer [*cheer up*] and let us go in search of the flocks, and **we will gather them together and bring them back unto the place of water;** and thus we will preserve the flocks unto the king and he will not slay us.

32 And it came to pass that **they went in search of the flocks, and they did follow Ammon**, and they rushed forth with much swiftness and did head [*head off*] the flocks of the king, and did gather them together again to the place of water.

It is a compliment to Ammon that these men followed his instructions, despite obvious feelings of fear and even confusion that no doubt filled their minds. Perhaps they sensed the Spirit upon Ammon without really knowing what it was. This is often the case with our missionaries today.

These troublemakers are in for a surprise!

33 And **those men again stood to scatter their flocks; but Ammon said unto his brethren: Encircle the flocks** round about that they flee not; **and I go and contend** [*fight*] **with these men** who do scatter our flocks.

34 Therefore, **they did as Ammon commanded** them, and **he went forth** and stood **to contend** with those who stood by the waters of Sebus; and they were in number not a few [*there were many of them*].

35 Therefore **they did not fear Ammon**, for they supposed that one of their men could slay him according to their pleasure, for **they knew not that the Lord had promised Mosiah that he would deliver his sons out of their hands**; neither did they know anything concerning the Lord; therefore **they delighted in the destruction of their brethren**; and for this cause they stood to scatter the flocks of the king.

36 But **Ammon stood forth and began to cast stones at them with his sling**; yea, with mighty power he did sling stones amongst them; and thus **he slew a certain number of them insomuch that they began to be astonished** at his power; nevertheless **they were angry** because of the slain of their brethren, and they were determined that he should fall; therefore, seeing that they could not hit him with their stones, **they came forth with clubs to slay him**.

37 But behold, every man that lifted his club to smite **Ammon**, he **smote off their arms with his sword**; for

he did withstand [*defend himself against*]
their blows by smiting their arms
with the edge of his sword, insomuch
that **they began to be astonished,**
and began to flee before him; yea,
and they were not few in number;
and he caused them to flee by the
strength of his arm.

38 Now **six of them had fallen** [*died*]
by the sling, but he slew none save it
were their leader with his sword; and
he smote off as many of their arms
as were lifted against him, and they
were not a few.

Imagine the feelings of the king's servants now! Perhaps they are already wondering who this Nephite, Ammon, really is (Alma 18:3).

39 And when he had driven them
afar off, he returned and **they wa-**
tered their flocks and returned
them to the pasture of the king,
and then went in unto the king,
bearing the arms which had been
smitten off by the sword of Ammon,
of those who sought to slay him; and
they were carried in unto the king for
a testimony of the things which they
had done.

ALMA 18

One of the greatest things you can do to progress in the gospel yourself is to serve others. In fact, one of the best ways to feel and retain the Spirit yourself is to serve others. As soon as you begin to serve, you feel the Spirit.

In this chapter, we will see the power of Ammon's service to the king and his fellow servants in preparing them to receive the gospel. Also, we will see the importance of teaching the basics of the plan of salvation as we help others to understand the whole purpose of the gospel and the Church.

Remember that Ammon, with the help of the Lord, saved the king's flocks when enemies attacked and scattered them. He defended his fellow servants as they gathered up the scattered animals and cut off several of the attackers' arms. As we begin this chapter, his fellow servants have gathered up the arms and brought them to the king and are telling him what Ammon did to protect the flocks.

1 AND it came to pass that **king**
Lamoni caused that his servants
should stand forth and testify to
all the things which they had seen
concerning the matter.

2 **And when** they had all testified to
the things which they had seen, and
he had learned of the faithfulness
of Ammon [*service*] in preserving his
flocks, and also of his great power in
contending against those who sought
to slay him, **he was astonished ex-**
ceedingly, and said: Surely, this is
more than a man. Behold, is not
this the Great Spirit who doth send
such great punishments upon this
people, because of their murders?

3 And **they answered** the king,
and said: **Whether he be the Great**
Spirit or a man, we know not; but
this much we do know, that he
cannot be slain by the enemies of
the king; neither can they scatter

the king's flocks when he is with us, because of his expertness and great strength; therefore, **we know that he is a friend to the king.** And now, O king, we do not believe that a man has such great power, for we know he cannot be slain.

4 And now, when **the king** heard these words, he **said** unto them: **Now I know that it is the Great Spirit;** and he has come down at this time to preserve your lives, that I might not slay you as I did your brethren. Now this is the Great Spirit of whom our fathers [*ancestors*] have spoken.

Ultimately, most people believe in God or at least some higher power. However, for many, this belief seems to place no restrictions upon what they do in their daily living. Such was apparently the case with Lamoni and his people.

5 Now **this was the tradition of Lamoni, which he had received from his father, that there was a Great Spirit. Notwithstanding** [*even though*] **they believed in a Great Spirit they supposed that whatsoever they did was right**; nevertheless, **Lamoni began to fear** exceedingly, with fear **lest** [*for fear that*] **he had done wrong in slaying his servants**;

6 For **he had slain** [*killed*] **many of them because their brethren** [*some Lamanites*] **had scattered their flocks** at the place of water; and thus, because they had had their flocks scattered they were slain.

7 Now **it was the practice of these Lamanites to** stand by the waters of Sebus to **scatter the flocks of the people, that thereby they might drive away many that were scattered unto their own land**, it being a practice of plunder [*stealing and taking valuable stuff from others*] among them.

8 And it came to pass that **king Lamoni inquired** of his servants, saying: **Where is this man that has such great power?**

9 And **they said** unto him: Behold, **he is feeding thy horses** [*service*]. Now the king had commanded his servants, previous to the time of the watering of their flocks, that they should prepare his horses and chariots, and conduct him forth to the land of Nephi; for there had been a great feast appointed at the land of Nephi, by the father of Lamoni, who was king over all the land.

Keep Lamoni's father in mind, because Aaron will get a chance to teach him the gospel in Alma 22, because of Ammon's good example.

10 Now when **king Lamoni** heard that Ammon was preparing his horses and his chariots he **was** more **astonished, because of the faithfulness of Ammon** [*trustworthiness; service*], saying: Surely there has not been any servant among all my servants that has been so faithful as this man; for even he doth remember all my commandments to execute them.

11 **Now I surely know that this is the Great Spirit**, and I would desire him that he come in unto me, but I durst [*dare*] not.

12 And it came to pass that **when Ammon** had made ready the horses and the chariots for the king and his servants, he **went in unto the king**, and **he saw that the countenance** [*the look on the face*] **of the king was changed**; therefore he was about to return out of his presence.

13 **And one of the king's servants said unto him**, Rabbanah, which is, being interpreted, powerful or great king, considering their kings to be powerful; and thus he said unto him: Rabbanah, **the king desireth thee to stay**.

14 Therefore **Ammon turned himself unto the king, and said** unto him: **What wilt thou that I should do for thee, O king** [*this is real service*]**?** And **the king answered him not for the space of an hour**, according to their time, for he knew not what he should say unto him.

15 And it came to pass that **Ammon said unto him again: What desirest thou of me?** But the king answered him not.

Next, we see once again that the Holy Ghost can inspire the servants of the Lord as to what is in the minds of those they serve. Thus, the Lord meets specific needs of His children through His faithful servants. First, Ammon is told by the Spirit that the king thinks he is the Great Spirit; therefore, he explains that he is not. Then, he will teach the king (and those listening) the basics of the plan of salvation.

You can learn much about Heavenly Father's plan for us by paying close attention to what Ammon teaches. It is the same thing our missionaries teach their investigators today.

16 And it came to pass that **Ammon, being filled with the Spirit of God, therefore he perceived the thoughts of the king.** And he said unto him: Is it because thou hast heard that I defended thy servants and thy flocks, and slew seven of their brethren with the sling and with the sword, and smote off the arms of others, in order to defend thy flocks and thy servants; behold, is it this that causeth thy marvelings?

17 I say unto you, what is it, that thy marvelings are so great? **Behold, I am a man,** and am thy servant; therefore, whatsoever thou desirest which is right, that will I do.

18 Now when the king had heard these words, he marveled again, for he beheld that Ammon could discern his thoughts; but notwithstanding this, **king Lamoni** did open his mouth, and **said** unto him: **Who art thou? Art thou that Great Spirit, who knows all things?**

19 **Ammon answered** and said unto him: **I am not.**

20 And the **king** said: **How knowest thou the thoughts of my heart?** Thou mayest speak boldly, and tell

me concerning these things; and also **tell me by what power ye slew** [*killed*] **and smote** [*cut*] **off the arms of my brethren that scattered my flocks—**

Next, Ammon has a chance to demonstrate to the king that he has something far more valuable to give the king than anything the king with his worldly power among his people could give Ammon in return.

21 And now, **if thou wilt tell me concerning these things, whatsoever thou desirest I will give unto thee;** and if it were needed, I would guard thee with my armies; but I know that thou art more powerful than all they; nevertheless, whatsoever thou desirest of me I will grant it unto thee.

22 Now **Ammon being wise, yet harmless, he said unto Lamoni: Wilt thou hearken** [*listen carefully*] **unto my words, if I tell thee by what power I do these things? And this is the thing that I desire of thee.**

23 And **the king** answered him, and **said: Yea**, I will believe all thy words. And thus he was caught with guile. [*In other words, under the inspiration of the Spirit, Ammon had maneuvered King Lamoni into a position where he truly wanted to be taught, without his knowing yet what had happened to him.*]

Watch now as Ammon begins at the very beginning, which is exactly what many people need. It is an example of the "milk before meat" principle. Ammon is skilled at using questions to involve his "student."

24 And **Ammon** began to speak unto him with boldness, and **said** unto him: **Believest thou that there is a God?**

25 And **he answered,** and said unto him: **I do not know what that meaneth.** [*Ammon will simplify even more.*]

26 And then **Ammon said: Believest thou that there is a Great Spirit?**

27 And **he said, Yea**.

28 And **Ammon said: This is God**. And Ammon said unto him again: **Believest thou that this Great Spirit, who is God, created all things which are in heaven and in the earth?**

29 And **he said: Yea**, I believe that he created all things which are in the earth; **but I do not know the heavens.** [*Lamoni is very open and honest.*]

30 And **Ammon said** unto him: **The heavens is a place where God dwells and all his holy angels**.

Now the king starts asking questions, which is a very good sign that he is listening carefully and is very interested.

31 And **king Lamoni said: Is it above the earth?**

32 And **Ammon said: Yea**, and he looketh down upon all the children of men; **and he knows all the thoughts and intents of the heart** [*this is why I know what you are thinking*];

for by his hand were they all created from the beginning.

33 And **king Lamoni said: I believe all these things** which thou hast spoken. **Art thou sent from God?**

> The king has already progressed to the point that Ammon can begin including other points of doctrine in the plan of salvation with his answers.

34 **Ammon said** unto him: I am a man; and **man in the beginning was created after the image of God,** and **I am called by his Holy Spirit to teach these things unto this people, that they may be brought to a knowledge of that which is just and true;**

35 And a portion of **that Spirit** dwelleth in me, which **giveth me knowledge,** and **also power according to my faith and desires which are in God.**

> Ammon now teaches the basics of the plan of salvation, including the Creation, the Fall, God's dealings with man, the mission of Christ, etc.

36 Now when **Ammon** had said these words, he **began at the creation** of the world, and also the creation of Adam, and told him all the things concerning **the fall** of man, and rehearsed and laid before him the records and **the holy scriptures** of the people, which had been spoken by the prophets, even down to the time that their father, Lehi, left Jerusalem.

37 And he also rehearsed unto them [*for it was unto the king and to his servants*] all **the journeyings of their fathers** [*ancestors; Lehi's family as they left Jerusalem*] **in the wilderness,** and all their sufferings with hunger and thirst, and their travail, and so forth.

38 And he also rehearsed unto them concerning **the rebellions of Laman and Lemuel, and the sons of Ishmael,** yea, all their rebellions did he relate unto them; and he expounded unto them all the records and scriptures from the time that Lehi left Jerusalem down to the present time.

39 But this is not all; for he expounded unto them **the plan of redemption** [*the plan of salvation*], which was **prepared from the foundation of the world** [*during our premortal life*]; and he also made known unto them concerning **the coming of Christ**, and **all the works of the Lord** did he make known unto them.

> Based on the king's response, in verses 40–41, next, Ammon had also taught him about faith, repentance, and forgiveness through the mercy of the Savior.

40 And it came to pass that after he had said all these things, and expounded [*explained*] them to the king, **that the king believed all his words.**

41 And he began to cry unto the Lord, saying: **O Lord, have mercy; according to thy abundant mercy which thou hast had upon the**

people of Nephi, have upon me, and my people.

What happens next will set the stage for a large-scale conversion of many people in King Lamoni's kingdom.

42 And now, when he had said this, **he fell unto the earth, as if he were dead.**

43 And it came to pass that his servants took him and carried him in unto his wife, and laid him upon a bed; and **he lay as if he were dead for the space of two days and two nights;** and his wife, and his sons, and his daughters mourned over him, after the manner of the Lamanites [*according to the customs of the Lamanites*], greatly lamenting [*mourning*] his loss.

ALMA 19

Ammon knows what is happening here (verse 6), and being "wise, yet harmless" (Alma 18:22), he patiently waits to be invited to help when the time is right. There is a principle for you to learn here, namely, that even though we may be ready for a step in the Lord's work, others may take longer to develop to the same point. We are wise not to push it upon them until they, too, are ready.

1 AND it came to pass that **after two days and two nights they were about to take his body and lay it in a sepulchre** [*a tomb*], which they had made for the purpose of burying their dead.

2 Now **the queen having heard of the fame of Ammon, therefore she sent and desired that he should come in unto her.**

3 And it came to pass that **Ammon** did as he was commanded, and went in unto the queen, and **desired to know what she would** [*wanted*] **that he should do.**

4 And she said unto him: **The servants of my husband have made it known unto me that thou art a prophet of a holy God, and that thou hast power to do many mighty works in his name;**

5 Therefore, if this is the case, **I would that ye should go in and see my husband**, for he has been laid upon his bed for the space of two days and two nights; and **some say that he is not dead, but others say that he is dead and that he stinketh**, and that he ought to be placed in the sepulchre; but as for myself, **to me he doth not stink.**

With a bit of humor intended, we might observe that the last phrase of verse 5, above, is good marriage counsel. Loyalty to one's spouse, when others are critical, can be helpful in strengthening marriage.

In verse 6, next, we are taught what happens deep in the heart of a person who changes from a life of unbelief and spiritual darkness to a life in which the Spirit can cause light and intelligence to come into the whole being. This is one of the reasons that converts to the Church or converts from inactivity in the Church are so happy.

6 Now, **this was what Ammon desired, for he knew that king Lamoni was under the power of God;**

he knew that **the dark veil of unbelief was being cast away from his mind,** and **the light** which **did light up his mind**, which was **the light of the glory of God,** which was **a marvelous light of his goodness**—yea, **this light** had **infused** [*put*] such **joy into his soul,** the **cloud of darkness** having been **dispelled**, and that **the light of everlasting life** was **lit up in his soul**, yea, **he knew that this had overcome his natural frame** [*his physical body*], and he was **carried away in God** [*symbolic of being carried into a whole new life, "born again"*]—

7 Therefore, what the queen desired of him was his only desire. **Therefore, he went in to see the king** according as the queen had desired him; and he saw the king, and **he knew that he was not dead**.

8 And **he said unto the queen: He is not dead,** but he sleepeth in God, and **on the morrow** [*tomorrow*] **he shall rise again; therefore bury him not.**

Based on verses 1 and 8, we calculate that King Lamoni was "gone" for a total of three days and three nights. This period of time could be symbolic of the death and resurrection of the Savior, and could represent the blessings of the Savior's Atonement upon Lamoni.

Next, we see the great faith of the Lamoni's wife. One of the gifts of the Spirit is the gift of believing on the words of others (D&C 46:14).

9 And **Ammon said unto her: Believest thou this?** And **she said** unto him: **I have had no witness save thy word, and the word of our servants**; nevertheless **I believe that it shall be according as thou hast said.**

10 And **Ammon said** unto her: **Blessed art thou because of thy exceeding faith;** I say unto thee, woman, there has not been such great faith among all the people of the Nephites.

11 And it came to pass that **she watched over the bed of her husband**, from that time even until that time on the morrow which Ammon had appointed that he should rise.

Because of her pure faith, Lamoni's wife will be well prepared for what her husband will announce the next day. As we watch him arise from the bed, we see that he has been taught the most important doctrine of all during his three days, namely that Jesus is the Christ.

12 And it came to pass that **he arose**, according to the words of Ammon; and as he arose, he stretched forth his hand unto the woman, **and said: Blessed be the name of God, and blessed art thou.**

13 For as sure as thou livest, behold, **I have seen my Redeemer; and he shall come forth, and be born of a woman, and he shall redeem all mankind who believe on his name.** Now, when he had said these words, his heart was swollen within him,

and **he sunk again with joy; and the queen also sunk down, being overpowered by the Spirit.**

14 Now **Ammon seeing the Spirit of the Lord poured out** according to his prayers upon the Lamanites, his brethren, who had been the cause of so much mourning among the Nephites, or among all the people of God because of their iniquities and their traditions, he **fell upon his knees, and began to pour out his soul in prayer and thanksgiving to God** for what he had done for his brethren; and **he was also overpowered with joy; and thus they all three had sunk to the earth.**

15 Now, when **the servants** of the king had seen that they had fallen, they **also began to cry unto God,** for the fear of the Lord had come upon them also, for it was they who had stood before the king and testified unto him concerning the great power of Ammon.

16 And it came to pass that they did call on the name of the Lord, in their might, **even until they had all fallen to the earth, save** [*except*] it were **one of the Lamanitish women**, whose name was **Abish**, she having been converted unto the Lord for many years, on account of a remarkable vision of her father—

Abish is an example of the visions and dreams, etc., that the Lord has given to individuals throughout time to prepare them to play a role in establishing the Church in their land when the gospel finally comes to that area.

As we continue reading, we will also see how quickly Satan steps in to squelch the good intentions of believers by stirring up others to stamp out the good that is about to grow.

17 Thus, having been converted to the Lord, and never having made it known, therefore, when she saw that all the servants of Lamoni had fallen to the earth, and also her mistress, the queen, and the king, and Ammon lay prostrate upon the earth, **she knew that it was the power of God**; and supposing that this opportunity, by making known unto the people what had happened among them, that by beholding this scene it would cause them to believe in the power of God, therefore **she ran forth from house to house, making it known unto the people.**

18 And they began to assemble themselves together unto the house of the king. And **there came a multitude**, and to their astonishment they beheld the king, and the queen, and their servants prostrate upon the earth, and they all lay there as though they were dead; and they also **saw Ammon,** and behold, **he was a Nephite.**

19 And now **the people began to murmur** among themselves; **some saying that it was a great evil that had come upon them**, or upon the king and his house, **because he had suffered** [*allowed*] **that the Nephite**

should remain in the land [*racial prejudice, a strong tool of the devil*].

20 But others rebuked [*criticized*] them, saying: **The king hath brought this evil upon his house, because he slew his servants who had had their flocks scattered** at the waters of Sebus.

Notice how quickly Satan is stirring things up to hide the fact that a beautiful miracle has taken place.

21 And they were also rebuked by **those men who had** stood at the waters of Sebus and **scattered the flocks which belonged to the king**, for they **were angry with Ammon** because of the number which he had slain of their brethren at the waters of Sebus, while defending the flocks of the king.

22 Now, **one of them**, whose brother had been slain with the sword of Ammon, being exceedingly angry with Ammon, **drew his sword and went forth that he might let it fall upon Ammon, to slay him**; and as he lifted the sword to smite him, **behold, he fell dead.**

23 Now **we see that Ammon could not be slain** [*the Lord keeps His promises*], **for the Lord had said unto Mosiah, his father: I will spare him**, and it shall be unto him according to thy faith—therefore, Mosiah trusted him unto the Lord.

24 And it came to pass that **when the multitude beheld** [*saw*] **that the man had fallen dead, who lifted the sword to slay Ammon**, fear came upon them all, and they durst not put forth their hands to touch him or any of those who had fallen; and **they began to marvel** again among themselves what could be the cause of this great power, or what all these things could mean.

You would think that all of them would now become believers. However, some do not. We see a principle demonstrated, namely, that deep personal wickedness does not promote rational thought—in other words, clear, correct thinking.

25 And it came to pass that there were **many** among them who **said that Ammon was the Great Spirit,** and **others said he was sent by the Great Spirit;**

26 But **others rebuked** [*scolded*] **them all, saying that he was a monster, who had been sent from the Nephites to torment them.**

27 And there were **some** who **said that Ammon was sent by the Great Spirit to afflict them because of their iniquities;** and that it was **the Great Spirit** that **had always attended the Nephites,** who had ever delivered them out of their hands; and they said that it was this Great Spirit who had destroyed so many of their brethren, the Lamanites.

28 And thus the **contention** [*arguing*] **began to be exceedingly sharp among them**. And while they were thus contending, **the woman** servant

[*Abish; see verse 16*] who had caused the multitude to be gathered together **came, and when she saw the contention which was among the multitude she was exceedingly** [*very*] **sorrowful**, even unto tears [*she began to cry*].

As you will see next, the queen has now had a conversion experience similar to that of her husband.

29 And it came to pass that **she went and took the queen by the hand**, that perhaps she might raise her from the ground; and as soon as she touched her hand **she arose** and stood upon her feet, **and cried with a loud voice, saying: O blessed Jesus, who has saved me from an awful hell! O blessed God, have mercy on this people!**

30 And when she had said this, she clasped her hands, being filled with joy, speaking many words which were not understood; and when she had done this, **she took the king, Lamoni, by the hand, and behold he arose and stood upon his feet.**

31 And **he**, immediately, seeing the contention among his people, **went forth and began to rebuke them, and to teach them** the words which he had heard from the mouth of Ammon; and **as many as heard** [*who humbly listened to*] **his words believed, and were converted unto the Lord.**

32 But **there were many among them who would not hear his words** [*the principle of agency at work*]; therefore they went their way [*refusing to listen to their king*].

33 And it came to pass that **when Ammon arose** he also administered unto them, and also did all the servants of Lamoni; and they did all declare unto the people the selfsame thing—that **their hearts had been changed; that they had no more desire to do evil** [*true conversion*].

34 And behold, **many** did declare unto the people that they **had seen angels and had conversed** [*talked*] **with them**; and thus they had told them things of God, and of his righteousness.

35 And it came to pass that there were **many that did believe in their words; and as many as did believe were baptized**; and they became a righteous people, and they did establish a church among them.

At the end of verse 36, next, Mormon points out a major message he wants us to understand from these events.

36 And thus the work of the Lord did commence [*begin*] among the Lamanites; thus the Lord did begin to pour out his Spirit upon them; and **we see that his arm is extended** [*reaches out*] **to all people who will repent and believe on his name.**

ALMA 20

One of the things you will see in this chapter is the power of Christlike love in overcoming the awful power of hatred and prejudice. We will also be taught a principle, which we will call "the short straw principle," as to why things sometimes go wrong for people who are living the gospel.

By way of background, Lamoni's father, who was the big king over all the land, and who had allowed his sons and others to serve as local kings under his authority, had invited Lamoni to come to a feast which he had prepared for his sons. Lamoni hadn't come because of his conversion to the gospel and the conversion of many of his people as well as the establishment of the Church in his land. Lamoni's father was furious when Lamoni didn't come to the feast, and, without Lamoni's knowledge, had determined to travel from his headquarters in the land of Nephi to see his son and find out why he had not come.

Also, in the land of Middoni, another part of the big king's territory, Aaron, Ammon's brother, and his missionary companions, Muloki and Ammah, have been suffering in prison for many days. They were not as fortunate as Ammon, and were immediately arrested and thrown in prison when they came to the land of Middoni to preach. They are patiently miserable at this point of the account.

As we continue, Lamoni would like Ammon to meet his father, the big king of the whole land.

1 AND it came to pass that when they had established a church in that land, that king **Lamoni desired that Ammon should go with him to the land of Nephi** [*his father's headquarters*], **that he might show him unto his father.**

2 And **the voice of the Lord came to Ammon, saying: Thou shalt not go up to the land of Nephi**, for behold, the king will seek thy life; **but thou shalt go to the land of Middoni; for behold, thy brother Aaron, and also Muloki and Ammah are in prison.**

3 Now it came to pass that **when Ammon had heard this, he said unto Lamoni: Behold, my brother and brethren are in prison at Middoni, and I go that I may deliver them.**

4 Now **Lamoni said** unto Ammon: I know, in the strength of the Lord thou canst do all things. But behold, **I will go with thee** to the land of Middoni; for **the king of the land of Middoni**, whose name is Antiomno, **is a friend** unto me; therefore I go to the land of Middoni, that I may flatter the king of the land, and he will cast thy brethren out of prison. Now Lamoni said unto him: **Who told thee that thy brethren were in prison?**

5 And **Ammon said** unto him: **No one hath told me, save** [*except*] it be **God**; and he said unto me—Go and deliver thy brethren, for they are in prison in the land of Middoni.

6 Now **when Lamoni had heard this** he caused that his servants should make ready his horses and his chariots.

7 And **he said unto Ammon: Come, I will go with thee down to the land of Middoni**, and there I will plead with the king that he will cast thy brethren out of prison.

Next, Lamoni and Ammon unexpectedly meet his father as they travel toward Middoni. His father is still furious. He was obviously embarrassed when Lamoni didn't show up at the feast and is now coming to find out why.

8 And it came to pass that as Ammon and Lamoni were journeying thither, **they met the father of Lamoni**, who was king over all the land.

9 And behold, **the father of Lamoni said** unto him: **Why did ye not come to the feast** on that great day when I made a feast unto my sons, and unto my people?

Lamoni's father is shocked to see his son in company with a Nephite, and his hatred and prejudice show in what he says next.

10 And he also said: **Whither art thou going with this Nephite, who is one of the children of a liar?** [*The false tradition of the Lamanites was that Nephi and others had lied, cheated, and wronged Laman and Lemuel out of leadership positions as well as the brass plates and other treasures, etc.; see verse 13, also Mosiah 10:12–13.*]

11 And it came to pass that **Lamoni rehearsed unto him whither** [*where*] **he was going,** for he feared to offend him.

12 And **he also told him all the cause of his tarrying** [*staying*] **in his own kingdom, that he did not go unto his father to the feast which he had prepared.**

13 And now when Lamoni had rehearsed unto him all these things, behold, to his astonishment, **his father was angry** with him, **and said: Lamoni, thou art going to deliver** [*free them from prison*] **these Nephites, who are sons of a liar.** Behold, he [*Nephi, etc.*] robbed our fathers [*ancestors; Laman and Lemuel, etc.*]; and now his children [*descendants*] are also come amongst us that they may, by their cunning and their lyings, deceive us, that they again may rob us of our property.

14 Now **the father of Lamoni commanded him that he should slay Ammon** with the sword. And **he also commanded him that he should not go to the land of Middoni,** but that he should return with him to the land of Ishmael.

Next, Lamoni bears testimony to his father. We suspect that Lamoni's father was also a great and noble spirit, loyal to Christ in the premortal life, but just doesn't realize it yet because of his upbringing.

15 But **Lamoni said** unto him: **I will not slay Ammon, neither will I return to the land of Ishmael, but I go to the land of Middoni that I may release the brethren of Ammon**, for **I know that they are just** [*righteous*] **men and holy prophets of the true God.**

16 Now **when his father had heard these words, he was angry with**

him, and he drew his sword that he might smite him to the earth.

What happens next would make an exciting scene in a movie. Also, Ammon will say some things that will puzzle the king and will give the Spirit a chance to work on his mind over time.

17 But **Ammon stood forth and said unto him: Behold, thou shalt not slay thy son**; nevertheless, **it were better that he should fall than thee, for behold, he has repented of his sins; but if thou shouldst fall at this time, in thine anger, thy soul could not be saved.**

18 And again, **it is expedient** [*absolutely necessary*] **that thou shouldst forbear** [*hold back*]; for **if thou shouldst slay thy son, he being an innocent man, his blood would cry from the ground** to the Lord his God, for vengeance to come upon thee; and **perhaps thou wouldst lose thy soul.**

19 Now when Ammon had said these words unto him, **he answered him**, saying: I know that if I should slay my son, that I should shed innocent blood; for **it is thou that hast sought to destroy him.** [*By teaching him the Nephite religion. The king completely missed the point that Ammon was trying to teach him.*]

20 And **he stretched forth his hand to slay Ammon. But Ammon withstood** [*resisted*] **his blows, and also smote his arm** that he could not use it.

21 Now when **the king** saw that Ammon could slay him, he **began to plead with Ammon that he would spare his life.**

22 But **Ammon** raised his sword, and **said** unto him: **Behold, I will smite thee except thou wilt grant unto me that my brethren may be cast out of prison.**

23 Now the **king**, fearing he should lose his life, **said: If thou wilt spare me I will grant unto thee whatsoever thou wilt ask, even to half of the kingdom.**

What Ammon says next, showing his deep love for his brethren and for Lamoni, the king's son, opens the door for the Spirit to prepare the king's mind to hear the gospel. See verses 26–27, also Alma 22:3.

24 Now when **Ammon** saw that he had wrought upon the old king according to his desire, he **said** unto him: **If thou wilt grant that my brethren may be cast out of prison, and also that Lamoni may retain his kingdom**, and that ye be not displeased with him, but **grant that he may do according to his own desires** in whatsoever thing he thinketh, **then will I spare thee; otherwise I will smite thee to the earth**.

25 Now when Ammon had said these words, **the king began to rejoice** because of his life.

26 And when **he saw that Ammon had no desire to destroy him**, and when **he also saw the great love he had for his son Lamoni,** he was astonished exceedingly, and said: Because this is all that thou hast desired,

that I would release thy brethren, and suffer that my son Lamoni should retain his kingdom, behold, I will grant unto you that my son may retain his kingdom from this time and forever; and I will govern him no more—

27 And I will also grant unto thee that thy brethren may be cast out of prison, and thou and thy brethren may come unto me, in my kingdom; for **I shall greatly desire to see thee. For the king was greatly astonished at the words which he had spoken, and also at the words which had been spoken by his son Lamoni, therefore he was desirous to learn them.**

28 And it came to pass that **Ammon and Lamoni proceeded on their journey towards the land of Middoni**. And Lamoni found favor in the eyes of the king of the land; therefore **the brethren of Ammon were brought forth out of prison.**

These missionaries had suffered much, but were patient in their afflictions. This is an indicator that they had the gift of perspective.

29 And when Ammon did meet them he was exceedingly sorrowful, for behold **they were naked, and their skins were worn exceedingly because of being bound with strong cords** [*ropes*]. And they also had suffered **hunger**, **thirst**, and all kinds of afflictions; **nevertheless they were patient in all their sufferings**.

Next, we come to what we could perhaps refer to as the "short straw principle." Remember that when people are trying to decide who goes first or whatever, they sometimes draw straws to see who gets the short straw and, thus, goes first. This principle is that, sometimes, when things keep going wrong, faithful Saints keep trying to figure out what they are doing wrong and how they should repent. They search their attitudes, behaviors, and lives and, although they are not perfect, they still find no big sins of commission or even of omission. Thus, they are baffled as to why it seems they are being punished, while other Saints seem to be getting all the blessings.

In the case we are studying, Ammon got a pleasant reception among Lamoni and his people, and was even offered the hand of one of the king's daughters in marriage. Whereas Aaron and his companions were put in prison and treated badly. Was it because Aaron and his brethren were less righteous than Ammon? Mormon tells us in verse 30 that such was not the case.

In verse 30, we are taught a simple but very important principle, namely, that sometimes bad things simply happen. It is not God's plan to stop every bad or negative thing that happens to the righteous. It would ruin our test here on earth and our opportunity for growth.

30 And, **as it happened, it was their lot** [*they simply got the "short straw" this time, whereas Ammon got the "long straw"*] to have fallen into the hands of a more hardened and a more stiffnecked people; therefore they would not hearken [*listen*] unto their words, and they had cast them out, and had smitten them,

and had driven them from house to house, and from place to place, even until they had arrived in the land of Middoni; and there they were taken and cast into prison, and bound [*tied up*] with strong cords, and kept in prison for many days, and were delivered [*set free*] by Lamoni and Ammon.

ALMA 21

Chapters 21–26 contain an account of the experiences of Ammon's brother, Aaron, and those with him, after the brothers first entered Lamanite territory to start their missions. Aaron himself went to a city called Jerusalem, which was built by the Lamanites and others and was named after the city from which Laman and Lemuel came.

Aaron will meet some apostate Nephites ("apostates" are people who used to be members of the Church but now have left it), called Amalekites and Amulonites, who are very hardened, as far as spiritual things are concerned. There is a bit of a lesson in this, namely, that once people who have the gospel leave it, they generally become more hardened than those who have never had it.

1 NOW when Ammon and his brethren separated themselves in the borders of the land of the Lamanites, behold **Aaron took his journey towards the land which was called by the Lamanites, Jerusalem**, calling it after the land of their fathers' [*ancestors; Laman and Lemuel*] nativity [*birth*]; and it was away joining the borders of Mormon [*apparently the land where Alma and his people had lived for twenty-four years before they escaped to Zarahemla; see Mosiah 18:4 and 24:18–25*].

2 Now the Lamanites and the Amalekites [*apostate Nephites; see Index, under "Amalekites"*] and the people of Amulon [*descendants of the leader of the wicked priests of King Noah; see Mosiah 23:31–32*] **had built a great city, which was called Jerusalem**.

3 Now **the Lamanites of themselves were sufficiently hardened, but the Amalekites and the Amulonites were still harder** [*more resistant to spirituality and the gospel*]**;** therefore **they did cause the Lamanites that they should harden their hearts,** that they should wax [*grow*] strong in wickedness and their abominations.

In Alma, chapter 1, we met Nehor, an influential apostate who preached to become popular and to gain wealth. This is known as "priestcraft" (see Alma 1:16). It is very damaging and had spread from there into many areas, including the area where Aaron came to preach. Thus, we see the damage that one man can do—in this case, Nehor.

4 And it came to pass that **Aaron came to the city of Jerusalem,** and **first began to preach to the Amalekites**. And he began to preach to them in their synagogues, for they had built synagogues after the order of the Nehors; for **many of the Amalekites and the Amulonites were after the order of the Nehors** [*those who practiced priestcraft, preaching for popularity and wealth, like Nehor had done*].

Watch, next, as one of the Amalakites ridicules Aaron and his teaching, in effect saying that Aaron thinks he is better than they are and his message is an insult to them. Who is Aaron to say that his religion is better than their religion? Who are you to say what righteousness is? And so forth.

5 Therefore, as Aaron entered into one of their synagogues to preach unto the people, and as he was speaking unto them, behold there arose **an Amalekite** and **began to contend** [*argue*] **with him, saying:** What is that thou hast testified? Hast thou seen an angel? **Why do not angels appear unto us?** Behold **are not this people as good as thy people?**

6 Thou also sayest, except we repent we shall perish. How knowest thou the thought and intent of our hearts? **How knowest thou that we have cause to repent? How knowest thou that we are not a righteous people?** Behold, we have built sanctuaries [*we have churches too*], and **we** do assemble ourselves together to **worship God. We do believe that God will save all men** [*exactly what Nehor taught; see Alma 1:4*].

7 Now **Aaron said** unto him: **Believest thou that the Son of God shall come to redeem mankind from their sins?**

What the Amalekite man says next to Aaron is sadly representative of the thinking of many people in our day; namely, they consider our belief in the Bible to be foolish tradition, and that prophets cannot know the future.

8 And **the man said** unto him: **We do not believe that thou knowest any such thing. We do not believe in these foolish traditions. We do not believe that thou knowest of things to come,** neither do we believe that thy fathers and also that our fathers did know concerning the things which they spake, of that which is to come.

9 Now **Aaron began to open** [*explain*] **the scriptures unto them concerning the coming of Christ**, and also **concerning the resurrection of the dead,** and that there could be no redemption for mankind save it were through the death and sufferings of Christ, **and the atonement** of his blood.

One of Satan's effective tools is to impress people to get angry at truth and that which is good.

10 And it came to pass as he began to expound [*teach and explain*] these things unto them **they were angry with him, and began to mock** [*make fun of him*] **him**; and they would not hear the words which he spake.

11 **Therefore**, when he saw that they would not hear his words, **he departed out of their synagogue, and came over to a village** which was called Ani-Anti, and there he **found Muloki** preaching the word unto them; **and also Ammah and his brethren**. And they contended [*debated*] with many about the word.

12 And it came to pass that **they saw that the people would harden their hearts, therefore they departed and came over into the land of Middoni.** And they did preach the word unto many, **and few believed** on the words which they taught.

13 Nevertheless, **Aaron and a certain number of his brethren were taken and cast into prison,** and the remainder of them fled out of the land of Middoni unto the regions round about.

14 And those who were cast into prison **suffered many things, and they were delivered by the hand of Lamoni and Ammon, and they were fed and clothed.**

So far, Aaron and those with him have not had much success and have had much of opposition and misery. It would be easy to give up, especially when they are doing the Lord's work and nothing much seems to be going right. Nevertheless, they keep trying, and eventually, things begin going better. There seems to be a lesson in this for us, too.

15 And **they went forth again to declare the word**, and thus they were delivered for the first time out of prison; and thus they had suffered.

16 And they went forth whithersoever they were **led by the Spirit of the Lord**, preaching the word of God in every synagogue of the Amalekites, or in every assembly of the Lamanites where they could be admitted.

17 And it came to pass that **the Lord began to bless them, insomuch that they brought many to the knowledge of the truth**; yea, they did convince many of their sins, and of the traditions of their fathers, which were not correct.

Mormon will take a moment now to tell us what Lamoni and Ammon did, after freeing Aaron and his companions from prison in Middoni. Then, he will return to the account of Aaron and the great opportunity he had to teach Lamoni's father, who, as you may remember, is the big king over the whole land of the Lamanites.

18 And it came to pass that **Ammon and Lamoni returned from the land of Middoni to the land of Ishmael** [*Lamoni's home*], which was the land of their inheritance.

19 And **king Lamoni would not suffer** [*permit*] **that Ammon should serve him, or be his servant.**

20 But **he caused that there should be synagogues** [*churches*] **built** in the land of Ishmael; **and** he caused **that his people**, or the people who were under his reign [*rule*], **should assemble themselves together**.

21 And he did rejoice over them, **and he did teach them many things**. And he did also declare unto them that they were a people who were under him, and that they were a free people, that they were free from the oppressions of the king, his father; for that his father had granted unto him that he might reign over the

people who were in the land of Ishmael, and in all the land round about.

In addition to giving his people much more freedom than they had before Ammon came, King Lamoni provides freedom of religion as a matter of the law of the land.

22 And **he also declared unto them that they might have the liberty of worshiping the Lord their God according to their desires**, in whatsoever place they were in, if it were in the land which was under the reign of king Lamoni.

23 And **Ammon did preach unto the people of king Lamoni**; and it came to pass that he did teach them all things concerning things pertaining to righteousness. And he did exhort them daily, with all diligence; **and they gave heed unto his word** [*they believed and followed his teaching in their own lives*], and they were zealous for [*very faithful in*] keeping the commandments of God.

ALMA 22

Aaron, who went through much trouble and persecution at the first of his mission, will now have the privilege of teaching the king of all the Lamanites, Lamoni's father. He and his companions will travel to the land of Nephi, to the palace of the king. Ammon's generosity and love for Lamoni have been on this powerful king's mind, since his first encounter with Ammon in Alma 20:8–26. He is prepared to hear the gospel.

1 NOW, as Ammon was thus teaching the people of Lamoni continually, **we will return to the account of Aaron and his brethren;** for after he departed from the land of Middoni **he was led by the Spirit to the land of Nephi, even to the house of the king which was over all the land save** [*except*] **it were the land of Ishmael;** [*because he had given Lamoni the right to be an independent king over that part of Lamanite territory*] and he was **the father of Lamoni.**

2 And it came to pass that **he went** in unto him **into the king's palace, with his brethren,** and bowed himself before the king, and said unto him: Behold, O king, we are the brethren of Ammon, whom thou hast delivered out of prison.

3 And now, O king, if thou wilt spare our lives, we will be thy servants. **And the king said** unto them: Arise, for I will grant unto you your lives, and I will not suffer [*allow*] that ye shall be my servants; but **I will insist that ye shall administer unto me** [*help me with some personal needs*]; **for I have been somewhat troubled in mind because of the generosity and the greatness of the words of thy brother Ammon;** and **I desire to know** the cause **why he has not come up out of Middoni with thee**.

4 And **Aaron said** unto the king: Behold, **the Spirit of the Lord has called him another way**; he has gone to the land of Ishmael, to teach the people of Lamoni.

You have probably noticed that almost every time missionaries in the Book of Mormon have taught someone so far, they have taught them the basics of the plan of salvation, including the Creation, the Fall, and the Atonement. There is certainly a message for us in this, namely, that the basics of Heavenly Father's plan are what we need to teach others also. This is what Aaron will do now for Lamoni's father.

5 Now **the king said** unto them: **What is this that ye have said concerning the Spirit of the Lord?** Behold, this is the thing which doth trouble me.

6 And **also, what is this that Ammon said—If ye will repent ye shall be saved, and if ye will not repent, ye shall be cast off at the last day?**

7 And **Aaron** answered him and **said** unto him: **Believest thou that there is a God?** And **the king said**: I know that the Amalekites say that there is a God, and I have granted unto them that they should build sanctuaries, that they may assemble themselves together to worship him. And **if now thou sayest there is a God, behold I will believe** [*simple, uncluttered faith*].

8 And now **when Aaron heard this, his heart began to rejoice, and he said** [*Aaron bears simple testimony*]: Behold, **assuredly as thou livest, O king, there is a God.**

Both in the case of Ammon teaching Lamoni (Alma 18:31–33 and beyond) and here with Aaron teaching Lamoni's father, these missionaries move quickly to the point where their "investigators" are asking questions.

9 And **the king said: Is God that Great Spirit that brought our fathers out of the land of Jerusalem?**

10 And **Aaron said** unto him: **Yea, he is that Great Spirit, and he created all things both in heaven and in earth. Believest thou this?**

11 And **he said: Yea, I believe that the Great Spirit created all things, and I desire that ye should tell me concerning all these things, and I will believe thy words.**

Now the door is opened for teaching the plan of salvation.

12 And it came to pass that when Aaron saw that the king would believe his words, he began from **the creation of Adam**, reading the scriptures unto the king—how **God created man after his own image,** and that **God gave him commandments,** and that **because of transgression, man had fallen.**

13 And Aaron did expound unto him the scriptures from the creation of Adam, laying **the fall of man** before him, and **their carnal** [*worldly*] **state and also the plan of redemption** [*the plan of salvation*], which was prepared from the foundation of the world, **through Christ, for all whosoever** [*whoever*] **would believe on his name.**

14 And **since man had fallen he could not merit anything of himself** [*could not save himself*]; but **the**

sufferings and death of Christ atone for their sins, through faith and repentance, and so forth; and that **he breaketh the bands of death** [*provides resurrection for all*], that the grave shall have no victory, and that the sting of death should be swallowed up in the hopes of glory; and Aaron did expound [*teach and explain*] all these things unto the king.

There could be no greater joy for a missionary than to have an investigator respond the way the king does now.

15 And it came to pass that after Aaron had expounded these things unto him, **the king said: What shall I do that I may have this eternal life of which thou hast spoken? Yea, what shall I do that I may be born of God, having this wicked spirit rooted out of my breast, and receive his Spirit, that I may be filled with joy, that I may not be cast off at the last day** [*the Final Judgment*]**?** Behold, said he, **I will give up all that I possess, yea, I will forsake my kingdom, that I may receive this great joy.**

16 But **Aaron said** unto him: If thou desirest this thing, if thou wilt **bow down before God** [*be completely humble*], yea, if thou wilt **repent of all thy sins**, and will bow down before God, and **call on his name in faith,** believing that ye shall receive, **then shalt thou receive the hope** [*encouragement*] **which thou desirest.**

17 And it came to pass that when Aaron had said these words, **the king did bow down before the Lord**, upon his knees; yea, even he did prostrate himself upon the earth, and cried mightily, saying:

Verse 18, next, contains one of the great teaching verses of the Book of Mormon. It is a vital lesson for all of us.

18 O God, Aaron hath told me that there is a God; and if there is a God, and if thou art God, wilt thou make thyself known unto me, and **I will give away all my sins to know thee, and that I may be raised from the dead, and be saved at the last day.** And now when the king had said these words, he was struck as if he were dead.

These wonderful Lamanite people seem to be so humble and close to the Spirit when they receive the gospel, that they are easily overcome by it. Here again, as was the case with Lamoni and his wife and others (Alma 19:13–16), the situation will be understood by some and badly misinterpreted by others.

19 And it came to pass that **his servants ran and told the queen** all that had happened unto the king. **And she came in unto the king; and when she saw him lay as if he were dead, and also Aaron and his brethren standing as though they had been the cause of his fall, she was angry with them, and commanded that her servants, or the servants of the king, should take them and slay them.**

20 Now **the servants had seen the cause of the king's fall, therefore they durst not** [*didn't dare*] **lay their hands on** [*take hold of*] **Aaron and his brethren;** and they pled with the queen saying: Why commandest thou that we should slay these men, when behold one of them is mightier than us all? Therefore we shall fall before them.

21 Now **when the queen saw the fear of the servants she also began to fear exceedingly,** lest there should some evil come upon her. And **she commanded her servants that they should go and call the people, that they might slay Aaron and his brethren.**

This situation will be handled differently than was the case with Lamoni and his people. Each circumstance has it own individual needs and the Spirit will direct how it is to be handled.

22 Now **when Aaron saw the determination of the queen**, he, also knowing the hardness of the hearts of the people, feared lest that a multitude should assemble themselves together, and there should be a great contention and a disturbance among them; therefore **he put forth his hand and raised the king from the earth, and said unto him: Stand. And he stood upon his feet, receiving his strength.**

23 Now this was done in the presence of the queen and many of the servants. And when they saw it they greatly marveled, and began to fear. And **the king stood forth, and began to minister unto them. And he did minister unto them, insomuch that his whole household were converted unto the Lord.**

24 Now **there was a multitude gathered** together because of the commandment of the queen, **and there began to be great murmurings among them because of Aaron and his brethren.**

25 **But the king stood forth** among them and administered unto them [*took care of their concerns*]. **And they were pacified** towards Aaron and those who were with him.

26 And it came to pass that when **the king** saw that the people were pacified, he **caused that Aaron and his brethren** should stand forth in the midst of the multitude, and that they **should preach the word** [*the gospel*] **unto them.**

27 And it came to pass that **the king sent a proclamation throughout all the land** [*this thought will be finished in chapter 23, verse 1*], amongst all his people who were in all his land, who were in all the regions round about, which was bordering even to the sea, on the east and on the west, and which was divided from the land of Zarahemla by a narrow strip of wilderness, which ran from the sea east even to the sea west, and round about on the borders of the seashore, and the borders of the wilderness which was on the north by the land of Zarahemla, through the borders of Manti, by the head of the river Sidon, running from

the east towards the west—and thus were the Lamanites and the Nephites divided.

As you can see, Mormon chose this part of the plates to engrave a rather detailed description of the geography of the area, as well as giving other historical details. In verse 35, he tells us that at that point, he will return to the account of the four sons of Mosiah and their missionary companions.

28 Now, **the more idle part of the Lamanites lived in the wilderness**, and dwelt in tents; and they were spread through the wilderness on the west, in the land of Nephi; yea, and also on the west of the land of Zarahemla, in the borders by the seashore, and on the west in the land of Nephi, in the place of their fathers' first inheritance, and thus bordering along by the seashore.

29 And also there were **many Lamanites on the east by the seashore**, whither the Nephites had driven them. And thus the Nephites were nearly surrounded by the Lamanites; nevertheless the Nephites had taken possession of all the northern parts of the land bordering on the wilderness, at the head of the river Sidon, from the east to the west, round about on the wilderness side; on the north, even until they came to the land which they called Bountiful.

30 And **it bordered upon the land which they called Desolation**, it being so far northward that it came into the land which had been peopled and been destroyed, of whose bones we have spoken [*the remains of the Jaredites; see Mosiah, chapter 8, heading*], which was discovered by the people of Zarahemla, it being the place of their first landing.

31 And they came from there up into the south wilderness. Thus **the land on the northward was called Desolation, and the land on the southward was called Bountiful**, it being the wilderness which is filled with all manner of wild animals of every kind, a part of which had come from the land northward for food.

32 And now, **it was only the distance of a day and a half's journey for a Nephite**, on the line Bountiful and the land Desolation, **from the east to the west sea**; and thus the land of Nephi and the land of Zarahemla were nearly surrounded by water, there being a small neck of land between the land northward and the land southward.

33 And it came to pass that the Nephites had inhabited the land Bountiful, even from the east unto the west sea, and thus **the Nephites in their wisdom, with their guards and their armies, had hemmed in the Lamanites on the south**, that thereby they should have no more possession on the north, that they might not overrun the land northward.

34 **Therefore the Lamanites could have no more possessions only in the land of Nephi**, and the

wilderness round about. Now this was wisdom in the Nephites—as the Lamanites were an enemy to them, they would not suffer their afflictions on every hand, and also that they might have a country whither they might flee, according to their desires.

35 And **now I** [*Mormon*], after having said this, **return again to the account of Ammon and Aaron, Omner and Himni, and their brethren** [*missionary companions*].

ALMA 23

Religious freedom is a necessary part of being free to choose and to exercise our agency. Wherever true freedom exists, it includes religious freedom. As we continue, Lamoni's father sends a proclamation throughout his kingdom guaranteeing such freedom to all his people, and thousands join the Church. These Lamanite converts will call themselves Anti-Nephi-Lehies.

1 BEHOLD, now it came to pass that **the king of the Lamanites** [*Lamoni's father*] **sent a proclamation among all his people, that they should not lay their hands on Ammon, or Aaron, or Omner, or Himni, nor either** [*any*] **of their brethren** [*missionary companions*] who should go forth preaching the word of God, in whatsoever place they should be, in any part of their land.

2 Yea [*indeed*], **he sent a decree** among them, that they should not lay their hands on them to bind them, or to cast them into prison; neither should they spit upon them, nor smite them, nor cast them out of their synagogues, nor scourge [*whip*] them; neither should they cast stones at them, but **that they should have free access to their houses, and also their temples, and their sanctuaries** [*churches*].

The gospel of Christ is the only real and lasting solution to the world's problems of ethnic hatred in which children are taught to hate the people their parents and relatives hate. Such hatred is a devastating tradition. The last half of verse 3, next, teaches this principle—namely, the role of the gospel in solving this problem.

3 And thus they might go forth and preach the word according to their desires, for **the king had been converted unto the Lord, and all his household;** therefore **he sent his proclamation throughout the land** unto his people, that the word of God might have no obstruction, but that it might go forth throughout all the land, **that his people might be convinced concerning the wicked traditions of their fathers,** and **that they might be convinced that they were all brethren,** and that they ought not to murder, nor to plunder, nor to steal, nor to commit adultery, nor to commit any manner of wickedness.

4 And now it came to pass that when the king had sent forth this proclamation, that **Aaron and his**

brethren went forth from city to city, and from one house of worship to another, establishing churches, and consecrating priests and teachers throughout the land among the Lamanites, to preach and to teach the word of God among them; and thus they began to have great success.

5 And **thousands were brought to the knowledge of the Lord**, yea, thousands were brought to believe in the traditions [*righteous traditions*] of the Nephites; and they were taught the records [*the scriptures*] and prophecies which were handed down even to the present time.

6 And as sure as the Lord liveth, so sure as many as believed, or as many as were brought to the knowledge of the truth, through the preaching of Ammon and his brethren, according to the spirit of revelation and of prophecy, and the power of God working miracles in them—yea, I [*Mormon*] say unto you, as the Lord liveth, **as many of the Lamanites as believed in their preaching, and were converted unto the Lord, never did fall away.**

7 For **they became a righteous people**; they did lay down the weapons of their rebellion, that they did not fight against God any more, neither against any of their brethren.

8 Now, **these are they who were converted** unto the Lord:

Mormon will now tell us of the seven lands and cities in which these converts lived.

9 The people of the Lamanites who were in **the land of Ishmael;**

10 And also of the people of the Lamanites who were in **the land of Middoni;**

11 And also of the people of the Lamanites who were in the **city of Nephi;**

12 And also of the people of the Lamanites who were in **the land of Shilom**, and who were in **the land of Shemlon,** and in the **city of Lemuel**, and in the **city of Shimnilom.**

13 And these are the names of the cities of the Lamanites which were converted unto the Lord; and **these are they that laid down the weapons of their rebellion, yea, all their weapons of war; and they were all Lamanites.**

Next, we see the powerful influence which parents who apostatize from the Church can have on their posterity. The Amalekites and the Amulonites were descended from apostate Nephites and were apparently so hardened against the Spirit that the great conversion did not work among them. They also influenced many Lamanites to reject the missionaries' message.

14 And **the Amalekites were not converted, save** [*except*] **only one; neither were any of the Amulonites;** but they did harden their hearts, and also the hearts of the Lamanites in that part of the land wheresoever

they dwelt, yea, and all their villages and all their cities.

15 Therefore, **we have named all the cities of the Lamanites in which they did repent** and come to the knowledge of the truth, and were converted.

Next, these Lamanite converts choose to give themselves a name which will set them apart from those who did not join the Church. While we don't know anything for sure about the purpose of this name, other than what is given in verse 16, we wonder if perhaps the fact that King Benjamin gave his people another name might have played a role in their desire to have a special name for themselves. King Benjamin told his people the purpose for their distinguishing name: "that thereby they may be distinguished above all the people which the Lord God hath brought out of the land of Jerusalem . . . because they have been a diligent people in keeping the commandments of the Lord" (Mosiah 1:11).

16 And now it came to pass that **the king and those who were converted were desirous that they might have a name, that thereby they might be distinguished** [*so that people could tell them apart*] **from their brethren;** therefore the king consulted with Aaron and many of their priests, concerning the name that they should take upon them, that they might be distinguished.

17 And it came to pass that **they called their names Anti-Nephi-Lehies**; and they were called by this name and were no more called Lamanites.

We do not have any authoritative explanation as to what the name Anti-Nephi-Lehies means, other than what is given in verse 16, above, namely, that it set them apart from others in their lands. Perhaps one possibility along this line of thinking might be that the new standards and lifestyle of these converts were "anti" or opposite of the lifestyles of others who had rejected the gospel and who lived in the lands of Nephi and Lehi. There is really no point in speculating further. Perhaps we will have to wait until we get a chance to talk to Mormon in the next life to find out why they chose the name Anti-Nephi-Lehies. At any rate, the positive results of large-scale conversion and becoming a society of Saints are very predictable and are summarized next in verse 18.

18 And they began to be a **very industrious** people; yea, and they **were friendly with the Nephites;** therefore, they did open a correspondence with them, and **the curse of God** [*spiritual darkness; see also 1 Nephi 12:23*] **did no more follow them.**

ALMA 24

In this chapter, we see these new Lamanite converts to the gospel wrestle with whether or not to defend themselves against those who have become their enemies because they have joined the Church. They are more afraid of losing their souls by going back to their old bloodthirsty ways than afraid for their lives. They fear that if they take up weapons and fight, they might go back to their old ways of delighting in bloodshed and hating their enemies. They determine to avoid the risk of reverting to their old lifestyle, at all costs. There is a lesson for us in this, as we seek to make significant changes in our lives which will bring us closer to Christ.

1 AND it came to pass that **the Amalekites** [*apostate Nephites*] and the **Amulonites** [*apostate Nephites*] and the **Lamanites** who were in the land of Amulon, and also in the land of Helam, and who were in the land of Jerusalem, and in fine [*summary*], in all the land round about, **who had not been converted** and had not taken upon them the name of Anti-Nephi-Lehi, **were stirred up by the Amalekites and by the Amulonites to anger against their brethren** [*who had been converted to the Church; thus we see that apostates can do much damage in stirring up public sentiment against the Saints*].

Verse 2, next, reminds us that wicked people cannot stand a righteous leader in their government.

2 And their hatred became exceedingly sore against them, even insomuch that **they began to rebel against their king** [*who had converted to the gospel*], insomuch that **they would not** [*didn't want*] **that he should be their king;** therefore, they took up arms against the people of Anti-Nephi-Lehi.

3 Now **the king conferred the kingdom upon his son, and he called his name Anti-Nephi-Lehi.**

4 And **the king** [*Lamoni's father*] **died** in that selfsame year that the Lamanites began to make preparations for war against the people of God.

5 Now when Ammon and his brethren and all those who had come up with him saw the preparations of the Lamanites to destroy their brethren [*converts*], they came forth to the land of Midian, and there Ammon met all his brethren [*the other Nephite missionaries*]; and from thence they came to the land of Ishmael that they might hold a council with Lamoni and also with his brother Anti-Nephi-Lehi, **what they should do to defend themselves against the Lamanites.**

6 Now **there was not one soul among all the people who had been converted unto the Lord that would take up arms against their brethren;** nay, they would not even make any preparations for war; yea, and also **their king commanded them that they should not.**

In the gospel, we are taught to stay away from evil and to avoid putting ourselves into a position wherein we might be seriously tempted to violate the covenants we have made. In the next several verses, these great Lamanite converts set a marvelous example for us in following this principle.

7 Now, **these are the words which he said** unto the people concerning the matter: **I thank my God, my beloved people, that our great God has in goodness sent these our brethren, the Nephites, unto us to**

preach unto us, and to convince us of the traditions of our wicked fathers.

8 And behold, **I thank my great God** that he has given us a portion of his Spirit to soften our hearts, that we have opened a correspondence with these brethren, the Nephites.

9 And behold, **I also thank my God**, that by opening this correspondence [*association with the Nephite missionaries*] we have been convinced of our sins, and of the many murders which we have committed.

10 And **I also thank my God**, yea, my great God, that he hath granted unto us that we might repent of these things, and also that he hath forgiven us of those our many sins and murders which we have committed, and taken away the guilt from our hearts, through the merits of his Son [*the Atonement*].

11 And now behold, my brethren, **since it has been all that we could do,** [*as we were the most lost of all mankind*] **to repent of all our sins and the many murders which we have committed, and to get God to take them away from our hearts,** for it was all we could do to repent sufficiently before God that he would take away our stain—

12 Now, my best beloved brethren, since God hath taken away our stains, and our swords have become bright, **then let us stain our swords no more with the blood of our brethren.**

13 Behold, I say unto you, Nay, let us retain [*keep from using*] our swords that they be not stained with the blood of our brethren; for **perhaps, if we should stain our swords again they can no more be washed bright through the blood of the Son of our great God, which shall be shed for the atonement of our sins.**

14 And **the great God has had mercy on us, and made these things known unto us** that we might not perish; yea, and he has made these things known unto us beforehand, because he loveth our souls as well as he loveth our children; therefore, in his mercy he doth visit us by his angels, that the plan of salvation might be made known unto us as well as unto future generations.

15 Oh, how merciful is our God! And now behold, **since it has been as much as we could do to get our stains** [*past sins*] **taken away from us, and our swords are made bright, let us hide them away that they may be kept bright, as a testimony to our God at the last day, or at the day that we shall be brought to stand before him to be judged, that we have not stained our swords in the blood of our brethren since he imparted his word unto us and has made us clean thereby.**

16 And now, my brethren, if our brethren seek to destroy us, behold, **we will hide away our swords, yea, even we will bury them deep in the earth, that they may be kept bright, as a testimony that we have**

never used them, at the last day [*final Judgment Day*]; and if our brethren destroy us, behold, we shall go to our God and shall be saved.

> Perhaps you know of members who have thrown away their cigarettes, burned their pornographic materials, disconnected their computers from the internet, or found other friends or employment, etc., in order to avoid becoming involved again with former sins that were destroying their spirituality.

17 And now it came to pass that when the king had made an end of these sayings, and all the people were assembled together, **they took their swords, and all the weapons which were used for the shedding of man's blood, and they did bury them up deep in the earth.**

> Making covenants with God is a powerful way to voluntarily strengthen resolve to stay on the covenant path toward exaltation. It is a privilege to make such covenants, and the souls of these converts were saved because of it.
>
> You will see in verse 18, next, that they did much more than covenant not to take up weapons of war again.

18 And **this they did,** it being in their view **a testimony to God, and also to men,** that they never would use weapons again for the shedding of man's blood; and this they did, **vouching** [*promising*] **and covenanting with God**, that **rather than shed the blood of their brethren they would give up their own lives; and rather than take away from a brother they would give unto him; and rather than spend their days in idleness they would labor abundantly with their hands.**

19 And **thus we see** [*Mormon's commentary to us*] that, when these Lamanites were brought to believe and to know the truth, they were firm, and would suffer even unto death rather than commit sin; and thus we see that they buried their weapons of peace, or they buried the weapons of war, for peace.

20 And it came to pass that their brethren, **the Lamanites, made preparations for war, and came up to the land of Nephi** for the purpose of destroying the king, and to place another in his stead, and also of destroying the people of Anti-Nephi-Lehi out of the land.

21 Now when the people saw that they were coming against them they went out to meet them, and prostrated themselves [*laid down*] before them to the earth, and began to call on the name of the Lord; and thus they were in this attitude when **the Lamanites began to fall upon them, and began to slay them with the sword.**

22 And thus **without meeting any resistance, they did slay a thousand and five of them;** and we know that they are blessed, for they have gone to dwell with their God.

23 Now **when the Lamanites saw that their brethren would not flee from the sword,** neither would they turn aside to the right hand or to the

left, but that they would lie down and perish, and praised God even in the very act of perishing under the sword—

The example of these converts, even in death, was such that many more Lamanites were converted.

24 Now when the Lamanites saw this they did forbear [*stop*] from slaying them; and **there were many whose hearts had swollen in them** [*they developed strong feelings of sympathy*] **for those of their brethren who had fallen** under the sword, for **they repented of the things which they had done.**

25 And it came to pass that they threw down their weapons of war, and they would not take them again, for **they were stung for the murders which they had committed**; and they came down [*they lay down*] even as their brethren, relying upon the mercies of those whose arms were lifted to slay them.

26 And it came to pass that **the people of God were joined that day by more than the number who had been slain**; and **those who had been slain were righteous people, therefore we have no reason to doubt but what they were saved.**

27 And **there was not a wicked man slain among them; but there were more than a thousand brought to the knowledge of the truth**; thus we see [*Mormon's commentary, telling us what he hopes we learn from this account*] that the Lord worketh in many ways to the salvation of his people.

28 Now **the greatest number** [*the majority*] **of those of the Lamanites who slew so many of their brethren were Amalekites and Amulonites**, the greatest number of whom were after the order of the Nehors.

29 Now, **among those who joined the people of the Lord, there were none who were Amalekites or Amulonites, or who were of the order of Nehor, but they were actual descendants of Laman and Lemuel.**

Next, Mormon clearly warns of the hardness that comes upon those who have had testimonies, and who then leave the Church and the gospel.

30 And thus we can plainly discern, that **after a people have been once enlightened by the Spirit of God, and have had great knowledge of things pertaining to righteousness, and then have fallen away into sin and transgression, they become more hardened, and thus their state** [*condition*] **becomes worse than though they had never known these things.**

ALMA 25

Let me remind you that, during the time that Ammon, Aaron, Omner, and Himni (the four sons of King Mosiah II) and their missionary companions have been on their missions among the Lamanites (which will be a total of fourteen years), Alma the Younger, who is now the President of the Church, has been preaching and setting the Church in order in the land of Zarahemla. He and Amulek have converted some citizens in the wicked city of Ammonihah. Zeezrom, who was one of the chief wicked lawyers, has been converted. Angry citizens who refused to be converted have driven the convert men out of the city and burned their wives and children.

At the same time, in the land of Nephi, the Lamanites have killed many of their own people who were converted by the four sons of Mosiah and their missionary companions. But, as you just read in chapter 24, these Lamanites got sick of killing their own people and quit doing it. But they were still angry, so they decided to go kill some Nephites instead. This is one of Satan's ways of leading the wicked to commit more sins. They traveled to the borders of the land of Zarahemla where Nephites lived and completely destroyed the first city of Nephites they found, which was the wicked city of Ammonihah. Remember, these were the people who spit on Alma and kicked him out of their city when he came to preach to them and bragged that they didn't need God and that nobody could destroy them.

1 AND behold, now it came to pass that **those Lamanites were more angry because they had slain their brethren** [*the Anti-Nephi-Lehies*]; **therefore they swore vengeance upon the Nephites;** and they did no more attempt to slay the people of Anti-Nephi-Lehi at that time.

2 But **they took their armies and went over into the borders of the land of Zarahemla, and fell upon the people who were in the land of Ammonihah and destroyed them.**

3 And **after that, they had many battles with the Nephites**, in the which they were driven and slain.

4 And **among the Lamanites who were slain were almost all the seed of Amulon and his brethren, who were the priests of Noah,** and they were slain by the hands of the Nephites;

Verse 5, next, is a direct fulfillment of the prophecy of Abinadi as found in Mosiah 17:15.

5 And **the remainder** [*of Amulon's descendants*], **having fled into the east wilderness, and having usurped the power and authority over the Lamanites, caused that many of the Lamanites should perish by fire because of their belief—**

In verse 6, we are shown that God's punishments upon the wicked can lead to conversion.

6 For **many of them** [*the Lamanites who rejected conversion at first*], **after having suffered much loss and so many afflictions, began to be stirred up in remembrance of the words which Aaron and his brethren had preached to them in their land; therefore they began to disbelieve the traditions of their fathers, and to believe in the Lord**, and that he gave great power unto the Nephites; and **thus there were many of them converted** in the wilderness.

7 And it came to pass that **those rulers who were the remnant of the children of Amulon caused that**

they should be put to death, yea, all those that believed in these things.

8 Now **this martyrdom** [*being killed because of something you believe*] **caused that many of their brethren should be stirred up to anger**; and there began to be contention in the wilderness; and **the Lamanites began to hunt the seed** [*descendants*] **of Amulon** [*one of King Noah's wicked priests*] and his brethren and began to slay them; and they fled into the east wilderness.

9 And behold **they are hunted at this day** by the Lamanites. **Thus the words of Abinadi were brought to pass** [*fulfilled*], which he said concerning the seed of the priests who caused that he should suffer death by fire.

10 For he said unto them: **What ye shall do unto me shall be a type** [*symbolic*] **of things to come** [*Mosiah 13:10*].

11 And now **Abinadi was the first that suffered death by fire because of his belief in God**; now this is what he meant, that many should suffer death by fire, according as he had suffered.

12 And **he said unto the priests of Noah that their seed should cause many to be put to death, in the like manner as he was**, and that they should be scattered abroad and slain, even as a sheep having no shepherd is driven and slain by wild beasts; and now behold, these words were verified, for they were driven by the Lamanites, and they were hunted, and they were smitten.

Many more converts came later.

13 And it came to pass that **when the Lamanites saw that they could not overpower the Nephites they returned again to their own land; and many of them came over to dwell in the land of Ishmael and the land of Nephi, and did join themselves to the people of God, who were the people of Anti-Nephi-Lehi.**

14 And they did also bury their weapons of war, according as their brethren had, and **they began to be a righteous people;** and they did walk in the ways of the Lord, and did observe to keep his commandments and his statutes.

These people were still keeping the Law of Moses (the rules for worshipping God during the Old Testament), even though they knew of Christ, because He had not yet come to earth and done away with the outward performances and daily sacrifices, etc., required by that law.

15 Yea, and **they did keep the law of Moses**; for it was expedient [*necessary*] that they should keep the law of Moses as yet, **for it was not all fulfilled**. But notwithstanding [*even though they kept*] the law of Moses, **they did look forward to the coming of Christ**, considering that **the law of Moses was a type** [*symbolic*] **of his coming**, and believing that they must keep those outward performances until the time that he should be revealed unto them.

Mormon is teaching us a powerful lesson on the purpose of the Law of Moses in these verses. Most of the Jews at the time of Christ failed to understand this.

16 Now **they did not suppose that salvation came by the law of Moses; but the law of Moses did serve to strengthen their faith in Christ;** and thus they did retain a hope through faith, unto eternal salvation, relying upon the spirit of prophecy, which spake of those things to come.

17 And now behold, **Ammon, and Aaron, and Omner, and Himni, and their brethren did rejoice exceedingly, for the success which they had had among the Lamanites**, seeing that the Lord had granted unto them according to their prayers, and that he had also verified his word unto them in every particular [*detail*].

ALMA 26

It appears now to be getting close to the end of the fourteen-year missions of the sons of Mosiah and their companions among the Lamanites. Mormon takes time here to tell us about the rejoicing of Ammon with his brothers and the others who came with them on this mission. It could appear at first that Ammon is boasting. In fact, his brother, Aaron, will think so, but such is not the case. As we listen to Ammon's words, we too can rejoice in the work of the Lord to reclaim His children and bring them safely back home to the gospel.

1 AND now, **these are the words of Ammon to his brethren,** which say thus: My brothers [*Aaron, Omner, and Himni*] and my brethren [*their missionary companions*], behold I say unto you, **how great reason have we to rejoice**; for could we have supposed when we started from the land of Zarahemla that God would have granted unto us such great blessings?

2 And now, **I ask, what great blessings has he bestowed upon us?** Can ye tell?

3 Behold, **I answer** for you; for **our brethren, the Lamanites**, were in darkness, yea, even in the darkest abyss [*deepest gulf; hell*], but behold, how many of them **are brought to behold the marvelous light of God!** And this is the blessing which hath been bestowed upon us, that **we have been made instruments in the hands of God to bring about this great work**.

4 Behold, **thousands of them do rejoice, and have been brought into the fold** [*church*] **of God**.

5 Behold, **the field was ripe** [*ready to harvest*], and blessed are ye, for ye did thrust in the sickle [*a sharp-bladed tool for harvesting grain*], and did reap [*harvest*] with your might, yea, all the day long did ye labor; and behold the number of your sheaves [*bundles of grain stocks*]! And they shall be gathered into the garners [*barns; symbolic of being taken to heaven*], that they are not wasted.

Next, Ammon uses many symbols from his agricultural society to describe how these converts will be saved and protected by the Lord. Picture fields of grain (symbolic of converts) ready for harvest in your mind as you continue to read.

6 Yea, **they shall not be beaten down by the storm** at the last day [*on Final Judgment Day*]; yea, **neither shall they be harrowed** [*torn*] **up by the whirlwinds**; but **when the storm cometh they shall be gathered together in their place, that the storm cannot penetrate to them**; yea, **neither shall they be driven with fierce winds whithersoever the enemy** [*Satan*] **listeth** [*desires*] **to carry them.**

7 But behold, **they are in the hands of the Lord of the harvest**, and they are his; and he will raise them up [*exalt them*] at the last day [*Judgment Day*].

8 **Blessed be the name of our God**; let us sing to his praise, yea, let us give thanks to his holy name, for he doth work righteousness forever.

9 For **if we had not come up out of the land of Zarahemla, these our dearly beloved brethren, who have so dearly beloved us, would still have been racked with hatred against us, yea, and they would also have been strangers to God.**

At this point, Aaron felt that Ammon was boasting.

10 And it came to pass that when Ammon had said these words, his brother **Aaron rebuked** [*scolded*] **him, saying: Ammon, I fear that thy joy doth carry thee away unto boasting.**

11 But Ammon said unto him: **I do not boast in my own strength**, nor in my own wisdom; but behold, my joy is full, yea, my heart is brim with joy, and **I will rejoice in my God**.

12 Yea, I know that I am nothing; as to my strength I am weak; therefore **I will not boast of myself, but I will boast of my God**, for in his strength I can do all things; yea, behold, many mighty miracles we have wrought in this land, for which we will praise his name forever.

13 Behold [*look at*], **how many thousands of our brethren has he loosed from the pains of hell**; and they are brought to sing redeeming love, and this because of the power of his word which is in us, therefore **have we not great reason to rejoice?**

14 Yea, **we have reason to praise him forever**, for he is the Most High God, and has loosed our brethren from the chains of hell [*spiritual darkness and bondage to the devil*].

15 Yea, **they were encircled about with everlasting darkness and destruction**; but **behold, he has brought them into his everlasting light, yea, into everlasting salvation**; and they are encircled about with the matchless bounty [*reward; abundance*] of his love; yea, and we have been instruments in his hands of

doing this great and marvelous work.

16 **Therefore, let us glory, yea, we will glory in the Lord**; yea, we will rejoice, for our joy is full; yea, we will praise our God forever. Behold, **who can glory too much in the Lord?** Yea, who can say too much of his great power, and of his mercy, and of his long-suffering towards the children of men? Behold, I say unto you, **I cannot say the smallest part which I feel.**

17 **Who could have supposed that our God would** have been so merciful as to have **snatched us from our awful, sinful, and polluted state?**

18 Behold, **we went forth even in wrath**, with mighty threatenings **to destroy his church** [*see Mosiah 27:10*].

19 Oh then, why did he not consign us [*turn us over*] to an awful destruction, yea, **why did he not let the sword of his justice fall upon us**, and doom us to eternal despair?

20 Oh, my soul, almost as it were, fleeth at the thought. Behold, he did not exercise his justice upon us, but in **his great mercy hath brought us over that everlasting gulf of death and misery**, even **to the salvation of our souls**.

Next, Ammon exclaims that none but those who are spiritually awake and have felt the redeeming love of Christ can possibly understand the joy about which he is speaking.

21 And now behold, my brethren, **what natural man is there that knoweth these things?** I say unto you, there is none that knoweth these things, save it be the penitent [*the repentant*].

22 Yea, **he that repenteth and exerciseth faith, and bringeth forth good works, and prayeth continually** without ceasing—**unto such it is given to know the mysteries of God** [*the basics of the gospel, such as faith, repentance, baptism, gift of the Holy Ghost, priesthood ordinances, doctrines of the plan of salvation, etc.; see Bible Dictionary, page 736, under "Mystery"*]; yea, unto such it shall be given to reveal things which never have been revealed; yea, and it shall be given unto such to bring thousands of souls to repentance, even as it has been given unto us to bring these our brethren to repentance.

23 Now **do ye remember, my brethren, that we said unto our brethren in the land of Zarahemla, we go up to the land of Nephi, to preach unto our brethren, the Lamanites, and they laughed us to scorn?**

24 For they said unto us: **Do ye suppose that ye can bring the Lamanites to the knowledge of the truth?** Do ye suppose that ye can convince the Lamanites of the incorrectness of the traditions of their fathers, as stiffnecked [*stubborn*] a people as they are; whose hearts delight in the shedding of blood; whose days have been spent in the grossest iniquity; whose ways have been the ways of a transgressor from the beginning? Now my brethren, ye remember that this was their language.

There is a saying that goes something to the effect that if you want to destroy your enemy, make him your friend. The same principle is demonstrated in the next few verses.

25 And moreover **they did say: Let us take up arms against them, that we destroy them and their iniquity out of the land, lest they overrun us and destroy us.**

26 **But behold, my beloved brethren, we came into the wilderness not with the intent to destroy our brethren, but with the intent that perhaps we might save some few of their souls.**

27 Now when our hearts were depressed, and we were about to turn back, behold, **the Lord comforted us**, and said: Go amongst thy brethren, the Lamanites, and bear with patience thine afflictions, and I will give unto you success.

As mentioned previously, because we have been called by the Lord to fulfill a certain task or mission, it does not guarantee that it will be easy. Often, we learn patience and love through affliction, attributes that we may not develop otherwise. It is helpful to keep in mind that we are gods in training. And patience, love, and perseverance in the face of rejection are necessary attributes for gods to have.

Next, Ammon mentions several of the trials that he and his missionary companions endured.

28 And now behold, we have come, and been forth amongst them; and **we have been patient in our sufferings**, and **we have suffered every privation** [*lack of comfort and basic needs*]; yea, we have traveled from house to house, relying upon the mercies of the world—not upon the mercies of the world alone but upon the mercies of God.

29 And we have entered into their houses and taught them, and we have taught them in their streets; yea, and we have taught them upon their hills; and we have also entered into their temples and their synagogues and taught them; and **we have been cast out**, and **mocked**, and **spit upon**, and **smote upon our cheeks**; and we have been **stoned**, and taken and **bound with strong cords**, and **cast into prison**; and through the power and wisdom of God we have been delivered again.

30 And **we have suffered all manner of afflictions**, and **all this, that perhaps we might be the means of saving some soul**; and we supposed that our joy would be full if perhaps we could be the means of saving some.

Verse 30, above, is a reminder of the value of each individual soul. Another place we are taught this is in D&C 18:10–15.

31 Now behold, we can look forth and see the fruits of our labors; and are they few? I say unto you, Nay, they are many; yea, and **we can witness of their sincerity, because of their love towards their brethren and also towards us.**

32 **For behold, they had rather sacrifice their lives than even to take the life of their enemy; and they have buried their weapons of war deep in the earth, because of their love towards their brethren.**

33 And now behold I say unto you, **has there been so great love in all the land?** Behold, I say unto you, **Nay, there has not**, even among the Nephites.

34 For behold, they would take up arms against their brethren; they would not suffer [*permit*] themselves to be slain. But behold how many of these have laid down their lives; and **we know that they have gone to their God**, because of their love and of their hatred to sin.

35 Now **have we not reason to rejoice? Yea, I say unto you, there never were men that had so great reason to rejoice as we, since the world began; yea, and my joy is carried away, even unto boasting in my God;** for he has all power, all wisdom, and all understanding; he comprehendeth all things, and he is a merciful Being, even unto salvation, to those who will repent and believe on his name.

36 Now **if this is boasting, even so will I boast**; for this is my life and my light, my joy and my salvation, and my redemption from everlasting wo. Yea, blessed is the name of my God, who has been mindful [*is always aware*] of this people, who are a branch of the tree of Israel, and has been lost from its body [*the rest of Israel* in a strange land [*the Americas*]; yea, I say, blessed be the name of my God, who has been mindful of us, wanderers in a strange land.

37 Now my brethren, we see that **God is mindful of every people**, whatsoever land they may be in; yea, he numbereth his people [*He knows every one of His children*], and his bowels [*deep feelings*] of mercy are over all the earth. **Now this is my joy, and my great thanksgiving; yea, and I will give thanks unto my God forever.** Amen.

ALMA 27

As you know, there were many Lamanites who did not join the Church. They were stirred up by the Amalekites and the Amulonites to fight against the Lamanite converts (Alma 24:1), who had chosen the name Anti-Nephi-Lehies so that others could tell them apart from the other Lamanites. When they came to war against them, the converts offered no resistance (Alma 24:21–22), and finally, after killing 1,005 of the converts, they stopped. Several more Lamanites joined the church, but those who did not decided to kill some Nephites to satisfy their lust for blood. They traveled swiftly to the borders of Nephite territory and destroyed all of the inhabitants of the wicked city of Ammonihah (where Alma had been spit upon and driven out, had returned, met Amulek, preached, and been imprisoned and so forth).

These angry Lamanites had attempted

to destroy many more Nephites, but had ultimately been driven back, and as we begin this chapter, they have returned home to the land of Nephi. We said before that it is Satan's way to be angry at someone, and, as indicated in verse 2, below, the Amalekites once again stir up anger against the Lamanite converts.

1 NOW it came to pass that when
**those Lamanites who had gone
to war against the Nephites** had
found, after their many struggles to
destroy them, that it was in vain [*use-
less*] to seek their destruction, they **re-
turned again to the land of Nephi**.

2 And it came to pass that **the Ama-
lekites, because of their loss, were
exceedingly angry.** And **when they
saw that they could not seek re-
venge from the Nephites, they be-
gan to stir up the people in anger
against their brethren, the people
of Anti-Nephi-Lehi**; therefore they
began again to destroy them.

3 Now **this people again refused to
take their arms, and they suffered
themselves to be slain** according to
the desires of their enemies.

4 Now when Ammon and his breth-
ren saw this work of destruction
among those whom they so dearly
beloved, and among those who had
so dearly beloved them—for they
were treated as though they were an-
gels sent from God to save them from
everlasting destruction—therefore,
**when Ammon and his brethren
saw this great work of destruction,
they were moved with compassion,
and they said unto the king**:

You can sense the serious problem faced by the Anti-Nephi-Lehies. If they remain in their own land, they will be slaughtered. If they go to the land of Zarahemla, where they themselves have killed Nephites before their conversion to the Church, they will likely face destruction, too. It is in this setting that we are taught of true brotherly love on the part of the members of the Church in Zarahemla, where Alma is the President of the Church.

Next, Ammon and his brethren suggest a plan to the king of the converted Lamanites (Alma 24:3–5).

5 **Let us gather together this people
of the Lord** [*the converted Lamanites*],
**and let us go down to the land
of Zarahemla** to our brethren the
Nephites, and flee out of the hands
of our enemies, that we be not de-
stroyed.

6 **But the king said unto them: Be-
hold, the Nephites will destroy us,
because of the many murders and
sins we have committed against
them.**

7 And **Ammon said: I will go and
inquire of the Lord, and if he say
unto us, go down unto our breth-
ren, will ye go?**

8 And **the king said** unto him: **Yea,
if the Lord saith unto us go, we
will go down unto our brethren,
and we will be their slaves** until we
repair unto them the many murders
and sins which we have committed
against them.

9 But **Ammon said** unto him: **It is against the law** of our brethren, which was established by my father, **that there should be any slaves among them**; therefore **let us go down and rely upon the mercies of our brethren** [*the Nephites*].

10 But **the king said** unto him: **Inquire of the Lord** [*ask the Lord*], **and if he saith unto us go, we will go; otherwise we will perish in the land.**

11 And it came to pass that Ammon went and inquired of the Lord, and **the Lord said** unto him:

12 **Get this people out of this land**, that they perish not; for Satan has great hold on the hearts of the Amalekites [*apostate Nephites*], who do stir up the Lamanites to anger against their brethren to slay them; therefore get thee out of this land; and blessed are this people in this generation, for I will preserve them.

13 And now it came to pass that **Ammon went and told the king** all the words which the Lord had said unto him.

14 And **they gathered together** all their people, yea, **all the people of the Lord**, and did gather together all their flocks and herds, and departed out of the land, and came into the wilderness which divided the land of Nephi from the land of Zarahemla, and came over near the borders of the land.

Unknown to Ammon and his companions, Alma was at this moment heading south from the land of Gideon, where he had been teaching and strengthening the Church among the Nephites (Alma 17:1). In a short while, they will run into each other as the missionaries head north to Zarahemla.

15 And it came to pass that **Ammon said unto them: Behold, I and my brethren will go forth into the land of Zarahemla, and ye shall remain here until we return**; and **we will try the hearts** [*check out the feelings*] **of our brethren** [*members of the Church in Zarahemla*], whether [*if*] they will [*desire*] that ye shall come into their land.

16 And it came to pass that **as Ammon was going forth into the land, that he and his brethren met Alma**, over in the place of which has been spoken; and behold, **this was a joyful meeting** [*understatement*].

Next, Mormon describes this great joy.

17 Now **the joy of Ammon was so great even that** he was full; yea, he was swallowed up in the joy of his God, even to the exhausting of his strength; and **he fell again to the earth**.

18 **Now was not this exceeding joy? Behold, this is joy which none receiveth save it be the truly penitent and humble seeker of happiness.**

19 Now **the joy of Alma in meeting his brethren was truly great**, and **also the joy of Aaron, of Omner,**

and Himni; but behold their joy was not that to exceed their strength [*in other words, they did not pass out*].

20 And now it came to pass that **Alma conducted** [*accompanied*] **his brethren back to the land of Zarahemla**; even to his own house. And they went and told the chief judge all the things that had happened unto them in the land of Nephi, among their brethren, the Lamanites.

Next, the people vote whether or not to allow the Lamanite converts to enter their land and settle among them.

21 And it came to pass that **the chief judge sent a proclamation throughout all the land, desiring the voice of the people** [*asking the people to vote*] **concerning the admitting their brethren, who were the people of Anti-Nephi-Lehi.**

22 And it came to pass that the voice of the people came [*the results of the voting came in*], saying: Behold, **we will give up the land of Jershon**, which is on the east by the sea, which joins the land Bountiful, which is on the south of the land Bountiful; and this land Jershon is the land which we will give **unto our brethren for an inheritance.**

This was a very Christlike act on the part of the Saints in the land of Zarahemla. It was not only a matter of generously giving up good land, but also a matter of defending them in battles against the Lamanites, since all of the Anti-Nephi-Lehies had made a covenant with the Lord never to take up weapons and shed blood again. In about ten to twelve years, we will see two thousand stripling warriors, the children of these Anti-Nephi-Lehies, go to war with Captain Moroni's armies, under the leadership of Helaman (Alma's son). Helaman persuaded their parents to keep their covenant to not go to war, and these young warriors went in their place. We will read about them beginning in Alma 53.

23 And behold, **we will set our armies between the land Jershon and the land Nephi, that we may protect our brethren in the land Jershon**; and this we do for our brethren, on account of their fear to take up arms against their brethren lest they should commit sin; and this their great fear came because of their sore [*deep and difficult*] repentance which they had, on account of their many murders and their awful wickedness.

The Nephites wisely placed an important condition on defending the new converts from Lamanite enemies, namely, that the Anti-Nephi-Lehies would provide supplies and material support for the Nephite armies.

24 And now behold, this will we do unto our brethren, that they may inherit the land Jershon; and **we will guard them from their enemies with our armies, on condition that** [*if*] **they will give us a portion of their substance** [*food and whatever else is needed*] **to assist us that we may maintain our armies.**

Imagine how Ammon felt as he returned to the Lamanite converts with this wonderful news!

25 Now, it came to pass that **when Ammon had heard this, he returned to the people of Anti-Nephi-Lehi, and also Alma with him**, into the wilderness, where they had pitched their tents, **and made known unto them all these things**. And Alma also related unto them his conversion, with Ammon and Aaron, and his brethren. [*This must have been a great meeting!*]

In verse 26, next, the Anti-Nephi-Lehies are given another name by the Nephites: "the people of Ammon." They are also referred to as "Ammonites."

26 And it came to pass that it did cause great joy among them. And they went down into the land of Jershon, and took possession of the land of Jershon; and **they were called by the Nephites the people of Ammon**; therefore they were distinguished [*known*] by that name ever after.

27 And they were among the people of Nephi, and also numbered among the people who were of the church of God. And they were also distinguished for their zeal towards God, and also towards men; for **they were perfectly honest and upright in all things; and they were firm in the faith of Christ, even unto the end.**

28 **And they did look upon shedding the blood of their brethren with the greatest abhorrence** [*disgust, horror*]**; and they never could be prevailed upon** [*convinced*] **to take up arms against their brethren; and they never did look upon death with any degree of terror, for** [*because of*] **their hope and views of Christ and the resurrection**; therefore, death was swallowed up to them by the victory of Christ over it.

29 Therefore, **they would suffer death in the most aggravating and distressing manner** which could be inflicted by their brethren, **before they would take the sword or cimeter to smite them** [*to defend themselves*].

30 And **thus they were a zealous** [*energetic in living the gospel*] **and beloved people**, a **highly favored** [*much blessed*] **people of the Lord**.

ALMA 28

Sometimes we wonder why the enemies of the Church can't just leave us alone, yet, they don't seem to be capable of it. Perhaps it is because the devil is their master, often without their knowing it, and his goal is to destroy the work of God. At any rate, he is a master of stirring people up with an irrational and unreasonable hatred against righteous people.

This terrible hatred is demonstrated as the unconverted Lamanites follow the Anti-Nephi-Lehies all the way to the land of Zarahemla with the intent of destroying them. In the resulting battle, many Nephites will give their lives defending their land and the new converts against their common enemies, the Lamanites.

1 AND now it came to pass that **after the people of Ammon were established in the land of Jershon**, and a church also established in the land of Jershon, **and the armies of the Nephites were set round about the land of Jershon**, yea, in all the borders round about the land of Zarahemla; **behold the armies of the Lamanites had followed their brethren** [*the Anti-Nephi-Lehies, or the people of Ammon*] **into the wilderness.**

2 And thus **there was a tremendous battle**; yea, even such an one as never had been known among all the people in the land from the time Lehi left Jerusalem; yea, and **tens of thousands of the Lamanites were slain** and scattered abroad.

3 Yea, and **also there was a tremendous slaughter among the people of Nephi**; nevertheless, the Lamanites were driven and scattered, and the people of Nephi returned again to their land.

4 And now **this was a time that there was a great mourning and lamentation** [*weeping for the loss of loved ones*] heard throughout all the land, among all the people of Nephi—

5 Yea, the cry of widows mourning for their husbands, and also of fathers mourning for their sons, and the daughter for the brother, yea, the brother for the father; and **thus the cry of mourning was heard among all of them, mourning for their kindred** [*relatives*] **who had been slain**.

6 And now surely **this was a sorrowful day**; yea, **a time of solemnity** [*being very serious about life*], and **a time of much fasting and prayer**.

Mormon now concludes his account of the missions of the sons of Mosiah and their companions among the Lamanites. He points out several lessons he hopes we learn from this account.

7 And **thus endeth the fifteenth year of the reign of the judges** over the people of Nephi [*it has been 15 years since King Mosiah II set up the new form of government for the Nephites, namely a democratic government with judges*];

8 And **this is the account of Ammon and his brethren**, their journeyings in the land of Nephi, **their sufferings** in the land, their **sorrows**, and their **afflictions**, and their **incomprehensible joy, and the reception and safety of the brethren in the land of Jershon**. And now may **the Lord, the Redeemer of all men, bless their souls forever.**

9 And **this is the account of the wars and contentions among the Nephites, and also the wars between the Nephites and the Lamanites**; and the fifteenth year of the reign of the judges is ended.

10 And from **the first year to the fifteenth has brought** to pass the **destruction** of many thousand lives; yea, it has brought to pass **an awful scene of bloodshed**.

11 And the bodies of many thousands are laid low in the earth, while

the bodies of many thousands are moldering in heaps upon the face of the earth; yea, and **many thousands are mourning for the loss of their kindred, because they have reason to fear, according to the promises of the Lord, that they are consigned to a state of endless wo** [*the final state of the wicked*].

12 While **many thousands of others truly mourn for the loss of their kindred, yet they rejoice and exult** [*have joyous feelings*] **in the hope, and even know, according to the promises of the Lord, that they are raised to dwell at the right hand of God** [*are saved in heaven*], **in a state of never–ending happiness** [*the final state of the righteous*].

13 And **thus we** see how great the inequality of man is because of sin and transgression, and the power of the devil, which comes by the cunning plans which he hath devised to ensnare the hearts of men.

14 And **thus we see** the great call of diligence of men to labor in the vineyards of the Lord [*the importance of missionaries*]; and thus we see the great reason of sorrow, and also of rejoicing—sorrow because of death and destruction among men, and joy because of the light of Christ unto life.

ALMA 29

This is one of the better-known chapters in the Book of Mormon. The first verses have even been set to beautiful music. Alma knows the joy that comes from accepting and living the gospel with deep conviction and commitment. He has seen the results in his own life and in the lives of countless others, including his friends, Ammon, Aaron, Omner, and Himni, who have just returned from tremendously successful missions to the Lamanites.

Alma's heart and soul find expression in inspired words as he tells of his deep desire to take the gospel to all people.

1 **O that I were an angel, and could have the wish of mine heart, that I might go forth and speak with the trump of God, with a voice to shake the earth, and cry repentance unto every people!**

2 Yea, **I would declare unto every soul**, as with the voice of thunder, **repentance and the plan of redemption** [*the doctrines of the plan of salvation*], that they should repent and come unto our God, **that there might not be more sorrow upon all the face of the earth**.

3 But behold, I am a man, and do sin in my wish; for **I ought to be content** with the things which the Lord hath allotted unto me.

4 I ought not to harrow up in my desires, the firm decree of a just God, for **I know that he granteth unto men according to their desire, whether it be unto death or unto life** [*all people are given agency, and I must not violate it*]; yea, I know that he allotteth unto men, yea, decreeth unto them decrees which are unalterable [*can't be changed, such as the*

laws of justice and mercy], according to their wills [*agency*], whether they be unto salvation or unto destruction.

5 Yea, and I know that good and evil have come before all men; he that knoweth not good from evil is blameless; but **he that knoweth good and evil, to him it is given according to his desires, whether he desireth good or evil, life or death, joy or remorse of conscience**.

6 Now, seeing that I know these things, **why should I desire** more than to perform the work to which I have been called?

7 **Why should I desire** that I were an angel, that I could speak unto all the ends of the earth?

Next, Alma emphasizes that everyone will get the opportunity to understand the gospel in language and circumstances that are completely fair, and then accept or reject it. From latter-day revelation, we know that for some, this will be in the spirit world mission field. See D&C 138.

8 For behold, **the Lord doth grant unto all nations, of their own nation and tongue, to teach his word**, yea, in wisdom, all that he seeth fit that they should have; therefore we see that the Lord doth counsel in wisdom, **according to that which is just and true**.

9 I know that which the Lord hath commanded me, and I glory in it. I do not glory of myself, but I glory in that which the Lord hath commanded me; yea, and **this is my glory, that perhaps I may be an instrument in the hands of God to bring some soul to repentance; and this is my joy.**

10 And behold, **when I see many of my brethren truly penitent** [*repentant*]**, and coming to the Lord their God, then is my soul filled with joy**; then do I remember what the Lord has done for me, yea, even that he hath heard my prayer; yea, then do I remember his merciful arm which he extended towards me.

In verse 10, above, Alma reminds us of the importance of remembering past blessings from the Lord. This is a great stabilizing factor in the lives of true Saints.

11 Yea, and **I also remember** the captivity of my fathers; for I surely do know that the Lord did deliver them out of bondage, and by this did establish his church; yea, the Lord God, the God of Abraham, the God of Isaac, and the God of Jacob, did deliver them out of bondage.

12 Yea, **I have always remembered** the captivity of my fathers; and that same God who delivered them out of the hands of the Egyptians did deliver them out of bondage.

13 Yea, and **that same God did establish his church among them**; yea, and **that same God hath called me by a holy calling, to preach the word unto this people, and hath given me much success, in the which my joy is full**.

14 But **I do not joy in my own success alone**, but my joy is more full because of the success of my brethren [*including Ammon, Aaron, Omner, and Himni*], who have been up to the land of Nephi.

15 Behold, **they have labored exceedingly** [*worked very hard*], and have brought forth much fruit [*a rich harvest of converts*]; and how great shall be their reward!

16 Now, **when I think of the success of these my brethren** my soul is carried away, even to the separation of it from the body, as it were, so great is my joy.

> As the President of the Church, Alma leaves a wonderful blessing upon these missionaries and converts in verse 17, next. Perhaps you have been in congregations when our Prophet today has left such blessings upon the Saints.

17 And now **may God grant unto these, my brethren, that they may sit down in the kingdom of God** [*in celestial glory*]; yea, and also all those who are the fruit of their labor [*all their converts*] that they may go no more out [*that they may be with God eternally*], but that they may praise him forever. And may God grant that it may be done according to my words, even as I have spoken. Amen.

ALMA 30

As we begin chapter 30, it has been about two years since the Lamanite converts left their own lands and followed Ammon and his brothers to Zarahemla, where the Nephites gave them the land of Jershon in which to settle. As reported in Alma 28:1, the unconverted Lamanites were still wicked and followed these Anti-Nephi-Lehies (or people of Ammon, as they will be called from now on in the Book of Mormon) to the land of Zarahemla and a tremendous battle with the Nephites followed (Alma 28:3).

In this chapter, we will meet another "Anti-Christ." We met one by the name of Nehor in Alma, chapter one. The one in this chapter is named Korihor. An Anti-Christ is a person who teaches the people that there will be no Christ. Anti-Christs usually teach other very damaging false doctrines such as: we can do whatever we want because there will be no Judgment Day, there is no need for repentance and baptism, no one can know what will happen in the future, there is no such thing as good and evil, and so forth.

Alma chapters 30 through 42 are especially rich in doctrine and counsel for daily living. And so, I will provide even more notes and commentary than usual. You may wish to put several of these notes into your own scriptures, plus others which you come up with yourself as you study. These chapters are excellent examples of why we call our scriptures the "standard works." They are the "standards" by which we can measure all philosophies, doctrines, ideas, etc., in order to avoid being deceived and led astray by Satan.

1 BEHOLD, now it came to pass that **after the people of Ammon**

were established in the land of Jershon, yea, **and also after the Lamanites were driven out of the land**, and their dead were buried by the people of the land—

2 Now **their dead were not numbered** [*counted*] because of the greatness of their numbers; neither were the dead of the Nephites numbered—but it came to pass after they had buried their dead, and also after the days of fasting, and mourning, and prayer, (and it was in the sixteenth year of the reign of the judges over the people of Nephi) **there began to be continual peace throughout all the land.**

3 Yea, and **the people did observe to keep the commandments of the Lord**; and they were strict in observing the ordinances of God, according to the law of Moses; for they were taught to keep the law of Moses until it should be fulfilled.

4 And thus the people did **have no disturbance in all the sixteenth year** of the reign of the judges over the people of Nephi.

5 And it came to pass that in the commencement of the seventeenth year of the reign of the judges, **there was continual peace**.

6 But it came to pass in the latter end of the seventeenth year, **there came a man** [*Korihor; see verse 12*] **into the land of Zarahemla, and he was Anti-Christ**, for **he began to preach unto the people against the prophecies** which had been spoken by the prophets, concerning the coming of Christ.

As is the case with Korihor, many in our day take advantage of laws that protect religious freedom in order to gain wealth and popularity. In so doing, they undermine the basic strengths of society, and thus it becomes obvious that they are working for Satan, either knowingly or without being aware of it.

7 Now **there was no law against a man's belief** [*their government gave them religious freedom*]; for it was strictly contrary to [*against*] the commands of God that there should be a law which should bring men on to unequal grounds [*would make people unequal in the eyes of the law*].

8 For thus saith the scripture: **Choose ye this day, whom ye will serve**.

9 Now if a man desired to serve God, it was his privilege; or rather**, if he believed in God it was his privilege to serve him; but if he did not believe in him there was no law to punish him**.

In our society today, all but one of the crimes mentioned in verse 10, next, are punished by law.

10 But **if he murdered** he was punished unto death; and **if he robbed** he was also punished; and **if he stole** he was also punished; and **if he committed adultery** he was also punished; yea, for all this wickedness they were punished.

Unfortunately, adultery is not considered a crime by many today, even though it undermines the spiritual and moral fiber of a nation, which leads to destruction. Satan has scored a major victory through his widespread deception on this matter.

11 For **there was a law that men should be judged according to their crimes.** Nevertheless, there was no law against a man's belief; therefore, a man was punished only for the crimes which he had done; therefore all men were on equal grounds.

We will now go through verses 12–31, **bolding** the main teachings, philosophies, and attitudes taught by Korihor. He uses emotionally powerful words and phrases to lead people away from God and the Church. Notice how many are around us today. When we are finished with this, we will repeat these verses and point out a few more things.

Korihor's major teachings, philosophies, attitudes and ridicule of the true gospel of Christ

12 And **this Anti–Christ, whose name was Korihor**, (and the law could have no hold upon him) **began to preach** unto the people that there should be **no Christ.** And after this manner did he preach, saying:

13 O ye that are bound down under a **foolish and a vain hope**, why do ye **yoke yourselves** with such **foolish things**? **Why do ye look for a Christ?** For **no man can know of anything which is to come** [*there is no such thing as prophets and prophecy*].

14 Behold, these things **which ye call** [*sarcasm*] prophecies, **which ye say** are handed down by holy prophets, behold, **they are foolish traditions** [*righteous traditions*] of your fathers.

15 **How do ye know** of their surety? Behold, **ye cannot know of things which ye do not see**; therefore **ye cannot know that there shall be a Christ.**

16 **Ye look forward and say that ye see a remission** [*forgiveness*] **of your sins.** But behold, it is **the effect of a frenzied** [*over-excited, crazy*] **mind**; and this **derangement** [*messed up condition*] of your minds comes because of the **traditions of your fathers**, which lead you away into a **belief of things which are not so**.

17 And many more such things did he say unto them, telling them that **there could be no atonement** made for the sins of men, but **every man fared** [*gets along*] **in this life according to the management of the creature** [*however he or she wants to run his or her life; situational ethics; there are no absolute rules*]; therefore **every man prospered according to his genius**, and that **every man conquered according to his strength**; and **whatsoever a man did was no crime** [*there is no such thing as right and wrong, good and evil, sin*].

18 And thus he did preach unto them, leading away the hearts of many, causing them to lift up their heads in their wickedness, yea, leading away many women, and also men, to commit whoredoms—telling them that

when a man was dead, that was the end thereof [*no life after death, therefore, no ultimate accountability*].

19 Now **this man** [*Korihor*] **went over to the land of Jershon also, to preach** these things among the people of Ammon, who were once the people of the Lamanites.

20 But behold **they were more wise** than many of the Nephites; for they took him, and bound him, and carried him before Ammon, who was a high priest over that people.

21 And it came to pass that he caused that he should be carried out of the land. And **he came over into the land of Gideon, and began to preach** unto them also; and here he did not have much success, for he was taken and bound and carried before the high priest, and also the chief judge over the land.

22 And it came to pass that the high priest said unto him: **Why do ye go about perverting** [*changing*] **the ways of the Lord?** Why do ye teach this people that there shall be no Christ, to interrupt their rejoicings? Why do ye speak against all the prophecies of the holy prophets?

23 Now the high priest's name was Giddonah. And **Korihor said** unto him: Because **I do not teach the foolish traditions of your fathers** [*ancestors*], and because I do not teach this people to bind themselves down under the **foolish ordinances and performances** which are **laid down by ancient priests, to usurp** [*take*] **power and authority over them, to keep them in ignorance** [*to keep people from knowing much*], **that they may not lift up their heads** [*to keep them depressed and destroy their happiness*], **but be brought down according to thy words** [*ancient priests did this to keep their people in bondage, to keep them under their thumb*].

For the next few verses, Korihor will use a rather powerful and cunning technique, namely the "I say . . . you say, you say . . . but I say" method of persuading the people to believe his teachings.

24 **Ye say** [*sarcasm*] that **this people is a free** people. Behold, **I say they are in bondage. Ye say** that those ancient **prophecies are true**. Behold, **I say** that **ye do not know that they are true**.

25 **Ye say** that **this people is a guilty and a fallen people**, because of the transgression of a parent [*the fall of Adam and Eve*]. Behold, **I say** that **a child is not guilty because of its parents.**

Did you notice that Korihor just tossed in a true doctrine to make his false doctrines sound true? At the end of verse 25, above, he, in effect, gave the second article of faith: "We believe that men will be punished for their own sins, and not for Adam's transgression."

26 And **ye also say** that **Christ shall come.** But behold, **I say** that **ye do not know that there shall be a Christ.** And **ye say** also that **he shall**

be slain for the sins of the world—

27 And thus **ye lead away this people after the foolish traditions of your fathers**, and according to your own desires; and **ye keep them down**, even as it were **in bondage**, that ye may **glut yourselves** [*live high and mighty*] **with the labors of their hands**, that **they durst** [*dare*] **not look up** with boldness [*they don't even dare look up because of your grip on them*], and that **they durst not enjoy their rights and privileges.**

28 Yea, **they durst not make use of that which is their own** lest they should offend their priests, who do **yoke them** according to their desires, and have brought them to believe, by their **traditions** and their **dreams** and their **whims** and their **visions** and their **pretended mysteries**, that they should, if they did not do according to their words, **offend some unknown being, who they say is God**—a being **who never has been seen or known, who never was nor ever will be.**

29 Now when the high priest and the chief judge saw the hardness of his heart, yea, when they saw that he would revile even against God, they would not make any reply to his words; but they caused that he should be bound; and they delivered him up into the hands of the officers [*they arrested him*], and **sent him to the land of Zarahemla, that he might be brought before Alma**, and the chief judge who was governor over all the land.

30 And it came to pass that **when he was brought before Alma** and the chief judge, **he did go on in the same manner** [*say the same things*] as he did in the land of Gideon; yea, he went on to blaspheme [*speak disrespectfully of God*].

31 And he did rise up in great swelling words before Alma, and did revile against [*strongly criticize*] the priests and teachers, **accusing them of leading away the people after the silly traditions** of their fathers, for the sake of **glutting** on the labors of the people.

We see much ridicule of that which is good and righteous and much emotional debate against the standards upheld by the Saints of God in our day. As stated previously, Satan's methods do not change. We would do well to use what Mormon has pointed out to us in these verses as a "standard" against which to measure such things that confront us in our lives.

We will now repeat verses 12–31 and explain some more things this time through.

VERSES 12–31 REPEATED

12 And this **Anti–Christ, whose name was Korihor**, [*and the law could have no hold upon him*] **began to preach unto the people that there should be no Christ**. And after this manner did he preach, saying:

13 O ye that are bound down under a foolish and a vain [*useless*] hope, why do ye yoke yourselves with such foolish things? **Why do ye look for**

a Christ? For **no man can know of anything which is to come.**

In saying that no one can know the future, at the end of verse 13, Korihor has just contradicted what he said in verse 12 wherein he claims to know the future sufficiently to know that there will be no Christ!

14 Behold, **these things which ye call prophecies**, which ye say are handed down by holy prophets, behold, they **are foolish traditions of your fathers.**

15 **How do ye know of their surety** [*how do you know that they are true*]? Behold, **ye cannot know of things which ye do not see**; therefore ye cannot know that there shall be a Christ.

One of the devil's powerful tools is to convince children to break away from the righteous "traditions" of their parents and grandparents. We see this in Korihor's teaching in verse 16, next.

16 Ye look forward and say that ye see a remission of your sins. But behold, it is the effect of a frenzied mind; and **this derangement** [*confusion*] **of your minds comes because of the traditions of your fathers**, which lead you away into a belief of things which are not so.

17 And many more such things did he say unto them, telling them that there could be **no atonement** made for the sins of men, but **every man fared** [*gets along*] **in this life according to the management of the creature** [*according to his own strength and abilities*]; therefore every man prospered according to his genius, and that every man conquered according to his strength; and **whatsoever a man did was no crime.**

18 And thus he did preach unto them, leading away the hearts of many, causing them to lift up their heads in their wickedness, yea, **leading away many women, and also men, to commit whoredoms** [*various types of sexual immorality*]—**telling them that when a man was dead, that was the end thereof** [*there is no life after death so don't worry about any accountability or consequences for what you do*].

One of the most basic and successful tools Satan uses to lead people astray is sexual immorality, as pointed out in verse 18, above. Some people wonder why sexual sin is so devastating and so effective in tearing people away from God. The answer is simple. It is found in D&C 42:23 as follows:

Doctrine and Covenants 42:23

23 And he that looketh upon a woman to lust after her shall deny the faith, and **shall not have the Spirit**; and if he repents not he shall be cast out.

Thus, sexual immorality of any kind offends and drives away the Spirit. And when we lose the Spirit, we are extremely vulnerable to Satan's influence.

19 **Now this man** [*Korihor*] **went over to the land of Jershon** also [*a foolish thing to do, since these Lamanite converts are so strong in the gospel*], to preach these

things among the people of Ammon, who were once the people of the Lamanites.

20 But behold **they were more wise than many of the Nephites**; for they took him, and bound him, and carried him before Ammon, who was a high priest over that people.

21 And it came to pass that he caused that he should be carried out of the land. And **he came over into the land of Gideon**, and began to preach unto them also; and **here he did not have much success**, for he was taken and bound and carried before the high priest, and also the chief judge over the land.

22 And it came to pass that **the high priest said** unto him: Why do ye go about perverting [*changing, corrupting*] the ways of the Lord? Why do ye teach this people that there shall be no Christ, to interrupt their rejoicings? **Why do ye speak against all the prophecies of the holy prophets?**

23 Now the high priest's name was Giddonah. And **Korihor said** unto him: Because I do not teach the foolish traditions of your fathers, and because I do not teach this people to bind themselves down under the foolish ordinances and performances which are laid down by ancient priests, to usurp power and authority over them, to keep them in ignorance, that they may not lift up their heads, but be brought down according to thy words.

24 **Ye say** that this people is a free people. Behold, **I say** they are in bondage [*in slavery because of what you teach them*]. **Ye say** that those ancient [*old*] prophecies are true. Behold, **I say** that ye do not know that they are true [*you don't really have a testimony*].

25 **Ye say** that this people is a guilty and a fallen people [*in other words, the people need the Atonement of Christ*], because of the transgression of a parent [*because of the Fall of Adam and Eve*]. Behold, **I say** that a child is not guilty because of its parents.

26 And **ye also say** that Christ shall come. But behold, **I say** that ye do not know that there shall be a Christ. And **ye say** also that he shall be slain [*killed*] for the sins of the world—

27 And thus **ye lead away this people** after the foolish traditions of your fathers, and **according to your own desires** [*to satisfy your own selfish motives*]; and **ye keep them down** [*you oppress them*], even as it were in bondage, **that ye may glut yourselves** [*live in wealth and ease with what you take from them*] with the labors of their hands, that they durst not look up with boldness, **and that they durst not enjoy their rights and privileges** [*you take their basic rights and freedoms from them*].

28 Yea, **they durst not make use of that which is their own lest** [*for fear that*] **they should offend their priests**, who do yoke [*burden, subject*] them according to their desires, and have brought them to believe, by their traditions and their dreams and their whims [*things they imagine*]

and their visions and their pretended mysteries, that they should, if they did not do according to their words, offend **some unknown being, who they say is God—a being who never has been seen or known, who never was nor ever will be** [*here, Korihor is acting like he knows the future*].

29 **Now when the high priest and the chief judge saw the hardness of his heart,** yea, **when they saw that he would revile** [*oppose*] **even against God, they would not make any reply to his words**; but they caused that he should be bound [*tied up*]; and they delivered him up into the hands of the officers, and **sent him to the land of Zarahemla, that he might be brought before Alma** [*the President of the Church*], and **the chief judge** [*in effect, the president of the nation*] who was governor over all the land.

30 And it came to pass that when **he was brought before Alma and the chief judge**, he did go on in the same manner as he did in the land of Gideon; yea, he went on to blaspheme [*to speak with total disrespect of sacred things and God*].

31 And **he did rise up in great swelling words** [*big fancy vocabulary words, trying to impress Alma*] **before Alma**, and did revile [*speak*] against the priests and teachers, accusing [*false accusations are a powerful tool of the devil*] them of leading away the people after the silly traditions of their fathers, for the sake of glutting on the labors of the people.

Alma now replies to the false accusations of Korihor. We will watch as Korihor maintains his arrogant and prideful attitude, and then begins to retreat when faced with the inescapable realities of what he has done. In effect, he will have an experience similar to the Final Judgment.

32 Now **Alma said** unto him: **Thou knowest that we do not glut ourselves** [*make ourselves rich*] **upon the labors of this people**; for behold I have labored even from the commencement of the reign of the judges [*for the last seventeen years*] until now, with mine own hands for my support, notwithstanding [*in spite of*] my many travels round about the land to declare the word of God unto my people.

33 And notwithstanding the many labors which I have performed in the church, I have never received so much as even one senine [*a day's wages for a judge; see Alma 11:3*] for my labor; neither has any of my brethren, save [*except*] it were in the judgment-seat; and then **we have received** [*our pay*] **only according to law for our time**.

34 And now, **if we do not receive anything for our labors in the church, what doth it profit us to labor in the church save** [*except*] **it were to declare the truth, that we may have rejoicings in the joy of our brethren?**

35 Then **why sayest thou that we preach unto this people to get gain** [*to get money, to get rich*], **when thou, of thyself, knowest that we receive no**

gain? [*In other words, why have you lied?*] And now, **believest thou that we deceive** [*fool*] **this people, that causes such joy in their hearts?** [*In other words, why are they so happy if we are so bad for them?*]

36 And **Korihor** answered him, **Yea.**

37 And then **Alma said** unto him: **Believest thou that there is a God?**

38 And he answered, **Nay.**

In verse 38, above, Korihor is a professed atheist (one who denies the existence of God). By the time we get to verse 48, he will soften his position and become an agnostic (one who claims no one can know whether or not there is a God). And so, we see the basic instability of people such as Korihor.

39 Now **Alma said** unto him: **Will ye deny again that there is a God, and also deny the Christ?** For behold, I say unto you, **I know there is a God, and also that Christ shall come.**

40 And now **what evidence have ye that there is no God, or that Christ cometh not?** I say unto you that ye have none, save it be your word only.

The question that Alma asks Korihor in verse 40, above—namely, what evidence does he have that there is no God?—is a powerful question. You have no doubt noticed that there is far more evidence all around us in support of the existence of God than there is supposed evidence against the fact. Moses 6:63 informs us that everything is designed to bear witness of God. It reads as follows:

Moses 6:63

63 And behold, all things have their likeness, and **all things are created and made to bear record of me**, both things which are temporal, and things which are spiritual; things which are in the heavens above, and things which are on the earth, and things which are in the earth, and things which are under the earth, both above and beneath: **all things bear record of me.**

41 But, behold, **I have all things as a testimony that these things are true**; and **ye also have all things as a testimony unto you that they are true**; and **will ye deny them?** Believest thou that these things are true?

Next, through the power of the Spirit, Alma lets us see inside Korihor's mind and what has happened to him. Korihor will bluff again and ask for a sign, and soon his entire bluff and blustery attitude will break down.

42 Behold, **I know that thou believest**, but **thou art possessed with a lying spirit** [*you are denying what I know you know, namely, that God exists*], and **ye have put off the Spirit of God** [*pushed the Spirit away, an agency choice*] that it may have no place in you; but **the devil has power over you, and he doth carry you about, working devices** [*using you as a tool*] **that he may destroy the children of God.**

43 And now **Korihor said** unto Alma: If thou wilt **show me a sign**, that I may be convinced that there is a God, yea, show unto me that he

hath power, and then will I be convinced of the truth of thy words.

44 But **Alma said** unto him: **Thou hast had signs enough**; will ye tempt your God? Will ye say, Show unto me a sign, when **ye have the testimony of all these thy brethren**, and also **all the holy prophets**? The **scriptures** are laid before thee, yea, and **all things denote there is a God**; yea, even **the earth**, and **all things that are upon the face of it**, yea, and **its motion**, yea, and also **all the planets which move in their regular form** do **witness that there is a Supreme Creator.**

45 And yet do ye go about, leading away the hearts of this people, testifying unto them there is no God? And yet **will ye deny against all these witnesses?** And **he said: Yea**, I will deny, **except ye shall show me a sign**. [*In other words, it is up to God to prove to me that He exists.*]

46 And now it came to pass that **Alma said** unto him: Behold, **I am grieved** [*saddened and disturbed*] **because of the hardness of your heart**, yea, that ye will still resist the spirit of the truth, that thy soul may be destroyed.

What Alma says next must have startled Korihor a bit, especially since we know from previous verses that he secretly believed in God.

47 But behold, **it is better that thy soul should be lost than that thou shouldst be the means of bringing many souls down to destruction**, by thy lying and by thy flattering words; therefore if thou shalt deny again, behold **God shall smite thee, that thou shalt become dumb** [*unable to speak, a devastating blow to one who has gained power and popularity through his skill at public speaking*], that **thou shalt never open thy mouth** [*talk*] **any more**, that thou shalt not deceive this people any more.

Next, Korihor begins to back off, but we know from verse 55 that he is not sincere.

48 Now **Korihor said** unto him: **I do not deny the existence of a God, but I do not believe that there is a God**; and I say also, that **ye do not know that there is a God**; and **except ye show me a sign, I will not believe.**

49 Now **Alma said** unto him: **This will I give unto thee for a sign, that thou shalt be struck dumb**, according to my words; and I say, that in the name of God, ye shall be struck dumb, that ye shall no more have utterance [*be able to talk*].

50 Now when Alma had said these words, **Korihor was struck dumb**, that he could not have utterance, according to the words of Alma.

Based on verse 51, next, it appears that Korihor was struck both deaf and dumb.

51 And now when **the chief judge** saw this, he put forth his hand and **wrote unto Korihor**, saying: Art thou convinced of the power of God? In whom did ye desire that Alma should show forth his sign? Would

ye that he should afflict others, to show unto thee a sign? Behold, he has showed unto you a sign; and now will ye dispute more?

Korihor now admits he was lying.

52 And **Korihor** put forth his hand and **wrote**, saying: **I know that I am dumb**, for **I cannot speak**; and I know that nothing save [*except*] it were the power of God could bring this upon me; yea, and **I always knew that there was a God.**

What Korihor says in verse 53, next is pretty interesting. Remember that in verses 37 and 38, he claimed there is no God. In verse 18, he taught that there is no life after death. In effect, he is saying that there is nothing beyond earth life. Yet, Satan appeared to him, from an unseen world beyond earth life, and, in effect, told him that there is no such thing as anything except this life. And he believed him! Wickedness does not help people think clearly!

53 But behold, **the devil hath deceived me**; for **he appeared unto me in the form of an angel**, and said unto me: Go and reclaim this people, for they have all gone astray after an unknown God. And **he said unto me: There is no God**; yea, and he taught me that which I should say. And **I have taught his words**; and I taught them because they were pleasing unto the carnal mind; and I taught them, even until I had much success, **insomuch that I verily** [*actually*] **believed that they were true**; and for this cause I withstood [*taught against*] the truth, even until I have brought this great curse upon me.

There is also a strong warning about lying in verse 53. It is that if we lie enough, we may well begin to believe our own lies.

54 Now when he had said this, **he besought** [*requested*] **that Alma should pray unto God, that the curse might be taken from him.**

55 But **Alma said** unto him: **If this curse should be taken from thee thou wouldst again lead away the hearts of this people** [*in other words, Korihor hadn't truly repented*]; therefore, it shall be unto thee even as the Lord will.

56 And it came to pass that **the curse was not taken off of Korihor**; but **he was cast out, and went about from house to house begging for his food.**

57 Now **the knowledge of what had happened unto Korihor was immediately published throughout all the land**; yea, the proclamation was sent forth by the chief judge to all the people in the land, declaring unto those who had believed in the words of Korihor that they must speedily repent, lest the same judgments would come unto them.

58 And it came to pass that **they were all convinced of the wickedness of Korihor; therefore they were all converted again unto the Lord**; and this put an end to the iniquity after the manner of Korihor

[*the kind of wickedness Korihor taught*]. And Korihor did go about from house to house, begging food for his support [*to stay alive*].

Next, in verse 59, we are introduced to the Zoramites. Korihor will be trampled to death by them. Keep them in mind, because in chapter 31, Alma will take an "all-star" cast of missionaries to preach the gospel to them. Among other things, they will be startled to find the Zoramites saying prayers on a Rameumptom tower.

59 And it came to pass that as **he went forth among the** people, yea, among a people who had separated themselves from the Nephites and called themselves **Zoramites**, being led by a man whose name was Zoram—and as he went forth amongst them, behold, **he was run upon and trodden down** [*stomped on*], **even until he was dead.**

Next, in verse 60, Mormon summarizes a major point he hopes we learn from chapter 30.

60 And **thus we see the end of him who perverteth** [*twists and changes*] **the ways of the Lord**; and thus we see that **the devil will not support his children** [*followers*] **at the last day** [*when they desperately need his help*], **but doth speedily drag them down to hell.**

ALMA 31

The Zoramites, who trampled Korihor to death, were apostate Nephites. The word "apostate" means they had left the Church and no longer believed the gospel, meaning the teachings of Christ. They had become hardened and were considered by Alma's people to be a threat to their national security because they were very likely to join the Lamanites and fight against them. Since the gospel is the only peaceful way to solve problems of this type, Alma will gather a group of very powerful missionaries and take the gospel to these Zoramites. He and his fellow missionaries are in for some surprises and we stand to learn much from what happens.

1 NOW it came to pass that after the end of Korihor, Alma having received tidings [*news*] that **the Zoramites were perverting the ways** [*changing the true teachings*] **of the Lord, and that Zoram, who was their leader, was leading the hearts of the people to bow down to dumb idols** [*idols that are obviously not alive, can't speak*], his heart again began to sicken because of the iniquity [*wickedness*] of the people.

2 For it was the cause of great sorrow to **Alma** to know of iniquity among his people; therefore his heart **was exceedingly sorrowful because of the separation** [*apostasy as well as physical separation*] **of the Zoramites from the Nephites.**

3 Now **the Zoramites had gathered themselves** together in a land which they called Antionum, which was **east of the land of Zarahemla**, which lay nearly bordering upon the seashore, which was south of the land of Jershon, which also bordered upon the wilderness south, which wilderness was full of the Lamanites.

4 Now **the Nephites greatly feared that the Zoramites would enter into a correspondence** [*alliance; treaty*] **with the Lamanites**, and that it would be the means of great loss on the part of the Nephites.

Next, Mormon reminds us of the power of preaching the gospel as a means of solving problems among people.

5 And now, **as the preaching of the word** [*the true gospel of Jesus Christ*] **had a great tendency to lead the people to do that which was just** [*right*]—yea, **it had had more powerful effect upon the minds of the people than the sword, or anything else**, which had happened unto them—therefore Alma thought it was expedient [*necessary*] that they should try the virtue [*power*] of the word of God.

Just look at the "all-star" cast of missionaries that Alma chose to preach to the Zoramites, in verses 6 and 7.

6 Therefore he took **Ammon,** and **Aaron**, and **Omner** [*three of the four sons of Mosiah, who had served a fourteen-year mission among the Lamanites*]; and Himni he did leave in the church in Zarahemla; but the former three he took with him, and also **Amulek** [*the "inactive" member who had fed Alma in Ammonihah, and who became a powerful missionary*] and **Zeezrom** [*the converted lawyer from Ammonihah*], who were at Melek; and he also took two of his sons.

7 Now the eldest of his sons he took not with him, and his name was Helaman; but the names of those whom he took with him were **Shiblon** [*Alma's middle son*] and **Corianton** [*Alma's youngest son*]; and these are the names of those who went with him among the Zoramites, to preach unto them the word.

8 Now **the Zoramites were dissenters** [*apostates*] **from the Nephites**; therefore **they had had the word of God preached unto them** [*they knew the gospel but had rejected it*].

9 But **they had fallen into great errors**, for they would not observe to keep the commandments of God, and his statutes [*laws*], according to the law of Moses [*they were in open rebellion*].

10 **Neither would they observe the performances** [*rites and rituals*] **of the church, to continue in prayer** and supplication to God daily, that they might not enter into temptation.

11 Yea, in fine [*in summary*], **they did pervert the ways of the Lord in very many instances**; therefore, for this cause [*this is why*], **Alma and his brethren went into the land to preach the word unto them**.

12 Now, when they had come into the land, behold, to their astonishment they found that **the Zoramites had built synagogues** [*buildings in which to worship*], and that they did gather themselves together on one day of the week, which day they did call the day of the Lord; **and they did worship after a manner which Alma and his brethren had never beheld** [*seen*];

13 For **they had a place built up in the center of their synagogue**, a place **for standing** [*the Rameumptom; see verse 21*], **which was high above the head**; and the top thereof **would only admit one person**.

14 Therefore, **whosoever desired to worship must** go forth and **stand upon the top thereof, and stretch forth his hands** towards heaven, **and cry with a loud voice, saying:**

> Verses 15–18, next, are what can be referred to as the "Rameumptom prayer." You will notice that it contains truths mixed with errors.

15 **Holy, holy God**; we believe that **thou art God** [*true*], and we believe that **thou art holy** [*true*], and that **thou wast a spirit** [*true, until He was sent to an earth and gained a body*], and that **thou art a spirit** [*false*], and that **thou wilt be a spirit forever** [*false*].

16 Holy God, we believe that **thou hast separated us from our brethren** [*false; they did it through apostasy*]; and we do not believe in the tradition of our brethren, which was handed down to them by the childishness of their fathers; but we believe that **thou hast elected us to be thy holy children** [*false; this is typical of Satan's imitation of the true gospel*]; and also thou hast made it known unto us that **there shall be no Christ** [*false*].

17 But **thou art the same yesterday, today, and forever** [*true; God uses the same gospel always to save His children*]; and **thou hast elected us that we shall be saved** [*false; this is predestination*], whilst **all around us are elected to be cast by thy wrath down to hell** [*false*]; for the which holiness, O God, we thank thee; and we also thank thee that **thou hast elected us** [*false*], that we may not be led away after the **foolish traditions of our brethren** [*false*], which doth bind them down to a belief of Christ, which **doth lead their hearts to wander far from thee** [*false*], our God.

18 And again we thank thee, O God, that **we are a chosen and a holy people** [*false*]. Amen.

> One of the fatal flaws in the belief system of these Zoramites, as evidenced in their Rameumptom prayer, is that they have redefined God according to their own beliefs rather than according to the truth. We see much of this in religious beliefs today.

19 Now it came to pass that after **Alma and his brethren and his sons** had heard these prayers, they **were astonished** [*surprised*] **beyond all measure.**

20 For behold, **every man did go forth and offer up these same prayers**.

21 Now the place was called by them **Rameumptom**, which, being interpreted, is **the holy stand**.

22 Now, from this stand **they did offer up, every man, the selfsame** [*the exact same*] **prayer** unto God, thanking their God that they were chosen of him, and that he did not lead them away after the tradition of their

brethren [*the gospel taught by the Nephites*], and that their hearts were not stolen away to believe in things to come [*in the future, like the coming of Christ*], which they knew nothing about.

23 Now, after the people had all offered up thanks after this manner, **they returned to their homes, never speaking of their God again until they had assembled themselves together again** to the holy stand, to offer up thanks after their manner.

24 Now **when Alma saw this his heart was grieved** [*very worried*]; for he saw that they were a wicked and a perverse people [*had moved far away from God's teachings*]; yea, he saw that **their hearts were set upon gold, and upon silver, and upon all manner of fine goods** [*they were caught up in materialism*].

25 Yea, and he also saw that their hearts were lifted up unto great boasting, in their **pride**.

According to 1 Nephi 13:7–9, three major temptations used by the devil to very good advantage are materialism, pride, and sexual immorality. Here among the Zoramites, Mormon points out two of these tools: materialism and pride.

Next, we see Alma almost overwhelmed by sorrow at seeing such open and extreme apostate worship.

26 And **he lifted up his voice to heaven, and cried**, saying: O, how long, O Lord, wilt thou suffer that thy servants shall dwell here below in the flesh, to behold such gross wickedness among the children of men?

27 Behold, O God, they cry unto thee, and yet their hearts are swallowed up in their **pride**. Behold, O God, they cry unto thee with their mouths, while they are puffed up, even to greatness, with the **vain** [*of no real, lasting value*] **things of the world**.

28 Behold, O my God, their **costly apparel**, and their **ringlets**, and their **bracelets**, and their **ornaments of gold**, and all their **precious things** which they are ornamented with; and behold, **their hearts are set upon them**, and yet they cry unto thee and say—We thank thee, O God, for we are a chosen people unto thee, while others shall perish.

29 Yea, and **they say that thou hast made it known unto them that there shall be no Christ**.

What Alma says next in his prayer is a bit unexpected for most of us. Normally, we ourselves would probably pray for them to change their ways, which is certainly a proper thing to pray for. But Alma prays that the Lord will soften and strengthen his own heart so that he will not be so critical of the Zoramites that he can't work with them.

30 O Lord God, how long wilt thou suffer that such wickedness and infidelity shall be among this people? **O Lord, wilt thou give me strength, that I may bear with mine infirmities** [*perhaps meaning, among other things, the infirmity of being judgmental and critical of these people*]. **For I am infirm, and such wickedness among this people doth pain my soul.**

31 O Lord, my heart is exceedingly sorrowful; wilt thou comfort my soul in Christ. O Lord, wilt thou **grant unto me that I may have strength, that I may suffer** [*put up with*] **with patience these afflictions which shall come upon me, because of the iniquity of this people.**

32 O Lord, wilt thou **comfort my soul**, and **give unto me success, and also my fellow laborers who are with me**—yea, Ammon, and Aaron, and Omner, and also Amulek and Zeezrom and also my two sons—yea, even all these wilt thou comfort, O Lord. Yea, wilt thou comfort their souls in Christ.

33 Wilt thou **grant unto them that they may have strength**, that they may bear their afflictions which shall come upon them because of the iniquities of this people.

34 O Lord, wilt thou **grant unto us that we may have success in bringing them again unto thee in Christ**.

35 Behold, O Lord, **their souls are precious**, and many of them are our brethren; therefore, give unto us, O Lord, power and wisdom that we may bring these, our brethren, again unto thee.

36 Now it came to pass that when Alma had said these words, that **he clapped his hands** [*laid his hands*] **upon all them who were with him**. And behold, as he clapped his hands upon them, **they were filled with the Holy Spirit**.

In the 1828 edition of the Noah Webster Dictionary (which reflects English usage in the days of the Prophet Joseph Smith), the word "clapped" is defined as "to thrust or put on." Thus, our definition and understanding of the word "clapped" as used in verse 36, above.

37 And after that **they did separate themselves one from another** [*they went different directions among the Zoramites to preach*], taking no thought for themselves what they should eat, or what they should drink, or what they should put on.

38 And **the Lord provided for them that they should hunger not, neither should they thirst; yea, and he also gave them strength, that they should suffer no manner of afflictions, save it were swallowed up in the joy of Christ.** [*The Spirit of the Lord can give us perspective that minimizes trials and afflictions.*] **Now this was according to the prayer of Alma; and this because he prayed in faith**.

ALMA 32

You can learn many things from this chapter. Alma 32 is one of the best-known and oft-quoted chapters in the Book of Mormon. Perhaps you have heard of the seed that is planted, then nourished with faith, and then eventually grows into a tree, providing a feast of gospel fruit.

As Alma and the other missionaries begin to preach among the Zoramites, as mentioned in chapter 31, they soon find that the wealthy Zoramites have treated the poorer Zoramites very badly, refusing to allow them to worship in the church buildings that they helped build. Soon Alma turns his attention to these poverty-stricken citizens who have been humbled by their circumstances, and a great sermon follows in which we, too, are taught how to develop strong faith.

1 AND it came to pass that **they did go forth, and began to preach the word of God unto the people**, entering into their synagogues [*church buildings*], and into their houses; yea, and even they did preach the word in their streets.

2 And it came to pass that **after much labor** [*work*] **among them, they began to have success among the poor class of people**; for behold, they were cast out of the synagogues because of the coarseness of their apparel [*roughness of their clothing*]—

3 **Therefore** [*because of this*] **they were not permitted to enter into their synagogues to worship God**, being esteemed [*considered, thought of*] as filthiness; therefore they were poor; yea, they were esteemed by their brethren as dross [*worthless trash*]; therefore **they were poor as to things of the world; and also they were poor in heart** [*humble*].

4 Now, **as Alma was teaching** and speaking unto the people upon the hill Onidah, **there came a great multitude unto him**, who were those of whom we have been speaking, **of whom were poor in heart**, because of their poverty as to the things of the world.

5 And they came unto Alma; and the one who was the foremost among them [*the leader*] said unto him: **Behold, what shall these my brethren do**, for **they are despised** [*looked down upon; thought badly of*] of all men because of their poverty, yea, and more especially **by our priests**; for they **have cast us out of our synagogues which we have labored abundantly to build with our own hands**; and they have cast us out **because of our exceeding** [*extreme, terrible*] **poverty**; and **we have no place to worship our God; and behold, what shall we do?**

The leader of these poorer people has asked a key question: how can they worship God since they are not allowed in the synagogues where they have Rameumptom towers for worship? Alma's answer, starting with verse 9, below, will be a bit startling to them at first, but will become a great relief to them.

6 And now **when Alma heard this, he turned him about** [*around*], his face immediately towards him, and he beheld with great joy; for **he beheld** [*saw*] **that their afflictions had truly humbled them, and that they were in a preparation to hear the word.**

7 Therefore **he did say no more to the other multitude**; but **he stretched forth his hand, and cried unto those** [*the poor people*] **whom he beheld, who were truly penitent** [*willing to repent*], and said unto them:

8 **I behold** [*see*] **that ye are lowly in heart** [*humble*]; and if so, blessed are ye.

9 Behold **thy brother hath said, What shall we do?—for we are cast out of our synagogues, that we cannot worship our God.**

10 Behold I say unto you, **do ye suppose that ye cannot worship God save** [*except*] **it be in your synagogues only?**

11 And moreover, I would ask, **do ye suppose that ye must not worship God only** [*except*] **once in a week?**

12 I say unto you, **it is well** [*good*] **that ye are cast out of your synagogues**, that ye may be humble, and that ye may learn wisdom; for it is necessary that ye should learn wisdom; for it is because that ye are cast out, that ye are despised of [*not respected by*] your brethren because of your exceeding poverty, that ye are brought to a lowliness of heart; **for ye are necessarily brought to be humble**.

Next, Alma points out that it can work for a person to be humbled by circumstances to the point that he repents and is saved. He will then go on to point out that a more pleasant approach to being saved is to be humble in the first place.

13 And now, **because ye are compelled** [*forced*] **to be humble blessed are ye; for a man sometimes, if he is compelled to be humble, seeketh repentance**; and now surely, **whosoever repenteth shall find mercy; and he that findeth mercy and endureth** [*remains faithful to the gospel*] **to the end the same shall be saved.**

14 And now, as I said unto you, that because ye were compelled to be humble ye were blessed, **do ye not suppose that they are more blessed who truly humble themselves** because of the word [*the gospel*]?

15 **Yea** [*yes*], he that truly humbleth himself, and repenteth of his sins, and endureth to the end, the same shall be blessed—yea, much more blessed [*because he has a good attitude to begin with*] than they who are compelled to be humble because of their exceeding poverty.

16 Therefore, blessed are they who humble themselves without being compelled to be humble; or rather, in other words, **blessed is he that believeth in the word of God, and is baptized without stubbornness of heart, yea, without being brought to know the word, or even compelled to know, before they will believe**.

Next, Alma begins the transition into the topic of faith.

17 Yea, there are **many** who do **say: If thou wilt show unto us a sign from heaven, then we shall know of a surety; then we shall believe.**

18 Now I ask, **is this faith?** Behold, I say unto you, **Nay**; for if a man knoweth a thing he hath no cause to believe, for he knoweth it.

Next, Alma teaches the principle of knowledge and accountability. Those who have a knowledge of the gospel are more accountable than those who do not.

19 And now, **how much more cursed is he that knoweth the will of God and doeth it not, than he that only believeth, or only hath cause to believe, and falleth into transgression?**

20 **Now of this thing ye must judge** [*you decide*]. Behold, I say unto you, that it is on the one hand even as it is on the other; and it shall be unto every man according to his work.

Verses 21 through 43 contain five simple steps you can use to help your faith become very strong.

Five steps that can lead to strong faith

Step 1

Hope that the gospel is true, then look for evidence. If you "hope" that the gospel is true, you will look for evidence that it is. If you look for evidence, you will find it. And you will have the beginnings of faith. You will start to believe.

21 And now as I said concerning faith—**faith is not to have a perfect knowledge of things**; therefore if ye have faith ye **hope for things which are not seen, which are true.**

22 And now, behold, I say unto you, and I would that ye should remember, that **God is merciful unto all who believe on his name; therefore he desireth, in the first place, that ye should believe**, yea, even on his word.

23 And now, **he imparteth** [*teaches*] **his word** [*gospel*] by angels unto men, yea, not only men but women also. Now this is not all; little children do have words given unto them many times, which confound [*surprise, sometimes overwhelm*] the wise and the learned.

24 And now, my beloved brethren, **as ye have desired to know of me what ye shall do because ye are afflicted and cast out**—now I do not desire that ye should suppose that I mean to judge you only according to that which is true—

25 For I do not mean that ye all of you have been compelled to humble yourselves; for **I verily believe that there are some among you who would humble themselves, let them be in whatsoever circumstances they might** [*no matter what circumstances they find themselves in*].

26 Now, as I said concerning **faith**—that it was **not a perfect knowledge**—even so it is with my words. **Ye cannot know of their surety** [*you cannot be certain that they are true*] **at first**, unto perfection, any more than faith is a perfect knowledge.

Step 2

"Test drive" the gospel. In other words, try it out. Test it thoroughly. Alma instructs these Zoramites to "experiment" with the gospel.

27 But behold, if ye will awake and **arouse your faculties** [*your abilities to think and do*], even to an **experiment**

upon my words, and exercise a particle of faith, yea, even if ye can no more than desire to believe, let this desire work in you, even until ye believe in a manner that ye can give place for a portion of my words.

28 Now, **we will compare the word unto a seed**. Now, if ye **give place** [*make room in your life to try the gospel out*], **that a seed may be planted in your heart**,

Step 3

Learn how to recognize it when the Spirit is working with you. Don't rush it. If your expectations are too high, you will miss this step and the experiment will fail.

[*verse 28 continued*] behold, if it be a true seed, or a good seed, if ye **do not cast it out by your unbelief,** that ye will resist the Spirit of the Lord, behold, **it will begin to swell within your breasts**; [*In other words, it will feel good. You will have warm feelings.*] and when you feel these swelling motions, **ye will begin to say within yourselves—It must needs be that this is a good seed**, or that the word is good, for it **beginneth** to enlarge my soul [*you feel better about yourself*]; yea, it **beginneth** to enlighten my understanding [*life and its purposes begin to make sense*], yea, it **beginneth** to be delicious to me [*it begins to feel very good and you don't want to lose the feeling*].

Notice that we **bolded** the words "begin" and "beginneth" in verse 28, above. This is to emphasize again that these are very tender beginnings of personal faith and require careful attention and noticing what is going on.

29 Now behold, **would not this increase your faith?** I say unto you, **Yea**; nevertheless it hath not grown up to a perfect knowledge [*you don't have to have a perfect knowledge for these feelings to arise in your heart*].

Remember, you can't rush spiritual things, so patience is very necessary.

30 But behold, **as the seed** swelleth, and sprouteth, and **beginneth to grow**, then you must needs say that the seed is good; for behold it swelleth, and sprouteth, and **beginneth to grow**. And now, behold, will not this strengthen your faith? Yea, it will strengthen your faith: for ye will say I know that this is a good seed; for behold it sprouteth and **beginneth to grow.**

31 And now, behold, **are ye sure that this is a good seed?** I say unto you, **Yea**; for every seed bringeth forth unto its own likeness [*if it were not a good seed, in other words, if the gospel were not true, you wouldn't feel so good*].

32 Therefore, **if a seed groweth it is good**, but if it groweth not, behold it is not good, therefore it is cast away.

33 And now, behold, **because ye have tried the experiment, and planted the seed, and it swelleth and sprouteth, and beginneth to grow, ye must needs know that the seed is good.** [*As you continue to "test*

drive" the gospel, it begins to change your life for the better and you know that it is good for you.]

At this point in the experiment, even though it may be small, you have definite knowledge, rather than faith, that the gospel is improving your life. This may sound almost too simple, but it is the simple things in life that people often miss while looking for something more spectacular.

34 And now, behold, **is your knowledge perfect? Yea, your knowledge is perfect in that thing** [*that the gospel is improving your life and that you are feeling it and feeling much better about yourself*], and your faith is dormant; and this **because you know**, for **ye know that the word hath swelled your souls**, and ye also know that it hath sprouted up, that **your understanding doth begin to be enlightened**, and **your mind doth begin to expand** [*for instance, you find that you are beginning to understand more about God and His purposes for you here on earth*].

35 O then, **is not this real?** I say unto you, **Yea, because it is light; and whatsoever is light, is good, because it is discernible** [*noticeable*], **therefore ye must know that it is good**; and now behold, after ye have tasted this light **is your knowledge perfect?**

36 Behold I say unto you, **Nay**; neither must ye lay aside your faith [*don't quit the experiment at this point*], for ye have only exercised your faith to plant the seed that ye might try the experiment to know if the seed was good. [*You are just getting a good start at this point.*]

Step 4

Don't stop now. Keep nourishing your faith and feelings by continuing to live the gospel. Your faith is still very young and tender and it is at this point that many people stop nourishing it and it dies. Remember that this is an agency choice and that God will not force the gospel upon you. You must keep inviting the Spirit to work with you by your actions as well as words.

37 And behold, as the tree beginneth to grow, ye will say: Let us **nourish it with great care, that it may get root, that it may grow up**, and bring forth fruit unto us. And now behold, **if ye nourish it with much care it will get root, and grow up, and bring forth fruit.** [*This is a promise from God.*]

38 But **if ye neglect the tree, and take no thought for its nourishment, behold it will not get any root; and when the heat of the sun cometh and scorcheth it, because it hath no root it withers away, and ye pluck it up and cast it out.**

39 Now, **this is not because the seed was not good**, neither is it because the fruit thereof would not be desirable; **but it is because your ground is barren, and ye will not nourish the tree**, therefore ye cannot have the fruit thereof.

40 And thus, **if ye will not nourish the word**, looking forward with an eye of faith to the fruit thereof, **ye can never pluck of the fruit of the**

tree of life [*you can never have the wonderful results of faith in your life*].

In the next three verses, Alma emphasizes the importance of continuing to try and patience. This is an important theme in this whole chapter.

41 But **if ye will nourish the word**, yea, nourish the tree as it beginneth to grow, by your faith with great **diligence** [*faithfully continuing to try*], and with **patience**, looking forward to the fruit thereof, **it shall take root**; and behold **it shall be a tree springing up unto everlasting life** [*eventually getting you to heaven and exaltation*].

Step 5

Once you have nourished the seed to the point that it has become a tree, then be sure to "feast" on the fruit (the gospel) the rest of your life. Don't just nibble. This will continue to strengthen your faith and your knowledge throughout your life.

42 And **because of your diligence** and your **faith** and your **patience** with the word in nourishing it, that it may take root in you, behold, by and by [*eventually*] **ye shall pluck the fruit** thereof [*a promise*], which is most precious, which is sweet above all that is sweet, and which is white above all that is white, yea, and pure above all that is pure; and ye shall **feast upon this fruit even until ye are filled, that ye hunger not, neither shall ye thirst.**

43 Then, my brethren, **ye shall reap the rewards of your faith**, and your **diligence**, and **patience**, and **long-suffering, waiting for the tree to bring forth fruit unto you.**

Again, at the very end of the chapter, we see the caution to patiently wait for the end results of your (1) hoping, (2) experimenting (test driving), (3) learning how to recognize when the Spirit is working with you, (4) nourishing the seed, and (5) feasting on the results. As mentioned previously, too many people tend to want to rush this process. You cannot rush spiritual things. When you attempt to do so, you set yourself up for deception by the devil.

ALMA 33

After Alma had taught these poor Zoramite outcasts the concept of planting the seed of faith and nourishing it until it develops into a full-grown tree with gospel fruit (Alma 32), they asked for more help as to how they should go about planting the seed, or how to begin exercising their tender faith. Alma gives them at least three answers to their question.

1. You must study the scriptures so that you know correct doctrine about who God is and how you can worship Him.

2. You must study the scriptures to find out how and where you can pray (in other words, you are not limited to your church buildings and the Rameumptom tower for saying prayers).

3. You must keep God in mind constantly, all week long instead of just on Sunday, which will make you

want to pray often throughout the day, no matter where you are.

As we now proceed to study chapter 33, you will see that these humble Zoramites ask three good questions in verse 1.

1 NOW after Alma had spoken these words, they [*the poor among the Zoramites*] sent forth unto him [*passed some questions to him*] desiring to know **whether they should believe in one God**, that they might obtain this fruit of which he had spoken, or **how they should plant the seed**, or the word of which he had spoken, which he said must be planted in their hearts; or **in what manner they should begin to exercise their faith**.

2 And **Alma said** unto them: Behold, **ye have said that ye could not worship your God because ye are cast out of your synagogues**. But behold, I say unto you, **if ye suppose that ye cannot worship God, ye do greatly err** [*you are completely wrong*], and **ye ought to search the scriptures**; if ye suppose that they have taught you this, ye do not understand them.

Alma's response, "ye do greatly err . . . ye ought to search the scriptures," is a direct reminder to us that the scriptures are indeed the standard works, and that we should measure all teachings, philosophies, ideas, things we hear others teach, including in school, on TV, social media, etc., against them in order to keep our own thinking in line with eternal truth.

Next, Alma will quote Zenos (verses 4–11) to emphasize the importance of prayer, anytime, anywhere. Zenos was an Old Testament prophet whose teachings have been left out of the Bible but are mentioned in the Book of Mormon.

3 **Do ye remember** to have read **what Zenos**, the prophet of old, has **said concerning prayer or worship?**

4 For he said: Thou art merciful, O God, for **thou hast heard my prayer**, even when I was **in the wilderness**; yea, thou wast merciful when I prayed concerning those who were mine enemies, and thou didst turn them to me.

5 Yea, O God, and thou wast merciful unto me when I did cry unto thee **in my field**; when I did cry unto thee in my prayer, and thou didst hear me.

6 And again, O God, when I did turn to **my house** thou didst hear me in my prayer.

7 And when I did turn unto **my closet**, O Lord, and prayed unto thee, thou didst hear me.

8 Yea, **thou art merciful unto thy children when they cry** [*pray*] **unto thee**, to be heard of thee and not of men, and thou wilt hear them.

9 Yea, O God, thou hast been merciful unto me, and heard my cries **in the midst of thy congregations.**

10 Yea, and thou hast also heard **me when I have been cast out** and have been **despised by mine enemies** [*this fits these Zoramite outcasts especially well*];

yea, thou didst hear my cries, and wast angry with mine enemies, and thou didst visit them in thine anger with speedy destruction.

11 And thou didst hear me because of mine afflictions and my sincerity; and it is because of thy Son that thou hast been thus merciful unto me, therefore **I will cry unto thee in all mine afflictions** [*troubles*], for in thee is my joy; for thou hast turned thy judgments away from me, because of thy Son [*You have forgiven me because of the Atonement of Christ*].

12 And now **Alma said** unto them: **Do ye believe those scriptures** which have been written by them of old? [*Alma wants a commitment out of them on this.*]

13 Behold, **if ye do, ye must believe what Zenos said**; for, behold he said: **Thou hast turned away thy judgments because of thy Son.**

Now, Alma is beginning a transition into teaching these people about the Atonement of Christ.

14 Now behold, my brethren, I would ask if ye have read the scriptures? If ye have, **how can ye disbelieve on the Son of God?**

15 For it is not written that Zenos alone spake of these things, but **Zenock also spake of these things** [*Alma is using the law of having at least two witnesses to prove teachings of the gospel*]—

16 For behold, he said: Thou art angry, O Lord, with this people, because they will not understand **thy mercies which thou hast bestowed upon them because of thy Son**.

17 And now, my brethren, ye see that **a second prophet of old has testified of the Son of God**, and because the people would not understand his words they stoned him to death.

18 But behold, **this is not all; these are not the only ones who have spoken concerning the Son of God.**

19 Behold, **he** [*Christ*] **was spoken of by Moses**; yea, and behold a type [*a brass serpent, on a pole, symbolic of the Savior and his Atonement; see Numbers 21:6–9*] was raised up in the wilderness, that whosoever would look upon it might live. And many did look and live.

20 But few understood the meaning of those things, and this because of the hardness of their hearts. But there were many who were so hardened that they would not look, therefore they perished. Now **the reason they would not look is because they did not believe** that it would heal them.

As you can see, in the preceding verses as well as the next, Alma is answering their question as to how to plant the seed of faith. He is basically telling them that it is so simple that many will not be willing to do it. All they have to do is allow themselves to begin believing. This simple step is very difficult for many people because of pride and a lack of childlike faith.

21 O my brethren, **if ye could be healed by merely casting about**

your eyes that ye might be healed, would ye not behold [*look*] **quickly** [*if you knew the power of "planting the seed" you would plant it very quickly*], or would ye rather harden your hearts in unbelief, and be slothful, that ye would not cast about your eyes, that ye might perish?

22 If so, wo [*trouble*] shall come upon you; but if not so [*if you are not hard-hearted and unbelieving*], then cast about your eyes and **begin to believe in the Son of God** [*this is how to plant the seed*], that he will come to redeem his people, and that he shall suffer and die to atone for their sins; and that he shall rise again from the dead, which shall bring to pass the resurrection, that all men shall stand before him, to be judged at the last and judgment day, according to their works.

Alma now summarizes his answer to the question they asked in verse 1 of this chapter.

23 And now, my brethren, I desire that ye shall **plant this word in your hearts**, and as it beginneth to swell even so **nourish it by your faith.** And behold, **it will become a tree, springing up in you unto everlasting life** [*leading you to eternal exaltation in the celestial kingdom*]. And then may God grant unto you that your burdens may be light [*a very discernable result of the growing seed*], through the joy of his Son. And even all this can ye do if ye will [*if you desire to and are willing*]. Amen.

ALMA 34

After Alma finished teaching these poor and humbled Zoramites how to get faith in the gospel, Amulek took over and will now teach them about the Savior Jesus Christ and how His Atonement can help them move forward in their lives by exercising faith and repenting of their sins.

As you know, all of these things apply to you and me also, so pay close attention to what Amulek says.

1 AND now it came to pass that **after Alma had spoken these words unto them he sat down** upon the ground, **and Amulek arose and began to teach them**, saying:

2 My brethren, **I think that it is impossible that ye should be ignorant** [*have no knowledge*] **of the things which have been spoken concerning the coming of Christ**, who is taught by us to be **the Son of God**; yea, I know that these things were taught unto you bountifully [*abundantly*] before your dissension from among us [*before you apostatized and left the Church*].

3 And as ye have desired of my beloved brother [*Alma*] that he should make known unto you what ye should do, because of your afflictions [*troubles*]; and **he hath spoken somewhat unto you to prepare your minds**; yea, and he hath exhorted [*taught and urged*] you unto **faith** and to **patience**—

4 Yea, even **that ye would have so much faith as even to plant the**

word in your hearts, that ye may **try the experiment** of its goodness.

Next, Amulek replies to the question asked by these Zoramites in Alma 33:1 as to whether they should believe in just one God, meaning that they had been taught by their priests that there was only one God and that there would be no Christ (Alma 31:16).

5 And we [*Alma and Amulek*] have beheld that **the great question which is in your minds is whether the word be in the Son of God** [*whether or not the gospel is focused on Christ*], **or whether there shall be no Christ.**

6 And ye also beheld that **my brother** [*Alma*] **has proved unto you**, in many instances [*using many quotes from the scriptures*], **that the word is in Christ unto salvation**. [*In other words, there will be a Christ, and the only way you can be saved is through Him.*]

7 My brother [*Alma*] has called upon the words of [*has quoted*] Zenos, that **redemption** [*being saved from our sins*] **cometh through the Son of God**, and also upon the words of Zenock; and also he has appealed unto [*quoted*] Moses, to prove that these things are true.

Next, Amulek adds his own testimony to that of Alma and prophets in the scriptures. By the way, you may have already noticed that when you bear your own testimony of the gospel, the Holy Ghost adds real power to your words.

8 And now, behold, **I will testify unto you of myself that these things are true.** Behold, I say unto you, that **I do know that Christ shall come among the children of men, to take upon him the transgressions of his people, and that he shall atone for the sins of the world**; for the Lord God hath spoken it.

9 For **it is expedient** [*absolutely necessary*] **that an atonement should be made**; for according to the great plan of the Eternal God [*the plan of salvation*] there must be an atonement made, or else all mankind must unavoidably perish; yea, all are hardened; yea, all are fallen and are lost, and must perish except it be through the atonement which it is expedient should be made. [*Without the Atonement of Christ, we would all be lost. Compare with 2 Nephi 9:7–9.*]

All of this is in response to the question in verse 5, above, as to whether or not there will be a Christ.

10 For **it is expedient that there should be a great and last sacrifice**; yea, not a sacrifice of man, neither of beast, neither of any manner of fowl; for it shall not be a human sacrifice; but **it must be an infinite and eternal sacrifice.**

11 Now **there is not any man that can sacrifice his own blood which will atone** [*pay*] **for the sins of another**. Now, if a man murdereth, behold will our law, which is just, take the life of his brother? I say unto you, Nay.

12 But the law requireth the life of him who hath murdered; therefore

there can be nothing which is short of an infinite atonement which will suffice [*be enough to pay*] **for the sins of the world.**

13 Therefore, **it is expedient** [*necessary*] **that there should be a great and last sacrifice** [*the Atonement of Christ*], and then shall there be, or it is expedient there should be, a stop to the shedding of blood [*an end to the daily animal sacrifices under the Law of Moses*]; then shall the law of Moses be fulfilled; yea, it shall be all fulfilled [*by Christ*], every jot and tittle [*every tiny bit of it*], and none shall have passed away [*there is not one bit of the Law of Moses that will not have been fulfilled by Christ*].

Amulek is giving us a very valuable summary of the purposes of the Law of Moses.

14 And behold, **this is the whole meaning of the law** [*of Moses*], every whit [*bit*] **pointing to** that great and last sacrifice; and **that great and last sacrifice will be the Son of God**, yea, infinite and eternal.

15 And thus [*this is how*] **he shall bring salvation to all those who shall believe on his name**; this being the intent [*the purpose*] of this last sacrifice [*of the Savior's Atonement*] to bring about the bowels of mercy [*the tenderest, deepest mercy*], which overpowereth justice, and bringeth about means unto men **that they may have faith unto repentance**.

In verse 15, above, Amulek makes reference to both the law of mercy and the law of justice. Briefly stated, the law of justice is that whenever a law is broken, a penalty must be paid. The law of mercy is that Christ paid the price necessary to satisfy the law of justice, and that He can let us pay Him rather than having to pay justice ourselves, which would bring inexpressible agony to us (see D&C 19:15–19). The way we pay Him is by repenting and progressing. As you can see, this is very "merciful." This is why it is called "the law of mercy."

In verses 16 and 17, next, Amulek summarizes what he has taught so far about mercy and justice, and ties it in with "planting the seed."

16 And **thus mercy can satisfy the demands of justice**, and encircles them in the arms of safety, while **he that exercises no faith unto repentance is exposed to the whole law of the demands of justice**; therefore **only unto him that has faith unto repentance is brought about the great and eternal plan of redemption** [*only those who exercise faith in Christ and repent of their sins will have the Atonement work for them*].

17 Therefore may God grant unto you, my brethren, that ye may begin to **exercise your faith unto repentance**, that ye begin [*plant the seed*] to **call upon his holy name, that he would have mercy upon you**;

Remember that one of Alma's answers to the Zoramite question in Alma 33:1 (how to plant the seed, how to begin to exercise faith) was that they should pray. Alma emphasized this by quoting Zenos (Alma 33:3–11). Amulek will now add his testimony of the need to pray (verse 17 and verses 18–27).

18 Yea, **cry** [*pray*] **unto him for mercy**; for he is mighty to save.

19 Yea, humble yourselves, and **continue in prayer unto him**.

20 **Cry** [*pray*] **unto him** when ye are **in your fields**, yea, **over all your flocks**.

21 Cry unto him **in your houses**, yea, **over all your household, both morning, mid–day, and evening**.

22 Yea, cry unto him **against the power of your enemies.**

There is an important lesson for us in verse 22, above. Amulek did not teach us to pray against our enemies. He said to pray "against the **power** of [*our*] enemies." This is an important distinction. We are taught to pray **for** our enemies (Matthew 5:44). The devil is an exception to this rule (see verse 23, next), since he is permanently evil and God has said that he has been cast out forever. If we were to pray for the devil, it would, in effect, be praying against God's righteous judgment of Lucifer.

23 Yea, cry unto him **against the devil**, who is an enemy to all righteousness.

24 Cry unto him **over the crops of your fields**, that ye may prosper in them.

25 Cry **over the flocks of your fields**, that they may increase.

26 But this is not all; ye must **pour out your souls** [*in prayer*] **in your closets, and your secret places, and in your wilderness.**

In other words, you Zoramites can pray anytime, anywhere, about anything you want to. It is not true that you can only pray on the Rameumptom tower, like you have been taught by your priests and teachers.

Next, Amulek helps us understand what it means to "pray always" (D&C 10:5).

27 Yea, and **when you do not cry unto the Lord** [*when you are not actually praying*], **let your hearts be full, drawn out in prayer unto him continually** for your welfare, and also for the welfare of those who are around you.

Again, remember that Alma and Amulek have been responding to the Zoramite's question as to how to "plant the seed." Next, Amulek teaches them and us a very necessary lesson about effective prayer. Basically, he will say that if we want our prayers answered, we must answer the requests for help from others whom we are in a position to help. Otherwise, our prayers are useless and we are hypocrites.

28 And now behold, my beloved brethren, I say unto you, **do not suppose that this is all** [*don't think that all you have to do is pray and believe in Christ*]; for after ye have done all these things, **if ye turn away the needy**, and **the naked** [*those who do not have adequate clothing*], and **visit not the sick and afflicted**, and **impart** [*give*] **of your substance, if ye have, to those who stand in**

need—I say unto you, **if ye do not any of these things, behold, your prayer is vain** [*useless*], and availeth you nothing [*doesn't help you at all*], and **ye are as hypocrites who do deny the faith** [*your words may say that you have faith in Christ, but your actions overrule your words*].

29 Therefore, **if ye do not remember to be charitable, ye are as dross** [*slag, cinders; the useless rock which is thrown away after the gold is melted out of it*], which the refiners do cast out, (it being of no worth) and is trodden under foot of men [*it is used to make paths to be walked on*].

We are now entering some Book of Mormon verses that are much-quoted, including "this life is the time for men to prepare to meet God." It is important that we understand these verses in context (in the background of the verses around them). Otherwise, we would not be able to accept that there is a great work of conversion going on in the spirit world mission field. See D&C 138.

The context for these verses is that these people have already been taught the gospel. They apostatized from it and are now being taught again by Alma and Amulek. Verse 30 says that they "have received so many witnesses." In other words, we are probably safe to believe that many of these people have had the Holy Ghost testify to them of the truth of the gospel many times, and are getting their full set of chances to receive the gospel here on earth. If they still reject it, or do not live it with full commitment, then the highest they can go after Final Judgment is the terrestrial kingdom (D&C 76:71, 74, and 79).

In fact, Amulek will tell these people very plainly that if they "do not improve . . . while in this life, then cometh the night of darkness wherein there can be no labor performed" (see verse 33). Most of us would probably do well to consider that we are getting our full set of chances in this life, too. Those who do not get a fair chance in this life will get a completely fair chance in the spirit world mission field after this mortal life, so that at the Final Judgment they will be on equal footing with all others.

30 And now, my brethren, I would that, **after ye have received so many witnesses**, seeing that the holy scriptures testify of these things, ye come forth and bring fruit unto repentance.

31 Yea, I would that ye would come forth and **harden not your hearts any longer**; for behold, **now is the time and the day of your salvation**; and therefore, if ye will repent and harden not your hearts, immediately shall the great plan of redemption be brought about unto you.

The word "immediately" is an interesting word in verse 31, above. Perhaps you've noticed that as soon as you make a choice to do better, to repent sincerely when needed, you "immediately" feel better. The Lord, in effect, is giving you a hug!

32 For behold, **this life is the time for men to prepare to meet God; yea, behold the day of this life is the day for men to perform their labors.**

33 And now, as I said unto you [*the Zoramites as well as many of us*] before, **as ye have had so many witnesses** [*so much evidence and testimony that the gospel is true*], therefore, I beseech of you that ye **do not procrastinate** [*put off*] **the day of your repentance until the end; for after this day of life, which is given us to prepare for eternity, behold, if we do not improve our time while in this life, then cometh the night of darkness wherein there can be no labor performed.**

Among many other important words in verse 33, above, a key word can assure us of salvation. The word is "improve." If we do not improve, then our eternal progression is stopped. However, if we do improve, sincerely, continuously, verse 36 will apply to us. Namely, that our "garments (symbolic of our lives) should be made white through the blood of the Lamb." In other words, the key to successfully preparing to meet God, in this life, is to exercise faith and keep trying such that we continue to improve throughout our lives. That enables the Savior to make us clean and spotless (2 Nephi 33:7) on Judgment Day, so that we can enter celestial exaltation and continue progressing until we learn everything we need to know and do as gods (see *Teachings of the Prophet Joseph Smith,* 348).

Elder Marvin J. Ashton of the Quorum of the Twelve Apostles gave a talk in the April 1989 general conference, in which he taught this principle of improving. Among other things, he said, ". . . the speed with which we head along the straight and narrow path isn't as important as the direction in which we are traveling." You may wish to find and read the rest of his address.

Next, Amulek teaches us that people remain basically the same upon dying as they were here on earth. In other words, they don't suddenly change just because they die and discover that there is life after death.

34 Ye cannot say, when ye are brought to that awful crisis [*when you die and face God*], that I will repent, that I will return to my God. Nay, ye cannot say this; for **that same spirit which doth possess your bodies at the time that ye go out of this life, that same spirit will have power to possess your body in that eternal world** [*the next life*].

Verse 35, next, contains a powerful doctrinal point. It is a fair warning to us to use our agency to choose to follow God rather than Satan.

35 For behold, **if ye have procrastinated** [*put off*] **the day of your repentance even until death**, behold, **ye have become subjected to the spirit of the devil**, and **he doth seal you his**; therefore, **the Spirit of the Lord hath withdrawn from you, and hath no place in you**, and **the devil hath all power over you**; and **this is the final state of the wicked** [*sons of perdition; see D&C 76:31–49*].

36 And this I know, because **the Lord** hath said he **dwelleth not in unholy temples** [*in evil people*], but in the hearts of the righteous doth he dwell; yea, and he has also said that **the righteous shall sit down in his kingdom** [*celestial*

glory], to go no more out [*permanently*]; but **their garments** [*their clothes, symbolic of their lives*] **should be** [*will be*] **made white** [*cleansed*] **through the blood of the Lamb** [*Christ*].

37 And now, my beloved brethren, I desire that ye should **remember these things**, and that ye should work out your salvation with fear before God, and that ye should no more deny the coming of Christ [*as you have been taught to do by your false religion; see Alma 31:16*];

38 That ye **contend** [*fight*] **no more against the Holy Ghost** [*don't resist the promptings of the Holy Ghost; it will leave investigators if they resist it; see D&C 130:23*], but that ye **receive it**, and **take upon you the name of Christ** [*make covenants, including baptism, in the name of Jesus Christ*]; that **ye humble yourselves** even to the dust, **and worship God, in whatsoever place ye may be in** [*wherever you are*]**, in spirit and in truth**; and that ye **live in thanksgiving daily** [*show gratitude*], for the many mercies and blessings which he doth bestow upon you.

39 Yea, and I also exhort you, my brethren, that ye **be watchful unto prayer continually** [*don't forget your daily prayers*], **that ye may not be led away by the temptations of the devil,** that he may not overpower you, that ye may not become his subjects at the last day; for behold, he rewardeth you no good thing [*the devil's reward to his followers has nothing good at all in it*].

40 And now my beloved brethren, I would exhort you to **have patience**, and that ye **bear with all manner of afflictions**; that ye **do not revile against those who do cast you out because of your exceeding poverty**, lest [*for fear that*] ye become sinners like unto them [*don't hate others and try to get even, or you will become sinners like they are; see D&C 64:9–11*];

41 But that ye **have patience**, and **bear with** those **afflictions**, with a **firm hope** that ye shall one day rest from all your afflictions [*don't let afflictions sour you on life; keep the perspective that the gospel gives*].

ALMA 35

In this chapter you will see the trickery of the wicked prominent Zoramites as they ask questions to find out which of their people believe the words of Alma and Amulek and their missionary companions (Alma 31:6–7). They hide the true purpose of the questions so that the people do not realize what they intend to do with the results. After finding out who the believers are, they drive them out of their land.

Not only do they drive them out, but they also threaten the people of Ammon in the land of Jershon, who welcome the converted Zoramites to live among them. When their threats do not work, they go among the Lamanites and stir them up to join them in war against the Lamanite converts (formerly known as the Anti-Nephi-Lehis) in the land of Jershon.

It seems that Satan can't leave members of the Church alone. It is the devil's way to be angry at someone, and the Zoramites who were not converted fell right into this trap.

After finishing their successful preaching among the poorer Zoramites (Alma, chapters 31–34), Alma and his missionary companions left and traveled to the people of Ammon (the Lamanite converts to the Church from the 14-year mission of Ammon and his brothers) in the land of Jershon (in Nephite territory).

1 NOW it came to pass that **after Amulek had made an end of these words** [*had finished teaching*], they [*Alma and Amulek*] withdrew themselves from the multitude and came over into the land of Jershon.

2 Yea, and **the rest of the brethren** [*Ammon, Aaron, Omner, Zeezrom, Shiblon, and Corianton*], **after they had preached** the word unto the Zoramites, **also came over into the land of Jershon**.

Next, we see the plotting of the prominent, unbelieving Zoramites.

3 And it came to pass that **after the more popular part of the Zoramites** had **consulted together concerning the words which had been preached** unto them, **they were angry because of the word** [*the gospel the missionaries preached*], for **it did destroy their craft** [*it destroyed their priestcraft and the wealth and popularity they gained from it*]; therefore they would not hearken unto the words.

Now, we see the sly survey, or opinion poll, they conducted to see who believed the missionaries.

4 And **they sent and gathered together throughout all the land all the people, and consulted with them concerning the words which had been spoken.**

5 Now **their rulers and their priests and their teachers did not let the people know concerning their desires**; therefore they found out privily [*secretly; in a round about way*] the minds of all the people.

6 And it came to pass that **after they had found out the minds of all the people, those who were in favor of the words which had been spoken by Alma and his brethren** were **cast out of the land**; and they were many; and **they came over also into the land of Jershon**.

7 And it came to pass that **Alma and his brethren did minister unto them**.

Next, we see the attempt by the Zoramite leaders to bully the Lamanite converts in the land of Jershon.

8 Now the people of the Zoramites were angry with the people of Ammon who were in Jershon, and **the chief ruler of the Zoramites**, being a very wicked man, **sent over unto the people of Ammon desiring them that they should cast out of their land all those who came over from them** [*the Zoramites*] **into their land.**

9 And **he breathed out many threatenings against them**. And now **the people of Ammon did not**

fear their words; therefore **they did not cast them out**, but they **did receive all the poor of the Zoramites** that came over unto them; and they **did nourish them, and did clothe them, and did give unto them lands for their inheritance**; and they did administer unto them according to their wants.

10 Now **this did stir up the Zoramites to anger against the people of Ammon, and they began to mix with the Lamanites and to stir them up also to anger against them.**

11 And thus **the Zoramites and the Lamanites began to make preparations for war** against the people of Ammon, and also against the Nephites [*who had promised to defend them, because they had made a covenant never to take up weapons again; see Alma 24:16–18*].

12 And **thus ended the seventeenth year** of the reign of the judges over the people of Nephi.

Because of the coming battle with the Zoramites and Lamanites, the Ammonites now have to relocate again to make room for the Nephite armies. They are joined by the Zoramite converts to defend that border.

13 And **the people of Ammon departed out of the land of Jershon**, and came over into the land of Melek, and **gave place in the land of Jershon for the armies of the Nephites, that they might contend** [*fight*] **with the armies of the Lamanites and the armies of the Zoramites**; and thus commenced a war betwixt the Lamanites and the Nephites, in the eighteenth year of the reign of the judges; and an account shall be given of their wars hereafter [*beginning with Alma 43:3 and continuing basically until the end of the Book of Alma*].

14 And **Alma, and Ammon, and their brethren, and also the two sons of Alma returned to the land of Zarahemla**, after having been instruments in the hands of God of **bringing many of the Zoramites to repentance**; and as many as were brought to repentance were driven out of their land; but they have lands for their inheritance in the land of Jershon, and **they have taken up arms to defend themselves, and their wives, and children, and their lands.**

Alma will now set the stage to speak to each of his sons, fortifying them against the many evils of their day. We will learn much from his counsel to them, because the evils of our day are the same tools the devil used in their day.

Remember, Alma is the President of the Church.

15 Now **Alma, being grieved** [*worried and pained*] for the iniquity of his people, yea for the wars, and the bloodsheds, and the contentions which were among them; and having been to declare the word, or sent to declare the word, among all the people in every city; and seeing that **the hearts of the people began to wax hard** [*to grow hard against religion and spiritual things*], **and that they began to be**

offended because of the strictness of the word [*they wanted the rules of the Church to be "relaxed" so that they could commit sins and still feel like they were religious*], his heart was exceedingly sorrowful.

16 Therefore, **he caused that his sons should be gathered together, that he might give unto them every one his charge, separately, concerning the things pertaining** [*that apply*] **unto righteousness.** And we have an account of his commandments, which he gave unto them according to his own record. [*Mormon will be quoting Alma now from chapter 36 through chapter 42.*]

ALMA 36

Alma, chapter 36, is one of the best chapters to read to learn how to tell if you have been forgiven of sins you have repented of.

In this chapter, Alma interviews and teaches his oldest son, Helaman. As he does so, he tells him about his younger days when he rebelled against the Church and went around with his four friends, the sons of King Mosiah II, trying to destroy the Church. He tells about his conversion when an angel appeared to him and his friends and how he knew he had been forgiven after very deep and sincere repentance.

1 **MY son, give ear to my words** [*listen carefully*]; for I swear [*promise*] unto you, that **inasmuch** [*if*] **as ye shall keep the commandments of God ye shall prosper** [*do well*] in the land.

First, Alma will prepare Helaman to better understand what he wants to tell him by teaching him to remember past blessings from the Lord. This will help him to understand how powerful repenting and being forgiven of sins is in progressing in living the gospel.

2 **I would** [*want*] **that ye should do as I have done, in remembering the captivity of our fathers** [*ancestors*]; for **they were in bondage** [*captivity, slavery*], and **none could deliver them except it was the God of Abraham, and the God of Isaac, and the God of Jacob** [*another way of saying Jesus Christ, who was the God of the Old Testament under Heavenly Father's direction*]; and he surely did deliver them in their afflictions. [*Remember past blessings from the Lord.*]

Next, we are reminded that a righteous life is not free from troubles and trials. The difference, though, is the fact that the righteous are supported by the Lord during their trials, while the wicked tend to try to go it alone.

3 And now, O my son Helaman, behold, thou art in thy youth, and therefore, I beseech of thee that thou wilt hear my words and learn of me; for I do know that **whosoever shall put their trust in God shall be supported in their trials, and their troubles, and their afflictions**, and shall be lifted up [*exalted in celestial glory*] at the last day [*on Judgment Day*].

4 And **I would not that ye think that I know of myself**—not of the temporal but of the spiritual, not of the carnal [*worldly*] mind **but of God.**

[*Mine is not an academic witness, rather a spiritual testimony.*]

5 Now, behold, I say unto you, if **I had not been born of God** [*if I had not gone through godly sorrow and completely repented and changed and become a new person through the Atonement*] **I should not** [*would not*] **have known these things**; but God has, by the mouth of his holy angel, made these things known unto me, not of any worthiness of myself;

Alma will now tell about his conversion, giving Helaman many details and teaching many lessons to him and us.

6 For **I went about with the sons of Mosiah, seeking to destroy the church of God** [*Mosiah 27:10*]; but behold, **God sent his holy angel to stop us** by the way [*as we were on our way to cause more trouble*].

7 And behold, **he spake** [*spoke*] **unto us, as it were the voice of thunder, and the whole earth did tremble** beneath our feet; and **we all fell to the earth**, for the fear of the Lord came upon us.

8 But behold, **the voice said unto me: Arise**. And **I arose and stood up, and beheld** [*saw*] **the angel.**

9 And **he said** unto me: **If thou wilt of thyself be destroyed** [*if you want to be destroyed yourself, go ahead and keep being wicked; you have your agency*], **seek no more to destroy the church of God**.

10 And it came to pass that **I fell to the earth**; and it was for the space of **three days and three nights** that **I could not open my mouth, neither had I the use of my limbs** [*arms and legs*].

In verse 10, above, Alma speaks of the three days and three nights. Some people become a bit confused because Mosiah 27:23 speaks of two days and two nights. What they don't remember is that the account in Mosiah speaks of the two days and two nights, after Alma had been brought to his father and after his father had assembled others to join him in fasting for his son. In other words, in Alma 36, he is speaking of the total time that he was being born again, and the account in Mosiah refers only to two of the three days and nights.

11 And **the angel spake more things unto me, which were heard by my brethren** [*friends who were with him*], **but I did not hear them**; for **when I heard the words**—If thou wilt be destroyed of thyself, seek no more to destroy the church of God—**I was struck with such great fear and amazement lest perhaps I should be destroyed, that I fell to the earth and I did hear no more.**

It has been said that when we stop making excuses for current bad behavior, personal progress begins. One of the very important messages for us in the next verses is that Alma accepted full responsibility for his sinful behavior. He perhaps could have blamed his friends, the four sons of Mosiah, for what he was doing since they were participating with him. He did not. Watch as he blames only himself, making no excuses.

12 But **I was racked** [*severely pained*] **with eternal torment** [*suffering*], for **my soul was harrowed** [*torn*] **up** to the greatest degree and racked **with all my sins.**

13 Yea, **I did remember all my sins and iniquities** [*wickedness*], for which **I was tormented with the pains of hell**; yea, I saw that **I had rebelled against my God**, and that **I had not kept his holy commandments.**

14 Yea, and **I had murdered many of his children, or rather led them away unto destruction** [*spiritual destruction*]; yea, and in fine [*in summary*] so great had been my iniquities, that **the very thought of coming into the presence of my God did rack my soul with inexpressible horror.**

Alma is experiencing what we call "godly sorrow." Paul teaches about this in the Bible in 2 Corinthians 7:8–11, as follows:

2 Corinthians 7:8–11

8 For though I made you sorry with a letter [*even though I caused you sorrow when I scolded you in my last letter to you (First Corinthians)*], I do not repent [*I don't take back what I said because you needed it*], though I did repent [*though I did regret hurting your feelings*]: for I perceive that the same epistle [*that letter*] hath made you sorry, though it were but for a season [*even though you got over it after a while*].

9 Now I rejoice, not that ye were made sorry [*not because I caused you pain*], but that ye sorrowed to repentance [*but because you actually repented because of what I said to you*]: for ye were made **sorry after a godly manner** [*my letter caused you to have "godly sorrow" so that you truly repented*], that ye might receive damage by us in nothing [*so that, as it ultimately turned out, we did not hurt you in any way*].

Paul now defines "godly sorrow," which is a necessary part of truly repenting.

10 For **godly sorrow** worketh repentance [*causes us to repent*] to salvation [*and thus obtain exaltation*] not to be repented of [*and leaves us with no regrets*]: but **the sorrow of the world** [*being sorry you got caught, or sorry because you are embarrassed, or sorry that your opportunity to continue committing that sin has been taken away, etc.*] **worketh death** [*leads to spiritual death*].

Now, Paul describes some components of "godly sorrow" that make it effective in cleansing us from sin and leading to a true change of heart.

11 For behold this selfsame thing [*this godly sorrow, the very thing I'm teaching you about*] that **ye sorrowed** [*were sorry for sins*] **after a godly sort** [*in the way God wants you to*], what **carefulness** [*sincerity, anxiety*] it wrought [*caused*] in you, yea, what **clearing of yourselves** [*eagerness to become clear of the sin*], yea, what **indignation** [*irritation, anger at yourself for committing the sin*], yea, what **fear** [*alarm; fear for your salvation*], yea, what **vehement desire** [*strong desire to change*], yea, what **zeal** [*enthusiasm to change*], yea,

what **revenge** [*punishment; suffering whatever is necessary to make permanent change*]! In all things ye have approved yourselves to be clear in this matter [*in everything you have done you have demonstrated that you understand godly sorrow*].

We will now return to Alma's account. With very serious sin, people sometimes wish that they could be extinct, in other words, simply cease to exist so that they don't have to face themselves or God. Keep in mind that the Atonement will overcome Alma's desire to become extinct and will replace it with "exquisite joy" (verse 21). This is one of the miracles that accompanies forgiveness.

15 **Oh, thought I, that I could be banished and become extinct both soul and body, that I might not be brought to stand in the presence of my God, to be judged of my deeds.**

16 And now, **for three days and for three nights was I racked, even with the pains of a damned soul** [*godly sorrow*].

Watch now as the Atonement of Christ begins to work in Alma's tormented soul. A "seed" was planted long ago by Alma's father's righteous teachings.

17 And it came to pass that as I was thus racked with torment, while I was harrowed [*torn*] up by the memory of my many sins, behold, **I remembered also to have heard my father prophesy unto the people concerning the coming of one Jesus Christ, a Son of God, to atone** [*pay*] **for the sins of the world.**

18 Now, **as my mind caught hold upon this thought, I cried within my heart: O Jesus, thou Son of God, have mercy on me**, who am in the gall [*a very bitter fluid*] of bitterness, and am encircled about by the everlasting chains of death.

Some have come to believe that as long as one can remember past sins, forgiveness has not been granted. This is false. They are perhaps confused by D&C 58:42–43, where the Lord tells us that He remembers them no more. In other words, they will not be brought up again, unless we repeat them (D&C 82:7). They won't even be brought up on Judgment Day (2 Nephi 9:14, last half of verse).

Alma obviously remembers his past sins or he wouldn't be discussing this with Helaman. However, something has changed. The pain of the past is gone. This is what forgiveness does for us. Pay close attention to what replaces this pain and agony for past sins, as Alma continues teaching Helaman.

19 And now, behold, when I thought this, **I could remember my pains no more** [*the pain was gone*]; yea, I was harrowed [*torn*] up by the memory of my sins no more.

20 And oh, **what joy**, and **what marvelous light** I did behold; yea, **my soul was filled with joy** as exceeding as was my pain [*to the same degree that pain previously filled my soul*]!

21 Yea, I say unto you, my son, that there could be nothing so exquisite and so bitter as were my pains. Yea, and again I say unto you, my son,

that on the other hand, **there can be nothing so exquisite** [*intense and wonderful*] **and sweet as was my joy.**

22 Yea, **methought I saw**, even as our father Lehi saw, **God sitting upon his throne**, surrounded with numberless concourses of angels, in the attitude of singing and praising their God; yea, **and my soul did long to be there** [*a complete turnabout from verses 14 and 15, where he couldn't stand the thought of being in the presence of God*].

23 But behold, my limbs did receive their strength again, and I stood upon my feet, and did manifest unto the people that **I had been born of God.** [*Alma is now a completely new person.*]

24 Yea, and from that time even until now, I have labored without ceasing, that I might bring souls unto repentance; that I might bring them to taste of **the exceeding joy of which I did taste**; that they might also be born of God, and be **filled with the Holy Ghost**.

25 Yea, and now behold, O my son, the Lord doth give me **exceedingly great joy** in the fruit of my labors;

Alma goes on to remind Helaman of another principle that accompanies true repentance, namely, the principle of restitution. It is that we do all we can to undo the damage that we have caused. Beyond that, the Atonement takes over and we are cleansed, even of things that we can never repair or make right. Alma and the sons of Mosiah did all they could to repair the damage they had caused (Mosiah 27:35), and he now tells Helaman of the many who have been brought to Christ as a result of their continuing efforts.

26 For **because of the word which he has imparted unto me, behold, many have been born of God** [*have been brought into the Church, been baptized, and each has become a new and different person, compared to their old selves before conversion and baptism*], **and have tasted as I have tasted**, and have seen eye to eye as I have seen; therefore **they do know of these things of which I have spoken, as I do know**; and the knowledge which I have is of God.

27 And **I have been supported under trials and troubles of every kind**, yea, and in all manner of afflictions [*troubles and difficulties*]; yea, God has delivered me from prison, and from bonds, and from death; yea, and I do put my trust in him, and he will still deliver me.

Another thing true repentance brings is deep confidence in attaining celestial exaltation. This is not arrogance. This is simply true, for the righteous.

28 And **I know that he will raise me up at the last day** [*on Judgment Day*], **to dwell with him in glory**; yea, and I will praise him forever, for he has brought our fathers out of Egypt, and he has swallowed up the Egyptians in the Red Sea; and he led them by his power into the promised land; yea, and he has delivered them out of bondage and captivity from time to time.

29 Yea, and he has also brought our fathers out of the land of Jerusalem; and he has also, by his everlasting power, delivered them out of bondage and captivity, from time to time even down to the present day; and **I have always retained in remembrance their captivity; yea, and ye also ought to retain in remembrance, as I have done, their captivity.** [*I have always remembered what God did for them and what will happen to me if I revert back to my sinful ways of the past.*]

30 But behold, my son, this is not all; for **ye ought to know as I do know, that inasmuch as ye shall keep the commandments of God ye shall prosper in the land; and ye ought to know also, that inasmuch as ye will not keep the commandments of God ye shall be cut off from his presence.** Now this is according to his word.

ALMA 37

In this chapter, Alma turns the records over to his oldest son, Helaman, including the large plates of Nephi, the brass plates of Laban, the twenty-four gold plates containing the record of the Jaredites, as well as the Urim and Thummim. Helaman thus becomes the record keeper and the one assigned to continue making a record of his people. Alma continues giving counsel and instruction.

1 AND now, my son Helaman, I command you that ye **take the records which have been entrusted with me**;

2 And I also command you that ye **keep a record of this people, according as I have done, upon the plates of Nephi** [*the large plates of Nephi*], and keep all these things sacred which I have kept, even as I have kept them; for it is for a wise purpose that they are kept.

3 And these **plates of brass**, which contain these engravings, which have the records of the holy scriptures upon them [*basically, the Old Testament, up to and including Jeremiah*], which have the genealogy of our forefathers, even from the beginning—

From verse 4, next, we learn that the contents of the brass plates will someday go forth to all nations.

4 Behold, it has been prophesied by our fathers, that **they** [*the brass plates*] **should be kept** and handed down from one generation to another, and be kept and preserved by the hand of the Lord **until they should go forth unto every nation, kindred, tongue, and people**, that they shall know of the mysteries contained thereon.

5 And now behold, if they are kept they must retain their brightness; yea, and **they will retain their brightness**; yea, and also shall all the plates which do contain that which is holy writ.

6 Now ye may suppose that this is foolishness in me; but behold I say unto you, that **by small and simple things are great things brought to pass; and small means in many instances doth confound the wise.**

7 And **the Lord God doth work by means to bring about his great and eternal purposes**; and by very small means the Lord doth confound the wise and bringeth about the salvation of many souls.

Next, Alma reminds us of the value and purpose of the scriptures.

8 And now, it has hitherto [*up to now*] been wisdom in God that these things should be preserved; for behold, **they have enlarged the memory of this people, yea, and convinced many of the error of their ways, and brought them to the knowledge of their God unto the salvation of their souls.**

9 Yea, I say unto you, were it not for these things that these records do contain, which are on these plates, Ammon and his brethren could not have convinced so many thousands of the Lamanites of the incorrect tradition of their fathers; yea, **these records** [*the scriptures*] and their words **brought them unto repentance; that is, they brought them to the knowledge of the Lord their God, and to rejoice in Jesus Christ their Redeemer.**

10 And **who knoweth but what they will be the means of bringing many thousands** of them, yea, and also many thousands of our stiffnecked [*stubborn and prideful*] brethren, the Nephites, who are now hardening their hearts in sin and iniquities, **to the knowledge of their Redeemer?**

Verse 11, next, is quite well known and contains good advice to all of us regarding teaching our own opinions as doctrine. There are some things that we simply don't know yet.

11 **Now these mysteries are not yet fully made known unto me; therefore I shall forbear** [*I won't say any more about them*].

12 And it may suffice if I only say **they are preserved for a wise purpose**, which purpose is known unto God; for he doth counsel in wisdom over all his works, and his paths are straight, and his course is one eternal round. [*In other words, God knows what he is doing and everything will work out as it should, even though we may not understand it all.*]

13 O **remember, remember, my son Helaman, how strict are the commandments of God**. And he said: If ye will keep my commandments ye shall prosper in the land—but if ye keep not his commandments ye shall be cut off from his presence.

14 And now remember, my son, that **God has entrusted you with these things** [*these records*], which are sacred, which he has kept sacred, and also which he will keep and preserve for a wise purpose in him, that he may show forth his power unto future generations.

15 And now behold, **I tell you by the spirit of prophecy, that if ye transgress the commandments of God, behold, these things which are**

sacred shall be taken away from
you by the power of God, and ye
shall be delivered up unto Satan, that
he may sift you as chaff before the
wind.

The imagery at the end of verse 15, above, has to do with harvesting grain in ancient times. As the plants grow and mature, the heads of grain are enclosed in husks, and in order to harvest the grain, the husks are walked on or rolled together to separate the actual grain from the husks. At this point, the husks are called "chaff." The piles of intermixed grain and chaff are tossed up into the wind. Since the chaff is very light, it blows away easily in the wind, and the heads of grain fall back to the threshing floor. Thus, the imagery of being sifted by Satan as chaff in the wind is that those who transgress God's laws are easy for Satan to influence and "blow" wherever he wants.

16 But **if ye keep the command-**
ments of God, and do with these
things which are sacred according to
that which the Lord doth command
you, [*for you must appeal unto the Lord for*
all things whatsoever ye must do with them]
behold, **no power of earth or hell**
can take them from you, for God
is powerful to the fulfilling of all his
words.

As Alma bears testimony that God fulfills His promises, he gives a specific example, next.

17 For he will fulfil all his promises
which he shall make unto you, for **he**
has fulfilled his promises which he
has made unto our fathers [*ancestors;*
prophets such as Lehi, Nephi and others].

18 For **he promised unto them that**
he would preserve these things [*these*
scriptural records] for a wise purpose in
him, **that he might show forth his**
power unto future generations.

19 And now behold, **one purpose**
hath he fulfilled, even to the res-
toration of many thousands of the
Lamanites to the knowledge of the
truth; and he hath shown forth his
power in them, and he will also still
show forth his power in them unto
future generations; therefore they
shall be preserved.

20 Therefore **I command you, my**
son Helaman, that ye **be diligent**
[*faithful*] in fulfilling all my words,
and that ye **be diligent** in keeping
the commandments of God as they
are written.

21 And now, **I will speak unto you**
concerning those twenty–four
plates [*containing the record of the Jaredites;*
see Mosiah 8:8–9; the book of Ether], that ye
keep them, that the mysteries and the
works of darkness, and their secret
works, or the secret works of those
people who have been destroyed,
may be made manifest unto this peo-
ple; yea, all their murders, and rob-
bings, and their plunderings, and all
their wickedness and abominations,
may be made manifest unto this peo-
ple; yea, **and that ye preserve these**
interpreters [*the Urim and Thummim*
which Mosiah II had; see Mosiah 8:13; see also
Topical Guide under "Urim and Thummim"].

22 For behold, **the Lord saw that**
his people began to work in

darkness [*spiritual darkness*], yea, work secret murders and abominations; therefore the Lord said, **if they did not repent they** [*the Jaredites*] **should be destroyed** from off the face of the earth.

23 And the Lord said: **I will prepare unto** [*for*] **my servant Gazelem, a stone** [*a Urim and Thummim; see* Mormon Doctrine, *by Bruce R. McConkie, 1966, 307–8*], which shall shine forth in darkness unto light, that I may discover [*uncover; reveal*] unto my people who serve me, that I may discover [*uncover; reveal*] unto them the works of their brethren, yea, their secret works, their works of darkness, and their wickedness and abominations.

We don't know for sure what the name "Gazelem" means or whether or not it refers to an ancient prophet who was able to translate by means of a Urim and Thummim. We will have to wait for further knowledge on the matter. It is interesting to note that in earlier editions of the Doctrine and Covenants, Joseph Smith was referred to as "Gazelam" (different spelling) in D&C 82:11.

24 And now, my son, **these interpreters** [*Urim and Thummim*] **were prepared that the word of God might be fulfilled**, which he spake, saying:

25 I will bring forth out of darkness unto light [*I will expose*] all their secret works and their abominations; and except they repent I will destroy them from off the face of the earth; and **I will bring to light all their secrets and abominations**, unto every nation that shall hereafter possess the land.

26 And now, my son, we see that **they** [*the Jaredites*] **did not repent**; therefore they have been destroyed, and thus far the word of God has been fulfilled; yea, their secret abominations have been brought out of darkness and made known unto us [*see Ether 8, for example*].

Next, Alma commands Helaman not to reveal the actual oaths, covenants, and specific details of the agreements that the Jaredites made among themselves as they became entangled in secret combinations.

27 And now, my son, **I command you that ye retain all their oaths, and their covenants, and their agreements in their secret abominations; yea, and all their signs and their wonders ye shall keep from this people, that they know them not, lest peradventure they should fall into darkness also and be destroyed.**

28 For behold, there is a curse upon all this land, that destruction shall come upon all those workers of darkness, according to the power of God, **when they are fully ripe**; therefore I desire that this people might not be destroyed.

The phrase "fully ripe" as used in verse 28, above, means when there is no hope left of reclaiming them, because they have become so thoroughly involved in wickedness.

29 Therefore **ye shall keep these secret plans of their oaths and their covenants from this people, and only their wickedness and their murders and their abominations**

shall ye make known unto them; and ye shall **teach them to abhor such wickedness and abominations and murders; and ye shall also teach them that these people were destroyed on account of their wickedness and abominations and their murders.**

30 For behold, **they murdered all the prophets of the Lord who came among them** to declare unto them concerning their iniquities; and the blood of those whom they murdered did cry unto the Lord their God for vengeance upon those who were their murderers; and thus the judgments of God did come upon these workers of darkness and secret combinations.

In a very real sense, we are seeing "secret combinations" functioning today in the form of terrorist networks whose basic purpose is to terrorize and destroy in order to attain their evil goals. The false promises made to suicide bombers in concert with their oaths to give their lives for the cause of revenge and terror are just one manifestation of the depths to which Satan leads his followers as he counterfeits oaths and covenants of God.

31 Yea, and **cursed be the land forever** and ever unto those workers of darkness and secret combinations, even unto destruction, **except they repent before they are fully ripe**.

32 And now, my son, remember the words which I have spoken unto you; trust not [*do not reveal*] those secret plans unto this people, **but teach them an everlasting hatred against sin and iniquity**.

Next, Alma shows us the exact opposites of the elements of secret combinations.

33 Preach unto them **repentance**, and **faith on the Lord Jesus Christ**; teach them to **humble themselves** and to **be meek and lowly in heart**; teach them to **withstand every temptation of the devil, with their faith on the Lord Jesus Christ.**

34 Teach them to **never be weary of good works**, but to be meek and lowly in heart; for such shall find rest to their souls.

Verses 35 and 37, next, are two of the best-known verses in the Book of Mormon. Alma defines wisdom as keeping the commandments and constantly counseling with God.

35 **O, remember, my son, and learn wisdom in thy youth; yea, learn in thy youth to keep the commandments of God.**

36 Yea, and cry unto God for all thy support; yea, let all thy doings be unto the Lord, and whithersoever thou goest let it be in the Lord; yea, **let all thy thoughts be directed unto the Lord**; yea, let the affections of thy heart be placed upon the Lord forever.

37 **Counsel with the Lord in all thy doings, and he will direct thee for good**; yea, when thou liest down at night lie down unto the Lord, that he may watch over you in your sleep; and when thou risest in the morning let thy heart be full of thanks unto

God; and if ye do these things, ye shall be lifted up at the last day [*you will be exalted at the Final Judgment*].

One of the lessons we can learn from what Alma teaches Helaman, next, is that after the major covenants and ordinances are in place in our lives, salvation is found in the little things, because they are what mainly make up this life. Alma will use the Liahona as an object lesson. Remember, Lehi found the Liahona, which was described as a ball or compass, outside his tent door one day. It guided them on their journey and had the word of God on it from time to time.

38 And **now, my son, I have somewhat to say concerning the thing which our fathers** [*ancestors*] **call a ball, or director**—or our fathers called it **Liahona**, which is, being interpreted, **a compass**; and **the Lord prepared it**.

39 And behold, there cannot any man work after the manner of so curious a workmanship [*such excellent craftsmanship*]. And behold, **it was prepared to show unto our fathers the course which they should travel in the wilderness**.

40 And **it did work for them according to their faith in God**; therefore, **if they had faith to believe that God could cause that those spindles should point the way they should go, behold, it was done**; therefore they had this miracle, and also many other miracles wrought by the power of God, **day by day**.

41 Nevertheless, **because those miracles were worked by small means it did show unto them marvelous works**. They were slothful, and forgot to exercise their faith and diligence and then those marvelous works ceased, and they did not progress in their journey;

42 Therefore, **they tarried in the wilderness, or did not travel a direct course, and were afflicted** with hunger and thirst, **because of their transgressions**.

43 And now, my son, **I would that ye should understand that these things are not without a shadow** [*there was symbolism in these things*]; for **as our fathers were slothful to give heed to** [*pay attention and obey*] **this compass** [*now these things were temporal*] **they did not prosper; even so it is with things which are spiritual**.

44 For behold, **it is as easy to give heed to the word of Christ, which will point to you a straight course to eternal bliss** [*happiness*], **as it was for our fathers to give heed to this compass, which would point unto them a straight course to the promised land**.

45 And now I say, is there not a type [*symbolism*] in this thing? For **just as surely as this director did bring our fathers, by following its course, to the promised land, shall the words of Christ, if we follow their course, carry us beyond this vale of sorrow** [*this earthly life*] **into a far better land of promise** [*heaven*].

46 O my son, **do not let us be slothful because of the easiness of the way**; for so was it with our fathers; for so was it prepared for them, that **if they would look they might live**; even so it is with us. **The way is prepared** [*by Christ*], **and if we will look** [*to Him for direction*] **we may live forever** [*in eternal life and exaltation*].

47 And now, my son, see that ye take care of these sacred things, yea, **see that ye look to God and live**. Go unto this people and declare the word, and be sober [*be serious about things that matter eternally*]. My son, farewell.

ALMA 38

Next, Alma gives counsel to his middle son, Shiblon. You will find much good counsel for daily living in his message.

One of the major lessons we can learn from this chapter is that we should bridle (control) our passions (verse 12). "Passions" are strong feelings about various things, such as music, art, hunting, fishing, cycling, skateboarding, horses, sex, caring for the poor, politics, and so forth. Some religions teach that passions are evil and should be done away with as completely as possible. This is false doctrine. True doctrine is that we should "bridle" them. When powerful horses are controlled by means of a bridle, they bring pleasure to the owner and rider. Passions, likewise, when bridled according to the laws and counsels of God, provide much satisfaction and enjoyment. For example, one could have great passion for beautiful landscapes but could spend so much time painting them that the necessities of life are not provided for the family. One could have a passion for great music, but could get so caught up in it that other aspects of life are not kept in reasonable balance. Even the powers of procreation are associated with sweet passion, respect, and love. When used within the covenant of marriage, these passions are clean and proper. However, when not "bridled," they are destructive to the soul and to society.

1 MY son, give ear to my words, for I say unto you, even as I said unto Helaman, that **inasmuch as ye shall keep the commandments of God ye shall prosper in the land; and inasmuch as ye will not keep the commandments of God ye shall be cut off from his presence.**

Parents are entitled to have joy because of their children. Shiblon is an example of this as expressed by his father, Alma, in the next verses.

2 And now, my son, **I trust that I shall have great joy in you, because of your steadiness and your faithfulness unto God**; for as you have commenced [*begun*] in your youth to look to the Lord your God, even so I hope that you will continue in keeping his commandments; for blessed is he that endureth to the end.

3 I say unto you, my son, that **I have had great joy in thee already, because of thy faithfulness and thy diligence, and thy patience and**

thy long-suffering among the people of the Zoramites [*the people with the Rameumptom; Alma 31–35*].

Next, we see that the mission to the Zoramites was not an easy one for Shiblon.

4 For I know that **thou wast in bonds** [*tied up*]; yea, and I also know that **thou wast stoned** [*hit with rocks*] for the word's [*gospel's*] sake; and **thou didst bear all these things with patience because the Lord was with thee**; and now thou knowest that the Lord did deliver thee [*you have a strong testimony*].

5 And now my son, Shiblon, I would that ye should remember [*I want you to remember*], that **as much as ye shall put your trust in God even so much ye shall be delivered out of your trials, and your troubles, and your afflictions**, and ye shall be lifted up at the last day [*exalted on Judgment Day*].

6 Now, my son, **I would not that ye should think that I know these things of myself, but it is the Spirit of God which is in me** which maketh these things known unto me; for **if I had not been born of God** [*if I had not become a new man through the Atonement of Christ*] **I should** [*would*] **not have known these things.**

Next, Alma briefly tells Shiblon of his conversion. For more details, see Alma 36 or Mosiah 27.

7 But behold, **the Lord in his great mercy sent his angel to declare unto me that I must stop the work of destruction among his people**; yea, and **I have seen an angel face to face**, and he spake with me, and his voice was as thunder, and it shook the whole earth.

8 And it came to pass that **I was three days and three nights in the most bitter pain and anguish of soul**; and **never, until I did cry out unto the Lord Jesus Christ for mercy, did I receive a remission of my sins** [*forgiveness of my sins*]. But behold, **I did cry unto him and I did find peace to my soul.**

9 And now, my son, **I have told you this that ye may learn wisdom**, that ye may learn of me that **there is no other way or means whereby man can be saved, only in and through Christ. Behold, he is the life and the light of the world. Behold, he is the word of truth and righteousness.**

10 And now, as ye have begun to teach the word even so I would that ye should continue to teach; and I would that ye would **be diligent and temperate** [*not extreme*] **in all things.**

11 **See that ye are not lifted up unto pride**; yea, see that ye **do not boast in your own wisdom, nor of your much strength.**

12 **Use boldness, but not overbearance** [*pushiness*]; and also see that ye **bridle all your passions**, that ye may be filled with love [*both love for God and the love of God*]; **see that ye refrain from idleness.**

13 **Do not pray** as the Zoramites do, for ye have seen that they pray **to be heard of men**, and to be praised for their wisdom.

14 **Do not say: O God, I thank thee that we are better than our brethren; but rather say: O Lord, forgive my unworthiness, and remember my brethren in mercy**—yea, acknowledge your unworthiness before God at all times.

15 And **may the Lord bless your soul, and receive you at the last day** [*at the Final Judgment*] **into his kingdom** [*celestial glory*], to sit down in peace. Now go, my son, and **teach the word** [*the gospel*] **unto this people**. Be sober [*be serious about serious things*]. My son, farewell.

ALMA 39

Remember, as recorded in Alma, chapters 31–34, that Alma, as President of the Church, took two of his sons, Shiblon and Corianton, along with some other missionaries on a mission to preach to the Zoramites. The Zoramites had left the Church (apostatized). Perhaps you remember the strange prayer tower they used, called the Rameumptom. While they were all on this mission to try to convert the Zoramites back to the gospel, Corianton, Alma's youngest son, set a terrible example and got sexually involved with a lady named Isabel. He broke the law of chastity. His behaviors as a missionary, committing fornication with this popular harlot (prostitute), caused a lot of trouble for Alma and the other missionaries. When the people saw what Corianton was doing, they wouldn't believe the preaching of the other missionaries, including Alma.

Chapters 39 through 42 are the account of Alma's counsel to his son, Corianton, trying to help him repent and return to being a faithful member of the Church. The problem right now is that Corianton doesn't believe that what he did was all that bad.

There are many important doctrines and teachings in these four chapters and many possible approaches to studying them. In addition to providing notes and commentary on many of these doctrines, we will approach our study of these chapters from the standpoint of Corianton's "basic belief system" through which he has allowed himself to stray from God's commandments and the instructions of his mission president father, Alma. We will note how Alma, with skill and inspiration, helps Corianton change his flawed basic belief system such that ultimately, he repents and becomes a faithful servant of the Lord.

First, just a brief explanation of what we mean by "basic belief system." Much of our thinking and behavior is directed by our basic beliefs. For example, if a member of the Church believes that it is extremely difficult to attain celestial glory, let alone exaltation, he or she might be inclined not to try very hard to live the gospel. On the other hand, if members understand D&C 76:67, wherein the Lord says that "innumerable" people will achieve that reward on Judgment Day, they will be much more inclined to strive to be faithful.

A basic belief of the Lamanites was that their ancestors, Laman and Lemuel, had been robbed and cheated by Nephi and his people (Mosiah 10:11–17), and thus they taught their children to hate the Nephites. A basic belief of the sons of Mosiah was that the Lamanites were precious children of God, and so they risked everything to take the gospel to them (Mosiah 28:1–3).

In the case of Corianton, he had several incorrect basic beliefs that served as his guidance system as far as living the gospel was concerned and led to trouble and grief. We will list some of them here and then watch how Alma deals with them in these four chapters. Corianton believed:

1. "I can handle it."
2. "I know more than my leaders."
3. "I can occasionally set aside rules, commitments, and covenants. I don't have to be religious all the time."
4. "Everybody is doing it, so it can't be that bad."
5. "Maybe there is no resurrection or life after death. If so, there is no such thing as Judgment Day and accountability. So I can do what I want to here on earth. It really doesn't matter."
6. If God is so merciful and kind, He won't really punish me that bad."
7. "Wickedness is happiness."
8. "I'm not really a bad person. What I'm doing isn't really wicked, just experimentation, gaining experience."
9. "God is fair and nice, so He wouldn't do something that mean to me on Judgment Day."

We will point out these basic belief problems in these chapters by <u>underlining</u> them and putting (B.B.), in other words, "basic belief," next to them.

As we begin chapter 39, we will quote Apostle Boyd K. Packer as he taught the importance of our understanding true doctrine. He said (**bold** added for emphasis): "**True doctrine, understood, changes attitudes and behavior**. The study of the doctrines of the gospel will improve behavior quicker than a study of behavior will improve behavior" (October 1986 general conference of the Church). Alma will use many "true doctrines" successfully, as he teaches and helps Corianton to see why what he has done is very serious sin and he needs to repent and change.

1 AND now, my son, **I have somewhat more to say unto thee than what I said unto thy brother** [*Shiblon*]; for behold, have ye not observed the steadiness of thy brother, his faithfulness, and his diligence in keeping the commandments of God? Behold, has he not set a good example for thee?

> The reason we know that Alma is referring to Corianton's brother, Shiblon, here rather than Helaman, is that Helaman did not go with them on the mission to the Zoramites (Alma 31:7).

2 For thou didst not give so much heed unto my words as did thy brother, among the people of the

Zoramites. **Now this is what I have against thee**; thou didst go on unto boasting in thy strength [*B.B. "I can handle it."*] and thy wisdom [*B.B. "I know more than my leaders."*].

3 And **this is not all**, my son. Thou didst do that which was grievous [*very painful and serious*] unto me; for thou didst forsake the ministry [*you left your missionary work*], and did go over into the land of Siron among the borders of the Lamanites, after the harlot Isabel [*B.B. "I can occasionally set aside rules, commitments, and covenants. I don't have to be religious all the time."*].

4 Yea, she [*the prostitute Isabel*] did steal away the hearts of many; but this was no excuse for thee, my son [*B.B. "Everybody is doing it so it can't be that bad."*]. Thou shouldst have tended to the ministry [*kept doing your missionary work*] wherewith thou wast entrusted.

Next, Alma teaches pure doctrine as to the seriousness of the sexual sins of fornication and adultery. He informs Corianton that first degree murder and to sin against the Holy Ghost are the only sins that are more serious than what he had done.

5 Know ye not, my son, that **these things are an abomination** [*very, very serious sin*] **in the sight of the Lord; yea, most abominable above all sins save it be the shedding of innocent blood or denying the Holy Ghost?**

The doctrine of the seriousness of sexual immorality has been reconfirmed time and time again by modern prophets. One such First Presidency statement follows (**bold** added for emphasis):

"The doctrine of this Church is that sexual sin—the illicit sexual relations of men and women—**stands, in its enormity, next to murder.**

"The Lord has drawn no essential distinctions between fornication, adultery, and harlotry or prostitution. Each has fallen under His solemn and awful condemnation.

"You youths of Zion, you cannot associate in non-marital, illicit sex relationships, which is fornication, and escape the punishments and the judgments which the Lord has declared against this sin. The day of reckoning will come just as certainly as night follows day. They who would palliate (downplay; make excuses for) this crime and say that such indulgence is but a sinless gratification of a normal desire, like appeasing hunger and thirst, speak filthiness with their lips. Their counsel leads to destruction; their wisdom comes from the father of lies.

"You husbands and wives who have taken on solemn obligations of chastity in the holy temples of the Lord and who violate those sacred vows by illicit sexual relations with others, you not only commit the vile and loathsome sin of adultery, but you break the oath you yourselves made with the Lord Himself before you went to the altar for your sealing. You become subject to the penalties which the Lord has prescribed for those who breach their covenants with Him" (Heber J. Grant, J. Reuben Clark, Jr., and

David O. McKay, in Conference Report, Oct. 1942, p. 11).

Some years ago, when I was serving as a bishop, the question was asked in the priests quorum as to whether or not the sin Corianton committed could be forgiven. Eight out of the ten priests in class replied that it could not be. That is not true. See Alma 39:8–9, where Corianton is instructed to repent. In the discussion which followed, these young men came to understand that while it requires very deep repenting and change, it can be forgiven completely. In fact, Elder Theodore M. Burton taught that chastity can be restored. He said, "Jesus Christ can restore that virtue and he can thus show you mercy. . . . Jesus has power to restore virtue and make your victim (the person with whom you commit sexual transgression) absolutely clean and holy" (BYU Devotional, March 26, 1985).

Next, Alma explains more about the other two sins mentioned in verse 5.

6 For behold, **if ye deny the Holy Ghost** when it once has had place in you, **and ye know that ye deny it**, behold, **this is a sin which is unpardonable**; yea, and **whosoever murdereth against the light and knowledge of God, it is not easy for him to obtain forgiveness**; yea, I say unto you, my son, that it is not easy for him to obtain a forgiveness.

Next, in verses 7 and 8, sexual sin is referred to as a "crime." This is a reminder of how serious it is in the eyes of God.

7 And now, my son, **I would to God** [*I very much wish*] **that ye had not been guilty of so great a crime**. I would not dwell upon **your crimes**, to harrow up [*stir up; cause severe pain to*] your soul, if it were not for your good.

8 But behold, **ye cannot hide your crimes from God**; and **except** [*unless*] **ye repent** they will stand as a testimony against you at the last day [*Final Judgment*].

9 Now my son, I would that ye should **repent and forsake** [*stop*] **your sins**, and go no more after the lusts of your eyes, but **cross yourself** [*turn yourself around; repent*] **in all these things**; for except ye do this ye can in nowise [*in no way*] inherit the kingdom of God. Oh, remember, and take it upon you, and **cross yourself in these things**.

In verse 9, above, the phrase "cross yourself" is used twice. It can mean to turn your life around, to switch directions, to deny yourself of sin, to control yourself and no longer give in to these sins. The Joseph Smith Translation of the Bible, Matthew 16:26, helps us understand this. It reads: "And now for a man to take up his cross, is to deny himself of all ungodliness, and every worldly lust, and keep my commandments."

10 And **I command you** to take it upon you to **counsel with your elder brothers** [*Helaman and Shiblon*] in your undertakings [*the things you do*]; for behold, thou art in thy youth [*you are young*], and ye stand in need to be nourished by your brothers. And give heed [*listen*] to their counsel.

Next, in verse 11, Alma reminds Corianton how much damage he has done to their missionary efforts among the Zoramites by his sinful behavior.

11 **Suffer not** [*don't allow*] **yourself to be led away by any vain** [*prideful*] **or foolish thing**; suffer [*let*] not the devil to lead away your heart again after those wicked harlots [*women who invite men to get involved with them sexually, usually for money*]. Behold, O my son, **how great iniquity** [*wickedness*] **ye brought upon the Zoramites; for when they saw your conduct they would not believe in my words.**

Some people may feel that Alma's language to his son is too strong. Obviously, it is not, because he is being inspired by the Holy Ghost. This is a reminder to all of us that we, as members of the Church, have extra accountability because of the knowledge we have of the gospel and God's commandments.

12 And now **the Spirit of the Lord doth say unto me: Command thy children to do good**, lest they lead away the hearts of many people to destruction; therefore **I command you, my son**, in the fear of God, **that ye refrain from your iniquities** [*stop your wickedness*];

13 That ye **turn to the Lord with all your mind, might, and strength**; that ye **lead away the hearts of no more to do wickedly**; but rather **return unto them, and acknowledge your faults and that wrong which ye have done** [*the "law of restitution," meaning do your best to repair the damage you have done*].

14 **Seek not after riches** [*wealth*] **nor the vain** [*unimportant*] **things of this world; for behold, you cannot carry them with you** [*to heaven*].

In the final verses of this chapter, Alma will tenderly teach Corianton one of the things he needs most—namely, that Christ's perfect Atonement can work for him. He can still repent.

15 And **now, my son, I would say somewhat unto you concerning the coming of Christ.** Behold, I say unto you, that it is **he** that **surely shall come to take away the sins of the world**; yea, he cometh to declare glad tidings [*this is "good news"*] of salvation unto his people.

At this point in the Book of Mormon, the birth of Christ to Mary in Bethlehem is about seventy-three years in the future. The ministry of the Savior among the Nephites is about one hundred and six years in the future. Alma tells Corianton in verse 16, next, that the children of those who are alive now among the Nephites will have the privilege of hearing the gospel from the Savior Himself at the time of His coming to them. This implies that the youngest children of the current generation, many of whom will not be born for several years, will see the Savior when He comes to them.

16 And now, my son, **this was the ministry unto which ye were called, to declare these glad tidings** [*this happy news, namely, about Christ and His future coming to the Nephites*] **unto this people**, to prepare their minds; or rather that salvation might come unto them, **that they may prepare the minds of their children to hear the word at the time of his coming.**

It appears that Corianton just gave his father a quizzical look about what he had just been told. Next, Alma puts his mind at ease.

17 And now **I will ease your mind somewhat on this subject.** Behold, you marvel [*you are wondering*] why these things [*the Atonement of Christ, the gospel, etc.*] should be known so long beforehand. Behold, I say unto you, **is not a soul at this time as precious unto God as a soul will be at the time of his coming?**

18 **Is it not as necessary that the plan of redemption should be made known unto this people as well as unto their children?** [*In other words, doesn't everyone need the Atonement?*]

19 **Is it not as easy at this time for the Lord to send his angel** to declare [*teach and explain*] these glad tidings **unto us as unto our children**, or as after the time of his coming?

The above verses are a reminder that the Atonement was in effect before it was actually performed by the Savior. We know from D&C 76:24 that it even works for the inhabitants of other worlds. It is truly miraculous and infinite!

ALMA 40

In this chapter, we, along with Corianton, will be taught more plan of salvation doctrines, especially about resurrection and what happens to the spirit between death and resurrection. We will also be taught that all people will be held accountable before God for their use of their agency to make bad choices.

It may be that Corianton has been wondering whether or not there really is life after death. If there is, then he will be in trouble unless he repents. If not, then there is ultimately nothing to worry about. In verse 1, next, Alma knows that his son is wondering about the topic of resurrection, and so he teaches the true doctrine that "all shall rise from the dead" (verse 5) and that all shall "be brought to stand before God, and be judged according to their works" (verse 21).

Based on this emphasis, we can perhaps conclude that one of Corianton's basic beliefs is "Maybe there is no resurrection or life after death. If so, there is no such thing as Judgment Day and accountability. And if that is the case, I am not really in any trouble." Watch now as Alma teaches more doctrines of the plan of salvation, which will ultimately change Corianton's basic beliefs and thus change his behaviors and save his soul.

1 NOW my son, here is somewhat more I would say unto thee; for **I perceive** [*can tell*] **that thy mind is worried concerning the resurrection of the dead.** [*It appears that Corianton is worried about whether or not he is going to be resurrected and have to face God.*]

2 Behold, I say unto you, that **there is no resurrection**—or, I would say, in other words, that this mortal [*mortal body*] does not put on immortality, this corruption [*corruptible body, which deteriorates when it dies*] does not put on incorruption [*eternal permanence*]—**until after the coming of Christ**

[*Doctrine: there is no resurrection on this world until the resurrection of Christ*].

3 Behold, **he bringeth to pass the resurrection of the dead**. But behold, my son, the resurrection is not yet [*no one has been resurrected yet*]. Now, I unfold unto you a mystery; nevertheless, there are many mysteries which are kept, that no one knoweth them save God himself. But I show unto you one thing which **I have inquired** [*asked*] **diligently of God that I might know—that is concerning the resurrection**.

Now Alma will teach several correct doctrines of which the Holy Ghost can bear witness to Corianton.

4 Behold, there is a time appointed that **all shall come forth from the dead** [*everyone will be resurrected*]. Now when this time cometh no one knows; but God knoweth the time which is appointed.

5 Now, whether there shall be one time, or a second time, or a third time, that men shall come forth from the dead, it mattereth not; for God knoweth all these things; and it sufficeth me to know that this is the case—that **there is a time appointed that all shall rise from the dead**.

We are told that many doctrinal details have been revealed in our day (the dispensation of the fulness of times) that were not known in many previous dispensations. For instance, according to verse 5, above, Alma does not know for sure if there will be several resurrections or just one. We know more detail because of the Doctrine and Covenants.

We know of at least five resurrections: 1. The resurrection of the righteous (celestial quality people) from Adam and Eve down to Christ, at the time of Christ's resurrection (D&C 133:54–55). 2. The resurrection of the righteous at the Second Coming (D&C 88:97–98). 3. The resurrection of terrestrial quality people near the beginning of the Millennium (D&C 88:99). 4. The resurrection of telestial quality people at the end of the Millennium (D&C 88:100–101). 5. The resurrection of those who were born on earth and then became sons of perdition (D&C 88:102), at the end of the Millennium after the telestial resurrection.

Quite a bit more has been revealed, for instance, that Peter, James, and Moroni have already been resurrected, and that there will be an ongoing resurrection during the Millennium (D&C 101:31).

Next, Alma will teach about what happens to our spirit when we die. He will teach about paradise and prison in the spirit world.

6 Now **there must needs be a space betwixt** [*between*] **the time of death and the time of the resurrection.**

7 And now I would inquire **what becometh of the souls of men from this time of death to the time appointed for the resurrection?**

8 Now whether there is more than one time appointed for men to rise it mattereth not; for all do not die at once, and this mattereth not; all is as one day with God, and **time only is measured unto men**.

9 Therefore, there is a time appointed unto men that they shall rise [*be*

resurrected] from the dead; and **there is a space between the time of death and the resurrection.** And now, concerning this space of time, what becometh of the souls of men is the thing which I have inquired diligently of the Lord to know; and this is the thing of which I do know.

10 And when the time cometh **when all shall rise, then shall they know** that God knoweth all the times which are appointed unto man.

Having set the stage, Alma now teaches more specific doctrine.

11 Now, **concerning the state of the soul** [*the spirit*] **between death and the resurrection**—Behold, it has been made known unto me by an angel, that **the spirits of all men, as soon as they are departed from this mortal body, yea, the spirits of all men, whether they be good or evil, are taken home to that God who gave them life**.

Next, Alma describes paradise (in the spirit world), where righteous people go when they die.

12 And then shall it come to pass, that the spirits of those who are righteous are received into **a state of happiness**, which is **called paradise**, a state of **rest**, a state of **peace**, where they shall **rest from all their troubles and from all care, and sorrow.**

Now he describes spirit prison. This has particular meaning for Corianton, because unless he repents, this is where he will go when he dies.

13 And then shall it come to pass, that **the spirits of the wicked,** yea, who are evil—for behold, they **have no part nor portion of the Spirit of the Lord**; for behold, **they chose evil works rather than good**; therefore the spirit of the devil did enter into them, and take possession of their house—and **these shall be cast out into outer darkness**; there shall be **weeping**, and **wailing**, and **gnashing of teeth** [*a term that means grinding one's teeth together because of agony and grief*], and this because of their own iniquity [*wickedness*], being led captive by the will of the devil.

The phrase "outer darkness" as used in verse 13, above, is not the final, permanent dwelling place of the sons of perdition. Rather, it is a Book of Mormon term for spirit prison. This "outer darkness" or spirit prison situation is a temporary state for them as taught in verse 14, next.

14 Now this is the state of the souls of the wicked, yea, in darkness, and a state of awful, fearful looking for the fiery indignation of the wrath of God upon them; thus **they remain in this state, as well as the righteous in paradise, until the time of their resurrection.**

In verses 15–18, next, Alma straightens out some confusion on the part of people in his day, about whether or not the spirit leaving the body at the time of death and then being assigned either to paradise or prison can properly be termed a "resurrection."

15 Now, **there are some that have understood that this state of**

happiness [*paradise*] **and this state of misery** of the soul [*prison*], **before the resurrection, was a first resurrection.** Yea, I admit it may be termed a resurrection [*some people refer to it as a resurrection*], the raising of the spirit or the soul and their consignation [*being assigned*] to happiness or misery, according to the words which have been spoken.

16 And behold, again [*on the other hand*] it hath been spoken [*you hear it said*], that there is a first resurrection, a resurrection of all those who have been, or who are, or who shall be, down to the resurrection of Christ from the dead. [*In other words, you have heard two usages of the term "resurrection" including that when Christ is resurrected, everyone since Adam and Eve will be resurrected. (By the way, it was only the righteous who were resurrected with Christ.)*]

Next, Alma straightens out this misconception, teaching Corianton that the word "resurrection" refers to the reuniting of the body and the spirit, not simply the spirit leaving the body at the time of death.

17 Now, **we do not suppose that this first resurrection** [*the resurrection of the righteous from Adam to Christ*], **which is spoken of in this manner, can be the resurrection of the souls and their consignation** [*being assigned*] **to happiness or misery. Ye cannot suppose that this is what it meaneth.**

18 Behold, I say unto you, **Nay**; but **it meaneth the reuniting of the soul with the body**, of those from the days of Adam down to the resurrection of Christ.

There are many different scriptural words and phrases that refer to the resurrection of those who are going to receive celestial glory. They are often used interchangeably in our gospel discussions. For example: "the resurrection of the just," "those who come forth in the first resurrection," "the morning of the first resurrection," "the resurrection of the righteous," etc.

19 Now, **whether the souls** [*spirits*] **and the bodies of those of whom has been spoken shall all be reunited at once, the wicked as well as the righteous** [*modern revelation teaches that they will not be resurrected together; see D&C 88:97–102*], **I do not say**; let it suffice, that I say that they all come forth; or in other words, their resurrection cometh to pass before the resurrection of those who die after the resurrection of Christ.

Verses 19–21 are an example of keeping verses of scripture in their context. If you were to stop reading at the end of verse 19, you would have the idea that everybody, righteous and wicked, who lived before Christ, will be resurrected before those who die after Christ's resurrection. We know from D&C 88:100–101, that none of the wicked will be resurrected before the end of the Millennium.

If you keep reading, and keep these verses together, you find in verses 20 and 21 that Alma tells Corianton that he is giving his opinion concerning this aspect of the resurrection. They did not then have D&C 88:100–101.

20 Now, my son, **I do not say that their** [*the righteous and the wicked*] **resurrection cometh at the resurrection of Christ**; but behold, **I give it as my opinion, that the souls and the bodies are reunited, of the righteous**, at the resurrection of Christ, and his ascension into heaven. [*It was indeed the righteous who were resurrected with the Savior; see D&C 133:54–55.*]

21 But whether it be at his resurrection or after, I do not say [*I don't know for sure*]; but this much I say [*this much I do know*], that **there is a space between death and the resurrection of the body, and a state of the soul** [*spirit*] **in happiness or in misery until the time which is appointed of God that the dead shall come forth, and be reunited, both soul and body, and be brought to stand before God, and be judged according to their works.**

22 Yea, **this bringeth about the restoration of those things of which has been spoken by the mouths of the prophets**.

Verse 23, next, is a rather famous quote from the Book of Mormon defining what it means to be resurrected. It is very comforting.

23 **The soul** [*spirit*] **shall be restored to the body, and the body to the soul**; yea, and every limb and joint shall be restored to its body; yea, even a hair of the head shall not be lost; but **all things shall be restored to their proper and perfect frame.**

The last phrase of verse 23, above, is doctrinally significant. People hear that "a hair of the head shall not be lost" and imagine some rather grotesque images of resurrected beings with every hair they ever had, or every fingernail clipping, etc. Obviously, this would not be "their proper and perfect frame."

Some want to know what "the perfect" age is. Opinions vary, but if you stop to think about it, since we are all mortal, we have never had a truly "proper and perfect frame." The point is that "perfect age" doesn't really fit. We will all be very pleasantly surprised when we are resurrected and discover what the words "perfect" and "proper" mean with respect to us.

Alma now summarizes what he has taught Corianton on the absolute certainty of life after death.

24 And **now, my son, this is the restoration** of which has been spoken by the mouths of the prophets—

25 And **then shall the righteous shine forth in the kingdom of God.**

26 But behold, **an awful death** [*spiritual death*] **cometh upon the wicked**; for they die as to things pertaining to things of righteousness; for they are unclean, and **no unclean thing can inherit the kingdom of God**; but they are cast out, and consigned [*assigned by God*] to partake of the fruits of their labors or their works [*the law of the harvest; in other words, what you plant, you harvest*], which have been evil; and they drink the dregs [*the bitter matter that has sunk to the bottom of the cup*] of a bitter cup. [*In other words, they own and have to live with the results of their choices for eternity.*]

ALMA 41

As Alma continues trying to help his son, Corianton, understand why the sins he committed while on their mission to the Zoramites were so wrong and why he needs to repent, he will discuss three more false basic beliefs that Corianton has. These three false basic beliefs are:

1. "If God is so merciful and kind, He will give us better than we have earned on Judgment Day."
2. "Wickedness is happiness."
3. "I'm not really a bad person. What I am doing isn't really wicked, just experimentation and gaining experience."

To help Corianton understand why these three ways of thinking won't work if we want to get to heaven, Alma teaches him about the doctrine of restoration. This doctrine is that if we lived a good, righteous life here on earth, we will be given a good reward on Judgment Day. On the other hand, if we intentionally lived a wicked life, we will be given an unpleasant reward. In other words, we will be restored to good or we will be restored to evil on Final Judgment Day, depending on what lifestyle we chose during this time of learning and testing on earth.

1 AND now, my son, **I have somewhat to say concerning** the **restoration** of which has been spoken; for behold, some have wrested [*twisted; misinterpreted*] the scriptures, and have gone far astray because of this thing [*because they have misunderstood the doctrine of restoration*]. And **I perceive that thy mind has been worried also concerning this thing. But behold, I will explain it unto thee.**

Next, Alma defines the law of restoration. He will give examples, including the "restoration" of the body to the spirit in the process of resurrection, and also at the Final Judgment that the lifestyle we chose on earth will be "restored" or reflected in the judgment we receive.

It is significant, in this context especially, that those who live a telestial lifestyle will receive a telestial, resurrected body. Those who live worthy of terrestrial glory will receive a terrestrial body, and those whose lives earn celestial glory will receive a celestial body, which is a natural body. (See D&C 88:28–32.) In other words, on Judgment Day, they will be "restored," eternally, to the type of resurrected body they have earned. The law of restoration is indeed the law of the harvest. "Whatsoever ye sow [*plant*], that shall ye also reap [*harvest*]" (D&C 6:33).

2 I say unto thee, my son, that the **plan of restoration is requisite with the justice of God** [*the law of restoration is required by the law of justice*]; for it is requisite [*required*] that **all things should be** [*must be*] **restored to their proper order.** Behold, it is requisite and just [*required and fair; proper*], **according to the** power and **resurrection** of Christ, **that the soul** [*spirit*] of man **should be restored to its body**, and that every part of the body should be restored to itself.

3 And **it is requisite** [*required*] with

the justice of God **that men should be judged according to their works** [*what they did on earth*]; and **if their works were good in this life, and the desires of their hearts were good, that they should also, at the last day** [*on Judgment Day*], **be restored unto that which is good.**

There is extra encouragement for us in verse 3, above. We will be judged by the desires of our hearts as well as our works. For instance, if someone wants to be baptized, but his or her parents will not allow it, such people will be judged by the desires of their hearts. See also D&C 137:9, and D&C 124:49.

4 And **if their works are evil they shall be restored unto them for evil**. Therefore, **all things shall be restored to their proper order** [*the basic law of restoration*], every thing to its natural frame—mortality raised to immortality, corruption to incorruption—raised **to endless happiness** to inherit the kingdom of God, **or to endless misery** to inherit the kingdom of the devil, the one on one hand, the other on the other—

The pure doctrine being taught here by Alma is vital for Corianton. It will work.

5 **The one raised to happiness** according to his desires of happiness, **or good** according to his desires of good; and **the other to evil** according to his desires of evil; for as he has desired to do evil all the day long **even so shall he have his reward of evil** when the night cometh [*when it is too late to make changes in how you are living*].

You may have noticed in the above verses that a key issue is the desire of our hearts. If the desire of our hearts is to be righteous, we try to keep the commandments of God. If we desire evil, we don't keep the commandments. This is beautifully simple. Truth is simple.

What Alma says next is very encouraging to Corianton.

6 And so it is on the other hand. **If he hath repented of his sins, and desired righteousness until the end of his days, even so he shall be rewarded unto righteousness.**

7 These are **they** that **are redeemed of** [*by*] **the Lord**; yea, these are they that are taken out [*of spiritual darkness and taken away from punishment for sins*], that are delivered [*set free by Christ's Atonement*] from that endless night of darkness [*when it is too late to repent*]; and **thus they stand or fall**; for behold, **they are their own judges, whether to do good or do evil**.

As given in verse 7, above, the law of restoration says that we are our own judges because we are "writing the script for our own final judgment," so to speak, by choosing righteousness or wickedness in this time of preparation to meet God.

8 Now, **the decrees** [*laws and commandments*] **of God are unalterable** [*can't be changed*]; therefore, the way is prepared that whosoever will [*desires to*] may walk therein [*in the gospel of Christ*] and be saved.

Those who do not understand or accept true doctrine often do not know what they are risking, especially as far as eternity is concerned, when they break God's commandments. Corianton is being taught correct doctrine and now knows what the risks of continuing to choose wickedness are.

9 And now behold, my son, **do not risk one more offense against your God upon those points of doctrine, which ye have hitherto risked to commit sin.**

10 Do not suppose, because it has been spoken concerning restoration, that ye shall be restored from sin to happiness. [*B.B. "If God is so merciful and kind, He will give me better than I earn."*] Behold, I say unto you, wickedness never was happiness. [*B.B. "Wickedness is happiness."*]

Next, Alma will remind Corianton that he is not alone in needing to repent. Many others are choosing evil also. They may not realize it, but they are miserable and have the need to repent and to prepare for Final Judgment, at which time they will be "restored" to righteousness eternally in the presence of God. Of course, righteousness also pays off right now in this life.

11 And now, my son, **all men that are in a state of nature, or I would say, in a carnal** [*worldly*] **state** [*who are choosing wickedness*], **are in the gall of bitterness and in the bonds of iniquity** [*they are chained down with wickedness*]; **they are without God** [*a very vulnerable situation*] in the world, and **they have gone contrary to** [*against*] **the nature of God** [*they don't think like He does, desire what He does, act toward others like He does, etc.*]; therefore, they are in a state contrary to the nature of happiness [*this is eternal truth, doctrine, reality*].

As he summarizes his teachings about the law of restoration, Alma now asks Corianton a very important question and then answers his own question.

12 And now behold, **is the meaning of the word restoration to take a thing of a natural state and place it in an unnatural state, or to place it in a state opposite to its nature?** [*For instance, if you were naturally evil and desired evil on a daily basis, would you feel comfortable eternally with righteous people in the presence of God?*]

13 O, my son, **this is not the case**; but **the meaning of the word restoration is to bring back again evil for evil, or carnal for carnal, or devilish for devilish—good for that which is good; righteous for that which is righteous; just** [*being honest and fair*] **for that which is just; merciful for that which is merciful.**

Corianton is invited, as is the case with all of us, to demonstrate the righteous desires of the heart with actions, as explained next.

14 Therefore, my son, **see that you are merciful** unto your brethren; **deal justly** [*be honest and fair*], **judge righteously**, and **do good continually**; and **if ye do all these things** then shall ye receive **your reward**; yea, **ye shall have mercy restored unto you again**; ye shall have **justice restored unto you again**; ye shall have **a righteous judgment restored**

unto you again; and **ye shall have good rewarded unto you again**.

In finishing up this major explanation of the law of restoration, Alma reminds Corianton once more that it makes no difference who you are—you cannot justify intentional sin or ignore the seriousness of it. If your basic belief is that you can commit serious sin without being a wicked person, you are wrong.

15 For that which ye do send out shall return unto you again, and be restored; therefore, the word restoration more fully condemneth the sinner, and justifieth him not at all. [*B.B. "I'm not really a bad person. What I'm doing isn't really wicked. I'm just gaining experience."*]

ALMA 42

This is the last of four chapters recording Alma's interview with his youngest son, Corianton. He has been teaching his son pure doctrine in order to change his basic belief system that has led to sin. In this chapter, our agency to choose right or wrong is a basic topic. As he discusses agency, Alma will use Adam and Eve in the Garden of Eden as an example of the use of agency and ownership of consequences. In addition, he will teach the laws of justice and mercy, and the fact that even God cannot break the laws of justice and mercy for Corianton or any of us. Alma continues to be inspired by the Holy Ghost to know what is troubling his son and to address the problem effectively with the power of true doctrine.

1 AND **now, my son, I perceive there is somewhat more which doth worry your mind**, which ye cannot understand—which is **concerning the justice of God in the punishment of the sinner**; for ye do try to suppose that it is injustice that the sinner should be consigned [*assigned*] to a state of misery. [*B.B. "God is fair and nice, so He wouldn't do something so mean to me on Judgment Day."*]

As mentioned above, agency and ownership of consequences of our own choices are major topics here. In order to help Corianton understand that he can't blame God if his reward on Judgment Day is less than what he wanted, Alma will teach agency, using Adam and Eve as examples.

2 Now behold, my son, **I will explain this thing** [*"the justice of God in the punishment of the sinner" in verse 1*] **unto thee**. For behold, after the Lord God sent our first parents [*Adam and Eve*] forth from the garden of Eden [*a consequence of their agency choice*], to till [*farm*] the ground, from whence [*where*] they were taken—yea, he drew out the man, and he placed at the east end of the garden of Eden, cherubim [*angelic being*], and a flaming sword which turned every way, to keep the tree of life [*to keep Adam and Eve from eating the fruit of the tree of life after having eaten of the tree of knowledge of good and evil*]—

3 Now, we see that **the man had become as God, knowing good and evil** [*a good consequence of Adam and Eve's agency choice in the Garden of Eden*]; **and**

lest he should put [*to keep him from putting*] **forth his hand, and take also of the tree of life, and eat and live forever, the Lord God placed cherubim and the flaming sword, that he should not partake of the fruit—**

4 And thus we see, that **there was a time granted unto man to repent, yea, a probationary time** [*a time to be tested to see if you will choose the right*]**, a time to repent and serve God.** [*Mortality is Corianton's "probationary time" and his chance "to repent and serve God."*]

Many people have wondered what would have happened if Adam and Eve had immediately eaten of the tree of life. Alma explains the answer next.

5 For behold, **if Adam had put forth his hand immediately, and partaken of the tree of life, he would have lived forever**, according to the word of God, **having no space for repentance**; yea, and also the word of God [*God's promise that we would have time to prepare to meet Him, before Judgment Day*] would have been void, **and the great plan of salvation would have been frustrated** [*would not have worked*].

Remember that those who do not have a fair chance to prepare to meet God during their lives here on earth are given this opportunity in the spirit world and before the Final Judgment. Thus, by the time of the Final Judgment, everyone will have had a completely fair opportunity to understand the gospel and use their agency to prepare to meet Him. It appears that Corianton is perhaps getting a major portion of his opportunity now.

6 But behold, **it was appointed unto man to die** [*it was part of the plan that we would die*]—therefore, as they were cut off from the tree of life they should be cut off from the face of the earth [*they would die*]—and man became lost forever, yea, they became fallen man. [*In other words, they needed the Atonement just as Corianton needs it.*]

In the overall "big picture," it is a great blessing and privilege to die. Lucifer and the one third who followed him will never have this blessing. It paves the way to resurrection and immortality.

Next, Alma will teach that the choices given Adam and Eve in the Garden of Eden put them in a position to use their agency and their choice got things moving. Also, the Fall was good. It is said that they "fell forward."

7 And now, ye see by this [*the Fall*] that our first parents were cut off both temporally [*physically*] and spiritually from the presence of the Lord; and **thus we see they became subjects to follow after their own will** [*they were now able to use their own agency and choose to do right or wrong*]**.**

8 Now behold, **it was not expedient** [*not necessary*] **that man should be reclaimed from this temporal death** [*physical death; the death of the body*], for **that would destroy the great plan of happiness** [*the plan of salvation; verse 5*]. [*In other words, the Fall was good.*]

9 Therefore, as **the soul** [*spirit*] **could**

never die, and the fall had brought
upon all mankind a spiritual death
[*being cut off from the direct physical presence
of God; see below*] as well as a temporal
[*physical death*], that is, **they were cut
off from the presence of the Lord**,
it was **expedient** [*necessary*] **that man-
kind should be reclaimed** [*saved;
brought back*] **from this spiritual
death** [*which sets the stage for the need for
an atonement*].

Next, Alma explains that this mortal world brings with it the possibility to make agency choices that lead to wickedness; see verse 12.

10 Therefore, as **they had become**
[*by choices some people make*] **carnal, sen-
sual**, and **devilish**, by nature, **this
probationary state became a state
for them to prepare; it became a
preparatory state** [*a time to prepare to
meet God*].

11 And now remember, my son, **if it
were not for the plan of redemp-
tion** [*including the Atonement*], [*laying it
aside*] as soon as they were dead **their
souls were** [*would have been*] **misera-
ble**, being cut off from the presence
of the Lord.

Remember, Alma is setting the stage in Corianton's mind for the desperate condition mankind would be in without the Atonement. It is also setting things up for Corianton to realize the desperate condition he will be in if he does not exercise his agency to choose repentance and personal righteousness.

12 And now, **there was no means to
reclaim men from this fallen state,
which man had brought upon
himself because of his own disobe-
dience**;

13 Therefore, **according to justice**
[*the law of justice*], **the plan of redemp-
tion could not be brought about,
only** [*except*] **on conditions of repen-
tance of men in this probationary
state, yea, this preparatory state**;
for **except it were for these condi-
tions** [*repentance and forgiveness offered by
the Atonement of Christ*], **mercy** [*the law of
mercy*] **could not take effect except
it should destroy the work of jus-
tice.** Now **the work of justice could
not be destroyed; if so, God would
cease to be God.**

The phrase "God would cease to be God" is repeated three times in this chapter (verses 13, 22, and 25). Corianton must understand that if God tried to bend the rules so that he could be forgiven without repenting, "God would cease to be God."

14 And **thus we see that all man-
kind were fallen, and they were
in the grasp of justice** [*the law of jus-
tice*]; yea, the justice of God, which
consigned them forever to be cut off
from his presence [*which is what will hap-
pen to Corianton unless he repents sincerely. By
the way, he will*].

Having set the stage for the need of an Atonement for us all, Alma now introduces the Atonement of Christ into the lesson.

15 And now, **the plan of mercy
could not be brought about except
an atonement should be made;
therefore God** [*Christ*] **himself**

atoneth for the sins of the world, to bring about the plan of mercy, to appease the demands of justice, that God [*the Father*] might be a perfect, just God, and a merciful God also. [*In other words, the Savior's Atonement made it possible to satisfy the law of justice and still offer mercy to those who repent.*]

Remember that Corianton's concern, at the beginning of this chapter was that he didn't feel that it was fair for God to send sinners into a condition of misery for eternity. Alma will use another doctrine here, the doctrine of opposites, to explain why punishing the unrepentant sinner is necessary. He will teach that repentance would be meaningless unless there were an eternal punishment in place for the unrepentant.

The next verses illustrate that pure truth, understood in the context of the "big picture," is pure logic.

16 Now, **repentance could not come unto men except** [*unless*] **there were a punishment, which also was eternal as** [*would last as long as*] **the life of the soul should be, affixed opposite to the plan of happiness, which was as eternal also as the life of the soul.**

17 Now, **how could a man repent except he should sin? How could he sin if there was no law? How could there be a law save there was a punishment?**

18 Now, **there was a punishment affixed** [*attached*], **and a just law given, which brought remorse** [*sorrow*] **of conscience unto man.**

19 Now, **if there was no law given—if a man murdered he should die—would he be afraid he would die if he should murder?**

20 And also, **if there was no law given against sin men would not be afraid to sin.**

21 And **if there was no law given, if men sinned what could justice do, or mercy either, for they would have no claim upon the creature?**

Having built a framework of inspired logic for Corianton, Alma now bears testimony of what we might term the "law of opposites."

In other words, the law of punishment is opposite the law of repentance, and so forth.

22 But **there is a law given, and a punishment affixed**, **and a repentance granted**; which repentance, mercy claimeth [*the law of mercy can claim the sinner who repents, because Christ paid the penalty for sin required by the law of justice*]; **otherwise, justice claimeth the creature** [*the sinner*] and executeth the law [*carries out the law of punishment*], and the law inflicteth [*applies*] the punishment; **if not so** [*if this were not the case*], the works of justice would be destroyed, and **God would cease to be God.**

Now, Alma summarizes everything he has been teaching Corianton, and then gives him another chance to prove that he can be wise and repent and serve God.

23 **But God ceaseth not to be God** [*a simple fact*], and **mercy claimeth the penitent** [*repentant*], and **mercy cometh because of the atonement**; and

the atonement bringeth to pass the resurrection of the dead; and **the resurrection of the dead bringeth back men into the presence of God**; and **thus they are restored into his presence, to be judged according to their works, according to the law and justice.**

24 For behold, **justice exerciseth all his demands** [*the law of justice gets completely satisfied*], and also **mercy claimeth all which is her own**; and thus, **none but the truly penitent** [*repentant*] **are saved.**

Perhaps you noticed in verse 24, above, that justice is referred to as masculine, and mercy is referred to as feminine. Just an interesting observation, perhaps reminding us that mercy is tender and nurturing.

25 What, **do ye suppose that mercy can rob justice? I say unto you, Nay; not one whit** [*not one bit*]. **If so, God would cease to be God.**

26 And **thus** [*using the laws of justice and mercy, combined with the Atonement*] **God bringeth about his great and eternal purposes** [*"to bring to pass the immortality and eternal life of man," as stated in Moses 1:39*], which were prepared from the foundation of the world [*in the premortal life*]. And **thus cometh about the salvation and the redemption** [*salvation*] **of men, and also their destruction and misery** [*the law of opposites, again*].

Next, Alma again emphasizes that we all have God-given agency to choose between right and wrong.

27 Therefore, O my son, **whosoever will** [*desires to*] **come may come** and partake of the waters of life [*the gospel, including the Atonement*] freely; and **whosoever will not come the same is not compelled** [*forced*] **to come; but in the last day** [*on Judgment Day*] **it shall be restored unto him according to his deeds** [*he will get what he has earned*].

28 **If he has desired to do evil, and has not repented in his days, behold, evil shall be done unto him, according to the restoration of God.**

29 And now, my son, I desire that ye should let these things trouble you no more, and only **let your sins trouble you, with that trouble** [*godly sorrow; see 2 Corinthians 7:8–11*] **which shall bring you down unto repentance.**

30 O my son, I desire that ye should **deny the justice of God no more. Do not endeavor to excuse yourself in the least point because of your sins, by denying the justice of God; but do you let the justice of God, and his mercy, and his long-suffering** [*patience*] **have full sway** [*have full influence*] **in your heart; and let it bring you down to the dust in humility.**

Next, Alma gives Corianton another chance to continue on his mission.

31 **And now, O my son, ye are called of God to preach the word** [*the gospel*] **unto this people**. And now, my son, **go thy way**, declare the word with truth and soberness,

that thou mayest bring souls unto repentance, that the great plan of mercy may have claim upon them. And may God grant unto you even according to my words. Amen.

Alma's efforts to teach Corianton and help him understand the gospel worked. Mormon tells us in Alma 43:1–2 that the sons of Alma went forth preaching the gospel, along with their father. In Alma 48:17–18, he says that Alma and his sons were "all men of God." In Alma 49:30, we find Corianton listed as one who was teaching the word of God, in other words, had gone back on his mission and was being a successful missionary.

ALMA 43

Perhaps you remember that, in Alma, chapter 31, Alma took two of his sons, Shiblon and Corianton along with several other missionary companions to preach to the Zoramites, most of whom had left the Church. These missionaries were startled to see that the Zoramites had built their own church buildings and had a Rameumptom prayer tower and said the same prayer every time they worshipped their god. The wealthier Zoramites refused to listen to the gospel message, but the poor Zoramites did. Many of them were converted and baptized.

But the wealthy and wicked Zoramites drove the male members of the Church out of town and burned their wives and children. After they did this, they helped stir the Lamanites up against the Nephites and talked them into going to war against the Nephites. From now to the end of the book of Alma, we will be reading about these wars.

The first two verses of this chapter tell us that after Alma finished counseling with each of his sons, Helaman, Shiblon, and Corianton (Alma, chapters 36–42), he and his sons went forth again among the people and taught the gospel.

1 AND now it came to pass that **the sons of Alma did go forth among the people, to declare the word** [*the gospel*] **unto them. And Alma, also, himself, could not rest, and he also went forth.**

2 Now we shall say no more concerning their preaching, except that **they preached the word, and the truth, according to the spirit of prophecy and revelation**; and they preached after the holy order of God by which they were called.

As mentioned before, Mormon told us (in Alma 35:10–13) that the Zoramites who did not join the Church stirred the Lamanites up to go to war against the Nephites. He told us that he would eventually return to the topic of these wars between the Nephites and the Lamanites. Now he does so.

3 And **now I return to an account of the wars between the Nephites and the Lamanites**, in the eighteenth year of the reign of the judges [*eighteen years after Alma became the President of the Church and about seventy-four years before the birth of the Savior to Mary in Bethlehem*].

4 For behold, it came to pass that

the Zoramites [*the apostates who had the Rameumptom prayer tower; see Alma 31*] **became Lamanites**; therefore, in the commencement [*beginning*] of the eighteenth year the people of **the Nephites saw that the Lamanites were coming upon them; therefore they made preparations for war**; yea, they gathered together their armies in the land of Jershon [*where the Anti-Nephi-Lehies had originally settled after their conversion*].

The Anti-Nephi-Lehies (later referred to as the people of Ammon) were the Lamanite converts who had been forced to flee to the land of Zarahemla after joining the Church. They had made a covenant never to take up weapons of war again. Alma and his people gave them the land of Jershon. Later they moved to another area in order to make room for the Nephite armies to defend their country against the Lamanites.

5 And it came to pass that **the Lamanites came with their thousands**; and **they came into** the land of Antionum, which is **the land of the Zoramites**; and a man by the name of **Zerahemnah was their leader**.

As a matter of military strategy, Zerahemnah appointed bitter apostates (former members of the Church) who hated the Nephites as chief captains over the Lamanite armies. He chose these leaders from among the Amalekites (apostates who adopted Nehor's teachings; see Alma 1; and who rejected Aaron and his missionary companions; see Alma 21:3–11) and from the apostate Zoramites (see Alma 31–35).

6 And now, **as the Amalekites were of a more wicked and murderous disposition than the Lamanites were, in and of themselves, therefore, Zerahemnah appointed chief captains over the Lamanites, and they were all Amalekites and Zoramites.**

7 Now **this he did that he might preserve their hatred towards the Nephites**, that he might bring them into subjection [*under his rule*] to the accomplishment of his designs [*plans, plots*].

Next, we see the true motives of Zerahemnah. They are the same as bullies and tyrants, anytime, anywhere.

8 For behold, his designs [*plans*] were to stir up the Lamanites to anger against the Nephites; **this he did that he might usurp** [*seize; unrighteously gain*] **great power over them** [*the Lamanites*], **and also that he might gain power over the Nephites by bringing them into bondage** [*slavery*].

In contrast to the motives of Zerahemnah, we see the motives of the Nephites next, in verse 9.

9 And now **the design** [*plan and purpose*] **of the Nephites was to support their lands**, and their **houses**, and their **wives**, and their **children**, that they might **preserve them from the hands of their enemies**; and also that they might **preserve their rights and their privileges, yea, and also their liberty, that they might worship God according to their desires.**

10 For **they knew that if they should fall into the hands of the Lamanites**, that whosoever should worship God in spirit and in truth, the true and the living God, the Lamanites would destroy.

In the above verses, Mormon taught us when it is appropriate to go to war. As we continue, he explains what would happen if the righteous Nephites refused to go to war.

11 Yea, and **they also knew the extreme hatred of the Lamanites towards their brethren, who were the people of Anti-Nephi-Lehi, who were called the people of Ammon**—and they would not take up arms, yea, they had entered into a covenant and they would not break it—therefore, **if they should fall into the hands of the Lamanites they would be destroyed.**

12 And **the Nephites would not suffer** [*allow*] **that they should be destroyed;** therefore they gave them lands for their inheritance.

13 And the people of Ammon did give unto the Nephites a large portion of their substance to support their armies; and thus **the Nephites were compelled, alone, to withstand** [*fight*] **against the Lamanites**, who were a compound [*a combination of descendants*] of Laman and Lemuel, and the sons of Ishmael, and all those who had dissented [*apostatized*] from the Nephites, who were Amalekites and Zoramites, and the descendants of the priests of Noah.

14 Now those descendants were as numerous, nearly, as were the Nephites; and **thus the Nephites were obliged** [*required*] **to contend with their brethren, even unto bloodshed.**

15 And it came to pass as **the armies of the Lamanites had gathered together in the land of Antionum**, behold, the armies of **the Nephites were prepared to meet them in the land of Jershon**.

Next, we are introduced to Captain Moroni, the young leader of the Nephite armies.

16 Now, **the leader of the Nephites,** or the man who had been appointed to be **the chief captain** over the Nephites—now the chief captain took the command of all the armies of the Nephites—and his name **was Moroni**;

17 And Moroni took all the command, and the government of their wars. And **he was only twenty and five years old** when he was appointed chief captain over the armies of the Nephites.

18 And it came to pass that he met the Lamanites in the borders of Jershon, and **his people were armed with swords, and with cimeters** [*a relatively short curved sword*]**, and all manner of weapons of war**. [*They had prepared themselves to defend their people against the threat of outside enemies.*]

19 And when the armies of the Lamanites saw that the people of Nephi,

or that **Moroni, had prepared his people with breastplates** and with **arm–shields,** yea, and also **shields to defend their heads**, and also they were dressed with **thick clothing**—

20 Now **the army of Zerahemnah was not prepared with any such thing**; they had only their swords and their cimeters, their bows and their arrows, their stones and their slings; and they were naked, save it were a skin which was girded about their loins; yea, all were naked, save it were the Zoramites and the Amalekites [*apostate Nephites*];

21 But they were not armed with breastplates, nor shields—**therefore, they were exceedingly afraid of the armies of the Nephites** because of their armor, notwithstanding [*even though*] their number being so much greater than the Nephites.

You can see that Captain Moroni was a wise and inspired leader.

22 Behold, now it came to pass that **they durst not** [*did not dare*] **come against the Nephites in the borders of Jershon** [*where they were well defended*]; therefore they departed out of the land of Antionum into the wilderness, and took their journey round about in the wilderness, away by the head of the river Sidon, that they might come into the land of Manti and take possession of the land; for they did not suppose that the armies of Moroni would know whither [*where*] they had gone.

Next, we see the benefits of having a commander in chief who is himself a man of God.

23 But it came to pass, as soon as they had departed into the wilderness Moroni sent spies into the wilderness to watch their camp; and **Moroni, also, knowing of the prophecies of Alma, sent certain men unto him, desiring him that he should inquire of the Lord whither** [*where*] **the armies of the Nephites should go to defend themselves against the Lamanites.**

24 And it came to pass that **the word of the Lord came unto Alma, and Alma informed the messengers of Moroni**, that the armies of the Lamanites were marching round about in the wilderness, that they might come over into the land of Manti, that they might commence an attack upon the weaker part of the people. And those messengers went and delivered the message unto Moroni.

Watch Moroni's strategy now as he responds to the word of the Lord from the prophet, Alma. Note also the advantage that advanced preparation for potential war gave the Nephites (verse 26).

25 Now Moroni, **leaving a part of his army in the land of Jershon**, lest by any means a part of the Lamanites should come into that land and take possession of the city, **took the remaining part of his army and marched over into the land of Manti.**

26 And **he caused that all the people in that quarter of the land should gather themselves together to battle against the Lamanites**, to defend their lands and their country, their rights and their liberties; therefore **they were prepared against the time of the coming of the Lamanites.**

27 And it came to pass that **Moroni caused that his army should be secreted** [*hidden*] in the valley which was near the bank of the river Sidon, which was on the west of the river Sidon in the wilderness.

28 And **Moroni placed spies** round about, that he might know when the camp of the Lamanites should come.

29 And now, as **Moroni knew the intention of the Lamanites**, that it was their intention to destroy their brethren, or to subject them and bring them into bondage that they might establish a kingdom unto themselves over all the land;

30 And **he also knowing that it was the only desire of the Nephites to preserve their lands, and their liberty, and their church**, therefore he thought it **no sin** that he should **defend them by stratagem**; therefore, he found by his spies which course the Lamanites were to take.

The fact that Mormon is giving us considerable detail about Moroni's military strategy is evidence that he wants us to understand that it is not a sin or unfair to come up with ways to outwit and subdue the enemies of our rights and freedoms. Perhaps there is a major side message in this for us today: the rights of criminals and enemies to society should not be elevated above the rights of law-abiding citizens.

We will continue to observe Moroni's strategy.

31 Therefore, **he divided his army** and **brought a part over into the valley, and concealed** [*hid*] **them** on the east, and on the south of the hill Riplah;

32 And **the remainder he concealed in the west valley**, on the west of the river Sidon, and so down into the borders of the land Manti.

33 And thus having placed his army according to his desire, **he was prepared to meet them** [*the Lamanites*].

34 And it came to pass that **the Lamanites came** up on the north of the hill, where a part of the army of Moroni was concealed.

35 And **as the Lamanites had passed the hill Riplah** [*where part of Moroni's army was hiding*], and came into the valley, **and began to cross the river Sidon**, the army which was concealed on the south of the hill, which was led by a man whose name was **Lehi**, and he **led his army forth and encircled the Lamanites** about on the east in their rear.

36 And it came to pass that **the Lamanites**, when they saw the Nephites coming upon them in their rear, **turned them about** [*turned around*] **and began to contend with the army of Lehi.**

37 And **the work of death commenced on both sides**, but it was more dreadful on the part of the Lamanites, for their nakedness was exposed to the heavy blows of **the Nephites with their swords and their cimeters**, which **brought death almost at every stroke**.

38 While on the other hand, there was **now and then a man fell among the Nephites**, by their swords and the loss of blood, they being shielded from the more vital parts of the body, or the more vital parts of the body being shielded from the strokes of the Lamanites, by their breastplates, and their armshields, and their headplates; and thus the Nephites did carry on the work of death among the Lamanites.

There is an interesting reminder, in verse 38, above, that the record from which Joseph Smith translated was indeed engraved on metal plates. It appears that perhaps Mormon was a bit distracted as he engraved this part of his account. He first engraved that the Nephite soldiers were "shielded from the more vital parts of the body" when he meant to engrave "the more vital parts of the body being shielded from the strokes of the Lamanites."

Of course, Mormon couldn't simply erase or highlight and then delete text on his gold plates like we do on our computers. This is a small but important internal evidence that the Book of Mormon was indeed translated from a record engraved on metal plates. And Joseph Smith stuck precisely to what was on the plates.

We will continue now to read as Mormon describes the strategy used by Moroni's armies to defeat the Lamanites.

39 And it came to pass that **the Lamanites became frightened**, because of the great destruction among them, even until they **began to flee towards the river Sidon.**

40 And **they were pursued by Lehi and his men**; and they were driven by Lehi into the waters of Sidon [*the river named Sidon*], and **they crossed the waters of Sidon**. And **Lehi retained** [*kept*] **his armies upon the bank** of the river Sidon that they should not cross.

41 And it came to pass that **Moroni and his army met the Lamanites** in the valley, **on the other side of the river Sidon**, and began to fall upon them and to slay them.

42 And **the Lamanites did flee** again before them, **towards the land of Manti**; and **they were met again by the armies of Moroni.**

43 Now in this case **the Lamanites did fight exceedingly** [*very hard*]; yea, never had the Lamanites been known to fight with such exceedingly great strength and courage, no, not even from the beginning.

44 And they were **inspired by the Zoramites and the Amalekites**, who were their chief captains and leaders [*and who hated the Nephites*], **and by Zerahemnah**, who was their chief captain, or their chief leader and

commander; yea, they did fight like dragons, and **many of the Nephites were slain** [*killed*] by their hands, yea, for they did smite in two many of their head-plates, and they did pierce many of their breastplates, and they did smite off many of their arms; and thus the Lamanites did smite in their fierce anger.

45 Nevertheless [*however*], **the Nephites were inspired by a better cause**, for they were not fighting for monarchy nor power but they were fighting for their homes and their liberties, their wives and their children, and their all, yea, for their rites of worship and their church.

In verses 46 and 47, next, we see what is often referred to as "the law of self-defense." In fact, the Lord refers to it in D&C 98:32–33 in which He says, "This is the law I gave unto my servant Nephi . . ." (you will need to read the whole section). This is a very important law for us to understand. Otherwise, we may be led aside by people with good intentions in our day who completely oppose war under all circumstances.

46 And they were doing that which they felt was the duty which they owed to their God; for **the Lord had said unto them, and also unto their fathers** [*ancestors*], **that: Inasmuch as ye are not guilty of the first offense, neither the second, ye shall not suffer** [*allow*] **yourselves to be slain by the hands of your enemies.**

47 And again, **the Lord has said that: Ye shall defend your families even unto bloodshed** [*even if it means killing your enemies*]. Therefore for this cause were the Nephites contending [*fighting*] with the Lamanites, to defend themselves, and their families, and their lands, their country, and their rights, and their religion.

48 And it came to pass that **when the men of Moroni saw the fierceness and the anger of the Lamanites, they were about to shrink and flee from them**. And **Moroni**, perceiving their intent [*seeing what they were about to do*], sent forth and **inspired their hearts with these thoughts**—yea, the thoughts of **their lands, their liberty**, yea, **their freedom from bondage** [*key issues in determining when to go to war*].

49 And it came to pass that **they turned upon the Lamanites, and they cried** with one voice **unto the Lord their God, for their liberty** and their **freedom from bondage.**

50 And **they began to stand against the Lamanites with power**; and in that selfsame hour that they cried unto the Lord for their freedom, **the Lamanites began to flee** before them; and they fled even to the waters of Sidon.

51 Now, **the Lamanites were more numerous, yea, by more than double** the number of the Nephites; nevertheless, they were driven insomuch that they were gathered together in one body in the valley, upon the bank by the river Sidon.

As we read the next three verses, in which the Lamanites are surrounded by Moroni's armies, we will see one of Captain Moroni's great, Christlike virtues—mercy.

52 Therefore **the armies of Moroni encircled them** about, yea, even on both sides of the river, for behold, on the east were the men of Lehi.

53 Therefore when Zerahemnah saw the men of Lehi on the east of the river Sidon, and the armies of Moroni on the west of the river Sidon, that they were encircled about by the Nephites, **they were struck with terror**.

54 **Now Moroni, when he saw their terror, commanded his men that they should stop shedding their blood.**

ALMA 44

As the battle continues, we see Captain Moroni show mercy to the enemies by commanding his men to stop killing the Lamanites, who are trembling with terror. He will explain to Zerahemnah that the Nephites do not want war and that if the Lamanites will stop fighting, surrender their weapons to the Nephites, go home and not come back and fight anymore, Moroni's armies will let them go.

1 AND it came to pass that they did stop and withdrew a pace from them. And **Moroni said unto Zerahemnah:** Behold, Zerahemnah, that **we do not desire to be men of blood**. Ye know that ye are in our hands, yet we do not desire to slay you.

2 Behold, **we have not come out to battle against you that we might shed your blood for power; neither do we desire to bring any one to the yoke of bondage** [*we don't want to make you our slaves*]. But this is the very cause [*these are your exact motives*] for which ye have come against us; yea, and **ye are angry with us because of our religion**.

Simply put, Zerahemnah's motives are basically the same as Satan's. He wants to make us miserable and have full control over us. Moroni continues, explaining that the forces of evil cannot ultimately triumph over the forces of good.

3 But now, ye behold [*see*] that **the Lord is with us**; and ye behold that he has delivered you into our hands. And now I would that ye should understand that this is done unto us **because of our religion and our faith in Christ.** And now ye see that **ye cannot destroy this our faith.**

4 Now ye see that **this is the true faith of God**; yea, **ye see that God will support, and keep, and preserve us, so long as we are faithful unto him, and unto our faith, and our religion; and never will the Lord suffer** [*allow*] **that we shall be destroyed except we should fall into transgression** [*sin*] **and deny our faith.**

Next, Moroni explains to Zerahemnah how he and his men can preserve their lives. As you read these next verses, you will see that Captain Moroni is strong-willed and a no-nonsense leader. Either Zerahemnah agrees to strict terms or the battle continues. You will also see the foundation upon which faithful Saints can stand when forced into a position of self-defense.

5 And now, Zerahemnah, I command you, in the name of that all–powerful God, who has strengthened our arms that **we have gained power over you, by our faith**, by **our religion**, and by **our rites of worship**, and by **our church**, and **by the sacred support which we owe to our wives and our children, by that liberty which binds us to our lands and our country**; yea, and **also by the maintenance of** [*by living according to*] **the sacred word of God, to which we owe all our happiness**; and by all that is most dear unto us—

6 Yea, and **this is not all; I command you** by all the desires which ye have for life, that ye **deliver up your weapons of war unto us, and we will seek not your blood**, but **we will spare your lives, if ye will go your way and come not again to war against us**.

The "if" phrase at the end of verse 6, above, is a very important part of the potential agreement. Moroni is an example that it is appropriate for righteous people to be very tough when necessary, as evidenced by the second half of the agreement, starting with "if" in verse 7.

7 And now, **if ye do not this, behold, ye are in our hands, and I will command my men that they shall fall upon you, and inflict the wounds of death in your bodies, that ye may become extinct**; and then we will see who shall have power over this people; yea, we will see who shall be brought into bondage.

Watch next, as Zerahemnah attempts to bluff Moroni into letting him and his warriors get away. It could be easy for Moroni to be pulled into an eventual trap by respecting Zerahemnah's "honor" in refusing to make a promise which he and his men would not keep. The deeper issue here is the ultimate protection of Moroni's people and their freedoms. A mark of an inspired, wise military leader is that he can see the deeper issues at stake and take appropriate action.

8 And now it came to pass that **when Zerahemnah had heard these sayings he came forth and delivered up his sword and his cimeter, and his bow into the hands of Moroni, and said** unto him: Behold, **here are our weapons of war; we will deliver them up** [*surrender them*] **unto you, but we will not suffer ourselves** [*agree*] **to take an oath** [*make a promise*] unto you, **which we know that we shall break**, and also our children; **but take our weapons of war, and suffer** [*allow*] **that we may depart** into the wilderness; otherwise we will retain our swords, and we will perish or conquer.

9 Behold, **we are not of your faith; we do not believe that it is God that has delivered us into your hands**; but we believe that it is your cunning that has preserved you from our swords. Behold, it is your breastplates and your shields that have preserved you.

Moroni refuses to be taken in by Zerahemnah's smooth and seemingly noble stance. Satan is a master of deception and such counterfeit integrity has claimed many victims over the centuries.

10 And now when Zerahemnah had made an end of speaking these words, **Moroni returned the sword and the weapons of war**, which he had received, unto Zerahemnah, saying: Behold, we will end the conflict [*we will begin fighting again and finish the matter*].

11 Now I cannot recall [*take back*] the words which I have spoken, therefore **as the Lord liveth** [*the strongest oath or promise in the Nephite culture*], **ye shall not depart except** [*unless*] **ye depart with an oath that ye will not return again against us to war**. Now as ye are in our hands **we will spill your blood upon the ground, or ye shall submit to the conditions which I have proposed.**

12 And now when Moroni had said these words, **Zerahemnah** retained [*kept*] his sword, and he **was angry with Moroni, and he rushed forward that he might slay Moroni; but as he raised his sword, behold, one of Moroni's soldiers smote** [*struck*] **it even to the earth, and it broke by the hilt**; and **he also smote Zerahemnah that he took off his scalp** and it fell to the earth. And Zerahemnah withdrew from before them into the midst of his soldiers.

13 And it came to pass that **the soldier** who stood by, who smote off the scalp of Zerahemnah, **took up the scalp** from off the ground by the hair, **and laid it upon the point of his sword, and stretched it forth unto them, saying unto them with a loud voice**:

14 **Even as this scalp has fallen to the earth**, which is the scalp of your chief, **so shall ye fall to the earth except ye will deliver up your weapons of war and depart with a covenant of peace**. [*In other words, unless you make an oath of permanent peace with us, you will die.*]

15 Now there were **many**, when they heard these words and saw the scalp which was upon the sword, that were struck with fear; and many **came forth and threw down their weapons of war at the feet of Moroni, and entered into a covenant of peace**. And as many as entered into a covenant they suffered [*allowed*] to depart into the wilderness.

16 Now it came to pass that **Zerahemnah was exceedingly wroth** [*very, very, angry*], and he did stir up the remainder of his soldiers to anger, to contend [*fight*] more powerfully against the Nephites.

This is quite a scene! You can imagine Zerahemnah without his scalp, yelling to his soldiers to continue the fight!

Next, you will see Captain Moroni become angry. There is a major difference between Zerahemnah's anger (verse 16) and that of Moroni. Zerahemnah's anger is based on evil, bitterness, and hatred of that which is good and honorable. Moroni's anger is what is often called "righteous indignation," in other words, righteous anger against evil. These two types of anger are opposites.

17 And now **Moroni was angry**, because of the stubbornness of the Lamanites; **therefore he commanded his people that they should fall upon them and slay them**. And it came to pass that they began to slay them; yea, and the Lamanites did contend [*fight*] with their swords and their might.

18 But behold, **their naked skins and their bare heads were exposed to the sharp swords of the Nephites**; yea, behold they were pierced and smitten, yea, and did fall exceedingly fast before the swords of the Nephites; and they began to be swept down, even as the soldier of Moroni had prophesied.

Next, Zerahemnah will change his mind, and Moroni will again show mercy.

19 Now **Zerahemnah**, when he saw that they were all about to be destroyed, **cried mightily unto Moroni, promising that he would covenant** [*make a promise, a strong agreement*] **and also his people with them, if they would spare the remainder of their lives, that they never would come to war again against them.**

20 And it came to pass that **Moroni caused that the work of death should cease again** among the people. And he took the weapons of war from the Lamanites; and after they had entered into a covenant with him of peace **they were suffered** [*permitted*] **to depart into the wilderness**.

21 Now **the number of their dead was not numbered** [*counted*] because of the greatness of the number; yea, the number of their dead was exceedingly great, both on the Nephites and on the Lamanites.

22 And it came to pass that **they did cast their dead into the waters of Sidon** [*into the River Sidon*], and they have gone forth and are buried in the depths of the sea.

23 And **the armies of the Nephites**, or of Moroni, returned and **came to their houses and their lands**.

24 And thus ended the eighteenth year of the reign of the judges over the people of Nephi. And **thus ended the record of Alma** [*which began with Alma, chapter 1; see heading at the beginning of the Book of Alma*], **which was written upon the plates of Nephi**.

ALMA 45

In Alma 37:1–2, Alma gave his oldest son, Helaman, the records of the Nephites, including the plates of Nephi and the brass plates of Laban. He instructed Helaman to continue keeping a record of the people.

As we continue, Mormon uses the records kept by Helaman to engrave his ongoing account of the wars between the Nephites and the Lamanites (see note above the heading of Alma 45, in your Book of Mormon).

In chapter 45, Alma the Younger will leave and never be heard from again. Many believe he was translated (taken up to heaven without dying) because there is no record of his being buried (see Alma 45:18–19).

Next, the armies of Captain Moroni return to their homes and families. They do not forget to express gratitude to the Lord. In fact, as they do so, we are taught that it is good on occasions to fast to show Heavenly Father that you are thankful for His blessings. In other words, fasting is not necessarily only to go along with requests for blessings from the Lord, but may also be used as a sincere means of expressing gratitude.

1 BEHOLD, now it came to pass that the people of Nephi were exceedingly rejoiced, because the Lord had again delivered them out of the hands of their enemies; therefore **they gave thanks unto the Lord their God**; yea, and **they did fast much and pray much, and they did worship God with exceedingly great joy.**

Next, Alma reviews with his son, Helaman, the responsibility he has accepted to continue keeping the Nephite records.

2 And it came to pass in the nineteenth year of the reign of the judges over the people of Nephi, that **Alma came unto his son Helaman and said** unto him: **Believest thou the words which I spake unto thee** [*Alma 37:1–2*] **concerning those records** [*the plates of Nephi, etc.*] which have been kept?

3 And **Helaman said** unto him: **Yea, I believe.**

4 And **Alma said** again: **Believest thou in Jesus Christ, who shall come?**

5 And **he said: Yea, I believe all the words which thou hast spoken.**

6 And **Alma said** unto him again: **Will ye keep my commandments?**

7 And **he said**: **Yea, I will keep thy commandments with all my heart.**

8 Then **Alma said** unto him: **Blessed art thou; and the Lord shall prosper thee in this land.**

Next, Alma the Younger, who has been serving as President of the Church for many years, gives a very specific prophecy concerning the Nephites, after the Savior appears to them.

9 But behold, **I have somewhat to prophesy unto thee**; but what I prophesy unto thee ye shall not make known; yea, what I prophesy unto thee shall not be made known, even until the prophecy is fulfilled; therefore write the words which I shall say.

10 And **these are the words:** Behold, I perceive [*see, understand*] that this very people, **the Nephites**, according to the spirit of revelation which is in me, **in four hundred years from the time that Jesus Christ shall**

manifest himself unto them, shall dwindle in unbelief [*will gradually fall away from the Church and the gospel of Jesus Christ*].

11 Yea, and **then shall they see wars and pestilences** [*all kinds of troubles and problems*], **yea, famines and bloodshed, even until the people of Nephi shall become extinct**—

> Next, Alma explains what caused the destruction of the Nephites. The same things have destroyed numerous civilizations and continue to destroy societies as well as individuals today.

12 Yea, and this **because they shall dwindle in unbelief** and **fall into the works of darkness** [*get caught up in committing sins and doing evil*], and **lasciviousness** [*sexual immorality of all kinds*], and **all manner of iniquities** [*every kind of wickedness*]; yea, I say unto you, that because they shall sin against so great light and knowledge, yea, I say unto you, that from that day, even the fourth generation shall not all pass away before this great iniquity shall come.

13 And **when that great day cometh**, behold, the time very soon cometh that those who are now, or the seed of those who are now numbered among **the people of Nephi, shall no more be numbered** [*counted*] **among the people of Nephi**.

14 **But** whosoever remaineth, and is not destroyed in that great and dreadful day, **shall be numbered among the Lamanites, and shall become like unto them**, all, save it be a few who shall be called the disciples of the Lord; and them shall the Lamanites pursue even until they shall become extinct. And now, **because of iniquity** [*wickedness*], **this prophecy shall be fulfilled**.

> After having prophesied the destruction of the Nephites, both by wars and by being absorbed into the wicked culture and practices of the Lamanites, Alma gives his sons a final blessing. He is about to leave and never be seen again.

15 And now it came to pass that **after Alma had said these things to Helaman, he blessed him, and also his other sons**; and he also blessed the earth for the righteous' sake.

16 And **he said: Thus saith the Lord God—Cursed shall be the land, yea, this land** [*the Americas*], **unto every nation, kindred, tongue, and people, unto destruction, which do wickedly, when they are fully ripe** [*when they have become so wicked that the righteous don't have a chance*]; and as I have said so shall it be; for this is the cursing and the blessing of God upon the land, for **the Lord cannot look upon sin with the least degree of allowance.**

17 And now, **when Alma had said these words he blessed the church**, yea, all those who should stand fast [*stay faithful*] in the faith from that time henceforth.

18 And **when Alma had done this he departed out of the land of Zarahemla, as if to go into the land of Melek. And it came to pass that**

he was never heard of more; as to his death or burial we know not of.

We have now said goodbye to Alma the Younger. It will be exciting to meet him and his father in the next life.

Verse 19, next, has several facets. First, we are reminded one more time of the power of the Atonement of Christ to cleanse and heal. As you recall, when we first met Alma the Younger, he was the rebellious son of Alma the Elder and was attempting to destroy the Church. As he leaves this earth, he is a righteous man.

Concerning Moses, the Bible says that he was "buried by the hand of the Lord" (Deuteronomy 34:6), but from modern revelation, including Alma 45:19, we know that he was translated (see Bible Dictionary, 735). "Translated" means taken up without dying in order to do more work for the Lord. Then being resurrected later.

19 Behold, this we know, that **he was a righteous man**; and the saying went abroad in the church that he was taken up by the Spirit, or buried by the hand of the Lord, even as Moses. But behold, **the scriptures saith the Lord took Moses unto himself; and we suppose that he has also received Alma in the spirit, unto himself**; therefore, for this cause we know nothing concerning his death and burial.

20 And now it came to pass in the commencement of the nineteenth year of the reign of the judges over the people of Nephi, that **Helaman** [*Alma's oldest son*] **went forth among the people to declare the word unto them**.

21 For behold, because of their wars with the Lamanites and the many little dissensions and disturbances which had been among the people, **it became expedient that the word of God should be declared among them**, yea, and that a regulation should be made throughout the church.

22 **Therefore, Helaman and his brethren went forth to establish the church again in all the land**, yea, in every city throughout all the land which was possessed by the people of Nephi. And it came to pass that they did appoint priests and teachers throughout all the land, over all the churches.

23 And now it came to pass that after Helaman and his brethren had appointed priests and teachers over the churches that **there arose a dissension** [*argument*] **among them, and they would not give heed to the words of Helaman and his brethren**;

24 But **they grew proud**, being **lifted up in their hearts** [*prideful*], because of their exceedingly great riches; therefore **they grew rich in their own eyes,** and would not give heed to their words, to walk uprightly [*to live righteously*] before God.

ALMA 46

This chapter is famous because of the title of liberty. It is here that Captain Moroni raises the banner or title of liberty to rally his people to battle. Many artists who are members of the Church have depicted this scene in their paintings.

As we begin this chapter, we see that it has come down to war between those who do not believe in Christ and those who do. This is perhaps symbolic of the battle that began with the war in heaven between those who followed Lucifer and those who followed Christ. We are told that in the last days before the Second Coming of the Savior, it will once again come down to the basic battle between good and evil, believers and unbelievers. Speaking of our day, D&C 1:35–36 says, "And the devil shall have power over his own dominion. And also the Lord shall have power over his saints."

Once again, the leader of the unbelievers was a large man who easily attracted people to listen to him. His basic motive was to gain power over people. His name was Amalickiah.

1 AND it came to pass that **as many as would not hearken** [*listen*] **to the words of Helaman and his brethren** [*the unbelievers*] **were gathered together against their brethren** [*the believers*].

2 And now behold, **they** [*the unbelievers*] **were exceedingly wroth** [*angry*], insomuch that they were determined to slay them.

3 Now **the leader of those who were wroth against their brethren** [*the believers*] **was a large and a strong man; and his name was Amalickiah.**

One of the great values for us in this part of the Book of Mormon is that we are taught and cautioned about motives, trends, political issues, and philosophies in our day. In verse 4 you will see that the political system and government had become filled with people whose basic motive was power over others rather than seeking the best interests of the people. Such selfish and power-hungry officials are quick to support individuals like Amalickiah in hopes that he will give them positions of power under him.

4 And **Amalickiah was desirous to** [*wanted to*] **be a king**; and **those people who were wroth** [*angry at the believers*] **were also desirous that he should be their king; and they were the greater part** [*the majority*] **of them the lower judges of the land, and they were seeking for power.**

5 And **they had been led by the flatteries of Amalickiah, that if they would support him and establish him to be their king that he would make them rulers over the people.**

6 Thus **they were led away by Amalickiah to dissensions** [*apostasy*], notwithstanding [*in spite of*] the preaching of Helaman and his brethren, yea, notwithstanding their exceedingly great care over the church, for they were high priests over the church.

7 And **there were many in the church who believed in the flattering words of Amalickiah, therefore they dissented** [*apostatized; left*] **even from the church**; and **thus were the affairs of the people of Nephi exceedingly precarious** [*off balance*] **and dangerous**, notwithstanding their great victory which they had had over the Lamanites, and their great rejoicings which they had had because of their deliverance by the hand of the Lord.

Whenever you see the phrase "thus we see," as in verse 8, next, be aware that it is Mormon pointing out what he wants us to learn from what he has just told us.

8 **Thus we see** how quick the children of men do forget the Lord their God, yea, how quick to do iniquity, and to be led away by the evil one.

9 Yea, and **we also see** the great wickedness one very wicked man [*like Amalickiah*] can cause to take place among the children of men.

10 Yea, **we see** that Amalickiah, because he was a man of cunning device and a man of many flattering words, that he led away the hearts of many people to do wickedly; yea, and to seek to destroy the church of God, and to destroy the foundation of liberty which God had granted unto them, or which blessing God had sent upon the face of the land for the righteous' sake.

11 And now it came to pass that **when Moroni**, who was the chief commander of the armies of the Nephites, **had heard of these dissensions, he was angry** [*righteous anger; righteous indignation*] **with Amalickiah**.

Next comes the famous scene in which Moroni raises the title of liberty.

12 And it came to pass that **he rent** [*tore*] **his coat; and he took a piece thereof, and wrote upon it—In memory of our God, our religion, and freedom, and our peace, our wives, and our children**—and **he fastened it upon the end of a pole**.

13 And **he fastened on his head-plate, and his breastplate, and his shields, and girded on** [*put on*] **his armor about his loins; and he took the pole, which had on the end thereof his rent coat**, (and he called it **the title of liberty**) and he bowed himself to the earth, **and he prayed mightily unto his God for the blessings of liberty to rest upon his brethren**, so long as there should a band of **Christians** remain to possess the land—

14 For **thus were all the true believers of Christ, who belonged to the church of God, called** by those who did not belong to the church.

Mormon takes a moment here, in verses 13–15, to explain the beginning of the use of the word "Christians" to refer to the believers. It is interesting that the first use of "Christians" to refer to members of the Church in the New Testament is found in Acts 11:26. It is suggested in the Bible Dictionary under

"Christians," that this term may at first have been used in a negative way by non-members to refer to followers of Christ. If such is the case, it is not surprising that Satan would sponsor its use in both the Old World and the New World.

15 And those who did belong to the church were faithful; yea, **all those who were true believers in Christ took upon them, gladly, the name of Christ, or Christians** as they were called, **because of their belief in Christ** who should come.

16 And therefore, at this time, **Moroni prayed that the cause of the Christians, and the freedom of the land might be favored**.

Next, Moroni, as commander in chief of the Nephite armies, defines the boundaries of the land that were to be defended against the enemies of freedom.

17 And it came to pass that when he had poured out his soul to God, he named all the land which was south of the land Desolation, yea, and in fine, all the land, both on the north and on the south—**A chosen land, and the land of liberty**.

In verse 18, next, we are reminded that the only way in which the people of the Lord can be destroyed as a group is through transgression.

18 And he said: Surely God shall not suffer [*allow*] that we, who are despised because we take upon us the name of Christ, shall be trodden down and destroyed, **until we bring it upon us by our own transgressions**.

19 And when **Moroni** had said these words, he **went forth among the people, waving the rent part** [*torn piece*] **of his garment** [*his coat; see verse 12*] **in the air**, that all might see the writing which he had written upon the rent part, and **crying with a loud voice, saying**:

20 Behold, **whosoever will maintain this title upon the land, let them come forth in the strength of the Lord, and enter into a covenant that they will maintain their rights, and their religion, that the Lord God may bless them**.

There is powerful symbolism in verse 20, above, in the fact that Moroni invited those who were willing, to come forth and make a covenant to preserve their freedom. Perhaps you have already noticed that the highest freedoms and protections against Satan and the evil around us are gained through the voluntary making of covenants in temples.

In verse 21, next, we see the words "token" and "covenant" used in association with freedom from bondage and captivity. These words are significant to endowed Latter-day Saints.

21 And it came to pass that when Moroni had proclaimed these words, behold, the people came running together with their armor girded about their loins, rending their garments in **token**, or as a **covenant**, that they would not forsake the Lord their God; or, in other words, if they should transgress the commandments of God, or fall into

transgression, and be ashamed to take upon them the name of Christ, the Lord should rend them even as they had rent their garments.

22 Now **this was the covenant which they made**, and they cast their garments at the feet of Moroni, saying: We covenant with our God, that we shall be destroyed, even as our brethren in the land northward, if we shall fall into transgression; yea, he may cast us at the feet of our enemies, even as we have cast our garments at thy feet to be trodden under foot, if we shall fall into transgression.

Next, we are informed of some details about Joseph's coat of many colors, which are not mentioned elsewhere in scripture. Joseph was sold into Egyptian slavery at the age of seventeen, by his brothers, who, among other things, were jealous of his special coat.

Moroni is a master of using symbolism and objects to teach and rally support for the cause of freedom.

23 Moroni said unto them: Behold, we are a remnant of the seed [*descendants*] of Jacob; yea, **we are a remnant of the seed of Joseph, whose coat was rent** [*torn*] by his brethren into many pieces; yea, and now behold, **let us remember to keep the commandments of God, or our garments shall be rent by our brethren** [*the Lamanites and apostate Nephites who have gathered around Amalickiah*], and we be cast into prison, or be sold, or be slain.

As Moroni continues to rally his forces, we learn that a part of Joseph's coat of many colors has been preserved. No doubt, someday the faithful from all ages will be privileged to see it. This remnant of Joseph's coat is symbolic of the remnant of his descendants that was preserved by the Lord from utter destruction.

In verses 24 and 25, we are privileged to read some of the words of Jacob that have been left out of Genesis in the Bible.

24 Yea, let us preserve our liberty as a remnant of Joseph; yea, **let us remember the words of Jacob, before his death**, for behold, he saw that a part of the remnant of the coat of Joseph was preserved and had not decayed. And **he** [*Jacob*] **said—Even as this remnant of garment of my son** [*Joseph*] **hath been preserved, so shall a remnant of the seed** [*descendants*] **of my son be preserved by the hand of God, and be taken unto himself, while the remainder of the seed of Joseph shall perish, even as the remnant of his garment.**

25 **Now behold, this giveth my soul sorrow; nevertheless, my soul hath joy in my son, because of that part of his seed which shall be taken unto God.**

26 Now behold, **this was the language of Jacob.** [*The words of Jacob quoted above by Moroni, may fit nicely into Genesis 37:33 and its context.*]

Moroni now suggests a possibility as to how a remnant of the descendants of Joseph may be destroyed, thus fulfilling, in part, the prophecy of Jacob quoted above.

27 And now **who knoweth but what the remnant of the seed of Joseph, which shall perish as his garment, are those** [*apostates*] **who have dissented from us** [*left the Church*]**?** Yea, and even **it shall be ourselves if we do not stand fast in the faith of Christ.**

Next, we see a great gathering of the faithful out from among the wicked. This has symbolic elements which can remind us of the great gathering of the righteous from among the wicked lifestyles around us in our last days.

28 And now it came to pass that when **Moroni** had said these words he **went forth, and** also **sent forth** in all the parts of the land where there were dissensions, **and gathered together all the people who were desirous to maintain their liberty, to stand against Amalickiah and those who had dissented, who were called Amalickiahites.**

Next, we see another answer to a current question, namely, whether or not it is justified, on occasions, to send soldiers to capture and eliminate an individual or group of individuals whose declared purpose is to destroy the God-given freedoms of a nation, and who pose an imminent threat.

We will watch what Captain Moroni does when it becomes obvious that Amalickiah and his followers are going to go among the Lamanites and recruit others to join the fight against Moroni's people.

29 And it came to pass that when **Amalickiah** saw that the people of Moroni were more numerous than the Amalickiahites—and he also saw that his people were doubtful concerning the justice of the cause in which they had undertaken [*they had doubts as to whether or not it was right to fight against the Nephites*]—therefore, fearing that he should not gain the point, he **took those of his people who would** [*who agreed to follow him*] **and departed into the land of Nephi** [*where the Lamanites lived*].

30 Now **Moroni thought it was not expedient** [*it was not wise to allow*] **that the Lamanites should have any more strength; therefore he thought to cut off the people of Amalickiah, or to take them and bring them back, and put Amalickiah to death**; yea, for he knew that he would stir up the Lamanites to anger against them, and cause them to come to battle against them; and this he knew that Amalickiah would do that he might obtain his purposes.

31 Therefore **Moroni** thought it was expedient that he should take his armies, who had gathered themselves together, and armed themselves, and entered into a covenant to keep the peace—and it came to pass that he **took his army and marched out with his tents into the wilderness, to cut off the course of Amalickiah in the wilderness.**

32 And it came to pass that **he** did according to his desires, and **marched**

forth into the wilderness, and headed [*confronted; faced*] **the armies of Amalickiah**.

33 And it came to pass that **Amalickiah fled with a small number of his men**, and the remainder were delivered up into the hands of Moroni and were taken back into the land of Zarahemla.

As is often the case with tyrants and individuals who lust for power over others, they have no real loyalty to their followers. When faced with capture, they quickly desert and seek their own safety. Amalickiah deserted his soldiers and escaped. But we have not seen the last of him.

Next, we see that the righteous are sometimes obligated to take a very tough stand against evil military enemies. Without such guidelines as those given by Mormon, and holding Captain Moroni up as an example, many well-meaning people today could support causes and philosophies that ultimately undermine God-given freedoms.

34 Now, **Moroni** being a man who was appointed by the chief judges and the voice of the people, therefore he **had power** [*authority*] according to his will with the armies of the Nephites, **to establish and to exercise authority over them**.

35 And it came to pass that **whomsoever of the Amalickiahites that would not enter into a covenant to support the cause of freedom, that they might maintain a free government, he caused to be put to death**; and there were but few who denied [*refused to make*] the covenant of freedom.

36 And it came to pass also, that **he caused the title of liberty to be hoisted upon every tower which was in all the land, which was possessed by the Nephites**; and thus Moroni planted the standard of liberty among the Nephites.

Next we see that Moroni's tough stance and strategy had the desired effect in preserving peace and freedom.

37 And **they began to have peace again in the land**; and thus they did maintain peace in the land until nearly the end of the nineteenth year of the reign of the judges.

38 And **Helaman and the high priests did also maintain order in the church**; yea, even **for** the space of **four years** did they have much peace and rejoicing in the church.

39 And it came to pass that **there were many who died, firmly believing that their souls were redeemed by the Lord Jesus Christ**; thus they went out of the world rejoicing.

Next, Mormon points out that the Creator placed many plants and resources on earth for people to discover and use for medicinal purposes.

40 And there were some who died with fevers, which at some seasons of the year were very frequent in the land—but not so much so with fevers, because of the excellent qualities of the **many plants and roots which**

God had prepared to remove the cause of diseases, to which men were subject by the nature of the climate—

41 But there were many who died with old age; and **those who died in the faith of Christ are happy** in him, as we must needs suppose [*as we have every reason to believe*].

ALMA 47

In this chapter, Mormon will point out many things, including the fact that when members of the Church leave the standards of the gospel, after they have once had a testimony of the truthfulness of the Church, they often become more wicked and dangerous to the Lord's work than those who never knew the gospel.

This is probably one of the most action-packed chapters of the Book of Mormon. Amalickiah is certainly a "type" of the devil, meaning that what he does is similar to what Satan does and stands for, including deception, treachery, greed, lust for power, and total lack of care or feeling for those who stand in his way. Amalickiah uses people to get what he wants for himself without a trace of conscience.

When we last saw Amalickiah, he had deserted his soldiers and fled with a small group of followers (Alma 46:33). Mormon now returns to him and his plots as he works his plan to use the Lamanites to accomplish his selfish goals.

1 **NOW we will return in our record to Amalickiah and those who had fled with him into the wilderness**; for, behold, **he had taken those who went with him, and went up in the land of Nephi among the Lamanites, and did stir up the Lamanites to anger against the people of Nephi**, insomuch [*so much so*] that the king of the Lamanites sent a proclamation [*a message*] throughout all his land, among all his people, that they should gather themselves together again to go to battle against the Nephites.

The Lamanites find themselves in a real worrisome situation as Amalickiah inspires their king to command them to go again to fight against the Nephites. Their fear causes the majority of them to refuse to obey the command of their king. This fear plays into the cunning hands of Amalickiah.

2 And it came to pass that when the proclamation had gone forth among them **they were exceedingly afraid; yea, they feared to displease the king, and they also feared to go to battle against the Nephites** lest they should lose their lives. And it came to pass that they would not, or the more part of them would not, obey the commandments of the king.

3 And now it came to pass that **the king** was wroth because of their disobedience; therefore he **gave Amalickiah the command of that part of his army which was obedient unto his commands**, and commanded him that he should go forth

and compel them to arms [*force the other Lamanites to go to war*].

4 Now behold, **this was the desire of Amalickiah; for he being a very subtle** [*crafty, sly*] **man to do evil therefore he laid the plan in his heart to dethrone the king of the Lamanites.**

> Watch how cunning and sly Amalickiah is. He almost competes with the devil himself as far as being evil is concerned. Satan seeks power over people so that he can force them to do his evil will. God respects agency and does everything possible to preserve it for His faithful Saints but will never force people against their will.

5 And now **he had got the command of those parts of the Lamanites who were in favor of the king**; and **he sought to gain favor of those who were not obedient**; therefore he went forward to the place which was called Onidah, for thither [*there*] had all the Lamanites [*who had disobeyed the king*] fled; for they discovered the army coming, and, supposing that they were coming to destroy them, therefore they fled to Onidah, to the place of arms.

6 And **they had appointed a man to be a king and a leader over them**, being fixed in their minds with a determined resolution that they would not be subjected [*forced*] to go against the Nephites.

7 And it came to pass that **they had gathered themselves together upon the top of the mount** which was called Antipas, **in preparation to battle.**

8 Now **it was not Amalickiah's intention to give them battle according to the commandments of the king; but behold, it was his intention to gain favor with the armies of the Lamanites, that he might place himself at their head and dethrone the king and take possession of the kingdom.**

9 And behold, it came to pass that **he caused his army to pitch their tents** in the valley which was **near the mount Antipas** [*where the frightened Lamanites had gathered*].

10 And it came to pass that **when it was night he sent a secret embassy** [*messenger or messengers*] **into the mount Antipas, desiring that the leader of those who were upon the mount**, whose name was Lehonti, that he **should come down to the foot of the mount**, for he desired to speak with him.

11 And it came to pass that when **Lehonti** received the message **he durst not** [*did not dare*] **go down** to the foot of the mount. And it came to pass that **Amalickiah sent again the second time**, desiring him to come down. And it came to pass that **Lehonti would not**; and **he sent again the third time**.

12 And it came to pass that **when Amalickiah found that he could not get Lehonti to come** down off from the mount, **he went up** into the mount, **nearly to Lehonti's camp;**

and he sent again the fourth time his message unto Lehonti, desiring that he would come down, and that he would bring his guards with him.

Next, we see the extreme cunning of Amalickiah as he promises Lehonti that he can become the leader of all the Lamanite armies, as long as he keeps Amalickiah as his second in command. This reminds us of what Satan said to Cain in Moses 5:30 when he promised Cain that he could be the leader. Satan is quick to promise his potential victims whatever is necessary to lure them into his trap. So also does Amalickiah. As Lehonti agrees, he basically sets things up for his own death and Amalickiah prepares to spring the trap.

13 And it came to pass that **when Lehonti had come down** with his guards to Amalickiah, that **Amalickiah desired him to come down with his army in the night–time, and surround those men in their camps over whom the king had given him command, and that he would deliver them up into Lehonti's hands, if he would make him** [*Amalickiah*] **a second leader over the whole army.**

14 And it came to pass that **Lehonti came down with his men and surrounded the men of Amalickiah**, so that before they awoke at the dawn of day they were surrounded by the armies of Lehonti.

15 And it came to pass that **when they saw that they were surrounded, they plead with Amalickiah that he would suffer** [*allow*] **them to fall in** [*join*] **with their brethren, that they might not be destroyed. Now this was the very thing which Amalickiah desired.**

16 And it came to pass that **he delivered his men** [*turned his soldiers over to Lehonti*], **contrary to** [*against*] **the commands of the king**. Now this was the thing that Amalickiah desired, that he might accomplish his designs [*plot*] in dethroning the king [*removing the Lamanite King from power*].

Next, Mormon gives us a hint of what Amalickiah is planning to do to Lehonti.

17 Now **it was the custom among the Lamanites, if their chief leader was killed, to appoint the second leader to be their chief leader.**

18 And it came to pass that **Amalickiah caused that one of his servants should administer poison by degrees to Lehonti, that he died.**

19 Now, **when Lehonti was dead, the Lamanites appointed Amalickiah** to be **their leader and their chief commander.**

20 And it came to pass that **Amalickiah marched with his armies** [*for he had gained his desires*] **to the land of Nephi** [*where the Lamanites lived*], to the city of Nephi, which was the chief city.

21 And **the king came out to meet him** with his guards, for he supposed that Amalickiah had fulfilled his commands, and that

Amalickiah had gathered together so great an army to go against the Nephites to battle.

22 But behold, as the king came out to meet him **Amalickiah caused that his servants should go forth to meet the king.** And **they** went and **bowed themselves before the king,** as if to reverence [*to show respect and honor for*] him because of his greatness.

23 And it came to pass that **the king put forth his hand to raise them**, as was the custom with the Lamanites, as a token of peace, which custom they had taken from the Nephites.

24 And it came to pass that **when he had raised the first from the ground, behold he stabbed the king to the heart**; and he fell to the earth.

25 Now **the servants of the king fled**; and **the servants of Amalickiah raised a cry, saying:**

26 **Behold, the servants of the king have stabbed him to the heart**, and he has fallen and they have fled; behold, come and see.

27 And it came to pass that Amalickiah commanded that his armies should march forth and see what had happened to the king; and when they had come to the spot, and found the king lying in his gore, **Amalickiah pretended to be wroth** [*angry*], **and said: Whosoever loved the king, let him go forth, and pursue his servants that they may be slain.**

28 And it came to pass that **all they who loved the king**, when they heard these words, came forth and **pursued** [*ran*] **after the servants of the king**.

29 Now when **the servants of the king** saw an army pursuing after them, they were frightened again, and **fled** into the wilderness, **and came over into the land of Zarahemla and joined the people of Ammon** [*the Lamanites who had been converted to the gospel several years ago by the sons of Mosiah and their missionary companions*].

30 And the army which pursued after them returned, having pursued after them in vain [*unsuccessfully*]; and thus **Amalickiah, by his fraud, gained the hearts of the people.** [*In other words, now the people love him. All he has left to do is to marry the queen.*]

31 And it came to pass **on the morrow** [*the next day*] **he entered the city Nephi with his armies, and took possession of the city**.

32 And now it came to pass that **the queen**, when she had **heard that the king was slain**—for Amalickiah had sent an embassy [*message, messenger, or messengers*] to the queen informing her that the king had been slain by his servants, that he had pursued them with his army, but it was in vain [*unsuccessful*], and they had made their escape—

33 Therefore, **when the queen had received this message she sent unto Amalickiah**, desiring him that he would spare the people of the city;

and she also desired him that he should come in unto her; and she also desired him that he should bring witnesses with him to testify concerning the death of the king.

34 And it came to pass that Amalickiah took the same servant that slew the king, and all them who were with him, and went in unto the queen, unto the place where she sat; and **they all testified unto her that the king was slain by his own servants**; and they said also: They have fled; does not this testify against them? And thus they satisfied the queen concerning the death of the king.

35 And it came to pass that **Amalickiah sought the favor of the queen, and took her unto him to wife**; and thus by his fraud [*faking and lying*], and by the assistance of his cunning servants, he obtained the kingdom; yea, **he was acknowledged king throughout all the land, among all the people of the Lamanites**, who were composed of the Lamanites and the Lemuelites and the Ishmaelites, and all the dissenters of the Nephites, from the reign of Nephi down to the present time.

There are strong parallels between Amalickiah and Satan. Amalickiah now has evil and cunning followers who think like he does and have the same motives. He also has a great number of followers who have foolishly followed the crowd because they have no gospel standards or knowledge against which to measure the actions of others, including Amalickiah.

As Mormon points out next, the reason they have no such anchors for their choices is that they have intentionally rejected the gospel. Having apostatized from the gospel, they have set themselves adrift to be blown about by the prevailing winds of public sentiment, guided by the fog of personal wickedness.

36 Now **these dissenters** [*apostates*], **having the same instruction and the same information of the Nephites, yea, having been instructed in the same knowledge of the Lord**, nevertheless, it is strange to relate, **not long after their dissensions** [*apostasy*] **they became more hardened and impenitent** [*unrepentant*]**, and more wild, wicked and ferocious than the Lamanites—drinking in with the traditions of the Lamanites**; giving way to **indolence** [*lack of work ethic*], and all manner of **lasciviousness** [*sexual immorality of all kinds*]; yea, **entirely forgetting the Lord their God.**

ALMA 48

This chapter provides another opportunity to compare a man of God with a man of evil. In a very real way, Amalickiah is a "type" of Lucifer (in other words, can be compared to Lucifer, another name for Satan), and Moroni is a "type" of Christ (can be compared to Christ, in other words, is Christlike). Thus, we can see the ways of the devil in Amalickiah as Mormon describes him, and we can see the ways of the Lord as he describes Moroni.

In Amalickiah, we see patterns and approaches typical of dictators and tyrants throughout the ages. First, in verse 1, we will see his attempts to use constant government-sponsored messages to make the Lamanites hate the Nephites.

1 AND now it came to pass that, as soon as Amalickiah had obtained the kingdom he began to inspire the hearts of the Lamanites against the people of Nephi; yea, **he did appoint men to speak unto the Lamanites from their towers, against the Nephites.**

2 And **thus he did inspire their hearts against the Nephites**, insomuch that in the latter end of the nineteenth year of the reign of the judges, he having accomplished his designs thus far, yea, having been made king over the Lamanites, **he sought also to reign over all the land, yea, and all the people who were in the land, the Nephites as well as the Lamanites** [*similar to Satan's goal of ruling over all people*].

Next, we see that Amalickiah's methods are similar to those of Lucifer.

3 Therefore he had accomplished his design [*plan; plot*], for **he had hardened the hearts of the Lamanites** and **blinded their minds**, and **stirred them up to anger**, insomuch that he had gathered together a numerous host to go to battle **against the Nephites** [*against the righteous*].

4 For **he was determined**, because of the greatness of the number of his people, to overpower the Nephites and **to bring them into bondage** [*slavery*].

Just as the devil uses especially wicked men and women to accomplish his goal of leading many to destruction, so also Amalickiah used extra hardened and wicked apostates, the Zoramites, to lead others in the cause of evil.

5 And thus **he did appoint chief captains of the Zoramites** [*apostates who used to be Nephites*], they being the most acquainted with the strength of the Nephites, and their places of resort, and the weakest parts of their cities; therefore he appointed them to be chief captains over his armies.

6 And it came to pass **that they took their camp, and moved forth toward the land of Zarahemla** [*where the Nephites and the Lamanite converts lived*] in the wilderness.

Verse 7, next, is the transition verse, changing topics from Amalickiah to Captain Moroni.

7 Now it came to pass that **while Amalickiah had thus been obtaining power by fraud and deceit, Moroni, on the other hand, had been preparing the minds of the people to be faithful unto the Lord their God.**

8 Yea, **he had been strengthening the armies of the Nephites**, and erecting small forts, or places of resort [*to go for safety*]; throwing up banks of earth round about to enclose his

armies, and also building walls of stone to encircle them about, round about their cities and the borders of their lands; yea, all round about the land.

9 And in their weakest fortifications he did place the greater number of men; and thus **he did fortify and strengthen the land which was possessed by the Nephites**.

10 And thus **he was preparing to support their liberty, their lands, their wives, and their children, and their peace, and that they might live unto the Lord their God, and that they might maintain that which was called by their enemies the cause of Christians.**

11 And **Moroni was a strong and a mighty man**; he was **a man of a perfect understanding**; yea, a man that **did not delight in bloodshed**; a man **whose soul did joy in the liberty and the freedom of his country, and his brethren from bondage and slavery;**

Among other things, we are taught here that one way to keep personal spiritual balance, even in the midst of the terrible conditions and duties of war, is to have gratitude to God.

12 Yea, **a man whose heart did swell with thanksgiving** [*gratitude*] **to his God, for the many privileges and blessings which he bestowed upon his people**; a man who did labor exceedingly for the welfare and safety of his people [*Moroni's basic reason for going to war*].

13 Yea, and **he was a man who was firm in the faith of Christ**, and **he had sworn with an oath** [*made a covenant*] **to defend his people, his rights, and his country, and his religion, even to the loss of his blood.**

Next, Mormon points out again the things that make it okay to go to war. This must be a very important message to us in our day, or he would not point it out so often in these chapters.

14 Now **the Nephites were taught to defend themselves against their enemies, even to the shedding of blood** [*the killing of enemies*] **if it were necessary; yea, and they were also taught never to give an offense, yea, and never to raise the sword except it were against an enemy, except it were to preserve their lives.**

15 And **this was their faith, that by so doing God would prosper** [*bless*] **them in the land, or in other words, if they were faithful in keeping the commandments of God that he would prosper them in the land; yea, warn them to flee, or to prepare for war, according to their danger;**

In other words, by following their prophet, they would know whether to move or to stay and fight. This was a prominent pattern in the early history of The Church in our day. Time and time again, the Saints moved. They moved from New York to Ohio, from Ohio to Missouri, from Missouri to Illinois, then from Illinois to Utah. But in Utah, they first moved from Salt Lake City to surrounding areas but then fought back against Johnston's army and thus remained.

16 And also, that **God would make it known unto them whither** [*where*] **they should go to defend themselves against their enemies, and by so doing, the Lord would deliver them**; and **this was the faith of Moroni**, and his heart did glory in it; not in the shedding of blood but in doing good, in preserving his people, yea, in keeping the commandments of God, yea, and resisting iniquity.

You are probably aware that Mormon named his son Moroni after Captain Moroni. In the next verses, Mormon describes his admiration for this great Nephite general and man of God.

17 Yea, verily, verily I [*Mormon*] say unto you, **if all men had been, and were, and ever would be, like unto Moroni, behold, the very powers of hell would have been shaken forever**; yea, the devil would never have power over the hearts of the children of men.

As Mormon continues praising Moroni's virtues, he compares him to other great men of God in the Book of Mormon. One of the beautiful things about this is that Corianton (see Alma 49:30) is included in these righteous and stalwart men. After one has truly repented of grievous sin, he or she is forgiven completely and is not a "second-class" citizen in the Church. Elder Richard G. Scott spoke about this directly in his general conference talk of October 7, 2000, entitled "The Path to Peace and Joy." He said:

"If you have repented from serious transgression and mistakenly believe that you will always be a second-class citizen in the kingdom of God, learn that is not true. The Savior said:

"'Behold, he who has repented of his sins, the same is forgiven, and I, the Lord, remember them no more.

"'By this ye may know if a man repenteth of his sins—behold, he will confess them and forsake them' (D&C 58:42–43).

"Find encouragement in the lives of Alma the Younger and the sons of Mosiah. They were tragically wicked. Yet their full repentance and service qualified them to be considered as noble as righteous Captain Moroni (Alma 48:17–18)."

18 Behold, **he was a man like unto Ammon**, the son of Mosiah, yea, and **even the other sons of Mosiah**, yea, and **also Alma and his sons, for they were all men of God**.

The battle for the protection of the Nephites is actually being fought on two fronts: the physical (led by Captain Moroni) and the spiritual (led by Helaman, Shiblon, Corianton, and others). Next, Mormon points out how important the spiritual battle is.

19 Now behold, **Helaman and his brethren were no less serviceable** [*useful and important*] **unto the people than was Moroni**; for **they did preach the word of God**, and **they did baptize** unto repentance all men whosoever would hearken unto their words.

20 And thus **they went forth, and the people did humble themselves**

because of their words, insomuch that [*so that*] **they were highly favored** [*very blessed*] **of the Lord, and thus they were free from wars and contentions among themselves, yea, even for the space of four years.**

21 But, as I [*Mormon*] have said, in the latter end of the nineteenth year, yea, notwithstanding [*in spite of*] their peace amongst themselves, **they were compelled reluctantly to contend** [*fight*] **with their brethren, the Lamanites**.

The word "reluctantly" in verse 21, above, is another key to spiritual survival in times of fighting.

22 Yea, and in fine [*in summary*], **their wars never did cease for the space of many years with the Lamanites** [*as is the case with us with our enemies in the last days*], **notwithstanding their much reluctance** [*even though they really did not want to go to war with anyone*]**.**

23 Now, **they were sorry to take up arms against the Lamanites**, because **they did not delight in the shedding of blood**; yea, and this was not all—**they were sorry to be the means of sending so many of their brethren out of this world into an eternal world** [*the next life*]**, unprepared to meet their God.**

Here again, Mormon teaches us that there are circumstances under which men of God must take up weapons of war and use them.

24 Nevertheless, **they could not suffer** [*allow themselves*] **to lay down their lives, that their wives and their children should be massacred** [*In other words, they could not allow themselves not to fight because if they did, their families would be destroyed.*] by the barbarous cruelty of those who were once their brethren [*such as the Zoramites*], yea, and had dissented [*apostatized*] from their church, and had left them and had gone to destroy them by joining the Lamanites.

25 Yea, **they could not bear that their brethren should rejoice over the blood of the Nephites** [*they couldn't stand to have Lamanites enjoying killing Nephites*], so long as there were any who should keep the commandments of God, for the promise of the Lord was, **if they should keep his commandments they should prosper in the land**.

The last part of verse 25, above, is a sobering reminder that we must do all that we can as a part of qualifying to prosper through the blessings of God.

ALMA 49

Mormon now tells us about the next battle. We will see the worry and desperation of the wicked people who go along with the crowd in doing evil and the bravery of those who fight to defend God-given freedom.

1 AND now it came to pass in the eleventh month of the nineteenth year, on the tenth day of the month, **the armies of the Lamanites were seen approaching towards the land**

of Ammonihah [*the border city of Nephite territory which was previously destroyed in one day by Lamanites; see Alma 16:9–10*].

2 And behold, **the city had been rebuilt**, and **Moroni had stationed an army by the borders of the city**, and they had cast up dirt round about to shield them from the arrows and the stones of the Lamanites; for behold, they fought with stones and with arrows.

3 Behold, I said that the city of Ammonihah had been rebuilt. I say unto you, yea, that **it was in part rebuilt**; and because **the Lamanites** had destroyed it once because of the iniquity of the people [*they were the ones who burned the women and children while they made Alma and Amulek watch; see Alma 14:8–11*], they **supposed that it would again become an easy prey for them** [*would be easy for them to conquer*].

4 But behold, **how great was their disappointment**; for behold, the Nephites had dug up a ridge of earth round about them, which was so high that the Lamanites could not cast their stones and their arrows at them that they might take effect, neither could they come upon them save it was by their place of entrance.

5 Now at this time **the chief captains of the Lamanites were astonished exceedingly**, because of the wisdom of the Nephites in preparing their places of security.

6 Now **the leaders of the Lamanites had supposed, because of the greatness of their numbers** [*because they had so many fighting men*], yea, **they supposed that they should** be privileged to **come upon them as they had hitherto done** [*as they had done up to now*]; yea, and **they had also prepared themselves with shields, and with breastplates** [*like the Nephites had last time they fought them; see Alma 43:19–20*]; and they had also prepared themselves with garments of skins, yea, **very thick garments** [*clothing*] to cover their nakedness.

7 And being thus prepared **they supposed that they should easily** overpower and subject their brethren [*the Nephites*] to the yoke of bondage, or slay and massacre them according to their pleasure.

8 But behold, **to their uttermost astonishment**, **they** [*the Nephites*] **were prepared for them**, in a manner which never had been known among the children of Lehi. Now they were prepared for the Lamanites, to battle after the manner of the instructions of Moroni [*a truly inspired leader*].

9 And it came to pass that **the Lamanites, or the Amalickiahites, were exceedingly astonished** at their manner of preparation for war.

10 Now, if **king Amalickiah** had come down out of the land of Nephi, at the head of his army, perhaps he would have caused the Lamanites to have attacked the Nephites at the city of Ammonihah; for behold, he **did care not for the blood of his people.**

11 But behold, **Amalickiah did not come down himself to battle**. And

behold, **his chief captains durst not** [*didn't dare*] **attack the Nephites at the city of Ammonihah**, for Moroni had altered the management of affairs among the Nephites, insomuch that the Lamanites were disappointed in their places of retreat and they could not come upon them.

12 Therefore **they** [*the Lamanites*] **retreated** into the wilderness, and took their camp **and marched towards the land of Noah**, supposing that to be the next best place for them to come against the Nephites.

Next, you will see the chief officers of the Lamanite armies make an oath to destroy the Nephite city of Noah. In their culture, once a person had made an oath (the most serious promise possible), they were bound by it, in this case, either until success or until death. As a result, retreat or surrender is no longer an option. All these chief captains will die in battle, leading many of their soldiers to their deaths also.

13 For **they knew not that Moroni had fortified, or had built forts of security, for every city** in all the land round about; therefore, they marched forward to the land of Noah with a firm determination; yea, **their chief captains came forward and took an oath that they would destroy the people of that city.**

14 But behold, **to their astonishment, the city of Noah**, which had hitherto been a weak place, **had now, by the means of Moroni, become strong**, yea, even to exceed the strength of [*even stronger than*] the city Ammonihah.

15 And now, behold, **this was wisdom in Moroni; for he had supposed that** they would be frightened at the city Ammonihah; and as the city of Noah had hitherto been the weakest part of the land, therefore they would march thither [*over there*] to battle; and thus it was according to his desires [*it happened like Moroni had planned*].

16 And behold, **Moroni had appointed Lehi to be chief captain over the men of that city**; and it was that same Lehi who fought with the Lamanites in the valley on the east of the river Sidon.

17 And now behold it came to pass, that when **the Lamanites** had found that Lehi commanded the city they were again disappointed, for they **feared Lehi exceedingly; nevertheless their chief captains had sworn with an oath to attack the city; therefore, they brought up their armies.**

18 Now behold, **the Lamanites could not get into their forts of security by any other way save** [*except*] **by the entrance**, because of the highness of the bank which had been thrown up, and the depth of the ditch which had been dug round about, save it were by the entrance.

19 And **thus were the Nephites prepared to destroy all such as should attempt to climb up to enter the fort by any other way**, by casting over stones and arrows at them.

20 Thus **they were prepared**, yea,

a body of their strongest men, with their swords and their slings, to smite down all who should attempt to come into their place of security by the place of entrance; and thus were they prepared to defend themselves against the Lamanites.

21 And it came to pass that **the captains of the Lamanites brought up their armies before the place of entrance**, and began to contend with the Nephites, to get into their place of security; but behold, they were driven back from time to time, insomuch that **they were slain with an immense** [*huge*] **slaughter**.

22 Now when they found that they could not obtain power over the Nephites by the pass, **they began to dig down their banks of earth that they might obtain a pass to their armies**, that they might have an equal chance to fight; but behold, in these attempts **they were swept off by the stones and arrows** which were thrown at them; and **instead of filling up their ditches by pulling down the banks of earth, they were filled up in a measure with their dead and wounded bodies.**

23 Thus **the Nephites had all power over their enemies**; and thus **the Lamanites did attempt to destroy the Nephites until their chief captains were all slain**; yea, and **more than a thousand of the Lamanites were slain**; while, on the other hand, **there was not a single soul of the Nephites which was slain.**

24 **There were about fifty who were wounded**, who had been exposed to the arrows of the Lamanites through the pass, but they were shielded by their shields, and their breastplates, and their head–plates, insomuch that their wounds were upon their legs, many of which were very severe.

25 And it came to pass, that **when the Lamanites saw that their chief captains were all slain they fled into the wilderness**. And it came to pass that **they returned to the land of Nephi, to inform their king, Amalickiah, who was a Nephite by birth, concerning their great loss.**

26 And it came to pass that **he was exceedingly angry** with his people, because he had not obtained his desire over the Nephites; he had not subjected them to the yoke of bondage [*Similar to Satan's anger when he is defeated by the forces of righteousness; see, for example, Moses 1:22.*]

27 Yea, **he was exceedingly wroth** [*very angry*], and **he did curse God, and also Moroni, swearing with an oath that he would drink his blood** [*a reminder of the intense hatred of the righteous that Satan puts in the hearts of extremely wicked people as they become more like him*]; and this because Moroni had kept the commandments of God in preparing for the safety of his people.

Here again, Mormon points out the big contrast between the very wicked and the faithful Saints of God.

28 And it came to pass, that **on the other hand, the people of Nephi**

did thank the Lord their God, because of his matchless power in delivering them from the hands of their enemies.

29 And thus ended the nineteenth year of the reign of the judges over the people of Nephi.

> There is a bit of symbolism in what Mormon tells us next. Just as righteousness of the Saints, as a group, brings literal prosperity here on earth, so also righteousness brings spiritual prosperity on earth and in heaven.

30 Yea, and **there was continual peace** among them, and exceedingly **great prosperity** in the church because of their heed and diligence which they gave unto the word of God, which was **declared unto them by Helaman**, and **Shiblon**, and **Corianton**, and **Ammon and his brethren**, yea, and by all those who had been ordained by the holy order of God, being baptized unto repentance, and sent forth to preach among the people.

> Once again, we see that Corianton repented successfully (see Alma 39–42) as Mormon specifically mentions him with others who were teaching the word of God among Moroni's people.

ALMA 50

As you well know by now, one of the biggest reasons for studying the Book of Mormon is to find ways it applies to us in our own personal lives and the lives of family and friends. One of the most significant messages for us in this chapter is found in verse 23 where Mormon tells us that "there never was a happier time" among the faithful Saints than during this time of wars. This is a direct message to us in our day that we can have happiness in our time of constant "wars and rumors of war" all over the world. In other words, no matter what is going on around us in our lives, if we try our best to live the gospel faithfully, we can have deep inner happiness. Happiness is much more a result of personal faithfulness to God than of things that are going on around us.

> In verses 1-6, we see that Captain Moroni was wise to have his armies keep preparing things they needed for defending themselves for future battles with the Lamanites, even though it was a time of peace.

1 And now it came to pass that **Moroni did not stop making preparations for war**, or to defend his people against the Lamanites; for he caused that his armies should commence in the commencement of the twentieth year of the reign of the judges, that they should commence in digging up **heaps of earth round about all the cities**, throughout all the land which was possessed by the Nephites.

2 And upon the top of these ridges of earth he caused that there should be timbers, yea, **works of timbers built up to the height of a man, round about the cities.**

3 And he caused that upon those works of timbers there should be a frame of **pickets built upon the**

timbers round about; and they were strong and high.

4 And **he caused towers to be erected** that overlooked those works of pickets, and he caused **places of security** to be built **upon those towers**, that the stones and the arrows of the Lamanites could not hurt them.

5 And **they were prepared** that they could cast stones from the top thereof, according to their pleasure and their strength, and slay him who should attempt to approach near the walls of the city.

6 Thus **Moroni did prepare strongholds against the coming of their enemies, round about every city in all the land.**

7 And it came to pass that **Moroni caused that his armies should go forth into the east wilderness; yea, and they went forth and drove all the Lamanites who were in the east wilderness into their own lands**, which were south of the land of Zarahemla.

8 And the land of Nephi did run in a straight course from the east sea to the west.

9 And it came to pass that when Moroni had driven all the Lamanites out of the east wilderness, which was north of the lands of their own possessions**, he caused that the inhabitants who were in the land of Zarahemla and in the land round about should go forth into the east wilderness**, even to the borders by the seashore, **and possess the land**.

10 And **he also placed armies on the south, in the borders of their possessions, and caused them to erect fortifications** that they might secure their armies and their people from the hands of their enemies.

11 And thus **he cut off all the strongholds of the Lamanites** in the east wilderness, yea, and also on the west, fortifying the line between the Nephites and the Lamanites, between the land of Zarahemla and the land of Nephi, from the west sea, running by the head of the river Sidon—the Nephites possessing all the land northward, yea, even all the land which was northward of the land Bountiful, according to their pleasure.

12 **Thus Moroni, with his armies**, which did increase daily because of the assurance of protection which his works did bring forth unto them, **did seek to cut off the strength and the power of the Lamanites** from off the lands of their possessions, that they should have no power upon the lands of their possession.

13 And it came to pass **that the Nephites began the foundation of a city, and they called the name of the city Moroni**; and it was by the east sea; and it was on the south by the line of the possessions of the Lamanites.

14 And **they also began a foundation for a city between the city of**

Moroni and the city of Aaron, joining the borders of Aaron and Moroni; and they called the name of the city, or the land, Nephihah.

15 And **they also began in that same year to build many cities on the north**, one in a particular manner which they called Lehi, which was in the north by the borders of the seashore.

16 And **thus ended the twentieth year**.

Once again, we are reminded that prosperity comes to a people as a result of keeping the commandments of God, no matter what circumstances are elsewhere.

17 And **in these prosperous circumstances were the people of Nephi** in the commencement of the twenty and first year of the reign of the judges over the people of Nephi.

18 And **they did prosper exceedingly, and they became exceedingly rich; yea, and they did multiply and wax** [*grow*] **strong in the land.**

Just a quick reminder, as mentioned before, whenever you see "thus we see," as in verse 19, next, or words to that effect, you can know that it is Mormon pointing out what he hopes you will learn from what he has just written.

19 And **thus we see** how merciful and just are all the dealings of the Lord, to the fulfilling of all his words unto the children of men; yea, we can behold that his words are verified [*shown to be true*], even at this time, which he spake unto Lehi, saying:

20 Blessed art thou and thy children; and they shall be blessed, **inasmuch as** [*if*] **they shall keep my commandments they shall prosper in the land**. But remember, inasmuch as they will not keep my commandments they shall be cut off from the presence of the Lord.

Next, as Mormon continues with his "thus we see" teaching emphasis, he reminds us again that wars and destruction come upon the people of the Lord when they, themselves, fall into wickedness.

21 And **we see** that these promises have been verified to **the people of Nephi**; for it has been **their quarrelings** and their **contentions,** yea, their **murderings**, and their **plunderings**, their **idolatry**, their **whoredoms** [*sexual sins*], and their **abominations**, which were **among themselves**, which **brought upon them their wars and their destructions.**

Mormon again reminds us of the contrast between those who keep the commandments and those who fall away from the Lord into sin.

22 And **those who were faithful in keeping the commandments of the Lord were delivered at all times**, whilst **thousands of their wicked brethren** [*apostate Nephites*] **have been consigned to bondage** [*put in slavery*]**, or to perish by the sword, or to dwindle in unbelief, and mingle with the Lamanites.**

The phrase "mingle with the Lamanites" in verse 22, above, can be symbolic of our adopting the fashions and behaviors of the world today that are not in harmony with the counsel and commandments of the Lord.

As pointed out previously, verse 23, next, is most significant for us. President Gordon B. Hinckley was well-known for constantly reminding modern Saints that these last days are a wonderful time to be alive. For instance, in the Church News for the week ending July 22, 1995, President Hinckley spoke of "the marvelous age in which we live," and went on to say, "What a great time to be alive, in this time in the world's history."

23 But behold **there never was a happier time among the people of Nephi, since the days of Nephi, than in the days of Moroni**, yea, even at this time, in the twenty and first year of the reign of the judges.

24 And it came to pass that **the twenty and second year of the reign of the judges also ended in peace**; yea, and **also the twenty and third year**.

Next, we see the problems caused by internal trouble and contention among the members of the Church themselves. In the case which Mormon will now point out, we will also be reminded of the damage which one bad-tempered and hot-headed leader can cause. In this case, it is a man by the name of Morianton.

25 And it came to pass that in the commencement [*at the beginning*] of the twenty and fourth year of the reign of the judges, **there would also have been peace among the people of Nephi had it not been for a contention** which took place among them concerning the land of Lehi, and the land of Morianton, which joined upon the borders of Lehi; both of which were on the borders by the seashore.

26 For behold, the people who possessed the land of Morianton did claim a part of the land of Lehi; therefore **there began to be a warm contention between them**, insomuch that **the people of Morianton took up arms** [*weapons*] **against their brethren, and they were determined by the sword to slay them.**

27 But behold, **the people who possessed the land of Lehi** fled to the camp of Moroni, and appealed unto him for assistance; for behold **they were not in the wrong.**

28 And it came to pass that when **the people of Morianton**, who **were led by a man whose name was Morianton**, found that the people of Lehi had fled to the camp of Moroni, they were exceedingly fearful lest the army of Moroni should come upon them and destroy them.

29 Therefore, **Morianton put it into their hearts that they should flee to the land which was northward**, which was covered with large bodies of water, and take possession of the land which was northward.

30 And behold, **they would have carried this plan into effect**, (which would have been a cause to have

been lamented) **but** behold, **Morianton** being **a man of much passion**, therefore **he was angry with one of his maid servants, and he fell upon her and beat her much.**

31 And it came to pass that **she fled, and came over to the camp of Moroni, and told Moroni all things concerning the matter**, and also concerning their intentions to flee into the land northward.

32 Now behold, the people who were in the land Bountiful, or rather Moroni [*the land of Moroni or the city of Moroni; see verse 13*], feared that they would hearken to [*listen to and believe*] the words of Morianton and unite with his people, and thus he would obtain possession of those parts of the land, which would lay a foundation for serious consequences among the people of Nephi, yea, **which consequences would lead to the overthrow of their liberty**.

Here again, Mormon teaches us another aspect of appropriate military strategy and common sense in times of war and threats to homeland security from outside sources.

33 Therefore **Moroni sent an army**, with their camp, to head [*overtake; get in front of*] the people of Morianton, **to stop their flight** [*running away*] **into the land northward.**

34 And it came to pass that **they did not head** [*stop*] **them until they had come to the borders of the land Desolation**; and there they did head them, by the narrow pass which led by the sea into the land northward, yea, by the sea, on the west and on the east.

Next, we are introduced to one of the quiet heroes of the Book of Mormon, namely, Teancum.

35 And it came to pass that the army which was sent by Moroni, which was led by a man whose name was **Teancum**, did meet the people of Morianton; and so stubborn were the people of Morianton, (being **inspired by his wickedness and his flattering words**) that **a battle commenced** between them, in the which **Teancum did slay Morianton and defeat his army**, and took them prisoners, and returned to the camp of Moroni. And thus ended the twenty and fourth year of the reign of the judges over the people of Nephi.

It is interesting that Moroni's strategy did not include prisoner of war camps, at this point, with the accompanying drain on manpower and financial resources to maintain them. Instead, he employs the rule of agency choice and consequences. He gave the renegade people of Morianton the option of covenanting to keep the peace between themselves and Moroni's forces or take the consequences. They accepted and went home to their own lands and residences, thus sparing Moroni's troops and people much trouble and expense.

36 And thus were the people of Morianton brought back. And **upon their covenanting to keep the peace they were restored to the land of Morianton**, and a union took place between

them and the people of Lehi; and they were also restored to their lands.

37 And it came to pass that in the same year that the people of Nephi had peace restored unto them, that **Nephihah** [*the man who took over from Alma, as chief judge or president of the country; see Alma 4:15–18*], the second chief judge, **died**, having filled the judgment-seat with perfect uprightness before God. [*He had served as president of the Nephite nation for about sixteen years.*]

38 Nevertheless, **he had refused** [*turned down the offer from*] Alma **to take possession of those records and those things** [*the large and small plates of Nephi, the brass plates, the twenty-four gold plates (record of the Jaredites), the Liahona, etc.; see Alma 37*] **which were esteemed** [*considered*] **by Alma and his fathers** [*ancestors*] **to be most sacred**; therefore Alma had conferred them upon [*given them to*] his son, Helaman.

Next, the Nephites get another chief judge to replace Nephihah. He is Nephihah's son, and his name is Pahoran. He would be the political equivalent of the president of the United States.

39 Behold, it came to pass that **the son of Nephihah was appointed to fill** [*possess*] **the judgment-seat**, in the stead of [*in place of*] his father; yea, he was appointed chief judge and governor over the people, with an oath and sacred ordinance to judge righteously, and to keep the peace and the freedom of the people, and to grant unto them their sacred privileges to worship the Lord their God, yea, to support and maintain the cause of God all his days, and to bring the wicked to justice according to their crime.

40 Now behold, **his name was Pahoran.** And Pahoran did fill the seat of his father, and did commence his reign in the end of the twenty and fourth year, over the people of Nephi.

Keep Pahoran in mind for future reference. He is a good man who will have much trouble from people within the Nephite nation who refuse to support Captain Moroni and the cause of freedom. In fact, they will take pleasure when Moroni and the nation have trouble. We see such things in our nation today.

ALMA 51

In this chapter, we will be introduced to the "king-men" who seek to destroy the Nephite democracy and set up a king. We will also be introduced to the "freemen" who want to preserve the Nephite democracy that King Mosiah set up about 24 years ago. One thing you might keep in mind is that successful democracy requires a high degree of personal integrity and responsibility on the part of citizens. It also requires an educated and wise citizenry. A major component of wisdom is the ability to think ahead. In attempting to set up a king, the king-men are encouraging a step backward for the Nephite nation such that citizens would have less responsibility, less agency, and less accountability—consequently, less personal progression (compare with D&C 101:77–78).

1 AND now it came to pass **in the commencement of the twenty and fifth year of the reign of the judges** over the people of Nephi, they having established peace between the people of Lehi and the people of Morianton concerning their lands, and having commenced the twenty and fifth year in peace;

As you will see, one of the first steps the king-men take is to attempt to change the "constitution" of their democracy by changing some of the laws upon which it was based, as established by King Mosiah II in Mosiah 29.

2 Nevertheless, they did not long maintain an entire peace in the land, for **there began to be a contention among the people concerning the chief judge Pahoran**; for behold, there were a **part of the people** who **desired that a few particular points of the law should be altered** [*changed*].

3 But behold, **Pahoran would not alter nor suffer** [*allow*] **the law to be altered**; therefore, he did not hearken [*give in*] to those who had sent in their voices with their petitions concerning the altering of the law.

4 Therefore, **those** [*the king-men*] **who were desirous that the law should be altered were angry with him, and desired that he should no longer be chief judge over the land**; therefore there arose a warm dispute concerning the matter, but not unto bloodshed.

5 And it came to pass that those who were desirous that Pahoran should be dethroned from the judgment-seat were called **king-men**, for they were desirous that the law should be altered in a manner to overthrow the free government and to establish a king over the land.

6 And those who were desirous that Pahoran should remain chief judge over the land took upon them the name of **freemen**; and thus was the division among them, for the freemen had sworn or covenanted to maintain their rights and the privileges of their religion by a free government.

The dispute as to which kind of government to have, a kingdom or a democracy, finally came to a point. A national election was held to choose a form of government. The majority chose democracy rather than having a king.

7 And it came to pass that **this matter of their contention was settled by the voice of the people**. And it came to pass that **the voice of the people came in favor of the freemen**, and Pahoran retained the judgment-seat, which caused much rejoicing among the brethren of Pahoran and also many of the people of liberty, who also put the king-men to silence, that they durst not oppose but were obliged to maintain the cause of freedom.

Next, we see the true motives of many of the king-men. They wanted power over people. This is similar to what Satan wants.

8 Now **those who were in favor of kings were those of high birth** [*those who were high up in society*], **and they sought** [*wanted*] **to be kings**; and **they were supported by those who sought power and authority over the people.**

> This internal contention and lack of unity within the Nephite nation came at a very bad time, as Mormon explains next.

9 But behold, **this was a critical time for such contentions to be among the people of Nephi**; for behold, **Amalickiah** [*the apostate Nephite (Alma 49:25) who had become king of the Lamanites by fraud and deception (Alma 47) and who had vowed to drink Captain Moroni's blood (Alma 49:27)*] **had again stirred up the hearts of the people of the Lamanites against the people of the Nephites**, and he was gathering together soldiers from all parts of his land, and arming them, and preparing for war with all diligence; for he had sworn to drink the blood of Moroni.

10 But behold, we shall see that his promise which he made was rash [*foolish*]; nevertheless, **he did prepare himself and his armies to come to battle against the Nephites**.

11 Now **his armies were not so great as they had hitherto** [*up to now*] **been**, because of the many thousands who had been slain by the hand of the Nephites; **but notwithstanding** [*in spite of*] **their great loss, Amalickiah had gathered together a wonderfully** [*a surprisingly*] **great army**, insomuch that he feared not to come down to the land of Zarahemla.

> Perhaps you will remember that the last time that King Amalickiah sent his Lamanite subjects to battle against the Nephites, he did not lead them, but rather stayed home in the city of Nephi in Lamanite territory, where he had become the king of the Lamanites. See Alma 49:10–11. This time, he comes with his armies, leading them against the Nephites. They are a real threat to the Nephite nation.

12 Yea, even **Amalickiah did himself come down, at the head of the Lamanites.** And it was in the twenty and fifth year of the reign of the judges; and it was at the same time that they had begun to settle the affairs of their contentions [*arguing and fighting among themselves*] concerning the chief judge, Pahoran.

> Sadly, the king-men among the Nephites were secretly pleased with this external threat to their nation. It gave them satisfaction to see the president of their nation, whom they disliked intensely, and those who supported his policies, have trouble.

13 And it came to pass that **when the** men who were called **king-men** had **heard that the Lamanites were coming down to battle against them, they were glad in their hearts**; and they refused to take up arms, for they were so wroth with the chief judge, and also with the people of liberty, that **they would not take up arms** [*weapons*] **to defend their country**.

Every democratic nation established upon the laws of God and faced with war from outside enemies, has at one time or another had to confront the issue of citizens who refuse to fight to defend the very freedoms they enjoy. Watch what Captain Moroni does about this problem.

14 And it came to pass that **when Moroni saw this** [*the refusal of the king-men to help defend the nation*], and also saw that the Lamanites were coming into the borders of the land, **he was exceedingly wroth** [*very, very, angry; righteous anger; righteous indignation*] **because of the stubbornness of those people whom he had labored with so much diligence to preserve**; yea, he was exceedingly wroth; his soul was filled with anger against them.

What Captain Moroni does next is indeed no-nonsense. It can answer questions raised about this issue in our day. You have no doubt noticed already that our Church supports its members in serving in the armed forces of the nations in which they live.

15 And it came to pass that **he sent a petition**, with the voice of the people, **unto the governor** of the land [*Pahoran*], **desiring that he should read it, and give him** [*Moroni*] **power to compel** [*force*] **those dissenters** [*those who would not join his army to defend the nation*] **to defend their country or to put them to death.**

Next, Mormon teaches us that internal disagreement and contention are more dangerous to a nation than outside enemies.

16 For **it was his first care to put an end to such contentions and dissensions among the people**; for behold, this had been hitherto [*up to now*] a cause of all their destruction. And it came to pass that **it was granted according to the voice of the people** [*the people voted for it*].

17 And it came to pass that **Moroni commanded that his army should go against those king-men, to pull down their pride and their nobility and level them with the earth, or they should take up arms and support the cause of liberty.**

18 And it came to pass that **the armies did march forth against them**; and they did pull down their pride and their nobility, insomuch that as they did lift their weapons of war to fight against the men of Moroni they were hewn down and leveled to the earth.

19 And it came to pass that **there were four thousand of those dissenters who were hewn** [*cut*] **down by the sword**; and those of their leaders who were not slain in battle were taken and cast into prison, for there was no time for their trials at this period.

20 And **the remainder of those dissenters**, rather than be smitten down to the earth by the sword, yielded to the standard of liberty, and **were compelled** to hoist the title of liberty upon their towers, and in their cities, and **to take up arms in defence of their country**.

21 And **thus Moroni put an end to those king-men**, that there were not any known by the appellation [*name*] of king-men; and thus he put an end to **the stubbornness** and the **pride** of those people who professed [*claimed*] the blood of nobility; but they were brought down to humble themselves like unto their brethren, and to fight valiantly for their freedom from bondage.

As we continue, we are shown the danger posed by citizens who shortsightedly or with evil intent seek to undermine their own democratic government. While Moroni is busy putting down internal threats to national security, Amalickiah successfully leads his Lamanite armies in taking several Nephite cities.

22 Behold, it came to pass that **while Moroni was thus breaking down the wars and contentions among his own people**, and subjecting them to peace and civilization, and making regulations to prepare for war against the Lamanites, behold, **the Lamanites had come into the land of Moroni**, which was in the borders by the seashore.

23 And it came to pass that **the Nephites were not sufficiently strong** in the city of Moroni; therefore **Amalickiah did drive them, slaying many. And it came to pass that Amalickiah took possession of the city, yea, possession of all their fortifications.**

24 And **those who fled out of the city of Moroni came to the city of Nephihah; and also the people of the city of Lehi gathered themselves together**, and made preparations and were ready to receive the Lamanites to battle.

25 But it came to pass that **Amalickiah would not suffer** [*permit*] **the Lamanites to go against the city of Nephihah** to battle, but kept them down by the seashore, **leaving men in every city to maintain and defend it.**

26 And **thus he went on, taking possession of many cities**, the city of Nephihah, and the city of Lehi, and the city of Morianton, and the city of Omner, and the city of Gid, and the city of Mulek, all of which were on the east borders by the seashore.

27 And **thus had the Lamanites obtained, by the cunning of Amalickiah**, so **many cities**, by their numberless hosts, all of which were strongly fortified after the manner of the fortifications of Moroni; all of which afforded strongholds for the Lamanites.

28 And it came to pass that **they marched to the borders of the land Bountiful, driving the Nephites before them and slaying many.**

Next, we meet Teancum again, a righteous Nephite commander serving under Captain Moroni.

29 But it came to pass that **they were met by Teancum**, who had slain Morianton and had headed his people in his flight.

30 And it came to pass that **he headed** [*stopped*] **Amalickiah also, as he was marching forth with his numerous army** that he might take possession of the land Bountiful, and also the land northward.

31 But behold he met with a disappointment by being repulsed by Teancum and his men, for they were great warriors; for **every man of Teancum did exceed the Lamanites in their strength and in their skill of war**, insomuch that they did gain advantage over the Lamanites.

32 And it came to pass that they did harass them, insomuch that **they did slay them even until it was dark. And it came to pass that Teancum and his men did pitch their tents** in the borders of the land Bountiful; and Amalickiah did pitch his tents in the borders on the beach by the seashore, and after this manner were they driven.

Next, Mormon tells us of Teancum's courage and daring in putting his life on the line for the benefit of the cause.

33 And it came to pass that **when the night had come, Teancum and his servant stole forth and went out by night, and went into the camp of Amalickiah**; and behold, sleep had overpowered them because of their much fatigue, which was caused by the labors and heat of the day.

34 And it came to pass that **Teancum stole privily** [*secretly*] **into the tent of the king** [*Amalickiah*], **and put a javelin to his heart**; and he did cause the death of the king immediately that he did not awake his servants.

35 And **he returned again privily to his own camp**, and behold, his men were asleep, and he awoke them and told them all the things that he had done.

36 And **he caused that his armies should stand in readiness**, lest the Lamanites had awakened and should come upon them.

37 And thus endeth the twenty and fifth year of the reign of the judges over the people of Nephi; and **thus endeth the days of Amalickiah.**

ALMA 52

Remember that Amalickiah was a Nephite who had led a rebellion against the Church among the Nephites. He wanted to be king over the Nephites and had led many away from Helaman and other leaders of the Church (Alma 46:1–11). He was not successful, so he fooled the Lamanites into making him their king so he could use them to fight against the Nephites.

Now Amalickiah is dead, and his brother, Ammoron, becomes the next king of the Lamanites. His strategy is to keep the Nephite cities that the Lamanites had already taken under the leadership of Amalickiah. This becomes a problem for Moroni's armies because he had fortified these cities very well, and they now have become strongholds for the Lamanite armies. Teancum is the commander of the Nephite armies in this part of the country. Moroni can't bring reinforcements because he has to try to repel Lamanite attacks in another part of the land of Zarahemla.

1 AND now, it came to pass in the twenty and sixth year of the reign of the judges over the people of Nephi, behold, **when the Lamanites awoke** on the first morning of the first month, behold, **they found Amalickiah was dead** in his own tent; and **they also saw that Teancum was ready to give them battle on that day**.

2 And now, when the Lamanites saw this they were affrighted; and **they** abandoned their design in marching into the land northward, and **retreated with all their army into the city of Mulek**, and sought protection in their fortifications.

3 And it came to pass that **the brother of Amalickiah was appointed king over the people; and his name was Ammoron**; thus king Ammoron, the brother of king Amalickiah, was appointed to reign in his stead [*in his place*].

4 And it came to pass that **he did command that his people should maintain those cities** [*Nephite cities*], **which they had taken by the shedding of blood**; for they had not taken any cities save they had lost much blood.

5 And now, **Teancum saw that the Lamanites were determined to maintain those cities** which they had taken, and those parts of the land which they had obtained possession of; and also seeing the enormity of their number, **Teancum thought it was not expedient** [*not a good idea*] **that he should attempt to attack them in their forts.**

Perhaps you've noticed that the word "expedient" (verse 6, above) is used much in the scriptures and that it has many fine shades of meaning, according to context. For example, it can mean necessary, vital, wise, urgent, and so forth.

6 But **he kept his men round about, as if making preparations for war**; yea, and truly he was preparing to defend himself against them, by casting up walls round about and preparing places of resort.

Next, we see that Teancum was hoping for reinforcements from Moroni.

7 And it came to pass that **he kept thus preparing for war until Moroni had sent a large number of men to strengthen his army.**

Part of Moroni's strategy this time around is to keep Lamanite prisoners of war to exchange for Nephite prisoners.

8 And **Moroni also sent orders unto him that he should retain all the prisoners who fell into his hands**; for as the Lamanites had taken many prisoners, that he should retain all the prisoners of the Lamanites **as a ransom for those whom the Lamanites had taken**.

9 And **he also sent orders unto him**

that he should fortify the land Bountiful, and secure the narrow pass which led into the land northward, lest [*for fear that*] the Lamanites should obtain that point and should have power to harass them on every side.

10 And **Moroni also sent unto him, desiring him that he would be faithful in maintaining that quarter of the land**, and that he would seek every opportunity to scourge [*harass*] the Lamanites in that quarter, as much as was in his power, that perhaps he might take again by stratagem or some other way those cities which had been taken out of their hands; and that he also would fortify and strengthen the cities round about, which had not fallen into the hands of the Lamanites.

11 And **he** [*Moroni*] also **said** unto him, **I would come unto you, but behold, the Lamanites are upon us in the borders of the land by the west sea; and behold, I go against them, therefore I cannot come unto you.**

12 Now, **the king** [*Ammoron*] **had departed out of the land of Zarahemla**, and had made known unto the queen concerning the death of his brother, and had gathered together a large number of men, and had marched forth against the Nephites on the borders by the west sea.

Ammoron is good at plotting ways to succeed against the Nephites, as Mormon points out to us in the next verses.

13 And thus **he was endeavoring to harass the Nephites, and to draw away a part of their forces to that part of the land, while he had commanded those whom he had left to possess the cities which he had taken, that they should also harass the Nephites on the borders by the east sea**, and should take possession of their lands as much as it was in their power, according to the power of their armies.

14 And **thus were the Nephites in those dangerous circumstances in the ending of the twenty and sixth year** of the reign of the judges over the people of Nephi.

15 But behold, it came to pass **in the twenty and seventh year** of the reign of the judges, that Teancum, by the command of **Moroni**—who had established armies to protect the south and the west borders of the land, and **had begun his march** towards the land Bountiful, **that he might assist Teancum** with his men in retaking the cities which they had lost—

16 And it came to pass that **Teancum had received orders to make an attack upon the city of Mulek, and retake it if it were possible.**

17 And it came to pass that Teancum made preparations to make an attack upon the city of Mulek, and march forth with his army against the Lamanites; **but he saw that it was**

impossible that he could overpower them while they were in their fortifications; therefore he abandoned his designs and **returned again to the city Bountiful, to wait for the coming of Moroni, that he might receive strength to his army.**

This battle has been going on for about two years now. Moroni and his chief captains will now hold a planning session to come up with possible ways to lure the Lamanites out of their strongholds in the Nephite cities they took.

18 And it came to pass that **Moroni did arrive with his army at the land of Bountiful, in the latter end of the twenty and seventh year** of the reign of the judges over the people of Nephi.

19 And in the commencement of the twenty and eighth year, **Moroni and Teancum and many of the chief captains held a council of war—what they should do to cause the Lamanites to come out against them to battle; or that they might by some means flatter them out of their strongholds**, that they might gain advantage over them and take again the city of Mulek.

20 And it came to pass **they sent embassies** [*messengers*] **to the army of the Lamanites, which protected the city of Mulek, to their leader, whose name was Jacob**, desiring him that he would come out with his armies to meet them upon the plains between the two cities. But behold, **Jacob**, who **was a Zoramite** [*an apostate Nephite*], would not come out with his army to meet them upon the plains.

Moroni now comes up with a plan to lure the Lamanites out of their fortified city.

21 And it came to pass that **Moroni**, having no hopes of meeting them upon fair grounds, therefore, he **resolved upon a plan that he might decoy** [*lure*] **the Lamanites out of their strongholds.**

22 Therefore **he caused that Teancum should take a small number of men and march down near the seashore**; and **Moroni and his army, by night, marched in the wilderness**, on the west of the city Mulek; and thus, on the morrow [*the next day*], **when the guards of the Lamanites had discovered Teancum, they ran and told it unto Jacob**, their leader. [*Moroni's plan is working.*]

23 And it came to pass that **the armies of the Lamanites did march forth against Teancum**, supposing by their numbers to overpower Teancum because of the smallness of his numbers. And **as Teancum saw the armies of the Lamanites coming out against him he began to retreat** down by the seashore, northward.

24 And it came to pass that **when the Lamanites saw that he began to flee, they took courage and pursued them with vigor** [*energy*]**.** And **while Teancum was thus leading**

away the Lamanites who were pursuing them in vain [*without success*], **behold, Moroni commanded that a part of his army who were with him should march forth into the city, and take possession of it.**

25 And thus **they did** [*the plan worked*], **and slew** [*killed*] **all** those who had been left to protect the city, yea, all those **who would not yield up their weapons of war**. [*Again, Moroni was tough when he had to be and merciful when he could be.*]

26 And **thus Moroni had obtained possession of the city Mulek with a part of his army, while he marched with the remainder to meet the Lamanites when they should return from the pursuit of** [*chasing after*] **Teancum.**

27 And it came to pass that **the Lamanites did pursue Teancum until they came near the city Bountiful, and then they were met by Lehi and a small army**, which had been left to protect the city Bountiful.

Imagine how tired the Lamanite armies are by now. The strategy of Moroni and his generals is working.

28 And now behold, **when the chief captains of the Lamanites had beheld** [*had seen*] **Lehi with his army coming against them, they fled in much confusion, lest perhaps they should not obtain the city Mulek before Lehi should overtake them**; for **they were wearied because of their march, and the men of Lehi were fresh.**

29 Now **the Lamanites did not know that Moroni had been** [*coming up*] **in their rear with his army**; and **all they feared was Lehi and his men.**

30 Now **Lehi was not desirous to overtake them till they should meet Moroni and his army.**

31 And it came to pass that **before the Lamanites had retreated far they were surrounded by the Nephites, by the men of Moroni on one hand, and the men of Lehi on the other, all of whom were fresh and full of strength**; but **the Lamanites were wearied because of their long march.**

32 And **Moroni commanded his men that they should fall upon** [*attack*] **them until they had given up their weapons of war** [*until they surrendered*].

33 And it came to pass that **Jacob, being their leader, being also a Zoramite**, and having an unconquerable spirit, he **led the Lamanites forth to battle with exceeding fury against Moroni**.

34 Moroni being in their course of march, therefore **Jacob was determined to slay them and cut his way through to the city of Mulek**. But behold, Moroni and his men were more powerful; therefore they did not give way before the Lamanites.

35 And it came to pass that they fought on both hands with exceeding fury; and there were many slain on both sides; yea, and **Moroni was wounded and Jacob was killed**.

36 And **Lehi pressed upon their rear with such fury with his strong men, that the Lamanites in the rear delivered up their weapons of war** [*surrendered*]; and the remainder of them, being much confused, knew not whither [*where*] to go or to strike.

> Captain Moroni is not a man who delights in bloodshed. Next, he will extend the hand of mercy to his enemies. Many will surrender.

37 Now **Moroni** seeing their confusion, he **said** unto them: **If ye will bring forth your weapons of war and deliver them up, behold we will forbear** [*stop*] **shedding your blood.**

38 And it came to pass that when the Lamanites had heard these words, **their chief captains**, all those who were not slain, came forth and **threw down their weapons of war at the feet of Moroni, and also commanded their men that they should do the same.**

39 But behold, there were **many** that **would not**; and those who would not deliver up their swords **were taken and bound, and their weapons of war were taken from them**, and they were compelled to march with their brethren forth into the land Bountiful.

40 And now **the number of prisoners who were taken exceeded more than the number of those who had been slain**, yea, more than those who had been slain on both sides. [*In other words, there are now a very large number of prisoners of war. Moroni will put them to work.*]

ALMA 53

In this chapter we are introduced for the first time to the "two thousand stripling soldiers" (verse 22), the sons of the people of Ammon, whom Helaman leads into battle. We will hear more about them in chapters 56, 57, and 58. Theirs is a great story of faith and courage, a story of complete dedication to a righteous cause even though their lives were in danger. If you read Mormon's description of them carefully, at the end of this chapter, you will sense that he had very tender feelings for them.

First, we will see what Moroni does with their prisoners of war. He will put them to work instead of just feeding and guarding them so they don't escape.

1 AND it came to pass that **they did set guards over the prisoners** of the Lamanites, **and did compel** [*force*] **them to go forth and bury their dead, yea, and also the dead of the Nephites who were slain**; and Moroni placed men over them to guard them while they should perform their labors.

2 And **Moroni went to the city of Mulek** [*which had been recaptured from the*

Lamanites] **with Lehi, and took command of the city and gave it unto Lehi.** Now behold, this Lehi was a man who had been with Moroni in the more part [*majority*] of all his battles; and he was a man like unto Moroni, and they rejoiced in each other's safety; yea, they were beloved by each other, and also beloved by all the people of Nephi.

Having buried the dead of the Lamanites as well as of the Nephites, the prisoners are now put to work fortifying the city of Bountiful and building a walled enclosure in which the Nephite guards could more easily keep their Lamanite prisoners under control. Moroni also found that it was easier to guard the prisoners when they were kept busy.

3 And it came to pass that **after the Lamanites had finished burying their dead and also the dead of the Nephites,** they were marched back into the land Bountiful; and Teancum, by the orders of **Moroni, caused that they should commence** [*begin*] **laboring in digging a ditch round about the land, or the city, Bountiful.**

4 And he caused that they should build a breastwork of timbers upon the inner bank of the ditch; and they cast up dirt out of the ditch against the breastwork of timbers; and thus **they did cause the Lamanites to labor until they had encircled the city of Bountiful round about with a strong wall of timbers and earth, to an exceeding height** [*it was very tall*].

5 And this city became an exceeding stronghold ever after; and **in this city they did guard the prisoners of the Lamanites; yea, even within a wall which they had caused them to build with their own hands.** Now Moroni was compelled to cause the Lamanites to labor, because **it was easy to guard them while at their labor**; and he desired all his forces when he should make an attack upon the Lamanites.

6 And it came to pass that Moroni had thus gained a victory over one of the greatest of the armies of the Lamanites, and had obtained possession of the city of Mulek, which was one of the strongest holds of the Lamanites in the land of Nephi; and **thus he had also built a stronghold to retain his prisoners.**

7 And it came to pass that he did no more attempt a battle with the Lamanites in that year, but **he did employ his men in preparing for war, yea, and in making fortifications to guard against the Lamanites, yea, and also delivering their women and their children from famine and affliction, and providing food for their armies.**

It seems that evil never rests, and that there are always those among the Lord's people who succumb to the temptation to break His commandments and thus weaken the harmony and peace of the righteous. We see this next, as apostates among the Nephites jeopardize their security and safety.

8 And now it came to pass that **the armies of the Lamanites**, on the west sea, south, while in the absence of Moroni **on account of some intrigue amongst the Nephites, which caused dissensions amongst them, had gained some ground over the Nephites,** yea, insomuch that **they** had **obtained possession of a number of their cities** in that part of the land.

9 And thus **because of iniquity** [*sin and wickedness*] **amongst themselves, yea, because of dissensions** [*disagreements*] **and intrigue** [*plotting*] **among themselves they were placed in the most dangerous circumstances** [*symbolic also of spiritual danger, which comes through personal wickedness*].

Mormon will now set the stage to introduce us to the two thousand stripling warriors, who are the sons of the Ammonites, the people of Ammon.

Remember that the sons of Mosiah, after their conversion (Mosiah 27), went on a mission to the Lamanites in the land of Nephi. Over time, there were large numbers of baptisms. These new members of the Church made an oath, a very serious promise and covenant, never to take up weapons of war again, and also took upon themselves the name Anti-Nephi-Lehies (Alma 23:17). They later became known as the people of Ammon, no doubt because he was the leader of the missionaries who brought them the gospel.

Over one thousand of these converts were killed (Alma 24:20–22) by their own people, the Lamanites who refused to accept the gospel. Ultimately, Ammon and his missionary companions led the converts to the land of Zarahemla, where the Nephites generously accepted them into their midst. The agreement was that these converts, who had covenanted with God that they would never take up weapons of war again, would provide food and supplies for the Nephites who had to fight to defend them.

However, as these Ammonites watched valiant Nephite soldiers losing their lives in order to defend them, they began to wonder if they should break their oath and take up weapons again. It was a difficult problem for them, as Mormon tells us, next.

10 And now behold, **I** [*Mormon*] **have somewhat to say concerning the people of Ammon, who, in the beginning, were Lamanites; but by Ammon and his brethren, or rather by the power and word of God**, they **had been converted** unto the Lord; and they had been **brought down into the land of Zarahemla**, and had ever since been **protected by the Nephites**.

11 And **because of their oath they had been kept from taking up arms** [*weapons of war*] against their brethren; for **they had taken an oath that they never would shed blood more**; and according to their oath they would have perished; yea, they would have suffered [*allowed*] themselves to have fallen into the hands of their brethren, had it not been for the pity and the exceeding love which Ammon and his brethren had had for them.

12 And **for this cause** [*this is the reason*] **they were brought down into the land of Zarahemla**; and they ever had been protected by the Nephites.

13 **But** it came to pass that **when they saw the danger, and the many afflictions and tribulations** [*difficulties*] **which the Nephites bore for them, they were moved with compassion** [*felt sorry for them*] **and were desirous to take up arms in the defence of their country.**

14 **But** behold, **as they were about to take their weapons of war**, they were **overpowered** [*convinced*] **by the persuasions of Helaman and his brethren**, for they were about to break the oath which they had made.

15 And **Helaman feared lest by so doing they should lose their souls**; therefore all those who had entered into this covenant were compelled to behold their brethren wade through their afflictions, in their dangerous circumstances at this time.

16 But behold, it came to pass **they had many sons, who had not entered into a covenant that they would not take their weapons of war to defend themselves against their enemies**; therefore they did assemble themselves together at this time, as many as were able to take up arms, and they called themselves Nephites.

17 And **they entered into a covenant to fight for the liberty of the Nephites**, yea, to protect the land unto the laying down of their lives; yea, even they covenanted that they never would give up their liberty, but they would fight in all cases to protect the Nephites and themselves from bondage.

18 Now behold, **there were two thousand of those young men**, who entered into this covenant and took their weapons of war to defend their country.

19 And now behold, as they never had hitherto been a disadvantage to the Nephites, **they became now at this period of time also a great support; for they took their weapons of war, and they would that Helaman should be their leader.** [*They requested that Helaman become the military leader of their group.*]

As previously mentioned, Mormon's tender feelings for these valiant young men are very apparent in the next verses.

20 And **they were all young men**, and they were **exceedingly valiant for courage**, and also **for strength and activity** [*in excellent physical condition*]; but behold, **this was not all—they were men who were true at all times in whatsoever thing they were entrusted** [*they were completely trustworthy*].

21 Yea, **they were men of truth** and **soberness** [*they were honest and serious about serious things*], for **they had been taught to keep the commandments of God and to walk uprightly** [*righteously*] **before him.**

22 And now it came to pass that **Helaman did march at the head of his two thousand stripling soldiers**, to the support of the people in the borders of the land on the south by the west sea.

23 And **thus ended the twenty and eighth year** of the reign of the judges over the people of Nephi.

ALMA 54

The issue in this chapter is the exchange of prisoners of war. We will see the tough side of Moroni's righteous personality. And, as we read Ammoron's letter (he is the apostate Nephite who is king of the Lamanites), we see speech typical of today's tyrants and cruel leaders attempting to convince themselves and others that they are in the right. They fulfill the prophecy of Isaiah as they "call evil good, and good evil" (Isaiah 5:20).

As we begin, Mormon points out an issue that we commonly see in our world today: evil dictators and leaders often use women and children as pawns and victims in their schemes to gain power and control, whereas military leaders whose values reflect God's standards do not.

1 AND now it came to pass **in the commencement of the twenty and ninth year** of the judges [*Captain Moroni is now about thirty-six years old*], that **Ammoron** [*the apostate Nephite who took over as king of the Lamanites after his brother, Amalickiah, was killed by Teancum; see Alma 51:33–34*] **sent unto Moroni desiring that he would exchange prisoners.**

2 And it came to pass that **Moroni felt to rejoice exceedingly at this request**, for he desired the provisions which were imparted for the support of the Lamanite prisoners for the support of his own people; and he also desired his own people for the strengthening of his army.

3 Now **the Lamanites had taken many women and children, and there was not a woman nor a child among all the prisoners of Moroni**, or the prisoners whom Moroni had taken; therefore **Moroni resolved upon a stratagem** [*a plan with a specific goal in mind*] **to obtain as many prisoners of the Nephites from the Lamanites as it were possible.**

4 **Therefore he wrote an epistle** [*a letter*], and sent it by the servant of Ammoron, the same who had brought an epistle to Moroni. Now **these are the words which he wrote unto Ammoron, saying**:

We will now read Captain Moroni's letter to Ammoron. Moroni points out the real reasons for this war and expresses little hope that Ammoron will acknowledge them and repent. It may well be that the Lord, through Moroni, is giving Ammoron another chance to rethink and repent. As mentioned previously, Moroni can be a tough and no-nonsense negotiator when conditions and wisdom require it. Perhaps this is an important message for us in our day, when very few world leaders hold firmly to high standards and principles when striving to negotiate with enemies to bring peace.

5 Behold, Ammoron, **I have written unto you somewhat concerning this war which ye have waged against my people, or rather which thy brother hath waged against them** [*Moroni is giving Ammoron an "out" to take if he will; in other words, Moroni is laying the blame for the war on Ammoron's brother, Amalickiah, the previous king of the Lamanites, rather than Ammoron, which gives Ammoron a way to save face if he chooses to end the war*], and which ye are still determined to carry on after his death.

Perhaps you have noticed that very few world leaders nowadays ever even mention God or the standards set by the scriptures. It is not politically correct to do so. It is refreshing when one does mention Him. Moroni has no hesitation in including the Lord and the eternal standards set by the gospel, in his letter. You will also note a bit of a challenge to "wake up and think straight," in Moroni's words to Ammoron.

6 Behold, **I would tell you somewhat concerning the justice of God, and the sword of his almighty wrath** [*anger*], **which doth hang over you except ye repent** and withdraw your armies into your own lands, or the land of your possessions, which is the land of Nephi.

7 Yea, **I would tell you these things if ye were capable of hearkening unto them** [*if you were capable of waking up*]; yea, I would tell you **concerning that awful hell that awaits to receive such murderers as thou and thy brother have been, except ye repent** and withdraw your murderous purposes, and return with your armies to your own lands.

Based on what Moroni says next at the beginning of verse 8, we come to understand that Ammoron was also an apostate Nephite, as was his brother, Amalickiah (Alma 46:3–8). Thus, he had known the gospel and had "dissented," in other words, had left it, apostatized from it (Alma 46:7). This increases his level of accountability before God.

8 But **as ye have once rejected these things** [*the gospel*], and have fought against the people of the Lord, even **so I may expect you will do it again.**

9 And now behold, **we are prepared to receive you** [*we are ready for you*]; yea, and except [*unless*] you withdraw your purposes, behold, **ye will pull down the wrath of that God whom you have rejected upon you, even to your utter destruction.**

10 But, **as the Lord liveth** [*Moroni is making an oath, a most solemn promise, which Ammoron understands in his culture*], **our armies shall come upon you except ye withdraw**, and **ye shall soon be visited with death**, for **we will retain our cities and our lands**; yea, and **we will maintain our religion and the cause of our God.**

Watch, now, as Moroni expresses his feeling that Ammoron is beyond any concerns about the gospel and presents Ammoron with a tough bit of negotiating to get Nephite families back safely.

11 But behold, **it supposeth me that I talk to you concerning these**

things in vain [*without success*]; or **it supposeth me** [*I suspect*] **that thou art a child of hell**; therefore I will close my epistle [*letter*] by telling you that **I will not exchange prisoners, save** [*except*] it be on conditions that **ye will deliver up** [*exchange*] **a man and his wife and his children, for one prisoner** [*for one of our Lamanite prisoners of war*]; if this be the case that ye will do it, I will exchange.

12 And behold, **if ye do not this, I will come against you with my armies; yea, even I will arm** [*give weapons to*] **my women and my children, and I will come against you, and I will follow you even into your own land, which is the land of our first inheritance** [*where Lehi, Sariah, Nephi, etc., first settled*]**; yea, and it shall be blood for blood, yea, life for life; and I will give you battle even until you are destroyed from off the face of the earth.**

Moroni expresses his righteous indignation, his righteous anger, to Ammoron. He summarizes the difference in motives between the two leaders of armies and warns that the time for trying to make peace is about up.

13 Behold, **I am in my anger** [*I'm mad!*], and also my people; **ye have sought** [*tried*] **to murder us**, and **we have only sought to defend ourselves**. But behold, **if ye seek to destroy us more we will seek to destroy you**; yea, and we will seek our land, the land of our first inheritance [*the land of Nephi, the land first settled by Lehi's colony as they arrived in the Americas, which, over time, had been taken over completely by the Lamanites*].

14 Now **I close my epistle. I am Moroni**; I am a leader of the people of the Nephites.

Did you notice Moroni's humility in verse 14, above? Instead of signing his letter to Ammoron as the "commander in chief" of the Nephite armies, which he is, Moroni humbly refers to himself as "a leader" of the Nephites. In other words, he considers himself to be just one of many who are helping the cause of freedom.

15 Now it came to pass that **Ammoron, when he had received this epistle, was angry**; and he wrote another epistle [*letter*] unto Moroni, and these are the words which he wrote, saying:

Ammoron typifies tyrants and wicked leaders throughout history who claim to have been wronged by their intended victims, and know better. Mormon will point this out in Alma 55:1. It boils down to the fact that such people as Ammoron are liars and bullies seeking justification in the eyes of others for their cruelties against others. They are learning to think and act like Satan. Pay attention to the sly wording and bold false accusations that Ammoron uses in his letter to Moroni.

16 **I am Ammoron**, the king of the Lamanites; **I am the brother of Amalickiah whom ye have murdered**. Behold, **I will avenge his blood** [*I will get revenge*] **upon you**, yea, and I will come upon you with my

armies for **I fear not your threatenings.**

17 For behold, **your fathers** [*ancestors; Nephi, Sam, Jacob, Joseph, etc.*] **did wrong their brethren** [*Laman, Lemuel, etc.*], insomuch that **they did rob them of their right to the government when it rightly belonged unto them.** [*These are the false traditions that Laman and Lemuel passed down through the ages to their descendants.*]

18 And now behold, **if ye will lay down your arms, and subject yourselves to be governed by those to whom the government doth rightly belong**, then will I cause that my people shall lay down their weapons and shall be at war no more.

19 Behold, **ye have breathed out many threatenings against me and my people; but behold, we fear not your threatenings.**

Next, Ammoron agrees to exchange a Nephite family for each Lamanite soldier in a prisoner of war exchange. But Moroni will not agree to it because of what Ammoron says immediately after agreeing to the exchange.

20 Nevertheless, **I will grant to exchange prisoners according to your request**, gladly, **that I may preserve my food for my men of war; and we will wage a war which shall be eternal, either to the subjecting the Nephites to our authority or to their eternal extinction.**

Remember, as stated above, Ammoron is lying to himself, to Moroni, and to God in what he says next. His accountability level is high.

21 And **as concerning that God whom ye say we have rejected, behold, we know not such a being; neither do ye**; but if it so be that there is such a being, we know not but that he hath made us as well as you. [*Another way of saying, in effect, who are you to think that your ways are right and our ways are wrong?*]

22 And **if it so be that there is a devil and a hell, behold will he not send you there to dwell with my brother** [*Amalickiah*] whom ye have murdered, whom **ye have hinted that he hath gone to such a place**? But behold these things matter not.

23 **I am Ammoron, and a descendant of Zoram** [*the servant of Laban who gave Nephi the brass plates, and who accompanied Nephi out of Jerusalem and into the wilderness; 1 Nephi 4*], whom your fathers pressed [*forced to come with them*] and brought out of Jerusalem.

24 And behold now, **I am a bold Lamanite** [*he has completely rejected his gospel heritage as a Nephite*]; behold, **this war hath been waged to avenge their wrongs** [*the Nephite wrongs against the Lamanites*], and to maintain **and to obtain their rights to the government**; and I close my epistle to Moroni.

ALMA 55

As Moroni receives Ammoron's cocky reply to his letter about exchanging prisoners (chapter 54), he determines to rescue the Nephite prisoners of war rather than exchanging them.

As we begin this chapter, perhaps we see a response to a question some members of the Church ask. It concerns whether most wicked leaders, who fight against truth and light, really know what they are doing. This question can also apply to terrorist groups today whose stated goal is to destroy Western democracy. Mormon answers the question next, at least in the case of Ammoron.

1 NOW it came to pass that when **Moroni** had received this epistle he **was more angry, because he knew that Ammoron had a perfect knowledge of his fraud** [*lying and cheating to get what you want*]; yea, **he knew that Ammoron knew that it was not a just** [*fair, righteous*] **cause that had caused him to wage a war against the people of Nephi**.

2 And he said: Behold, **I will not exchange prisoners with Ammoron save** [*unless*] **he will withdraw his purpose** [*to destroy the Nephites*], as I have stated in my epistle; for I will not grant unto him that he shall have any more power than what he hath got.

> Moroni now puts a plan in place to rescue Nephite prisoners. He also states his intent to defend his country with a strong offense against the enemies who have clearly stated the intent to destroy his people.

3 Behold, **I know the place where the Lamanites do guard my people whom they have taken prisoners;** and as Ammoron would not grant unto me mine epistle, behold, I will give unto him according to my words; yea, **I will seek death among them until they shall sue** [*ask*] **for peace.**

4 And now it came to pass that when **Moroni** had said these words, he **caused that a search should be made among his men, that perhaps he might find a man who was a descendant of Laman among them.**

5 And it came to pass that **they found one, whose name was Laman**; and he was one of the servants of the king who was murdered by Amalickiah.

6 Now **Moroni caused that Laman and a small number of his men should go forth unto the guards who were over the Nephites** [*the Nephite prisoners of war*].

7 Now **the Nephites were guarded in the city of Gid**; therefore Moroni appointed Laman and caused that a small number of men should go with him.

8 And **when it was evening Laman went to the guards who were over the Nephites**, and behold, they saw him coming and they hailed him [*called out to him to identify himself*]; but **he saith unto them**: Fear not; behold, **I am a Lamanite**. Behold, **we have escaped from the Nephites**, and they sleep; and behold **we have taken of their wine and brought with us**.

9 Now when **the Lamanites** heard these words they **received him with joy**; and they said unto him: **Give us**

of your wine, that we may drink; we are glad that ye have thus taken wine with you for we are weary.

Watch next, as the age-old strategy of reverse psychology works for Laman and his fellow soldiers.

10 But **Laman said** unto them: **Let us keep of our wine till** [*let's not drink any wine until*] **we go against the Nephites** to battle. But **this saying only made them more desirous to drink of the wine;**

11 For, said they: We are weary, therefore **let us take of the wine**, and by and by we shall receive wine for our rations, which will strengthen us to go against the Nephites.

12 And **Laman said** unto them: **You may do according to your desires.** [*In other words, whatever you want.*]

13 And it came to pass that **they did take of the wine freely**; and it was pleasant to their taste, therefore **they took of it more freely**; and **it was strong**, having been prepared in its strength [*the Nephites had made it extra strong to get them drunk quickly*].

14 And it came to pass they did drink and were merry, and **by and by they were all drunken.**

15 And now **when Laman and his men saw that they were all drunken, and were in a deep sleep**, **they returned to Moroni** and told him all the things that had happened.

16 And now **this was according to the design** [*plan*] **of Moroni**. And **Moroni had prepared his men with weapons of war; and he went to the city Gid, while the Lamanites were in a deep sleep and drunken, and cast in** [*threw over the wall*] **weapons of war unto the prisoners, insomuch that they were all armed;**

17 Yea, **even to their women**, and all those of their **children**, as many as were **able to use a weapon of war**, when Moroni had armed all those prisoners; and **all those things were done in a profound** [*very careful*] **silence**.

18 But **had they awakened the Lamanites**, behold they were drunken and **the Nephites could have slain them**.

19 **But behold, this was not the desire of Moroni; he did not delight in murder or bloodshed, but he delighted in the saving of his people from destruction**; and for this cause he might not bring upon him injustice, he would not fall upon the Lamanites and destroy them in their drunkenness.

20 But **he had obtained his desires**; for he had armed those prisoners of the Nephites who were within the wall of the city, and had given them power to gain possession of those parts which were within the walls.

21 And **then he caused the men who were with him to withdraw a pace from them, and surround the armies of the Lamanites.**

22 Now behold **this was done in the**

night-time, so that **when the Lamanites awoke in the morning they beheld that they were surrounded** by the Nephites without [*outside the city*], and that their prisoners were armed within.

23 And thus they saw that the Nephites had power over them; and in these circumstances they found that it was not expedient [*not wise*] that they should fight with the Nephites; therefore **their chief captains demanded their weapons of war, and they brought them forth and cast them at the feet of the Nephites, pleading for mercy.**

24 Now behold, this was the desire of **Moroni**. He **took them prisoners of war**, and took possession of the city, and **caused that all the prisoners should be liberated, who were Nephites**; and they did join the army of Moroni, and **were a great strength to his army.**

Once again, Moroni will put his prisoners of war to work constructively for the cause of Nephite freedom.

25 And it came to pass that **he did cause the Lamanites, whom he had taken prisoners, that they should commence a labor in strengthening the fortifications round about the city Gid.**

26 And it came to pass that **when he had fortified the city Gid**, according to his desires, **he caused that his prisoners should be taken to the city Bountiful** [*which other prisoners of war had fortified and where they had built a secure area in which to hold Lamanite prisoners; see Alma 53:5*]; and he also guarded that city with an exceedingly strong force.

27 And it came to pass that **they did**, notwithstanding all the intrigues [*in spite of all the attempts*] of the Lamanites, **keep and protect all the prisoners** whom they had taken, and **also maintain all the ground and the advantage which they had retaken.**

Captain Moroni's strategy is beginning to turn things in favor of the Nephites.

28 And it came to pass that **the Nephites began again to be victorious, and to reclaim their rights and their privileges.**

29 **Many times did the Lamanites attempt to encircle them about by night**, but in these attempts they did lose many prisoners.

30 And **many times did they attempt to administer of their wine to the Nephites**, that they might destroy them with poison or with drunkenness.

31 But behold, **the Nephites were not slow to remember the Lord their God in this their time of affliction**. They could not be taken in their snares; yea, **they would not partake of their wine, save they had first given to some of the Lamanite prisoners**.

32 And **they were thus cautious**

that no poison should be administered among them; for if their wine would poison a Lamanite it would also poison a Nephite; and thus they did try [*test*] all their liquors.

Just a quick reminder that the Word of Wisdom (D&C 89) was not given until 1833, and even then, it was about one hundred years before keeping the Word of Wisdom became a temple recommend item under President Heber J. Grant. Furthermore, it was given because of special problems that exist in our days (D&C 89:4). Therefore, it was not against the Word of Wisdom for the Nephites to drink wine because they didn't have the Word of Wisdom.

33 And now it came to pass that **it was expedient** [*necessary*] **for Moroni to make preparations to attack the city Morianton** [*which had been taken by the Lamanites about four years ago; see Alma 51:26*]; for behold, **the Lamanites had, by their labors, fortified the city Morianton until it had become an exceeding stronghold** [*very difficult to attack*].

34 And **they were continually bringing new forces** into that city, and **also new supplies** of provisions.

35 And **thus ended the twenty and ninth year** of the reign of the judges over the people of Nephi.

ALMA 56

This chapter is a favorite of many members of the Church because it contains the verses in which the two thousand stripling (meaning quite young) soldiers report that their mothers had taught them to have great faith in the Lord and His help in times of danger and trouble.

In Alma 53:16–22, we were introduced to these two thousand stripling soldiers, young sons of the people of Ammon, who pledged to go to war to help defend the Nephites who were defending their parents. Their parents, Lamanite converts formerly known as Anti-Nephi-Lehies (Alma 23:17), had made a covenant never to take up weapons again. Their sons volunteered to take their place in defending the Nephites and these converts against the Lamanites.

At the request of these young Ammonite warriors, Helaman, the oldest son of Alma the Younger, was appointed to lead them into battle (Alma 53:19). Mormon now quotes a letter to Captain Moroni from Helaman in which Helaman reports what has happened with these stripling soldiers over the past three to four years as they joined the Nephite forces in battle. His letter or epistle, as it is called by Mormon, covers Alma, chapters 56, 57, and 58.

First, Helaman reviews the conditions that led up to these young men's joining the Nephite army.

1 AND now it came to pass **in the commencement of the thirtieth year** of the reign of the judges [*sixty-two years before the birth of Christ to Mary in Bethlehem*], on the second day in the first month, **Moroni received an epistle** [*a letter*] **from Helaman,**

stating the affairs of the people in that quarter [*part*] of the land.

2 And **these are the words which he wrote**, saying: **My dearly beloved brother, Moroni**, as well in the Lord as in the tribulations [*troubles*] of our warfare; behold, my beloved brother, **I have somewhat to tell you concerning our warfare in this part of the land**.

3 Behold, **two thousand of the sons of those men whom Ammon brought down out of the land of Nephi**—now ye have known that these were **descendants of Laman**, who was the eldest son of our father [*ancestor*] Lehi;

4 Now **I need not rehearse unto** [*remind*] **you concerning their traditions or their unbelief**, for thou knowest concerning all these things—

5 Therefore it sufficeth me [*it is sufficient*] that I tell you that **two thousand of these young men have taken their weapons of war, and would that I should** [*wanted me to*] **be their leader; and we have come forth to defend our country**.

6 And now **ye also know concerning the covenant which their fathers made, that they would not take up their weapons of war against their brethren to shed blood.**

7 But **in the twenty and sixth year**, when they [*the fathers of the two thousand young men*] saw our afflictions and our tribulations for them, **they were about to break the covenant which they had made and take up their weapons of war in our defence**.

8 **But I** [*Helaman*] **would not suffer** [*permit*] **them that they should break this covenant** which they had made, supposing [*having faith*] that God would strengthen us, insomuch [*to the extent*] that we should not suffer more because of the fulfilling the oath which they had taken.

9 But behold, here is one thing in which we may have great joy. **For behold, in the twenty and sixth year** [*about four years ago*], **I, Helaman, did march at the head of these two thousand young men to the city of Judea, to assist Antipus,** whom ye had appointed a leader over the people of that part of the land.

You will see, as we continue, that these young stripling soldiers were thrown into the thick of battle where they were badly needed and where death was extremely likely.

10 And **I did join my two thousand sons, (for they are worthy to be called sons) to the army of Antipus, in which strength Antipus did rejoice exceedingly**; for behold, **his army had been reduced by the Lamanites because their forces had slain a vast number of our men**, for which cause we have to mourn.

11 Nevertheless, we may console ourselves in this point, that **they have died in the cause of their country**

and of their God, yea, and they are happy [*a brief course in eternal perspective*].

12 And **the Lamanites had also retained many prisoners**, all of whom are chief captains, for none other have they spared alive. And we suppose that they are now at this time in the land of Nephi; it is so if they are not slain.

13 And now **these are the cities of which the Lamanites have obtained possession by the shedding of the blood of so many of our valiant men;**

14 The land of Manti, or the city of **Manti**, and the city of **Zeezrom** [*apparently, there was a Nephite city named after Zeezrom, the lawyer who debated Alma and Amulek in the wicked city of Ammonihah; see Alma 11; Zeezrom was converted and became a powerful missionary; see Alma 31:6*], and the city of **Cumeni**, and the city of **Antiparah**.

15 And these are the cities which they possessed **when I arrived at the city of Judea; and I found Antipus and his men toiling with their might to fortify the city.**

16 Yea, and **they were depressed in body as well as in spirit**, for they had fought valiantly by day and toiled by night to maintain their cities; and thus **they had suffered great afflictions of every kind.**

17 And now **they were determined to conquer in this place or die**; therefore **you may well suppose that this little force which I brought with me, yea, those sons of mine, gave them great hopes and much joy.**

18 And now it came to pass that **when the Lamanites saw that Antipus had received a greater strength to his army**, they were compelled by the orders of Ammoron [*the apostate Nephite who had become the king of the Lamanites; see Alma 52:3 and Alma 49:25–27*] to not come against the city of Judea, or against us, to battle.

19 And **thus were we favored of the Lord; for had they come upon us in this our weakness they might have perhaps destroyed our little army; but thus were we preserved.**

20 **They were commanded by Ammoron to maintain those cities which they had taken**. And thus ended the twenty and sixth year. And **in the commencement of the twenty and seventh year** we had prepared our city and ourselves for defence.

Next, Helaman shares with Moroni the military strategy he and his two thousand helped carry out to lure one of the most powerful Lamanite armies out of their strongly fortified city.

21 Now **we were desirous that the Lamanites should come upon us**; for we were not desirous to make an attack upon them in their strongholds.

22 And it came to pass that **we kept spies out** round about, **to watch the movements of the Lamanites, that they might not pass us by night nor by day to make an attack upon**

our other cities which were on the northward.

23 For **we knew in those cities they were not sufficiently strong to meet them**; therefore **we were desirous, if they should pass by us, to fall upon them in their rear, and thus bring them up in the rear at the same time they were met in the front**. We supposed that we could overpower them; but behold, **we were disappointed in this our desire.**

24 **They durst not** [*didn't dare*] **pass by us with their whole army**, neither durst they with a part, lest they should not be sufficiently strong and they should fall.

25 **Neither durst they march down against the city of Zarahemla; neither durst they cross the head of Sidon, over to the city of Nephihah**.

26 And thus, with their forces, **they were determined to maintain those cities which they had taken.**

27 And now it came to pass **in the second month of this year**, there was brought unto us many provisions from the fathers of those my two thousand sons.

28 And **also there were sent two thousand men unto us** from the land of Zarahemla. And thus we were prepared with ten thousand men, and provisions for them, and also for their wives and their children.

29 And **the Lamanites, thus seeing our forces increase daily, and provisions arrive for our support, they began to be fearful, and began to sally forth** [*come out of their strongholds*], **if it were possible to put an end to our receiving provisions and strength.**

Next, Helaman describes a key part of their strategy.

30 Now when we saw that the Lamanites began to grow uneasy on this wise, **we were desirous to bring a stratagem into effect upon them**; therefore **Antipus ordered that I should march forth with my little sons to a neighboring city, as if we were carrying provisions to a neighboring city.**

31 And **we were to march near the city of Antiparah, as if we were going to the city beyond**, in the borders by the seashore.

32 And it came to pass that **we did march forth, as if with our provisions, to go to that city.**

33 And it came to pass that **Antipus did march forth with a part of his army, leaving the remainder to maintain the city. But he did not march forth until I had gone forth with my little army, and came near the city Antiparah.**

34 And now, **in the city Antiparah were stationed the strongest army of the Lamanites; yea, the most numerous.**

35 And it came to pass that when they had been informed by their

spies, **they came forth with their army and marched against us**. [*The strategy worked.*]

36 And it came to pass that **we did flee before them, northward. And thus** [*this is how*] **we did lead away the most powerful army of the Lamanites**;

37 Yea, even to a considerable distance, insomuch that **when they saw the army of Antipus pursuing them, with their might, they did not turn to the right nor to the left, but pursued their march in a straight course after us; and, as we suppose, it was their intent to slay us before Antipus should overtake them, and this that they might not be surrounded by our people.**

38 And now **Antipus, beholding** [*seeing*] **our danger, did speed the march of his army**. But behold, **it was night**; therefore **they did not overtake us, neither did Antipus overtake them**; therefore **we did camp for the night**.

39 And it came to pass that **before** the **dawn** of the morning, behold, **the Lamanites were pursuing us. Now we were not sufficiently strong to contend** [*fight*] **with them; yea, I would not suffer that my little sons should fall into their hands**; therefore we did continue our march, and **we took our march into the wilderness**.

40 Now they durst not [*did not dare*] turn to the right nor to the left lest they should be surrounded; neither would I turn to the right nor to the left lest they should overtake me, and we could not stand against them, but be slain, and they would make their escape; and thus **we did flee all that day into the wilderness, even until it was dark.**

41 And it came to pass that again, **when the light of the morning came we saw the Lamanites upon us, and we did flee before them.**

42 But it came to pass that **they did not pursue us far before they halted**; and it was in the morning of the third day of **the seventh month**.

43 And now, **whether they were overtaken by Antipus we knew not**, but I said unto my men: Behold, we know not but they have halted for the purpose that we should come against them, that they might catch us in their snare; [*In other words, they might be setting a trap for us.*]

One can almost see tender tears in Helaman's eyes as he reports to Moroni what happened next as he put the question of what to do directly to his stripling warriors.

44 Therefore **what say ye, my sons, will ye go against them to battle?**

45 And now **I say unto you, my beloved brother Moroni, that never had I seen so great courage,** nay, not amongst all the Nephites.

46 For as I had ever called them my sons [*for they were all of them very young*] even so **they said unto me: Father,**

behold our God is with us, and he will not suffer [*allow*] **that we should fall; then let us go forth**; we would not slay our brethren if they would let us alone; therefore let us go, lest they should overpower the army of Antipus.

In these famous verses (47 and 48), we see the great influence of righteous mothers.

47 Now **they never had fought, yet they did not fear death**; and they did think more upon the liberty of their fathers than they did upon their lives; yea, **they had been taught by their mothers, that if they did not doubt, God would deliver them.**

48 And they rehearsed unto me the words of their mothers, saying: **We do not doubt our mothers knew it.**

Next, Helaman and his young men, who had never fought in a battle before (verse 47, above), turned around and headed straight for the Lamanite army.

49 And it came to pass that **I did return with my two thousand against these Lamanites who had pursued us. And now behold, the armies of Antipus had overtaken them, and a terrible battle had commenced.**

50 **The army of Antipus being weary, because of their long march in so short a space of time, were about to fall into the hands of the Lamanites; and had I not returned with my two thousand they would have obtained their purpose.**

51 For **Antipus had fallen by the sword, and many of his leaders, because of their weariness** [*because they were so tired*], which was occasioned [*caused*] by the speed of their march—therefore **the men of Antipus**, being confused because of the fall of their leaders, **began to give way before the Lamanites.**

It appears that Mormon is summarizing some of what Helaman told Moroni, in verses 52 and 53, next; then he resumes quoting Helaman as of verse 54.

52 And it came to pass that the Lamanites took courage, and began to pursue them; and thus were the Lamanites pursuing them with great vigor **when Helaman came upon their rear with his two thousand**, and began to slay them exceedingly, insomuch that **the whole army of the Lamanites halted and turned upon Helaman.**

53 Now **when the people of Antipus saw that the Lamanites had turned them about**, they gathered together their men and **came again upon the rear of the Lamanites**.

54 And now it came to pass that **we, the people of Nephi, the people of Antipus, and I with my two thousand, did surround the Lamanites**, and did slay them; yea, insomuch that they were compelled to deliver up their weapons of war and also themselves as prisoners of war.

Next, Helaman recounts the miracle of survival of his two thousand young Ammonite soldiers.

55 And now it came to pass that **when they had surrendered** themselves up unto us, behold, **I numbered** [*counted*] **those young men who had fought with me, fearing lest there were many of them slain.**

56 But behold, **to my great joy, there had not one soul of them fallen to the earth** [*not one of them had been killed*]; yea, and they had fought as if with the strength of God; yea, never were men known to have fought with such miraculous strength; and with such mighty power did they fall upon the Lamanites, that they did frighten them; and for this cause [*because of the two thousand stripling warriors*] did the Lamanites deliver themselves up as prisoners of war.

57 And as **we had no place for our prisoners, that we could guard them** to keep them from the armies of the Lamanites, **therefore we sent them to the land of Zarahemla**, and a part of those men who were not slain of Antipus, with them; and the remainder I took and joined them to my stripling Ammonites, and took our march back to the city of Judea.

ALMA 57

Next, Helaman tells Captain Moroni of an offer from Ammoron, the apostate Nephite king of the Lamanites, to exchange the Nephite city of Antiparah for the large number of Lamanite prisoners taken in the battle in chapter 56.

1 AND now it came to pass that **I** [*Helaman*] **received an epistle** [*letter*] **from Ammoron**, the king, **stating that if I would deliver up those prisoners of war whom we had taken that he would deliver up the city of Antiparah unto us.**

2 But **I sent an epistle unto the king, that we were sure our forces were sufficient to take the city of Antiparah by our force; and by delivering up the prisoners for that city we should suppose ourselves unwise**, and that **we would only deliver up our prisoners on exchange.**

3 And **Ammoron refused** mine epistle, for he would not exchange prisoners; **therefore we began to make preparations to go against the city of Antiparah**.

4 **But the people** [*Lamanites who had taken possession*] **of Antiparah did leave the city, and fled to their other cities**, which they had possession of, to fortify them; and **thus the city of Antiparah fell into our hands**.

5 And **thus ended the twenty and eighth year** of the reign of the judges. [*Helaman and his two thousand young Ammonites have been serving in the army for about two years now.*]

In verse 6, next, sixty more Ammonite stripling soldiers join Helaman's band of two thousand.

6 And it came to pass that **in the**

commencement of the twenty and ninth year, we received a supply of provisions, and also an addition to our army, from the land of Zarahemla, and from the land round about, to the number of six thousand men, besides **sixty of the sons of the Ammonites who had come to join their brethren, my little band of two thousand**. And now behold, we were strong, yea, and we had also plenty of provisions [*supplies*] brought unto us.

7 And it came to pass that **it was our desire to wage a battle with the army which was placed to protect the city Cumeni** [*a Nephite city that had been taken over by the Lamanites*].

Next, Helaman shares with Moroni the strategy he used to take back the city of Cumeni.

8 And now behold, I will show unto you that **we soon accomplished our desire**; yea, with our strong force, or **with a part of our strong force, we did surround, by night, the city Cumeni, a little before they were to receive a supply of provisions**.

9 And it came to pass that **we did camp round about the city for many nights**; but **we did sleep upon our swords** [*with our swords right by us*], **and keep guards, that the Lamanites could not come upon us by night and slay us, which they attempted many times; but as many times as they attempted this their blood was spilt.**

10 At length **their provisions did arrive**, and they were about to enter the city by night. And we, instead of being Lamanites, were Nephites; therefore, **we did take them and their provisions**.

11 And notwithstanding **the Lamanites being cut off from their support after this manner, they were still determined to maintain** [*keep*] **the city**; therefore it became expedient [*necessary*] that we should take those provisions and send them to Judea, and our prisoners to the land of Zarahemla.

12 And it came to pass that not many days had passed away before **the Lamanites began to lose all hopes of succor** [*help and support*]; therefore **they yielded up the city unto our hands**; and thus we had accomplished our designs in obtaining the city Cumeni.

By now, prisoners of war have become a real problem for Helaman's forces.

13 But it came to pass that **our prisoners were so numerous** [*many*] **that**, notwithstanding the enormity [*largeness*] of our numbers, **we were obliged to employ all our force to keep them, or to put them to death.**

14 For behold, **they would break out in great numbers, and would fight with stones, and with clubs, or whatsoever thing they could get into their hands, insomuch that** [*so that*] **we did slay upwards of**

two thousand of them after they had surrendered themselves prisoners of war.

15 Therefore **it became expedient** [*necessary*] **for us, that we should put an end to their lives, or guard them, sword in hand, down to the land of Zarahemla**; and also our provisions were not any more than sufficient for our own people, notwithstanding [*in spite of*] that which we had taken from the Lamanites.

16 And now, in those critical circumstances, **it became a very serious matter to determine** [*make a decision*] **concerning these prisoners of war**; nevertheless, **we did resolve to send them down to the land of Zarahemla; therefore we selected a part of our men, and gave them charge over our prisoners to go down to the land of Zarahemla.**

17 **But** it came to pass that **on the morrow** [*the next day*] **they did return.** And now behold, we did not inquire of them concerning the prisoners; [*we will be told what happened, starting with verse 28*] for behold, **the Lamanites were upon us**, and they returned in season to save us from falling into their hands. For behold, **Ammoron** [*the king of the Lamanites*] **had sent to their support a new supply of provisions and also a numerous** [*big*] **army of men.**

18 And it came to pass that **those men whom we sent with the prisoners did arrive in season** [*at just the right time*] **to check** [*stop*] **them**, as they were about to overpower us.

Next, Helaman tells Moroni about his two thousand and sixty young Ammonite soldiers as they fought in this intense battle. Remember, another sixty had joined his group of two thousand (see verse 6).

19 But behold, **my little band of two thousand and sixty fought most desperately**; yea, they were firm before the Lamanites, and did administer death unto all those who opposed them.

20 And **as the remainder of our army were about to give way before the Lamanites, behold, those two thousand and sixty were firm and undaunted** [*unstoppable*].

21 Yea, and **they did obey and observe to perform every word of command with exactness; yea, and even according to their faith it was done unto them**; and **I did remember the words which they said unto me that their mothers had taught them.**

22 And now behold, **it was these my sons, and those men who had been selected to convey** [*take*] **the prisoners, to whom we owe this great victory**; for it was they who did beat the Lamanites; therefore they were driven back to the city of Manti.

Next, we will see that this was a terrible battle with much loss of life. It is in this context that Helaman bears testimony to Captain Moroni concerning the results of the faith of the two thousand and sixty stripling warriors.

23 And we retained our city Cumeni, and were not all destroyed by the sword; nevertheless, **we had suffered great loss** [*we had lost many of our soldiers*].

24 And it came to pass that **after the Lamanites had fled**, I immediately gave orders that my men who had been wounded should be taken from among the dead, and caused that their wounds should be dressed [*taken care of*].

25 And it came to pass that **there were two hundred, out of my two thousand and sixty, who had fainted because of the loss of blood**; nevertheless, **according to the goodness of God**, and to our great astonishment, and also the joy of our whole army, **there was not one soul of them who did perish** [*die*]; yea, and **neither was there one soul among them who had not received many wounds.**

26 And now, **their preservation** [*not being killed*] **was astonishing** [*very surprising*] **to our whole army**, yea, **that they should be spared while there was a thousand of our brethren who were slain.** And **we do justly ascribe it** [*give credit*] **to the miraculous power of God, because of their exceeding faith in that which they had been taught to believe**—that there was a just God, and whosoever did not doubt, that they should be preserved by his marvelous power.

27 **Now this was the faith of these of whom I have spoken; they are young, and their minds are firm, and they do put their trust in God continually.**

Next, Helaman reports what happened with the Lamanite prisoners of war (verses 16–17) who were supposed to be taken to the land of Zarahemla under a group of Nephite guards, commanded by Gid.

28 And now it came to pass that after we had thus taken care of our wounded men, and had buried our dead and also the dead of the Lamanites, who were many, behold, **we did inquire of Gid concerning the prisoners whom they had started to go down to the land of Zarahemla with.**

29 Now **Gid was the chief captain over the band who was appointed to guard them** down to the land.

30 And now, **these are the words which Gid said unto me**: Behold, **we did start to go down to the land of Zarahemla with our prisoners**. And it came to pass that **we did meet the spies of our armies**, who had been sent out to watch the camp of the Lamanites.

31 And **they** [*the Nephite spies*] **cried unto us**, saying—Behold, **the armies of the Lamanites are marching towards the city of Cumeni; and behold, they will fall upon them, yea, and will destroy our people.**

32 And it came to pass that **our prisoners did hear their cries**, which caused them to take courage;

and they did rise up in rebellion against us.

33 And it came to pass because of their rebellion **we did cause that our swords should come upon them.** And it came to pass that **they did in a body** [*as a group*] **run upon our swords, in the which, the greater number of them were slain; and the remainder of them broke through and fled from us.**

34 And behold, when they had fled and **we could not overtake them, we took our march with speed towards the city Cumeni; and behold, we did arrive in time that we might assist our brethren in preserving the city.**

One of the great qualities of these Nephite soldiers is that they never forget to give gratitude to God for their blessings. This is an important lesson for us. You may wish to read D&C 59:21 to see how important it is to express gratitude to our Father in Heaven.

35 And behold, **we are again delivered out of the hands of our enemies.** And **blessed is the name of our God; for behold, it is he that has delivered us; yea, that has done this great thing for us.**

36 Now it came to pass that **when I, Helaman, had heard these words of Gid, I was filled with exceeding joy because of the goodness of God in preserving us, that we might not all perish**; yea, and **I trust that the souls of them who have been slain have entered into the rest of their God.**

Perhaps you have noticed several times so far, in these chapters about the wars between the Nephites and the Lamanites, that we are told that the righteous who lose their lives in defending their country are in a place where we no longer need to worry about their well-being. In other words, they have gone to paradise in the spirit world.

ALMA 58

Helaman's letter to Captain Moroni about his 2,060 stripling warriors ends at the close of this chapter. We will see that, despite the intense battles in which the two thousand and sixty stripling soldiers fought, not one of them lost his life.

What if someone you know has lost a loved one in war? How would you counsel them as they read about the miraculous preservation of these young Ammonite warriors? What if they have a difficult time reading it? What if they are wondering why their loved one was not protected in battle, whereas these were? What if they are wondering if perhaps their lost one was not as righteous as these? Difficult questions indeed, but perhaps there has been an answer all along, in these chapters.

Many righteous Nephites were also killed in these battles. At the end of Alma 57:36, Helaman uses the phrase, "entered into the rest of their God." The Doctrine and Covenants gives us a fine-tuned definition of the word "rest" as it applies to the next life. In D&C 84:24, we read this definition as follows (**bold** added for emphasis): ". . . which

rest is **the fulness of his glory**." We know that the "fulness of his glory" is exaltation in the highest degree of glory in the celestial kingdom (see D&C 131:1–4). In other words, becoming gods and living in our own family unit forever. Therefore, in the bigger perspective of things, both the two thousand and sixty young men and the righteous who gave their lives in battle are in the best of condition, and that is what ultimately counts. It would be foolish to attempt to judge who is more worthy, because worthiness is not an issue here.

Helaman continues now with his report to Moroni.

1 AND behold, now it came to pass that **our next object** [*goal*] **was to obtain the city of Manti** [*get the city of Manti back from the Lamanites*]**; but behold, there was no way that we could lead them out of the city by our small bands** [*groups of soldiers*]. For behold, they remembered that which we had hitherto done [*how we had tricked them before*]; therefore **we could not decoy them away from their strongholds.**

2 And **they were** so **much more numerous than was our army** that we durst not go forth and attack them in their strongholds.

Helaman's forces are so small, relative to the large numbers of Lamanite soldiers, that he decides that his strategy will be to hold on to the cities and lands that they have taken back from the Lamanites, and then wait for reinforcements. As you will see, this will be a very long and difficult period of several months. In fact, before it is over, Helaman and his forces, including his two thousand and sixty young soldiers, will come close to starving to death. This could perhaps serve as a reminder to us that things do not necessarily always go well for those doing the work of the Lord.

3 Yea, and **it became expedient** [*necessary; wise*] **that we should employ our men to the maintaining those parts of the land which we had regained of our possessions**; therefore it became expedient that we should wait, that we might receive more strength from the land of Zarahemla and also a new supply of provisions.

4 And it came to pass that **I** thus **did send an embassy** [*a message or a messenger*] **to the governor of our land**, to acquaint him concerning the affairs of our people. And it came to pass that **we did wait to receive provisions and strength from the land of Zarahemla**.

5 But behold, **this did profit us but little** [*it didn't do us much good*]; for the Lamanites were also receiving great strength from day to day, and also many provisions; and thus were our circumstances at this period of time.

6 And **the Lamanites were sallying forth** [*coming out*] **against us from time to time, resolving by stratagem to destroy us**; nevertheless we could not come to battle with them, because of their retreats and their strongholds.

7 And it came to pass that **we did wait in these difficult circumstances for the space of many months,**

even until we were about to perish for the want [*lack*] **of food.**

8 But it came to pass that **we did receive food, which was guarded to us** [*brought to us under guard*] by an army of two thousand men to our assistance; **and this is all the assistance which we did receive, to defend ourselves and our country from falling into the hands of our enemies, yea, to contend** [*fight*] **with an enemy which was innumerable** [*so many that you couldn't count them*]**.**

9 And now the cause of these our embarrassments [*probably meaning embarrassed at the lack of support from their government*], or **the cause** [*reason*] **why they did not send more strength** unto us, **we knew not**; therefore **we were grieved** [*very concerned*] **and also filled with fear, lest by any means the judgments of God should come upon our land, to our overthrow and utter** [*complete*] **destruction.**

10 **Therefore we did pour out our souls in prayer to God**, that he would strengthen us and deliver us out of the hands of our enemies, yea, and also give us strength that we might retain our cities, and our lands, and our possessions, for the support of our people.

The word "hope" as used in the Book of Mormon is a much stronger word than "hope" as used in modern English. An example of this is found in the context of verse 11, next. The words "assurances," "peace," and "great faith" lead up to the word "hope."

11 Yea, and it came to pass that **the Lord our God did visit** [*bless*] **us with assurances** that he would deliver us; yea, insomuch that he did speak **peace to our souls**, and did grant unto us **great faith**, and did cause us that we should **hope** for our deliverance in him.

Another example of the power of the word "hope" as used in the Book of Mormon is found in 2 Nephi 31:20, where it is used in the context of obtaining eternal life (exaltation). Quoting from 2 Nephi 31:20, we see "press forward with a steadfastness in Christ, having a **perfect brightness of hope.**" In other words, we are encouraged to plan on achieving eternal life rather than merely hoping that we make it.

In verse 12 we see another application to our daily lives: even though our own resources may be little, with the help of the Lord we can overcome all our "enemies," including sin, shortcomings, and inadequacies.

12 And **we did take courage** with our small force which we had received, **and were fixed with a determination to conquer our enemies**, and to maintain our lands, and our possessions, and our wives, and our children, and the cause of our liberty.

13 And thus **we did go forth with all our might against the Lamanites, who were in the city of Manti**; and we did pitch our tents by the wilderness side, which was near to the city.

14 And it came to pass that on the

morrow [*the next day*], that when **the Lamanites** saw that we were in the borders by the wilderness which was near the city, that they **sent out their spies round about us that they might discover the number and the strength of our army.**

15 And it came to pass that when **they saw that we were not strong, according to our numbers**, and fearing that we should cut them off from their support except they should come out to battle against us and kill us, and also **supposing that they could easily destroy us with their numerous hosts** [*many soldiers*], therefore **they began to make preparations to come out against us to battle.**

16 And when we saw that they were making preparations to come out against us, behold, **I caused that Gid, with a small number of men, should secrete** [*hide*] **himself in the wilderness**, and **also that Teomner and a small number of men should secrete themselves also in the wilderness.**

17 Now **Gid and his men were on the right and the others on the left**; and when they had thus secreted [*hidden*] themselves, behold, **I** [*Helaman*] **remained, with the remainder of my army, in that same place** where we had first pitched our tents against the time [*in preparation for the time*] that the Lamanites should come out to battle.

18 And it came to pass that **the Lamanites did come out with their numerous army against us.** And when they had come and were about to fall upon us with the sword, **I caused that my men, those who were with me, should retreat into the wilderness.**

19 And it came to pass that **the Lamanites did follow after us with great speed**, for they were exceedingly desirous to overtake us **that they might slay us**; therefore they did follow us into the wilderness; and **we did pass by in the midst of Gid and Teomner, insomuch that they were not discovered by the Lamanites.**

20 And it came to pass that **when the Lamanites had passed by**, or when the army had passed by, **Gid and Teomner did rise up from their secret places, and did cut off the spies of the Lamanites that they should not return to the city.**

21 And it came to pass that **when they had cut them off, they ran to the city and fell upon the guards who were left to guard the city, insomuch that they did destroy them and did take possession of the city.**

22 Now **this was done because the Lamanites did suffer** [*allow*] **their whole army, save** [*except*] **a few guards only, to be led away into the wilderness.**

23 And it came to pass that **Gid and Teomner by this means had obtained possession of their strongholds**. And it came to pass that

we took our course, after having traveled much in the wilderness towards the land of Zarahemla [*the headquarters of Nephite territory*].

24 And **when the Lamanites saw that they were marching towards the land of Zarahemla, they were exceedingly afraid**, lest there was a plan laid to lead them on to destruction; therefore **they began to retreat** into the wilderness again, yea, even back by the same way which they had come.

25 And behold, **it was night and they did pitch their tents**, for the chief captains of the Lamanites had supposed that the Nephites were weary because of their march; and supposing that they had driven their whole army therefore **they took no thought concerning the city of Manti** [*which was now possessed by Nephite soldiers under the direction of Gid and Teomner*].

26 Now it came to pass that **when it was night, I caused that my men should not sleep, but that they should march forward by another way towards the land of Manti.**

27 And because of this our march in the night-time, behold, **on the morrow we were beyond the Lamanites, insomuch that we did arrive before them at the city of Manti.**

28 And thus it came to pass, that **by this stratagem we did take possession of the city of Manti without the shedding of blood**.

29 And it came to pass that **when the armies of the Lamanites did arrive near the city, and saw that we were prepared to meet them, they were astonished exceedingly and struck with great fear, insomuch that they did flee into the wilderness.**

30 Yea, and it came to pass that the armies of the Lamanites did flee out of all this quarter of the land. **But behold, they have carried with them many women and children out of the land.**

By this time, Helaman and the other Nephite captains, with their soldiers, have succeeded in taking back all the Nephite cities in that area, which had been taken by the Lamanites. They have a great concern, though, for the Nephite prisoners that had been taken by the Lamanites as they retreated.

31 And **those cities which had been taken by the Lamanites, all of them are at this period of time in our possession**; and our fathers and our women and our children are returning to their homes, **all save it be those who have been taken prisoners and carried off by the Lamanites.**

32 But behold, **our armies are small** to maintain so great a number of cities and so great possessions.

As mentioned at the beginning of these "war chapters," in Alma 43, there are many messages in this part of the Book of Mormon for us in our day, as we go through the ever-present plagues of war, terrorism, and troubles that, according to

D&C 84:97, will not cease until the Second Coming of Christ. One of these messages is found in verse 33, next; namely, do not stop trusting in God, no matter what.

33 But behold, **we trust in our God** who has given us victory over those lands, insomuch that we have obtained those cities and those lands, which were our own.

In verse 9 of this chapter, Helaman was wondering why he and his armies did not get more help from their government. Next, in verse 34, he expresses this concern again. In verse 35, he wonders if perhaps Moroni has needed all the extra help available from the government. If so, Helaman does not wish to complain. However, in verse 36, he brings up the possibility that there may be trouble with the government. There is, and Moroni will use his no-nonsense approach to it in chapters 59 through 62.

34 Now **we do not know the cause that the government does not grant us more strength**; neither do those men who came up unto us know why we have not received greater strength.

35 Behold, **we do not know but what ye are unsuccessful, and ye have drawn away the forces into that quarter of the land; if so, we do not desire to murmur.**

36 And **if it is not so, behold, we fear that there is some faction** [*split*] **in the government**, that they do not send more men to our assistance; for **we know that they are more numerous than that which they have sent** [*we know that they could send many more soldiers to help us than they have so far*].

37 But, behold, **it mattereth not—we trust God will deliver us, notwithstanding** [*in spite of*] **the weakness of our armies, yea, and deliver us out of the hands of our enemies.**

38 Behold, **this is the twenty and ninth year, in the latter end**, and we are in the possession of our lands; and the Lamanites have fled to the land of Nephi [*the land that Nephi and his followers settled (see 2 Nephi 5:1–8) after Laman and Lemuel and their followers threatened to kill Nephi. Later, the Lamanites took over the land of Nephi after Mosiah I and his people fled from them (see Omni 1:12–14)*].

39 And **those sons of the people of Ammon** [*the two thousand and sixty stripling soldiers*], **of whom I have so highly spoken, are with me in the city of Manti**; and **the Lord had supported them, yea, and kept them from falling by the sword, insomuch that even one soul has not been slain.**

Helaman's stripling soldiers are indeed role models for all of us, as they remain true to God no matter what. Helaman summarizes some of their attributes next.

40 But behold, they have received many wounds; nevertheless **they stand fast in that liberty wherewith God has made them free; and they are strict to remember the Lord their God from day to day; yea, they do observe to keep his statutes** [*laws*], **and his judgments,**

and his commandments continually; and their faith is strong in the prophecies concerning that which is to come.

The phrase "that which is to come," in verse 40, above, is also used in Mosiah 4:11, in reference to Christ's birth and earthly mission (see Mosiah 3:5). Therefore, we understand that the strength of Helaman's stripling soldiers comes from their faith in Christ, who will be born to Mary in Bethlehem in sixty-two years from this time.

Helaman now finishes his epistle (letter) to his great friend Captain Moroni. We can feel his tender feelings for this humble and powerful leader.

41 And now, **my beloved brother, Moroni, may the Lord our God, who has redeemed us and made us free, keep you continually in his presence**; yea, and may he favor this people, even that ye may have success in obtaining the possession of all that which the Lamanites have taken from us, which was for our support. And now, behold, **I close mine epistle. I am Helaman, the son of Alma.**

ALMA 59

This is a rather short chapter, but it contains a very important message. While Moroni, Helaman, and their faithful soldiers have been risking their lives and giving their lives in defense of their country's freedom, many Nephite citizens have been sinking into sin and wickedness. Sin is the most dangerous "enemy" of all. And as we continue, we will see that these great commanders and their men are afraid that the behavior of the citizens of their country will stop the blessings of God, and as a result, their sacrifices will be in vain, in other words, will not do any good.

1 NOW it came to pass **in the thirtieth year** of the reign of the judges over the people of Nephi [*these wars have been going on for about twelve years now*], **after Moroni had received and had read Helaman's epistle, he was exceedingly rejoiced** because of the welfare, yea, the exceeding success which Helaman had had, in obtaining those lands which were lost.

2 Yea, and **he did make it known unto all his people**, in all the land round about in that part where he was, that they might rejoice also.

Captain Moroni had read of Helaman's concern about not getting enough reinforcements and supplies from the central government of the nation (Alma 58:34–36), so he begins doing something about it next, in verse 3.

3 And it came to pass that **he immediately sent an epistle** [*a letter*] **to Pahoran** [*the chief judge or president of the Nephite nation*], **desiring that he should cause men to be gathered together to strengthen Helaman, or the armies of Helaman**, insomuch that he might with ease maintain that part of the land which he had been so miraculously prospered [*blessed*] in regaining.

After having written to Pahoran, Moroni turns his attention to recapturing the rest of the Nephite cities and territory that the Lamanites had taken.

4 And it came to pass when **Moroni** had sent this epistle to the land of Zarahemla, he **began again to lay a plan that he might obtain the remainder of those possessions and cities which the Lamanites had taken from them**.

5 And it came to pass that **while Moroni was thus making preparations** to go against the Lamanites to battle, behold, **the people of Nephihah**, who were gathered together from the city of Moroni and the city of Lehi and the city of Morianton, **were attacked by the Lamanites.**

6 Yea, even **those who had been compelled to flee from the land of Manti, and from the land round about, had come over and joined the Lamanites in this part of the land.**

7 And thus being exceedingly numerous, yea, and receiving strength from day to day, by the command of Ammoron **they came forth against the people of Nephihah, and they did begin to slay them with an exceedingly great slaughter.**

8 And their armies were so numerous that **the remainder of the people of Nephihah were obliged to flee before them** [*had to run for their lives*]**; and they came even and joined the army of Moroni.**

Moroni had thought that his government would send plenty of reinforcements and supplies for the city of Nephihah to be easily protected from Lamanite invaders. They didn't. As we continue, we sense that Moroni is beginning to seriously suspect that things are not right at home with his government.

9 And now as **Moroni had supposed that there should be men sent to the city of Nephihah,** to the assistance of the people to maintain that city, and knowing that it was easier to keep the city from falling into the hands of the Lamanites than to retake it from them, **he supposed that they would easily maintain that city.**

10 **Therefore he retained all his force to maintain those places which he had recovered** [*from the Lamanites*].

11 And now, **when Moroni saw that the city of Nephihah was lost he was exceedingly sorrowful** [*very sad*]**, and began to doubt, because of the wickedness of the people** [*the Nephites*]**, whether they should not fall into the hands of their brethren** [*the Lamanites*]**.**

12 Now this was the case with **all his chief captains.** They **doubted and marveled also because of the wickedness of the people**, and this because of the success of the Lamanites over them.

13 And it came to pass that **Moroni was angry with the government, because of their indifference** [*because

they didn't seem to care] **concerning the freedom of their country.**

The indifference spoken of at the end of verse 13, above, is a very serious issue in many democracies today, and Mormon no doubt included this verse as a warning to us.

ALMA 60

By now you are well enough acquainted with Moroni to know that when action is needed, he takes action. First, in this chapter, he will write to Pahoran (the president of the Nephite nation) and express in no uncertain terms his concerns about the condition in the government which has led to lack of support for his armies. In chapter 61, Pahoran, who is a good man, will reply and explain what has happened back home. In chapter 62, Moroni will take strong, needed action.

Moroni's letter skillfully comes straight to the point, then builds to a powerful conclusion.

1 AND it came to pass that **he** [*Moroni*] **wrote again to the governor of the land, who was Pahoran**, and these are the words which he wrote, **saying**: Behold, **I direct mine epistle** [*letter*] **to Pahoran**, in the city of Zarahemla, who is the chief judge and the governor over the land, **and also to all those who have been chosen by this people to govern and manage the affairs of this war**.

2 For behold, **I have somewhat to say unto them by the way of condemnation** [*strong criticism*]; for behold, **ye yourselves know that ye have been appointed to gather together men, and arm them** with swords, and with cimeters, and all manner of weapons of war of every kind, **and send forth against the Lamanites**, in whatsoever parts they should come into our land.

3 And now behold, I say unto you that **myself, and also my men, and also Helaman and his men, have suffered exceedingly great sufferings**; yea, even hunger, thirst, and fatigue, and all manner of afflictions of every kind.

4 But behold, **were this all we had suffered we would not murmur nor complain**.

5 But behold, **great has been the slaughter among our people; yea, thousands have fallen by the sword, while it might have otherwise been if ye had rendered** [*given*] **unto our armies sufficient strength and succor** [*support, aid*] **for them.** Yea, **great has been your neglect towards us.**

6 And now behold, **we desire to know the cause of this exceedingly** [*very, very*] **great neglect**; yea, we desire to know **the cause of your thoughtless state.**

7 **Can you think to sit upon your thrones in a state of thoughtless stupor** [*lack of thinking, complete lack of awareness*], **while your enemies are spreading the work of death around you?** Yea, while they are murdering thousands of your brethren—

8 Yea, even **they who have looked up to you for protection** [*in other words, my armies*], **yea** [*indeed*], **have placed you in a situation that ye might have succored** [*helped*] **them**, yea, **ye might have sent armies unto them, to have strengthened them, and have saved thousands of them from falling by the sword.**

9 But behold, **this is not all—ye have withheld** [*held back*] **your provisions** [*supplies*] **from them**, insomuch that many have fought and bled out their lives because of their great desires which they had for the welfare of this people; yea, and **this they have done when they were about to perish with hunger, because of your exceedingly great neglect towards them**.

10 And now, **my beloved brethren—for ye ought to be beloved**; yea, and **ye ought to have stirred yourselves more diligently for the welfare and the freedom of this people**; but behold, **ye have neglected them insomuch that the blood of thousands shall come upon your heads for vengeance**; yea, for known unto God were all their cries, and all their sufferings [*you will be in big trouble when you meet God*]—

11 Behold, **could ye suppose that ye could sit upon your thrones, and because of the exceeding goodness of God ye could do nothing and he would deliver you** [*save you from our enemies*]**?** Behold, if ye have supposed this ye have supposed in vain [*it won't do you any good to suppose this*].

12 **Do ye suppose that, because so many of your brethren have been killed it is because of their wickedness? I say unto you, if ye have supposed this ye have supposed in vain**; for I say unto you, **there are many who have fallen by the sword; and behold it is to your condemnation** [*damnation; deep trouble with God*];

Next, Moroni gives us major insight into the suffering of righteous people caused by the wicked. It has to do with the law of witnesses.

13 For **the Lord suffereth the righteous to be slain that his justice and judgment may come upon the wicked**; therefore ye need not suppose that the righteous are lost because they are slain; but behold, **they do enter into the rest** [*heaven*] **of the Lord their God**.

14 And now behold, I say unto you, **I fear exceedingly that the judgments** [*punishments*] **of God will come upon this people, because of their exceeding slothfulness** [*lack of action*], **yea, even the slothfulness of our government, and their exceedingly great neglect towards their brethren, yea, towards those who have been slain.**

15 For **were it not for the wickedness which first commenced at our head** [*in our government leaders*], **we could have withstood** [*succeeded against*] **our enemies that they could have gained no power over us**.

16 Yea, **had it not been for the war**

which broke out among ourselves; yea, **were it not for these king-men** [*the Nephites who wanted to have a king again, see Alma 51*], who caused so much bloodshed among ourselves; yea, at the time we were contending [*fighting*] among ourselves, if we had united our strength as we hitherto have done; yea, **had it not been for the desire of power and authority which those king-men had over us**; had they been true to the cause of our freedom, and united with us, and gone forth against our enemies, instead of taking up their swords against us, which was the cause of so much bloodshed among ourselves; yea, if we had gone forth against them in the strength of the Lord, **we should have dispersed** [*won against*] **our enemies, for it would have been done, according to the fulfilling of his word.**

Moroni is giving us a major message here, namely, that the only way a great nation, which was founded upon the laws of God, as was the case with the Nephites (see Mosiah 29), can be destroyed is through the corruption and wickedness of its citizens. In other words, such a nation cannot be destroyed by outside enemies while the people are righteous. It can only fall when the people themselves choose wickedness.

17 But behold, **now the Lamanites are coming upon us,** taking possession of our lands, and they are murdering our people with the sword, yea, our women and our children, and also carrying them away captive, causing them that they should suffer all manner of afflictions, **and this because of the great wickedness of those who are seeking for power and authority, yea, even those king-men.**

Moroni is very direct when the occasion demands it.

18 **But why should I say much concerning this matter? For we know not but what ye yourselves are seeking for authority. We know not but what ye are also traitors to your country.**

19 **Or is it that ye have neglected us because ye are in the heart of our country and ye are surrounded by security**, that ye do not cause food to be sent unto us, and also men to strengthen our armies?

In Biblical culture, something repeated three times is the most, the maximum, the best, the worst, whatever the topic being discussed is. In verse 20, next, Moroni uses the word "forgotten" three times. This is an extra strong warning in the culture of these people.

20 Have ye **forgotten** the commandments of the Lord your God? Yea, have ye **forgotten** the captivity of our fathers? Have ye **forgotten** the many times we have been delivered out of the hands of our enemies?

21 Or **do ye suppose that the Lord will still deliver us** [*save us from our enemies*], **while we sit upon our thrones and do not make use of the means which the Lord has provided for us?**

In verses 22 and 23, you will also notice that Moroni uses the word "sit" three times. Again, this is the strongest emphasis in his culture.

22 Yea, will ye **sit in idleness** while ye are surrounded with thousands of those, yea, and tens of thousands, who do also **sit in idleness**, while there are thousands round about in the borders of the land who are falling by the sword, yea, wounded and bleeding?

23 Do ye suppose that God will look upon you as guiltless while ye **sit still** and behold these things? Behold I say unto you, Nay. Now **I would that ye should remember that God has said that the inward vessel shall be cleansed first, and then shall the outer vessel be cleansed also.**

Moroni gives a very strong warning and promise of action in the next verses.

24 And now, **except** [*unless*] **ye do repent of that which ye have done, and begin to be up and doing, and send forth food and men unto us**, and also unto Helaman, that he may support those parts of our country which he has regained, and that we may also recover the remainder of our possessions in these parts, behold **it will be expedient** [*it will become necessary*] **that we contend** [*fight*] **no more with the Lamanites until we have first cleansed our inward vessel, yea, even the great head of our government** [*our government leaders*]**.**

25 And **except ye grant mine epistle** [*give me what I'm asking*]**, and come out and show unto me a true spirit of freedom, and strive to strengthen and fortify our armies**, and grant unto them food for their support, behold **I will leave a part of my freemen to maintain this part of our land**, and **I will leave the strength and the blessings of God upon them**, that none other power can operate against them—

26 And **this because of their exceeding faith, and their patience in their tribulations** [*in their troubles*]—

27 And **I will come unto you, and if there be any among you that has a desire for freedom, yea, if there be even a spark of freedom remaining, behold I will stir up insurrections** [*uprisings, rebellions*] **among you, even until those who have desires to usurp** [*grab, take*] **power and authority shall become extinct.**

28 Yea, behold **I do not fear your power nor your authority, but it is my God whom I fear**; and it is according to his commandments that I do take my sword to defend the cause of my country, and **it is because of your iniquity that we have suffered so much loss.**

29 Behold it is time, yea, the time is now at hand, that **except ye do bestir yourselves** [*get moving*] **in the defence of your country and your little ones, the sword of justice doth hang over you; yea,**

and it shall fall upon you and visit you even to your utter destruction.

30 Behold, **I wait for assistance from you; and, except ye do administer unto** [*take action for*] **our relief, behold, I come unto you, even in the land of Zarahemla, and smite you with the sword, insomuch that ye can have no more power to impede** [*stop*] **the progress of this people in the cause of our freedom.**

31 For behold, **the Lord will not suffer** [*permit*] **that ye shall live and wax** [*grow*] **strong in your iniquities to destroy his righteous people.**

32 Behold, **can you suppose that the Lord will spare you and come out in judgment against the Lamanites**, when it is the tradition of their fathers that has caused their hatred, yea, and it has been redoubled by those who have dissented from us, **while your iniquity** [*sin and wickedness*] **is for the cause of** [*is because of*] **your love of glory and the vain** [*worthless*] **things of the world**?

33 **Ye know that ye do transgress the laws of God, and ye do know that ye do trample them under your feet. Behold, the Lord saith unto me: If those whom ye have appointed your governors do not repent of their sins and iniquities, ye shall go up to battle against them.**

34 And now behold, I, Moroni, am constrained, according to the covenant which I have made to keep the commandments of my God; therefore **I would that ye should adhere to** [*obey*] **the word of God, and send speedily unto me of your provisions** [*supplies*] **and of your men, and also to Helaman.**

35 And behold, **if ye will not do this I come unto you speedily**; for behold, God will not suffer that we should perish with hunger; therefore he will give unto us of your food, even if it must be by the sword. **Now see that ye fulfil the word of God**.

Next, Moroni reassures the government officials at home that his motives are not selfish.

36 Behold, **I am Moroni**, your chief captain. **I seek not for power, but to pull it down. I seek not for honor of the world, but for the glory of my God, and the freedom and welfare of my country.** And thus I close mine epistle.

ALMA 61

As mentioned before, Pahoran, the Nephite nation's leader, is a righteous man. His national capitol, the city of Zarahemla, has been taken over by rebels, and he and others have been forced to flee to the land of Gideon. We feel the greatness of Pahoran as we read his tender reply and bold invitation to Moroni to bring troops and join him in ridding the government of the king-men who are destroying it and refusing to send help and supplies to Moroni and his armies.

1 BEHOLD, now it came to pass that **soon after Moroni had sent his epistle** [*letter*] **unto the chief governor, he received an epistle from Pahoran, the chief governor.** And these are the words which he received:

2 **I, Pahoran**, who am the chief governor of this land, do send these words unto Moroni, the chief captain over the army. Behold, I say unto you, Moroni, that I **do not joy in your great afflictions, yea, it grieves** [*pains*] **my soul**.

> Perhaps it is a bit strong to say, but just as in the case of the people in verse 3, next, there are those in our nation who take pleasure when our military men and women meet disaster and death. They are of the same mean spirit and philosophy of the king-men who have caused Pahoran's government so much grief. They shortsightedly abuse and treat badly the very freedoms that allow them to disagree with their government, as they mock those who are putting their lives on the line to protect these freedoms.

3 But behold, **there are those** [*the king-men*] **who do joy in your afflictions,** yea, insomuch that **they have risen up in rebellion against me**, and **also those of my people who are freemen**, yea, and those who have risen up [*rebelled against us*] are exceedingly numerous [*there are lots of them*].

4 And **it is those who have sought to take away the judgment-seat from me that have been the cause of this great iniquity**; for they have used great flattery, and they have led away the hearts of many people, which will be the cause of sore affliction [*very bad trouble*] among us; **they have withheld our provisions, and have daunted** [*intimidated; bullied*] **our freemen that they have not come unto you.**

5 And behold, **they have driven me out** before them, and **I have fled to the land of Gideon, with as many men as it were possible that I could get.**

6 And behold, I have sent a proclamation throughout this part of the land; and behold, **they** [*the freemen, see Alma 51:6*] **are flocking to us daily, to their arms, in the defence of their country and their freedom**, and to avenge our wrongs.

7 And **they have come unto us, insomuch that those who have risen up in rebellion against us** are set at defiance, yea, insomuch that they **do fear us and durst not come out against us to battle**.

> It is amazing how fast those who wanted a different form of government gained control in Zarahemla. Perhaps we are being warned by the Book of Mormon that rapid disintegration of sound government can happen in our day too.

8 **They have got possession of the land, or the city, of Zarahemla; they have appointed a king over**

them, and he hath written unto the king of the Lamanites, in the which he hath joined an alliance with him; in the which alliance he hath agreed to maintain the city of Zarahemla, which maintenance he supposeth will enable the Lamanites to conquer the remainder of the land, and he shall be placed king over this people when they shall be conquered under the Lamanites. [*These were Amalickiah's goals when he first became king of the Lamanites by fraud and deceit; see Alma 48:2. Now, his brother, Ammoron, king of the Lamanites, feels he is getting close to this goal.*]

Next, we see the greatness of Pahoran's soul as he responds to Moroni's strong words.

9 And now, **in your epistle you have censured** [*strongly criticized*] **me**, but **it mattereth not; I am not angry, but do rejoice in the greatness of your heart.** I, Pahoran, do not seek for power, save only to retain my judgment-seat that I may preserve the rights and the liberty of my people. My soul standeth fast in that liberty in the which God hath made us free.

10 And now, behold, **we will resist wickedness even unto bloodshed** [*even if we have to give our lives*]**. We would not shed the blood of the Lamanites if they would stay in their own land.**

11 **We would not shed the blood of our brethren** [*the king-men*] **if they would not rise up in rebellion and take the sword against** [*try to kill us*] **us.**

12 **We would subject ourselves to the yoke of bondage** [*slavery*] **if it were requisite** [*required*] with the justice of God, or if he should command us so to do.

13 But behold **he doth not command us that we shall subject ourselves to our enemies, but that we should put our trust in him, and he will deliver us.**

There are inspired, important guidelines in verse 14, next, for god-fearing people with respect to if and when to go to war.

14 Therefore, my beloved brother, Moroni, let us resist evil, and **whatsoever evil we cannot resist with our words, yea, such as rebellions and dissensions, let us resist them with our swords, that we may retain our freedom**, that we may rejoice in the great privilege of our church, and in the cause of our Redeemer and our God.

15 Therefore, **come unto me speedily with a few of your men,** and leave the remainder in the charge of Lehi and Teancum; give unto them power to conduct the war in that part of the land, according to **the Spirit of God**, which **is also the spirit of freedom** which is in them.

16 Behold **I have sent a few provisions** [*supplies*] **unto them**, that they may not perish until ye can come unto me.

17 **Gather together whatsoever force ye can upon your march**

hither [*here*], **and we will go speedily against those dissenters** [*those who have rebelled against our government*], **in the strength of our God according to the faith which is in us.**

18 And we will take possession of the city of Zarahemla, that we may obtain more food to send forth unto Lehi and Teancum; yea, **we will go forth against them in the strength of the Lord** [*with the blessings of the Lord*], and we will put an end to this great iniquity [*wickedness*].

Next, Pahoran confides in Moroni that he had been a bit worried as to whether it was justifiable to go to war against the citizens of his own country. But Moroni's words in his letter to Pahoran took care of this worry, as stated in verse 20.

19 And now, Moroni, I do joy in receiving your epistle, for **I was somewhat worried concerning what we should do, whether it should be just in us** [*righteous; okay with God*] **to go against our brethren** [*our own citizens*].

20 **But ye have said, except** [*unless*] **they repent the Lord hath commanded you that ye should go against them.**

21 See that ye strengthen Lehi and Teancum in the Lord; tell them to fear not, for **God will deliver them, yea, and also all those who stand fast in that liberty wherewith God hath made them free.** And now I close mine epistle to my beloved brother, Moroni.

ALMA 62

As you know, from the chapters you've already read, the Nephite government has become so corrupt by this time that the Nephite democracy is in a big mess. It appears that the majority of citizens have become so wicked that they can't stand to have good and honorable people in responsible government positions. Therefore, they have driven Pahoran and others out and replaced them with a king (Alma 61:8). The king's name is Pachus (Alma 62:6).

As you also know, Captain Moroni is a man of God and a man of action. Times of serious trouble require direct action. We will watch and be taught by Moroni's actions.

1 AND now it came to pass that **when Moroni had received this epistle** [*letter from Pahoran, the ousted chief judge of the Nephites*] **his heart did take courage** [*he was very encouraged*], **and was filled with exceedingly great joy because of the faithfulness of Pahoran**, that he was not also a traitor to the freedom and cause of his country [*like the king-men were*].

2 **But he did also mourn exceedingly** [*he was very sad*] **because of the iniquity** [*wickedness*] **of those who had driven Pahoran from the judgment-seat**, yea, in fine [*in summary*] **because of those who had rebelled against their country and also their God.**

3 And it came to pass that **Moroni took a small number of men,**

according to the desire of Pahoran, and **gave Lehi and Teancum command over the remainder of his army, and took his march towards the land of Gideon** [*where Pahoran and the other freemen had gathered*].

4 And **he did raise the standard of liberty** [*the "title of liberty;" see Alma 46:36*] in whatsoever [*whatever*] place he did enter, **and gained whatsoever force** [*as many followers as*] **he could in all his march towards the land of Gideon**.

It is comforting to know that there are still thousands of Nephites who want a democracy and who want to uphold high standards in government. To have such a government requires willingness to sacrifice on the part of the people, and we see this in verse 5, next.

5 And it came to pass that **thousands did flock unto his standard**, and did take up their swords in the defence of their freedom, that they might not come into bondage.

6 And thus, **when Moroni had gathered together whatsoever men he could in all his march, he came to the land of Gideon; and uniting his forces with those of Pahoran they became** exceedingly strong, even **stronger than the men of Pachus, who was the king of those dissenters** who had driven the freemen out of the land of Zarahemla and had taken possession of the land.

7 And it came to pass that **Moroni and Pahoran went down with their armies into the land of Zarahemla**, and went forth against the city, **and did meet the men of Pachus, insomuch that they did come to battle.**

One problem that always follows apostasy from the gospel is lack of decisiveness—in other words, lack of ability to make a decision and then stick with it. Satan's way is often to keep people in an indecisive mode regarding important issues. People who have few or no firm standards themselves have difficulty supporting decisive actions on a national level by leaders who support high standards.

Perhaps one of the major messages for us in this chapter is that leaders who have wisdom and high standards themselves must sometimes take very decisive action, rather than continuing in endless dialogue and debate on national issues. Moroni and Pahoran are examples of such leaders.

8 And behold, **Pachus was slain and his men were taken prisoners, and Pahoran was restored to his judgment-seat.**

9 And **the men of Pachus received their trial, according to the law, and also those king-men who had been taken and cast into prison; and they were executed according to the law; yea, those men of Pachus and those king-men, whosoever would not take up arms in the defence of their country, but would fight against it, were put to death.**

Next, Mormon points out what he wants us to learn from what he has just told us.

10 And **thus it became expedient**

[*essential, necessary*] **that this law should be strictly observed for the safety of their country**; yea, and whosoever was found denying their freedom was speedily executed according to the law.

11 And **thus ended the thirtieth year** of the reign of the judges over the people of Nephi; **Moroni and Pahoran having restored peace to the land of Zarahemla, among their own people**, having inflicted death upon all those who were not true to the cause of freedom.

Having taken definite and swift action against the internal wickedness and corruption in the government and nation, Moroni now turns his attention to the needs of Helaman and others who are still defending the nation against external dangers from the Lamanites.

By the way, it has now been nearly 31 years since righteous king Mosiah II changed the Nephites' form of government from having a king to having a type of democracy with a chief judge, elected by the people, at the head of their government.

12 And it came to pass **in the commencement of the thirty and first year** of the reign of the judges over the people of Nephi, **Moroni immediately caused that provisions should be sent, and also an army of six thousand men should be sent unto Helaman**, to assist him in preserving that part of the land.

13 And **he also caused that an army of six thousand men, with a sufficient quantity of food, should be sent to the armies of Lehi and Teancum.** And it came to pass that this was done **to fortify the land against the Lamanites**.

14 And it came to pass that **Moroni and Pahoran, leaving a large body of men in the land of Zarahemla, took their march with a large body of men towards the land of Nephihah, being determined to overthrow the Lamanites in that city.**

15 And it came to pass that **as they were marching towards the land, they took a large body of men of the Lamanites**, and slew many of them, and took their provisions and their weapons of war.

Once again, we see that all these years of intense battle and the horrors of war have not taken mercy from Moroni's heart. Next, he shows mercy to thousands of Lamanite soldiers if they will promise to fight no more against the Nephites.

It is interesting that this can be symbolic of the laws of mercy and justice in action. Normally, the law of justice would demand that the Lamanite soldiers pay for their actions against the Nephites. However, Moroni gave them an opportunity to use their agency to obtain mercy. In order to obtain it, they had to make a covenant, a very serious promise, that they would permanently change from their former lifestyle of sin and wickedness against the Nephites, or people of God. In choosing mercy, these Lamanites chose freedom and went to join other Lamanite converts, who were the people of Ammon. Thus, because of their choice of mercy, they were allowed to live among the Saints of God.

16 And it came to pass **after they had taken them, they caused them to enter into a covenant** that they would **no more take up their weapons of war against the Nephites**.

17 And **when they had entered into this covenant they sent them to dwell with the people of Ammon**, and they were in number **about four thousand** who had not been slain.

Next, Moroni and Pahoran turn their attention to freeing the city of Nephihah from the Lamanites. Again, careful strategy is required to avoid loss of life among the Nephite soldiers. This is quite a contrast compared to Amalickiah, the former king of the Lamanites, who "did care not for the blood of his people" (Alma 49:10).

18 And it came to pass that when they had sent them away **they pursued their march towards the land of Nephihah**. And it came to pass that **when they had come to the city of Nephihah**, they did pitch their tents in the plains of Nephihah, which is near the city of Nephihah.

19 Now **Moroni was desirous** [*wanted*] **that the Lamanites should come out to battle against them, upon the plains**; but the Lamanites, knowing of their exceedingly great courage, and beholding the greatness of their numbers [*seeing how many soldiers the Nephites had*], therefore they durst not [*did not dare*] come out against them; therefore **they did not come to battle in that day.**

20 And when the night came, **Moroni went forth in the darkness of the night, and came upon the top of the wall to spy** out in what part of the city the Lamanites did camp with their army.

21 And it came to pass that they were on the east, by the entrance; and they were all asleep. And now **Moroni returned to his army, and caused that they should prepare in haste** [*quickly*] strong cords [*ropes*] and ladders, to be let down from the top of the wall into the inner part of the wall.

22 And it came to pass that **Moroni caused that his men should march forth and come upon the top of the wall, and let themselves down into that part of the city,** yea, even on the west, **where the Lamanites did not camp with their armies.**

23 And it came to pass that **they were all let down into the city by night**, by the means of their strong cords and their ladders; thus when the morning came they were all within the walls of the city.

24 And now, **when the Lamanites awoke and saw that the armies of Moroni were within the walls, they were affrighted exceedingly, insomuch that they did flee** out by the pass.

25 And now **when Moroni saw that they were fleeing before him, he did cause that his men should march forth against them, and slew many, and surrounded many others, and took them prisoners;**

and the remainder of them fled into the land of Moroni, which was in the borders by the seashore.

26 **Thus had Moroni and Pahoran obtained the possession of the city of Nephihah without the loss of one soul** [*of his army*]; and there were many of the Lamanites who were slain.

Again, Moroni demonstrates mercy, as shown in verses 27–29, allowing the Lamanite prisoners to choose to enter a life of freedom, peace, and productivity.

27 Now it came to pass that **many of the Lamanites that were prisoners were desirous to join the people of Ammon and become a free people.**

28 And it came to pass that as many as were desirous, unto them **it was granted** according to their desires.

29 Therefore, **all the prisoners of the Lamanites did join the people of Ammon,** and did begin to labor exceedingly, **tilling** [*farming*] **the ground, raising all manner of** [*all kinds of*] **grain, and flocks and herds of every kind**; and thus were the Nephites relieved from a great burden; yea, insomuch that they were relieved from all the prisoners of the Lamanites. [*This is a great way to relieve the country from the burden of taking care of prisoners!*]

Moroni is a great example of one who does not stop until the job is finished.

30 Now it came to pass that **Moroni, after he had obtained possession of the city of Nephihah**, having taken many prisoners, which did reduce the armies of the Lamanites exceedingly [*very much*], and having regained many of the Nephites who had been taken prisoners, which did strengthen the army of Moroni exceedingly; therefore **Moroni went forth from the land of Nephihah to the land of Lehi.**

31 And it came to pass that **when the Lamanites saw that Moroni was coming against them, they were again frightened and fled** before the army of Moroni.

32 And it came to pass that **Moroni and his army did pursue them from city to city, until they were met by Lehi and Teancum; and the Lamanites fled** from Lehi and Teancum, even down upon the borders by the seashore, **until they came to the land of Moroni**.

Next, we meet Ammoron again, the apostate Nephite who took over as king of the Lamanites after his wicked brother, Amalickiah, was killed.

33 And **the armies of the Lamanites were all gathered together,** insomuch that they were all in one body **in the land of Moroni**. Now **Ammoron, the king of the Lamanites, was also with them.**

34 And it came to pass that **Moroni and Lehi and Teancum did encamp with their armies round about in the borders of the land of Moroni**, insomuch that [*so that*] the

Lamanites were encircled about in the borders by the wilderness on the south, and in the borders by the wilderness on the east.

Next, we lose a great man in the cause of freedom. Teancum, one of Moroni's most trusted military leaders, killed Amalickiah (Alma 51:34) and he will use the same approach to kill Amalickiah's wicked brother, Ammoron. He will again use a javelin.

35 And thus they did encamp for the night. For behold, **the Nephites and the Lamanites also were weary** [*tired*] because of the greatness of the march; **therefore they did not resolve upon any stratagem** [*plans to carry out*] **in the night-time, save it were** [*except for*] **Teancum**; for **he was exceedingly angry with Ammoron**, insomuch that **he considered** [*felt*] **that Ammoron, and Amalickiah his brother** [*who were both apostate Nephites, in other words, had both left God and the Nephites and become leaders of the Lamanites against the Nephites*], **had been the cause of this great and lasting war** between them and the Lamanites, which had been the cause of so much war and bloodshed, yea, and so much famine.

36 And it came to pass that **Teancum in his anger did go forth into the camp of the Lamanites**, and did let himself down over the walls of the city. And he went forth with a cord [*rope*], from place to place, insomuch that **he did find the king; and he did cast a javelin at him, which did pierce him near the heart. But behold, the king did awaken his servants before he died, insomuch that they did pursue Teancum, and slew** [*killed*] **him**.

37 Now it came to pass that **when Lehi and Moroni knew that Teancum was dead they were exceedingly sorrowful**; for behold, he had been a man who had fought valiantly for his country, yea, a true friend to liberty; and he had suffered very many exceedingly sore afflictions. But behold, he was dead, and had gone the way of all the earth.

38 Now it came to pass that **Moroni marched forth on the morrow, and came upon the Lamanites, insomuch that they did slay them with a great slaughter; and they did drive them out of the land; and they did flee, even that they did not return at that time against the Nephites.**

39 And **thus ended the thirty and first year** of the reign of the judges over the people of Nephi; and thus they had had wars, and bloodsheds, and famine, and affliction, for the space of many years [*about fourteen years*].

Next, Mormon teaches us that a few righteous people can keep a nation from total destruction.

40 And **there had been murders, and contentions, and dissensions** [*rebellions*], **and all manner of iniquity** [*wickedness*] **among the**

people of Nephi; nevertheless for the righteous' sake, yea, because of the prayers of the righteous, they were spared.

Next, we see that people react and respond differently to times of war and stress. Some become hardened and some become softer and kinder. Personal humility seems to be the determining factor.

41 But behold, because of the exceedingly great length of the war between the Nephites and the Lamanites **many had become hardened**, because of the exceedingly great length of the war; and **many were softened** because of their afflictions, insomuch that **they did humble themselves before God, even in the depth of humility.**

The war is over; the stability of the government has been restored; and Captain Moroni and Helaman can now return home.

42 And it came to pass that after **Moroni** had fortified those parts of the land which were most exposed to the Lamanites, until they were sufficiently strong, he **returned to the city of Zarahemla**; and also **Helaman returned to the place of his inheritance**; and there was once more **peace established among the people of Nephi**.

Moroni will now turn the position of commander in chief of the Nephite armies over to his son, Moronihah.

43 And **Moroni yielded up the command of his armies into the hands of his son**, whose name was **Moronihah**; and **he retired to his own house that he might spend the remainder of his days in peace**.

44 And **Pahoran did return to his judgment-seat**; and **Helaman did take upon him again to preach unto the people the word of God**; for because of so many wars and contentions it had become expedient [*necessary*] that a regulation should be made again in the church [*the Church needed to be strengthened and set in order again*].

45 Therefore, **Helaman and his brethren went forth, and did declare the word of God with much power unto the convincing of many people of their wickedness, which did cause them to repent of their sins and to be baptized unto the Lord their God.**

46 And it came to pass that **they did establish again the church of God, throughout all the land.**

47 Yea, and **regulations were made concerning the law. And their judges, and their chief judges were chosen**.

Next, Mormon reviews with us how individuals as well as nations can remain righteous under conditions of prosperity where things go very well for them and they get rich.

48 And **the people of Nephi began to prosper again** in the land, and began to multiply [*had families*] and to wax exceedingly strong again in the land. And **they began to grow exceedingly rich.**

49 But notwithstanding [*in spite of*] their riches, or their strength, or their prosperity, **they were not lifted up in** the **pride** of their eyes; **neither were they slow to remember the Lord their God**; but **they did humble themselves** exceedingly before him.

50 Yea, **they did remember how great things the Lord had done for them**, that he had delivered them from death, and from bonds, and from prisons, and from all manner of afflictions [*troubles and problems*] and he had delivered them out of the hands of their enemies.

51 And **they did pray unto the Lord their God continually**, insomuch that the Lord did bless them, according to his word, so that they did wax [*grow*] strong and prosper in the land.

52 And it came to pass that all these things were done. And **Helaman died**, in the thirty and fifth year of the reign of the judges over the people of Nephi.

ALMA 63

We are now coming to the end of the book of Alma. Basically, the book has covered from the first year of the reign of the judges (Alma 1:1) to the thirty-ninth year of the reign of the judges (Alma 63:10), or about thirty-nine years. We will be saying goodbye to Moroni and watching as some Nephites spread out to settle other lands.

First, Mormon reports that Shiblon, Alma's second son, takes over his brother Helaman's work as the record keeper for the Nephites (Alma 62:52).

1 AND it came to pass in the commencement of the thirty and sixth year of the reign of the judges over the people of Nephi, that **Shiblon took possession of those sacred things which had been delivered unto Helaman by Alma.**

2 And **he was a just** [*a righteous*] **man**, and **he did walk uprightly before God**; and he **did observe to do good continually, to keep the commandments of the Lord** his God; and also did his brother.

Next, Moroni dies at about age forty-two or forty-three. He was twenty-five years old when he was appointed to be commander-in-chief of all the Nephite armies (Alma 43:17) in the eighteenth year of the reign of the judges (Alma 43:4), and he died seventeen or eighteen years later, in the thirty-sixth year of the reign of the judges (Alma 63:3).

3 And it came to pass that **Moroni died** also. And **thus ended the thirty and sixth year** of the reign of the judges.

As mentioned previously, there was considerable out-migration and colonizing at this point among the Nephites.

4 And it came to pass that **in the thirty and seventh year of the reign of the judges, there was a large company of men, even** to the

amount of **five thousand and four hundred men, with their wives and their children, departed out of the land of Zarahemla into the land which was northward.**

We understand that Hagoth, mentioned next, led people to the islands of the South Pacific, and that the Polynesians are his descendants.

5 And it came to pass that **Hagoth**, he being an exceedingly curious man, therefore he went forth and **built him an exceedingly** [*very*] **large ship**, on the borders of the land Bountiful, by the land Desolation, **and launched it forth into the west sea**, by the narrow neck which led into the land northward.

6 And behold, there were **many of the Nephites who did enter therein and did sail forth** with much provisions, and also many women and children; and they took their course northward. And **thus ended the thirty and seventh year**.

Next, we see that Hagoth also sponsored other migrations to the north.

7 And in the thirty and eighth year, **this man** [*Hagoth*] **built other ships. And the first ship did also return, and many more people did enter into it; and they also took much provisions** [*many supplies*]**, and set out again to the land northward.**

8 And it came to pass that **they were never heard of more**. And we suppose that they were drowned in the depths of the sea. And it came to pass that **one other ship also did sail forth; and whither she did go we know not**.

9 And it came to pass that **in this year there were many people who went forth into the land northward**. And thus ended the thirty and eighth year.

10 And it came to pass in the thirty and ninth year of the reign of the judges, **Shiblon died** also, and **Corianton had gone forth to the land northward in a ship**, to carry forth provisions unto the people who had gone forth into that land.

Verse 11, next, sets the stage for the book of Helaman, which comes next in the Book of Mormon. It is the record kept by Helaman, the son of Helaman—in other words, Alma the Younger's grandson.

11 Therefore **it became expedient** [*necessary*] **for Shiblon to confer** [*give*] **those sacred things, before his death, upon the son of Helaman, who was called Helaman, being called after the name of his father.**

12 Now behold, **all those engravings** [*the scriptures and other records*] which were in the possession of Helaman **were written and sent forth among the children of men throughout all the land**, save [*except*] it were those parts which had been commanded by Alma should not go forth [*the specific records of the covenants and signs, etc., used by secret combinations; see Alma 37:27*].

13 Nevertheless, **these things were to be kept sacred, and handed down from one generation to another**; therefore, in this year, **they had been conferred upon Helaman, before the death of Shiblon.**

14 And it came to pass also **in this year that there were some dissenters** [*rebel Nephites*] **who had gone forth unto the Lamanites; and they were stirred up again to anger against the Nephites.**

15 And also **in this same year they came down with a numerous army to war against the people of Moronihah, or against the army of Moronihah, in the which they were beaten and driven back again to their own lands**, suffering great loss.

16 And **thus ended the thirty and ninth year** of the reign of the judges over the people of Nephi.

17 And **thus ended the account of Alma, and Helaman his son, and also Shiblon, who was his son.**

SOURCES

Anderson, Richard Lloyd. *Investigating the Book of Mormon Witnesses.* Salt Lake City: Shadow Mountain, 1989.

Authorized King James Version of the Bible. Salt Lake City: The Church of Jesus Christ of Latter-day Saints, 1979.

Book of Mormon Student Manual, Religion 121 and 122. Salt Lake City: The Church of Jesus Christ of Latter-day Saints, 1989.

Church History in the Fulness of Times, Religion 341–43. Salt Lake City: The Church of Jesus Christ of Latter-day Saints, 1980.

Collier, John. *The Indians of the Americas.* New York: W. W. Norton, 1947.

Dibble, Johnathan A. "Delivered by the Power of God: The American Revolution and Nephi's Prophecy." *Ensign,* Oct. 1987.

Doctrine and Covenants Student Manual, Religion 324 and 325. Salt Lake City: The Church of Jesus Christ of Latter-day Saints, 1981.

Holland, Jeffrey R. "'This Do in Remembrance of Me.'" *Ensign,* Nov. 1995.

Jacobs, Wilbur R. *The Frontier in American History.* Tuscon, Arizona: University of Arizona Press, 1986.

Jacobs, Wilbur R. "The Indian and the Frontier in American History—A Need for Revision." *Western Historical Quarterly.* Jan. 1973.

Journal of Discourses. 26 vols. London: Latter-day Saints' Book Depot., 1854–86.

Kimball, Spencer W. "Our Paths Have Met Again." *Ensign,* Dec. 1975.

Kimball, Spencer W. "The Blessings and Responsibilities of Womanhood." *Ensign,* Mar. 1976.

Kimball, Spencer W. *The Miracle of Forgiveness.* Salt Lake City: Bookcraft, 1969.

Latourette, Kenneth Scott. *A History of the Expansion of Christianity, The Great Century.* Vol. 4. New York: Harper and Brothers, 1941.

Library of Aboriginal American Literature. Edited by Daniel Garrison Brinton. 8 vols. Philadelphia: William F. Fell, 1890.

Ludlow, Daniel H. *A Companion to Your Study of The Book of Mormon.* Salt Lake City: Deseret Book, 1976.

Martin Luther edition of the German Bible, which Joseph Smith said was the most correct of any then available.

Maxwell, Neal A. "On Being a Light." Address delivered at the Salt Lake Institute of Religion, Jan. 2, 1974.

Maxwell, Neal A. "According to the Desire of [Our] Hearts." *Ensign*, Nov. 1996.

McConkie, Bruce R. *Millennial Messiah.* Salt Lake City: Deseret Book, 1983.

McConkie, Bruce R. *Mormon Doctrine.* 2nd ed. Salt Lake City: Bookcraft, 1966.

Moldenke, Harold and Alma Moldenke. *Plants of the Bible.* Mineola, New York: Dover Publications, 1986.

Nibley, Hugh. *Since Cumorah: The Book of Mormon in the Modern World.* Salt Lake City: Deseret Book, 1970.

Old Testament Student Manual, 1 Kings through Malachi, Religion 302. Salt Lake City: The Church of Jesus Christ of Latter-day Saints, 1981.

Petersen, Mark E. *The Great Prologue.* Salt Lake City: Deseret Book, 1976.

Reynolds, George and Janne M. Sjodahl. *Commentary on the Book of Mormon.* 7 vols. Salt Lake City: Deseret Press, 1976.

Richards, LeGrand. "Prophets and Prophecy." In Conference Report, Oct. 1975; or *Ensign*, Nov. 1975.

Richards, LeGrand. *Israel! Do You Know?* 4th ed. Salt Lake City: Shadow Mountain, 1990.

Smith, George Albert. In Conference Report, Apr. 1918.

Smith, Joseph. *History of The Church of Jesus Christ of Latter-day Saints.* Edited by B. H. Roberts. 2d ed. rev., 7 vols., Salt Lake City: The Church of Jesus Christ of Latter-day Saints, 1932–51.

Smith, Joseph. *Messenger and Advocate*, Apr. 1835.

Smith, Joseph. *Teachings of the Prophet Joseph Smith.* Selected and arranged by Joseph Fielding Smith. Salt Lake City: Deseret Book, 1976.

Smith, Joseph F., Anthon H. Lund, and John Henry Smith. First Presidency Statement. *Improvement Era*, Aug. 1916.

Smith, Joseph F., John R. Winder, and Anthon H. Lund. First Presidency Message. *Messages of the First Presidency of The Church of Jesus Christ of Latter-day Saints.* 6 vols. Compiled by James R. Clark. Salt Lake City: Bookcraft, 1965.

Smith, Joseph Fielding. *Answers to Gospel Questions.* Compiled by Joseph Fielding Smith. 5 vols. Salt Lake City: Deseret Book, 1957–66.

Smith, Joseph Fielding. *Church History and Modern Revelation.* 4 vols. Salt Lake City: Deseret Book, 1947.

Smith, Joseph Fielding. *Doctrines of Salvation.* Compiled by Bruce R. McConkie. 3 vols. Salt Lake City: Bookcraft, 1954–56.

Smith, Lucy Mack. *History of Joseph Smith by His Mother.* Salt Lake City: Stevens & Wallis, 1945.

Talmage, James E. *Articles of Faith.* Salt Lake City: Deseret Book, 1981.

"The Family: A Proclamation to the World." First Presidency and Council of the Twelve Apostles. *Family Guide Book.* Salt Lake City: Church of Jesus Christ of Latter-day Saints, 1995.

Wasserman, Jacob. *Columbus: Don Quixote of the Seas.* Translated by Eric Sutton. Boston: Little, Brown, and Co., 1930.

Young, Brigham. *Discourses of Brigham Young.* Compiled by John A. Widtsoe. Salt Lake City: Deseret Book, 1954.

NOTES

NOTES

NOTES

NOTES

NOTES

NOTES

NOTES

NOTES

NOTES

ABOUT THE AUTHOR

David J. Ridges taught for the Church Educational System for thirty-five years and has taught for several years at BYU Campus Education Week. He taught adult religion classes and Know Your Religion classes for BYU Continuing Education for many years. He has also served as a curriculum writer for Sunday School, seminary, and institute of religion manuals.

He has served in many callings in the Church, including Gospel Doctrine teacher, bishop, stake president, and patriarch. He and Sister Ridges served a full-time eighteen-month mission, training senior CES missionaries and helping coordinate their assignments throughout the world.

Brother Ridges and his wife, Janette, are the parents of six children and make their home in Springville, Utah.

Scan to visit

www.davidjridges.com